GENESIS 12–50

GENESIS 12–50

A Narrative-Theological Commentary

James Chukwuma Okoye, CSSp

CASCADE *Books* • Eugene, Oregon

GENESIS 12–50
A Narrative-Theological Commentary

Copyright © 2020 James Chukwuma Okoye. All rights reserved. Except for brief quotations in critical publications or reviews, no part of this book may be reproduced in any manner without prior written permission from the publisher. Write: Permissions, Wipf and Stock Publishers, 199 W. 8th Ave., Suite 3, Eugene, OR 97401.

Cascade Books
An Imprint of Wipf and Stock Publishers
199 W. 8th Ave., Suite 3
Eugene, OR 97401

www.wipfandstock.com

PAPERBACK ISBN: 978-1-5326-7397-9
HARDCOVER ISBN: 978-1-5326-7398-6
EBOOK ISBN: 978-1-5326-7399-3

Cataloguing-in-Publication data:

Names: Okoye, James Chukwuma, author.
Title: Genesis 12–50 : a narrative-theological commentary / James Chukwuma Okoye.
Description: Eugene, OR: Cascade Books, 2020 | Includes bibliographical references and index.
Identifiers: ISBN 978-1-5326-7397-9 (paperback) | ISBN 978-1-5326-7398-6 (hardcover) | ISBN 978-1-5326-7399-3 (ebook)
Subjects: LCSH: Bible.—Genesis, XII–L—Commentaries | Bible.—Genesis, XII–L—Criticism, interpretation, etc.
Classification: BS1235.3 O36 2020 (print) | BS1235.3 (ebook)

Manufactured in the U.S.A. FEBRUARY 24, 2022

The Scripture texts of Genesis 12–50 in this commentary, unless otherwise stated, are from the New American Bible Revised Edition © 2011 (USCCB).

Cum permissu superiorum
Very Rev. Jeff Duaime, CSSp
Provincial, Province of the United States of America
July 18, 2019

Dedicated to

Lady Rose Ibeme (née Okoye)

With a Prayer for her Heavenly Repose

Table of Contents

Foreword ix
Preface xi
Abbreviations xiii
Chapter 1. A Narrative Theology of the Book of Genesis 1
Chapter 2. Genesis 12: The LORD Calls Abram Forth to Be Blessing for All Families 33
Chapter 3. Genesis 13–14: Abraham and Lot 54
Chapter 4. Genesis 15: Covenant Between the Pieces 69
Chapter 5. Genesis 16: Sarai and Hagar 82
Chapter 6. Genesis 17: The Covenant of Circumcision 91
Chapter 7. Genesis 18–19: Abraham, Lot, and Sodom 108
Chapter 8. Genesis 20: The Ancestress in Danger 127
Chapter 9. Genesis 21: Isaac Is Born; Ishmael Is Expelled 134
Chapter 10. Genesis 22: "The One You Love" 147
Chapter 11. Genesis 23: Abraham Acquires the Cave of Machpelah in the Land of Canaan 162
Chapter 12. Genesis 24: Transmitting the Blessing; A Wife for Isaac 168
Chapter 13. Genesis 25:1–18: Death of Abraham; Genealogy of Ishmael 180
Chapter 14. The Jacob Cycle: Esau and Jacob 186
Chapter 15. Genesis 26: Traditions of Isaac 195
Chapter 16. Genesis 27: Jacob Deceives Isaac, Receives Esau's Blessing 208
Chapter 17. Genesis 28: Divine Encounter at Bethel 219
Chapter 18. Genesis 29–31: Jacob and Laban; The Twelve Tribes of Israel 231
Chapter 19. Genesis 32–33: Jacob Renamed Israel; Jacob Encounters Esau 249

Chapter 20. Genesis 34: Dinah at Shechem 266
Chapter 21. Genesis 35–36: Jacob Becomes Israel; Esau Becomes Edom 284
Chapter 22. Genesis 37: The Joseph Narrative; Joseph Is Sold into Egypt 298
Chapter 23. Chapter 38: Judah and Tamar 314
Chapter 24. Genesis 39: Joseph and Potiphar's Wife 324
Chapter 25. Genesis 40–41: From Prison to Power 335
Chapter 26. Genesis 42–44: Joseph Encounters His Brothers 347
Chapter 27. Genesis 45: Joseph Reveals Himself to His Brothers 364
Chapter 28. Genesis 46: Jacob Migrates to Egypt 371
Chapter 29. Genesis 47: Israel Settles in Goshen; Joseph's Agrarian Policy 377
Chapter 30. Genesis 48: Jacob Adopts Joseph's Sons; Ephraim and Manasseh 386
Chapter 31. Genesis 49: The Testament of Jacob 394
Chapter 32. Genesis 50: The Joseph Story Dovetails with the Jacob Story; Reconstruction of Memory 407
Chapter 33. By Way of Conclusion: Some Themes of the Narrative 414

Bibliography 427
Subject Index 447
Scripture Index 483

Foreword

One could ask for no better guide through the book of Genesis than James Chukwuma Okoye. He brings to this study an enviable breadth of knowledge from his scholarly research into the biblical text from both Jewish and Christian perspectives, along with his own deep spirituality as a missionary priest in the Congregation of the Holy Spirit and his keen pastoral sensitivity shaped by his many years of teaching, preaching, and leadership in diverse contexts around the globe. For the student new to the study of Scripture, his thorough explanations give a firm foundation for understanding the text exegetically. But more than that, his narrative theological approach unfolds the manifold ways that the biblical story intersects with the deepest human questions of each age, illuminating the constancy of the divine presence in the search for meaning and direction. For the seasoned scholar, teacher, and preacher as well, Okoye's work is a treasure trove, offering fresh insights and direction toward holistic meaning-making and spirituality.

Rare are the studies of Genesis that use a literary and theological approach; most previous studies have opened up the text from historical-critical perspectives. While completely adept at historical study, Okoye forges new pathways of understanding with his attention to the narrative dynamics: the words, form, content, literary themes, patterns, and rhetorical features of the ancient Hebrew text. He attends to the characters and their actions, including God, as he analyzes plot and point of view. He points out, without always trying to resolve, ambiguities in the text as he guides the reader to reflect on ambiguities in our own lives concerning our relationships with God, other people, creatures, and our world. He shows that there are multiple approaches to the text, each of which opens new ways to theological meaning and relevancy.

It is a great delight to see that Okoye's profound insights on Genesis (along with the first volume, on Genesis 1–11, published in 2018) are now available to a wider audience beyond the students who flocked to his courses when we were colleagues at Catholic Theological Union in Chicago. Great profit awaits those who allow Okoye to break open for you the stories from Babel to Noah to the patriarchs and matriarchs to the death of Joseph, and let them speak to your life.

Barbara E. Reid, OP, PhD
Professor of New Testament Studies
Catholic Theological Union
Chicago

Preface

The reception given the first volume, *Genesis 1–11: A Narrative Theological Commentary* (2018) showed a need for this type of commentary. I have made this one even more accessible to the ordinary reader by putting more of the discussion in the footnotes. Two features are added that readers may skip if they wish. First, necessary details of a more technical nature are indented and put in smaller print. Second, I added a new section for deeper reflection, "Further Reflections," indented but not in smaller print. These delve more deeply into the theology of the text. Great effort was made to assure that the interpretation does not obscure the flow of the story.

I have always wanted to write this type of commentary. I was enriched by the effort and hope the experience will be similar for the reader. The fathers of the church and the early rabbis are models in making Scripture speak to the concrete circumstances of the life of their times, even if some of their methods of interpretation may not pass muster today.

This work is written in thanksgiving to God for his mercies and graces during fifty years of ordination as a priest. My particular assignment in God's Vineyard has been the service of administration for my brothers and sisters and the teaching of sacred Scripture. For the past few years, I have been engaged in researching and disseminating Spiritan history, charism, and mission.

It is already evening; and soon will be, hopefully not night, but endless light. May the good Lord accept this work as a pleasing sacrifice to the glory of his Name!

James Chukwuma Okoye, CSSp

Abbreviations

1 En.	1 Enoch (Ethiopian Enoch)
ACCS	Genesis 12–50, edited by Mark Sheridan, Ancient Christian Commentary on Scripture, Old Testament 2 (Downers Grove: InterVarsity, 2001)
ANET	Ancient Near Eastern Texts Relating to the Old Testament, edited by James B. Pritchard, 3rd ed. (Princeton, NJ: Princeton University Press, 1969)
Ant.	Antiquities of the Jews, by Flavius Josephus, in The Works of Josephus: Complete and Unabridged, translated by William Whiston, 27–542, new updated ed. (Peabody, MA: Hendrickson, 1987)
AUSS	Andrews University Seminary Studies
BBR	Bulletin for Biblical Research
BDB	Brown, Francis, with S. R. Driver and Charles A. Briggs, A Hebrew and English Lexicon of the Old Testament (Oxford: Clarendon Press, 1951)
Bib	Biblica
BibInt	Biblical Interpretation
BibSac	Bibliotheca Sacra
BN	Biblische Notizen
BTB	Biblical Theology Bulletin
Catechism	Catechism of the Catholic Church (1998)
CBQ	Catholic Biblical Quarterly
CBQMS	Catholic Biblical Quarterly Monograph Series
CBR	Currents in Biblical Research
CTM	Concordia Theological Monthly

CTQ	*Concordia Theological Quarterly*
CV	*Communio Viatorum*
ERev	*Ecumenical Review*
ETR	*Etudes Théologiques et Religieuses*
EuroJTh	*European Journal of Theology*
FC	*Fathers of the Church*
Gen. Rab.	*Midrash Rabbah: Genesis*, edited by H. Freedman and Maurice Simon (London: Soncino, 1977)
HAR	*Hebrew Annual Review*
HBT	*Horizons in Biblical Theology*
IDB	*Interpreters' Dictionary of the Bible*, edited by George Arthur Buttrick, 4 vols., with *Supplementary Volume* edited by Keith Crim (Nashville: Abingdon, 1962, 1976)
Int	*Interpretation*
JANES	*Journal of the Ancient Near Eastern Society*
JBL	*Journal of Biblical Literature*
JBQ	*Jewish Biblical Quarterly*
JBT	*Jahrbuch für Biblische Theologie*
JECS	*Journal of Early Christian Studies*
JEH	*Journal of Ecclesiastical History*
JETS	*Journal of the Ecumenical Theological Society.*
JJS	*Journal of Jewish Studies*
JNES	*Journal of Near Eastern Studies*
JP	*Journal for Preachers*
JQR	*Jewish Quarterly Review*
JR	*Journal of Religion*
JSJ	*Journal for the Study of Judaism.*
JSOT	*Journal for the Study of the Old Testament.*
JSOTSup	*Journal for the Study of the Old Testament: Supplement Series*
JSQ	*Jewish Studies Quarterly*
JTI	*Journal of Theological Interpretation*
JTSA	*Journal of Theology for Southern Africa*

Jub.	*Jubilees*
L.A.B.	*Liber Antiquitatuum Biblicarum* / *The Book of Biblical Antiquities*
LTJ	*Lutheran Theological Journal*
LXX	Septuagint
NABRE	New American Bible, Revised Edition (2011)
NIV	New International Version
NJB	New Jerusalem Bible (1985)
NRSV	New Revised Standard Version
NTS	*New Testament Studies*
OTP	*Old Testament Pseudepigrapha*, edited by James H. Charlesworth, 2 vols. (New York: Doubleday, 1985)
PRS	*Perspectives in Religious Studies*
RB	*Revue Biblique*
REB	*Revised English Bible.*
ResQ	*Restoration Quarterly*
SEÅ	*Svensk exegetisk årsbok*
SJOT	*Scandinavian Journal of Old Testament*
StPatr	*Studia Patristica*
TDNT	*Theological Dictionary of the New Testament*, edited by Gerhard Kittel and Gerhard Friedrich, translated by Geoffrey W. Bromiley, 10 vols. (Grand Rapids: Eerdmans, 1964–76)
TDOT	*Theological Dictionary of the Old Testament*, edited by G. Johannes Botterweck and Helmer Ringgren, translated by Geoffrey W. Bromiley et al., 14 vols. (Grand Rapids: Eerdmans, 1974–2004)
Tg. Neof.	*Targum Neofiti 1: Genesis*, The Aramaic Bible, translated by Martin McNamara (Collegeville, MN: Liturgical, 1992)
Tg. Onq.	*Targum Onqelos to Genesis*, The Aramaic Bible 6, translated by Bernard Grossfeld (Collegeville, MN: Liturgical, 1988)
Tg. Ps.-J.	*Targum Pseudo-Jonathan: Genesis*, The Aramaic Bible, translated by Michael Maher (Collegeville, MN: Liturgical, 1992)

TNK	Jewish Publication Society TANAKH translation of the Hebrew Scriptures
TS	*Teologiese Studies / Theological Studies*
TynBul	*Tyndale Bulletin*
VT	*Vetus Testamentum*
VTSup	Vetus Testamentum Supplements
WMANT	Wissenschaftliche Monographien zum Alten und Neuen Testament
WTJ	*Westminster Theological Journal*
WW	*Word and World*
ZAW	*Zeitschrift für die alttestamentliche Wissenschaft*

CHAPTER 1

A Narrative Theology of the Book of Genesis

Introduction

MULTIPLE COMMENTARIES ON GENESIS of differing levels and approaches there certainly are. Genesis is one of the books of the Hebrew Bible most commented upon.[1] Narrative commentaries exist on Judges, Samuel, and Kings,[2] but precious little on Genesis.

The new approach, called "Narrative Art" or "Hebrew Poetics," that focuses on "the distinctive principles of the Bible's narrative art,"[3] has been developing for some time. Umberto Cassuto was broadly in this tradition of commentary, even if not *ex professo*.[4] Two Israeli scholars, Menakhem Perry and Meir Sternberg, caused a stir in 1968 when they launched the conscious approach to narrative art with "The King through Ironic Eyes,"[5] analyzing the story of David and Bathsheba. The following are important works in this genre; they are listed in historical order.

---

1. This chapter updates the preface and chapter 1 of Okoye, *Genesis 1–11*.

2. For example, Gunn, *Fate of Saul*; Garsiel, *First Book of Samuel*; Amit, *Book of Judges*; Fokkelman, *Narrative Art and Poetry in the Books of Samuel*.

3. Alter, *Art of Biblical Narrative*, 2011, xiii; see also x–xii, 14–18.

4. Cassuto, *Commentary on the Book of Genesis*, 2 vols. Both volumes have been reprinted several times.

5. Perry and Stenberg, "King through Ironic Eyes." The piece is now incorporated into Sternberg, *Poetics of Biblical Narrative* as chapter 6, "Gaps, Ambiguity, and the Reading Process."

Jan P. Fokkelman, *Narrative Art in Genesis: Specimens of Stylistic and Structural Analysis* (Assen: Van Gorcum, 1975) (knowledge of Hebrew is needed for this book) was an early protagonist.

Robert Alter, *The Art of Biblical Narrative* (New York: Basic, 1981; 2nd ed. 2011) was also among the first to illustrate this art.

Meir Sternberg, *The Poetics of Biblical Narrative: Ideological Literature and the Drama of Reading* (Bloomington: Indiana University Press, 1985) has become a quasi-classic in the field.

Robert Alter and Frank Kermode, eds., *The Literary Guide to the Bible* (Cambridge, MA: Harvard University Press, 1987).

Luis Alonso Schökel, *A Manual of Hebrew Poetics* (Rome: Editrice Pontificio Istituto Biblico, 1988) illustrated the technique with inciting comments.

Shimeon Bar-Efrat, *Narrative Art in the Bible* (Sheffield: Almond, 1989).

David Gunn and Danna Fewell, *Narrative in the Hebrew Bible* (New York: Oxford University Press, 1993).

Adele Berlin, *Poetics and Interpretation of Biblical Narrative* (Winona Lake, IN: Eisenbrauns, 1994).

Jan P. Fokkelman, *Reading Biblical Narrative: An Introductory Guide* (Louisville: Westminster John Knox, 1999).

Yairah Amit, *Reading Biblical Narratives. Literary Criticism and the Hebrew Bible* (Minneapolis: Fortress, 2001).

Narrative English commentaries on Genesis are few, as far as I know.[6] Here are some.

Robert Alter, *Genesis: Translation and Commentary* (New York: Norton, 1997) is more literary than theological.

David Cotter, *Genesis*, Berit Olam (Collegeville, MN: Liturgical, 2003) is a narrative commentary, with greater focus on elements of structure.[7]

James Chukwuma Okoye, *Genesis 1–11: A Narrative-Theological Commentary* (Eugene, OR: Cascade, 2018).

Two narrative commentaries that span the entire Pentateuch are the following.

---

6. Brueggemann, *Genesis* is a discourse analysis that does theology from a Christian perspective. Coats, *Genesis* treats narrative as a species of form criticism; he invests in structure, genre, setting, and intention.

7. The author asserts on page xxiv: "as far as I know, there is no commentary that applies the tools of narrative analysis to the book as an integral whole." That was 2003.

Thomas Mann, *The Book of the Torah: The Narrative Integrity of the Pentateuch* (Atlanta: John Knox, 1988; 2nd ed., Eugene, OR: Cascade, 2013).

John H. Sailhamer, *The Pentateuch as Narrative: A Biblical-Theological Commentary* (Grand Rapids: Zondervan, 1992) is an Evangelical approach (more on him later).

The present commentary is both narratival and theological. It does not stop at the formal elements of language and style, but also investigates what is portrayed of the nature of God, the life of humans, creation, and the interaction between all of these. Some of the literary features resist description in translation. Under "Tradition," I seek to show how Jewish and Christian faith have interpreted the text of Scripture in various contexts in their history.

This commentary is written for students who long for access to the Hebrew Bible and its message. Pastors and ministers who have to preach the word of God will find much help herein. Well-informed readers will find engagement with questions they bring to their reading. Although the apparatus has been kept to a minimum, fellow academics will find herein a dialogue partner.

A Narrative Approach

Methods chosen are usually relevant to goals sought. Each commentator brings a certain perspective to the text. He or she approaches the text with certain presuppositions, questions, and concerns or is already convinced of the effectiveness of some method for the exegetical task at hand.

Most commentators on the book of Genesis use some form of the *historical critical approach*—form or tradition criticism, social science criticism, or some other. In the historical approach, meaning derives from the author and is generally sought in the author's intentions within his or her historical context. Many of these commentators have recourse to the Documentary Hypothesis[8] or some recent adaptation or replacement of

---

8. The Documentary Hypothesis is the theory of four *written* sources combined in the current Pentateuch as systematized in 1878 in the Graf-Wellhausen Hypothesis. The four sources are Yahwist (siglum J), assigned to the tenth century BCE; Elohist (siglum E), assigned to the late ninth century; Deuteronomy (siglum D), seventh century; and Priestly (siglum P), mid-sixth century. A redactor in the P tradition is supposed to have spliced these sources. This hypothesis is under attack; the dating of the sources, their nature and extent, are under negotiation, but no consensus has so

it, for example, the Yahwist as postexilic, the entire material as divided into Priestly and non-Priestly, or D-Komposition and P-Komposition. For current trends in this area, the advanced reader may consult Dozeman et al., *The Pentateuch*. Nicholson's *The Pentateuch in the Twentieth Century* analyzed the trends till 1998 and came to the conclusion that there were indeed legitimate questions, the hypothesis is shaken, but still has largely stood up. Levin adds for the period till 2011: "the truth is that everyone who denies the Documentary Hypothesis as such will be drowned in the flood or, like the Egyptians, in the sea."[9]

Some commentators use *reader-response approaches* that privilege the reader. The reader consciously brings his or her convictions and points of view to bear; the meaning of the text is "meaning for me." Strands of this approach are ideological criticism, liberation and feminist criticism, postcolonial criticism, and so on.

An increasing number of commentators have recourse to *literary approaches*. These derive meaning from the structure of the text itself and how it intends to mean. They pay close attention to how it does things with words, both the form (the *how*) and the content (the *what*). Intentionally distancing himself from the author of the text to focus on the narrator, the interpreter constructs the meaning of the Hebrew text as a process[10]—as one reads, multiple possibilities suggest themselves and are weighed over against the meaning of the whole.[11] Strands of this approach are structuralism, rhetorical criticism, and narrative criticism. Meaning is never divorced from the participation of the reader.

> The maker has written his text with the express intention of being outlived by it . . . What is essential? That which the text itself provides, the world it evokes and the values it embodies, and then, the confrontation, the interplay, the friction and sometimes the clash between all this and the reader's world and values.[12]

Nor is text ever divorced from context. To begin with, the text of Genesis is in ancient Hebrew and this has built-in conventions and

---

far been reached.
9. Levin, "Righteousness in the Joseph Story," 226.
10. See Iser, *Art of Reading*; idem, "Reading Process."
11. See Floriani, "Benefits and Pitfalls of Narrative Criticism," 9.
12. Fokkelman, *Reading Biblical Narrative*, 23.

patterns of meaning.[13] The text itself has had a history and there may be textual riddles to be deciphered and apparent contradictions to be resolved. A synchronic reading thus cannot dispense with all historical or source-oriented inquiries[14]: "diachronic reading may show how any synchronic reading of a text is a choice."[15] For this reason, I sometimes call upon the so-called Pentateuchal "sources," for example, in Genesis 17 (Priestly theology) or Genesis 18 (Abraham and his visitors, Yahwist theology)—the diachronic in the service of the synchronic.

For the non-specialist, some concepts in narrative criticism may need brief explanation. In this commentary, I shall do much "showing" and less "telling," that is, I shall present the features at work, without always invoking the technical terms, trusting that the reader recognizes the narrative art in operation.

The Narrator

The voice telling the story is called the narrator, to be distinguished from the writer of the story. The narrator is also to be distinguished from the characters of the story. Sometimes the narrator's voice merges with that of the characters; sometimes it diverges or stands in opposition to it. Sometimes indeterminacy may result from irony, the implied author undermining the narrator.[16] In any case, the narrator wants to bring the reader to his point of view (in the context of Genesis, the writer was most probably male, so I use the masculine pronoun). The narrator knows everything, even the future and what is in the mind of God and not just of people, and so scholars call him the "omniscient narrator." Such omniscience is, in the first place, understood in a literary, not a theological

---

13. "Nobody is likely to regard the grammar and semantics of biblical Hebrew as irrelevant to a literary approach." Sternberg, *Poetics of Biblical Narrative*, 11.

14. Kawashima, "Sources and Redaction," *Reading Genesis*, 70: "Awareness of the sources and redaction of biblical texts ... far from obscuring or neglecting or denying literary art ... makes possible the retrieval of the intentions of the biblical writers and redactors, which have been lost with the passing of the centuries and obscured by modern notions of the single-author book." See also Carr, *Reading the Fractures of Genesis*, 7, 9, who argues for combining focus on the final form with a "geological approach," since the final form includes many meaning levels next to and in one another.

15. Carr, *Reading the Fractures of Genesis*, 334.

16. Gunn, "New Directions," 72.

sense: "it is not necessary to consider such a statement 'historically reliable' and assume a prior phonecall from the Holy Ghost to the writer."[17]

God as a Character

In narrative theory, "God" within the narrative is, in the first place, a character created by the narrator. "One writer's image of God is totally different than that of the other."[18]

> The God of the books of Samuel is not exactly the same as the God of Moses . . . and something else entirely than the God of Ecclesiastes. Add to this the fact that the God of a devout Jew or Christian will always be different and greater than the image that anyone has of God. So let us . . . not immediately lock the narrator of the Hebrew story inside our assumption that he, the maker of the character God, entertains the same values.[19]

Amit comments on the impact of the image of God and the characterization of the human personae: "when God is portrayed as distant, there seems to be greater scope, or living space, for human motives and their complexities."[20] One should distinguish the God of faith from the God who functions in different parts of the Bible. Yet, the *biblical* narrator presents the character God as omniscient and omnipotent, always trustworthy.[21] Jewish and Christian faith equates the God of the Bible with the Creator; Christian faith further presents him as the Father of our Lord Jesus Christ. The literary and theological points of view can be in some tension. For how this commentary navigates this conundrum, see "The Approach of This Commentary" below.

---

17. Fokkelman, *Reading Biblical Narrative*, 56.
18. Fokkelman, *Reading Biblical Narrative*, 58.
19. Fokkelman, *Reading Biblical Narrative*, 153.
20. Amit, *Reading Biblical Narratives*, 84. The entire section, "The Character of God and Its Implications for Human Characters," 82–87, is worth reading.
21. Alter, *Art of Biblical Narrative*, 196 reluctantly concedes that "in some of the oldest narrative documents, it appears at times that God's knowledge, in contrast to that of the narrator, has its limits."

Characters

The writer propels the story forward through characters who speak, act, and interact with one another—Cain and Abel, Lamech, Abraham ... Characters are generally *round* (complex, with many traits, developing through the narrative) or *flat* (represents a trait or an idea, behaves in a stereotypical manner). Berlin works with three categories: the *full-fledged* character (round character), the *type* (flat character), and the *agent* (a mere functionary). "An agent has no personality at all, but simply functions to move the story along."[22] As example of the agent, Berlin invokes Abishag, the beautiful girl who ministered to David in 1 Kings 1–2 but with whom the king had no sexual relations.[23]

Characters are revealed through what they do and say, and how they feel, intend, or desire. Character profiles are rare. Characters are also revealed through appearance, gestures, posture, costume, and their comments on other characters in the story.[24] The characters of the biblical story are to be distinguished from the historical individual: "Abraham in Genesis is not a real person any more than a painting of an apple is a real fruit."[25]

Narration and Dialogue

Biblical writers generally avoid indirect speech: "when speech is involved in a narrative event, it is presented as direct speech."[26] Dialogue has primacy over narration; speech, especially "inward speech" ("he said to himself," or "he said in his heart"), is a window to the character's true intentions and objectives. Revelatory also is the way in which a character's statements diverge from the narrator's report or when there is tension between what a character says and what he or she does.[27]

---

22. Sandy and Giese Jr., *Cracking Old Testament Codes*, 74.
23. Berlin, *Poetics and Interpretation*, 23, 27.
24. See Alter, *Art of Biblical Narrative*, 146–47.
25. Berlin, *Poetics and Interpretation*, 13.
26. Alter, *Art of Biblical Narrative*, 83.
27. Alter, *Art of Biblical Narrative*, 82, 85.

Plot

The plot is the sequence of events that make up the story. In Genesis 1, the ordering of creation is in a sequence of seven days. Sometimes the narrator anticipates or foreshadows events, as in the oracle at Gen 25:23, "two nations are in your womb . . . and the older will serve the younger." The narrator may also connect with the past through a flashback, or forge links in the story through prospection and retrospection. A common plot is to break up the story into *complication* and *change* leading to *denouement*; another is to break it up into scenes.

Point of View

The point of view is the perspective from which a story or part thereof is told, whose vision or interest is being portrayed. It compares with the camera eye in filming.[28] The camera man (here the narrator) trains the camera on this and then on that; the viewer absorbs the story by following the camera as it shifts. The narrator tells the story from his point of view, sometimes breaking out of the story to comment on it, show his attitude towards it. But he sometimes yields the perspective to a character to present his or her interest in the story. The term *hinneh* (behold) points to a character's perspective, what he or she is seeing. For example, Jacob had a dream and behold, a stairway (Gen 28:12; NABRE unfortunately omitted "behold"). "Irony occurs when we speak from one point of view, but make an evaluation from another point of view."[29] The interplay of perspectives can be illustrated from Genesis 37: "because it is told from several perspectives, Gen 37 is fraught with ambiguity. There is no clear right and wrong. Each character's actions are justified from his point of view."[30] To Joseph, his dreams portend future greatness and dominance over his brothers. To the brothers, it elicited the sarcastic, "are you really

---

28. Berlin, *Poetics and Interpretation*, 44. Berlin devotes the entire chapter 3 to the point of view. She speaks of the perceptual (perspective through which events of the narrative are perceived), conceptual (perspective of attitudes, conceptions, worldview), and interest (perspective of someone's benefit or disadvantage) points of view (47). See also Fokkelman, *Reading Biblical Narrative*, 139–48.

29. Berlin, *Poetics and Interpretation*, 51.

30. Berlin, *Poetics and Interpretation*, 50.

going to make yourself king over us?" The father found all this puzzling, yet intriguing—are the dreams hinting at what the future has in store?[31]

Naming

How a character is named and the epithets given to him or her can be significant. In the story of Cain and Abel, Gen 4:1–16, the word "brother" appears seven times, underlining the heinousness of the deed—fratricide. When his brothers spotted Joseph from a distance, they said, "here comes that dreamer" (Gen 37:19)—the dreams, not the relationship as brother, dominate the perspective. The brothers left Canaan as "sons of Israel," but arrive in Egypt in Gen 42:5, 6 as "Joseph's brothers."

Gaps and Ambiguities

"A gap is a lack of information about the world–an event, motive, causal link, character trait, plot structure, law of probability–contrived by a temporal displacement."[32] Sternberg distinguishes between "gaps," which demand closure, and "blanks," which may be disregarded without loss, because not relevant to the narrator's purview or interest.

Gen 6:4 contains a couple of gaps: "the Nephilim appeared on earth in those days, as well as later, after the sons of God had intercourse with the daughters of human beings, who bore them sons." Who are the Nephilim (literally, "fallen ones")? Are they the product of the mixing of the sons of God and the daughters of human beings? The text does not clearly say so. If the flood cleared all humans except Noah and his sons, how could Nephilim appear "as well later," as in Num 13:33 ("there we saw the Nephilim")? Gen 37:28 introduces ambiguity by having the Midianites pull Joseph out of the cistern. It becomes unclear who sold Joseph to the Ishmaelites; the brothers are somehow saved from the charge of kidnapping or murder, which in Exod 21:16 and Deut 24:7 draws a death sentence.[33]

---

31. Humphreys, *Joseph and his Family*, 102.
32. Sternberg, *Poetics of Biblical Narrative*, 235.
33. Coats, *From Canaan to Egypt*, 17.

Showing and Telling

In biblical narrative, character profiles are rare; characters are generally portrayed as acting, speaking, and reacting. Put another way, there is much "showing," less "telling." The narrator does not tell the reader what to see, but rather lets the story itself create the impact on the reader. When Jesus gave the Parable of the Sower (Matt 13:1–9), that was "showing." The explanation (Matt 13:18–23) is "telling." A usual illustration is the contrast between "John was angry with his wife," and "John looked at his wife, his eyebrows pursed, his lips contracted, his fists clenched. Then he got up, banged the door and left the house."[34]

The other elements of narrative art the interested reader may look up in one of the introductions to narrative criticism.

A Narrative Theology of Genesis

One third of the Hebrew Bible consists of stories. One criticism of narratology has been that moving from narrative to theology has been conspicuous by its absence.[35] But what is theological reading of the Bible and how does it relate to historical critical exegesis? Theological exegesis cannot be something completely different than historical exegesis; it is best informed when appropriately incorporating the insights of a seriously performed historical exegesis:

> historical critical exegesis becomes implausible when it misjudges the theological gravity of the biblical texts; theological interpretation of the Bible degenerates structurally into docetism when it relegates the historical X of textual interpretation to a place after a theological Y coefficient. In conclusion, historical exegesis is only then truly and responsibly historical when carried out with theological sensibility.[36]

Allow me to illustrate the drama of theological reading from the text of the New Testament, "sell what you have and give to the poor . . . then come follow me" (Matt 19:21).[37] But one cannot sell all one has and keep a family. Did Jesus intend the abolition of family life? He did not require

---

34. Rimmon-Kenan, *Narrative Fiction: Contemporary Poetic*, 109.
35. Kelly, "Discuss and Evaluate," 1.
36. Schmid, "Historical and Theological Exegesis?," 19, 18.
37. Kling, *Bible in History*, 13–43.

Zacchaeus (Luke 19:8-9) to sell all he had, yet he said that "it is easier for a camel to pass through the eye of a needle than for one who is rich to enter the kingdom of God" (Matt 19:24). Anthony of Egypt (251-356) took the words in their rigor. Hearing this text, he divested himself of his inherited wealth and withdrew to the desert. Desert monks imitated the ideal of the early Christian community. Francis of Assisi (1180-1226) heard the same text of Matthew and forsook his wealth to embrace Lady Poverty.

Another solution was to take the words in their rigor, but apply them only to those called to the way of counsels. Ambrose of Milan (339-397) distinguished the precepts (for all Christians) and counsels (for the chosen few).

Still another solution: the text's rigor is for all Christians. Anabaptist Hetterites (sixteenth century till today) insist that Christ meant communal ownership and that private property is not Christian.

A fourth solution: the text preaches poverty of spirit. Clement of Alexandria (150-215), speaking of the salvation of the rich man, insists that "what matters is poverty of spirit, not poverty of possessions." Martin Luther interprets the text to mean, "you shall have no gods before me" (when riches become idols).

A fifth solution is to regard riches as a blessing (Calvin)! For him, the injunction was relevant to this rich man alone. Gospel of wealth televangelists preach that God wills riches for Christians, for "whatever you ask in my name I will do" (John 14:13). What a diversity of theological readings of the same text!

Coming home to the Old Testament, a text like Genesis 34 illustrates how perplexing a theological reading can be. I place in italics some words and phrases that propel the reader in one direction or the other.

Dinah, Jacob's daughter from Leah, went out to see the women of the land. Shechem, son of Hamor the Hivite, saw her, seized her, and lay with her *by force*. But then he was attracted to her, and *in love with her*, and wanted her for wife. Jacob heard that Shechem had *defiled* his daughter Dinah, yet said nothing; his sons were out in the field. When they returned from the field, they were indignant—Shechem had *committed an outrage* in Israel, a *thing not done*. Shechem proposed marriage with the girl and that the two groups intermarry. Jacob's sons insisted on *circumcision* of all males. Shechem and Hamor convinced their people saying, among other things, "would not their livestock, their property, and all their animals then be ours?" The people agreed. On the third day, when the pain was greatest, Simeon and Levi, brothers of Dinah, slaughtered all the men, including Shechem and Hamor, and took Dinah from Shechem's house. The other sons of Jacob sacked the city, and took the women and children, *because their sister had been defiled*. To Jacob's complaint that they had made him repugnant to the inhabitants of the land, Simeon and Levi retorted, "*Should our sister be treated like a prostitute?*" God meantime asked Jacob to move to Bethel. A *great terror* fell upon the surrounding towns so that no one pursued the sons of Jacob. Is God siding with Jacob, saying nothing about the abuse of circumcision, breach of contract, and wholesale and disproportionate massacre of a people? And the narrator? Is he conflicted? He tells us that Shechem took Dinah by force and defiled her, yet was strongly attracted to her, in love, and spoke affectionately to her. Was Shechem's love sincere? Did he win her over? Was she detained in Shechem's house or was she there on her own volition? Jacob's sons slaughter a whole people who had agreed to circumcision in order to intermarry with them. The narrator tells us that Jacob's sons made this proposal "*with guile*, speaking as they did because he had *defiled their sister*, Dinah." Is the narrator condemning or excusing the subterfuge? Jacob obviously feared for the safety of his family, but was his inaction and the initiative taken by Simeon and Levi, Dinah's full brothers, because she was daughter of the unloved Leah? Wenham comments that by giving the last word to the brothers the narrator prevents moral closure, leaving the reader to ponder what should be done in a situation of competing moral imperatives, namely, which is more important now, pursuit of peace or the vindication of a sister?[38] In Gen 49:5–7, Jacob attempts some closure by dispossessing Simeon and Levi, but hardly. The reader may want to reread the story from Dinah's point of view, indeed the point of view of each of the characters, or give his/her own title to the unit, thus encapsulating his/her theological reading. How does your interpretation throw light on relevant issues in Christian ministry today, like rape, family conflict, violence, ethnic strife, self-defense, proportional response, or the virtues God's people should live by? You may also consider how this story fits into the whole, perhaps by checking texts that relate to the topic of the story, like Gen 35:22; 49:5–7; Exod 22:15–16; Deut 7:1–5; 22:28–29; 2 Sam 13:21; this is called intertextuality. We will delve more deeply into this chapter later in this commentary. But our perplexity with this text shows that the biblical text does not always give

---

38. See Wenham, "Some Problematic Tales," 119.

clear guidance to conduct, that theological interpretation is an ongoing drama in which one seeks to ponder God's word in relation to concrete circumstances that can sometimes be messy and unclear.

Theological interpretation is thus not reading texts to extract doctrines or *the* Bible teaching, as if the Bible consists of only clear-cut propositions of faith or only clearly articulated moral guidelines. I partly agree with Sternberg when he writes, "the whole idea of didacticism is alien, if not antipathetic, to the spirit of Israelite storytelling."[39] He gives examples: divine election and moral stature are not aligned; there is no automatic or at least intelligible system of rewards and punishments. The stories often are not written from a didactic and moralistic viewpoint. Sometimes they offer models, but generally they simply tell the story, "hold up a mirror before us to help us see ourselves and reflect on the way God is involved in our lives in their skewedness and ambiguity." "We discover such 'lessons' only by bringing priorities and criteria to the text and ignoring the dynamic of the stories' interest."[40] Besides, the text of the Bible is silent on many important areas of life. The Bible also contains diverse views on many issues, making the quest for the current will of God not always as easy and straightforward a quest as some might wish.

Partly because of the above reasons, scholars come at the theology of the Bible in diverse ways. Other facts come in for consideration. For one, the canon of Scripture differs. Protestants recognize sixty-six books as inspired, Catholics seventy-three (following more or less the Jewish canon of Alexandria, LXX), and the Orthodox a few more. The structure of the Bible and reading strategies differ. For Jews, the Prophets and Writings function to interpret Torah, the essential revelation for them, while Christians read Torah in light of the Prophets seen as heralds of Christ. Reading strategies differ also among Christians. I illustrate all this with the following six reading strategies.

Some Theological Reading Strategies

Moberly[41] reads the Old Testament as the *story of a people*; it tells of this people's life with its God. Theological interpretation reads the story with a view to articulating and practicing its enduring significance for human

---

39. Sternberg, *Poetics of Biblical Narrative*, 38.
40. Goldingay, *Israel's Gospel*, 286.
41. Moberly, *Theology of the Book of Genesis*, 17.

life under God. Moberly chooses to start from contemporary debates and appeals to the text of Scripture. His entry point is contemporary faith and spirituality, hence his may be called a *Christian* theology of the book of Genesis. The patriarchal narratives can be dubbed "the Old Testament of the Old Testament" in the sense that they retain a similar provisional relationship to the Mosaic revelation as the Mosaic revelation itself has to the revelation in Jesus Christ:

> The interpretive process primarily works from Jesus to the Old Testament and from Israel to Abraham; the normative traditions of Jesus and Israel provide the models by which God's earlier activity is to be understood.[42]

From Moberly we learn to bring our convictions and criteria to bear on the text and that what we find must have relevance for our life of faith today.

Brueggemann[43] sees the subject of a theology of the Bible as speech about God. Even when God speaks, the text is still Israel's testimony that God has spoken. The heuristic question then is: how does ancient Israel in this text speak about God? In focusing on speech, Brueggemann brackets out all questions of historicity—not what happened, but what was said. The *what* of Israel's talk of God is linked to the *how* of that speech (rhetoric). So he seizes upon testimony. Testimony happens in a *court of law*; witnesses are called upon to give their version of what is true, and on the basis of testimony alone the court must decide what is real, with no access to the "actual event" besides the testimony. Theologically said, testimony becomes revelation, that is, "human testimony is taken as revelation that discloses the true reality of God."[44] Israel as a community has rendered a verdict that accepts this testimony as reliable. But within her and outside of her, alternative construals of reality were always readily credible, and so attention to "Old Testament theology . . . refuses any reductionism to a single or simple articulation; it offers a witness that is enormously open, inviting, and suggestive, rather than one that yields settlement, closure, or precision."[45] The differing voices need not be reconciled with the core testimony and they destabilize the character of God, who is just

---

42. Moberly, *Old Testament of the Old Testament*, 145–46.

43. Brueggemann, *Theology of the Old Testament*. For this summary, I am indebted to Ollenburger, *Old Testament Theology*, 305–21.

44. Brueggemann, *Theology*, 121.

45. Brueggemann, *Theology*, 124.

a character in the story.⁴⁶ Brueggemann allows all voices in the text to speak, shutting down none for the sake of closure or certainty. He alerts us to the need to hold in tension all voices in the text as enshrining human experiences in the quest of meaning.

Goldingay⁴⁷ examines how the narrative of Genesis expresses "the faith implied in the Old Testament or the faith that emerges from the Old Testament . . . but to reflect on it analytically, critically and constructively . . . keep[ing] closer to the Old Testament's own categories of thought . . ." He writes,

> Yet I want to write on the Old Testament without looking at it through Christian lens or even New Testament lenses . . . a statement of what we might believe about God and us if we simply use the Old Testament or if we let it provide the lenses through which we look at Jesus.⁴⁸

Nevertheless, Goldingay, following the Christian attitude, does not consider the ritual commands of Torah. Yet, he teaches us to allow the Hebrew Bible and the New Testament to mutually illumine each other.

In one of his works, Sailhamer⁴⁹ posits a prophetic "second edition" as the rewrite of the "'first edition" Mosaic Pentateuch,⁵⁰ with the purpose not to teach a life of obedience to the law given to Moses at Sinai, but to "teach its readers about faith and hope in the new covenant (Deut 30:6)."⁵¹ The "'canonical Pentateuch' in our Bible today"⁵² was written after Israel's failures, and "it was given to tell Israel that the Sinai covenant had failed. As the prophet Hosea saw, the Pentateuch is primarily not about a wedding, but a divorce." In that respect, the Pentateuch is quite close in meaning to the NT book of Galatians. According to Galatians, the Sinai covenant failed. In the same way, the Pentateuch confronts its readers with the failure of the Sinai law and the hope of a new covenant."⁵³

---

46. Paul House judges that "Brueggemann's method leaves readers with no finally trustworthy witness, jurist, jury or judge . . ." in "God's Design and Postmodernism," 38.

47. Goldingay, *Israel's Gospel*.

48. Goldingay, *Israel's Gospel*, 20–21.

49. See Sailhamer, *Meaning of the Pentateuch*; idem, *Introduction to Old Testament Theology*. I chose the more recent (and more matured?) statement of his position.

50. Sailhamer, *Meaning of the Pentateuch*, 52.

51. Sailhamer, *Meaning of the Pentateuch*, 26.

52. Sailhamer, *Meaning of the Pentateuch*, 14.

53. Sailhamer, *Meaning of the Pentateuch*, 27.

Sailhamer here appears to assimilate the Old Testament to the New Testament (however, his actual interpretation in *Pentateuch as Narrative* tends to be more sensitive to the Old Testament meaning).

In 1987, Jon Douglas Levenson wrote, "Why Jews Are Not Interested in Biblical Theology." He wrote: "To the Christian, biblical theology is concerned with Christological issues in a way that excludes the Jew and finds no parallel in Judaism."[54] Christians look for one great idea that pervades and unifies the Hebrew Bible; Jewish biblical theology, if there were one, would be piecemeal observations appended to the text and subordinate to its particularity.[55] Judaism holds Torah as prior and normative; the Prophets only applied it: "it is hard to see how a biblical theology that did not respect the doctrine of the priority and normativity of the Pentateuch could be Jewish."[56] For the church, the sacred text is word (singular) demanding to be proclaimed. Judaism sees it as internally argumentative, a problem with many facets, each of which deserves attention, hence the midrash collections always invoke *dabar aḥer*, another interpretation—there is far higher tolerance for theological polydoxy. Point is, the personal stand of Jew or Christian includes postbiblical elements: "the message of the Hebrew Bible is a function of the tradition in which it is contextualized."[57] Jewish believers read the Hebrew Bible in relation to their own traditions in Midrash, the Mishnah, and Talmud. Two decades later, Sommer could affirm, "it is safe to say that Jews are interested in biblical theology,"[58] and Sweeney that "Jewish biblical theology has established itself as an important force in the larger field of biblical studies."[59] That is, as long as one respects the distinctive Jewish hermeneutical construction of the Bible (primacy of Torah over

---

54. Levenson, "Why Jews," 295.
55. Levenson, "Why Jews," 298.
56. Levenson, "Why Jews," 299.
57. Levenson, "Why Jews," 300.
58. Sommer, "Dialogical Biblical Theology." Such biblical theology is not totalizing and comprehensive, does not seek unity in a *Mitte* (overarching idea), and does not allow the voice of redactor, canonizer, or so-called final form to suppress the voice of discrete entities within the text. It is an "unambiguously confessional enterprise" (51) in that it constructs a discussion between biblical texts and a particular postbiblical theological tradition (21).
59. Sweeney, "Jewish Biblical Theology," 314. See also Kalimi, ed., *Jewish Bible Theology*.

Prophets and Writings) and "Oral Torah which represents the fullest form of divine instruction."[60]

Vatican II's *Dei Verbum* (Dogmatic Constitution on Divine Revelation) illustrates the Catholic position. Sacred Scripture is the word of God inasmuch as "divinely revealed realities . . . have been committed to writing under the inspiration of the Holy Spirit."[61] "To compose the sacred books, God chose certain men who, all the while he employed them in this task, made full use of their own faculties and powers so that, though he acted in them and by them, it was as true authors that they consigned to writing whatever he wanted written, and no more."[62] On the truth of Scripture, Vatican II concluded: "therefore, since everything asserted by the inspired authors or sacred writers must be held to be asserted by the Holy Spirit, it follows that the books of Scripture must be acknowledged as teaching solidly, faithfully and without error that truth which God wanted put into sacred writings for the sake of salvation."[63] For the relation of the Old Testament to the New, the Church cites St. Augustine: "*Novum Testamentum in Vetere latet, et in Novo Vetus patet.*"[64] However, the Church also teaches that the books of the Old Testament "are divinely inspired and retain a permanent value, for the Old Covenant has never been revoked."[65] The relationship is thus reciprocal: "the New Testament demands to be read in the light of the Old, but it also invites a 're-reading' of the Old in the light of the Jesus Christ (cf. Luke 24:45)."[66]

The Approach of This Commentary

It is clear from the foregoing that the diversity of approaches is not just between Jewish and Christian, but also among Christians themselves.

---

60. Sweeney, "Jewish Biblical Theology," 324.

61. Vatican II, *Dei Verbum*, no. 11.

62. *Catechism*, 106; Vatican II, *Dei Verbum*, no. 11.

63. Vatican II, *Dei Verbum*, no. 11.

64. Augustine, *Quaestiones in Heptateuchum*, 2, 73: The New Testament lies hidden in the Old, in the New the Old Testament is unveiled.

65. *Catechism*, 121.

66. Pontifical Biblical Commission, *Jewish People and Their Sacred Scriptures*, no. 19. This, even though the light of the events of Easter lends to certain texts of the Old Testament "a fullness of meaning previously unimaginable," even "relativizing very considerably its value as a system of salvation" Pontifical Biblical Commission, *Interpretation of the Bible*, III A. 2, pp. 88–92.

This commentary interprets the narratives of Genesis with a special eye on their theological and spiritual import following the Catholic canon.[67] It focuses specially on the relationship between the Testaments.

Belief in the inspiration and truth of Scripture makes some readers gloss over, or not take account of, difficulties and inconsistencies in the text. I am convinced that "When dealing with a topic like the inspiration of Scripture, it is better to begin with the text as it is and with facts that ground it in the human experience of the authors. We need also factor in the fact that the Bible contains variant forms of the text and some obscure passages that defy interpretation."[68] I draw attention to inconsistencies and even contradictions in the text, making it clear that inspiration did not necessarily bypass the normal processes of composition.

Pope Benedict XVI encouraged interpreters not to gloss over the "dark passages" of the Bible.

> Revelation is suited to the cultural and moral level of distant times and thus describes facts and customs, such as cheating and trickery, and acts of violence and massacre, without explicitly denouncing the immorality of such things. This can be explained by the historical context, yet it can cause the modern reader to be taken aback, especially if he or she fails to take account of the many "dark" deeds carried out down the centuries, and also in our own day.[69]

Recently, the Pontifical Biblical Commission[70] considered historical, ethical, and social problems in Scripture. On the relation of the Testaments, it affirms Christ as the center that sheds light on the whole of Scripture (no. 147). It insists on a canonical reading that evaluates passages in their relationship to the fullness of revelation in the person and work of Jesus (no. 135). Unfortunately, in my judgment, some of the applications made of this principle seem to "reconfigure the multiple witnesses of Scripture into some sort of coherent message,"[71] when "one of the characteristics of the Bible is precisely the absence of a sense of systematization and the presence . . . of things held in dynamic tension."[72]

---

67. I deal with the deuterocanonical books sometimes in the exegesis section, sometimes in the "Tradition" section.
68. Okoye, *Scripture in the Church*, 49.
69. Benedict XVI, *Verbum Domini*, no. 42.
70. Pontifical Biblical Commission, *Inspiration and Truth*, nos. 104–36.
71. Okoye, "PBC, the Old Testament," 77 (citing Davies, *Immoral Bible*, 94).
72. Pontifical Biblical Commission, *Interpretation of the Bible*, 90.

It must be recognized that the final form "as a whole does not include just one meaning level, but more levels next to and in one another."[73] And thus, "every layer of interpretation in the biblical materials must be sought out and recognized by the church as basis for speaking to the contemporary world. We cannot be satisfied with interpreting the biblical books in their present shape."[74]

For the theological meaning, some scholars prioritize the narrator—the narrator's statements, evaluations, silences, and manner of crafting the story. The biblical narrator accredits God with complete trustworthiness, so some authors argue that "both God and the narrator must be trustworthy and hence are the benchmark of trustworthiness for all other personae."[75] Some scholars even speak of the narrator's knowledge as divine in origin. That is, it is unlimited in extent and compels with divine authority: the biblical narrator "invests his dramatizations with the authority of an omniscience equivalent to God's own ... this omniscience itself ultimately goes back to God..."[76] However, the question is whether there is just one consistent narrator and whether his voice is but one of several.

> When Samuel-Kings is read alongside Chronicles, where is the reliable narrator? Where for that matter is the reliable narrator of the four Gospels? Or, to put it another way: Who among the four narrators is reliable? What *did* Jesus say?[77]

Narration is sometimes in tension with narration. For example, biblical images of God are not unitary. Gen 1:26 has God say, "let us create human beings in our image, after *our likeness*"; in Gen 3:22, God says, "See! The man has become *like one of us* . . ." The evaluation of human likeness to God differs in the two: in one, likeness to God is willed and established by God himself; in the other, it appears as something God looks askance at.[78] The image of the national God of Israel (Deuteronomy)

---

73. Carr, *Reading the Fractures of Genesis*, 7. As regards the Pentateuch, Carr concludes that it is as yet unproven that it was subjected to a systematic final redaction of the kind posited in some theories of canonical criticism.

74. Fretheim, "Jacob Traditions," 436.

75. Amit, *Reading Biblical Narratives*, 95.

76. Sternberg, *Poetics of Biblical Narrative*, 90.

77. Gunn, "New Directions," 71.

78. Some scholars detect here the differing images of God in P (Genesis 1) and J (Genesis 2–3).

varies somewhat from that of the unique and universal God and Creator of the world (Second Isaiah, Genesis 1). The biblical text contains millennia of human experiences of the Ineffable which it attempts to express in words; the diversity of times and contexts has led to a diversity of conceptualizations and even some polemics of text against text. The Hebrew Bible itself being polyphonic,[79] the editing allowed diverse voices across time to have their say, thus recording the people of God's diverse experiences of God and the world. Far from shying away from textual corruptions or inconsistencies in the text or trying to harmonize them forcefully, I allow the various voices their say, and I seek to understand each within its own context. The reader thus gains a better understanding of the realities of the text and a more nuanced view of Scripture as "word of God in the words of humankind." Christians are convinced that all this diversity did not devolve into chaos, rather God's Spirit internally guided the process unto God's final Word in Christ.

Because the texts of the Hebrew Scriptures "were recognized by the communities of the Former Covenant and by those of the apostolic age as the genuine expression of the common faith,"[80]

> Christians can and ought to admit that the Jewish reading of the Bible is a possible one, in continuity with the Jewish Sacred Scriptures from the Second Temple period, a reading analogous to the Christian reading which developed in parallel fashion. Both readings are bound up with the vision of their respective faiths, of which the readings are the result and expression. Consequently, both are irreducible.[81]

A promise-fulfillment pattern must allow the Old Testament room for fulfillment according to its particular logic, even if the New Testament discovers an additional meaning. Though the internal dynamism of the Old Testament finds its goal in Jesus, yet "this is a retrospective perception whose point of departure is not in the text as such, but in the events of the New Testaments proclaimed by the apostolic preaching."[82] So, "On

---

79. Amit, *Hidden Polemics*, xi: "this canon is by its nature polyphonic, and that the multiplicity of voices found therein is a function of the circumstances of its composition and shaping."

80. Pontifical Biblical Commission, *Interpretation of the Bible*, p. 91.

81. Pontifical Biblical Commission, *Jewish People and Their Sacred Scriptures*, no. 22.

82. Pontifical Biblical Commission, *Jewish People and Their Sacred Scriptures*, no. 21. See also the theme of promise and fulfillment in nos. 54-65 which consider the

the one hand, the New Testament demands to be read in the light of the Old, but it also invites a 're-reading' of the Old in the light of Jesus Christ (cf. Luke 24:45)."[83] Christians may "know the rest of the story," but "can come to a deeper appreciation of God's providential plan by attending to its intricate windings from its early stages with 'fresh eyes.' [thus] reading them 'both as Hebrew Scriptures and as the Old Testament.'"[84] The Christian meaning is a *parallel*, not a substitute, meaning.

Each chapter has thus two sections:

Commentary: the "plain meaning" or "literal sense" (not to be confused with literalistic sense).

Tradition: Jewish and Christian doctrine read out of the text.

I examine the early Jewish and Christian hermeneutics of the Old Testament. Patristic and rabbinic interpretations pinpoint how, in a particular age, the differing traditions negotiated the ancient text on behalf of godly living in relation to the issues of their time. Their interpretations model theological exegesis, without imposing their particular points of view on our modern age.[85] Rather, looking backwards and guided by them, we more easily navigate theological issues that the text raises for our context, even if our responses come from today's resources, knowledge, and faith.

A Common Treasure

The Old Testament itself embodies various interpretive processes. For example, Deuteronomy adapts Exodus–Numbers to the new conditions of life in the land; Chronicles reinterprets Kings. The Old Testament employed *typological* reading of Israel's history in which past events

---

themes of descent from Abraham, the Promised Land, the eternal and final salvation of Israel, the reign of God, and the son and successor of David. The conclusion (no. 64) highlights the elements of continuity, discontinuity/rupture, and progression.

83. Pontifical Biblical Commission, *Jewish People and Their Sacred Scriptures*, no. 19.

84. Kurz, "Patristic Interpretation of Scripture," 48–49.

85. Sommer, "Dialogical Biblical Theology," 21 explains "dialogical biblical theology" as follows: "dialogical biblical theology would attempt to construct a discussion between biblical texts and a particular postbiblical theological tradition." The goal is illuminating what the Bible invites us to attend to and examining how the various traditions pick up that invitation (43).

foreshadowed those to come. For example, Deutero-Isaiah speaks of the "New Exodus," and Esther makes the salvation of the Jews sound like one of the great events of the past, especially the story of Joseph in Pharaoh's court.[86]

Till about mid-second century CE, "Scripture" for synagogue and church meant mostly the Old Testament/Hebrew Scriptures. Judean Jews read it in Hebrew; Alexandrian Jews and the early church read it in Greek (the Greek translation, called the Septuagint, has seven books more than the Hebrew text, and also has additions to parts of some books). Jewish and early Christian hermeneutics were similar, though for Christians the real significance of the Old Testament was its witness to Christ. Both traditions allowed diverse currents of interpretation as long as orthodoxy was maintained.

With the growth of Christianity, the text of the Old Testament became the site of debate between Christians and Jews (for example, Justin Martyr and Trypho in Justin's *Dialogue with Trypho*). Especially when the Roman Empire became Christian (mid-fourth century), the Christian christological use of certain texts led the rabbis to "pre-emptive exegesis,"[87] that is, exegesis that implicitly rules out the Christian interpretation, rather than openly attacking it.

Detecting the points of emphasis or conflict in Jewish-Christian relations illumines each group's exegetical maneuvers. Confronting exegetical arguments by the "*minim*" (heretics, mainly Jewish Christians) and the Gnostics, Jews and Christians sometimes rejected paths of interpretation earlier seen as plausible. In dialogue with Jews, the church embraced allegory and typology as more easily enabling christological exegesis. Origen often characterized the literal sense of the Old Testament as "Jewish" or "Judaic." Yet, responding to Gnostic interpreters, the church sometimes shifted from allegory to the literal sense. Patristic exegesis was not monolithic; the fathers sometimes differed in their interpretation. Ambrose of Milan could still hold, with Justin Martyr, that the visitors of Genesis 18 were the Lord and two attending angels and that the three visitors and the three measures of flour symbolized God as Trinity.[88] Augustine at first held of the three that "it is not to be doubted were angels, although some think that one of them was Christ and assert

---

86. Cf. Kugel and Greer, *Early Biblical Interpretation*, 46, 47.
87. See Alexander, "Pre-Emptive Exegesis."
88. Ambrose, *On Abraham* 1.35, 33.

that he was visible before he put on flesh."[89] In face of the Arian crisis, he rejected this and argued for a Trinitarian interpretation (*On the Trinity*; see "Tradition" at Genesis 18–19).

Early Jewish Interpretation of the Old Testament

Jewish exegetes read the text closely and sought to fill in the gaps and/or reconcile contradictions. The stories were retold and expanded, the text was made to speak to changing situations of God's people, and new beliefs (for example, the resurrection of the dead) were integrated as outworkings of particular texts. The following early Jewish exegetical works are referenced in this commentary.

> The *Book of Jubilees* (second century BCE) retells the biblical story, taking the Mosaic Law for granted and deriving binding norms of behavior from the narrative. It stops in the early chapters of Exodus. The Ethiopian Orthodox Church considers it canonical.
>
> Qumran *Genesis Apocryphon* and others. The Qumran sectarians developed what is called *pesher*, reading Scripture as if a detailed prophecy of the events of their own time and interpreting it in the light of these events. This is very similar to what happens in the Gospels, especially in Matthew, who several times says, "this happened in order to fulfill what was said in . . ."
>
> Some works of Philo of Alexandria (20 BCE–40 CE). He used *allegory* to assimilate the Bible and Greek thinking.
>
> The works of Josephus (37/38–100 CE), especially the *Jewish Antiquities*, a history of the Jews which he prefaced with an interpretive paraphrase of the biblical account.
>
> The *Testament of the Twelve Patriarchs*. Because of the debate about whether it was originally Christian or Jewish, this work features little in this commentary.
>
> The *Mishnah* and *Tosephta* (200 CE) codified the system of laws based on traditional rabbinic interpretation. Commentaries on these produced the volumes of the Jerusalem *Talmud* (400 CE) and the

---

89. Augustine, *City of God* 16.29, in ACCS 2:61. Decisive for Augustine was Heb 13:2: "for through [hospitality] some have unknowingly entertained angels."

Babylonian *Talmud* (600 CE). These legal texts appear little in this commentary.

The *Targums* are Aramaic translations of the Hebrew Bible. They were simultaneous translations during the liturgy for a populace no longer comfortable with biblical Hebrew. They were eventually written down, some before the Christian era (as the Qumran fragments of the Targum on Leviticus and Job attest). The following are the four Targums on Genesis.

Targum Onkelos is the official targum of Babylonian Jewry (originated early second century CE in Palestine, but standardized in Babylon in the third century).

Palestinian *Targum Neofiti 1* (discovered in the Vatican Library in 1956) is so-called because it came from a college for neophytes, converts from Judaism, in Rome in the sixteenth century.

Targum Pseudo-Jonathan, a Targum with a pre-70 CE strand, revised not before the third century, and with additions some of which are post-Talmudic and even after the Muslim conquest.[90]

The *Fragmentary Targum*. This is rarely referenced since it mostly gives variants to the three above.

Jewish Midrash on Genesis is found in the following.

Midrash Rabbah: Genesis, edited by Harry Freedman and Maurice Simon (London: Soncino, 1977). *Genesis Rabbah* is a Palestinian compilation of about 400 CE, after Christianity had become the dominant political power. It is contemporary with Augustine, Jerome, Eusebius, and John Chrysostom. It collects earlier rabbinic interpretive activity, and often records diverse interpretations. Some interpretations consciously counter Christian exegesis of the Old Testament, some of which can be traced to early fathers of the church, especially Justin Martyr and Origen.[91]

Pentateuch: With Targum Onkelos, Haphtaroth and Rashi's Commentary, vol. 1, *Genesis*, translated by M. Rosenbaum and A. M. Silbermann (New York: Hebrew, 1935). Rashi (Rabbi Solomon Yitzhaqi, 1040–1105 CE) is the classical Jewish medieval commentator.

---

90. Okoye, "Genesis 1–11," 41–45. For example, it mentions the wife and daughter of Mohammed, Adisha, and Fatima at Gen 21:21.

91. Niehoff, "Circumcision as a Marker of Identity," 115.

Important secondary material in the study of rabbinic exegesis used in this commentary are the following.

James L. Kugel, *Traditions of the Bible: A Guide to the Bible as It Was at the Start of the Common Era* (Cambridge, MA: Harvard University Press, 1999) is a handy compilation of excerpts of rabbinic and patristic exegesis, with brief contexts and illuminating commentary. His *The Bible as It Was* (1997) is an abbreviated edition of the former.

Jacob Neusner, *The Theological Foundations of Rabbinic Midrash* (New York: University of America Press, 2006). He claims that his book "is the first systematic inquiry into the midrash documents in quest of the interiorities, the pervasive logic, that characterize and sustain a system."[92] Neusner is both prolific and perceptive, however, he may have oversystematized rabbinic exegesis, downplaying the general atomistic character of Midrash.

As concerns *Genesis Rabbah*, two other Neusner books provide good initiation: *Genesis and Judaism: The Perspective of Genesis Rabbah. An Analytical Anthology* (Atlanta: Scholars, 1985); and *A Theological Commentary to the Midrash*, vol. 2, *Genesis Rabbah* (Lanham, MD: University Press of America, 2001).

The title "rabbi" appeared in the first-century CE, later lending its name to what we call Rabbinic Judaism. By the first century CE, the Pharisees developed a body of interpretations called *"oral torah"* beside the *"written torah"*—both considered handed down from Moses. Because Scripture is regarded as its own best interpreter, and all Scripture seen as interrelated, the rabbis assimilated terms and phrases in various parts of the Bible. They applied two broad hermeneutic processes: *peshat* (the literal sense) and *derash* (deeper and multiple senses). They adduced multiple principles of interpretation, for example, that "Torah speaks in the language of humans," that is, words need be understood according to the linguistic usage of the time.

> Greek influence led to the elaboration of seven rules of interpretation (*middot*) of Hillel (turn of the Common Era), developed into thirteen rules by R. Ishmael (mid-second century CE). An example is *gezerah shavah*, that is, inference from analogous texts. Tradition arose that "no one may infer by *gezerah shavah* on his own authority," hence one must base such on authoritative

---

92. Neusner, *Theological Foundations*, xiv.

tradition. Jewish *midrash* focuses on conduct: the text is used to derive rules for conduct (*halakah*), and aspects of the narrative are freely developed for edification (*haggadah*). Midrash is often atomistic, inferring meanings from similar sounding words, often with little regard for the immediate context (similar to the Christian use of allegory, especially of the Alexandrian type).

Early Christian Hermeneutics of the Old Testament

The earliest Christian interpretation of Scripture was in the context of liturgy and catechesis—the sacred text as basis for preaching the gospel, formation in the faith, and instructing people for Christian living. The text availed also for theology and spirituality, and for disputes with Jews and heretics. As already mentioned, Jews and Christians shared similar hermeneutical processes, but the goals differed. Christians used the Old Testament to preach Christ and the Christian faith. The emerging New Testament treated the Old Testament as a prophecy fulfilled in the event of Jesus Christ. For Paul, "the law was our disciplinarian [*paidagōgos*] unto Christ, that we might be justified by faith" (Gal 3:24). He rejected the force of much of its legislation for his Gentile converts.

> New Testament texts found some details of the life of Jesus in the Old Testament, for example, the birth in Bethlehem. They sometimes wove the wording of the Old Testament into the story of Jesus; for example, Mark 15:24 (they divided his clothes) is in John 19:24 merely a quotation of Ps 22:18. They used *typology* to match persons and events in the two Testaments. For example, the crossing of the Red Sea became a type of Christ's victory, also of Christian baptism.[93] The Letter to the Hebrews sees the Old Testament as a shadow of the New.

The fathers memorized large portions of Scripture[94] and compared text with text on the premise that Scripture is best explained from Scripture. They read Scripture within the church. For them, the divine intention of Scripture was Christ, so Scripture serves for the development of Christology and Christian dogma.

---

93. Across the Red Sea Israel gained deliverance and was free from the shackles of slavery; across the waters of baptism the neophyte gained salvation and the freedom of the children of God.

94. To be noted is that their text was generally the Greek Old Testament (Septuagint, abbreviated LXX, the Latin siglum for seventy).

Marcion (c. 100–160 CE) rejected the entire Old Testament; in the New Testament, he selected only ten letters of Paul and a sanitized Luke. For Gnostics, the creator and god of the Old Testament was the demiurge, a lower god, who differed from the God of Jesus Christ. Gnostics added their secret works to the Bible and employed allegory as the method of interpretation. They initiated the commentary genre; in fact, the earliest Christian commentary was a Gnostic work: the Valentinian Heracleon's *Commentary on John's Gospel*, fragments of which are preserved in Origen's *Commentary on John*. The dual crisis of Marcion and the Gnostics forced the definition of the canon of the New Testament. It also led to greater attention to context, insistence on the unity of the Old and New Testaments, and a brief flight from allegory to the literal sense.

Justin Martyr's (100–165 CE) *Dialogue with Trypho* treated every part of the Old Testament as prophecy of Christ. Wherever God appeared in human form in the Old Testament, it was the Logos incarnate who appeared.

Irenaeus of Lyons (c. 125–202 CE) was the first to use the expression "New Testament" (*Against Heresies* 4.9.1). When the Arians enlisted the plain and grammatical meaning of the text in their arguments against Catholics, the wider church was led to rediscover analogy (language about God is symbolic). It developed the criterion of the *"rule of faith"* (first in Irenaeus).

Origen (c. 185–254) established Christian biblical hermeneutics as a real science (cf. *First Principles* 4.1–3). In *Against Celsus* 6.77, he compared the letter of the sacred text to the human body assumed by Christ, an envelope which encloses the divine Logos. The literal meaning is for him not the ultimate goal of Scripture, but only an educative starting point (*First Principles* 1, praef 3). That Scripture has a deeper spiritual sense over and above the literal sense is for him an article of faith: all Scripture has a spiritual sense, but not all have a literal sense.[95] He consistently worked with three senses of Scripture: the *literal*, the *moral*, and the *spiritual-mystical*.[96] Origen sometimes paid great attention to the

---

95. He gave the example of the Lord God planting a garden in Eden (*De Princ* 4, 3:5).

96. Origen's three senses of Scripture stood till John Cassian (360–432) writing for his monks distinguished historical from spiritual understanding (allegory), dividing allegory into three: *tropologia* (moral), *allegoria* (typology), and *anagoge* (from earthly to heavenly)—"as far as we know, this is the first instance of a fourfold distinction of the sense of Scripture, rather than three." Simonetti, *Biblical Interpretation*, 119.

literal sense, for example, for the *Song of Songs*, he first worked through the literal sense before the spiritual sense. He developed the *Hexapla* (compares the text in six columns) in which he tried to establish the correct text of Scripture. To counter the excessive allegorization of the Gnostics, he insisted that spiritual interpretation be connected with the literal sense and confirmed by other Scripture passages (*First Principles*, 4, 2:9; 4, 3:4, 5).

In the late third and early fourth centuries, two schools of Christian interpretation vied with each other: the allegorizing Alexandrian school, the icon of which was Origen, and the literalizing Antiochene school, of which the icon was Theodore, bishop of Mopsuestia (350–428).

Saint Jerome (347–420) prepared a fresh translation of the Old Testament directly from the Hebrew, the Vulgate (*vulgata* = commonly used). At first a disciple of Origen, he increasingly insisted on the literal sense.

Saint Augustine (354–430), a Latin rhetorician with no knowledge of Hebrew and who read Greek with difficulty, insisted that exegesis has only one task: to promote love (of God and neighbor) and lead to the enjoyment of God. As criteria for reducing ambiguity and discerning possible multiple senses, he used the analogy of Scripture, the analogy of faith, and the goal of love. Like Jerome, Augustine began interpretation as an Origenist, but later tempered the use of allegory for the greater use of the literal sense.

Saint Ambrose of Milan (333–397) was the teacher of St. Augustine. He remained close to the type of allegorical interpretation practiced by Philo and Origen.

> The patristic use of the term "allegory" was not consistent. The Greek fathers generally used two terms: *historia* (the literal sense) and *theoria* (deeper sense, allegory). But allegory can also be a division of *theoria* (as in note 93 above). Besides, allegory and typology are not synonyms. Typology is defined as "a prefiguration in a different stage of redemptive history that indicates the outline or essential features of the future reality and that loses its own significance when that reality appears."[97] The correspondence is seen to be historical, theological, in essential features (not accidentals), and divinely ordained. Allegory is correspondence between similar words understood as inspired symbols but removed from a historical context.[98]

---

97. Goppelt, *Typos*, 177.
98. Cf. VanMaaren, "Adam-Christ Typology in Paul," 277.

I have used the following easily accessible English translations or excerpts of the patristic exegesis of East and West.

The Fathers of the Church series, published by the Catholic University of America Press (now in the second revised edition).

Ancient Christian Commentary on Scripture: *Genesis 1–11*, edited by Andrew Louth; *Genesis 12–50*, edited by Mark Sheridan (Downers Grove, IL: InterVarsity, 2001).

William A. Jurgens, *The Faith of the Early Fathers*, 3 volumes (Collegeville, MN: Liturgical, 1970, 1979).

Christian Classics Ethereal Library at http://www.ccel.org/ccel/schaff/anf04.toc.html.

BiblIndex: Index of Biblical Quotations in Early Christian Literature at http://www.biblindex.info/. The material has been published in seven books in French (Paris: Éditions du Centre national de la recherche scientifique, 1975–1982) at reasonable prices.

Patristic Bible Commentary: Genesis at https://sites.google.com/site/aquinasstudybible/home/genesis.

Michael Graves's *The Inspiration and Interpretation of Scripture: What the Early Church Can Teach Us* is a useful discussion of how to use patristic exegesis today. He identified twenty principles of patristic exegesis; for example: Scripture is the supreme authority in Christian belief and practice; Scripture has multiple senses; divine illumination is required for biblical interpretation; Scripture's teaching is internally consistent; and Scripture's teaching must be worthy of God. For each of the twenty, he identifies how current exegesis might be in continuity or necessarily in discontinuity from patristic exegesis.[99] An example is the patristic (and rabbinic) belief that every detail of Scripture is meaningful[100] or that Scripture solves every problem we might put to it.[101]

---

99. "Some notions associated with inspiration in antiquity are no longer fully plausible from a modern standpoint." Graves, *Inspiration and Interpretation*, 131.

100. Graves, *Inspiration and Interpretation*, 22–26.

101. Graves, *Inspiration and Interpretation*, 26–32.

Translation Matters

Narrative criticism operates best on the original Hebrew text. Translation hampers narrative art in that it renders invisible much of the language games in the original through which the text produces some of its rhetorical effect. I will draw attention here and there to important language games, but in transliteration.

Translators often face the dilemma of choice between fields of meaning. They determine what is the global message of a section of the text and align their translations to this point of view. Look carefully at these translations of Gen 1:2.

> And a wind from God sweeping over the water (TNK)
>
> While a wind from God swept over the face of the waters (NRSV)
>
> and a mighty wind sweeping over the waters (NABRE)
>
> With a divine wind sweeping over the waters (NJB)
>
> And the spirit of God hovered over the surface of the water (REB)
>
> And the Spirit of God was hovering over the waters (NIV)

The original is *ruaḥ 'elohîm*. *Ruaḥ* can mean wind, breath, spirit. *'Elohīm* means God, or the plural, gods, but can used to refer to the height or grandeur of something (hence "mighty" wind, NABRE; "divine" wind; NJB makes out the wind as animate divine element). While "spirit of God" (REB) is ambiguous, "Spirit of God" (NIV) definitely Christianizes the text and understands it as expressing an action of the Holy Spirit. The root of the verb *meraḥephet* occurs again only in Deut 32:11, where it refers to an eagle hovering over its nest (hence REB and NIV). The other translations borrowed the analogy of Gen 8:1, where "God made a wind sweep [*ya'abar ruaḥ*—caused the wind to cross] over the earth, and the waters [of the flood] began to subside."

Now and then I refer to the original Hebrew to illumine the possible theological or moral fiber of a text. For it happens that a choice among apparent synonyms can give a slant to the meaning. Fokkelman[102] gives the example of 1 Sam 15:11.

> Samuel was *distressed* and he entreated the LORD all night long. (TNK)
>
> Samuel was *troubled*, and he cried out to the LORD all that night. (NIV)
>
> Samuel was *angry*; and he cried out to the LORD all night. (NRSV)

---

102. Fokkelman, *Reading Biblical Narrative*, 60.

The original is "*angry*"; the prophet was angry that at a stroke God was wiping out the entire project for which he worked so hard. The translation *distressed/troubled* aligns the prophet's feelings towards Saul; that of *angry* leaves open the possibility that prophet and God were not fully in sync and that the prophet may have had his own agenda in the matter.

Take Gen 6:6: "the Lord regretted making human beings on the earth, and his heart was grieved." Did he not foresee what would happen? Was he fickle? Can God change? Greek philosophy holds God immutable. The Greek translation (Septuagint) dissimulates the problem: "then God considered [*enethumēthē*] that he had made humankind on the earth, and he thought over it [*dienoēthē*]."

Transliteration Matters

It can thus be valuable in places to check the translation against other standard English and/or ancient versions. I dispense with Hebrew letters and use only transliteration when it is necessary to draw attention to features of the biblical text. The Bible text used is generally NABRE (New American Bible, Revised Edition, 2011); other versions are indicated when used. Occasionally I use my own translation.

Recurring Themes Propel the Story of Genesis

The story of Genesis is divided into four cycles: Primeval History (1–11), Abraham Cycle (12:1—25:18), Jacob Cycle (25:19—36:43), and Joseph Novella (37–50).

Certain recurring themes propel the story. In the first place, genealogies. Eleven *toledôt* phrases—"these are the descendants of" (5:1; 10:1; 11:10; 25:12; 36:1, 9) or "this is the story of" (2:4; 6:9; 11:27; 25:29; 37:2)—bind the text into a unity. The human race multiplies in segments from *Adam* till all families are wiped out in the flood except for Noah and his family. Noah is a new beginning. From *Noah* and his three sons, Shem, Ham, and Japheth, the earth is populated, seventy nations and peoples, God having scattered them after the incidence of the City and Tower (Genesis 11). The genealogy picks up the line of Shem and traces it through Terah to *Abram*, who becomes a sort of new beginning of the works of God. Abraham fathered Ishmael and Isaac; the younger Isaac is chosen. Isaac fathered Esau and Jacob; again the younger Jacob is chosen and his children become the twelve tribes of Israel.

Another unitive feature are the promises to the patriarchs—of blessing, descendants/great nation, land, political supremacy. Then there is the offer of covenant relationship. And all through, Israel is reflecting on her election, what it means to be blessed by God, and what relationship this dictates in relation to the nations and peoples of the earth. In short, the destiny of Israel vis-à-vis God and the rest of God's creation.

Setting

I place in italics the text of the Scripture being commented upon; other texts of Scripture are in quotation marks. That interpretation not obscure the story line, I have indented and placed in smaller print more complex aspects of exegesis. For some chapters, I have isolated these in an indented section marked as "Further Reflections." Besides the references, I have also placed in the footnotes discussion of the type useful for advanced readers.

CHAPTER 2

Genesis 12

The LORD Calls Abram Forth to Be Blessing for All Families

> Blessing and curse have been wrestling for dominance in the world . . . God declares that blessing will [win], first in Abram's family, but then through Abram's family in the wider world . . . YHWH's direct intent is blessing.[1]

Links with the Primeval History

TWO FEATURES MARK the literary structure of Genesis: *toledot* (begettings, genealogy) and *promise* texts. Eleven *toledot* phrases ("these are the descendants of," sometimes "this is the story of") plot "a genealogy of the world, which moves toward the teleological focus of the genealogy, the people of Israel."[2] Neighboring nations are shown in varying degrees of propinquity to Israel. The promise texts, which many scholars consider late, link the patriarchs, Abraham, Isaac, and Jacob; the only promise in the Joseph cycle is made to Jacob (Gen 46:3–4). The Genesis narrative unfolds in four sections: the Primeval History, the Abraham Cycle, the Jacob Cycle, and the Joseph Novella.

The Primeval History (Genesis 1–11)[3] posits three beginnings of humanity—Adam, Noah, and Abraham—each separated by ten

---

1. Goldingay, *Israel's Gospel*, 214.
2. Hendel, "Historical Context," 77.
3. See Okoye, *Genesis 1–11*.

generations. In *Adam*, relationship with the LORD[4] came to grief in a curse on the ground (Gen 3:17; 4:11). Adam's descendants caused divine regret and heartbreak; wickedness so increased on earth that the earth was "corrupt in the view of God and full of lawlessness" (Gen 6:11). For "every desire that their heart conceived was always nothing but evil" (Gen 6:11). The LORD singled out Noah: "Noah found favor with the LORD . . . Noah was a righteous man and blameless in his generation. Noah walked with God" (Gen 6:8–9). Except for Noah and the animals with him in the ark, God wiped out all living beings from the whole earth. After the flood, Noah's sacrifice assuaged the LORD's heart; he said, "never again will I curse the ground because of human beings, since the desires of the human heart are evil from youth; nor will I ever again strike down every living being, as I have done" (Gen 8:21). "The very reason for the flood (Gen 6:5) is now given for the promise of never again!"[5] The LORD commits to an imperfect world: "in spite of the motivation for a flood remaining present, God binds himself to take another course of action."[6] The descendants of Noah multiplied. They too came to grief at the building of the city and tower (Gen 11:1–9). The Lord scattered them from there over all the earth and they stopped building the city (Gen 11:8). Just as in the case of Noah, so now the Lord focused on a single person—*Abram*, ancestor of Israel.

The narrator depicts Abram's origins from peoples in Mesopotamia. The genealogical focus on the nations in Genesis 10–11 narrows down to the *toledot* of Shem[7] (Gen 11:10), "ancestor of all the children of Eber"[8] (Gen 10:21). Terah, father of Abram, a descendant of Eber, hailed from Ur of the Chaldeans (Gen 11:28).[9]

---

4. In biblical verses, "God" translates the Hebrew *Elohim*, "the LORD" translates the Hebrew *YHWH*. Source critics see in these names of God signals for the Yahwist and the Elohist writers in Genesis and the early part of Exodus. Narrative criticism may attend to sources where they seem to reveal intentionalities underlying the text.

5. Okoye, *Genesis 1–11*, 105. Hendel, "Historical Context," 76 put it this way: "YHWH's motivations draw together the destructive force of Enlil and the compassion of Enki . . . By this monotheistic revision of the older story, where one God now plays the roles of cosmic destroyer and wise savior, the J story yields a complex concept of God, who balances, sometimes precariously, the competing imperatives of justice and compassion."

6. Clines, "Theology of the Flood Narrative," 139–40.

7. The term Semite derives from this name.

8. The term Hebrew (*'ivrî*) possibly derives from the name Eber (*'ēver*).

9. An anachronism. The region was not so called till the Neo-Babylonian Era,

This agrees with Gen 15:7, where the LORD brought Abram from Ur of the Chaldeans. However, other traditions place the ancestral homeland in Haran. When Abraham asked his servant to "go to my own land and to my relatives to get a wife for my son Isaac" (Gen 24:4), he went to Haran.[10]

The editor harmonizes the two traditions by making them two different stages of a journey: "Terah took his son Abram, his grandson Lot . . . and his daughter-in-law Sarai, the wife of his son Abram, and brought them out of Ur of the Chaldeans, to go to the land of Canaan. But when they reached Haran, they settled there." The term *yashab* (settle down), not *gûr* (sojourn), implies permanent residence.

The narrator introduces an important detail of the plot: "Sarai was barren; she had no child." Most of the matriarchs of Israel were barren. Israel was like a fresh creation by God. Brueggemann reflects on this metaphor of barrenness: "barrenness is the way of human history. It is an effective metaphor for human hopelessness. There is no foreseeable future . . . this God speaks his powerful word directly into a situation of barrenness."[11]

The Abraham Cycle

In Gen 12:1–4a, a rather late theological introduction from different sources, the editor created a link between the Primeval History and the rest of the story. The Abraham Cycle (Gen 11:27—25:18)[12] narrates YHWH's call of Abram and the vicissitudes of YHWH's promise of an heir to parents past the age. Various obstacles blocking the fulfillment of this promise all give way to the persistent fidelity of YHWH. At last, at Gen 25:5, "Abraham gave everything that he owned to his son Isaac," having

---

late seventh to sixth century BCE. Hendel, "Historical Context," 62 comments that P makes Babylon where the Judean exiles were Abram's birthplace, hence the exiled Judeans' ancestral home.

10. For J, the patriarchal home was Haran, for P, Ur of the Chaldeans. The P editor tried to harmonize the two at Gen 11:28. P makes Babylon, where the Judean exiles were, Abram's birthplace: "the exile is in this sense a homecoming. At the same time, it is a home that Abram left, on God's command, in his journey to the Promised Land." Hendel, "Historical Context," 62.

11. Brueggemann, *Genesis*, 116–17.

12. The synagogue seder, *lek leka*, begins at Gen 12:1, highlighting the newness of God's word breaking through.

given gifts to the other sons and sent them off eastward, away from his son Isaac, left in secure possession of Canaan.

The "memory" of Abraham particularly enshrines the gratuitousness of God's choice of Israel (see "Further Reflections" below). However, call invites response; it is meant to transform the one called, it carries obligations towards the one calling.[13] The tradition accordingly notes a first act of obedience at Gen 12:4a, "Abram went as the LORD directed him"; it will narrate the supreme test of his obedience at Genesis 22.

Vocation and Blessing, 12:1-4

Blessing and curse have been wrestling for dominance in the world . . . God declares that blessing will [win], first in Abram's family, but then through Abram's family in the wider world . . . YHWH's direct intent is blessing.[14] The concept of blessing links together Abraham-Isaac-Jacob, each with a blessing for the whole of humanity.[15] This unit gathers together elements of the divine promises scattered throughout Genesis. The promises function to "give support and hope to exiles and later Jewish audiences after the loss of their national existence and the attendant threats to their religious and ethnical identity."[16]

The LORD said to Abram.

The call of Abram sounds like a bolt from the blue. The narrator has said nothing of any prior relationship with YHWH nor of Abram's righteousness, as he did in the case of Noah. The reader is entitled to ask, "Why Abram?" How did Abram discern this voice addressing him for the first time? How do we discern the voice of God?[17]

---

13. See Ben Zvi, "Memory of Abraham," 35.
14. Goldingay, *Israel's Gospel*, 214.
15. Rendtorff, *Problem of the Process*, 76. The promises are repeated at 13:14-17; 15:1-7, 18; 17:1-22; 18:9-19; 22:15-18; 26:4-5 (Isaac); 27:29; 28:14-15; 46:2-4 (Jacob)—see also Num 24:9 (Balaam); Isa 19:24-25 (Egypt and Assyria included in the blessing). They are never transmitted to Joseph. In the current southern shape of the text, though Joseph once ruled, the rule belongs to Judah (Gen 49:8-12).
16. Spiekermann and Carr, "Abraham," 152.
17. The name *YHWH* was not revealed till Moses (Exod 3:14; E). Exod 6:2 (P) says that God appeared as *El Shaddai* to Abraham, Isaac, and Jacob. For the narrator, *El Shaddai* was just a different name for the one God, *YHWH*.

> Perhaps God thinks, "You are going to be that kind of person, so I will relate to you on this basis now." Or, perhaps, "I want you to be that kind of person, so I will relate to you on this basis now so that you become that kind of person." Or perhaps, "I want you to be that kind of person, so I will relate to you on that basis now, because that is the kind of way that someone who wants this would behave." (Goldingay, *Israel's Gospel*, 199)

"In Gen 12:1, YHWH asks Abraham to leave his past. In Gen 22:2, God asks him to leave his future."[18] The order of words in both passages is not geographical, but emotional—in ascending order of difficulty.[19]

> *Go forth* (*lek leka*) from your land, your relatives,[20] and from your father's house to a land that I will show you. (Gen 12:1)

> Take your son, your only one, whom you love, Isaac, and *go forth* (*lek leka*) . . . one of the heights I will tell you. (Gen 22:2)

Lek leka, go for yourself, go by yourself—this is a journey you must undertake alone. Abram is called to take on a new identity determined only by his relationship to YHWH. There is something exclusive about this God; he demands preferential love, not unlike what Jesus in his turn demands of his disciples: "if any one comes to me without hating his father and mother, wife and children, brothers and sisters, and even his own life, he cannot be my disciple" (Luke 14:26). Abram must leave behind everything dear to him and set forth not knowing the goal of the journey. Grazing rights are a matter of survival to people who rear flocks and cattle. Yet, God is asking him to venture into a foreign land as an

---

18. Ska, "Call of Abraham," 64. See also Sarna, *Commentary on Genesis*, 150.

19. Friedman, *Commentary on Torah*, 49.

20. The term *môladti*, as in Gen 24:4, means "my birthplace." The translation "your relatives" tries to harmonize with the context where the call came to Abram in Haran, not in Ur of the Chaldeans. See Friedman, *Commentary on the Torah*, 48. In Gen 15:7, the call is portrayed as coming to Abram in his birthplace of Ur of the Chaldeans. This tradition is picked up by Stephen in Acts 7:2–3: "the God of glory appeared to our father Abraham while he was in Mesopotamia, before he had settled in Haran, and said to him, 'go forth from your land and [from] your kinsfolk to the land that I will show you.'"

"undocumented alien." This God he must trust absolutely and hope that he will deliver, will be found faithful.

The tradition is careful to highlight YHWH's unconditioned love at the very beginning:

> Scripture does not begin by reciting Abraham's merit, in order to indicate that the choice was a divine mystery and by God's will alone–a choice that would never be dissolved or denied. Israel will always remain the 'holy seed,' for though Israel sins, it remains Israel.[21]

Still, Abram's response of obedience is also noted.[22] He heard a voice and obeyed that voice. His first act was one of obedience. It is the "act of the birth of a nation."[23] That every verb in these verses is in the future tense means that the promises look beyond Abram to the people of Israel whose ancestor he is portrayed to be.

I will make of you a great nation.[24]

Before this can take place, Abram has to go forth: "go from your land ... so that I may make of you a great nation."[25] Faith and obedience are here portrayed in the metaphor of a journey. Abram was seventy-five,[26] Sarai sixty-five and barren. This God has not given him a child until now! Nation (*gôy*) is political, *'am* (people) is social and familial.

---

21. Plaut, *Torah*, 103 n. 26.

22. Chinpeng Ho, "Paragon of Faith?," 453 has some point when he comments that for people who do not have our concept of sedentary life or of "homeland" this would be no test of faith.

23. "The act of obedience that leads the patriarch to an unknown land is the act of the birth of a people. On Abraham's obedience depends the future of Israel. It really is a founding moment in 'history.'" Ska, "Narrative Program in Gen 12:1–4a," 55. See also idem, "Call of Abraham," 55.

24. The promise of "great nation" is made to Ishmael (Gen 17:20; 21:18). It recurs in respect of Abraham in Gen 18:18 and of Jacob in Gen 46:3. Twice, Exod 32:10 and Num 14:18, YHWH would destroy his disobedient people, offering to make of Moses a great nation. Each time, Moses refused, asking YHWH to be mindful of his promises to Abraham. Deut 4:6–8 interprets Israel's greatness in terms of wisdom and discernment in carefully observing Torah and of having a close relationship with YHWH.

25. Lambdin, *Introduction to Biblical Hebrew*, 119 n. 107b.

26. If Terah was seventy at the birth of Abraham and died at age two hundred and five, then Abram at seventy-five left his father, who would still live sixty-five years. Midrash has God respond to his worry by exempting him from the duty of honoring his parents. *Gen. Rab.* 39:7, citing Rabbi Isaac.

A great nation betokens an organized people having some autonomy and interrelating with the nations of the world. This promise was not fulfilled in the lifetime of Abraham. It receives no developed narration in the Pentateuch.[27] It functions to ground in Abraham the current hearers' hopes of autonomy. YHWH's speech makes the beginning of the "story of Abraham" the beginning of the "story of Israel."[28]

I will bless you; I will make your name great.

The men of the tower sought to "make a name for ourselves" (Gen 11:4); the LORD offers a great name to Abram as gift.

So that you will be a blessing. I will bless those who bless you and curse those who curse you. All the families of the earth will find blessing in you.

The NABRE translation, "will find blessing in you," is purposely ambiguous, so it can be understood in a passive or reflexive sense.[29]

> *Nibrekû* (here and at 18:18; 28:14) is usually passive, "shall be blessed in/through you" (niphal tense). The LXX used the passive, "shall be blessed" (*eneulogēthēsontai*). All Targums translate this verse in the passive.[30]
>
> We see such blessing operating through Joseph: "the Lord blessed the Egyptian's house for Joseph's sake: the Lord's blessing was on everything he owned, both inside the house and out" (Gen 39:5). Sir 44:21 is also in this tradition: "God promised him with an oath to bless the nations through his descendants, to make him numerous as grains of dust, and to exalt his posterity like the stars, giving them an inheritance from sea to sea, and from the River to the ends of the earth."
>
> It seems that the diverse understandings of the promise of blessing derive from varying contextualizations (see discussion at Gen 22:15–18). The sense of (passive) mediator of blessings is used with *mishpaḥah* (clan) and *ha-adamah* (the ground), while the (reflexive) example/model of blessing is used with

---

27. See Coats, *From Canaan to Egypt*, 2.

28. Blum, *Komposition*, 354 n. 3.

29. The NABRE translators comment that "since the term is understood in a passive sense in the New Testament (Acts 3:25; Gal 3:8), it is rendered here by a neutral expression that admits of both meanings." *Catholic Study Bible* (2016), 28.

30. "All the families of the earth will be blessed on account of you" (*Tg. Onq.*); "and in your merit all the families of the earth shall be blessed" (*Tg. Neof.*); "and in you all the families of the earth will be blessed" (*Tg. Ps.-J.*).

goyim (nations) and *ha-areṣ* (the earth). It enshrines recognition by foreigners of Abram's and his heirs' fame and blessing.[31] An exception to the pattern of usage is Gen 18:18 where *goyim* (nations) is used with *nibrekû* (blessed through you).[32]

Abram becomes a source or mediator of blessing to all families of the earth. The "great nation" will become a world empire not by war or conquest, but by becoming a blessing and mediator of blessings for all the families of the earth.[33] The New Testament, especially Paul, emphasizes this mediatorial role in relating Christ to Abraham.[34]

Elsewhere, in Gen 22:18; 26:4, the promise occurs in the clearly reflexive *hitbarekû*, "bless themselves." In this acceptation, Abram becomes a paradigm or model of blessing. It is as if "a man says to his son, 'mayest thou become as Abraham.'"[35]

A strand of the biblical text has all humankind blessed directly by God (Gen 1:28). In this strand, no one is blessed through Abraham, nor do any bless themselves by him.[36]

---

31. Carr, *Reading the Fractures*, 158, 187.

32. Carr, *Reading the Fractures*, 155 considers this verse a secondary addition to its context. See also Ben Zvi, "Dialogue between Abraham and Yahweh," 31.

33. Albertz, *Israel in Exile*, 257.

34. Kaminsky, "Election Theology," 40 is among recent Jewish voices that caution that such missional aspect of Israel's election must not be allowed to water down the special status of Abram and his line in the LORD's promise.

35. Rosenbaum, Silbermann, *Pentateuch*, 49. Gen 48:20 illustrates this understanding, though using *yebārēk*, the piel tense of the verb: "by you shall the people of Israel pronounce blessings, saying 'God make you like Ephraim and Manasseh.'" Jewish interpreters generally follow Rashi in this: Cassuto, *From Noah to Abraham*, 315: "the father of the Israelites will be privileged to become a source of benison to all the peoples of the world, and his merit and prayer will protect them before the Heavenly Court of Justice." However, several join the Targums in the mediatorial sense of the passage: Friedmann, *Commentary on Torah*, 50: "the result of the divine choice of Abraham is supposed to be some good for all humankind."

36. Carr, *Reading the Fractures of Genesis*, 323. The strand in question is the priestly writing (P) which links humanity and Israel, making Israel's fertility only an intense instance of God's blessing on humanity in general. See ibid., 131.

> **ISA 51:1–3**
> Look to the rock from which you were hewn, to the quarry from which you were taken; look to Abraham, your father, and to Sarah, who gave you birth; Though he was but one when I called him, I blessed him and made him many. Yes, the Lord shall comfort Zion, shall comfort all her ruins; her wilderness he shall make like Eden, her wasteland like the garden of the Lord; joy and gladness shall be found in her, thanksgiving and the sound of song.

Another strand stresses, not blessing but separation—Israel as a holy nation must separate from the nations. Deut 7:14 speaks of being blessed more than all the peoples, not as means of blessing to other peoples.[37]

The above variations mean that in the search for the word of God today biblical theology must reckon with the diversity of views on various topics and themes.

Those who curse you.

This is protection formula,[38] an assurance of protection. There seems a "curse in the blessing." The Lord will curse (*'rr*) all who hold Abram in disdain (*qalal*). Those who bless Abram/his family stand in positive relationship with the Lord, but those who curse him or his family will meet misfortune[39] or must separate from the source of their blessing.[40] The narrative will show Israelite identity being defined as various branches separate from the tree; the patriarchal stories are about the construction of Israelite identity, through and against the surrounding nations.[41] Abraham parts ways with Lot, Moab and Ammon are excluded, Ishmael is unchosen, Esau is sidelined.

But what is blessing and how does it operate? The meaning of Abram's blessing will become clearer as the narrative unfolds. In Genesis 1, blessing had creational sense, indicating the intensification of the powers of the soul and success in whatever one says and does. Blessing

---

37. See Van Seters, *Abraham in History and Tradition*, 272, 275.

38. Westermann, *Genesis 12–36*, 150.

39. Pharaoh, though unwitting, was struck with plagues for taking Abram's wife (Gen 12:10–20); the men of Sodom bear the consequences for attacking Lot (Gen 19:1–25).

40. See Coats, "Curse in God's Blessing," 39.

41. Kawashima, "Literary Analysis," 90.

confers the power of fertility (of humans, flock, and plants) and protection from danger; it enables wisdom and the ability to harness resources at hand.[42] Second Isaiah evokes the blessing to encourage the exiles despondent about flailing numbers (see text box on, "Isa 51:1–3"). However, since Abram's blessing relates to all families of the earth, that is, humankind, which was "corrupt in the view of God and full of lawlessness" (Gen 6:11), one expects it to function also as spiritual vitality to deal with the lawlessness and corruption. In Gen 17:7, blessing includes the covenant "to be your God and the God of your descendants after you." And at Gen 18:19, YHWH for the first time makes clear the spiritual nature of this blessing: YHWH chose Abraham that he may command his children and his household after him to keep the way of the Lord by doing what is right and just.[43] Having entered the history of a family, blessing becomes determinative for this family's self-consciousness, its relationship with others, and their relationship with God.

Abram went as the LORD directed him, and Lot went with him.

Was he hedging his bets? Did he consider Lot as possible heir? The LORD spoke of a "great nation," but how this will come about seemed open? It is easy to cast blame in hindsight, but a person in Abram's situation did not yet have experience of the life-giving power of God.

Further Reflections

Social memory is about the past constantly present within the community, the present of the community legitimized by the past. Abraham became a site of memory, evoking and reinforcing matters and images at the core of the community's identity and self-understanding.[44] As is the case with most stories in the Bible, "the stories of Abraham are theological texts, but they use the form of a historical narrative . . . these are literary stories dealing with the problems of their time in the form of stories of the past."[45] The Abraham living in exilic conditions

---

42. Paraphrasing Pedersen, "Blessing," 198.

43. However, it is an open question to what extent Gen 18:19 applies to Ishmael and the children of Keturah, seeing that the latter part of Genesis 17 seems to restrict the blessing of being their God to the offspring of Abraham through Isaac.

44. See Ben Zvi, "Memory of Abraham," 4, 6.

45. Bechmann, "Genesis 12 and the Abraham-Paradigm," 67, 68.

in the land promised him best conforms to the community of Persian Yehud in the sixth and fifth centuries BCE.

The preexilic prophets extolled the origins of Israel in Moses and the covenant of Sinai. After deliverance from Egypt, Israel stood with Moses on Mt. Sinai, accepted the obligations of God's covenant, and became his "treasured possession among all peoples" (Exod 19:5). Since this covenant was conditioned on obedience, the events of 722 and 586 BCE provoked severe soul-searching concerning Israel's very existence and her status as people of YHWH. In the "memory" of Abraham, Israel rediscovered unconditionality. YHWH's love for and call of Abraham—and Israel in him—was pure grace (to use a theological term). Care was taken not to ground Abraham's (thus Israel's) choice on merit. The same was done for the gift of the land of Canaan, the choice of Jerusalem, the site of the temple, and the Davidic dynasty. Even the exodus was provoked, not by merit, but because "God heard their moaning and God was mindful of his covenant with Abraham, Isaac, and Jacob" (Exod 2:24). Each time the election was left unexplained, except to point to divine good pleasure.

God's gifts are without repentance. Israel remains people of God, hence retain election and blessing. The people were elect before the State of Israel arose in 1948 and will still be elect should the state cease or mutate. Yet, as representing the people politically, the state also has a duty to be blessing for all families of the earth. Friedman wonders whether it involves light to the nations, for example, showing how a community can live, care for one another. Or would Abram's descendants benefit the species through inventions, literature, music, learning?[46]

Dispensationalist Evangelicals, like Jerry Falwell and John Hagee, founder of Christians United for Israel, find in Abram's blessing a mandate for blind U.S. support of the State of Israel. Hagee writes, "the support of Israel is a biblically based mandate for every Christian. All other nations were created by an act of men, but God himself established the boundaries of the nation of Israel."[47] This is an unfortunate twisting of Scripture. The point is "election reaches its fruition in a humble yet exalted divine service which benefits the elect and the non-elect alike." So, "Israel's election reaches its culmination when she

---

46. Friedman, *Commentary on Torah*, 50.
47. See Moberly, *Theology of Genesis*, 164.

fulfills her special responsibilities of divine service, a vocation that benefits the world as a whole."[48]

Abram in Canaan, 12:5–9

And the persons they had acquired,

Literally, the persons they made (*'asû*),[49] that is, slaves. Indigent and indebted farmers bargained themselves into servitude. The narrator takes it for granted that slaves counted as part of one's wealth. The law will later legislate on slaves (Exod 21:1–11; Deut 15:12–18). However, this was not chattel slavery based on color, as in the West.

Abram's movements and activities in Canaan foreshadow two things. First, the journey up and down the land and the dedication of memorial stones are symbolic acts of taking possession of the land and inscribing YHWH's lordship over this land. Second, extensive parallels show that here and in the descent to Egypt and exit with great wealth (12:10–20) the patriarchs foreshadow the experience of Israel.[50]

Bethel to the west and Ai to the east. He built an altar there.

Bethel and Shechem were ancient sacred places. The text knows nothing of the proscription of the Bethel sanctuary and the religion of Canaan. Abraham's travel puts him on a track similar to Jacob's in Gen 33:18; 35:4—one of the ways in which the southern and northern ancestors were assimilated to each other. They both built an altar at Bethel; Joshua will also build an altar there during the conquest (Josh 8:9, 12).

Invoked the LORD by name.

Calling YHWH by name, that is, true worship of YHWH, is a motif that links the ancestors of Israel (Abraham, 12:8; 13:4; 21:33; Isaac, 26:25) with the line of Enosh (Gen 4:26). He does not sacrifice for this

---

48. Kaminsky, "Reclaiming a Theology of Election," 152, 145.

49. *Tg. Onq.*: "and the persons whom they had subjected to the Law in Haran"; *Tg. Neof.*: "and the souls they had converted" (similar *Tg. Ps.-J.*). The verb *'asah* is strange in this context. It was used of creation in Genesis 1. So R. Leazar: "that is to teach you that he who brings a Gentile near [to God] is as though he created him" (*Gen. Rab.* 39:14; see also 84:4). In the same manner, "be thou a blessing/*berakhah*" was understood as "be thou a *berekhah*/pool"—just as a pool purifies the unclean, so do thou bring near [to Me] those who are afar (*Gen. Rab.* 39:11).

50. Cassuto, *From Noah to Abraham*, 304–5; See also Fretheim, *Genesis*, 105.

is pre-Sinai, but also because the reader (in the exile and after) lived in a context where prayer, not sacrifice, defines worship.

The Canaanites were then in the land (repeated in 13:7).

This betrays the point of view of one writing long after the time of the event. Abraham ibn Ezra (1089–1167) saw this as one indication that Moses did not write the whole Torah.

The LORD appeared to Abram. To your descendants I will give this land.

Before there was a voice, arriving at the goal there is presence. The manner of this presence is not indicated, but the parallel in Genesis 18 suggests human form. The promise becomes a covenant in Gen 15:18 (*"to your descendants I give* ['I have given' means I hereby give] *this land"*).

The boundaries in the latter text go from Egypt to the Euphrates, while at 13:14–15 it is merely all the land Abram can see from north and south, east and west. This promise is in some tension with the rights of the native peoples in the land. The patriarchs are, however, portrayed as merely *gerim* (resident aliens) in Canaan[51]; when they need a plot for burial (Genesis 23) or for wells (Gen 26:15–22), they negotiate and pay for it.

> One may ask whether the land is essential to biblical faith,[52] and what may be the meaning of the grant of this land *"forever"* in 13:15. Interesting is that both the boundaries of the Promised Land[53] and its necessity to Jewish identity fluctuated with Israel's experiences in history. Torah "[designates] . . . the Mosaic age as a constitutive and normative narrative."[54] Deuteronomy conditions the possession of the land upon obedience to the commandments of Torah. Moses dies outside the land. So whereas a specific land was promised to Israel, this promise came largely to symbolize a place or condition of perfect harmony with God. Heb 11:9 transfers all speech of the promised land to the heavenly homeland.[55]

---

51. Mann, *Book of Torah*, 45.

52. Goldingay, *Israel's Gospel*, 209.

53. Hebrew has no word for "to promise" (uses "to give"); the term "promised land" does not occur in the Old Testament; "land of promise" appears in the New Testament at Heb 11:9.

54. Fretheim, *Pentateuch*, 57, citing Blenkinsopp, *Pentateuch*, 51.

55. See Pontifical Biblical Commission, *Jewish People and Their Scriptures*, nos. 54–57.

Abram in Egypt, Ancestress in Danger, 12:10–20

Three "wife-sister" stories appear: Gen 12:10–20; Genesis 20; and Gen 26:1–11. They are categorized as "type-scenes."[56] The type-scene is a literary type familiar to the audience. It presents a scaffolding of similar traits across a set of scenes and is marked by differences in each particular realization. The similarities and differences illumine developments in plot and character. The first story is the most ethically compromised; the later stories seem to resolve certain issues in the first.

> Abram journeyed to the Negeb (Gen 12:9) and is in the Negeb at 13:2. This indicates that the story of his descent into Egypt (12:10–20) has been inserted (13:1 being a linking verse). The insertion muddied the waters a bit, for no sooner did YHWH promise the land than famine in that land drove Abram off to Egypt!

There was famine in the land/ba-aretz.

Eretz means "the world," though to an Israelite *ba-aretz* refers to Palestine.[57] Egypt is the natural refuge in famine for people in Canaan. It is watered by the Nile and not as dependent on scarce rain and dew.

Abram went down to Egypt to sojourn there. They will say, "she is his wife"; then they will kill me, but let you live.

The verb *gûr* indicates temporary stay; he is not turning his back on the Promised Land, rather seeking survival. What choices are open to a man who, like Abram, believes he is faced with mortal danger?[58] He apparently thinks he has no real choice: "it is either lie or die."[59] And Sarai? Were Bedouin women so devoted as to be willing to lose their honor to protect a husband's life?[60] Though it does not fully justify his action, we

---

56. Alter, *Art of Biblical Narrative* (rev. ed., 2011), 55–78.

57. See Koch, *Growth of the Biblical Tradition*, 111–32, here 116. Koch lays out the parallel texts in a table. The three wife-sister stories were originally independent oral narratives; they probably derive from a common source.

58. Plaut, *Torah*, 105. Jewish teaching holds that even under duress one may not intentionally kill, profane the Name, or commit a sexual crime on an innocent person.

59. Friedman, *Commentary on Torah*, 52.

60. See Koch, *Growth of the Biblical Tradition*, 127. In 1Qap Gen[ar], it was not Abram but Sarai who hoped to deceive Pharaoh, for she saw it as the only way to save Abraham's life.

may want to recall that the full concept of human dignity and equality was not yet articulated. Exod 20:17 regards the wife as a piece of a man's property. Nachmanides (Ramban, 1194–1270) faults Abram for leaving the land and placing Sarai in danger instead of trusting in God's averred protection. Abram misjudged these Egyptian foreigners. Pharaoh's reproach makes it clear he would not have touched Sarai had he known she was Abram's wife! While Abram was willing to compromise his wife in order to save his skin, Pharaoh, far from taking the woman by force, gave her "brother" dowry worthy of a prince—sheep, oxen, male and female servants, male and female donkeys, and camels! Abram devised the ruse "so that I may fare well on your account," using the root *yeṭab* (to be well with). The narrator, by using an inflexion of the same verb, confirms that indeed, *Abram fared well on her account*—witness the royal presents. Is there irony here? Was not "faring well" the very object of blessing by the LORD?

> Cassuto sees a parallel rather between "that it may go well with me" and "that I may live on account of you." He argues that Abram's motivation was survival, not material and social gain.[61]

But the LORD struck Pharaoh and his household with severe plagues.

Nagaʿ (afflict) and *negaīʿm* (plagues), Pharaoh and his household, recall the plagues of Exodus. Why would a just God strike the unwitting Pharaoh, and why include Pharaoh's household?[62] Is it because the family is so holy that even unwitting violation of marital fidelity brings misery?[63] Do we meet here remnants of the ancient "act-consequence" moral chain whereby "the workings of the moral order do not discriminate between those who commit sins knowingly or unknowingly."[64] We read above that the LORD will curse (*ʾarr*) all who hold Abram in disdain (*qalal*). Is this curse blind and in effect here? How long did it take Pharaoh to guess the

---

61. *Jub.* 13:10–12 has Abram live five years in Egypt before his wife was taken *by force*. That she was taken by force occurs also in *Gen. Apoc.* 20:10–16: "I, Abram, wept greatly . . . on the night that Sarah was taken from me *by force*." Both texts omit both the subterfuge of Sarai being Abram's sister and that Abram was enriched by it.

62. Westermann, *Genesis 12–36*, 166 suggests that "and his household" is a gloss from 20:17–18.

63. Westermann, *Genesis 12–36*, 166.

64. Fretheim, *Genesis*, 107.

truth? Did he touch Sarai in the meantime?[65] His reprimand to Abram for saying Sarai was his sister *"so that I took her for my wife"*[66] suggests that he did indeed relate to her as wife. Rashi builds on an opinion in *Gen. Rab.* 41:1 that Pharaoh was struck by severe skin disease and this made sexual intercourse difficult! Anyway, it was not Sarai, as announced, but Abram who told the lie. Pharaoh is indignant at the suggestion he would sexually exploit anyone; he accepts that even kings are subject to family ethics.[67] Abram had no response. The last word belongs to Pharaoh:

Here is your wife. Take her and leave.

The original is brusque, two verbs of command: *qaḥ wa-lek*, take and be gone! This points to Pharaoh's similar brusque command to Moses and Aaron in Exod 12:31: *qûmû ṣû'û mi-tôk 'ammî* (get up, go out from among my people). He evicts Abram from Egypt and brings him under guard to the border! I agree with Westermann that by giving Pharaoh the last word, the narrator shows that Pharaoh is really in the right.[68]

Abram came to Egypt fleeing severe famine in Canaan; he is sent back to the famine—we are never told the famine was over. His wealth upon exit recalls the despoiling of the Egyptians in Exod 12:35–36. Pharaoh was gracious enough to let Abram leave with all the gifts acquired on false pretenses. The narrator does not tell us whether Pharaoh's house recovered health.[69] The second wife-sister tale will address this issue explicitly.

The story raises concerns about Abram's ethical integrity and about the impartial justice of God. The second story of the "ancestress in

---

65. *Tg. Ps.-J.*: "and immediately a plague was unleashed against me and I did not approach her." This appears in the GenApoc 20:16–17 (first century BCE) and in Josephus, *Ant.* 1.164—an attempt to preserve the dignity of the ancestress. Augustine speaks of the calumnies of Faustus the Manichaean on this matter, saying, "and far be it from us to believe that she was defiled by lying with another. It is much more credible that, by these great afflictions, Pharaoh was not permitted to do this." Augustine, *City of God* 16.19, in ACCS 2:8.

66. Some scholars suggest that on the analogy of Genesis 20, the plagues must have functioned as warning that prevented Pharaoh from violating Sarai. However, Genesis 20 was constructed precisely in view of relativizing issues raised by the earlier account.

67. See Rashkow, "Intersexuality," 66.

68. Westermann, *Genesis 12–36*, 166.

69. Koch, *Growth of the Biblical Tradition*, 120.

danger" will deal with some of these concerns. We may ask, do migrants have any rights in a foreign country and does God defend them?[70]

Further Reflections

Is this a trickster story, the powerless underdog surviving by his wits?[71] Or the story of an "astoundingly successful lie which made a virtue out of necessity"?[72] Is there irony in this narrative: the very first encounter of one called to be blessing brings disaster to a whole household? Does it, like the books of Jonah and Ruth, "instruct prejudiced Israelites inclined to think of themselves as religiously and morally superior to foreign peoples?"[73] Biblical narratives do not portray the patriarchs as perfect models, but as mirrors that hold up the quests and stirrings of our hearts for inspection. The story may tell of the loyalty and protection of YHWH: "what is important is that God so ordered the world as to show favor to their ancestors."[74] Part of its significance may be to promote the need for the exiles to remain in the land and not go off to Egypt, a topic debated in Jeremiah 42–44 and dramatized in Jeremiah's purchase of a piece of property at Anatoth (Jeremiah 32) during the destruction of Jerusalem by the Babylonians.[75]

Tradition

> We do not fall in love with everyone; we do not love everyone in the same way. God's individual love for Israel is not the barrier to God's loving the world. It is a kind of paradigm, a promise that God can also love other peoples individually. (Goldingay, *Israel's Gospel*, 217)

---

70. Romer and Finkelstein, "Historical Background," 19 find that the story reflects the exilic period and the debate about "Egyptian exile" (should the defeated Judeans seek asylum in Egypt) found in Jeremiah 42–44.
71. Zoob, "Wife-Sister Stories in Genesis," 18.
72. Koch, *Growth of the Biblical Tradition*, 127.
73. Zoob, "Wife-Sister Stories in Genesis," 25.
74. Koch, *Growth of the Biblical Tradition*, 119.
75. Römer and Finkelstein, "Historical Background," 19.

The narrator says nothing of any prior relationship of Abraham with the LORD. Why Abram? Is God's election arbitrary or are there grounds for divine choice?[76] The story of the sacrifice of Isaac in Genesis 22 will grapple with the relation of divine election and God's reward of human obedience. In Isa 41:8 God calls Israel "offspring of Abraham, my friend" (*ōhabî*—one who loves me). 2 Chr 20:7 picks this up when it reminds the LORD of his gift of the land to "the seed of Abraham your friend forever" (*ōhabka*—the one who loves you). Had Abraham developed friendly relations with YHWH before his call? Jas 2:23 notes that "Abraham believed God, and it was credited to him as righteousness," and he was called "the friend of God." Heb 11:8 underlined his faith, though associating such faith with obedience: "by faith Abraham obeyed when he was called to go out to a place that he was to receive as an inheritance; he went out, not knowing where he was to go."

How inclusive was Israel's blessing? Sure, at certain times, especially under duress, Israel tended to stress her particularity. But many texts show remarkable inclusivity that easily opens up to outsiders. Clements[77] categorizes three such interpretations of the blessing of Abraham. There is the *political* arena in which Israel as imperial power brings peace and righteous government to the world. Ps 2:7 says of YHWH's king on Zion: "ask it of me, and I will give you the nations as your inheritance, and as your possession, the ends of the earth." Psalm 72 prays God to give his justice to the king's son, not only to "govern your people with justice" (v. 2), but "may he rule from sea to sea, from the River to the ends of the earth" (v. 8). The *religious* interpretation has the nations streaming to the LORD's mountain in Zion, "that he may instruct us in his ways, and we may walk in his paths. For from Zion shall go forth instruction [*torah*] and the word of the LORD from Jerusalem" (Isa 2:2–5//Mic 4:1–5). Isa 19:24–25 speaks of that day when "Israel shall be a third party with Egypt and Assyria, a blessing in the midst of the earth, when the LORD of Hosts gives this blessing: 'Blessed be my people Egypt, and the work of my hands Assyria, and my heritage Israel.'" On that day, "the LORD shall make himself known to Egypt, and the Egyptians shall know the LORD" (Isa 19:21). The prophet of Isa 56:1–8 foresees foreigners and

---

76. Kaminsky, "New Testament and Rabbinic Views," 134 asks: "is election by divine fiat, or is it due to human action, or is it finally some mysterious interaction that includes both a divine and human component?"

77. See Clements, *Old Testament Theology*, 95–96. Further on this in Okoye, *Israel and the Nations*, 46–55.

eunuchs joining themselves to the LORD and keeping his covenant of Sabbath. Exod 19:5–6 had already proclaimed Israel both "my own possession" and "a kingdom of priests"—Israel having a priestly role among the nations? This abuts in a third interpretation—*vicarious suffering*: "my servant, the just one shall justify the many, their iniquity he shall bear" (Isa 53:11).

With the advent of the Christian church the question became: "Who was the true descendant of Abraham?" Paul argues in Gal 3:16 that the promises were made to Abraham and his seed (singular), that is, Christ. Whoever is in Christ, Jew or Gentile, inherits the promises of Abraham.

Abraham believed in the LORD, who attributed it to him as an act of righteousness (Gen 15:6), and that was before the law of circumcision, given in Genesis 17. Rom 4:13–16 expounds:

> It was not through the law that the promise was made to Abraham and his descendants that he would inherit the world, but through the righteousness that comes from faith. For if those who adhere to the law are the heirs, faith is null and the promise is void . . . For this reason, it depends on faith, so that it may be a gift, and the promise may be guaranteed to all his descendants, not to those who only adhere to the law but to those who follow the faith of Abraham, who is the father of all of us.

The figure of Abraham incites discussion of the tension between grace and obedience, free gift and merit, faith and "works"! Gen 22:16 makes the promises freely given to Abraham in Gen 12:1–3 conditional upon obedience (see the commentary there).

Paul argues that the call of Abraham opens up the blessing to the Gentiles. "Scripture which saw in advance that God would justify the Gentiles by faith, foretold the good news to Abraham saying, 'through you shall all the nations be blessed.' Consequently, those who have faith are blessed along with Abraham who had faith" (Gal 3:8–9). Jas 2:17–22, on the other hand, throws out the challenge: "demonstrate your faith to me without works, and I will demonstrate my faith to you from my works . . . Was not Abraham our father justified by works when he offered his son Isaac upon the altar? You see that faith was active along with his works, and faith was completed by the works . . ."

Was Abraham at his call a worshipper of the LORD? His clan was polytheistic. Josh 24:2 has Terah, father of Abraham, and Nahor serving other gods, but the LORD brought your father Abraham from there.

Tradition arose that Abraham was chosen because he had become a monotheist. *Jub.* 11:16-17 recounted how as a child he began to realize the errors of the land, and separated from his father so that he might not worship the idols with him. Josephus maintained that he was the first person to argue that a single God is the creator of all things (*Ant.* 1.154-157).[78] This led to tension with his clan and their attempt to burn him in a furnace. Abraham was the first monotheist.

He survived a furnace ordeal. Isa 29:22 reads, "thus says the LORD ... who redeemed Abraham." *Padah* (redeem) suggests a saving and rescuing deed of some sort. And so, reading Gen 15:7, "I am the LORD who brought you from Ur of the Chaldeans," and the notation in Gen 11:28, that "Haran died before Terah, his father, in Ur of the Chaldeans," Ur of the Chaldeans came to be understood as referring to the *fire/furnace of the Chaldeans* (*'ûr* means fire). Stories arose of how Nimrod cast Abram into the furnace because he would not worship his idol (*Tg. Ps.-J.*; *Tg. Neof.*; *Gen. Rab.* 38:13, in the name of R. Hiyya, c. 180-230).[79] Jerome reported this tradition in *Hebrew Questions on Genesis*[80]; it occurs also in the Vulgate of Neh 9:7 in the prayer of the Levites: "you are the LORD God, who chose Abram and brought him out of the fire of the Chaldeans, and named him Abraham" (NIV).

Did Abraham observe the Torah? In Gen 18:19, the LORD singled Abraham out "that he may direct his children and his household in the future to keep the way of the Lord by doing what is right and just." In Gen 26:5, the LORD repeats to Isaac the promise of the land and of progeny: "this because Abraham obeyed me, keeping my mandate, my commandments, my ordinances, and my instructions [*tōrōtai*]." These terms are used for observance of the whole Torah. "What is right and just" morphs into observance of all the precepts of Torah! On this Mishnah Kidd 4:13 opines: "We find that Avraham our father performed the whole entire Torah before it had been given, as it says, "By reason that Avraham listened to my voice, and kept my safekeeping, my commandments, my statutes and teachings."[81]

---

78. Further for the material in this section, consult Kugel, *Bible as It Was*, 133-48.

79. See Okoye, *Genesis 1-11*, 137-38.

80. See ACCS 1:172-73.

81. B. Yoma 28b reports a discussion on this: Rab said: our father Abraham kept the whole Torah, as it is said: Because that Abraham hearkened to My voice [kept My charge, My commandments, My statutes, and My laws]. R. Shimi b. Hiyya said to Rab:

Modern exegetes read this as hyperbole. Some argue that the ways of Torah, one of seven things apparently created before the creation of the world, were planted in Abram's heart (cf. Jer 31:31–34).

Say, perhaps, that this refers to the seven laws?—Surely there was also that of circumcision! Then say that it refers to the seven laws and circumcision [and not to the whole Torah]?—If that were so, why does Scripture say: 'My commandments and My laws'?

CHAPTER 3

Genesis 13–14

Abraham and Lot

> How good and how pleasant it is, when brothers dwell together as one!
>
> —Psalm 133:1

Genesis 13–14 consider and drop Lot as possible heir to Abram.[1] In the process, Abram shows himself gracious and faithful, willing to take risks in defense of his nephew. He acts like a king and shows great military prowess against a coalition of Mesopotamian kings.

> The narrative of the descent to Egypt focused on Abram and Sarah; Lot was not mentioned. This shows that Gen 13:1 is transitional; Abram picks up Lot on his way from Egypt to the Negeb.

---

1. See Helyer, "Separation of Abraham and Lot," 81, 85.

Abram and Lot Separate, Genesis 13

> Farms have been built on ancient routes of a semi-nomadic community in Nigeria, causing violence that has already claimed hundreds of lives this year.
> The attack in Agatu was one of the most serious in Nigeria this year . . . These types of clashes between herdsmen and farmers are increasingly common in some parts of the country as the struggle over grazing rights and access to water becomes more acute...But land that was once unclaimed and, therefore, free to graze on is now being farmed, frequently triggering clashes . . . Hundreds of people have been killed in the violence in 2016. (Martin Patience, "Nigeria's Deadly Battle for Land: Herdsman v Farmers," *BBC News*, August 10, 2016)

Now Abram was very rich in livestock, silver and gold.

ABRAM'S WEALTH in flocks prepares for the conflict between the herders of Abram and Lot's herders. The reader belatedly learns that Abram's wealth includes silver and gold, discreetly not mentioned in Gen 12:16, though they were part of the presents from Pharaoh. They foreshadow the exodus experience (cf. Exod 12:35–36) of the Israelites departing from Egypt, who asked and received from their neighbors "articles of silver and gold." Silver and gold will help in waging the war in the next chapter.

From the Negeb he traveled by stages toward Bethel . . . where he had first built the altar.

This journey to the Negeb was mentioned already in Gen 12:9, a signal that 12:10–20; 13:1 are an insertion. Bethel was an important cultic site in what would later be the northern kingdom. Abram, the southern ancestor, is made to legitimize it, just as Jacob, the northern ancestor, would in Genesis 32 and 35.[2] However, Abram never sacrificed in Bethel or Hebron; he only called upon the name of YHWH.[3] His sole act of

---

2. This, in contrast to Deuteronomy and the Deuteronomistic History that inveighed against these northern shrines as syncretistic.

3. Albertz, *Israel in Exile*, 258 suggests that this foregrounds the element of word that had become characteristic of exilic worship. Albertz assigns this text to the exilic

sacrifice was on the mount in the land of Moriah, Genesis 22, which may allude to Jerusalem.[4]

Let there be no strife between you and me.

Lot was also rich in flocks and herds. Besides, the Canaanites and the Perizzites were living in the land, shrinking further the amount of space available for grazing. For the types of conflicts that can arise in such situations, see the above text box. Sometimes, kith and kin may choose to live apart in peace than live together in bickering feuds.

In contrast to the ideology of the books of Deuteronomy and Joshua, which call for forcefully dispossessing the native populations, Abram's response was one of sharing the land. In so doing, the patriarch became an example for exiles returning to Yehud and encountering Jewish remainees in the land and others. Abram graciously allowed his younger nephew the first choice:

If you prefer the left, I will go to the right.

Directions were taken facing the east—the left would be the north, the right the south. Abram was content to share the Promised Land with Lot. Rather than north or south, Lot looked eastward; his eyes caught the fertile Jordan Plain.[5] It was to him like the Garden of YHWH or like the land of Egypt watered by the Nile all year round.

> The Garden of YHWH occurs again in Isa 51:3, where it is in parallelism with Eden: "[Zion's] wilderness he shall make like Eden, her wasteland like the garden of the LORD." In Lot's eyes, the Jordan Plain was well irrigated, with luxurious growth for man and beast, just like the mythical Garden of Eden.

Abundantly watered . . . as far as Zoar.

This is prolepsis. Lot and family will receive permission from the messengers of YHWH to flee to Zoar from Sodom. The name Zoar (meaning "small") reflects Lot's basis for the request, "is it not a small place?" (Gen 19:20). Lot chose to settle in the cities of the plain, pitching his tents near Sodom.

first edition of the patriarchal history.

4. Römer and Finkelstein, "Historical Background," 18 suggest that this presupposes the cult centralization in the Deuteronomistic History.

5. Alter, *Genesis*, 69 remarks that archeologists have discovered traces of an ancient irrigation system in the plain of the Jordan.

This was before the Lord destroyed Sodom and Gomorrah.

The omniscient narrator knows that Lot "is headed in the wrong direction."[6] Besides, ever since Cain was driven east of Eden, whoever faces east drops out of the line of special election and blessing. Chrysostom draws a salvific lesson: "do you observe Lot having regard for the nature of the land and not considering the wickedness of the inhabitants? What good, after all, is fertility of the land and abundance of produce when the inhabitants are evil in their ways?"[7] Lot needed greater discernment. More importantly, offered a choice to share the Promised Land, Lot chose land outside the boundaries and thus effectively withdrew himself from contention for the inheritance of Abram.[8] The narrator implied this by contrasting Lot's abode with the land of Canaan:

Abram settled in the land of Canaan, while Lot settled among the cities of the Plain.

"While" in this translation renders the ubiquitous Hebrew conjunction *we-* (and), which in this context means "but." Abram is again alone with a barren Sarai; the problem of who will inherit Abram becomes even sharper.

All the land that you see I will give to you and your descendants forever.

After Lot had parted from him, YHWH repeats the promise to Abram and his descendants. No military or forceful expulsion of anyone is envisaged here. Besides, "your descendants" is inclusive of all offspring of Abraham; some restrictions begin to appear in Genesis 17 in respect of Ishmael.

Look about you . . . All the land that you see.

Literally, "lift up your eyes and see" (using the root *ra'ah*). At Gen 12:1 YHWH bid Abram go to a land that I will make you see (using the same root); here he shows Abram that land.[9] The extent of the Promised Land varies in many texts. Here Abram can see all of it from a hill—not much more than the postexilic province of Yehud! The returnees receive

---

6. Mann, *Book of Torah*, 45.

7. Chrysostom, *Homilies on Genesis* 33.15, in ACCS 2:17.

8. Fretheim, "Genesis," 109 argues that Abram saw what Lot saw, hence the choices of both were included within the Promised Land at this point, though Lot journeys to the eastern edge.

9. Albert, *Israel in Exile*, 251.

a subtle message to settle down, stop dreaming of something bigger, or revolting against Babylonian or Persian rule.[10] The focus is peaceful possession and ease of pasture in good relationship with neighbors. This is the first time that *"forever"* is attached to the promise of land. Gen 17:8 will refer to the gift as *'ahuzzat 'ôlām*, a permanent possession. *'Ad 'ôlām*, translated "forever," has a range of meanings, going from "perpetually," "for always," to "abiding," "in/to the distant past/future."[11] But divine intention always reckons with human volition and performance. So, what is given *ad 'ôlām* may in fact prove to be provisional, depending on human response. Deuteronomy conditions the possession of the land upon obedience to God's commandments in the Torah. The Torah itself was edited in such manner as to end with the people of Israel on the plains of Moab overlooking the Promised Land,[12] thus relativizing the significance of possession of this land and subjecting it to Israel's faith in her God. Moses himself died outside the land. So whereas a specific land was promised to Israel, this "land" came largely to symbolize a place or condition of security and perfect harmony with her God. Heb 11:9 transfers all speech of the Promised Land to the heavenly homeland.[13]

Get up and walk through the land . . . for I give it to you.

A few verses earlier the text had "to you and your descendants." Here it says "to you." Some scholars seize on this difference to argue that YHWH here and now conveys the land to Abram. However, the same verb is used in the same future tense, *'etnennah*, I will give.

Abram, the Four Kings, and Lot, Genesis 14

We see Abram in this chapter as we never saw him before, nor ever will. He is a sheik operating in an international context and commanding enough trained (*ḥānîk* is one trained in something) forces to counter an invasion of four kings from the north. He is a royal figure operating

---

10. Bechmann, "Genesis 12 and the Abraham-Paradigm," 73.

11. Preusss, "*ôlām*," especially 536, 539.

12. Hebrew has no word for "to promise" (uses "to give"); the term "promised land," does not occur in the Old Testament; "land of promise" appears in the New Testament at Heb 11:9.

13. See Pontifical Biblical Commission, *Jewish People and Their Scriptures*, nos. 54–57.

among other royal figures—perhaps the original narrative aimed to portray Abram as a royal figure who embodied aspects of the Davidic royalty then in abeyance.[14] The narrative also portrays him as loyal and courageous, willing to put himself at risk to rescue his nephew Lot who had separated from him.

> This unit is not linked to the context; further, it reintroduces Abram as the "*Hebrew*" (see below). In v. 12, Lot is described as Abram's nephew (*ben-āḥîw*).[15] Elsewhere (vv. 14, 16) Lot is called *āḥîw*, his brother; the naming presents Abram's affective point of view. That Lot is reintroduced when we already knew of him in Genesis 13 points to the independent nature of this unit.

The trajectory of the four kings from the north to El Paran, right to En Mishpat, and back north beyond Damascus (see Figure 1 below), follows the King's Highway, the route generally taken by armies invading Canaan from Mesopotamia. We learn that Abram has allies in Aner, Eshcol, and Mamre (vv. 12, 24), perhaps each with his own men. Note that Mamre here is a person, not a place. There is no historical record of the kings mentioned.[16] Shinar is Babylon (Gen 10:10).

Ancient cities lived within walls surrounded on the outskirts by stretches of farmland. The five kings of the plain may be such petty kings, though sometimes one city-king may succeed in imposing hegemony over a number of adjoining cities. From the report that

"The victors seized all the possessions and food supplies of Sodom and Gomorrah and then went their way."

---

14. See Römer and Finkelstein, "Historical Background of the Abraham Narrative," 21. The authors believe that Genesis 14 is a late, possibly postexilic, part of attempts at refounding Israel in the patriarch Abraham and God's covenant with him.

15. Van Seters, *Abraham in History and Tradition*, 298 argues cogently that "nephew of Abraham" is probably later addition to make story fit the priestly view of the relationship between Abraham and Lot.

16. Speiser, *Genesis*, 107 contends that linguistically the name Arioch is the same as *Arriwuk*, the name of a vassal of Zimri-lim of Mari, a contemporary of Hammunrabi (eighteenth century BCE).

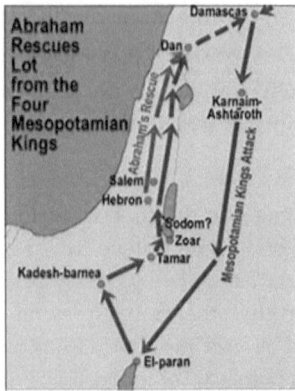

FIGURE 1: Abraham and the Four Kings[17]

It appears that only Sodom and Gomorrah were plundered. Perhaps these two cities headed the coalition of the kings of the plain? In fact, the king of Sodom may have been the leader, since it was he who would demand the captives of Abram. On the other hand, the narrative focus on Sodom may be because of Lot. The narrator continues the polemic against Sodom and Gomorrah by rendering the names of their kings pejoratively. The name of Bera, king of Sodom, signifies *be-ra'*, that is, "in evil"; Birsha, king of Gomorrah, means *be-resha'*, that is, "in wickedness."

The five kings of the Jordan Plain had been vassals of the northern kings for twelve years, but revolted in the thirteenth.[18] Earlier attempts to locate the story in the eighteenth century BCE, by identifying Amraphel with Hammurabi, have been abandoned. Consensus is growing to locate the setting of the entire unit in the late Persian era.[19] We do not know the bone of contention, but it may have been control over the copper mines south of the Dead Sea.[20] Surprisingly, the names of the peoples conquered by the northern coalition do not cohere with the names of the

17. Courtesy of Jesuswalk.com.

18. *Tg. Onq.*: twelve years they had served Chedorlaomer, and for thirteen years they had rebelled.

19. Van Seters, *Abraham in History and Tradition*, 305 suggests that the setting of the story is the late Persian Empire. Elam stands for Persia, the three kingdoms in league with Persia representing the major satrapies. The term Amorite apparently shifted in the Persian period from the indigenous population of Palestine to the Arab peoples, here the nomadic and pastoral peoples of southern Judah, including the region of Hebron.

20. Speiser, *Genesis*, 109.

cities of the plain, but rather with pre-Israelite peoples as mentioned in or about the same locations in Deut 2:9–14.[21]

> The Rephaim[22] are a race of giants in the area of Ammon. Deuteronomy regarded the mythical Rephaim as the ancient inhabitants of the whole of Transjordan.[23] Og, king of Bashan, belongs to this people. Deut 2:20 says that the Ammonites call them Zamzummim, perhaps reflected in the Zuzim[24] of our text. The Emim in Moab are said to be as tall as the Anakim, that is, the pre-flood giants (Deut 2:10). The Horites were said to be the former inhabitants of Seir, later dispossessed by the descendants of Esau (Deut 2:12).

Of the place names, Dan is the recent Israelite name for a place formerly called Laish.[25] El Paran is Elath, and En-Mishpat is Kadesh-barnea. Of the other double-barreled names, Ashtaroth-Karnaim and Shaveh-Kiriathaim, it appears that the second gives the name in more recent Israelite times.[26] According to 2 Chr 20:2, Hazazon-Tamar is Ein Gedi, on the western shore of the Dead Sea.

They took with them Abram's nephew Lot . . . A survivor came and brought the news to Abram the Hebrew.

The term *Hebrew* is applied to Israelites by outsiders (Gen 39:14, 17) or used for self-identification to foreigners (Jon 1:9, which belongs also the late Persian period).[27] Concern to rescue his nephew drew Abram

---

21. For what follows, see *Speiser, Genesis*, 102; and Westermann, *Genesis 12–36*, 196.

22. Elsewhere, Rephaim are the spirits of the dead (Ps 88:11).

23. See Van Seters, *Abraham in History and Tradition*, 303.

24. In fact, Symmachus rendered *Zoizommein* (Zamzummim) here and in Deut 2:20. See Westermann, *Genesis 12–36*, 196.

25. Judg 18:29: "the Danites then rebuilt the city and occupied it. They named it Dan after their ancestor Dan, who was born to Israel. But Laish was the name of the city formerly."

26. See Sarna, *Understanding Genesis*, 114. Sarna used these facts, among others, to try to prove that this account "preserves an authentic echo of a great military expedition which put an end to the Middle Bronze I settlements" (115). I do not buy into this, but rather believe with recent scholars that Genesis 14 is a late text that deliberately archaizes.

27. See Speiser, *Genesis*, 103. The identification with *Hapiru/Habiru*, which identified bands of landless outsiders during the Amarna Period, is disputed. LXX translated with *peratē*, one from across [the River], the emigrant. Hamilton, *Genesis 1–17*, 405 finds that the term occurs thirty-three times in the Hebrew Bible and believes that it is

into this conflict. Taking Aner, Eshcol, and Mamre, who were allies in covenant with him, perhaps with their forces, and 318[28] of his trained retainers, he went in pursuit of the northern kings as far as Dan. Deploying at night, Abram defeated them and pursued them as far as Hobah, north of Damascus.

He recovered all the possessions. He also recovered his kinsman Lot and his possessions, along with the women and the other people.

The story has reached its narrative resolution. Abram left Egypt enriched with gifts from Pharaoh obtained in questionable circumstances. His generous offer to Lot to choose grazing rights began the reinstatement of his character. To the king of Sodom, who asked him to keep the goods but give him the captives, Abram asserted:

"I have sworn to the LORD, God Most High, creator of heaven and earth, that I would not take so much as a thread or a sandal strap from anything that is yours, so that you cannot say, 'I made Abram rich.'"

> The god Elyon was the highest god who supervised the Canaanite pantheon. *El qn 'rṣ* (El, creator/possessor of earth[29]) was a distinct deity. The author combines the two titles and expands the latter to include both heaven and earth, achieving a complex title for the deity; v. 22 attributes all this title to YHWH.[30]

Abram's servants may take what is necessary for their sustenance. His coalition partners, Aner, Eshcol, and Mamre, may also take their share of the booty according to the laws of war. Abram makes it clear that brotherly loyalty, not possessions, was his motive. He will not invest himself in Lot's portion or become rich at Lot's expense.[31] Besides, unlike Lot, he will have nothing to do with Sin-City, of which we learn that

---

used primarily as an ethnic term, gentilic of Eber.

28. *Gen. Rab.* 43:2: "Rabbi Simeon ben Lakish said, 'it was Eliezer alone, the numerical value of Eliezer being three hundred and eighteen.'"

29. The Hebrew participle *qōneh* means "possessor," though in the context may mean "creator."

30. Van Seters, *Abraham in History and Tradition*, 307 remarks that "such a process was begun by [exilic] J and carried forward by P in their identifying forms of El with Yahweh, and it reached its culmination in Genesis 14."

31. Fretheim, "Genesis," 114.

The inhabitants of Sodom were wicked, great sinners against the Lord. (Gen 13:13)

The story teaches the virtues of courage, loyalty, and piety by Abraham's example."[32] In his blitz from the south to Dan in the north, Abram traversed the boundaries of the Promised Land, leaving him in virtual control of it.[33] There is a twist, however, perhaps even hidden polemic. Abram does not claim hegemony over the land or seek by force possession of the land God promised him. He even rejects booty for himself and returns the city's possessions and people to the king of Sodom. "The rejection of war and conquest contrasts to the tradition of holy war that dominates the story of Moses . . ."[34] In his relation to the land and the people of Canaan, Abram functions somewhat as counterfoil to Moses and Joshua. One task of biblical theology is to discern how contrasting views of godly living may yet respond to God's will for the respective time.

Abram and Melchizedek, 14:18–20

> There is near consensus that the unit of Gen 14:18-20, on Abram and Melchizedek, is an insertion. Melchizedek appears and leaves without preparation or introduction. The episode interrupts the meeting of Abram with the king of Sodom: he comes out to meet Abraham in v. 17, but does not speak until v. 21!

Melchizedek, king of Salem . . . a priest of God Most High.

The name Melchizedek means "king of righteousness"; it can also mean "my king of righteousness," that is, "my righteous king." Salem is in parallelism with Zion (Jerusalem) in Ps 76:3: "On Salem is God's tent, his shelter on Zion."[35]

The Valley of Shaveh, that is, the King's Valley.

---

32. Van Seters, *Abraham in History and Tradition*, 36, 306.
33. Fretheim, "Genesis," 112.
34. Dozeman et al., *Pentateuch*, 239.
35. Jerusalem in the Amarna letters is *uru-salim*.

> No other passage [in Genesis] values the notion that the pagan also has the true God. It is difficult to avoid the conclusion that the account regards the sanctuary and the priest-king of Shalem as the legitimate predecessors of the later Yahweh temple and priest-king of Jerusalem and that it thereby "assures the Jerusalem sanctuary the greatest age among all Israelite sanctuaries" (Westphal, 260). (Gunkel, *Genesis*, 280).

The King's Valley was a place near Jerusalem in which Absalom set up a pillar for himself (2 Sam 18:18). Josh 10:1, 3 refers to a pre-Israelite king of Jerusalem named Adonizedek—apparently *zedek*/righteousness was an element of the crown name of this city. The word used for priest, *kōhen*, is the term usual for Israelite priests; an idol priest would usually be designated as *kōmer*. "The Most High" is an epithet of the God of Israel, especially in poetry and the Psalms (Num 24:16; Deut 32:8), including the Psalms of Zion (Pss 46:5; 78:35, 56). The narrator thus presents Melchizedek as a worshipper of the true God. This priest-king celebrated the victory of Abram and his coalition by offering him and his soldiers bread and wine. He also blessed him:

And blessed be God Most High who delivered your foes into your hand.

Blessing is a priest's privilege. What so far was a victory report is now reinterpreted theologically as salvation from God.

> In so doing, the text plays with *māgēn* (shield). The intensive verb from it, *miggen*, is here used in the sense of delivering up Abram's adversaries. A few verses later, YHWH proclaims to Abram, "I am your shield" (Gen 15:1).

And he gave him a tenth of everything.

Who gave to whom? The subject of the verb is not defined, but the context suggests it was Abram who gave the priest-king a tenth of everything. This would be his share of the booty, but the interpolator has designated it as a tithe.[36] In giving a tithe, Abram recognizes both Melchizedek's priesthood and his God. There may also be allusion to the

---

36. Westermann, *Genesis 12-36*, 206: a tithe is never spoken of as tribute paid from something acquired on a particular occasion, but a tenth of the produce at regular intervals.

city's destiny as a cultic center to which Abram's offspring will in future bring tithes[37]—an element underlined by *Jub.* 13:25 (see below).[38]

Melchizedek appears again in the Old Testament only in the mysterious royal Ps 110:1–4: "the Lord said to my Lord, 'sit at my right hand . . . the Lord has sworn and will not waver: 'you are a priest of forever in the manner of Melchizedek.'" This translation takes verses 1 and 4 as referring to different persons.[39] YHWH addresses the king and proclaims him a priest in the manner of Melchizedek. Since the only other text on Melchizedek is Gen 14:18–20, the manner of Melchizedek may be that of being king and priest. It is interesting that the Hasmonean high priests who claimed kingship (Maccabean period, mid-second century BCE) took for themselves the title of "high priests of the God Most High."[40] 1 Macc 14:41 reports that "the Jewish people and their priests had decided the following: Simon shall be their leader and high priest forever until a trustworthy prophet arises." It was thus that in 142 BCE the high priest Simon Maccabeus assumed the title of king. Both Ps 110 and the insertion of Gen 14:18–20 may have served as Hasmonean foundation *muthoi*.[41]

Tradition

There were quarrels between the herders of Abram's livestock and the herders of Lot's livestock. Tg. Neof. (and more profusely *Tg. Ps.-J.*) used the

37. Amit, *Hidden Polemics*, 155.

38. Ska, "Abraham Cycle," 38: Gen 14:18–20 shows the patriarch paying tithes to Melchizedek—paradigmatic conduct suggesting submitting to the priesthood in Jerusalem. See also Fretheim, "Genesis," 111.

39. They can also be translated as referring to the same person. *'Al dibratî*, which occurs again only at Qoh 3:18; 7:14; and 8:2 with the meaning, "because of, for the sake of" (see BDB, 184), would be taken to mean, "according to my word," and Melchizedek would be vocative, "O Melchizedek." YHWH would be proclaiming and installing Melchizedek a priest. See Goldingay, *Psalms 90–150*, 291; Kugel, *Traditions of the Bible*, 279.

40. Josephus, *Ant.* 14.163.

41. Römer and Finkelstein, "Historical Background," 22. Van Seters, *Abraham in History and Tradition*, 308 remarks that "Melchizedek, then, represents the priesthood of the second temple." Gunkel, *Genesis*, 281 argues against Maccabean origins. For one, "the poet still dares to announce a divine oracle in the fashion of the earliest prophecy"—something no longer witnessed in the Maccabean period. He points out that Jethro was also priest and prince, and that Israel's kings occasionally functioned as priests.

incident to preach concern to do no harm and to respect the rights of the native populations. Abram's herdsmen muzzled their cattle until they reached the pastures, but Lot's herdsmen did not muzzle their cattle, but allowed them to graze freely and roam about. Besides, Abram commanded his herdsmen saying, "do not turn aside to the Canaanites."

Lot looked about and saw . . . (13:10). The text is literally, "and Lot lifted up his eyes and saw . . ." The same verb (*nś'*) was used of the wife of Potiphar lifting up her eyes to Joseph and saying, "lie with me" (Gen 39:7). Applying the meaning in one place to the other, *Tg. Ps.-J.* has, "and Lot lifted up his eyes with lustful desire," as if he already knew the vileness of Sodom. Ambrose of Milan[42] must have known of this strand when he wrote: "Lot, that is, deviation, 'chose for himself.' Indeed, God has placed before us good and evil, so that each may choose what he wishes. Let us not then choose that which is more pleasing at first sight but that which is truly better."

Melchizedek, king of Salem. Qumran scroll fragments of the first century BCE (11Q13 or 11QMelch) portray Melchizedek as a heavenly deliverer identical with the archangel Michael. The figure in Ps 110:1–4 who was summoned to sit on YHWH's right was named "Lord" and had his enemies subdued by YHWH. Referred to as Elohim, he is the head of the "sons of Heaven" and presides over the final judgment to occur on the Day of Atonement. He will atone for the sins of the righteous and execute judgment upon the wicked. His adversary and antinomy is Malchiresha (king of wickedness), also called Beliar and Satan. Here is a *pesher* (actualizing interpretation) on the text of Isa 61:1.

> *To proclaim liberty to captives* (Isa 61:1). Its interpretation is that he will assign them to the Sons of Heaven and to the inheritance of Melchizedek . . . and will proclaim to them liberty, forgiving them [the wrongdoings] of their iniquities . . .[43]

> He will proclaim to them the jubilee, thereby releasing th[em from the debt of a]ll their sins . . . this is the time decreed for "the year of Melchiz[edek]'s favor . . .[44]

---

42. Ambrose, *On Abraham* 2.6.35, in ACCS 2:17.
43. Vermes, *Complete Dead Sea Scrolls*, 500.
44. Abegg et al., *Dead Sea Scrolls*, 592.

Philo made Melchizedek into a high priest: the high priest of God Most High saw [Abraham] approaching and bearing his spoils.[45] In some traditions, Melchizedek became a high priest by divine appointment, not by heredity. Ps 110:1, 4 was interpreted as God personally setting up a priestly order (you are a priest *by my order*, O Melchizedek) headed by Melchizedek, hence he was a high priest by divine fiat. *Tg. Onq.* and *Tg. Ps.-J.*, however, deprived Melchizedek of the title of priest altogether, so as to invalidate Christian arguments that saw in Melchizedek a figure of Christ, the high priest, in Hebrews 5–7.[46]

> **THE ROMAN CANON**
> Be pleased to look upon these offerings with a serene and kindly countenance, and to accept them, as once you were pleased to accept the gifts of your servant Abel the just, the sacrifice of Abraham, our father in faith, and the offering of your high priest Melchizedek, a holy sacrifice, a spotless victim. (Eucharistic Prayer 1)

Ps 110 is the most quoted text of the Old Testament in the New Testament. The New Testament consistently reads Ps 110 in a messianic sense. This may derive from the messianic take on this psalm in the LXX. The NT reads verse 3, "from the womb of the dawn I have begotten you," as referring to the eternal generation of the Son by the Father. The author of Heb 1:13 argues that Jesus is a divine being: "for to which of the angels has [God] ever said, 'sit at my right hand until I make your enemies your footstool?'" LXX (followed by the Vulgate) rendered *'al dibratî malkî-zedek* of Ps 110:4 as "according to the order of Melchizedek" (*kata tēn taxin Melchisedek*). It was the LXX translation, expanding on Philo's take, that created the "order of Melchizedek." From this, Hebrews 5 and 7 make arguments for a high priestly Christology. The order of Melchizedek differs from the Aaronide—the former is by divine appointment, the latter by human heredity. Being from Judah, Jesus could not be high priest, but "was declared by God high priest according to the order of Melchizedek" (Heb 5:10).

---

45. *On Abraham*, 235. See Kugel, *Traditions of the Bible*, 279. *Tg. Neof.* on Gen 14:18: for he was the priest who ministered in the high priesthood before the Most High God.

46. See Maher, *Targum Pseudo-Jonathan*, 58 n. 44.

Melchizedek, contrary to custom in the Bible, appeared without ancestry, "without father, mother, or ancestry, without beginning or days or end of life, thus made to resemble the Son of God, he remains a priest forever" (Heb 7:3). That Melchizedek blessed Abram shows the superiority of Christ's priesthood and covenant (Heb 7:7). Aaronide priests were many because they were prevented by death from remaining in office. Christ, because he remains forever, has a priesthood that does not pass away. "Therefore, he is always able to save those who approach God through him, since he lives forever to make intercession for them" (Heb 7:25). Melchizedek got into Christian liturgy as high priest: "you [O God] are the one who appointed Melchizedek as a high priest in your service."[47] See also the text box above, "The Roman Canon."

The messianic sense of Ps 110 in the LXX suggests a pre-Christian Jewish eschatological messianic interpretation of this psalm.[48] Jewish tradition seems to have changed in reaction to Christian claims. Justin reproached Trypho that his teachers refer "sit thou at my right hand..." to Hezekiah, as if he was ordered to sit on the right side of the temple when the king of Assyria sent men with menacing messages.[49] Both *Tg. Neof.* and *Tg. Ps.-J.* identify Melchizedek with Shem, son of Noah (Melchizedek being perhaps an honorific title).[50] Jerome[51] and Ephrem knew of this Jewish tradition. Identification of Melchizedek as Abraham is not found in early rabbinic literature,[52] but occurs in *Sanh.* 108b and in Rashi.

For the Christian, the bread and wine offered by Melchizedek points forward to the Eucharist.[53]

---

47. *Apostolic Constitutions* 8.12.23. See Kugel, *Traditions of the Bible*, 279.

48. Teugels, "Anti-Christian Polemics," 190. See also Strack-Billerbeck, *Kommentar*, IV, I, 452.

49. Justin, *Dialogue with Trypho*, chap. 83.

50. According to the years allotted him, Shem would live two hundred and ten years after the birth of Abraham.

51. *Questions in Genesis*, Gen 14:18. Ephrem the Syrian: "This Melchizedek is Shem, who became a king due to his greatness; he was the head of the fourteen nations. In addition, 'he was a priest.' He received this from Noah, his father, through the right of succession. Shem lived not only to the time of Abraham, as Scripture says, but even to the time of Jacob and Esau." ACCS 2:26.

52. Strack and Billerbeck, *Kommentar*, 4.1.455.

53. See Cyprian, *Letters* 63.4, in ACCS 2:26.

CHAPTER 4

Genesis 15

Covenant Between the Pieces

> God commits to the promise at such a depth that God considers an experience of suffering and even death. This reveals...the divine willingness to become vulnerable for the sake of the promise [recalls] a comparable move that God makes in the incarnation and at the cross.[1]

The Promise of Progeny

GENESIS 15 is no narrative as such—it lacks a real plot that leads to tension and its resolution; it is theological reflection that achieves certain aims in context. It consists of dialogue between YHWH and Abram in two parallel panels, verses 1–6 and 7–21. Each comprises a divine promise with an "I am" identification by God (vv. 1, 7); an expression of apprehension by Abram, beginning with the invocation, "O LORD God" (vv. 2-2, 8); and a divine reassurance by verbal and symbolic action (vv. 4–5, 9–21).[2]

"Genesis 15 is a very conscious effort to substitute the election and covenant of Abraham for the exodus election and Sinai covenant..."[3]

---

1. Fretheim, "Genesis," 121.
2. See Sarna, *Genesis*, 111.
3. Seters, *Abraham in History and Tradition*, 292. See also Ska, "Groundwork of Gen 15," 77: Genesis 15 reinterprets the Sinai covenant; the covenant with Abraham

Gen 15:7, "I am the LORD who brought you from Ur of the Chaldeans to give you this land as a possession," replaces similar words in the Sinai context: "I am the LORD, your God, who brought you out of the land of Egypt, out of the house of slavery" (Exod 20:2). The shift from Egypt to Ur of the Chaldeans marks a fundamental shift in the election tradition: "Yahweh is now the God of Abraham and his offspring."[4] The text effects a refounding of the people Israel on the unconditional and irrevocable commitment of God to the fathers. In other words, grace, not merit, now rules the relationship of YHWH to his people. "The present chapter of Genesis addresses an audience awaiting the fulfillment of the promises to the fathers but who could see no present evidence of the fulfillment. They are like those whom Isaiah calls upon to 'wait on the Lord' (Isa 40:31.)[5] This chapter also lays down the foundations of the Pauline theology of grace.

Further Reflections

Genesis 15 is best interpreted against the background of the exile and the theological questions of the postexilic community.[6] The catastrophe of 586 and the exile shattered hopes founded on the bilateral Sinai covenant. The people of God had broken that covenant and the curses threatened in Deuteronomy 28 had taken effect. If they were to survive and continue as people of God, a fresh and different way to the heart of God must be found. Jer 31:31–34 held out a new covenant in which "I will place my law within them and write it upon their hearts; I will be their God and they shall be my people." This leaves the Sinai covenant in place, only that God's surgical operation will assure fidelity in the future; the danger of infringement remains. Deut 4:30–31[7] promised that "in your distress, when all these things shall have come upon you, you shall finally return to the LORD, your God, and listen to his voice. Since the LORD, your God, is a merciful God, he will not

---

preceded it and was unilateral and unconditioned. Römer, "Abraham, the Law and Prophets," 96: Genesis 15 anticipates the Sinai covenant; YHWH addressed himself to Abram with his name YHWH before the revelation of his name to Moses.

4. Seters, *Abraham in History and Tradition*, 264.
5. Sailhamer, *Pentateuch as Narrative*, 149.
6. Bechmann, "Genesis 12 and Abraham Paradigm," 67: "the stories of Abraham are theological texts, but they use the form of a historical narrative."
7. A postexilic addition to the Book of Deuteronomy.

abandon or destroy you, nor forget the covenant with your ancestors that he swore to them." This relies on the mercy of God, but also introduces a shift in the covenant. The basis of divine mercy is no longer the Sinai covenant, but *covenant as oath sworn* to the fathers[8] (not covenant cut with Moses and the exodus generation). The language of covenant as sworn oath is exactly what appears in Genesis 15!

The ritual described embodies the assertion by Fretheim that caps this chapter. It points to the depth of the divine commitment. It recalls the divine commitment to Noah, "never again will I curse the ground because of human beings, since the desires of the human heart are evil from youth; nor will I ever again strike down every living being, as I have done" (Gen 8:21). What has changed, since the desires of the human heart continue to be evil from youth? Point is, "in spite of the motivation for a flood remaining present, God binds himself to take another course of action."[9] Fretheim is right to see here traces of the path to the incarnation and the cross. God chooses to be long-suffering and patiently to absorb, even transform, the violence done by human disobedience.

The First Panel, 15:1–6

Sometime afterwards. The word of the LORD came to Abram.

The first panel deals with the promise of innumerable offspring. "Sometime afterwards" does not necessarily link up with what preceded, though the editor seems to have contrived some linkages.[10] The formula of the word-event to prophets is very common in Jeremiah and Ezekiel. That prophecy is in view is further indicated by the phrase, *in a vision*. The

---

8. Westermann, *Genesis 12–36*, 215 cites Perlittt, *Bundestheologie im Alten Testament* as demonstrating that the patriarchal oath (*berît*) as reinforcing the old and simple promise to the patriarchs belongs to the Deuteronomic theology, and in Genesis 12–50 is always related to the gift of the land.

9. Clines, "Theology of the Flood Narrative," 139–40.

10. Sarna, *Genesis*, 112 lists some of these. "I am your shield" (*māgēn*) recalls God delivering (*miggēn*) Abram's foes into his hand (14:20). Amorites as part of the owners of the land (15:21) recalls Mamre, the Amorite, an ally of Abram (14:13). Dammesek recalls Damascus (14:15), the only two places this city is mentioned in the Pentateuch. God makes a covenant, *berît*, with Abram, who in 14:13 had relied on human allies. Possessions, *rekûš*, also appears in 14:11, 12, 16, 21. To these one may add the Rephaim as among the inhabitants of the land, in 14:5 and 15:20.

reader prepares for a revelation of things to come or divine interpretation of present conditions. This being a *vaticinium ex eventu* (prophecy after the event),[11] the latter is given with the former.

Do not fear, Abram. I am your shield.

The formula "do not fear" usually gives assurance to the king (in an oracle of salvation) in the face of war or battle. Read against what preceded, one thinks of fear of renewed warfare by the kings.[12] However, the fear may relate to the issue at hand—Abram may fear dying without an heir, and in the circumstances he has reason to fear.

I will make your reward very great.

Śākār refers to the wages of a servant or of soldiers, reward for work done. But, what has Abram done to merit a reward? And how can humans claim credit over against God? Augustine's dictum is apposite: "if, then, your good merits are God's gifts, God does not crown your merits as your merits, but as his own gifts."[13] Some see YHWH rewarding Abram for spurning the booty in Gen 14:23. The reward is not specified, but may refer to Abram holding on to his trust in YHWH despite the non-fulfilment of the promise; as such, "*very great*" anticipates the countless progeny to come.

There is nothing like war for rudely awakening people to human mortality. Had Abram been struck down in battle, he would have died childless. The image conjured by the word ʻ*ārîrî* (stripped) is that of a fallen soldier stripped of all valuables and even of clothing. Whatever God gives Abram without giving him a son would still leave him so stripped. So far, God has dealt in promises only. The words of Abram's complaint are somewhat corrupt in the Hebrew.[14] The sense is that with no offspring of his and with Sarai barren and past the age of childbirth, some servant in his household, perhaps Eliezer of Damascus, will inherit everything. Verse 3 clarifies what verse 2 said obscurely:

---

11. The first timeline of four hundred years for the exile refers to the exodus setting, the second one of four generations refers to the current exilic situation.

12. R. Levi articulated the fear as follows: "perhaps the sons of the kings that I slew will collect troops and come and wage war against me" (*Gen. Rab.* 44:9).

13. Augustine, *On Grace and Free Will* 6.15.

14. LXX: "As for the son of Masek, my female homebred, he is Damascus Eliezer"; Vulgate: "and the son of the administrator of my house this [is] Damascus Eliezer" (*et filius procuratoris domus meae iste Damascus Eliezer*).

Look, you have given me no offspring, so a servant of my household will be my heir.

YHWH for the first time clarifies the promise of seed—your heir will be fruit of your own loins. Abram was seventy-five when he left Haran (Gen 12:5), so he too is past the age.

Look up at the sky and count the stars, if you can. Just so, he added, will your descendants be.

This points to a night scene. At Gen 13:16, YHWH had promised to make Abram's descendants like the dust of the earth for numbers. Here Abram's offspring will be as innumerable as the stars in the heavens. Second Isaiah had invited the exiles to "lift up your eyes on high and see who created these: he leads out their army and numbers them, calling them by name" (Isa 40:26)—a call to trust in the creative and regenerative power of God. So also our text calls for trust. Genesis 17 will make Abraham's "descendants" comprise more than the Jewish people, a point of vital political and theological interest.

The omniscient narrator breaks frame to add a comment on the story. He knows both the mind of Abram and YHWH's responding attitude towards Abram.

And Abram put his faith in the LORD, who attributed it to him as an act of righteousness.

The Hebrew says literally, "and he believed in the Lord, and he reckoned it to him righteousness." Who "reckoned" to whom? This is the basic text for justification by faith. As for the language of blessing in Gen 12:2-3, here also interpretations differ, beginning with Paul and James.

> The Targums[15] speak of merit, and this is reflected in the TNK: "and because he put his trust in the Lord, He reckoned it to his merit." The LXX, followed by the Vulgate, speak of faith itself as righteousness, using the passive, "and Abram believed God and it was reckoned to him as righteousness" (*kai elogisthē autō eis dikaiosunēn*), "and it was reputed to him for righteousness" (*et reputatum est ei ad iustitiam*, Vulgate).

---

15. And he trusted the Memra of the Lord and He considered it for him as a meritorious deed (*Tg. Onq.*); he had faith in the Memra of the Lord, and He reckoned it to him as merit because he did not speak rebelliously against him (*Tg. Ps.-J.*).

Sarna[16] is in line with the Jewish interpretive tradition in the matter. He argues that the Hebrew word *ṣedāqah*, usually rendered as righteousness, sometimes bears the sense of merit. It has this sense in Neh 9:7–8 and in Ps 106:30–31, which have similar phraseology.

> Because of Phinehas's act in the affair of Baal-peor (Num 25:6–13), God granted him a covenant of friendship: "this was counted for him as a righteous deed for all generations to come."[17] The covenant is that of priesthood for all time. His act of moral indignation secured the priesthood for his descendants. As in our passage, the verb, *ḥāšāb*, is used with the noun *ṣedāqah*. As pertaining to Phinehas, so also Abram's act of faith made him worthy of God's reward, secured through a covenant.[18]

The long prayer of confession in Nehemiah 9 seems to be in line with this interpretation; in verses 7–8 it reads: "you are the LORD God who chose Abram, who brought him from Ur of the Chaldees, who named him Abraham. You found his heart faithful in your sight,[19] you made the covenant with him to give the land of the Canaanites ... You fulfilled your promises, for[20] you are just."

Christian interpretation of the verse generally follows the LXX and the Vulgate. It finds here a divine pronouncement of faith as justifying one before God.

> *Ṣedāqah*, righteousness, justice, is a relational term, not an absolute norm. One is righteous who does justice to the claims of a particular relationship. Being righteous usually relates to moral integrity or keeping God's commandments. "Noah was a righteous man and blameless in his generation; Noah walked with God" (Gen 6:9). *Ṣaddiq tamîm* (righteous and blameless) refer to ethical integrity. The righteousness invoked of Abram

---

16. Sarna, *Genesis*, 113.

17. *Wa-tēḥašēb lô liṣdāqah ledōr wa-dōr 'ad-'ōlām* (Ps 106:31).

18. Moberly, "Abraham's Righteousness," 120 argues that "as Phinehas stands to the priesthood, so Abraham stands to Israel." His example of human faithfulness to YHWH calls forth YHWH's response in a way that is of enduring benefit to Israel (126). As in Gen 22:15–18, a promise previously grounded only in the will and purpose of YHWH is now grounded both in the will of YHWH and the obedience of Abraham. Henceforth, "Israel's existence as a people is dependent upon both Yahweh and Abraham" (126), citing also his "The Earliest Commentary on the Akedah," 320–21.

19. *Ne'emān le-panêka* (steadfast before you).

20. *Kî ṣaddîq 'ātah* (for you are righteous).

was not on ethical grounds. In the cultic background, *ṣedāqah* is what conforms to cultic requirements, hence is acceptable and pleasing to God.[21]

Our text transposes "to the sphere of a free and wholly personal relationship" whole-hearted acceptance of God's promise and commitment of one's life to it. This God-approved behavior sets humans on a right relationship with God. Van Seters comments that just as for Second Isaiah, the crisis of the moment was whether one believed there was a future for Israel any longer.[22] The fundamental concern was about God's desire and ability to restore his people once more. Personal faith in the promises was what kept Jewish hope and its religion alive.

> A line of interpretation attributed to Nachmanides (1194–1270) removes this text entirely from consideration of justification by faith. It arrives at the Jewish idea of the "merit of the fathers" by taking Abram as the subject of the accounting: and he [Abraham] put his trust in YHWH, and he [Abraham] counted it to him [YHWH] righteousness.[23]

The Second Panel: Land Grant as Sworn Oath, 15:7–12

The next scene occurred when "the sun was about to set" (v. 12). A resumptive repetition at verse 17, "when the sun had set and it was dark," picks up the story. This makes out verses 13–16 as later insertion, concerned with a different though germane theme. These verses will be considered latter.

The second panel also opens with YHWH's self-introduction. In contrast to the context of Exod 20:2, YHWH self-identifies as the one who brought Abram from Ur of the Chaldeans. In the commentary on Genesis 12, we noted that other traditions place Abram's homeland in Haran. When Babylon, where the Judean exiles lived, becomes Abram's home, "the exile is in this sense a homecoming. At the same time, it is a

---

21. Von Rad, "Faith Reckoned as Righteousness," 129.

22. Van Seters, Abraham in History and Tradition, 269.

23. Gaston, "Abraham and the Righteousness of God" expounds this interpretation. Neh 9:8 calls YHWH *ṣaddîq* (righteous) as one who fulfills promises made. The faith from which the righteous will live, Hab 2:4, is this faithfulness of God. When Abram believed God made a deposit in his account; this was counted out to him when God spared Isaac (Gen 22) and on other occasions.

home that Abram left, on God's command, in his journey to the Promised Land."[24] YHWH brought Abram from Mesopotamia to give him this land; his "exile" and "return" become a model for the exiles.

How will I know that I will possess it?

Does this show a tinge of doubt after the fulsome faith proclaimed a moment ago? Doubt is a necessary part of faith, genuine faith in God is always in the context of difficulties, some of which appear insurmountable.

Bring me a three-year-old female goat, a three-year-old ram, a turtle-dove, and a young pigeon.

Abram brought these, split them into two (except the birds), and put the pieces facing each other. Hence the naming of this covenant as "covenant between the pieces."

> A similar ritual appears in Jer 34:17-20, where during the siege the princes and the people entered into covenant to set free their slaves, their male and female servants (Jer 34:10).

The parties to the covenant walk in-between the pieces, invoking upon themselves the curse to suffer the fate of the split animals should they break their word.

Birds of prey swooped down on the carcasses, but Abram scared them away. Smoking fire pot and a flaming torch, which passed between those pieces.

These unclean birds may represent enemy nations.[25] Representing deity is the smoking fire and flaming torch; they recall the Sinai theophany and link up with it. Long before Moses, YHWH made a binding covenant with Abram to give the land to his descendants. God alone passed between the pieces in an undertaking to Abram. The usual language for a bilateral covenant is used, namely, *kārāt berît*, cut a covenant (15:18), but the reality is that of an unconditional and irrevocable commitment on the part of YHWH alone.

To your descendants I give this land.

---

24. Hendel, "Historical Context," 62. P is the first to invent a Mesopotamian origin for Abraham to make it easier for the golah to identify with him. Römer and Finkelstein, "Historical Background of Abraham Narratives," 20.

25. *Tg. Ps.-J.* interprets, "the nations, that are like unclean birds, came down to plunder the property of Israel; but the merit of Abram protected them."

The gift is for the future, Abraham himself will die in peace in old age and be buried as a sojourner on the land (15:15).

Two boundaries of the land appear. The first boundary reaches from the Wadi of Egypt to the River Euphrates (15:18). These most extensive borders of the land appear also in Deut 11:24 and Josh 1:4; they correspond to the borders of the Garden of Eden (2:10–14).[26]

> Earlier research thought of the Davidic-Solomonic empire, but that empire never attained such scope. Rather, the borders correspond to the Transeuphrates section of the Babylon-Transeuphrates satrapy before the conquest of Egypt by Cambysses (525 BCE).[27]

This means that the whole Persian province of Transeuphrates, the territory where the Jews lived, has become homeland for Abraham's offspring.[28] This is another way of saying that "the promise is fulfilled through the Diaspora, where Judeans—beginning to become the Jewish communities—could live all in all an acceptable life."[29]

The second boundary comprises a list of ten nations (usually seven are given) all within Palestine (15:19). The list opens with the Kenites, the Kennizites and the Kadmonites.

> These three, with the Rephaim,[30] are not mentioned in other lists. Jethro, the father-in-law of Moses, was called a Midianite in Exod 18:1, but Judg 1:16 speaks of the descendants of Hobab the Kenite, Moses' father-in-law, traveling with the Judahites. In Num 32:12, Joshua and Caleb, the Kennizite, were the only two to survive the generation of the wilderness. He received his portion of the land around Hebron (Josh 14:5–15). Kadmonites ("people of the east") appear only here.[31]

These three peoples are linked with Israel and are possibly Arab descendants of Abram. If this is so, the verb *yārāš*, possess, does not in this

---

26. See Sailhamer, *Pentateuch as Narrative*, 152.

27. Blenkinsopp, "Abraham as Paradigm," 235.

28. Römer, "Abraham, the Law and the Prophets," 95. See also Romer, "Exodus in Genesis," 19: "the whole Persian empire may be a homeland for Abraham's offspring."

29. Bechmann, "Genesis 12 and Abraham Paradigm," 74.

30. Elsewhere this name refers to the shades of the dead; here it refers to an ancient people occupying part of Canaan.

31. In *Gen. Rab.* 44:23, Rabbi identified these three peoples as Arabia, the Shalamite, and the Nabateans.

context imply the expulsion of the other peoples; rather the land is given to Abram and his offspring and all those who live in it.[32] The land theology of this text differs distinctively from the deuteronomistic conception of the Promised Land that requires the annihilation of the indigenous peoples.

> The tradition of migration and displacement is historically valuable as an authentic expression of Israel's sense of the meaning of its national existence. In all of its versions, this tradition says in effect: we are not the original inhabitants of this land; we are newcomers on the stage of history, the youngest of nations. We came here from afar; not long before coming here, we were subservient to others. In order for us to enter this land and take possession of it, the original occupants needed to be displaced; this was accomplished for our benefit by God in accord with a plan he conceived and of which he informed us in advance…the only logical explanation of this fact is that acknowledging and serving this deity is our raison d'être… these are not ours by right but as a sacred trust and charge…We exist not as other nations do, in order to subdue others and pursue greatness, but rather in order to carry out a divinely ordained task, and our continued existence depends on our carrying it out faithfully. (Schwartz, "Reexamining the Fate of the 'Canaanites' in the Torah Traditions," 152)

Foreshadowing of Exile, 15:13–16

A deep sleep fell upon Abram, and a great dark dread descended upon him. How will I know that I will possess it? Know for certain that your descendants will reside as aliens in a land not their own, where they shall be enslaved and oppressed for four hundred years.[33]

Tarddēmah is deep sleep such as fell upon Adam so YHWH would rip up one of his ribs (Gen 2:21). Abram will possess the land, but there will be some delay—not in his lifetime. The delay involves slavery in Egypt, which, because foreseen, does no prejudice to the divine promise of the

---

32. Römer, "Abraham, Law, and Prophets," 100.

33. However, Exod 12:40 says that "the time the Israelites had stayed in Egypt was four hundred and thirty years."

land. The allusion to Egypt and the exodus becomes clearer when we read,

But I will bring judgment on the nation they must serve, and after this they will go out with great wealth.

This alludes to the plagues of Egypt during the exodus and the despoiling of the Egyptians as Israel left Egypt (Exod 3:22 and 12:36). Verse 16 gives a different timeline:

In the fourth generation your descendants will return here.

Exegetes have wasted efforts trying to harmonize the two. Some posit that the ideal life span in Egypt is 110 years, so four generations would approximate to 400 years. Augustine tried his best, but after computations he arrived at 405 years, "or, as God chose to call it, 400."[34] We should read "four generations" as adaptation of the text to the hopes of the present exiles in Babylon, of which the Egyptian slavery in the past was merely a foreshadowing. The author's message is the same as the vibrant message of Second Isaiah: "Go up onto a high mountain, Zion, herald of good news! Cry out at the top of your voice, Jerusalem, herald of good news! Cry out, do not fear! Say to the cities of Judah: Here is your God! Here comes with power the Lord God, who rules by his strong arm; Here is his reward with him, his recompense before him" (Isa 40:9–10).

For the wickedness of the Amorites is not yet complete.

There is probably no factual evidence that the original inhabitants of the land were marked by licentiousness and incestuous relationships; according to Schwartz, "this tradition now seems, rather, to have risen out of polemic needs, as a means of stigmatizing the cultural 'others.'"[35] It may have been deviancy accusation arising out of polemics. The Amorites (in Akkadian, *Amurru* or "westerners" or "those of the west") were Semitic peoples whose territory in the third through the second millennium BCE stretched from western Mesopotamia (Syria) to the borders of Egypt. In the Hebrew Bible, the inhabitants of the hill country of Canaan were called Amorites. "Amorite" is a pseudonym for Jerusalem in Ezek 16:2, 45.[36] In the Persian period, the name may have shifted from its original meaning. It may have come to refer to the Arab people, the nomadic and

---

34. Augustine, *City of God* 16.24, in ACCS 2:36.
35. Schwartz, "Fate of the Canaanites," 169.
36. Römer, Thomas, "Genèse 15 et les tensions," 120.

pastoral peoples of southern Judah, including the region of Hebron. As such, it is possible that "Amorite" in this text refers to the hostile "people of the land" whom the returnees encountered. The term 'awōn can refer to sin or its judgment. The nature of the judgment is not specified; it can take any form—displacement, famine, natural disasters forcing the population to flee, plagues and other strikes by YHWH, military conquest, or annihilation. The text foregrounds delay of the promise of land; it also affirms that its possession is linked with righteous living—for the indigenous tribes as for Israel herself.

Further Reflections

Constant dialogue with YHWH is a feature of the Abraham narratives. Was YHWH's speaking an everyday event for Abram and should we expect such in our lives?[37] In Genesis 12, YHWH does not speak to chastise Abram; Pharaoh fulfills this role on YHWH's behalf. The normal human reality is for YHWH to expect people to use their human discernment as they look at their own lives and at other people's lives. The "voice" of God intervenes less and less as we enter the Jacob story; it becomes rare in the Joseph Novella, where it vacates the space to foreground human decisions and processes, while all remains under God. The Bible contains differing spiritualities of the presence of God.

Tradition

In Gal 3:16 Paul argues that the promises were made to Abraham and to his seed (singular[38]), that is, Christ. Whoever is in Christ, Jew or Gentile, inherits the promises of Abraham. Reading Gen 15:6 in the passive (with LXX), "thus Abraham believed God, and it was credited to him as righteousness," he connected this with the blessing of Abram in Gen 12:3 and affirms:

> realize then that it is those who have faith who are children of Abraham. Scripture which saw in advance that God would justify the Gentiles by faith, foretold the good news to Abraham saying, 'through you shall all the nations be blessed.' Consequently,

---

37. See Goldingay, *Israel's Gospel*, 247.

38. In the Hebrew, *zera'* is collective, meaning descendants, as numerous as the stars of heaven.

those who have faith are blessed along with Abraham who had faith. (Gal 3:7–9)

Abram believed and was justified before any law of circumcision (given in Genesis 17), so also the Galatians believed and were justified by their faith independent of circumcision. In Rom 4:13–16, Paul again reads Gen 15:6 in the light of Gen 12:3:

> It was not through the law that the promise was made to Abraham and his descendants that he would inherit the world, but through the righteousness that comes from faith. For if those who adhere to the law are the heirs, faith is null and the promise is void ... For this reason, it depends on faith, so that it may be a gift, and the promise may be guaranteed to all his descendants, not to those who only adhere to the law but to those who follow the faith of Abraham, who is the father of all of us.

James, however, read Gen 15:6 in the light of Gen 22:15–18, hence the challenge:

> demonstrate your faith to me without works, and I will demonstrate my faith to you from my works ... Was not Abraham our father justified by works when he offered his son Isaac upon the altar? You see that faith was active along with his works, and faith was completed by the works ... (Jas 2:17–22)[39]

This commentary will further pursue the dialectic of grace and merit at Genesis 22.

---

39. Moberly, "Abraham's Righteousness," 130 mentions Gen 15:6 as a case study of how different traditions developed differing implications of the text because of their differing theological contexts.

CHAPTER 5

Genesis 16

Sarai and Hagar

> The story of Hagar and Ishmael reminds us that the Bible is not simply a book of answers, but also a book of questions.[1]

THE STORY OF SARAI and Hagar has a doublet in Gen 21:9–21. The narrator allowed many voices who do not echo the main theme.[2] The differing portraits of Hagar and of her status in the household of Abram (slave? maid? wife?) leave questions concerning inheritance and fairness hanging in the air.

> There are signs of disunity in this chapter. Hagar is told to name the child (v. 11), but Abram names him (v. 15). The LORD's angel met Hagar by a spring (v. 7), but verse 14 speaks of a well. Hagar is consistently called "maidservant of Sarai," except in v. 3, which makes her wife of Abram. Three consecutive verses, 9, 10, and 11, open with, "and the LORD's angel said to her"—a classic signal of interpolation. It appears that verse 10, "I will make your descendants so numerous . . . ," is an addition—it precedes the announcement of the birth of a descendant! It is strange that the angel would declare that the LORD has heeded her oppression (v. 11) only to ask her to return and submit to the

---

1. Sherwood, "Hagar and Ishmael," 304.
2. Westermann, *Genesis 12–36*, 249.

oppression (v. 9), in both cases using forms of the verb *'innah*, "to oppress."[3] Hagar's interpretation of her experience of God in verse 13 seems to have been reworked (see later).

Birth of Ishmael, 16:1–6

Abram's wife Sarai had borne him no children.

The narrator informed us in Gen 11:30 that "Sarai was barren; she had no child." This barrenness becomes the fulcrum around which the plot of the Abraham cycle revolves. YHWH's promises of "descendants like the dust of the earth" (Gen 13:16) and innumerable more than the stars (Gen 15:5) were made to a man whose wife was both barren and past bearing age. Abram left Haran at seventy-five; he is now eighty-five. YHWH spoke of Abram's descendants ("your own offspring will be your heir," Gen 15:4), but has hitherto said nothing about who the mother would be. "Abram put his faith in the LORD" (Gen 15:6). Sarai, tiring of waiting, devised a way.

Now she had an Egyptian maidservant named Hagar.

Pharaoh gave Abram male servants and maidservants (Gen 12:16), though none were named.[4] The maidservant, *šiphḥah*, though standing at the beck and call of her mistress, is not necessarily a slave.

The LORD has kept me from bearing children . . . perhaps I will have sons through her.

The fruit of the womb was under divine power. Giving birth, especially to a male child, was considered the apex of womanhood. Sarai requested Abram to "go in to" (have sexual relations with) her maid.[5]

> A Nuzi marriage contract seems to suggest she had to do this: "if Gilimninu fails to bear children, Gilimninu shall get for Shennima a woman from the Lullu country (i.e., a slave girl) as

---

3. For some of this, see Römer, "Isaac et Ismaël," 165.

4. The connection is made in GenApoc 20.30–32 (dated 25 BCE–50 CE)—Pharaoh bestows gifts on Sarah (not Abraham as in Genesis) among which was Hagar. *Tg. Ps.-J.* and *Gen. Rab.* 45:1 take this up, but now Hagar is also Pharaoh's daughter.

5. Rachel would similarly give her maidservant Bilhah to Jacob saying, "have intercourse with her, and let her give birth on my knees, that I may have children through her" (Gen 30:3).

concubine. In that case, Gilimninu herself shall have authority over the offspring."[6] But this contract is concerned for the man.

Sarai is concerned for herself; she thought, "perhaps I will be built up through her," using the root *banah*, to build. "Hagar's role is to provide boy bricks for Sarah and Abraham's house."[7] The child will be Sarai's, not Hagar's; in other words, Hagar served somewhat as a modern surrogate mother. As I noted elsewhere, "Sarai is focused on herself. She needs to be built up–children will secure her identity and status. Hagar is seen as a possession, a disposable commodity that can exchange hands at the will of the owner . . . her feelings are of no consequence in the transaction."[8]

Thus after Abram had lived ten years in the land of Canaan, his wife Sarai took her maid, Hagar the Egyptian, and gave her to her husband Abram to be his wife.

This report (probably from another hand) says that Sarai gave Hagar to her *'ish*, man, to be *ishshah*, wife.[9] With Hagar as secondary wife, her offspring would have the right of inheritance. This strand of the Hagar narrative, as we shall see, consistently claims for Ishmael the right to inheritance and the blessing of Abraham.

He had intercourse with her and she became pregnant. As soon as Hagar knew she was pregnant, her mistress lost stature in her eyes.

It is as if one sexual act resulted in pregnancy. Hagar now showed she had feelings and a mind of her own. If modern surrogacy complications are any indication, she may already have started claiming rights over the child still in the womb. "Her mistress lost stature in her eyes" is a pregnant statement. For Gen 12:3 says, "I will bless those who bless you and curse those who curse you" using the same root, *qll*, to "make light of."

---

6. HSS V 67 cited in Speiser, *Genesis*, 120.
7. Sherwood, "Hagar and Ishmael," 296.
8. Okoye, "Sarah and Hagar," 167.
9. The strand here is usually identified as P (Priestly source). With Keturah, Hagar is *pilegesh*, concubine, at Gen 25:6, but then Keturah is *ishshah*, wife, in Gen 25:1. In Gen 35:22, Bilhah is Jacob's *pilegesh*, but his *ishshah* at Gen 30:4 and 37:2. See also Hamilton, *Genesis 1–17*, 446.

So Sarai said to Abram, "This outrage against me is your fault. I myself gave my maid to your embrace; but ever since she knew she was pregnant, I have lost stature in her eyes. May the LORD decide between you and me!"

To cry *ḥamas*, violence, is a legal formula of appeal for redress. Sarai calls upon YHWH to judge between her and Abram. This confirms that Abram took Sarai upon her word and treated Hagar as he would a wife. Conjugal relations have induced a reordering of family structure in Abram's household, and Sarai felt the loser for it.

Abram told Sarai: "Your maid is in your power. Do to her what you regard as right."

Literally, "what is good in your eyes." Abram washed his hands off the conflict between the two women, effectively restoring Hagar to the status of "maidservant of Sarai." Sarai's reaction was swift. Hagar was acting uppity; she needed to be put in her place. Sarai, no longer caring about the child Hagar was carrying, returned the favor by spurning mother-to-be and child in the womb. Through all this, the two women never spoke to each other.

Sarai then mistreated her so much that Hagar ran away from her.

The verb for "mistreated," *'innah*, stands out; Gen 15:13 used it in the prediction of Israel's oppression in Egypt. And Pharaoh will indeed oppress Israel in Exodus 1. "Sarai does to a child of Egypt . . . what the Egyptians would later do to Sarai's children."[10]

Hagar Receives a Theophany, 16:7–16

The Lord's angel found her by a spring in the wilderness, the spring on the road to Shur.

Hagar set her face towards autonomy in Egypt, her homeland. The last notice of the location of Abram was near the oak of Mamre, which is in Hebron. Fleeing from Hebron to Egypt, Hagar traverses the bare wilderness. Shur means "wall," and may refer to the Egyptian border forts. It was Israel's first stop when Moses led Israel from the Red Sea (Exod 15:22). *Mal'ak YHWH* (messenger/angel of YHWH) spoke to Hagar; but verse 13 says that she gave a name to YHWH who spoke to her. In earlier texts,

---

10. Tsevat, "Hagar and the Birth of Ishmael," 69.

YHWH would appear and speak, one would hear his footsteps (Gen 4:8). Later texts, refining the idea of divinity, use a variety of surrogates to remove YHWH from immediate consort with humans. One of these surrogates is the angel/messenger of YHWH, a form of the appearance of YHWH.[11] When the subject is a divine being, the verb *maṣa'*, "find," includes elements of encounter and divine election.[12] That is, YHWH sought Hagar out and found her in the wilderness.

Hagar, maid of Sarai, where have you come from and where are you going?

So far, no one has addressed Hagar by name; the messenger of YHWH not only knows her name, he knows what happened—her reduction from "wife of Abram" back to "maidservant of Sarai." But as in the garden of Eden, a question is meant to hit off a dialogue and allow the addressed to open up. Hagar answers the question of "whence"—fleeing from my mistress Sarai—but has no clue about "whither." Incidentally, *baraḥ*, "to flee," is also used of Israel in Egypt (Exod 14:5).

But the Lord's angel told her: Go back to your mistress and submit to her authority. I will make your descendants so numerous . . . that they will be too many to count. Then the Lord's angel said to her: You are now pregnant and shall bear a son; you shall name him Ishmael. For the Lord has heeded your affliction. He shall be a wild ass of a man, his hand against everyone, and everyone's hand against him; Alongside all his kindred shall he encamp.

Sarai oppressed (*'innah*) Hagar; the messenger of YHWH tells her to return and submit yourself to oppression (*hit'anneh*)! The reader is perplexed that a God who elsewhere responds to the cry of the oppressed here asks the oppressed to return to oppression. A different picture emerges in the name Ishmael, which proclaims that "God hears" and the announcement of the angel of YHWH that the LORD has heeded Hagar's oppression, that is, has heeded her cry under oppression. So was YHWH after all moved by mercy and compassion? The Septuagint sought to reconcile the two jarring pictures by softening "submit yourself to oppression" to "and humble yourself under her hands." Patristic exegesis will speak of the messenger appeasing Hagar and giving her a way forward.

---

11. Gunkel, *Genesis*, 186 points out how originally YHWH himself goes about in the night of the plagues (Exodus 11–12), but in a later view it was his messenger (2 Kgs 19:35); Jacob fought with a god at Penuel (Genesis 32), but in Hosea 12:5 it was with an angel.

12. McEvenue, "Comparison of Narrative Styles," 69.

The messenger then makes promises of great progeny similar to those made to Abram. In Genesis, such promises are made to patriarchs only. Hagar will equally give rise to nations, be progenitor of a vast multitude, just as Abram. The name Ishmael is predicated on *El* (El has heard) but interpreted as if predicated on YHWH (YHWH has heard). The equation of El and YHWH means that YHWH is God not only of Israel but also of Ishmael and Hagar and the Arabs! This is similar to the word of Amos 9:7, where the prophet denies that exodus was exclusive to Israel; rather, the Philistines and Arameans also had their exodus by the hand of the same YHWH.[13] Two types of relief are promised Hagar.[14] The child will be *hers*, not Abram's; her offspring will be enslaved by no one, he will hold his own against all. In Western idiom, the ass stands for stupidity or brutishness. But for desert folk, the ass is indomitable. Ishmael will submit to no one, will be a true son of her mother. "Alongside his kindred he will encamp" recognizes Ishmael as "brother" to the Israelites, but places him in the desert outside the land of Canaan. That way, any claim to the Promised Land is obviated. Gen 25:18 reports that in fact the Ishmaelites camped in the desert alongside their "brothers." The phrase *'al penē' kol-'eḥāw* can, however, have the pugilistic sense of "and he will set his face against all his brothers."[15] Desert folk sometimes survive by marauding their neighbors. Such constant conflict, though, does not materialize in the sequel of the text (it will appear in midrash). When Abraham died, his sons, Isaac and Ishmael, together buried him in the cave of Machpelah (Gen 25:9).[16]

To the LORD who spoke to her she gave a name, saying, "you are God who sees me"[17]; *she meant, "Have I really seen God and remained alive after he saw me?"*

---

13. Römer, "Isaac et Ismaël," 166.
14. Saner, "Of Bottles and Wells," 207.
15. Gunkel, *Genesis*, 188.
16. In this piece, Ishmael seemed still at home when Abraham died, Abraham having earlier sent eastwards all the children of his concubines, Gen 25:7.
17. This can also be translated, "God of seeing." *Gen. Rab.* 45:10: "you are a God of seeing [*El Roi*], for she said, "have I even here [*halom*] seen him that sees me."

The Vulgate[18] reworked the Hebrew text[19] to make Hagar see "the back" of God.[20] The reference is to God's appearance to Moses in Exod 33:23. Such reworking seemed called for, since otherwise Hagar would see and address YHWH before YHWH revealed his name to Moses!

The text states that Hagar saw and addressed YHWH and gave him a name from her particular experience of him. She is the only human ever to name God, and this is significant. The narrator means to say that the God she experienced as El Roi is actually the unique God, YHWH. As we experience God anew, we find new names for God that match our experience; that way, theology and the knowledge of God grow.

That is why the well is called Beer-lahai-roi. It is between Kadesh and Bered.

Beer-lahai-roi may be rendered "well of the living one who sees me."[21] We find Isaac in the same location in Gen 24:62; 25:11.[22] Kadesh was also the first stopping place of Israel fleeing from Egypt.

Hagar bore Abram a son, and Abram named the son whom Hagar bore him Ishmael.

The angel of YHWH spoke of the child as Hagar's, hence Hagar was to name him. This verse has Hagar bear Ishmael to Abram, not for Hagar, and certainly not for Sarai—nothing here about Sarai's initial desire to be "built up" through Hagar. Dissonant voices speak in this chapter. In naming the child, Abram effectively adopts Ishmael, thus securing his inheritance rights. The naming of Ishmael is closely patterned even in phraseology on that of Isaac in Gen 21:3: "Abraham gave the name Isaac to this son of his whom Sarah bore him."

Hagar saw and named YHWH according to her experience of him as the one who sought her out in her plight. She is constituted ancestor

---

18. Vulgate: "*Tu Deus qui vidisti me. Dixit enim: Profecto hic vidi posteriora videntis me*," that is, "'you are the God who has seen me'; for she said, indeed I have here seen the back of the one who has seen me." LXX: "Thou art God who sees me; for she said, For I have openly seen him that appeared to me."

19. It could read, "have I even seen after my seeing."

20. Hamilton, *Genesis 1–17*, 445 follows this: "Have I really seen the back of him who sees me?"

21. Sarna, *Genesis*, 122, on the basis of Arabic *hayy* meaning "clan," conjectures that it means, "well belonging to the clan of Roi."

22. Noth, *History of Pentateuchal Traditions*, 108 and n. 311 conjectures that the Isaac and Ishmael were brothers connected to the well of Lahai-Roi before traditions wove any genealogical link to Abraham or spoke of YHWH.

with a line of descendants, just like Abram. This was in her own right; the angel of YHWH in making the promises did not mention Abram or any relationship to Abram. It would have been a pure story of liberation had Hagar been left at Beer Lahai-roi; perhaps that was what happened when the Hagar story stood on its own. Instead, verse 9 makes her return to oppression, only to have her driven out into the same wilderness. Her story is incorporated into the Abraham-Isaac story and overwritten in the interests of the hereditary claims of Isaac, as becomes clear in Genesis 21.

Tradition

Patristic interpretation speaks here of the passionlessness (*apatheia*)[23] of Abraham and the moderation and virtue of Sarah. Hagar represents the studies and exercises preparatory to philosophy/wisdom: "Sarah represented virtue and a spiritual understanding of the Scriptures but . . . Hagar represented the introductory knowledge and the shadow."[24] Hagar lives the life of a beginner on the way to perfection. Her pregnancy symbolizes the gestation period of one who has begun to be educated according to God. The Master's word makes the promise that one will give birth, that is, bear fruit.[25] Chrysostom comments on the extreme restraint of "God's noble athlete" and his desire to tighten the bonds of harmony and peace when Sarai accused him of injustice. It was as if he said, "one thing alone concerns me, to keep you undisturbed, without distress, free from any sorrow and enjoying the highest respect."[26] Building on the LXX rendering, he opined that "Arrogant and self-important" Hagar fled, but the angel's words "adequately appeased her spirit, settled her thoughts, restrained her resentment and brought complete tranquility to her thinking."[27] This teaches us that "if we are alert, afflictions rather recommend us to the LORD, and that then we will succeed in winning favor from him when we approach him with anguish of spirit and warm

---

23. Augustine, *City of God* 16.25: "what he wrought he had not sought, that the access had been without excess, the fathering without philandery."
24. Didymus the Blind, *On Genesis* 242-43, in ACCS 2:46.
25. Didymus the Blind, *On Genesis* 245, in ACCS 2:46.
26. Chrysostom, "Homily 38," in *Homilies on Genesis 18-45*.
27. Chrysostom, "Homily 38," in *Homilies on Genesis 18-45*, 369.

tears. Let us not grieve in our afflictions but consider the advantage of afflictions and bear equally all occurrences."[28]

Did Abraham commit adultery? No, for "adultery, it seems, was not yet prohibited at this time . . . Abraham then cannot be said to have violated the law since he came before the law. Though in paradise God had praised marriage, he had not condemned adultery."[29] I treat Paul's allegory of Hagar and Sarah in Genesis 21.

Rabbinic midrash also polished Abram's image. His taking Hagar ten years after arriving in the land established the right of a man to remarry if the wife bore him no children after ten years (*Gen. Rab.* 45:3, R. Ammi in the name of Resh Lakish; see also b. Yeb 64a). Sarai set Hagar free before giving her to Abram, so he does not have children from a slave (*Tg. Ps.-J.*). Sarai "gave her to Abram . . . to be a wife . . . not a concubine" (*Gen. Rab.* 45:3)—giving Hagar marital rights and assuring the status of her son as child of Abraham. Sarai persuaded Hagar saying, "happy you are to be united to so holy a man" (*Gen. Rab.* 45:3). When Abram listened to the voice of Sarai, it was to the voice of the Holy Spirit moving her to speak (R. Jose in *Gen. Rab.* 45:2).

---

28. Chrysostom, "Homily 38," in *Homilies on Genesis 18–45*, 371.
29. Ambrose, *On Abraham* 1.4.23, in ACCS 2:42–43.

CHAPTER 6

Genesis 17

The Covenant of Circumcision

God orders Abraham (now representing Israel) to live his life before God in such a way that every single step is made with reference to God and every day experiences him close at hand.[1]

This chapter is not a real narrative, but consists of five divine speeches, with one question by Abram and a report of his carrying out the divine command. Multiple repetitions of "God said" (vv. 3, 9, 15, and 19), even though God remains the subject all through, show that the chapter strings together various traditions and comments on them.[2] There are also many repetitions, with variation.

Linguistic markers that indicate subsections are as follows: "for my part" (v. 4), "for your part" (v. 9), "as for Sarai, your wife" (v. 15), "now as for Ishmael" (v. 20). One notes that what God says to Abram in verese 4–8 is repeated for Sarai in verses 15–17 (including the change of name and its implication).[3]

---

1. Westermann, *Genesis 12–36*, 259.

2. Source critics identify the author as P, who supplements and redirects older tradition. Indeed, the chapter is full of P linguistic markers: El Shaddai, establish a covenant (with verb *qûm*), everlasting covenant . . . McEvenue, *Narrative Style of the Priestly Writer*, 145 opines that P has taken the narrative of Genesis 15 and the family tale of Gen 18:1–16, and turned the oath of the one and the promise of the other into a very solemn legal-theological statement.

3. McEvenue, *Narrative Style of the Priestly Writer*, 152–53 notes many linkages

When Abram was ninety-nine years old.

Abram was eighty-six at the end of the last chapter (Gen 16:16), hence thirteen years have passed. Abram now has a son from his own loins, Ishmael; is this the heir?

> This chapter develops from the general and vague to the specific and concrete.[4] "I will maintain my covenant between me and you and your descendants after you throughout the ages as an everlasting covenant" (v. 7, which embraces all born of Abram) narrows to "it is with [Isaac] that I will maintain my covenant as an everlasting covenant and with his descendants after him" (v. 19).

The covenant that at first appeared inclusive of all the offspring of Abram is restricted to a single line of descent. Church and synagogue will debate who is the true offspring of Abraham.

The LORD appeared to Abram and said.

The report of theophany (vv. 1–2) uses the divine name, YHWH, which the narrator equates with El Shaddai and Elohim, though the rest of the chapter uses the name God (Elohim). Only the speech event is noted; God does not appear in human form. The theophany concludes at verse 22: *when he had finished speaking with Abraham, God departed from him.*

I am God the Almighty.

"God Almighty" translates *El Shaddai*,[5] which should be rendered, "God of the Mountains."

> The gods are called mountains (*šdyn*) in the Deir 'Alla inscription of the seventh-century BCE. Gods are associated with mountains, the supreme god dwells on the cosmic mountain from which flow the cosmic waters that give life on earth.
>
> We encounter the divine name El Shaddai for the first time here. Exod 6:3 explains that "as God the Almighty [*El Shaddai*] I

---

between Gen 17:1–8 and 15:1–12, 17–18 and between Gen 17:15–22 (Abraham laughs) and Genesis 18 (Sarah laughs). See also van Seters, *Abraham in History and Tradition*, 282.

4. See McEvenue, *Narrative Style of the Priestly Writer*, 153.

5. The translation follows the Vulgate *omnipotens*. The self-introduction appears strange after that of Gen 15:7, but the explanation is that P is a different source.

appeared to Abraham, Isaac, and Jacob, but by my name, LORD [*YHWH*], I did not make myself known to them."[6]

Walk in my presence and be blameless.

"Walk before me" is idiom for a life lived consciously in the presence of God.[7] The second imperative, "be blameless," may have the force of result—and you will be blameless. *Tāmîm* is usual for sacrificial animals that must be without blemish to be acceptable as offering to God. Exod 12:5 prescribes that "your lamb must be a year old and without blemish." The term was used earlier of Noah, "a righteous man and blameless in his generation" (Gen 6:9). Is God gently admonishing Abram for having taken matters into his own hands in the matter of progeny?

Between you and me I will establish my covenant.

The Hebrew has, "and I will give/grant my covenant between me and you." Although "between me and you" indicates mutuality, "covenant" (*berît*) is here something granted and established by divine fiat alone. The issue at play, blessing of progeny, depends on divine power. It is divine promise, irrevocable and everlasting because predicated solely on divine assurance. There are no conditions and no reciprocal obligations, just as the covenant of Gen 9:8 (after the flood), which was solely the act of God. Later in the chapter, in the panel concerning Sarah, covenant is linked with blessing, thus underlining its gratuitous nature. So, while using the term *berît*, which usually refers to a bilateral treaty, the author redirected its meaning and import.[8] The judgment of exile meant that the bilateral Sinai covenant founded on law and obedience was no longer extant. The author bases new hopes on God's earlier and gratuitous commitment to the patriarchs (see my commentary on Genesis 15). The firm divine assurance has to do with progeny: *and I will multiply you exceedingly*. In Gen 1:28, the verbs *pārah* (increase) and *rābah* (multiply) are used for the blessing and power of fertility given to all humanity. *Rābah* appears

---

6. It appears that P assigned a different name for deity for each successive stage: *Elohim* (God) for the period from creation to Abraham, *El Shaddai* for the time of the patriarchs, *YHWH* from Moses onward. Van Seters, *Abraham in History and Tradition*, 288. See also McEvenue, *Narrative Style of the Priestly Writer*, 151 n. 12.

7. Sarna, *Genesis*, 123 refers to an Akkadian idiom for absolute loyalty to a king. Applied to God, it means, "to condition the entire range of human experience by the awareness of his presence and in response to his demands."

8. McEvenue, *Narrative Style of the Priestly Writer*, 155 and n. 19 notes how P suppressed all mention of *berît* in the revelation at Sinai. In P, what God gave at Sinai was the blueprint of the tabernacle. McEvenue translates *berît* here as oath.

here, *pārah* in verse 6. Abram will be a superlative instance of humanity's blessing of fertility.

For My Part, 17:4–8

Abram fell face down. For my part, here is my covenant with you: you are to become the father of a multitude of nations. I will make nations of you; kings will stem from you.

An act of worshipful recognition of divine presence. *Gôyîm* refers to a people organized politically, hence the talk about "kings." *'Ammîm*, on the contrary, refers to a people as a conglomeration of families and clans. *Hāmôn* refers to the din of a huge crowd, hence betokens multitudes. This blessing is further signified in a change of name.

> When Sailhamer interprets "I will make you a father of many nations" in the sense that they will be "children born not of natural descent, nor of human decision or a husband's will, but 'born of God' (John 1:13)," he allows the NT to elide the testimony of the OT (versus the two-stage interpretation outlined in my Introduction). Similarly, in respect of "kings will stem from you," he speaks of "a 'Christology' of Genesis."[9]

No longer will you be called Abram; your name will be Abraham, for I am making you the father of a multitude of nations.

A change of name signifies a new status or mission. Both names, Abram and Abraham, are dialectal variants and mean "exalted father" or "the father is exalted"; the new name produces assonance between the -*ham* syllable of Abraham and the *ham*- of *hāmôn* (multitude).[10] Genesis 25 reports the fulfillment of this promise in nations and princes springing from Ishmael and from the offspring of Abraham and Keturah—thus expanding the blessing in Gen 12:2.[11]

I will maintain my covenant between me and you and your descendants after you throughout the ages as an everlasting covenant, to be your God and the God of your descendants after you.

---

9. Sailhamer, *Pentateuch as Narrative*, 157, 158.

10. Spurrell, *Notes on the Hebrew Text*, 157.

11. The fathers of the church hear here transference to the Christian dispensation: "Abraham is made into nations, that is to say, his faith is transferred to the nations and to kings of the world, who have become believers . . ." Ambrose, *On Abraham* 2.10.77.

Two qualifications are added to the covenant: it is everlasting (*berît 'ôlām*) and it receives a new theological note. *'Ôlām* does not refer to eternity in the philosophical sense, rather to something that endures for the foreseeable future and whose end is not in sight. The new note is that this covenant makes God the God of Abraham and his descendants.

> The patristic tradition understood eternal to refer to the Christian covenant: "in what sense is the covenant eternal? One interpretation is that it is eternal according to the One promising, for the things of God are not time conditioned. But relative to us eternal things become time conditioned. Another interpretation is that even when the covenant with Israel was abolished, it was maintained for us, and we are God's [people] in place of them. Circumcision took over a second territory after the faith [came]."[12]

The so-called covenant formula, namely, "I will be your God, you will be my people," describes the reciprocal belonging of God and people. Elsewhere, it describes the reciprocal obligations of a bilateral covenant. In focusing solely on God's commitment, the author transforms the formula.[13] God is irrevocably committed to Abraham and his descendants and to their possession of living space.

[And] I will give to you and to your descendants after you the land in which you are now residing as aliens, the whole land of Canaan, as an [everlasting] possession; and I will be their God.[14]

We heard in Gen 13:15 of land given forever, but this was "all the land that you see." The land of Canaan, and even the entire Fertile Crescent, was given in Genesis 15, but that lacked the "everlasting" qualification.[15] Apparently in play are the fears and hopes of the exiles, who needed assurance that God was still their God even after the debacle of 586 BCE that implied the breach of the Sinai covenant. Belonging to God circumscribes land promise: "the only thing that is of vital importance

---

12. Cyril of Alexandria, *Catena on Genesis* 3.1026, in ACCS 2:53.

13. McEvenue, *Narrative Style of the Priestly Writer*, 155 n. 19 credits this to P theology, and points to Exod 6:7a (P), which states: "I will take you as my own people, and I will be your God."

14. I restored "and" to make clear that this sentence flows from the preceding; I also restored "everlasting" (*'ôlām*) for the possession of the land.

15. These seem to be from "sources" different from Genesis 17, which is P and tends to emphasize the everlasting nature of divine gifts and commitments, since secure from the side of the Lord.

is that God stand by the people, even if it is a people expelled from the land."[16] I suggested in the commentary on Genesis 15 that God being God of the people in the Diaspora could be one way God fulfilled the everlasting promise of land.

For Your Part, 17:9–14

"Jewish faith has a flesh-affirming, world-affirming bodiliness."[17] It can teach us Christians that "relationship with God does not express itself simply as a spiritual journey; it draws in the bodily dimensions of life to which God lays claim."[18] The "kingdom of God" means not only holiness, but also the absence of whatever harms human life.

For your part, you and your descendants must keep my covenant throughout the ages. . .every male among you shall be circumcised.

In verse 4, the covenant is, "you are to become the father of a multitude of nations"; here the covenant is the circumcision of every male. By the time of writing, the term *berît* had come to signify circumcision.[19]

> The midrash makes the connection: "hence with that member through which I will multiply thee exceedingly, I will make my covenant between me and thee."[20]

> God is demanding that Abram concede, symbolically, that fertility is not his own to exercise without divine let or hindrance . . . The organ and the power behind it now belong partly to God. (Miles, *God: A Biography*, 90).

In Isa 56:6 covenant refers to circumcision: "all who keep the Sabbath without profaning it and hold fast to my covenant, them I will bring to my holy mountain . . ." With the exiles living among uncircumcised folk,[21] circumcision took on confessional significance. No longer just a

---

16. Westermann, *Genesis 12–36*, 262.
17. Goldingay, "Significance of Circumcision," 3.
18. Fretheim, "Genesis 17:1–27," 130.
19. McEvenue, *Narrative Style of the Priestly Writer*, 171.
20. *Gen. Rab.* 46:4.
21. All peoples in Canaan, except the Philistines, were circumcised. It was in the

necessary part of culture, it depended on the free choice of Jewish fathers, who thus affirmed their belonging to the Jewish people and allegiance to their God.

Further Reflections

Circumcision came also to be understood metaphorically—there is spiritual circumcision and physical circumscription. Ezek 44:9 refers to the two circumcisions: "no foreigners, uncircumcised in heart and flesh, shall ever enter my sanctuary." Jer 9:24–25 speaks of those "circumcised in the foreskin[22]: Egypt and Judah, Edom and the Ammonites, Moab and those who live the wilderness and share their temples. For all the nations are uncircumcised, even the whole house of Israel is uncircumcised at heart."[23] Judah and the whole house of Israel are numbered among the uncircumcised in heart. The heart is the center of volition and decision and of the encounter with God and with fellow human beings.[24] Circumcision of heart comports whole-hearted listening and obedience to the word of God. This is spiritual and enabled by God. In an earlier work, I touched upon this when I traced the trajectory from circumcision as a human work to circumcision as divine work and gift.[25] Deut 10:16 commands, "circumcise therefore, the foreskin of your hearts, and be stiff-necked no longer."[26] The exilic Deut 30:6 makes this a result of divine action: "the Lord, your God, will circumcise your hearts and the hearts of your descendants, so that you will love the Lord, your God, with your whole heart and your whole being, in order that you may live." At play is the dynamic between human effort and grace.

Circumcise the flesh of your foreskin. That will be the sign of the covenant between me and you.

In yet another shift, circumcision becomes a sign of the covenant. In Gen 9:8, the rainbow in the sky is a sign to remind God of his

exile, that the difference could, and did, become an ethnic and confessional marker.

22. The text is more pungent—*mûl be-'orlah* means "circumcised in uncircumcision," having foreskin though circumcised! Derouchie, "Circumcision," 192.

23. See Okoye, *Israel and the Nations*, 97.

24. Okoye, *Israel and the Nations*, 93.

25. See Okoye, *Israel and the Nations*, 93–101, here 93.

26. The LXX brings out the spiritual meaning: "ye shall circumcise your hardness of heart."

commitment never again to destroy the world by a flood. It is also an assurance to humankind of God's commitment. It thus appears that as sign (*'ôt*) circumcision reminds God[27] of his undertaking to be the God of Abraham and his descendants and to multiply their seed.[28] However, because of the acquired confessional meaning, circumcision comes to remind the male Jew of his ethnic and confessional belonging, of God's sovereignty over everything connected with procreation, and of the demand to "walk before me and so be blameless."[29] Or, as the text says,

Thus my covenant will be in your flesh as an everlasting covenant. Every male among you, when he is eight days old, shall be circumcised.

The anomaly that only males are circumcised becomes glaring. However, in ancient times the father was the head and representative that embodies the entire family.[30] By moving back to childhood a rite that was practiced as preparation for marriage, the author frees it from its cultural moorings and invests it with ethnic and religious meanings.

Yes, both the house born slaves and those acquired with money must be circumcised.

The Passover legislation repeats some of the legislation: "no foreigner may eat of it. However, every slave bought for money you will circumcise, then he may eat of it" (Exod 12:43-44). The concern is family religion. Circumcision opened the door of the Jewish family to outsiders.[31]

---

27. The reader should remember the distinction in the introduction between the "god of the text" and the "God of faith." Unless we make nonsense of all the places God is said to "remember," or that something is a *zikkarôn* (reminder) to God, the god of the text must need these reminders.

28. Fox, "Sign of the Covenant," 584.

29. See Derouchie, "Circumcision," 185.

30. With the drive towards equality, modern Jewry has tried to establish something for the women. The Central Conference of American Rabbis introduced *berît ha-ḥayyîm* (covenant of life) for girls in 1975, also called *berît kedûšah* (covenant of holiness). Plaut, "Covenant of Circumcision," in *Torah*, 111.

31. Eventually, in the Common Era, it became one of the three requirements for the conversion of males to Judaism, namely, circumcision, immersion baptism with public witnesses, and a sacrifice in the temple (Mishna, 200 CE). Cf. Okoye, *Israel and the Nations*, 158.

If a male is uncircumcised . . . such a one will be cut off from his people, he has broken my covenant.

The covenant does not become conditional; rather, one who withdraws from circumscription withdraws himself from the people and the promises made to them: "honoring the rite of circumcision is not a condition of the oath, but rather a means of assuring blessing."[32] The Midrash sees cutting off (*karet*) as divine activity; for example, one may die childless or prematurely.[33] For a child of eight days, the onus lies on the father.

As for Sarai, Your Wife, 17:15–19

As for Sarai, your wife, do not call her Sarai; her name will be Sarah.

The meaning of the name change becomes evident in what follows. The -*ai* ending in Sarai is an ancient feminine form; both names mean "princess." Rashi comments: do not call her name Sarai which means "my princess" (princess to me and not to others), but Sarah—princess over all.[34]

I will bless her, and I will give you a son by her . . . she will give rise to nations, and rulers of peoples will issue from her.

God draws out the meaning of the name change. For the first time, God announces that Sarah will have a son. She will participate in the covenant of exceeding fertility that God made with Abram early in the chapter. The creative power of divine blessing will put an end to barrenness. Further, as princess, she will be mother to kings; peoples and nations will spring from her. This parallels the promise to Abram, "I will make nations of you; kings will stem from you" (v. 6). One easily understands the reference to nations and kings in relation to Abraham—Genesis 25 will tell of Abraham's sons by Keturah, and the nations and princes springing from Ishmael and from Abraham through Keturah. One searches the sequel in vain for nations and kings springing from Sarah![35]

---

32. McEvenue, *Narrative Style of the Priestly Writer*, 170.
33. Rosenbaum and Silbermann, *Pentateuch*, 1:67.
34. Rosenbaum and Silbermann, *Pentateuch*, 1:67.
35. Some readers point to the twelve tribes and the divided kingdoms of Israel and Judah.

Abraham fell face down and laughed . . . can a child be born to a man who is a hundred years old? Can Sarah give birth at ninety? So Abraham said to God, "if only Ishmael could live in your favor!"

"And laughed" (*wa-yiṣḥāq*) contains the name Isaac, *Yiṣḥāq*. The pun on the name will continue into the next chapter. This time Abraham's gesture is one of doubt. The omniscient narrator reports Abraham's thought: the prayer on behalf of Ishmael springs from disbelief.[36] The odds against what God is promising for Sarah are too great. God had better take back his words about her and confer the blessing on Hagar.

God replied: even so, your wife Sarah is to bear you a son, and you will call him Isaac. It is with him that I will maintain my covenant as an everlasting covenant and with his descendants after him.

The participle *yôledet* (about to give birth) may imply that Sarah is in fact pregnant—a statement of fact.[37] A restriction narrows the scope of the covenant! The result is that Ishmael, though circumcised and thus bearing the sign of the covenant, is nevertheless excluded from those aspects of the covenant that touch possession of the land and having YHWH as his God! This can only mean, as already pointed out, that the term covenant, *berît*, takes on different fields of meaning in different parts of this text.[38]

Now as for Ishmael, 17:20–22

Now as for Ishmael, I will heed you: I hereby bless him. I will make him fertile and will multiply him exceedingly.

God hearkens to Abraham's plea on behalf of Ishmael, even though he said this in disbelief. The blessing of Ishmael is couched in the same terms as for Abram at the beginning of the chapter. In Ishmael's case, the two terms of the blessing of "increase and multiply" (*pārah* and *rābah*) of Gen 1:28 appear together.

36. Westermann, *Genesis 12–36*, 268 comments: "what God has promised he does, independent of human attitudes. Abraham, therefore, is not the father in faith for P as he is in Gen 15:1–6."

37. Cf. McEvenue, *Narrative Style*, 173–74. He contends that this section depends on the story in Genesis 18, where, however, it was Sarah who laughed.

38. It may also mean that "verses 15–22 have been added to remove any doubt about the ascendancy of Isaac and his line over that of Ishmael," Blenkinsopp, "Abraham as Paradigm," 238.

He will become the father of twelve chieftains and I will make of him a great nation. But my covenant I will maintain with Isaac, whom Sarah will bear to you by this time next year.

The promise of "great nation" recalls the blessing of Abram in Gen 12:2. "Twelve chieftains" (princes, not *melākîm*/kings) may be subtle comparison to the twelve tribes of Israel. Ishmael indeed receives the blessing of Abraham and participates in the covenant, but his share of the covenant is only the blessing of great fertility and nationhood.

> There is something inherently troubling and dangerous when one people claims to be uniquely chosen by the one God. (Nelson-Pallmeyer, *Jesus Against Christianity*, 270)

Two currents clash in the image of Abraham in this chapter. There is the "ecumenical" patriarch, father of multitudes of nations who share in his blessing. There is, on the contrary, the Israelite patriarch whose blessings are channeled only through the line of Isaac. The contrast may reflect the divergence discussed in Genesis 12 between "in whom all families of the earth will be blessed" and "through whom all the nations of the earth will bless themselves." The danger of trying to hoard God's blessings for oneself is always real for Israel and the church.

Execution of the Command, 17:23–27

Then Abraham took his son Ishmael and all his slaves . . . and he circumcised the flesh of their foreskins that same day, as God had told him to do. Abraham was ninety-nine years old. . .and his son Ishmael was thirteen years old when the flesh of his foreskin was circumcised.

The command spoke of circumcising babes eight days old; Ishmael was thirteen years old. This "gap" suggests that the command of circumcision in verses 9–14 has probably been inserted.

For the reception of Abraham as "father of a multitude of nations" and Abraham as "ancestor of Israel" see the commentary at Genesis 25, the end of the Abraham cycle.

Tradition

> He who circumcises must recite: ". . . Who hast sanctified us with your commandments, and has commanded us concerning circumcision." The father of the infant recites, ". . . Who has sanctified us with your commandments and has commanded us to lead him into the covenant of our father Abraham." The bystanders exclaim, "Even as he has entered the covenant, so may he enter into the Torah, the marriage canopy, and good deeds." And he who pronounces the benediction recites: ". . . Who has sanctified the beloved one from the womb; he set a statute in his flesh, and his offspring he sealed with the sign of the holy covenant. Therefore, as a reward for this, O living God who are our portion, give command to save the beloved of our flesh from the pit, for the sake of your covenant which you have set in our flesh. Blessed art you, O Lord, who makes the covenant." (b. Shabb 137b)

In the exilic period, circumcision developed symbolic significance for whole-hearted listening to the word of God. It became the mark of Jewish identity and acceptance of the covenant of Torah. In the Hellenistic period, circumcision became a site of Jewish resistance. One of the decrees of Antiochus Epiphanes (167 BCE) was "to leave their sons uncircumcised" (1 Macc 1:48). The author reports that "in keeping with the decree, they put to death women who had their children circumcised, and they hung their babies from their necks; their families also and those who had circumcised them were killed" (1 Macc 1:60-61).[39]

About the same period, the book of *Jubilees* insisted that any uncircumcised Jew belonged not to the children of the covenant, but to the children of destruction, to be "rooted out of the land . . . for they have treated their members like the Gentiles, so that they may be removed and rooted out of the land" (*Jub.* 15:26, 28, 34). This text links circumcision to continuing to dwell in the land.

In Hellenistic Alexandria, Jews faced ridicule from Greeks and Romans for the rite. Some Jews avoided physical circumcision, although accepting its spiritual meaning. Philo (BCE 20-50 CE) as usual saw the essential meaning of circumcision as spiritual (the allegorical sense), yet

---

39. Emperor Hadrian (circa 130 CE) again made circumcision a capital crime. This was one of the reasons for the Second Jewish Revolt, the Bar Kockba Revolt, 130-135 CE, the end of which saw Jews banned from Jerusalem under pain of death.

he also held on to the physical rite (the literal sense) as marker of Jewish identity and the physical sign of belonging to the covenant of Abraham. Circumcision is the symbol of that *enkrateia* (self-control, self-perfecting) which is the purpose of Torah, and which brings one close to God. That is why "the circumcision of the skin is said to be a symbol ... as one indicating that it is proper to cut away all superfluous and extravagant desires, by studying continence and religion."[40] Pruned also is pride,[41] "a great wickedness and an associate of wickedness," including pride in generating, as if by the power of the male and not as divine gift.[42]

With Christianity and the influx of Gentiles into the church, circumcision began to stand for Judaism, as baptism for the faith.[43] After Peter received and baptized Cornelius (Acts 10), the circumcised believers confronted him: "you entered the house of uncircumcised people and ate with them" (Acts 11:4). Peter was able to allay their fears because of the (divine) prod given by the visions he had. Matters came to a head when emissaries from Judea arrived in Antioch to challenge the mission of Paul and Barnabas, saying, "unless you are circumcised according to the Mosaic practice, you cannot be saved" (Act 15:1). The consequent Council of Jerusalem made prescriptions to facilitate the concourse of Gentiles and Jews in the church (Act 15:28–29)—circumcision was not among them. The council accepted that Peter was entrusted with the gospel to the circumcised, as Paul to the uncircumcised (Gal 2:7). In Galatia, Paul faced down Judaizing apostles and had to warn his audience: "if you have yourselves circumcised, Christ will be of no benefit to you ... you are separated from Christ, you who are trying to be justified by law; you have fallen from grace" (Gal 5:2–4). Here circumcision stands for the entire Jewish dispensation of Torah.[44]

---

40. Philo, *Questions on Genesis* 3:48.

41. For the interpretation of Philo, I am beholden to Niehoff, "Circumcision as a Marker of Identity"; also Simkovich, "Interpretations of Abraham's Circumcision."

42. Philo's approach to circumcision as the spiritual pruning of the heart is similar to what we read in Col 2:11–13: "In him, you were also circumcised with a circumcision not administered by hand, by stripping off the carnal body, with the circumcision of Christ. You were buried with him in baptism, in which you were also raised with him through faith in the power of God, who raised him from the dead. And even when you were dead (in) transgressions and the uncircumcision of your flesh, he brought you to life along with him, having forgiven us all our transgressions."

43. Ignatius, *Ep. Phil* 6:1 characterized Judaism as "the circumcised," Christianity as "the uncircumcised."

44. In Galatians 3 and Romans 4, Paul argued that since Abraham believed God, who reckoned this to him as righteousness (Gen 15:6), and this before his circumcision

Whereas Philo had interpreted circumcision symbolically, yet held on to the rite itself as mark of Jewish identity, Paul exalted the circumcision of the heart as equivalent to the rite itself: "one is not a Jew outwardly. True circumcision is not outward, in the flesh. Rather, one is a Jew inwardly, and circumcision is of the heart, in the spirit, not the letter" (Rom 2:28–29). That is, "Jew and Gentile can equally count as circumcised before God, provided they are circumcised as to the heart."[45] The one is obedience to the written law, the other obedience effected by the Spirit of God.[46]

Circumcision continued to feature in Christian-Jewish polemics of the patristic period. Genesis Rabbah, a Palestinian fourth-century collection of rabbinic exegesis, often reacts to Christian interpretations. *Gen. Rab.* 46 stressed the physical circumcision of Abraham over against the Christian spiritual interpretation that made circumcision a sign of baptism. It renders "walk before me and be *tāmîm*" (Gen 17:1) as "walk before me and be thou whole"—understanding *tāmîm* in the cultic sense as "without blemish/defect." Example is given of a lady the nail of whose little finger is too long; when she removes the defect, she is whole. Four kinds of circumcision are referred to in Scripture—of ear, eye, heart, and foreskin. As a high priest, Abraham had the foreskin as the only defect he could remove and still be able to function as priest.[47]

Origen dismissed physical circumcision as flesh, not spirit. For him, the circumcision was symbol of the faith: "we therefore, familiar with the Apostle Paul, say that just as many other things were made in the figure and image of future truth, so also that circumcision of flesh was bearing the form of spiritual circumcision, about which it was worthy and fitting that 'the God of majesty' give precepts to mortals."[48] Justin Martyr reasoned that "the fact that females cannot receive circumcision of the flesh shows that circumcision was given as a sign, not as an act of justification."[49] In fact, the rite "was given to you as a distinguishing mark,

---

(in Genesis 17), it is faith that saves, not circumcision (see this commentary on Genesis 15).

45. Barclay, "Paul and Philo on Circumcision," 552.

46. Barclay, "Paul and Philo on Circumcision," 553.

47. *Gen. Rab.* 46:4, 5. Any cutting in ear, eye or heart makes the priest unable to serve.

48. Origen, *Homilies on Genesis* 3:4.

49. Justin Martyr, *Dialogue with Trypho* 23.

to set you off from other nations and from us Christians . . . that not one of you be permitted to enter your city of Jerusalem."⁵⁰

> **GOOD FRIDAY PRAYERS**
>
> Before 1955
> Let us pray also for the faithless Jews: that Almighty God may remove the veil from their hearts; so that they too may acknowledge Jesus Christ our Lord . . . Almighty and eternal God, who dost not exclude from thy mercy even Jewish faithlessness: hear our prayers, which we offer for the blindness of that people; that acknowledging the light of thy Truth, which is Christ, they may be delivered from their darkness. Through the same our Lord Jesus Christ, who lives and reigns with thee in the unity of the Holy Spirit, God, for ever and ever. Amen.
>
> 2011 Text
> Let us pray also for the Jewish people, to whom the Lord our God spoke first, that he may grant them to advance in love of his name and in faithfulness to his covenant . . . Almighty ever-living God, who bestowed your promises on Abraham and his descendants, hear graciously the prayers of your Church, that the people you first made your own may attain the fullness of redemption. Through Christ our Lord. Amen.

Theodoret of the school of Antioch, however, saw circumcision as a distinguishing mark more positively: "When [God] foretold the exile, he devised a protection for their religion so that, when mingling with pagans, they would not contaminate their noble descent, but rather, looking to the sign, keep an undying memory of the one who had conferred it."⁵¹ Aphrahat similarly sees Abraham's circumcision "as a sign and signification of the covenant, so that when his seed would multiply, they might be distinguished from all the peoples among whom they would go, so that they might not be mingled with their unclean deeds."⁵²

---

50. Justin Martyr, *Dialogue with Trypho* 16.
51. Theodoret, *Questions on the Octateuch* q. 69 (p. 141). Josephus, *Ant.* 1.192 already wrote: "[God] charged him, in order to keep his posterity unmixed with others, that they should be circumcised in the flesh of their foreskins."
52. Aphrahat, *Demonstrations* 11.3.

"A philosopher asked R. Hoshaya: 'if circumcision is so precious, why was it not given to Adam?'"[53] This reflects Justin Martyr's objection: "if as you claim circumcision had been necessary for salvation, God would not have created Adam uncircumcised; nor would he have looked with favor upon the sacrifice of the uncircumcised Abel..." The implication was that circumcision was not part of the original design of creation and therefore was both superfluous and temporary. Rabbi Hoshaya answered that, "whatever was created in the first six days required further preparation... and man too needs to be finished off." In other words, creation requires perfection through human effort. Circumcision inscribes the call "to retrieve a lost ideal and maintain a fragile victory over adverse, superfluous elements."[54]

Further Reflections: Catholic-Jewish Relations

Until modern times, Catholics regarded the Jewish covenant as replaced by the Christian one; this is called supersessionism. All through medieval times, Jews were accused of deicide, were isolated in ghettos, and suffered pogroms whenever there was a plague of any kind. Every Good Friday, the church prayed for the "perfidious Jews"[55] (see the text box "Good Friday Prayers" above). All that changed at the Second Vatican Council (1962–65) with the Declaration on the Relation of the Church to Non-Christian Religions, *Nostra Aetate*, no. 4 (dealing with Jews and Judaism). It developed doctrine in two ways, at least. Though the vast majority of Jews did not accept the gospel, "nevertheless, God holds the Jews most dear for the sake of their fathers; he does not repent of the gifts he makes or of the calls he issues." In other words, God's covenant with Israel is still intact. Further, "true, the Jewish authorities and those who followed their lead pressed for the death of Christ; still, what happened in his passion cannot be charged against all the Jews, without distinction, then alive, nor against the Jews of today."

Thereafter, the *Catechism* no. 121 clearly affirmed that the "books [of the Old Testament] are divinely inspired and retain a permanent value, for the Old Covenant has never been revoked." This actually

---

53. *Gen. Rab.* 11:6.

54. Niehoff, "Circumcision as a Marker of Identity," 106, citing Philo's answer to the question.

55. This was what I heard all my childhood.

reiterated the teaching of Saint John Paul II when meeting with Jewish representatives in Mainz (November 17, 1980). A recent document from the Commission for Religious Relations with the Jews[56] took up the theological implications of this assertion. That should mean that circumcision was word of God in Genesis 17 and still word of God for the Jews of our time. The 2011 Good Friday Prayer pleads "that he may grant them to advance in love of his name and in faithfulness to his covenant . . ." His covenant in this case is the Jewish covenant. Are there thus two paths to salvation, one for Jews through Torah, the other for Christians through Christ? The document answers that Christian faith proclaims that Christ's work is universal and involves all humankind (no. 25). There cannot, therefore, be two ways of salvation, since Christ is Redeemer of Jews and Gentiles alike (no. 37). That the Jews are participants in God's salvation is theologically unquestionable, but how that can be possible without confessing Christ explicitly is and remains an unfathomable divine mystery (no. 36). Meantime, the Church neither conducts nor supports any specific institutional mission work directed towards Jews, even if Christians are called to bear witness to their faith in Jesus Christ also to Jews. As already voiced by *Nostra Aetate*, "In company with the Prophets and the same Apostle, the church awaits that day, known to God alone, on which all peoples will address the Lord in a single voice and serve him shoulder to shoulder" (Zeph 3:9). *Nostra Aetate* drew out some pastoral guidelines: "Although the church is the new people of God, the Jews should not be presented as rejected or accursed by God, as if this followed from the Holy Scriptures. All should see to it, then, that in catechetical work or in the preaching of the word of God they do not teach anything that does not conform to the truth of the Gospel and the spirit of Christ."

---

56. Commission for Religious Relations with the Jews, *Reflection on the Theological Questions pertaining to Catholic-Jewish Relations*. I reviewed this document in *Spiritan Horizons* 11 (Fall 2016) 157.

CHAPTER 7

Genesis 18–19

Abraham, Lot, and Sodom

> Shall not the Judge of the whole Earth do Justice?
> —Genesis 18:25

GENESIS 18–19 FORM A literary unit; the same characters traverse the two chapters. The chapters are closely linked by literary and parallel panels, for example, between the hospitality of Abraham (Gen 18:1–8) and that of Lot (Gen 19:1–3).[1] They pick up the story of Abraham and his nephew Lot from Genesis 13–14. After this, Lot drops totally out of the picture, leaving offspring in Moabites and Ammonites to continue relationship with Israel. Gen 18:16–33 is an insertion, a theological reflection in the form of narrative.

The entire material easily divides as follows:[2]

Visit of YHWH to Abraham at Mamre (18:1–15)
YHWH's soliloquy and dialogue with Abraham (18:16–33)
Visit of the messengers to Lot at Sodom (19:1–23)
Destruction of Sodom and its aftermath (19:24–29)
The story of Lot and his daughters in the cave (19:30–38)

1. See the table in Lettelier, *Day in Mamre*, 39.
2. Letellier, *Day in Mamre*, 76.

The chapters manifest a dizzying shifting of singular and plural speakers. The crux, however, is 19:24: "the LORD rained down sulfur from the LORD out of heaven." If the LORD departed in 18:33, who is the LORD still in Sodom in 19:24? One begins to see why Jewish and Christian interpreters wrestle with this text, and how it would become one of the hot spots for the debate on the divinity of Christ (Justin Martyr), and later on the Trinity (Saint Augustine). See under "Tradition."

> The text begins with a notice, "the LORD appeared to Abraham" (18:1), which prepares the reader for a theophany. But then Abraham saw three men and ran towards them. He said, "Adonāi" (18:3, with long -ā), which usually refers to the LORD.[3] Is this Adonāi one of the "men?" Though he just addressed a singular person, he continued, "let some water be brought, that you [plural] may wash your [plural] feet..." "Very well" they replied, "do as you have said" (18:5). "Where is your wife," they asked him (18:9), but the dialogue continues with, "I will return to you about this time next year..." (18:10). This "I" is soon identified as YHWH: "but the LORD said to Abraham: 'why did Sarah laugh?'" (18:13). As Abraham escorted the men, YHWH (apparently one of the "men") considered, "shall I hide from Abraham what I am about to do..." (18:17). While YHWH was speaking with Abraham, "the two angels [no longer called "men"] reached Sodom in the evening" (19:1). Meantime, YHWH departed after speaking with Abraham (18:33). In 19:16, the two in Sodom become "the men" who seized Lot's hand and those of his family and led them outside Sodom. But Lot replied to them, "Oh no, Adonāi!" as usual for the LORD (NABRE renders, "Oh no, my lords!").

It appears that the author struggles to reconcile diverse yet important views of God: God can appear, yet his form cannot be seen (Exod 33:23). Use of singular and plural forms is such the "the three men always represent God's presence and can be identified with God's presence while remaining clearly distinct from him."[4]

---

3. NABRE has "Sir," though other versions render "my lords."
4. Sailhamer, *Pentateuch as Narrative*, 162, 163.

Hospitality at Mamre: Abraham Hosts YHWH, 18:1–15

> Rab Judah said in Rab's name: Hospitality to wayfarers is greater than welcoming the presence of the Shekinah, for it is written, And he said, "My lord, if now I have found favor in thy sight, pass not away . . ." (b. Shab 127a).
> On this interpretation, Abraham was speaking to God and begged him to remain while he saw to his guests.

The LORD appeared to Abraham by the oak [text: oaks] *of Mamre.*

This is possibly the narrator's heading for the unit. Abraham then saw three men, one of whom is later identified as YHWH.[5] Then follows an annunciation type-scene, in which a god or angel or holy person promises offspring to a barren couple, a promise that is fulfilled in conception and birth.[6] The LORD appeared in human form; he could stand with Abraham and dialogue with him, though no attempt is made to depict him. Abraham had settled near the Oak of Mamre, which is in Hebron (13:18). In 14:13, Mamre, the Amorite, hence a person, is one of the three allies of Abram in the battle against the four kings.

Abraham was at the entrance of his tent in the heat of the day, when travelers in desert areas were bound to look for shelter. He saw three men and ran to greet them; it was as if he was on the lookout for travelers. He prevailed upon them to accept hospitality, noting,

"For it is for this [kî 'al-kēn][7] *you have turned in to your servant."* (18:5)

As if overjoyed with their acceptance, he hurried into Sarah's tent to ask that she quickly bake bread, ran (rāṣ) to the herd to pick out a tender and choice calf, and gave it to the servant to prepare. With delicate touch, he spoke only of a morsel of bread (pat leḥem), something easily provided without bother, lest the guests might think they were a burden. What he

---

5. Some, like Gunkel, *Genesis*, 194 say that the heading is a conscious theologizing of an ancient pre-Israelite story of the visit of three gods to announce a birth. The shifting between YHWH and "the men" all through the unit may be part of the theologizing process.

6. See Alter, *Genesis*, 78.

7. NABRE: "now that you have come to your servant," misses the subtle coaxing.

actually offered was a sumptuous meal, while himself, not the servant, waited on the guests as they ate under the oak. An example of gracious hospitality.

One good turn deserves another. Hospitality in ancient cultures called for reciprocation. They ask Abraham the whereabouts of his wife, Sarah. The rejoinder:

"I will return to you about this time next year, and Sarah will then have a son."

An idiomatic manner of asserting conception and birth by the same time next year, not necessarily that he will revisit. Sarah was eavesdropping. The narrator reminds us that Abraham is old and Sarah was long past menopause.[8] She was tickled and laughed to herself,

"Now that I am worn out and my husband is old, am I still to have sexual pleasure?"

"She laughed," *tiṣḥaq*, is a play on the name *Yiṣḥaq* (Isaac); it recalls the laughter of Abraham in similar circumstances in Gen 17:17—both in derisive unbelief. This guest who can read the inward thoughts of people out of sight is no ordinary human. Perhaps at this point both Abraham and Sarah begin to realize they are dealing with divinity, or at least a prophet.

But the LORD said to Abraham, "why did Sarah laugh and say, 'will I really bear a child, old as I am?'"

Ignoring her subterfuge about pleasure, he addressed her real thought about the impossibility of conception in her age.

> Said R. Levi: "if you want to have a world, there can be no justice, and if justice is what you want, there can be no world. You are holding the rope at both ends, you want a world and you want justice. If you don't give in a bit, the world can never stand." Said the Holy One, blessed be He, to Abraham, "you have loved righteousness" (Ps 45:8): you have loved to justify my creatures; "and hated wickedness": you have refused to condemn them. (*Gen. Rab.* 49:9)

---

8. Messages of conception and birth to old couple usually requires they are childless—suggests that the independent tale did not know of Ishmael. See Römer, "Isaac (Patriarch)," 262.

Is anything too marvelous for the LORD to do?

Yippalē' combines the senses of "marvelous" and "difficult"; nothing is impossible with God.

Sarah lied, saying, "I did not laugh." But [the LORD] said, "Yes, you did."

The narrator tells us that Sarah lied because she was afraid. Scripture tells it as it is: the patriarchs are not presented as models for human conduct, but rather as mirrors of the human struggle for righteousness.

YHWH Dialogues with Abraham about Sodom, 18:16–33

Though couched in the form of a dialogue, this section is actually a theological reflection on a matter of importance to the community of its time. Blenkinsopp wrote: "Genesis 18:23–32 is a midrash on the destruction of Sodom occasioned by the destruction of Jerusalem in 586 BCE and the theological problems to which this event gave rise."[9] Questions of theodicy do not arise in the Hebrew Bible till the exilic period. Jer 12:1–6 ("why does the way of the wicked prosper," v. 2) was probably the first time this question was raised. Then come Ezek 14:12–20, Ezekiel 18, the book of Job, etc. The entire Deuteronomistic History is so patterned that God's judgment is consequent response to the wickedness of individuals and nations. God is not arbitrary in his dealings with people and nations. Abraham escorted the men on their way.

They set out from there and looked down toward Sodom. The LORD considered: shall I hide from Abraham what I am about to do?

The narrator externalizes divine internal locution. In sharing his plans, the LORD makes Abraham a participant in the drama. And that is precisely because, by the LORD's gift, Abraham will

become a great and mighty nation [-āṣûm can also mean numerous], and all the nations of the earth are to find blessing in him.[10]

The elect are given a role to play in God's dispositions for his world. What follows contains three firsts. For the first time, the LORD gives a reason for his call of Abram in Gen 12:1–3; for the first time, the spiritual

---

9. Blenkinsopp, "Abraham and the Righteous of Sodom," 129.

10. A variant translation is "will be blessed in him"; see the discussion in the commentary on Genesis 12.

nature of YHWH's election is adumbrated[11]; and for the first time (in canonical order), "the fulfillment of the covenantal promise is explicitly made contingent on moral performance."[12] This text is similar to Gen 22:15–18 and 26:5, both equally late additions to their context. Such conditioned promise is a feature of Deuteronomy and the works flowing from it, that condition promise of the possession of the land upon obedience to the Torah.[13]

Indeed, I have singled him out [literally, I have known him] *that he may direct* [literally, command] *his children and his household in the future to keep the way of the LORD by doing what is right and just, so that [le-ma'an] the LORD may put into effect for Abraham the promises he made about him.*

The LORD inducts Abraham into his role as "blessing." He will soon get an object lesson, in what happens to Sodom, of what happens when people flout God-given opportunities.

> Except for Isa 40:3 (prepare the way of the Lord), which refers to the divine pathway from Babylon with redeemed exiles, the way of the LORD (*derek YHWH*) occurs again, in Judg 2:22; Prov 10:29; and Jer 5:4, 5 (they do not know the way of the LORD, the justice [*mishpaṭ*] of their God) in the context of keeping the Torah of YHWH. Those whose way is blameless walk by the law of the LORD (Ps 119:1). The psalmist begs: "teach me the way of your statutes"; he promises to "run the way of your commandments" (Ps 119:33, 32).

Abraham is meant to teach his offspring fidelity to the paths of life that lead to God. *Derek* is also the way of being or the nature of a thing or being. As such, *derek YHWH* refers to conduct that corresponds to the nature of YHWH, conduct defined as *ṣedaqah u-mishpaṭ* (righteousness and justice).

> The inverse form, *mishpaṭ u-ṣedaqah*, is usual in the Hebrew Bible and connotes social justice. The form here, *ṣedaqah u-mishpaṭ*, recurs only in Prov 21:3 and Ps 33:5, "the LORD loves *ṣedaqah u-mishpaṭ*,"[14] which is to be translated, "YHWH

---

11. Lettelier, *Day in Mamre*, 114.
12. Alter, *Genesis*, 80.
13. Cf. Westermann, *Genesis 12–36*, 289.
14. It is parallel to *hesed YHWH* (the mercy of the LORD), "He loves *ṣedaqah u-mishpaṭ*. The earth is full of the mercy of the Lord."

loves mercy and justice" (not, "he loves justice and right," as NABRE).

Mercy and justice are the nature of YHWH. Abraham will teach his offspring the true nature of YHWH and how to live in imitation of it.[15] The root, ṣdq, "is not behavior in accordance with an ethical, legal, psychological, religious, or spiritual norm . . . rather righteousness is in the OT the fulfillment of the demands of a relationship be it with men or with God."[16] What it involves at any time depends on the particular relationship. As such, its meaning evolves. I wrote elsewhere:

> The Hebrew word pair *mishpaṭ/sedaqah* (justice and righteousness), which, in the Hebrew Bible, stands for social justice, abounds in Isaiah 1–39 (see, for example, Isa 16:5; 28:17; 32:16 and 33:5), but is lacking in Isaiah 40–55. In chapters 1–39, *ṣedaqah* (justice, righteousness) describes the activity of the people as they strive to live in accord with God's character and the commands of God's *torah*. In chapters 40–55, on the other hand, one meets only the word pair *ṣedaqah/yeshu'[ayin]â* (righteousness and salvation, cf. Isa 45:8 and 46:12–13), which pair is totally absent from chapters 1–39. *Ṣedaqah* in this section refers to God's own righteousness only, God's faithful performance of God's covenant promises. Though not strictly bound to do so, God had to deliver God's people if God is to act rightly toward them. Both John N. Oswalt and Rolf Rendtorff[17] suggest that Isaiah 56–66 had in mind, as one of the aims of that redaction, to synthesize these divergent views on righteousness in chapters 1–39 and 40–55. The synthesis appears already in Isa 56:1: "act with justice [*ṣedaqah*], for soon my salvation will come and my saving justice [*ṣedaqah*] be manifest."[18]

So the LORD said: the outcry against Sodom and Gomorrah is so great, and their sin so grave, that I must go down and see whether or not their actions are as bad as the cry against them that comes to me. I mean to find out.

---

15. MacDonald, "Listening to Abraham," 40–41 thus argues that the way of YHWH that Abraham must learn is the forgiving mercy of God, and that "Abraham may have saved Sodom had he asked for mercy."
16. Achtemeier, "Righteousness in the OT," 80.
17. Oswalt, "Righteousness in Isaiah"; Rendtorff, "Isaiah 56:1 as a Key."
18. Okoye, *Israel and the Nations*, 94–95.

This can also be translated as, "whether as the outcry that has come to me they have dealt destruction."[19] Once Lot chose the area of Sodom, the narrator informed us that "the inhabitants of Sodom were wicked, great sinners against the LORD" (13:13). *Za'aq/ṣa'aq* is the cry of the oppressed weaker party. The same formula is used for the voice of the blood of Abel crying to YHWH from the ground (Gen 4:10); this suggests oppressive violence as the sin of Sodom. As the men walked toward Sodom, Abraham remained standing with the LORD.[20]

Will you really sweep away the righteous with the wicked? Suppose there were fifty righteous people in the city . . . Far be it from you to do such a thing, to kill the righteous with the wicked, so that the righteous and the wicked are treated alike! Should not the judge of all the world do what is just?

While Job 9:22 affirmed that "both the innocent and the wicked he destroys," our text protests that it is against the very nature of YHWH to treat wicked and righteous alike.[21] YHWH is seen as the universal Lord and Judge. While polytheism solves the problem of evil by assigning good and evil to different gods or principles, monotheism is stuck with the one God who must answer for all that happens, good and evil. It is also assumed that real justice means individual retribution.[22] Against this background, Abraham proffered two requests: that the innocent not suffer with the guilty, and that the entire city be spared for the sake of an innocent minority.[23] The one request is based on the demands of justice, the other on mercy—the two attributes of YHWH invoked earlier. Unlike Jonah 3, the question of repentance is not raised, perhaps because the doctrine of repentance was yet to be formulated.

---

19. Alter, *Genesis*, 81, treating *kalah* as a noun, not adverbially, as meaning completely.

20. Here, one of the corrections of the scribes (*tikkunē sōpherîm*)—the text had YHWH standing by Abraham.

21. Said R. Aha: "[Abraham said to God,] 'You bound yourself by an oath not to bring a flood upon the world. Are you now going to act deceitfully against the clear intent of that oath? True enough, you are not going to bring a flood of water, but you are going to bring a flood of fire. If so, you will not faithfully carry out the oath!" (*Gen. Rab.* 49:9, translation Neusner).

22. Ben Zvi, "Dialogue between Abraham and YHWH," 38.

23. Sarna, *Genesis*, 132.

The Lord replied: if I find fifty righteous people in the city of Sodom, I will spare the whole place for their sake [using the verb *naśa'* (lift, forgive) as for Cain in Gen 4:7].

In six rounds of dialogue, Abraham continued to decrease the number till he arrived at ten:

"please do not let my Lord be angry if I speak up this last time. What if ten are found there?" "For the sake of the ten . . . I will not destroy it."

Abraham stopped here either because he thought there must be at least ten righteous in Sodom or the number ten was enough to save his nephew Lot's family.

The Lord departed as soon as he had finished speaking with Abraham.

He would have gone back to heaven.

What is the image of YHWH here? He came down to investigate, just as he did for the men of the tower (Gen 11:7); his investigation will confirm what he suspected. He responds, measure for measure, to the oppression of the weak, but only after ascertaining the facts. "He agrees that the righteous few can often save a city,"[24] thus launching the idea of vicarious redemption.[25] Yahweh had not decreed the punishment; the outcome was still open and depended on what the investigation would establish. Abraham's postulation with God was not in vain. YHWH's mercy will stop at destroying a city even for the sake of ten righteous people in it. If Sodom is eventually destroyed, that would mean that not even ten righteous people could be found in it. The reader hopes that this would not be the case.

The Two Angels in Sodom, 19:1–23

The two angels reached Sodom in the evening as Lot was sitting at the gate of Sodom. When Lot saw them, he got up to greet them, and bowed down with his face to the ground.

The narrator knows they are angels, but Lot saw just two men. Sodom is a city with city gates where elders adjudicate matters and foreigners may

---

24. Fretheim, "Genesis," 143.

25. However, in Ezek 14:14, YHWH maintains that "even if these three were in it, Noah, Daniel, and Job, they could only save themselves by their righteousness."

report. Lot is presented as eager to welcome visitors; in fact, he prevailed upon the reluctant visitors to accept his hospitality.

He prepared a banquet for them, baking unleavened bread, and they dined. Before they went to bed, the townspeople of Sodom, both young and old— all the people to the last man—surrounded the house.

An outcry reached the heavens from Sodom. The angels are about to see firsthand what's going on. Abraham lived in a tent, Lot in a house in a city with gates; this is city culture. From *na'ar* (young man, no longer a child) to *zāqēn* (old man) is merism—all sexually aware males of the city turned out. This is another way of saying the city is totally corrupt, to the last man. Women are not mentioned, perhaps because their fate is subsumed under that of the men. Surrounding the house is attack mode cutting off all avenues of escape.

Where are the men who came to your house tonight? Bring them out so that we may [know] them.

Lot alone encountered the visitors at the gate. We now know he was not alone; people were watching, even if with different intent. "That we may know them" is euphemism for sexual relations.

I beg you, my brothers, do not do this wicked thing! I have two daughters who have never [known] man. Let me bring them out to you, and you may do to them as you please. But do not do anything to these men, for they have come under the shelter of my roof.

What is "this wicked thing"? Lev 18:22 clearly views homosexual intercourse as abomination: "you shall not lie with a male as with a woman; such a thing is an abomination" (see also Lev 24:30). In this text, the only purpose of sexual intercourse is the generation of children, something homosexual union frustrates. Modern readers point out that generativity is not the unique end of marriage; still one needs to reckon with the implied morality of the text.

A second value, important for Eastern cultures, is at play here too. "This wicked thing" may equally refer to inhospitable violence perpetrated on a guest. Hospitality is sacred. The host is responsible for the welfare and safety of his guest. In defending his guests, Lot put himself in danger; he came out to them and shut the door behind him. He reasoned with them as follows: the men have turned in to me precisely for protection and safety. He went so far as to offer them his two daughters, who thereafter could not marry, were they even to survive the ordeal. At this stage of culture, daughters were considered part of the property of the father. Their violation would mean loss of dowry to him. To signal this cost, he pointedly referred to the girls' virginity. Many readers are shocked at Lot's offer of his daughters, perhaps rightly so. However, at the time the offer represented how much Lot was willing to suffer to protect and defend his guests.

Stand back! This man came here as a resident alien, and now he dares to give orders! We will treat you worse than them!

The resident alien or sojourner (*gēr*) does not have the rights of a citizen, nor even yet of the dweller (*yōshēb*). In resisting them, Lot proved himself righteous, and so deserving of rescue from the lot of the city.

They pressed hard against Lot, moving in closer to break the door . . . put out their hands, pulled Lot inside with them, and closed the door.

One can imagine Lot with his back to the door and the people pushing against him in an effort to open the door. The men (called angels at 19:1) struck the crowd with blinding light such that they could no longer find the doorway. They urged Lot to take out all that belonged to him, for

We are about to destroy this place, for the outcry reaching the LORD against those here is so great that the LORD has sent us to destroy it. So Lot went out and spoke to his sons-in-law.

Having themselves witnessed the "outcry" from Sodom, only divine retribution remained. The Septuagint assumes that Lot had two married daughters in the city. It would appear, however, that the reference is to those who betrothed Lot's daughters; the marriage rites had yet to be completed, and so the girls were still with their father. Since all the men of the city surrounded Lot's house, these sons-in-law would be among the crowd. Lot would have drawn them aside to communicate the news.

When he hesitated, the men, because of the LORD's compassion for him, seized his hand and the hands of his wife and his two daughters and led them to safety outside the city.

Why linger? Reluctance to leave behind his possessions and relationships? Attachment to the place he now called home? Because he did not fully believe the threat of destruction? Ambrose preaches flight from the world: "your flight is a good one if your heart does not act out the counsels of sinners and their designs . . ."[26] The image of the angels leading Lot's family by the hand is touching; it symbolizes the LORD's compassion for him.

Flee for your life! Do not look back or stop anywhere on the Plain . . . Oh, no, my lords! . . . You have already shown favor to your servant, doing me the great kindness of saving my life.

The Hebrew text has Adonāi (with *-ā* usual for the LORD) and the verbs and pronouns are in the singular. *Ḥesed* is not just kindness; in fact, it has no direct English equivalent. Translators usually render it as "faithful love" or "lovingkindness," one that goes beyond what one deserves or has a right to expect in a relationship. Lot feared disaster would overtake him in the nearby hills, so successfully pleaded to be saved in a small (*miṣ'ār*) town nearby. And so the town was called Zoar, a play on *miṣ'ār*. In effect, then, Zoar was spared for the sake of Lot.

The sun had risen over the earth when Lot arrived in Zoar, and the Lord rained down sulfur upon Sodom and Gomorrah, fire from the Lord out of heaven. He overthrew those cities and the whole Plain, together with the inhabitants of the cities and the produce of the soil.

The narrative of the destruction of Sodom has parallels with the story of the flood. God wipes out a whole population, sparing one family. The scourge is for moral depravity. That the LORD rained down (*himṭîr*) sulfur invokes comparison with the downpour of the rains and waters above the firmament in the story of the flood.[27] The surviving hero in both falls into drunkenness, during which state his offspring does something to him. Just as the flood wiped out all humanity on earth except for Noah's family, the daughters of Lot believed that only their family survived.

Destruction of Sodom, 19:24–29

"The LORD rained down sulfur . . . fire from the LORD out of heaven" (19:24) became a hotly disputed text between the early fathers of the church and the rabbis. It seemed to posit two Lords, one in heaven, the other in Sodom, addressed as Adonāi a few verses before this (see

---

26. Ambrose, *Flight from the World* 9.55–56, in ACCS 2:78.
27. Alter, *Genesis*, 88; Westermann, *Genesis 12–36*, 297.

under "Tradition"). The verb *haphak* (overturn, overthrow) is constant whenever the destruction of Sodom and Gomorrah is invoked. *Gophrît* is burning stone (brimstone), which would melt everything and set it on fire; *haphak* suggests an earthquake or a turning over of the earth. To overthrow the produce of the soil meant that the soil was rendered incapable of produce, though *Wis.* 10:7 has the plants bearing fruit that never ripens.

But Lot's wife looked back, and she was turned into a pillar of salt.

> The world is created for resurrection because it is created for human beings—and human beings for Christ . . . the whole of non-human creation will be incorporated in what is given to believers in the resurrection. (Lohfink, *Is This All There Is?*, 193, 224)

This suggests that salt was in the mix. In ancient warfare, a conquering army sometimes littered fields with salt to hinder produce. As in the flood story, it is as if creation became guilty by association with human beings. Ecologists protest. But can it be that such linkage articulates precisely both the dignity of humankind (for whom everything in the constellations seems directed) and humankind's dread responsibility for the life of creation? If all creation is groaning in labor pains (Rom 8:22), awaiting with eager expectation the revelation of the children of God (Rom 8:19), it must be that its being set free from the slavery of corruption hangs on sharing in the glorious freedom of the children of God (Rom 8:21).

When God destroyed the cities of the Plain, he remembered Abraham and sent Lot away from the upheaval.

This closing summary piece[28] attributes the salvation of Lot to YHWH's gracious fidelity to Abraham. The inner text showed Lot as the righteous one for whose sake Zoar was spared (unless Zoar was not occupied; see below). Was Lot's family less than ten, so divine justice could not spare Sodom for their sake? The narrator portrayed Lot as no citizen of Sodom. The men of the city regarded him as an alien (*gēr*), in fact one without rights. And the merism, from the young to the old, portrays the

---

28. Scholars see the hand of P in this repetition.

entire city as having not even one righteous person among them—*all* the men, young and old, surrounded Lot's door. The men rejected association with Lot, who in God's mercy could have gained reprieve for the city. So the foundations for the terms of Abraham's postulation with YHWH did not exist. There was not one righteous citizen in Sodom!

Origin of the Moabites and Ammonites, 19:30–38

Lot was afraid to stay in Zoar, he and his two daughters went up from Zoar and settled in the hill country . . . in a cave.

Now that the nearby hills were not overturned, Lot decided to dwell there, but in a cave, not in the open. He may have left Zoar precisely for fear of open spaces, or perhaps it was not inhabited. The daughters felt there was no man to give them offspring.

Our father is getting old and there is not a man in the land to have intercourse with us, as is the custom everywhere.

They concoct a plan to ply their father with wine and lie with him to beget offspring, *that we may ensure posterity by our father*. The narrator portrays the daughters sensitively—not lust, but desire to ensure posterity, drove them. Besides, they took the trouble to clear their father of guilt, making sure he is not a willing participant to incest, even if drunkenness is no virtue. The narrator manifests (snide?) interest in the origin of two neighbors, Moabites and Ammonites. The relationship is recognized in Deut 2:9: "do not show hostility to the Moabites or engage them in battle, for I will not give you possession of any of their land, since I have given Ar to the descendants of Lot as their possession." The same is said of Ammon in Deut 2:19-20. The modern reader poses the ethical question: can incest be permitted under any circumstances?[29]

No event in the Old Testament is mentioned as often as the destruction of Sodom and Gomorrah![30] Sodom and Gomorrah became ciphers for corporate sin and punishment, eventually of the ultimate destruction of the wicked. With the telling, the catalogue of sins increased. Isaiah calls the rulers of Jerusalem

---

29. Jub 16:8 (second century BCE) implicated even Lot: "and [Lot] and his daughters also committed sins upon the earth which were not committed on the earth from the days of Adam until his time because the man lay with his daughters."

30. Westermann, *Genesis 12-36*, 298.

> Someday God will raise up a single innocent one who does have the power to save the many unrighteous, not by resigning himself to that wickedness or ignoring it, but taking it into himself and exploding the powers of death from within [Isa 53:5, 10; Hos 11:8-9]. (Fretheim, "Genesis," 144)

"princes of Sodom," the people, "people of Gomorrah" (Isa 1:10). He accuses them: "your hands are full of blood . . . make justice your aim, redress the wronged, hear the orphan's plea, defend the widow" (Isa 1:15, 17). Jer 23:14 castigates the Jerusalem prophets for being like Sodom and Gomorrah, and cites "adultery, walking in deception, strengthening the power of the wicked, so that no one turns from evil." For Ezek 16:49-50, Sodom was "proud, sated with food, complacent in prosperity. They did not give any help to the poor and needy. Instead, they became arrogant and committed abominations before me, then, as you have seen, I removed them."[31] Among God's punishment of sinners, Sir 16:8 noted that God "did not spare the neighbors of Lot abominable in their pride." Wis 10:6 calls Lot "a righteous man" whom wisdom rescued from among the wicked who were being destroyed.[32]

Further Reflections

The Sodom story became one of the prime texts against homosexuality; "sodomy" designates unnatural sexual acts.[33] The narrator definitely wants to present the men as unnatural in their desires, to the point of turning aside even the offer of two virgins for the "two men." Lev 20:13 legislates that "if a man lies with a male as with a woman,

---

31. Philo, *On Abraham* 26: "The land of the Sodomites . . . was brimful of innumerable iniquities, particularly such as arise from gluttony and lewdness . . . The inhabitants owed this extreme license to the never-failing lavishness of their sources of wealth, for, deep-soiled and well-watered as it was, the land had every year a prolific harvest of all manner of fruits." Josephus, *Ant* 1.198: "they were overmuch proud of their numbers and their wealth. They showed themselves insolent to people and impious to the divinity. They hated foreigners and avoided any contact with others." *Tg. Ps.-J.*: "they oppress the poor and decree that whoever gives a morsel of bread to the needy shall be burned by fire."

32. In the NT, 2 Pet 2:6-8 speaks of God rescuing the "righteous Lot" greatly distressed by the licentiousness of the wicked.

33. Jude 7: they indulged in sexual promiscuity and practiced unnatural vice.

they have committed an abomination, the two of them shall be put to death, their blood-guilt is upon them." The general line in many parts of the Old Testament is to make the "natural" order of things also the moral order. An example: "you shall not wear cloth made from wool and linen woven together" (Deut 22:11). Genesis 1 insists on keeping the species apart and not mixing them. It can, however, be argued that in the foreground is lack of hospitality (one reason that the narrator stressed the gracious hospitality of Abraham and Lot), vitiated by the violence to and oppression of vulnerable strangers.

Tradition

The virtue of hospitality. Both the Christian and Jewish traditions read Genesis 18 as extolling the virtue of hospitality, with Abraham as model. For Philo, Abraham is filled with joy as he thinks about hosting the men. He enjoyed extending hospitality; for him it was a blessing.[34] Abraham would serve strangers food and drink, then ask them to bless the Lord of the universe. That way hospitality served for conversion (*Gen. Rab.* 49:4).

Paul exhorts the Roman community to "contribute to the needs of the holy ones, exercise hospitality" (Rom 12:13). The root of the verb *diōkontes* has the basic meaning of "to pursue"—not waiting for guests to appear but looking out for them, just as Abraham ran towards the strangers and invited them to his tent.[35] The writer of Heb 13:2 counsels: "do not neglect hospitality, for through it some have unknowingly entertained angels."

Who were Abraham's guests? Jews and Christians approached the text from diverse viewpoints. Both professed the absolute unicity of God as YHWH, however, Christians hailed the one God in three Persons. Both had some difficulty in YHWH (or the Father in Christian faith) appearing in human form and eating. Philo asserted the incorporeal nature of the visitors, who by a miracle took human form to do kindness to the man of worth (Abraham). In his allegorical section, he identified the visitors as the Father of the Universe along with his senior potencies—the creative and the kingly.[36] A Qumran text identified the three visitors as

---

34. Philo, *On Abraham* 107-18.

35. *Abot Rabbi Nathan*: Abraham built stately mansions on highways and left food and drink.

36. Philo, *On Abraham* 23, 24.

three angels.³⁷ *Tg. Neof.* put the meeting with the three angels before the meeting with the LORD. The rabbis generally isolated YHWH from the three identified as angels—Abraham saw the Shekinah *and* the angels (YHWH and his retinue, *Gen. Rab.* 48:9). When Abraham said, "let a little water be brought," he was speaking to Michael, the greatest of the three (the angels were identified in the Talmud as Michael, Raphael, and Gabriel). An angel is sent on earth to perform only one task and depart: Michael to announce the tidings to Abraham, Gabriel to overturn Sodom, and Raphael to rescue Lot. The crucial text of Gen 19:24, "the LORD rained down sulfur upon Sodom and Gomorrah, fire from the LORD out of heaven," refers to Gabriel calling for fire from YHWH out of heaven (*Gen. Rab.* 51:2), though the dissenting opinion of R. Isaac showed that "the LORD" in both cases could refer to YHWH. In summary, rabbinic tradition identified the three as angels, apart from YHWH. YHWH appeared to Abraham in Gen 18:1 before Abraham saw three "men" (this also in Justin Martyr, *Dialogue with Trypho* 56:5); later he dialogued with Abraham in 18:16–33 then departed.

The Christian tradition reckoned with John 8:56, 58: "Abraham your father rejoiced to see my day; he saw it and was glad . . . before Abraham came to be I AM." When did this happen? Justin Martyr posited that Abraham saw the Logos: "this very Person who was at the same time Angel and God and Lord and Man, and who was seen by Abraham and Jacob, also appeared and talked to Moses from the flame of the fiery bush."³⁸ He thus laid down a principle of Christian exegesis till the late fourth century, namely, all appearances of God in human form in the Old Testament referred to the Logos. No theophany is possible without the mediation of Christ.³⁹ So Irenaeus: Abraham saw two angels and the Son of God.⁴⁰ Origen, while holding the christological exegesis, planted two germs that flowered into the Trinitarian reading of the passage. In the Latin text by Rufinus, we read *tres vidit et unum adoravit* (he saw three, but worshiped one) as christological axiom that would later serve the Trinitarian acceptation.⁴¹ Further, Origen saw mystery in the three

---

37. 4Q180 *Pesher of the Periods* 2:3–4. See Kugels, *Traditions*, 341. The same in Josephus, *Ant.* 1.11.2; *Tg. Ps.-J.*: three angels in the form of men.

38. Justin Martyr, *Dialogue with Trypho*, 59.

39. Doerfler, "Entertaining the Trinity Unawares," 488. See also Grypeou and Spurling, "Abraham's Angels," 191.

40. Irenaeus, *Demonstrations*, 44.

41. See Bucur, "Early Christian Reception of Genesis 18," 252 n. 38; Kugel,

measures of flour, which he interpreted as "secret or hidden bread."⁴² The Greek *enkryphia* means "hidden things"—the flour was baked (hidden) in hot ashes.

The christological interpretation was almost universal till the late fourth century. The debate with the Arians showed a weakness of Justin's thesis—it was subordinationist and made Christ subordinate to God. The Arians seized upon this to deny Christ the title "God."⁴³ The First Council of Sirmium (347 CE) attempted a compromise with the Arians. Anathema 15–16, 5 has this:

> Whoever shall say that Abraham saw, not the Son, but the Ingenerate God or part of him, let him be anathema! Whoever shall say with Jacob, not the Son as man, but the Ingenerate God or part of him, has wrestled, let him be anathema . . . he it is to whom the Father said, "let us make man in our image, after our likeness" (Gen 1:26), who also was seen in his own Person by the patriarchs, gave the law, spoke by the prophets, and at last, became man . . .⁴⁴

The Council of Constantinople (381 CE) set on firm foundations the divinity of both the Son and the Holy Spirit. Justin's Logos-centric exegesis was now seen as deficient. Augustine, who earlier (*City of God* 16:29) had embraced the christological exegesis of Genesis 18 (Abraham saw God "in" the three), now argued against it in favor of a Trinitarian one. Why three, yet the LORD in the singular? It is because the Trinity is one Lord, not three Lords; the Trinity is one God, not three Gods; one substance, three persons.⁴⁵ In the treatise on the Trinity, he followed a critique of Justin's position with the Trinitarian affirmation:

> How, then, before he had done this [Virgin birth], did he appear as one man to Abraham? Or, was not that form a reality? I could put these questions, if it had been one man that appeared to Abraham, and if that one were believed to be the Son of God. But since three men appeared, and no one of them is said to be greater than the rest either in form, or age, or power, why should we not here understand, as visibly intimated by the

---

Traditions, 342.

42. Origen, *Homilies on Genesis* 4.1, in ACCS 2:65.
43. See Watson, "Abraham's Visitors," 5.
44. Text courtesy of Bucur, "Early Christian Reception of Genesis 18," 352.
45. Augustine, *Homilies on the First Letter of John* 7.6, on 1 John 4:4–12.

visible creature, the equality of the Trinity, and one and the same substance in three persons?[46]

Caesarius of Arles (470–543 CE), quite dependent on Origen, built on the term, *enkryphia*:

> He received the three men and served them loaves out of three measures. Why is this, brothers, unless it means the mystery of the Trinity? ... In the fact that he saw three, as was already said, he understood the mystery of the Trinity; but since he adored them as one, he recognized that there is one God in the three persons.[47]

The rabbinic side gave greater focus to the figure of Abraham as mediator of blessings to his descendants, something already in Genesis itself (Gen 18:19; 22:15–18; 26:3–6). Every aspect of Abraham's hospitality here yielded some merit for his descendants, in this world and in the age to come.[48] R. Hiyya:

> you have said, 'let a little water be brought.' By your life, I shall pay your descendants back for this... "And it shall come to pass in that day that living waters shall go out of Jerusalem" (Zech 14:8) ... "When the LORD will have washed away the filth of the daughters of Zion" (Isa 4:4) ...[49]

A theology of redemption developed, whereby Abraham's virtues and righteous acts gained a store of merits for the future descendants.

---

46. Augustine, *On the Trinity* 2.11.20 (NPNF). About the same time, Trinitarian interpretations appear in Cyril of Alexandria (375–444), *Against Julian*. Ambrose, *On Abraham* 1:35: the Lord and two attending angels; *On Abraham* 1:33: the three visitors and the three measures of flour point to God as Trinity.

47. Caesarious of Arles, *Sermon* 83.4, in ACCS 2:66.

48. See Neusner, *Theological Commentary*, 2:141, 143. The text is translated according to Neusner.

49 *Gen. Rab.* 48:10.

CHAPTER 8

Genesis 20

The Ancestress in Danger

> O Lord, would you kill an innocent man? . . . I acted with pure heart and with clean hands.
>
> —GENESIS 20:4, 5

THE STORY IN THIS chapter parallels that of Abram and Pharaoh in Egypt (Gen 12:10–12). There Abram claimed Sarai was his sister, Pharaoh took her, YHWH sent plagues, Abram was escorted to the border. The way that story was told raised questions about divine justice, the patriarch's integrity, and the purity of Sarah.[1] The present story of Abraham and Abimelech in Gerar is told from a more consciously religious perspective. It "seeks to answer certain important theological and moral issues that the narrator felt were inadequately treated in the earlier account."[2] Theological words abound: fear of God, the righteous (*ṣaddîq*), pure heart and clean hands, prophet, intercession, great sin/guilt, sin against God.[3] The narrator tells the story in such manner that most issues in the

---

1. See a succinct comparison of the ancestress in danger tales in Gunkel, *Genesis*, 223.
2. Van Seters, "Problem of the Beautiful Wife," in *Abraham in History and Tradition*, 172.
3. Cf. Koch, *Growth of the Biblical Tradition*, 123.

earlier story are resolved in favor of God and Abraham. There is a further complication. Already in Gen 15:4 the reader knows that the promised offspring will be from Abraham himself. Sarai's plan to have a child for Abraham through her maidservant Hagar fell through (Genesis 16). By Genesis 18, the reader expects Sarah herself to bear a child for Abraham within a year. Abimelech represents an intrusion that would put the paternity of this child in doubt, another hurdle to be overcome. Nothing is impossible with God.

Two dialogues structure the narrative: God's dialogue with Abimelech in a dream, and Abimelech's dialogue with Abraham.

God and Abimelech, 20:1–7

From there Abraham journeyed on to the region of the Negev.

Abraham's last station was by the Oak of Mamre, in Hebron (Gen 18:1). He went to Egypt because of a famine in the land; no motive is given for his migration to Gerar. Settling between Kadesh and Shur (on the way to Egypt), he sojourned (as *gēr*, resident alien) in Gerar.[4]

Abraham said of his wife Sarah, "she is my sister." [And] Abimelech, king of Gerar, sent and took Sarah. "

To take (*laqaḥ*) "a woman" is idiom for taking a wife. The juxtaposition of "she is my sister" and "Abimelech took" links the two together: he took her because he thought her unyoked to a man. He would not have touched her otherwise. Pharaoh's officials extolled Sarai's beauty; Pharaoh took Sarai because of her beauty. Here the "taking" is unmotivated. Upon "taking" Sarai, Pharaoh bestowed princely gifts on Abram; gifts will be given here later, but for a completely different reason. Who was inquiring about the status of Sarah, and why? Why pass off his wife as his sister? Why repeat a ruse that misfired earlier? These questions build up dramatic tension in the reader.

But God came to Abimelech in a dream one night and said to him, "you are about to die because of the woman you have taken, for she has a husband."

Literally: she is the possession of a master/husband. Abimelech is accused of robbery, or, at least, theft. All religions and faiths in the ancient world held adultery as a great sin. God intervenes right at the

---

4. Alliteration and play on words in *wa-yāgor bi-gerār*—became a *gēr* in *Gerar*.

beginning to warn about consequences. The ancients believed in the revelatory function of dreams. Even modern psychology has developed the interpretation of dreams as revealing our inner states.

Abimelech, who had not approached her, said: "O Lord, would you kill an innocent man? . . . I acted with pure heart and with clean hands."

The narrator vouches upfront for Sarah's purity. Abimelech did not touch her. Literally, Abimelech said, "would you kill even a righteous nation?" King and nation are bound together in righteousness or unrighteousness: a king who commits grave sin endangers his entire kingdom and people. Ps 24:3–4 asks, "who may go up the mountain of the Lord? Who can stand in his holy place?" The answer: "the clean of hand and pure of heart, who has not given his soul to useless things." Abimelech protests his innocence in the words of the psalmist. God should rather blame Abraham and Sarah who acted in concert to deceive.

God answered him in the dream: "yes, I know you did it with a pure heart. In fact, it was I who kept you from sinning against me; that is why I did not let you touch her."

God reaffirms Abimelech's innocence and the purity of Sarah; God prevented any marital relations. Adultery is a sin against God (not only against the woman's husband). Had Abimelech had relations with Sarah, he would have committed a sin against God. The ancients believed in punishable material sin, that is, sin transgresses the moral order even without the subject's knowledge or intent to do evil.

"So now, return the man's wife so that he may intercede for you, since he is a prophet, that you may live. If you do not return her, you can be sure that you and all who are yours will die."

Unlike the case of Pharaoh, God first warns the person going astray and affords the opportunity of repentance, before eventual judgment. God calls Abraham a prophet (*nābî'*) in the sense of a "man of God" who has power from and with God, in this case, the power of intercession. God expects and hears prayer; the prayer of one close to God works. Abimelech learns from God that Abraham is under God's protection and providence. God creates the space for Abraham to function as mediator of blessing to all families of earth. Now that Abimelech knows Sarah's real status, holding on to her would lead to internal guilt. But why no word to Abraham about his subterfuge? Is there irony in the deceiver being made intercessor? Is God associating Abraham in the cleaning up of the mess he caused?

Abimelech and Abraham, 20:8–18

Early the next morning Abimelech called all his servants and informed them of everything that had happened, and the men were filled with great fear.

Abimelech and his people do not merely have "fear of God," they have "great fear of God" and of his judgment; this gives the lie in advance to what Abraham soon adduces as his motive. "Abimelech plays the role of a 'righteous Gentile' with whom Abraham could live in peace and blessing."[5]

What wrong did I do to you that you would have brought such great guilt on me and my kingdom.

The translation "you would have brought" invokes more modern sentiments about guilt. Abimelech took it that "great sin" had been committed, even though he never intended to take a man's wife and never touched Sarah. He reproached Abraham saying, "deeds which are not done, you have done against us."

Abraham answered, "I thought there would be no fear of God in this place, and so they would kill me on account of my wife. Besides, she is really my sister, but only my father's daughter, not my mother's."

"Fear of God" is the basis of religion. It is that reverence for God and piety towards God that induce both worship and right conduct towards others, especially those for whom God is the only recourse and refuge. Abraham just witnessed the violent inhospitality of Sodom and Gomorrah, their proclivity towards abusing strangers (Genesis 19).[6] Even then, he appears to trade his wife for his own welfare, just as Lot offered his daughters. Chrysostom comes to his aid with psychology. When two passions affect the body at the same time, the stronger pain overwhelms us and does not allow us to feel anything of the lesser one. So "this just man in the present instance saw the fear of death affecting him and considered

---

5. Sailhamer, *Pentateuch as Narrative*, 174.
6. More on this in Sarna, *Genesis*, 140.

all other things tolerable."⁷ He rejoined that, thanks to God, the fear of death has been done away with by Christ. Unfortunately, this is no abstract question. The people of God in many parts of today's world live with similar radical choices (see "Tradition").

The genealogy of Sarah is never given, so we cannot check Abraham's assertion. Marriage of the type mentioned here was later prohibited in Ezek 22:11; Lev 20:19; and Deut 27:22.

When God sent me wandering from my father's house, I asked her . . . "in whatever place we come to, say: he is my brother."

His first excuse had to do with the character of the particular place: he thought there was no fear of God "in this place." Now he adduces a general habit that either invalidates that excuse or considers every place outside his own domains as devoid of the fear of God! The verb *ta'ah*, translated "to wander," usually means "to err," "to wander aimlessly." The majestic call of YHWH in Gen 12:1-3 appears stripped of all religious and vocational direction.⁸ The LXX naturally corrected the text to "when God brought me forth from my father's house." Jewish midrashic traditions use various strategies to resolve the "gap" (see "Tradition"). The reader learns with Abraham that the fear of God can indeed exist even outside Israel. God speaks and listens to a Canaanite king; that king and his court are moved by the fear of God in their conduct towards Abraham, a resident alien who was in fact guilty with regard to him. He honors this God and respects his "prophet."⁹

*Then Abimelech took flocks and herds and male and female slaves and gave them to Abraham; and he restored his wife Sarah to him . . . To Sarah he said, "I hereby give your brother a thousand shekels of silver. This will preserve your honor before all who are with you and will exonerate you before everyone."*¹⁰

Flocks and herds and male and female slaves were among the princely gifts Pharaoh gave Abram *before taking* Sarai in Genesis 12. Here

---

7. Chrysostom, *Homily on Genesis 18-45*, 472.

8. Besides, *Elohim* that usually takes a single verb when it refers to God, here takes a plural verb, as if referring to "the gods."

9. See Westermann, *Genesis 12-36*, 329.

10. The LXX renders the difficult final phrase as "and tell the whole truth." Chrysostom comments: "let everyone learn from you . . . that nothing wrong was done." *Homilies on Genesis* 45, in ACCS 2:480.

Abimelech gives them when *restoring* Sarah to Abraham. Only at the end does the narrator vouchsafe the delayed information that the presents were in gratitude for the healing power of Abraham's intercession.[11] Abimelech accepts Abraham's word about Sarah being his sister—or did he say this tongue-in-cheek? The gifts for Sarah, equally given to Abraham, are for *kesût 'ēnayîm*, covering of the eyes, that is, a propitiation that makes her blind to what happened, as though it had not happened[12]; the same for all in her household. R. Judah son of Ilai is reported as construing Abimelech's reproach thus: "you went to Egypt and made merchandise of her, and you came here and traded in her. If you desire money, here is money and cover up [your eyes] from her" (*Gen. Rab.* 52:12). That is, do not look at her to trade her, or cover people's eyes from her that they may not desire her.

Abraham then interceded with God, and God restored health to Abimelech, to his wife, and his maidservants, so that they bore children.

With Abraham's intercession, the narrator relays delayed information that gives sense to much that happened: God made Abimelech impotent so he could not function with his women. This was not punishment as for Pharaoh, rather the thwarting of a sin against God. The question of the justice of God in punishing an unwitting subject no longer arises.

For the LORD had closed every womb in Abimelech's household on account of Abraham's wife Sarah.

This closing sentence is at some variance with the preceding; here it is the women who are afflicted. Furthermore, it would take some time to ascertain that the wombs were closed, and this is in some tension with Abimelech being made impotent in the first place. Besides, the name YHWH/the LORD appears, whereas the divine name all through was Elohim/God.

Here, my land is at your disposal; settle wherever you please.

Pharaoh had Abram escorted to the Egyptian border; Abimelech accords him full citizenship rights. The next chapter relates a covenant between Abimelech and Abraham at Beersheba.

---

11. Westermann, *Genesis 12-36*, 327 suggest that "they express Abimelech's recognition of the God who spoke to him."

12. Spurrell, *Notes on Genesis*, 180.

Tradition

Following Philo and Origen, most of the fathers of the church interpret Sarah as virtue of the soul. Abimelech represents the studious and wise men of the world, who, by giving attention to philosophy, although they do not reach the complete and perfect rule of piety, nevertheless perceive that God is the Father and King of all things.[13] Abimelech could receive Sarah (virtue) because he was seeking with a pure heart, but time had not yet come. Virtue therefore remains with Abraham; it remains with circumcision, until the time should come that in Christ Jesus our Lord, in whom "dwells all the fullness of deity corporeally," complete and perfect virtue might pass over to the church of the Gentiles.[14]

When God sent me wandering from my father's house. The midrashic tradition kept to the basic meaning of the verb *t'h*, "to err." They applied it to the attempt of the nations or idolaters to mislead Abraham into idolatry, causing YHWH to call out to him to "get thee out . . . of thy father's house." Hence *Tg. Onq.*: "when the nations erred after the work of their hands and God brought me near to revering him from the house of my father . . ." The rabbis eventually decided when the law of self-preservation must give way to God's law: Rav Yochanan said in the name of Rav Shimon ben Yehotzadak: "It was decided by a vote in the loft of the house of Nitezeh in Lod: For all the sins in the Torah, if a person is told, 'transgress and you will not be killed,' they should transgress and not be killed, except for idol worship, sexual relations, and bloodshed."[15] The types of sexual immorality envisaged are incest, adultery, and bestiality.

---

13. Origen, *Homilies on Genesis* 6.2, in ACCS 2:85.
14. Origen, *Homilies on Genesis* 6.3, in ACCS 2:88.
15. b. Sanh 74a.

CHAPTER 9

Genesis 21

Isaac Is Born; Ishmael Is Expelled

The Hebrew Bible presents information on the individual who will not be the Israelite linear heir in the following generation.[1]

The Birth of Isaac, 21:1–13

The LORD took note of Sarah as he said he would . . . Sarah became pregnant and bore Abraham a son in his old age.

THE VERB *paqad* has the basic meaning, "to examine closely," "to take keen interest in."[2] God took care of Sarah's situation and gave new life to her organs. In Gen 17:6 God changed Sarai's name to Sarah, saying, "I will bless her, and I will give you a son by her . . . she will give rise to nations, and rulers of peoples will issue from her." This was the first time it became clear to Abraham that the promised son would be by Sarah. On this occasion, Abraham laughed to himself in doubt, "can Sarah give birth at ninety?" He pleaded for Ishmael to live in God's favor, that is, for God to confer the promised blessings on Ishmael. God, however, reaffirmed the promise of seed for Sarah: "your wife Sarah is to bear you a

---

1. Sternberg, "Sarah-Hagar Cycle," 42.
2. André, "Paqad," 30, 31.

son, and you shall call him Isaac. It is with him that I will maintain my covenant as an everlasting covenant and with his descendants after him" (Gen 17:19). Apparently, Abraham kept this news to himself. For when the visitors announced they would return at the same season, Sarah, eavesdropping, laughed her heart out, saying, "now that I am worn out and my husband is old, am I still to have sexual pleasure?" (Gen 18:12). The LORD is faithful. Nothing is impossible for God. The birth of Isaac was miraculous, fulfillment of a promise.

Abraham gave the name Isaac to this son of his whom Sarah bore him. Abraham circumcised him, as God had commanded. The child grew and was weaned, and Abraham held a great banquet on the day of the child's weaning.

The name Isaac is rooted in peals of laughter—of mother and father, of neighbors and all who hear of this birth. The patriarch is portrayed as prompt in obeying God's word and command. In traditional cultures, breastfeeding lasted three years. It was also a method of birth control, since lactation inhibits ovulation. Infant mortality was rampant then as now in some societies. It was great cause for joy for a son to survive the dangers of early childhood; the hereditary line was now assured.

In Genesis 16, Hagar is Sarai's maidservant (*shiphḥah*); here Hagar is Abraham's maid (*'amah*). These may or may not reflect dialectal choices for the same reality. The *'amah* is not necessarily a slave; she can be a concubine.[3] The narrator here posits no relationship with Sarah. Hagar is totally in Abraham's power. The pathos of the narrative is precisely in this that Ishmael is Abraham's son, hence with rights of inheritance. What is more, Ishmael was circumcised at age thirteen, hence bore the sign of belonging to God's covenant.

Sarah noticed the son whom Hagar the Egyptian had borne to Abraham playing with her son Isaac.

The phrase "with her son Isaac" is not in the Hebrew original, but taken from the LXX, followed by the Vulgate. The perspective is that of Sarah, what she saw. For her, Ishmael was "the son of Hagar the Egyptian, whom she bore to Abraham"—foreign blood in competition with native blood—while Isaac was "my son." The participle *meṣaḥēq* is denominative

---

3. In Gen 20:17, God healed Abimelech's wife and maids so they bore children.

of the name Isaac. Ishmael was "Isaacing," that is, "playing Isaac."[4] Sarah saw Ishmael displacing Isaac for the birthright. She may also have wanted to secure her own position in the household, since the dignity of a woman followed that of her son. Matters are complicated, however, for the narrator knows of God's decision, "but my covenant I will maintain with Isaac, whom Sarah shall bear to you by this time next year" (Gen 17:21), so adopts Sarah's perspective. But Sarah's laughter of doubt in Genesis 18 shows that she was not acting from that knowledge.

Drive out that [maid] and her son! No son of that [maid] is going to share the inheritance with my son Isaac.

I let stand the original "maid" (not slave)—the poignancy of the situation is that both Abraham and God accept that Ishmael is a "son of Abraham" with birthright (not son of a slave without it). God calls Israel "*this* people" when he feels distant from them in affection; "*that* maid" on Sarah's lips betokens both distance and disparagement. The verb *garēsh* is the imperative, without the usual softening suffix -*na'* to indicate a plea. It does double duty. It is the technical term for the divorce of a wife by the husband—Sarah is forcing Abraham to drive away Hagar and revoke his adoption of Ishmael. But the verb is used also both for Pharaoh's driving out Israel from Egypt and for Israel's driving out the indigenous peoples of Canaan. "The actions that Sarah wants Abraham to take will also effectively banish Ishmael from having a part in the possession of the Promised Land!"[5] To soften the blow, some readers hear Sarah asking Abraham to free Hagar in accordance with local law and custom, such as the Laws of Hammurabi 171 and the Code of Lipit-Ishtar 25: "if a man married his wife and she bears him a child and the child lives, and a slave woman also bears a child to her master, the father shall free the slave woman; the children of the slave woman will not divide the estate with the children of the master."[6] However, in this narrative, Hagar is no slave. Furthermore, Ishmael is circumcised and circumcision "is the sign of the covenant between me and you" (Gen 17:11). As

---

4. Coats, "Curse in the Blessing," 38. The same verb is used pejoratively in at least two other passages, leading some rabbis to a negative perception of Ishmael. It is used by Potiphar's wife: the Hebrew slave whom you brought us came to sport with me (Gen 39:17); at the scene of the Golden Calf, the people sat down to eat and drink, and rose up to play/revel (Exod 32:6).

5. Okoye, "Sarah and Hagar," 171.

6. *ANET* 160. See also Drey, "Role of Hagar in Genesis 16," 190.

mentioned in Genesis 17, it is anomalous that Ishmael is circumcised, yet cast out, against the very meaning of circumcision. Ishmael both belongs to YHWH and does not. The matter was very evil in the eyes of Abraham, for Ishmael was a son of his; Abraham was distraught. God intervenes to resolve the complication and sides with Sarah!

But God said to Abraham: Do not be distressed about the boy or about your [maid]. Obey Sarah, no matter what she asks of you, for it is through Isaac that descendants will bear your name. As for the son of the [maid], I will make a nation[7] of him also, since he too is your offspring.

"Hagar is powerless because God supports Sarah."[8] Abraham's moral indignation wilts before God's command. Chrysostom waxes eloquent about "the extraordinary considerateness of the loving God"[9] who wished to strengthen the bonds of harmony between Abraham and Sarah; he too took the side of Sarah. God begins to define what Abraham's being "the father of many nations" means. All children of Abraham do not share the same promises; as already announced in Genesis 17, election and covenant with YHWH are for Isaac and his line alone.[10] Election imports both preferential love and responsibility for God's purposes on earth. Ishmael shares in the blessing of Abraham, but must branch out from Abraham's household and steer clear of the promised land of Canaan.

---

7. LXX and some versions say "great nation," as in v. 18.
8. Trible, *Texts of Terror*, 28.
9. Chrysostom, *Homilies on Genesis* 46.5.
10. Dozeman, "Wilderness and Salvation," 42 is only partially right when he writes: "when read from the perspective of Israel, Ishmael represents an expansion of election beyond the boundaries of Israel, and as such Ishmael models the proselyte who undergoes circumcision." Rather than "expansion of election," he should say "expansion of blessing"; besides, nowhere in the text is Ishmael treated as "proselyte."

Hagar and Ishmael Are Cast Out, 21:14–21

FIGURE 2: Hagar and Ishmael, Gen 21

Early the next morning, Abraham got some bread and a skin of water and gave them to Hagar. Then placing the child on her back, he sent her away.[11]

There are unmistakable resonances with the near sacrifice of Isaac in the next chapter, Genesis 22. There too Abraham got up early in the morning, the messenger of YHWH intervenes, and the child is snatched from death.[12] Are these stories parallel hero accounts of the tribes springing from Ishmael and Isaac? Why only a loaf of bread and skin of water when

  11. *Tg. Ps.-J.*: "he sent her away with a bill of divorce."
  12. Sherwood, "Hagar and Ishmael," 292.

we hear in Gen 25:6 that Abraham gave gifts to the sons of his concubines and sent them away eastward, away from his son Isaac? The apparent meanness troubled some early readers who attributed it to some fault of Ishmael (see "Tradition"). If Ishmael was thirteen at circumcision (Gen 17:25), and Isaac was at least three years old at his weaning, then Ishmael was no child that could be put on Hagar's shoulders; this shows that neither story was written in relation to the other.[13] The verb *shalaḥ*, "to send away," has resonances in Pharaoh's sending away of the Hebrews in Exod 6:11.

As she roamed aimlessly in the wilderness of Beersheba, the water in the skin was used up. So she put the child down under one of the bushes, and then went and sat down opposite him, about a bowshot away, for she said to herself, "I cannot watch the child die." As she sat opposite him, she wept aloud.

Hagar did not "put the child down"; in desperation she cast (*shalak*) him down. She wept aloud helpless in face of the immediate danger of death for Ishmael.

God heard the boy's voice and God's angel called to Hagar from heaven. What is the matter, Hagar? Do not fear. God has heard the boy's voice in this plight of his.

It was Hagar who wept aloud, but God heard the boy's voice? The mother's loud weeping expressed the depths of the boy's suffering to which God now pays attention? "In this plight of his" can also be read as "in the place where he is"; later readers will derive theological meanings from this. God shows that the one expelled from Abraham's household is still under God's protection and care. Dozeman believes that here "expulsion is an act of liberation for the one being driven out, signifying release from slavery. The salvific character of expulsion for Hagar is made explicit when she receives a divine oracle of salvation in Gen 21:17, with the stereotyped formula that she 'fear not.'"[14] "God has heard" plays on the name Ishmael, as if to say, "your name is a prayer that God may hear (*Yishma'El*)," and indeed God has heard (*shama'El*). Having heard, God responds with salvation. God's angel continued:

---

13. Chrysostom simply said that "the maidservant took the bread and the bag of water and went off with her son." *Homilies on Genesis* 46.6.

14. Dozeman, "Wilderness and Salvation" 30.

Get up, lift up the boy and hold him by the hand; for I will make of him a great nation.

The promise of being a "great nation" made to Abram in Gen 12:2 is now given to Ishmael also.

Then God opened her eyes, and she saw a well of water.[15] *She went and filled the skin with water, and then let the boy drink. God was with the boy as he grew up.*

Was the well always there, or did God work a miracle in his favor? The fact of God's "being with" will be picked up by Abimelech (v. 22) in reference to Abraham; it will be a constant in the Jacob story. It indicates God's continuing providence and protection. "Both in his saving action and in his blessing, the God of Abraham remains with Ishmael, now driven from his family. God's grace is not restricted to Isaac's line."[16]

He lived in the wilderness and became an expert bowman. He lived in the wilderness of Paran. His mother got a wife for him from the land of Egypt.

Hagar in this story is in her own right an ancestor of the Ishmaelites, just as Abraham is of Israelites. Paran is one designation of YHWH's desert home (Deut 33:2; Hab 3:3)[17]; Ishmael, though not aggregated to Israel, is not foreign to the knowledge of YHWH.

Further Reflections

The reader of this narrative passes through a roller coaster of feelings and emotions, for and against the characters, including the God of the text. It is no wonder that the narrative has lent itself to varied and sometimes contradictory interpretations. Was the narrative intention Hagar's liberation and salvation or advocacy for the claims of Isaac? Is it another illustration of the saying that "the Hebrew Bible presents information on the individual who will not be the Israelite linear heir in the following generation"?[18]

---

15. LXX: a well of living water—a reading that conflates the well here with the "spring" of Gen 16:7. Both patristic and rabbinic exegesis will relate the word, "living," to fundamental aspects of their faiths.
16. Westermann, *Genesis 12–36*, 343.
17. See Dozeman, "Wilderness and Salvation," 36.
18. Sternberg, "Sarah-Hagar Cycle," 42.

> And God was with Ishmael. As God was with Isaac? Is this God's story? Perhaps there was no choice of one son over the other: rather, God chose both without taking into account that people cannot understand a logic of love that is not binary and supremacist. Is God's story one of conciliation which did not account for the human tendency toward animus? Is then a tradition that reads one over against the other, misreading God's story? (Cohen, "Hagar and Ishmael," 256)

Sherwood compares the story to an inverted exodus[19]:

> The expulsion of Hagar the Egyptian is told as an inverted exodus. Like the Israelites at the beginning of the Exodus, she is fertile and conceives easily. Oppressed in the Israelite house of bondage, the slave both flees and is forced out (just like the Israelites in the exodus: cf. Exod 12:33). She leaves the house of Abraham and ends up at Shur, on the borders of Egypt (Gen 16:7). She departs carrying bread on her shoulders (Gen 21:14; Exod 12:34) and enters the 'wilderness' (Gen 16:7; 21:14). She finds water in the desert and is found by a messenger/angel of God.[20]

Dozeman interprets Hagar as prototype of Moses:

> Each is a founder of a nation. The status of each is ambiguous: surrogate wife/slave (16:1–5) and Egyptian prince/Hebrew slave (Exod 2:1–10). Transition from slave to wife prompts oppression by Sarah, transition from Egyptian prince to Hebrew liberator a death threat from Pharaoh. Each flees (*baraḥ*) to a well in the wilderness to escape oppression. There each encounters a messenger of God, is commanded to return to the threatening situation, receives a word of promise and leaves with a special name for God. Upon return, each takes up a new role that leads to continued conflict abutting in expulsion into the wilderness.[21]

---

19. Sherwood, "Hagar and Ishmael," 290.

20. Perry, "Counter-Stories in the Bible," 286 speaks of Ishmael's banishment to the desert (Gen 21:4–21) as "Ishmael's Aqedah." He points to opposing details between the two culminating in the angel calling out from heaven in each. Abraham not to reach out his hand to the lad (Gen 22:12) contrasts with Hagar asked to lift up the lad and hold him by the hand (Gen 21:18).

21. Cf. Dozeman, "Wilderness and Salvation," 29–30.

Trible severely criticizes God's apparent partiality in favor of Sarah:

> Hagar foreshadows Israel's pilgrimage of faith through contrast. As a maid in bondage, she flees from suffering, Yet she experiences exodus without liberation, revelation without salvation, wilderness without covenant, wanderings without land, promise without fulfillment, and unmerited exile without return ... this Egyptian slave woman is stricken, smitten by God, and afflicted for the transgressions of Israel. She is bruised for the iniquities of Sarah and Abraham; upon her is the chastisement that makes them whole.[22]

It may be that, as in Job's story, the appropriate response is one of perplexity and question (see above text box). The fact is, "we do not fall in love with everyone; we do not love everyone in the same way. God's individual love for Israel is not the barrier to God's loving the world. It is a kind of paradigm, a promise that God can also love other peoples individually."[23]

Abraham and Abimelech: Covenant at Beersheba, 21:22–34

Abimelech and his commander Phicol appear without introduction. The story probably originally followed upon Genesis 20, where Abimelech, king of Gerar, is one of the central characters. In that story, Abraham was residing in Gerar as a resident alien. When Genesis 21 opens, Abraham was apparently in Beersheba (Gen 21:14) and it was thence that Abimelech went to meet with him before returning to the "land of the Philistines" (21:32). Verses 33–34 place Beersheba in the land of the Philistines, casting Abraham as a *gēr* (resident alien) in territory controlled by Abimelech. The narrative gives etiologies of Beersheba; even more, it recounts an oath of loyalty between the two for the present, and between their descendants in future. God's promise of an heir having been fulfilled, the narrative begins to focus on land and the welfare of Abraham's progeny.

At that time Abimelech, accompanied by Phicol, the commander of his army, said to Abraham: "God is with you in everything you do."

---

22. Trible, *Texts of Terror*, 28.
23. Goldingay, *Israel's Gospel*, 217.

The birth and weaning of Isaac fill in the passage of time. Abimelech was beneficiary of Abraham's closeness to God when by his prayer God opened the wombs of Abimelech's wife and maidservants. He has been able to observe since then that God is on Abraham's side and prospers him in everything.

So now, swear to me by God at this place that you will not deal falsely with me or with my progeny and posterity, but will act as loyally toward me and the land in which you reside as I have acted toward you. Abraham replied: "I so swear."

The root *šb‛* dominates the passage, occurring nine times. The narrative plays upon the double meaning of this root, "seven" and "to swear," giving two etiologies of the name Beersheba as "well of seven" and "well of the oath." Abimelech has acted towards Abraham with *ḥesed* (loyalty and kindness); this calls for a return.

Abraham, however, reproached Abimelech about a well that Abimelech's servants had seized by force.

Abraham gave him sheep and cattle and the two made a covenant (*berît*). The covenant goes beyond the question of wells. Abimelech seeks to secure blessings for his line and for his land by binding Abraham to a covenant of non-aggression. As in Genesis 14, Abraham appears here as a sort of chieftain, perhaps with military abilities (hence the presence of Abimelech's army commander), though the emphasis is placed on his power with God. The patriarch here represents the later nation of Israel: "it is only as other nations acknowledge Israel's destiny and the fact that YHWH is with Israel, that the nations can hope, through a covenant of peace, to obtain a blessing from Israel."[24] The reader should note how different from Deuteronomy is the attitude to the inhabitants of the land; Deuteronomy 7 and 20 forbid any covenants with the inhabitants of the land, rather they are to be put under the ban. Abraham put aside seven ewe lambs and explained that *the seven ewe lambs you shall accept from me that you may be my witness that I dug this well.* Abraham, the resident alien, secures his first piece of property in the land, and that through mutual transaction, as if at pains to renounce possession by force of arms, as in some strands of the tradition of Israel in Canaan.

---

24. Seters, "Covenants between Abimelech and the Patriarchs," 187.

Abraham planted a tamarisk at Beersheba, and there he invoked by name the LORD, God the Eternal. Abraham resided in the land of the Philistines for a long time.

One plants trees on secured property. In fact, the LXX, instead of tamarisk tree (*'ēshel*), has *arouran*, that is, a field. Abraham calls upon the name of YHWH wherever he pitches tent, that is, invokes his name in prayer. *El 'Olam*, God the Eternal, may be the name of the local god—in Genesis 14, both Abraham and Melchizedek, king of Salem, profess YHWH as *El Elyon*, God Most High. In either case, the narrator aggregates to YHWH the local name for God.

> The mention of the Philistines at this period is regarded as anachronistic, though some speak of the settlement of a first wave of Sea Peoples[25] before the main wave in the Iron Age (circa 1200 BCE).

Tradition

Paul invokes the case of Ishmael and Isaac to argue that Gentiles can share in the promise of Abraham, even while some Jews may find themselves left out:

> for not all who are of Israel are Israel, nor are they all children of Abraham because they are his descendants; but 'it is through Isaac that descendants shall bear your name.' This means that it is not the children of the flesh who are the children of God, but the children of the promise are counted as descendants. (Rom 9:7–8)

What matters is faith, "for there is no distinction between Jew and Greek; the same Lord is Lord of all, enriching all who call upon him" (Rom 10:12).

In Gal 4:21–31, Paul uses an allegory to address Christians tempted to accept circumcision in order to be saved. Hagar's children are children of the flesh, that is, born through natural processes. Sarah's children are children of the promise, that is, born through the gratuitous promise of God. Hagar, the slave, represents those in bondage to the Sinai covenant (who cling to circumcision as means of salvation); Sarah represents the freedom of God in the Jerusalem above. The former are slaves, like their

25. Hamilton, *Genesis 18–50*, 94.

mother; the latter freeborn, also like their mother. The Galatians are to choose freedom: "for freedom Christ set us free; so stand firm and do not submit again to the yoke of slavery" (Gal 5:1).

In the process, Paul says: "but just as then the child of the flesh persecuted the child of the spirit, it is the same now" (Gal 4:29). "He played with her son, Isaac. How did he injure or harm him if he was playing?" marveled Origen. How could Paul dub children's play a persecution "when certainly no persecution of Ishmael against Isaac is related to have been undertaken, except this play of the infant alone."[26] Origen thus understood the matter spiritually to refer to the conflict whereby the flesh (Ishmael born according to the flesh) seeks to entice the spirit, something which offends Sarah, who represents virtue. Paul judged allurements of this kind to be the most bitter persecution.

However, Paul, in speaking of the persecution of Isaac by Ishmael, may have depended on Jewish midrash now found in *Tg. Ps.-J.*: Sarah says: "cast out this maidservant . . . not possible . . . should inherit with my son, and (then) make war with Isaac." *Gen. Rab.* 53:11 reports that Ishmael tried to kill Isaac. Rabbi Azariah in R. Levi's name: Ishmael would ask Isaac to go with him to see their portions in the field[27]; then he would shoot arrows in Isaac's direction pretending to be playing. An anonymous patristic source[28] opined that while they were playing Ishmael struck Isaac. All these are attempts to justify Sarah and adduce a reason for her action to pass moral muster. Eusebius of Emesa (300–359) asked whether the just Abraham, with all the cattle he possessed, was inhumane, not supplying Hagar and the boy even a donkey; and why throw her out in the first place? The answer was that he would not have done it had God not asked him, besides, he believed God would protect the boy.[29]

The rabbis did not fault Abraham since he was obeying God. They, however, were troubled by Abraham's apparent meanness towards Ishmael and sought a reason for it. Some found it in the Hebrew text that said simply that Ishmael was *meṣaḥēq*, with no complement. This verb was used by Potiphar's wife: "the Hebrew slave whom you brought us came to *sport with* me" (Gen 39:17). Hence, Rabbi Akiba: making sport refers to nothing else but immorality (*Gen. Rab.* 53:11). At the scene of

---

26. Origen, *Homilies on Genesis* 7.3, in ACCS 2:93.
27. Echoes the Cain and Abel story?
28. *Catena on Genesis* 3.1206, in ACCS 2:94.
29. Eusebius of Emesa, *Catena on Genesis* 3.1216, in ACCS 2:96–97.

the golden calf, the people sat down to eat and drink, and rose up to *revel* (Exod 32:6, using the same term). Accordingly, *Tg. Onq.* found Ishmael jesting; in *Tg. Neof.* he was doing improper actions (such as jesting in a foreign cult). *Tg. Ps.-J.*: he was sporting with an idol and bowing down to it. These simply apply to the word here the meaning it had in another context.[30] However, Scripture regarded Ishmael positively; when Abraham died, he and Isaac together buried him (Gen 25:9). In fact, Isaac thereafter lived in the vicinity of Beer-lahai-roi (Gen 25:11), that is, precisely Ishmael's area in Gen 16:14.

The LXX read verse 19 as that Hagar saw "a well of living water." Cyril of Alexandria (375–444) applies this to the Jews. If, like Hagar, they should begin to weep and cry out to God, God will open their eyes to see the fountain of living water, that is, Christ.[31]

The original Hebrew text at 21:17 has: "God has heard the boy's voice in the place where he is." This connotes for his own sake, for a sick person's prayers on his own behalf are more efficacious than those of anyone else (*Gen. Rab.* 53:14). Another interpretation: I judge man only as he is at the moment. Rabbi Simon: The ministering angels protested to God that Ishmael would in future kill your children with thirst. To this, the Holy One, blessed be he, replied, "what is he now, righteous or wicked?" They replied, "righteous." He said to them, "according to his present deeds will I judge him" (*Gen. Rab.* 53:14). God takes account of the present condition of a person, leaving open the possibility of repentance in the future.[32]

Instead of a tamarisk tree, the LXX has Abraham plant an *arouran* (field, grove). R. Judah (*Gen. Rab.* 54:6) spoke of an orchard, R. Nehemiah of an inn. The story is told that Abraham would receive wayfarers and invite them to say grace after meals. When they asked what to say, he would instruct them to say, "blessed be the Everlasting God, of whose bounty we have eaten." Hence it is written, "and called there on the name of the Lord, the Everlasting God." Abraham was extremely hospitable and used hospitality to promote worship of and thanks to God.

---

30. Such type of interpretation is called *gezerah shavah* (verbal analogy).
31. Cyril of Alexandria, *Glaphyra on Genesis* 3.10, in ACCS 2:99.
32. Cf. Neusner, *Theological Commentary*, 2:156.

CHAPTER 10

Genesis 22

"The One You Love"

> At the beginning, Abraham is commanded to relinquish his past, and at the end, Abraham is commanded to relinquish his future.[1]

THE NARRATOR LETS THE reader in on a secret that Abraham does not yet know—this is a test by God. God wants to know if Abraham really fears God. Whatever the original intention,[2] the story is now told from a theological point of view. God's command strictly parallels God's first call of Abram.

> *Go forth* (*lek leka*) from your land, your relatives, and from your father's house to a land that I will show you. (Gen 12:1)

> Take your son, your only one, whom you love, Isaac, and *go forth* (*lek leka*)...one of the heights I will tell you. (Gen 22:2)

The two passages are bookends that together interpret the life of Abraham and his relevance for his descendants. Not only is there

---

1. Moberly, *Theology of the Book of Genesis*, 186.

2. Some scholars posit that God hereby mandates the transition from the sacrifice of the firstborn to animal sacrifice, or that the story originally served as etiology of a holy place. From the narrative point of view, this is a test in which the patriarch must, on behalf of his progeny, show that he is worthy of the blessings of God.

ascending gradation of psychological difficulty, both panels invite Abraham to journey into the unknown until God signals the destination—hence a journey of faith.

Much water has passed under the bridge in Abraham's relations with God. The call was an exercise of pure divine predilection. It was not premised on any virtues or qualities of Abram. Abraham needs to show that he is worthy of God's beneficence and that God's gifts are not arbitrary. The author (or redactor) redirects the original story to reflect on the dialogical relation between free gift and merit, grace and human endeavor, faith and works!

The Command, 22:1–14

Sometime afterward, literally, "after these things."

Which things? Was the narrator alluding to all the efforts to help God out with the production of an heir, or the lack of full trust in God displayed in passing Sarah off as his sister?[3] The reference to "only son," however, makes one think of the expulsion of Ishmael in the previous chapter.[4] Abraham was greatly distressed at Sarah's demand to drive out Hagar and Ishmael, "because it concerned a son of his." God took Sarah's side: "obey Sarah . . . for it is through Isaac that descendants will bear your name" (Gen 21:12). Abraham did not put up a fight, as he did for Sodom and Gomorrah. Now, the same God demands the sacrifice of Isaac also! Abraham is about to experience, as Hagar did, what it means to lose an only son. The story is one of "endangered promise,"[5] and crisis of trust. Postexilic Israel was undergoing an existential crisis of hope in her survival as a people. How far can she depend on God's promises to Abraham?

God put Abraham to the test.

When YHWH tests Israel, it is usually by affliction, for example, through the wanderings in the wilderness to see whether it was their intention to hold on to him and abide by his commandments (Deut 8:2).

3. More of this in Kuruvilla, "Aqedah (Genesis 22)," 497.

4. Chrysostom, *Homilies on Genesis* 47.3 comments on the LXX text, which rendered, "despite these things . . .": "despite these words of promise and despite his saying, 'your descendants will be called after him,' and he will be your successor—"despite these words God put Abraham to the test."

5. Schmid, "Abraham's Sacrifice and Von Rad," 271.

And said to him, "Abraham!"[6] "Here I am," he replied.

The medium of revelation is not given. Abraham has free access to God and his word. *Hinnēnî* means something like "awaiting orders."

Take your son, your only one,[7] whom you love, Isaac[8] and go to the land of Moriah. There offer him up as a burnt offering on one of the heights that I will point out to you.

> Rashi: And he said, "take, I pray you, your son." He said to him, "I have two sons." He said to him, "your only one." He said, "this is an only one to his mother, and this one is an only one to his father." "Whom you love." He said to him, "I love both of them." He said to him, "Isaac." (Rashi. See also *Gen. Rab.* 55:7)

A later homiletic midrash (see text box) beautifully illustrates the drama of the text. Ishmael is gone; Isaac is the only remaining son, repository of the promise. Even his birth was a miracle worked for a man a hundred years old, whose wife had been barren until then. Abraham has reasons not only to love Isaac, but to cling to him as his future. God is asking Abraham to relinquish this future, trust it entirely to the promising God. God knows what he is asking: to the verb "take," the original adds the enclitic *-na*, hence, "take, I pray you." The agony will be prolonged. The ascent of the mountain gives much time to think it over while journeying with the victim, perhaps even to backtrack.[9] Origen put it this way: "the ascent of the mountain is enjoined that . . . there might be a period of struggle between affection and faith, love of God and love of the flesh, the charm of things present and the expectation of things future."[10] Waiting for God—that is faith. A burnt offering is wholly consumed in fire, the smoke going up to heaven. The military equivalent is "burning your bridges." Moriah is not a known location, though 2 Chr 3:1 has Solomon build the house of the LORD in Jerusalem on Mount Moriah.[11]

---

6. LXX and some Hebrew manuscripts reduplicate: "Abraham, Abraham."

7. The LXX renders *ton agapēton*, your beloved.

8. I have recast the text according to the original Hebrew order which has "Isaac" at the end of the sentence.

9. That he has to make a pilgrimage to a place of sacrifice implies somewhat the late law of one central sanctuary. However, Abraham functions as priest of sacrifice, as fathers did in ancient Israel.

10. Origen, *Homilies on Genesis* 8.3, in ACCS 2:103.

11. The land of Moriah never recurs in the Bible. It is formed from the verb "to

Early the next morning, Abraham saddled his donkey, took with him two of his servants and his son Isaac, and after cutting the wood for the burnt offering set out for the place of which God had told him.

Early morning is the time to start journeys and get miles in before the sun burns too close to the skin. The charge is too heavy for words. The narrator lets actions speak volumes. In staccato fashion, like a man utterly dazed, Abraham sets about the task. He even cuts and brings along the wood, lest this lacks in the place.

On the third day, Abraham caught sight of the place from a distance. Stay here with the donkey, while the boy and I go on over there. We will worship and then come back to you.

FIGURE 3: **Abraham and Isaac, Gen 22**

How he knew it was the place, we are not told. "The boy and I," as if unable to bring himself to say "my son and I." The process of relinquishment is in motion.[12] Abraham spoke about worship, not about sacrifice.

---

see," Moriah could mean "vision"; hence Symmachus and the Vulgate have "the mount of vision." Verse 14 would then read: "on the mountain the LORD appears." It could also be formed from the other key verb in this passage, namely, "to fear [God]," hence, "the mount of *mōra'-yah*, fear of the Lord," as in the Targums. See Sarna, *Genesis*, 391.

12. Crenshaw, "Journey into Oblivion," 247: he already gave up his son in his heart.

One worshiped by prostrating oneself on the ground before deity. The story will teach that sacrifice itself is not the essential part of worship. Was Abraham telling a white lie when he said, "we will return to you"? Or did he hope that God would somehow find a way out, even by giving him another son? With sensitivity, he quit himself of the servants who might seek to weaken his resolve.

So Abraham took the wood for the burnt offering and laid it on his son Isaac, while he himself carried the fire and the knife. And the two walked on together.

He keeps to himself the destructive implements. Isaac was a boy who could carry the wood, and who knew what was required for a burnt offering. Isaac spoke to his father:

"Father . . . here are the fire and the wood, but where is the sheep for the burnt offering?" "God will provide the sheep for the burnt offering, my son.[13] *Then the two walked on together."*

The Hebrew for "will provide" is *yir'eh lô*, "will see for himself." The verb "to see" is a motif with various shades of meaning, not only in this story, but also in the story of Hagar in Genesis 16.[14] Is Abraham deliberately ambiguous? Is he expressing his faith in God's promise, because "he reasoned that God was able to raise even from the dead, and he received Isaac back as a symbol" (Heb 11:19)? Are we to read, "God will provide the sheep for the burnt offering, that is, you my son"? The refrain "the two walked on together" appeared above and will recur at the end. A basic meaning of the Hebrew word is "unitedly." Is the narrator suggesting a compromised unitedness or that Abraham's resolve held through and he did nothing to frighten his son?

The Sacrifice

Abraham built an altar there and arranged the wood on it. Next he bound his son Isaac, and put him on top of the wood on the altar. Then Abraham reached out and took the knife to slaughter his son.

Landy, "Narrative Techniques" speaks of the pain of possession and relinquishment for Abraham, also for God.

13. I have followed the Hebrew order that put "my son" at the end.
14. "You are God who sees me," Gen 16:13–14.

Abraham followed the ritual of sacrifice. The word "to bind," *'aqad*, means to tie up the hind feet of the animal of sacrifice. Jews refer to this event as the *Aqedah*, the Binding of Isaac. To slaughter is to slit the throat of the victim so that blood flows out.

But the angel of the LORD called to him from heaven, "Abraham, Abraham! . . . Do not lay your hand on the boy . . . do not do the least thing to him."

The angel of the LORD, a manifestation of YHWH, speaks from heaven at the critical time, just as the angel of God intervened, similarly from heaven, at the critical time to save Ishmael (Gen 21:17).[15]

For now, I know that you fear God, since you did not withhold from me your son, your only one.

The accent is on "your only one." Abraham is willing to forego his future when YHWH demands it. He shows steadfast and disinterested loyalty[16] to God. Israel learns that God is free to act with Israel however God wishes and Israel must respect that. Israel's existence is based on Abraham's fear of God.[17] Israel learns also that true sacrifice consists more in wholehearted devotion and obedience to God than the actual sacrifice.[18] God accepts Abraham's willingness as if he went through with the sacrifice. A minor detail is significant: the characterization of Isaac here lacks the phrase "the one you love."[19] His love for Isaac no longer rivals his preferential love of God. In fact, in the sequel of the narrative, Isaac disappears entirely.

Abraham looked up and saw a single[20] *ram caught by its horns in the thicket.*

He took it and offered it up in place of his son. Usually the animal for sacrifice must be from one's domestic flock, but the accent here is on the miraculous[21]—the appearance of the ram at the right moment

---

15. For tables illustrating the parallels between the rescue of Ishmael and that of Isaac, see Wenham, "Akedah," 99.
16. Sarna, *Understanding Genesis*, 163.
17. Schmid, "Abraham's Sacrifice and Von Rad," 274.
18. Chrysostom, *Homilies on Genesis* 47.13 articulated it this way: "take back your son ... After all, I am in the habit of rewarding the intention and giving recognition for the attitude."
19. See Kuruvilla, "Aqedah (Genesis 22)," 503.
20. The word translated as "single," can also be read as *'ahar*, behind him.
21. As already mentioned, the story may have been an etiology of the change from child sacrifice to animal sacrifice.

reminds one of the miraculous birth of Isaac. Incidentally, this prefigures the sacrificial ram giving its life for that of the offerer.

Abraham named that place Yahweh-yireh; hence people today say, "on the mountain the LORD will provide."[22]

Abraham forecast that YHWH will see (*yir'eh*) for himself the sheep for the burnt offering; YHWH has done so. The original Hebrew, still playing on the root, "to see," says that on the mountain of the LORD, it/he will appear—subject unclear. Some translate: "on the mountain of the LORD there is revelation." God's self-revelation and provision for those who fear him become a universal attribute of wherever God chooses to dwell.

Because You Obeyed My Command, 22:15–19

A second time the angel of the LORD called to Abraham from heaven and said.

The original reward of Abraham's obedience was the acceptance of his willingness and the return of his son Isaac.[23] The narrator now shows what the obedience of Abraham means for his descendants.

I swear by my very self–oracle of the LORD–that because you acted as you did in not withholding from me your son, your only one, I will bless you and make your descendants as countless as the stars of the sky and the sands of the seashore; your descendants will take possession of the gates of their enemies, and in your descendants all the nations of the earth will find blessing, because you obeyed my command.

Oracle of the LORD, *ne'um YHWH*, belongs to prophetic speech; divine oath belongs to Deuteronomic theology.[24] Both function to guarantee the future.[25] The focus is not so much on Abraham as on his descendants. "I will bless you" recaps Gen 12:2. "I will make your descendants as countless as the stars of the sky" recaps Gen 15:5. Like "the sands of the seashore" recalls Gen 13:16 (dust of the earth). New here is possession of

---

22. This etiology of a cultic place may have ended the narrative in an earlier form.
23. Carr, *Fractures of Genesis*, 155.
24. See Westermann, *Genesis 12–36*, 363. Deuteronomy links obedience with the fulfillment of God's promises.
25. Wenham, "Akedah," 102 opines that God's promises to the patriarchs have now become guarantees. Kuruvilla, "Aqedah (Genesis 22)," 101.

the gates of their enemies,[26] that is, conquest of their cities, military ascendancy. And with that a change is effected in the blessing motif. In Gen 12:3, "all the *families* of the earth will be blessed in you"—Abraham as medium of universal blessing. Here, "all the *nations* of the earth will *bless themselves* through your descendants." It is a prophecy for the far future, when Israel would have become a nation. The tension between blessing for the nations and victory over their cities demands that we read the blessing in the sense of Abraham's descendants as paragons of blessing.

Genesis 17 posited Abraham as "father of a multitude of nations," hence father of Jews and some non-Jews. As the story progresses, however, the narrative focus shifts more and more to that line of Abraham that issues in Jacob/Israel. Already at Gen 18:19, YHWH says he chose Abraham to command his children and his household in the future to keep the way of YHWH by doing what is right and just, *so that* YHWH may put into effect for Abraham the promises he made about him. At play is not only Abraham's personal reward and standing with God, but also the benefits that accrue to Israel as a nation because of God's fidelity to their father Abraham.[27] Neusner hit this on the nail: "Abraham's deeds would be matched by God's deeds in saving Israel in time to come. The merit that Abraham attained served his descendants later on."[28] Earlier, "Noah's sacrifice guaranteed humankind from the threat of a further deluge."[29] Scripture is establishing a pattern of redemption of many through the one.

Abraham then returned to his servants and they set out together for Beersheba, where Abraham lived.

Isaac is missing.[30] Abraham returns to Beersheba. Strangely, when we next hear of Sarah, she was dead in Hebron, not Beersheba.[31] And

26. The tension between blessing for the nations and victory over their cities demands that we read the blessing in the sense of Abraham's descendant as paragons of blessing.

27. This will be voiced more clearly at Gen 26:4–5.

28. Neusner, *Theological Commentary to the Midrash*, 163. He was commenting on the midrash, but what he says fits the actual text of Genesis.

29. Wenham, "Akedah," 102.

30. We suggested earlier that this may be artifice to show Abraham's total devotion to God. Some suggest, though, that in the original tale Abraham went through with the sacrifice, the substitution of the ram functioning as divine mandate that alters the sacrifice of firstborn sons.

31. *Tg. Ps.-J.*: "after Abraham had tied Isaac, Satan went and told Sarah that Abraham had slaughtered Isaac. And Sarah rose and cried out and was choked and died of

Abraham and Isaac never appear together till Isaac and Ishmael bury him in the cave of Machpelah.

Foreshadowing Rebekah, 22:20–24

Sometime afterward, the news came to Abraham: "Milcah too has borne sons to your brother Nahor."

We heard of Nahor and Milcah in Gen 11:29. Nahor stayed home and did not join the migration of his father Terah with Abraham and Haran, father of Lot. Genesis shunted off the Haran/Lot line at Genesis 19. Surprisingly, the genealogy focuses on a woman, Rebekah; the narrator soon recounts the wooing of Rebekah, daughter of Bethuel, son of Nahor (Genesis 24). Abraham learns of a possible wife for his son!

Further Reflections

Abraham did not know this was a test. He was ready to sacrifice his son because of a voice or a belief that he was hearing God speak to him. The question is: is something moral because God commands it, or does God command it because it is moral? That is, is God bound to moral norms? Kant insists that Abraham failed the test; he acted immorally, "for if the voice commands him to do something contrary to moral law . . . he must consider it an illusion."[32] The dilemma is diluted somewhat if, in Abraham's time and context, the sacrifice of the firstborn was a pious duty. Kierkegaard argued rather that Abraham's act is the best example of what true faith is about—suspending ethical judgments to fulfill what is seen as an absolute duty to God.[33]

At Genesis 21 I made clear the many contacts between "Ishmael's Aqedah"[34] and the Binding of Isaac. Is there deliberate contrast between the mother who reaches out her hand to her child who lies "under one of the bushes" and lifts him up and the father who grasps

---

anguish."

32. Kant, *Conflict of the Faculties*, 7:63. See the discussion by Palmquist and Rudisill, "Three Perspectives," 471.

33. Kierkegaard, *Fear and Trembling*, 1843. See also Römer, "Abraham's Righteousness and Sacrifice," 3.

34. Perry, "Counter-Stories in the Bible," 286. See also Sherwood, "Hagar and Ishmael," 290.

his son, binds him "on top of the wood," and reaches out his hand to slaughter him?[35] Both parents are dealing with objects of their love. How does the one image challenge or illumine the other?

The conditional nature of the promises here may suggest that "the promises made to him earlier are not simply reiterated but extended and reinforced."[36] This is hardly so, for it would mean that YHWH was not resolute in making the promises in the first place. Rather, the text posits a dialectic between free gift and merit, faith and works, grace and human endeavor! In the classic words of St. Augustine: "God who created you without you, will not save you without you."[37] We find grace and freedom juxtaposed in Phil 2:12-13: "work out your salvation with fear and trembling. For God is the one who, for his good purpose, works in you both to desire and to work." And when Paul in 2 Tim 4:7-8 speaks of the crown of righteousness awaiting him, Augustine rejoins that: "The crown simply comes to you from him; the work on the other hand comes from you, but only with him helping ... Or wasn't it by his gift that you were able to fight the good fight? ... So when God crowns your merits, he is not crowning anything but his own gifts."[38]

For the dialogue between Paul and James invoking Genesis 22 in the dialectic of faith and works, consult this commentary at Genesis 15.

What Abraham went through can be compared to the Dark Night of the Spirit. Proficients who have been purged of attachment to the consolations of the senses (Dark Night of the Senses) are led along this path. The difference between the two purgations is like that "between pulling up roots and cutting off a branch."[39] The saint describes the purgation of the spirit in these terms.

> God divests the faculties, affections, and senses, both spiritual and sensory, interior and exterior. He leaves the intellect in darkness, the will in aridity, the memory in emptiness, and the affections in supreme affliction, bitterness, and anguish, by depriving the soul of the feeling and satisfaction it previously obtained from spiritual blessings.[40]

---

35. Perry, "Counter-Stories in the Bible," 286, 314.
36. Kuruvilla, "Aqedah (Genesis 22)," 101.
37. Augustine, *Sermon* 169.13.
38. Augustine, *Sermon* 333.2, 5.
39. John of the Cross, *Dark Night*, bk. 2 (p. 331).
40. John of the Cross, *Dark Night*, bk. 2 (p. 333).

And what most grieves it is that it thinks that it will never be worthy, and that there are no more blessings for it . . . The soul at the sight of its miseries feels that it is melting away and being undone by a cruel spiritual death; it feels as if it were swallowed by a beast and being digested in the dark belly . . . But what the sorrowing soul feels most is the conviction that God has rejected it, and with an abhorrence of it cast it into darkness . . . A person also feels forsaken and despised by creatures, particularly by his friends . . . the soul feel[s] within itself the other extreme–its own intimate poverty and misery.[41]

The purpose is to bring the soul to complete self-abnegation, beyond self-love, to undivided love of God for his own sake and spiritual marriage. Abraham must forego what is dearest to him, even his hopes for the future, to rely solely on God.

We mentioned that the narrative begins to narrow the offspring of Abraham. Paul reflects two genealogies of Abraham—a biological genealogy and a theological genealogy[42]—and that makes his argument sometimes confusing. In Gal 3:7–9; 4:22–31 (Hagar as captive Sinai, Sarah as free Jerusalem), Abraham's descent is only through Isaac, Christ is the unique "seed" of Abraham, and faith is the only portal for entry into Abraham's family. Galatians seems to say that unbelieving Jews have no standing before God.[43] However, in Rom 4:11–13, 16 Paul operates with a double genealogy of Abraham: believers (Jew and non-Jew) are Abraham's children according to the spirit, but non-believing Jews are still Abraham's children (according to the flesh); they are beloved and elect for the sake of their fathers (Rom 11:28–30) and God has enduring concern for them. "Though a hardening has come upon Israel in part, until the full number of the Gentiles comes in, and thus all Israel will be saved" (Rom 11:26). In both cases, Abraham is the type of all who have faith and Gentiles are included in the promise God made to him.

In John 8, descent is not physical but has to do with behavior: "paternity is strictly a matter of behavior, so that those who act like 'the Jews' cannot be of Abrahamic or divine descent."[44]

---

41. John of the Cross, *Dark Night*, bk. 2 (pp. 336, 338).
42. Bakhos, "Family of Abraham," 122.
43. Bakhos, "Family of Abraham," 125.
44. Bakhos, "Family of Abraham," 125. For this she cites Levenson, *Inheriting Abraham*, 151.

It would seem that Rom 8:32 patterns the saving work of Christ according to Abraham's sacrifice of Isaac when it says, "he who did not spare his own son but handed him over for us all, how will he be not also give us everything along with him?" The claim that Pauline atonement theology is based on Jewish midrashic traditions of the sacrifice of Isaac is examined below.

Tradition

The fathers of the church wrestled with why the omniscient God should want to test Abraham. It was not ignorance on the part of God, but that people of the time and those from that time until now might be instructed in the same love as the patriarch and in showing obedience to the LORD's commands.[45] And when the angel of YHWH said, "for now I know that you fear God,"[46] it was not that YHWH only now came to know of the good man's virtue, rather that the good man has made clear to everyone how his fear of God is sincere.[47] When Isaac carried the wood for the sacrifice of himself, in this too he prefigured Christ our Lord, who carried his own cross to the place of his passion.[48]

Origen notes that the same things are repeated which were previously promised. The promises of Genesis 17 were made to him as father of those circumcised according to the flesh. This time the promises are made to him as father of those who are of faith and who come to the inheritance through the passion of Christ.[49] Chrysostom concluded that all this happened as a type of the cross. Christ was able to tell the Jews that Abraham rejoiced to see his day. He saw it in shadow. For just as the sheep was offered in place of Isaac, so here the rational lamb was offered for the world. There an only-begotten son, here an only-begotten son; dearly loved in that case, in this, my beloved son in whom I have found satisfaction; there offered as burnt offering by his father, here surrendered

---

45. Chrysostom, *Homilies on Genesis* 47.3

46. Jerome is perplexed; he asks, "have you just now known Abraham, Lord, with whom you have communicated for such a long time? Because Abraham had such great faith in sacrificing his own son, on that account God first began to know him . . . 'for the Lord knows the way of the just.'" Jerome, *Homilies on Psalms* 1, in ACCS 2:109.

47. Chrysostom, *Homilies on Genesis* 47.12. Already in the second century BCE, *Jub.* 18:16 had the same solution: "I have made known to everyone that you are faithful to me in everything that I have told you."

48. Caesarius of Arles, *Sermon* 84.3, in ACCS 2:104.

49. Origen, *Homilies on Genesis* 9.1, in ACCS 2: 112.

by the Father, who did not spare his son but handed him over for the sake of us all.[50]

Jewish tradition sees the sacrifice of Isaac as the last of ten trials of Abraham, though *Jubilees*, our most ancient source for the ten trials, lists it as the penultimate, the tenth being the death and burial of Sarah in Genesis 23 (*Jub.* 19:8). In a calque on Job, the test was provoked by Mastema who said to God that Abraham loves Isaac above all else. God should tell him to sacrifice Isaac and see whether he would obey and remain faithful (*Jub.* 17:15-18). Jdt 8:26-27 (second century BCE) relayed a tradition in which Isaac was also tested, hence was a willing victim: "recall how he dealt with Abraham, and how he tested Isaac." Similarly, that Abraham and Isaac went along together is interpreted in *Gen. Rab.* 56:4 as that they were united in the same spirit: "one to bind, the other to be bound, one to slaughter, the other to be slaughtered."

Further Reflections

The story of the near sacrifice of Isaac developed into a doctrine of the Aqedah, that is, "a haggadic presentation of the vicariously atoning sacrifice of Isaac in which he is said, e.g., to have shed his blood freely and/or to have been reduced to ashes."[51] Isaac was seen as a willing victim who requested to be well bound,[52] and who willingly shed his blood.[53] Such a doctrine appears in *L.A.B.* 32:3,[54] where Isaac says

---

50. Chrysostom, *Homilies on Genesis* 47.14.

51. Chilton and Davies, "Aqedah:," 515.

52. The rabbis give Isaac's age as twenty-six or thirty-seven: *Gen. Rab.* 56:8. *Tg. Neof.*: "Isaac answered and said to his father Abraham: 'Father, tie me well lest I kick you and your offering be rendered unfit and we be thrust down into the pit of destruction in the world to come.'"

53. See *Gen. Rab.* 56:8-10. *Tg. Neof.* has Abraham praying: "everything is manifest and known before you–that there was no division in my heart the first time that you said to me to offer my son Isaac, *to make him dust and ashes before you* . . . And now, when his sons are in the hour of distress you shall remember the Binding of their father Isaac, and listen to the voice of their supplication, and answer them and deliver them from all distress, so that the generations to arise after him may say: 'on the mountain of the sanctuary of the Lord Abraham sacrificed his son Isaac, and on this mountain the glory of the Shekinah of the Lord was revealed to him.'" Somewhat shorter in *Tg. Ps.-J.* and without the reference to "make him dust and ashes before you."

54. *L.A.B.* (*The Book of Biblical Antiquities*) is a recasting of the biblical narrative from Adam to Saul. It is an anonymous work handed down in Philo's name. It was composed in Hebrew, translated into Greek, then into Latin, in which language alone it is extant. It is to be dated between 70 and 100 CE. See Nickelsburg, *Jewish Literature*

that "peoples will understand because of me that the Lord has considered the life of a human being worthy [to be offered] in sacrifice." Here there appears the vicarious expiatory effect that constitutes the Aqedah doctrine. It appears clearly in the Mekilta of Rabbi Ishmael on Exod 12:13 on the Passover: "when I see the blood—blood of the sacrifice of Isaac."[55] This Mekilta is usually dated to the end of the second century CE.

L.A.B. is usually dated to 70–100 CE,[56] hence is not pre-Christian, according to Fitzmyer. Chilton and Davies argue that the Aqedah was in fact a deliberate reformulation of Jewish liturgy and doctrine during the second century CE; its matrix was in developments after 70 CE, its purpose to combat Christian claims of passion-atonement.[57] Vermes argues that the pre-Christian Qumran fragment 4Q225 or 4QPseudo-Jubilees[58] (late first century BCE) already contained elements of the Aqedah. Dating L.A.B. before the Christian era, he argues that "the Akedah theme, bound, as in Judaism, to the Servant motif, belongs to the oldest pre-Marcan stratum of the Christian kerygma." In this scenario, the purpose of all sacrifice was to remind God of the merit of him who bound himself upon the altar. As such, he argues that "it is reasonable . . . to wonder whether Jesus himself was conscious of his destiny as being the fulfillment of Isaac's sacrifice."[59]

The debate continues, but the evidence points to Jewish reformulation of doctrine in response to the Christian doctrine of atonement.[60] This may explain the oscillation between Passover and the New Year in the liturgical setting for Genesis 22.

---

between Bible and the Mishnah, 265–70.

55. "*And when I see the blood.* I see the blood of the sacrifice of Isaac. For it is said: 'And Abraham called the name of the place Adonai-jireh' (The Lord will see), e.t.c. (Gen 22:14) . . . What did he behold? He beheld the blood of the sacrifice of Isaac, as it is said: 'God will himself see the lamb,' e.t.c. (Gen 22:8)." Lauterbach, *Mekilta de-Rabbi Ishmael*, 57.

56. Fitzmyer, "Sacrifice of Isaac in Qumran," 223.

57. Chilton and Davies, "Aqedah," 536, 515.

58. Fitzmyer, "Sacrifice of Isaac in Qumran," argues that 4Q225 does reveal some steps in the developing tradition about the sacrifice of Isaac, but lacks the essential feature of atonement.

59. Vermes, "Redemption and Genesis XXII," 223.

60. Himmelfarb, "Abraham and the Messianism of Genesis Rabbah," 105 sees the shift of focus from Abraham to Isaac as a counter to the Christian treatment of the Aqedah.

By Amoraic times, Rosh Hashanah (rather than Passover) began to be associated with the Akedah. Rabbi Abahu (third century Palestinian Amora): "Why do we blow the horn of the ram? The Holy One (blessed be he) said: 'Blow the ram's horn before me so that I may remember for your benefit the Binding of Isaac, son of Abraham, and account it to you as if you had bound yourselves before me'" (b. Rosh HaShanah 16a).[61]

Kaunfer argues that the rabbis combated the Isaac-Jesus typology by moving the Akedah to the holiday of Rosh Hashanah. The clear break from the Christian calendar afforded an opportunity to further develop the "sacrifice" of Isaac (which may have been a pre-Christian concept) as alternative to the Christian understanding of the Akedah.[62] In sum, the development of the Akedah as the Rosh Hashanah reading is a result of rabbinic attempts to dissociate the Isaac narrative from the Jesus narrative. This liturgical development gave the rabbis a "weapon" used to eject Christians from the synagogue. But the association between Passover and the Akedah, while absent liturgically, remained in certain midrashic formulations. The rabbis may have developed these midrashim as a "second front" on the war with Christianity, proposing Isaac as a direct competition to the figure of Jesus.[63]

---

61. Kaunfer, "Torah Reading as a Weapon," 5.

62. Segal, "Sacrifice of Isaac," 129: "[I]t is not out of the question that rabbis continued to discuss this connection [with Passover] in competition with the Church-fathers' use of Isaac as a *typos* for Christ. The Amoraic traditions of the death and ashes of Isaac and his subsequent resurrection can be reasonably understood as an attempt to enrich Judaism with a figure that was as colorful as the one known to Christian exegesis."

63. Kaunfer, "Torah Reading as a Weapon," 13-14.

CHAPTER 11

Genesis 23

Abraham Acquires the Cave of Machpelah in the Land of Canaan

> Therefore my heart is glad, my soul rejoices; my body also dwells secure, For you will not abandon my soul to Sheol, nor let your devout one see the pit.
>
> —Psalm 16:9–10

How Read This Story?

This chapter is about a burial, the first burial in the Abraham story. The narrator leaves no one in doubt that this burial is important. "Bury your dead" rings out like a refrain all through the chapter. The burial is of no less a person than the first matriarch of Israel. Aspects of the narrative indicate there may be adjoining concerns. The inclusio of "in the land of Canaan" is significant: Sarah died in the land of Canaan (v. 2), Abraham buried her in the land of Canaan (v. 19). Canaan is land that God has been promising to Abraham and his descendants. The people of the land are called "sons of Heth," hence Hithites. Each of the lists of nations[1] that Israel is to displace in Canaan includes the Hithites, for example, Gen 15:20. In this chapter, the Hittites appear synonymous with the Canaanites. The drawn-out negotiations and the presence of "the people of the land" are significant. They signify the public nature of the transaction. All parties concerned endorse the deed so it is valid for generations to come. At Gen 21:22–33, Abraham secured wells in Beersheba. Does he begin symbolically to secure the future of Israel in the land? Abraham will also be buried here, so will Isaac and Jacob and some of the matriarchs. Did Ephron and the people of the land act with magnanimity or were they transactional?[2] Why does the narrator report this story in such detail? What is his intent?

The Narrative

After the near sacrifice of Isaac, Abraham returned to Beersheba. Strangely, when we next hear of Sarah she is dead in Hebron, not Beersheba.[3] *Jub.* 19:8 (second century BCE) sees the current story as the last of ten trials of Abraham. Having proven faithful in the trial to nullify the promise of seed, Abraham here confronts the promise of land. A double cave in a land not yet his own is a statement for the future, an act of faith. A sojourner with no rights in the place, Abraham needs ground to bury his wife (and himself eventually). In the next chapter (Gen 24:3, 6), he abjures his servant never to take a wife for Isaac from the daughters of the Canaanites and never, for any reason, take him back to the land from which he came. He stands on the promises of God.

The span of Sarah's life was one hundred and twenty-seven years. She died in Kiriath-arba—now Hebron—in the land of Canaan.

Sarah is the only matriarch whose age at death is given. Hebron is the current name of Kiriath-arba.[4] Josh 14:15 records that "Hebron was

---

1. There are eighteen such lists. See also Hamilton, *Genesis 18–50*, 127. He notes (n. 19) John van Seters's stand that all Pentateuch references to Hittites are from P.

2. Rashi cites the opinion in B. Metsia 87a that the name Ephron was written defectively to indicate that he lacked sincerity—promised much, but did not do even the least.

3. *Tg. Ps.-J.* explained the death as follows: "after Abraham had tied Isaac, Satan went and told Sarah that Abraham had slaughtered Isaac. And Sarah rose and cried out and was choked and died of anguish."

4. Literally, city of four—either four settlements or intersection of four roadways.

formerly called Kiryath-arba, for Arba, the greatest among the Anakim." David will establish his throne as king of Judah first in Hebron (2 Samuel 2).

And Abraham proceeded to mourn and weep for her.

In Gen 50:3, the Egyptians mourned for Jacob seventy days. In Deut 21:13, a female captive may mourn a full month for her father and mother.[5] The pain of death is accepted; there are mourning rites, like sitting on the ground, but excessive grief is prohibited, for example, one must not lacerate one's body for the dead (Lev 19:28). Abraham addressed the Hittites:

Although I am a resident alien among you, sell[6] me from your holdings a burial place, that I may bury my deceased wife.

What Abraham said translates better in NRSV: "give me property among you for a burial place."[7] He uses the verb *nātan*, which can mean "give" or "sell," though indicating with the noun *'aḥuzath-qever* (holding-grave) that he intends a permanent possession. A resident alien has no rights to land. Acquiring property in the place would also confer citizen rights. And Abraham was a crowd—he had a retinue of at least 318 people. This may be the reason the negotiation starts with the citizens of the village as a whole. The Hittites answered:

You are a mighty leader among us. Bury your dead in the choicest of our burial sites. None of us would deny you his burial ground for the burial of your dead.

$N^e\acute{s}\hat{\imath}$' *Elohim* means "a prince of God." The Hittites may be viewing Abraham as one in God's protection, or, as Abimelech said at Gen 21:22,

---

Josh 15:13, however, makes it the city of Arba—Caleb's portion among the Judahites fell on Kiryat-arba, the father of the giant(s) (*anak*), that is, Hebron.

5. Current Jewish practice is to have a period of mourning known as *shiva* (seven days) beginning on the day of burial and lasting until the morning of the seventh day after burial. This is followed by *shloshim* (thirty) because it lasts until the thirtieth day after burial. For parents, the final period of mourning is *avelut* which lasts for twelve months after the burial.

6. NIV and TNK also read "sell," but this destroys the dynamic of the ensuing negotiation. Sarna, *Genesis*, 158 points out that this verb is used seven times in the course of the negotiations and that its many meanings allow dialogue in a delicate, if contrived, politeness.

7. NJB: "let me have a burial site of my own here."

"God is with you in everything you do." The phrase can also mean "a great prince."[8] It would, as such, be an honor to give him a burial ground. Or perhaps their thinking was that such a great prince could surely pay for a burial plot, and handsomely too.[9] They seem to be saying, "you don't bury her in a land of your own. You bury her among us,"[10] otherwise let's negotiate. Abraham makes it clear he is prepared to buy the property. Prostrating himself before the Hittites, he said to the people of the land, the Hittites:

If you will allow me room for burial of my dead, listen to me! Intercede for me with Ephron, son of Zohar, so that he will sell me the cave of Machpelah that he owns; it is at the edge of his field. Let him sell it to me in your presence at its full price for a burial place.

The "people of the land" constitute the assembly of citizens; they will soon be called "all who entered the gate of his city."[11] The transaction has communal impact. The same verb, *nātan*, is used, but now in a context that clearly means "sell," and for the full price too. Machpelah means a double cave. "At the edge of the field" means that Abraham would not have to trespass Ephron's field or impinge upon it through right of entrance.

Ephron the Hittite replied to Abraham in the hearing of the Hittites . . . : please, sir, listen to me! I give you both the field and the cave in it; in the presence of my people I give it to you. Bury your dead!

Emphasis on this happening in the presence and hearing of his people invokes them as witnesses. For Ephron, it is a done deal: "I have given it to you" (*nᵉtattîha*)[12]; however, you must have both the field and the cave.[13] He said nothing about the price. Abraham again prostrated himself before the people, then addressed Ephron:

I will pay you the price of the field. Accept it from me, that I may bury my dead there. Ephron replied, *please, sir, listen to me! A piece of land worth*

---

8. *Elohim* is sometimes so used to mark a superlative.
9. See Lester, "Admiring Our Savvy Ancestors," 85.
10. Sternberg, "Double Cave," 85.
11. The city gate is the place for judicial and public transactions.
12. The perfect tense here expresses the future as if a finished and accomplished fact. See Grossfeld, *Targum Onkelos to Genesis*, 89 n. 4.
13. Hamilton, *Genesis 18–50*, 130 suggests that thereby Ephron would be quit of levies and feudal obligations on the field.

four hundred shekels of silver–what is that between you and me? Bury your dead!

Jeremiah paid seventeen shekels of silver for similar property (Jer 32:9). David paid fifty shekels for the threshing floor of Arauna on which the temple would be built (2 Sam 24:24). Because currency fluctuates so much in time and place, it is difficult to assess Ephron's price, but it looks high. Ephron mentioned the price casually, as if he was prepared to give the plot free. Abraham was prepared. He weighed out four hundred shekels of silver in the hearing of the Hittites! Besides, it was *at the current market value*,[14] that is, without depreciation.

Thus Ephron's field in Machpelah, facing Mamre,[15] *together with its cave and all the trees anywhere within its limits, was conveyed to Abraham by purchase in the presence of the Hittites, all who entered the gate of Ephron's city.*

The verb *qûm* is technical term for legal conveyance. It is also legal custom to indicate the trees that would accrue to the buyer of a field. The public and legal nature of the transaction and its attestation by the citizenry are stressed.

After this, Abraham buried his wife Sarah in the cave of the field of Machpelah, facing Mamre—now Hebron—in the land of Canaan.

It is surprising that Isaac is not mentioned at his mother's funeral.[16] The exact location is given because this is, as it were, a pledge of the promised ownership of the land of Canaan. "Abraham dies without knowing if the promise of land will ever be realized."[17] But this act of purchase seals his confidence in God. There his sons Isaac and Ishmael will bury him (Gen 25:9). There Jacob will ask to be buried, telling us that Isaac and his wife Rebekah, also Leah, were buried there (Gen 49:30; 50:13).

---

14. *Tg. Onq.*: "acceptable as merchandise in every country." Similar in *Tg. Neof*.

15. Here Mamre is a place; at Gen 14:13, 24 it is the name of an Amorite, ally of Abraham.

16. In fact, later Rebekah, his bride, arrives in Beer Lahai-roi, not at all to Beersheba and is not introduced to Abraham. Besides, after Sarah's death, not Isaac but a surrogate manages Abraham's estate. Perry, "Counter-Stories in the Bible," 288 suggests something shattered in Abraham's family.

17. Sternberg, "Double Cave," 92.

Narrative Intent?

Noting that Machpelah is the first piece of real estate in the Promised Land, Sarna opines that its acquisition presages the future possession of the entire land.[18] However, it is remarkable that the narrator never referred to God's promise of land. It may be that the story "dramatizes a problem that is central to the Bible. And that is the distance and sometimes a tension between what God promises and what happens. God's promises are finally realized, always! But sometimes the suffering that the beneficiary of the promise suffers on the way is really heart-rending. So the Bible in effect tells us, if what you expect is a promise by God and you expect a swift delivery, forget it! God acts in his own ways and he tries you all the time."[19] It is also possible that the story appeals to wealthy Jews of the Diaspora to buy back the Promised Land from the Edomites.[20]

Tradition

Heb 11:9 says that Abraham was so anchored on the things to come that he was content to dwell in tents: "by faith he sojourned in the promised land as in a foreign country, dwelling in tents with Isaac and Jacob, heirs of the same promise, for he was looking forward to the city with foundations whose architect and maker is God." Chrysostom points to how this counters those Christians who, despite such wonderful promises and guarantees of ineffable blessings, hanker for present realities, buying up property, ever concerned for their image, amassing all these possessions out of greed and avarice.[21]

---

18. Sarna, *Genesis*, 156.
19. Sternberg, "Double Cave," 92.
20. Van Seters, *Abraham in History*, 295, citing Vink, *Priestly Code*, 91.
21. Chrysostom, *Homilies on Genesis* 48.3–4. in ACCS 2:118.

CHAPTER 12

Genesis 24

Transmitting the Blessing: A Wife for Isaac

> Blessed be the Lord, the God of my master Abraham, who has not let his kindness and fidelity toward my master fail.
>
> —Genesis 24:27

Introduction

BEFORE ABRAHAM BOWS OFF the stage, he provides for the next generation and for the transmission of God's blessing. The story has elements of the betrothal type-scene, "meeting at the well."[1] Elements of the motif of "the faithful, prudent, and selfless steward" also occur and suggest that this may be an "example story" for the training of court officials.[2] However, the story is shot through with the themes of divine promise and divine guidance and now functions as a theological epilogue to the Abraham tradition.[3] "The divine agenda annexes to itself all the plots

---

1. Alter, *Art of Biblical Narrative* (2011), 62–65. A type-scene is a literary convention with a constellation of predetermined motifs; the particular one here is that of encounter with the future betrothed at a well. See also Jacob's encounter with Rachel at the well (Gen 19:1–10).

2. Roth, "Wooing of Rebekah," 117–87.

3. Aitken, "Wooing of Rebekah," 15, 17. "Ch. 24 then becomes a 'a guidance

beneath it and plays them off against one another. It 'intends' all of them, and especially the tensions between them."[4]

> Isaac was absent at the burial of Sarah in Hebron (Genesis 23); he was then at Beer Lahai-roi (Gen 24:62; 25:11).[5] Abraham commissions a trusted servant of his household to go to Aram Naharaim to fetch a wife for Isaac. Returning with Rebekah, this unnamed servant reported, not to Abraham in Beersheba, but to Isaac in the region of the Negeb by Beer Lahai-roi. The story clearly functions as a bridge between (originally separate?) patriarchal traditions of Abraham and Isaac.

The Commissioning, 24:1–9

At the beginning of Abraham's journey with God, YHWH assured him, "I will bless you" (Gen 12:2); now at the end of that journey, the narrator attests that YHWH has indeed been faithful:

The LORD had blessed him in every way.

It is time to provide for the future and for the transmission of blessing. This blessing becomes effective for the next generation in Gen 25:11: "after the death of Abraham, God blessed his son Isaac, who lived near Beer Lahai-roi." However, rather than bless Isaac and send him off to find a wife, as Isaac himself would do for Jacob (Gen 28:1–4), Abraham commissions

The oldest servant of his household who had charge of all his possessions.

---

narrative,' or a narrative whose purpose is to attest the hand of God in the life of a small community and thus in personal life." Westermann, *Genesis 12–36*, 382.

4. Perry, "Counter-Stories," 312.

5. Perry, "Counter-Stories," 288 suggests that the near-slaughter of Isaac in Genesis 22 shattered family relations. Abraham lived in Beersheba, Sarah in Hebron. Abraham had to travel thence for her funeral. Isaac does not show up for his mother's funeral. When a bride arrives, she is brought to Isaac at Beer Lahai-roi, not to Beersheba, nor is she introduced to Abraham. Father and son never meet till thirty years later, when "Abraham gave everything he owned to his son Isaac" (Gen 25:5).

> "Nevertheless don't take my son there." You see, I have no doubt that the Lord will take care of you. Showing how he trusted in God's power, Abraham forbade the servant to conduct Isaac there. (Chrysostom, *Homilies on Genesis* 48.12, in ACCS 2:123)

At Gen 15:2, the "servant of my household" was Eliezer of Damascus, who stood to inherit Abraham who was then childless. Here the servant is anonymous and is consistently called "the servant" or "the man." Abraham conjured[6] this servant by making him place his hand on his genitals (a similar oath occurs in Gen 47:29), an ancient rite of self-curse with childlessness should one break faith. He made him swear by *the LORD, the God of heaven and the God of earth*, never to bring Isaac back to his homeland for any reason. "YHWH himself promised this land to Abraham's seed; therefore he must remain in this land."[7] He was never to take a wife for him from among the Canaanites, rather from Abraham's land and birthplace; from Gen 22:23 Abraham already knew of at least one marriageable girl there, Rebekah, daughter of Bethuel. The "God of heaven" is a universal God and implies monotheistic belief; the purposes of this God are effective everywhere, to be obeyed by all. This divine title occurs nowhere else in Genesis, nor in preexilic literature,[8] but is characteristic of Jewish literature of the Persian period and later (Jon 1:9; Ezra 1:2 = 2 Chr 36:23; Ezra 5:12; 6:9–10; Dan 2:37). Such usage suggests that the interdiction of marriage with indigenes and the prohibition of abandoning the land addressed issues of tenancy and identity/survival as a people after the return from the exile.[9] For a threatened minority, intermarriage slowly leads to the loss of ethnic identity and peoplehood.

Abraham owned only a burial cave in the land YHWH promised him, but he steadfastly believed in future possession of this land of promise:[10]

---

6. Gunkel, *Genesis*, 245: the oath makes sense if he believed he would die shortly. If he expected to live he would not require an oath, he would give a command.

7. Gunkel, *Genesis*, 246.

8. Gunkel, *Genesis*, 249.

9. Rofé, "Betrothal of Rebekah," 36–37.

10. This differs from the dynamic in Deuteronomy (for example, Deut 7:3) that evokes the danger of idolatry and calls for the extermination of the local population.

The LORD . . . who took me from my father's house . . . and who confirmed by oath the promise he made to me . . . will send his angel before you, and you will get a wife for my son there. If the woman is unwilling to follow you, you will be released from this oath to me.

Abraham set two conditions: God's choice and the woman's will.[11] He wagered that the servant would find the appropriate wife and that the woman would agree to follow him to Canaan—all this by YHWH's guidance. Such guidance, here through the invisible promptings of the angel of YHWH, resembles the operation of divine providence in the Joseph Novella.

The Encounter, 24:10–33

The servant loaded ten camels with gifts and made his way to the city of Nahor in Aram Naharaim,[12] Aram of the Two Rivers (the Tigris and Euphrates). The narrator confirms God's providential guidance, but the servant does not know this yet. "City of Nahor" is ambivalent—is Nahor a person (brother of Abraham, Gen 11:27) or a city (Nahur, a city attested in Mari documents)?[13] In Gen 27:43, Rebekah identifies the city of her brother Laban as Haran. Near evening, the servant made the camels kneel by the well outside the city. The young girls would be coming to draw water.

> The betrothal type-scene calls for "travel to a foreign land, encounter there with the future bride (almost always referred to as *na'arah*, 'girl') at a well, drawing of water, 'hurrying' or 'running' to bring the news of the stranger's arrival, a feast at which a betrothal agreement is concluded."[14] "The well at an oasis is obviously a symbol of fertility and, in all likelihood, also a female symbol . . . The drawing of water from the well is the act that emblematically establishes a bond–male-female, host-guest, benefactor-benefitted–between the stranger and the girl . . ."[15]

---

11. Perry, "Counter-Stories," 304.
12. Another tradition, usually identified as P, calls Abraham's home Paddan-aram (Gen 25:20; 28:2, 6, 7; 35:9 . . .), that is, Field of Aram.
13. In Gen 11:31, Abraham's home was given as Ur of the Chaldeans.
14. Alter, *Genesis*, 115.
15. Alter, *Art of Biblical Narrative*, 62.

> This is the first prayer for guidance in the Bible, and it comes from the heart and mouth of a nameless individual. He asks for a sign, not a miracle; he uses neither magic nor divination and does not attempt to force God's hand . . . The biblical age had a deep conviction about God's role in human affairs. God was thought to be approachable, as near as prayer itself, a guide and guardian . . . Abraham's messenger did what most moderns still do: he looked for external manifestations of the Divine. (Plaut, *Torah*, 165)

The servant prayed to YHWH, the God of his master Abraham. He set a sign:

If I say to a young woman, "please lower your jug that I may drink," and she answers, "drink, and I will water your camels, too," then she is the one whom you have decided upon for your servant Isaac.

Was this a "shrewd character test"[16] of the grace and liberal hospitality befitting one to be associated with Abraham, or does it manifest the servant's trust in God's commitment to Abraham, foregrounding God's will and choice of "the one whom you have decided upon for your servant Isaac"? Or, did the servant dictate a test and oblige God to cooperate? Scarcely had he finished praying when Rebekah appeared with a jug on her shoulder. The narrator informs us that she was the daughter of Bethuel, son of Milcah, wife of Abraham's brother Nahor. She thus met a condition set by Abraham, though the servant does not yet know this.

The young woman was very beautiful, a virgin,[17] *untouched by man.*

This privileged information confirms that the girl was both nubile and strikingly beautiful. As she came up from filling her jug with water, the servant ran to meet her:

Please give me a sip of water from your jug. "Drink sir," she replied, and quickly lowering the jug into her hand, she gave him a drink.[18] *"I will draw water for your camels, too, until they have finished drinking."*

---

16. Sternberg, *Poetics of Biblical Narrative*, 137.

17. *Betulah* really refers to a young woman who has not given birth, hence the further qualification here "untouched by man." Wenham, "*Betulah*," 32–48.

18. In this particular type-scene, a surrogate represents the groom, and the girl

In the Hebrew, she said, "drink, my lord"—recognizing the man as a person of influence. She concentrates on the steward, ignoring the men with him. Is there flirting and courting going on here?[19] *Hagmî'înî-na'* calls for her to lower the jar into her hand and train the water into his mouth! She ran to and fro, filling her jug and emptying the water into the trough till she watered all the camels. Camels drink an enormous amount of water in one sitting, so this took time and energy.[20]

The man watched her the whole time, silently waiting to learn whether or not the Lord had made his journey successful. When the camels had finished drinking, the man took out a gold nose-ring weighing half a shekel and two gold bracelets weighing ten shekels for her wrists.

Discernment needs these periods of silent waiting and reviewing of events. Such expensive gifts before even ascertaining the identity and belonging of the woman are awkward.[21] However, fulfillment of the sign pointed to this girl as the possible bride. The servant needs to talk with her family. He asked her,

"Whose daughter are you? Tell me please. And is there a place in your father's house[22] for us to spend the night?" I am the daughter of Bethuel the son of Milcah, whom she bore to Nahor.

The process of discernment comes full circle: he has arrived at the family of Abraham! Slightly carried away, perhaps, he improperly asked a young girl about matters not under her control.

Blessed be the Lord, the God of my master Abraham, who has not let his kindness and fidelity toward my master fail. As for me, the Lord has led me straight to the house of my master's brother.

---

plays the man's conventional role of drawing water. Rebekah will prove the dominant partner in relation to Isaac. All through her life, she made the decisions and deluded Isaac to believe he made them. See Perry, "Counter-Stories," 300.

19. Perry, "Counter-Stories," 298 suggests that "from Rebekah's point of view the scene is indeed a meeting with a future bridegroom, who has come from a foreign territory."

20. Sarna, *Genesis*, 164: a single camel can drink twenty-five gallons of water to regain the weight it loses in the course of a long journey; it takes it about ten minutes to drink this amount.

21. They could be meant as bridal gifts in a form of the story where everything depended on the maiden's consent. See Gunkel, *Genesis*, 243.

22. If she still lived in her father's house, she would still be single.

Just as we say thanks to humans by verbally seeking their good (wealth, prosperity, long life and the like), so blessing God is "an expression of gratitude [that] suggests a kind of reciprocity, a verbal gift in return for the divine ... gift that has elicited the expression of thanks."[23] The reason for thanks is YHWH's *hesed* and *'emeth* toward Abraham—*hesed* is loving commitment not necessarily influenced by merit; *'emeth* is truth, standing by one's word and promise no matter the circumstances.

The young woman ran off and told her mother's household what had happened. When he saw the nose-ring and the bracelets on his sister's arms ... Come, blessed of the Lord![24] Why are you standing outside when I have made the house ready, as well as a place for the camels?

Her brother, Laban (in Gen 29:5, Laban is son of Nahor, not of Bethuel), rushed outside to the man at the spring. Laban is presented as selfish and greedy, with a sharp eye for gold, a characterization to be confirmed later in his dealings with Jacob. The verb *pinnah* means "to clear out of the way," "to free from obstacles." Laban uses the name of YHWH, and so Targum and midrash make him clear the house of idolatry so the servant will not hesitate to enter. He brought water for washing the feet of the servant and the men with him.

But when food was set before him, he said, "I will not eat until I have told my story." "Go ahead," they replied.

Their response to his tale will determine whether he stays or leaves, literally, whether he turns to the right or the left.

The Servant's Tale, 24:34–49

In the interest of persuasion, the servant modifies significantly what the narrator already told us.[25]

The LORD has blessed my master so abundantly ...

The narrator said that the LORD had blessed Abraham in every way (Gen 24:1). The servant sharpens the role and providence of God—this matter is God's choice and who would want to stand in the way? He

23. Miller, *They Cried to the Lord*, 180–81.
24. Gunkel, *Genesis*, 253: "Yahweh's blessed" (v. 31) must refer to him because he has a great deal of gold. The narrator also shares this theology, see verses 1 and 35.
25. See Sasson, "Servant's Tale," 257–60 for an illuminating comparison of the two.

builds Abraham up in the eyes of his audience by specifying the blessing in terms of wealth and possessions, but also in terms of God's gift of a son in his old age.

And he has given him everything he owns.

This conveyance does not happen till later (Gen 25:5)! The servant jumps the gun in the service of enticing the lady by laying it all out. Abraham asked him to go to "my land and my birthplace"; the servant narrows the circle *to my father's house, to my own family.* Abraham assured him that *the LORD, in whose presence I have always walked, will send his angel with you and make your journey successful.* God has brought him right to his master's family, and who wants to act against God? The servant omitted Abraham's strictures about not taking Isaac back to the land from which he came, everything about God's promise of the land of Canaan, lest he might be heard as suggesting that their land was inferior. Abraham's "if the woman is unwilling to follow you" becomes *if you go to my family and they refuse you*—shifting the burden for consent from the woman herself to her family. The oath becomes a dreaded curse.[26] He only asked her to *give me a little water from your jug* (nothing about lowering her jug so he may sip). Gone is his hesitation about the meaning of the events, his question about whether there is room in her father's house, and her affirmative answer. He conferred the expensive presents on her only *after* learning of her identity and belonging! Everything is from

> Your account shows the whole thing has happened by God's arrangement. So don't think we oppose the decisions of God; after all, it is beyond our powers to do it. Here, the maid is in your hands, "take her and be on your way, and she will be wife to your master's son, as the Lord has said. (Chrysostom, *Homilies on Genesis* 48.25. In ACCS, 134)

The Lord, the God of my master Abraham, who has led me on the right road to obtain the daughter of my master's kinsman for his son ... if you will act with kindness and fidelity toward my master, let me know, but if not, let me know that too.

---

26. He speaks consistently of a spring, *hā-'ayin* (24:42, 45) when the narrator juggled well, *b^{e}ēr* (42:11) and spring (42:13).

Yes, God has acted with kindness and fidelity (*hesed* and *'emeth*) with his master. He now asks them to follow in God's steps:

Laban and Bethuel said in reply: "this thing comes from the Lord; we can say nothing to you either for or against it. Here is Rebekah, right in front of you; take her and go, that she may become the wife of your master's son, as the Lord has said."

The men in the family give their consent (Bethuel, v. 50, is an awkward gloss; he does not appear again). "The wife of your master's son"—Rebekah and her family know only of Isaac's father. Isaac himself is never named, just as Abraham it was who organized the marriage.[27] The servant bowed before YHWH in worshipful thanksgiving; all through this account, the servant's piety is on display, praying before endeavors, discerning the hand of God, and rendering thankful praise in response to the felt guidance of God. The servant now brings out bridal gifts for Rebekah and makes presents to her brother and mother.[28] They eat and drink and go to bed.

A Wife for Isaac, 24:50–67

Next morning, the servant wanted to hit the road. But Laban and Rebekah's mother replied,

Let the young woman stay with us a short while, say ten days, after that she may go. They called Rebekah and asked her, "will you go with this man?" She answered, "I will." [29]

Yāmîm 'ô 'áśôr literally means "days or ten," perhaps an expression for a short period.[30] The servant insisted on leaving immediately. The last condition set by Abraham, the woman's consent, is now in place—the girl has given consent.

---

27. Boase, "Role and Function of Isaac," 317.

28. *Gen. Rab.* 60:12: where was Bethuel? He wished to hinder the marriage and so was smitten during the night, and died. The fact that the transactions are made in the mother's house and that Laban heads the discussions means that the father is dead.

29. Rashi: from here comes the Jewish practice that women are not to be married without their consent.

30. *Tg. Onq.* takes the expression to mean "a year or ten months." B. Keth 57a: after betrothal, a virgin was entitled to a period of twelve months before completing the marriage.

At this they sent off their sister Rebekah and her nurse[31] *with Abraham's servant and his men.* Rebekah's nurse is called Deborah (Gen 35:8). *They blessed Rebekah and said: Sister, may you grow into thousands of myriads. And may your descendants gain possession of the gates of their enemies.*

Gaining possession of the gates of enemies refers to political ascendancy and conquest of the cities of enemies—recalls the angel of YHWH's blessing of Abraham consequent at the Aqedah (Gen 22:18).

Meanwhile Isaac had gone from Beer Lahai-roi and was living in the region of the Negeb. One day toward evening he went out to walk in the field and caught sight of camels approaching.

> What *la-śûaḥ* means has been in debate; suggestions range from "to walk about," "to meditate/pray,"[32] "to mourn," "to relieve himself."[33] We already mentioned the anomaly that Isaac was absent at the burial of his mother, Sarah, and that Abraham commissioned the servant in Beersheba, but the servant returned to Isaac in Beer Lahai-roi. "At the beginning of the account, Abraham is still alive. At the end, when the servant returns to Isaac, he must be dead."[34]

Rebekah too caught sight of Isaac, and got down from her camel.[35] *She asked, "who is the man over there, walking through the fields toward us?" "That is my master," replied the servant. Then she took her veil and covered herself.*

This shows recognition of Isaac as her prospective husband. For in a marriage procession, the bride was veiled and took off the veil only in the bridal chamber. That was how Laban could substitute Leah for Rachel (Gen 29:23–25).[36]

---

31. However, in verse 61, Rebekah and her attendants (plural) mounted the camels and followed the man.
32. Targum and Midrash render "to pray."
33. See Hamilton, *Genesis 18–50*, 160 n. 3.
34. Gunkel, *Genesis*, 244.
35. The Hebrew has the verb *naphal*, "to fall." LXX renders *katepēdēsen*, "she leapt down."
36. Vaux, *Ancient Israel*, 34.

Then Isaac brought Rebekah into the tent of his mother Sarah. He took Rebekah as his wife. Isaac loved her and found solace after the death of his mother.

"He loved her" announces the success of the whole project. He never met this woman, nor had a hand in the negotiations for her hand, but she proved just the one for him—by divine providence. Rebekah takes the place of Sarah as the matriarch of the family.

> "Thus should one regard us: as servants of Christ and stewards of the mysteries of God. Now it is of course required of stewards that they be found trustworthy" (1 Cor 4:1–2)

The servant's report showcases the rhetorical strategies of a wise and able speaker who attends closely to the beliefs and foibles of an audience. The servant also embodies the piety, loyalty, and trustworthiness of a good steward; he is a mirror of stewardship whether in the earthly realm or concerning "the mysteries of God" (1 Cor 4:1).

Tradition

The rabbis discussed the propriety of setting up signs for God to fulfill. Four (the servant whom midrash equates with Eliezer, Caleb, Saul, and Jephthah) asked improperly, three were granted their request in a fitting manner, and the fourth in an unfitting manner. The way the servant set up the sign, the young woman could be a bondmaid, but God prepared Rebekah and granted his request in a fitting manner (*Gen. Rab.* 60:3). God is not bound to the terms we set for him in prayer; he sometimes purifies our request or responds in a different manner.

The fathers of the church generally see Rebekah as representing patience. "Rebekah came to the wells daily; she drew water daily. And because she spent time at the wells daily, therefore, she could be found by Abraham's servant and be united in marriage with Isaac. That servant is the prophetic word. Unless you have received it first, you cannot be married to Christ. Know, however, that no one untrained and inexperienced receives the prophetic word, but he who knows how to draw water from the depth of the well, who knows how to draw in such quantity that it may be sufficient also for those who appear irrational and perverse, whom the camels represent."[37]

Isaac took Rebekah and led her into the tent of his mother. "Christ also took the church and established it in place of the synagogue . . . He loved it so much that by this very love he tempered the grief that was occasioned by the death of his mother, the synagogue."[38]

---

37. Origen, *Homilies on Genesis* 10.2, in ACCS 2:126.
38. Caesarius of Arles, *Sermon* 85.5, in ACCS 2:137.

CHAPTER 13

Genesis 25:1–18

Death of Abraham; Genealogy of Ishmael

> It is the story of Jacob's struggle to come to terms with the God who befriends him despite his perversity, then fights with him despite his friendship.[1]

Abraham Dies; Isaac Sole Heir; Descendants of Ishmael, 25:1–18

THE NARRATOR ROUNDS OFF an account of the death of Abraham with notices concerning Isaac and the descendants of Ishmael. A "multitude of nations" (Gen 17:4) indeed sprang from Abraham. Two groupings of Arabian tribes are associated with him through a son or another wife.[2]

Two tendencies can be detected in this account: Abraham arranges to leave Isaac sole heir of the Promised Land, and YHWH proves faithful to the very end, just as the servant asserted in Gen 24:35. The genealogies evince fulfillment of the promise, "I will multiply you exceedingly" (Gen 17:2).

Abraham took another wife, whose name was Keturah.

---

1. Mann, *Book of the Torah* (rev. ed. 66), 52.
2. Westermann, *Genesis 12–36*, 399.

It is ironic that no sooner was the child of promise born than Abraham's fertility burst forth. He fathers six sons from a new wife![3] The drama of the Abraham story seems somewhat compromised—it hinged on the birth of a son from Abraham's loins and Sarah.

> The text seems aware of the problem. It first called Keturah a wife (*'ishshah*), but in verse 6 included her among Abraham's concubines (*pilagshîm*).[4] The concubines in question are possibly Keturah and Hagar, called "the Egyptian, Sarah's handmaid" (v. 12). Sons of concubines or secondary wives have no right to inherit, unless a father provides for this during his lifetime.
>
> Bilhah, Rachel's handmaid, is called Jacob's wife (Gen 30:4), but also his concubine (Gen 35:22). Zilpah, Leah's handmaid, is only called Jacob's wife (Gen 30:9).[5] Jacob assigns inheritance to the children of both women, along with those of Rachel and Leah.

The name Keturah is possibly a formation from *ketoret*, the Hebrew word for spices. In the manner of genealogies, a "geographic-ethnological table"[6] links with a Keturah as "mother" of the southern-eastern tribes, traders in incense and spices, who at some time had political and/or commercial relations with Israel. Of the six sons of Keturah, the Midianites will have longstanding relations with Israel. Jethro, father-in-law of Moses, was a priest of Midian (Exod 3:1).

> Sheba and Dedan are said to be sons of Cush and grandsons of Ham in Gen 10:7, though a variant has Sheba as grandson of Shem (Gen 10:28). The Asshurim (not to be confused with Assyrians), Letushim, and Leummim, all in gentilic plural, lack in the parallel list in 1 Chr 1:32; they may represent professions: peasants, smiths, and seminomads.[7]

---

3. Cf. Perry, "Counter-Stories," 288.

4. 1 Chr 1:32 also identifies Keturah as Abraham's concubine. Sarna, *Genesis*, 172 understands the use of the term concubine to point to a time of marriage before Sarah's death. *Gen. Rab.* 61:4 and *Tg. Ps.-J.* solve the difficulty by identifying Keturah and Hagar (so also Rashi), but Ibn Ezra rejected this.

5. See Hamilton, *Genesis 18–50*, 165.

6. Gunkel, *Genesis*, 256.

7. Sarna, *Genesis*, 173. *Tg. Onq.*: "camp and tent-dwellers, and island settlers"; *Tg. Ps.-J.*: "merchants, traders, and heads of peoples."

Abraham gave everything that he owned to his son Isaac. To the sons of his concubines, however, he gave gifts while he was still living, as he sent them away eastward, to the land of Kedem, away from his son Isaac.

That he sent the rest away from Canaan means that "everything he owned" includes especially the promised possession of the land of Canaan. God had assured Abraham he would maintain with Isaac "my covenant as an everlasting covenant and with his descendants after him" (Gen 17:19). Everything for Isaac runs counter to Deut 21:15–17, which allotted the inheritance to all sons (though a double portion to the firstborn). It seems that in earlier times the property remained undivided with the firstborn replacing the father,[8] or the father was at liberty to dispose of his inheritance according to his good pleasure. Isaac, in turn, wished to bless Esau with the inheritance (Genesis 27) and Jacob will disinherit Reuben, his firstborn (Gen 49:3–4).

The whole span of Abraham's life was one hundred and seventy-five years . . . His sons Isaac and Ishmael buried him in the cave of Machpelah.

YHWH promised he would die in ripe old age (Gen 15:15); the narrator relates that indeed Abraham *died at a ripe old age . . . and he was gathered to his people*. In Genesis 16 and 21, Hagar and Ishmael were expelled from Abraham's household and banished to the desert.[9] Here, Ishmael is still around to bury his father. Apparently in this tradition, Ishmael and Esau remain in the land, and legitimately so.[10]

> Abraham was 140 at the marriage of Isaac, and hence 160 at the birth of Esau and Jacob[11]; however, the biblical text records no encounter of Abraham and Isaac after his marriage with Rebekah, nor any meeting of Abraham and Jacob.

After the death of Abraham, God blessed his son Isaac, who lived near Beer Lahai-roi.

---

8. Gunkel, *Genesis*, 292. The firstborn was the apex of one's manhood and thus the "best." As such, every firstborn, of humankind and beasts, was God's.

9. Gunkel, *Genesis*, 272. Gunkel opines that P consciously corrected the tradition, refusing to accept that such quarreling and mistreatment could occur in the family of Abraham. Hamilton, *Genesis 18–50*, 168 wonders whether the brothers, deeply at odds with each other, had a real or artificial reunion at the death of their father.

10. Pury, "Jacob Story," 68.

11. See Hamilton, *Genesis 18–50*, 167.

The utterly faithful God now transmits the blessing to Isaac. Isaac lived in Beer Lahai-roi when Rebekah arrived (Gen 24:62). Hagar gave this name to the well of her encounter with YHWH, saying, "have I really seen God and remained alive?" (Gen 16:13). It turns out that Isaac and Ishmael lived in the same vicinity!

The narrator rounds off the Abraham story with an account of the line (*toledôt*) of Ishmael; the divine promises to him were also fulfilled.

> "Genealogies are records of perceived realities."[12] They have various functions depending on context. They define permissible marriages and regulate inheritance and succession. They demonstrate the continuity and legitimacy of a monarchy or dynasty. They may be adduced in claims to ownership of land or in claims to certain offices, both political and religious—hereditary priesthood, who are the bearers of the divine promise in the patriarchal narratives. They may signify ancestral names to be invoked. Telescoping may occur in the middle, since the names in the middle generally do not have vital function. The same person may be given divergent genealogies, for example, Enoch is son of Cain in the second generation (Gen 4:17), but son of Seth and in the seventh generation (Gen 5:18).

These are the descendants of Abraham's son Ishmael, whom Hagar the Egyptian . . . bore to Abraham . . . These are the sons of Ishmael, their names by their villages and encampments: twelve chieftains of as many tribal groups.

God's angel said of Ishmael, "I will make of him a great nation" (Gen 21:18, see also Gen 17:20), just as "great nation" was promised to Abraham himself (Gen 12:2). God also promised to multiply Ishmael and make him father of twelve chieftains (Gen 17:20). The narrator posits that all these promises were fulfilled. God's fidelity to Abraham overflowed to his descendants other than Isaac. Though for these others, blessing excludes a portion in the land of Canaan and the special religious commitment that would make YHWH their God and they "his people."

The Ishmaelites ranged from Havilah by Shur, which is on the border of Egypt . . . and they pitched camp alongside their various kindred.

> "They pitched camp alongside their various kindred" repeats the prophecy to Hagar in Gen 16:12, except for the verb *naphal*,

---

12. Wilson, "Anthropological Perspectives," 66.

which usually means "to fall." Some translate in the sense of "fall against," attack.[13]

At the end of the Abraham cycle, it can be said that:

> The basic idea of the Abraham narratives as compiled in the Yahwistic book is Yahweh's grace and wisdom. He chooses the patriarch; leads, protects, and blesses him through life; gives him the desired son who continues the line; brings the son the proper life-partner; and blesses the patriarch himself with a beautiful end . . . Abraham's deed, however, is unconditional obedience in which, confidently, he subjects himself to his God. Thus was Israel's original ancestor—so the book wants to say—and thus should you, his son, be too![14]

Tradition

Ever since God made Abraham "father of a multitude of nations" (Gen 17:5), the question of who belongs to the family of Abraham became complex. Jewish tradition accepted that he was physical father of non-Jews, but the spiritual father of Israel—a double genealogy of Abraham, biological and theological.[15] See this commentary at Genesis 22 ("Further Reflections").

Gen. Rab. does not have a homogeneous concept of Abraham as father, but rather responds variously to issues of the day. *Gen. Rab.* 63:3 calls Jacob, Isaac, and Abraham Israel. In contrast, the contemporary Sifre Deut and LevR 36:5 and the later b. Pesah 119b claim that Abraham produced unfit children—Ishmael and the children of Keturah; Isaac too fathered Esau. Jacob produced only righteous ones and is father of righteous Israel. *Gen. Rab.* 11:7 and 68:11 join them in this.[16] The midrashim may have been reacting to Christian claims of Abraham as father of those who have faith.

---

13. Speiser, *Genesis*, 188: "each made forays against his various kinsmen."

14. Gunkel, *Genesis*, 161. R. Nehemiah observed that the Hebrew for "concubines" (verse 6) is written defectively, that is, without the *yod* letter that indicates the plural; however, our critical texts have the plural. *Tg. Ps.-J.*: "Keturah, she is Hagar, who was bound to him from the beginning."

15. Bakhos, "Family of Abraham," 122.

16. Bakhos, "Family of Abraham," 117, 121.

The midrash generally interprets "another wife" as Hagar, whom Abraham took back.[17] Jerome says that Abraham had divorced Hagar and now takes her back.[18] Augustine used the event as an argument against those heretics opposed to second marriages, since the example of the very father of many nations proves that there is no sin in a second marriage that is made after one's wife is dead.[19] Ephrem gave another twist: Abraham took for himself a concubine after the death of Sarah, so that through the uprightness of his many sons who were to be scattered throughout the entire earth, knowledge and worship of the one God would be spread.[20]

Abraham gave everything to Isaac. R. Yehuda: he gave him the birthright; R. Nehemiah: the power of blessing. But the rabbis say he gave him the family vault and a deed—he did not give him the birthright or the blessing as customary at the end of one's life. Abraham argued: "if I bless Isaac, the children of Ishmael and of Keturah are included; while if I do not bless the children of Ishmael and of Keturah, how can I bless Isaac?" Abraham left the choice of blessing to God, "and God blessed his son, Isaac . . ." In other words, God himself, not Abraham, decided the recipient of the blessing of Abraham.[21] The story is told of Ishmaelites coming before Alexander the Great to dispute the birthright of Israel. They based their case on Deut 21:17: "he shall recognize as his firstborn the son of the unloved wife, giving him a double share of whatever he happens to own." The defense counsel, Gebiah, son of Kosem, said, "cannot a man do as he wishes to his sons?" He then cited the text of Abraham giving all he had to Isaac, but gifts to the sons of his concubines. The case was dismissed.

17. *Gen. Rab.* 61:4.
18. Jerome, *Hebrew Questions on Genesis* 25:1.
19. Augustine, *City of God* 16.34, in ACCS 2:140.
20. Ephrem the Syrian, *Commentary on Genesis* 22.1, in ACCS 2:140.
21. *Gen. Rab.* 61:6.

CHAPTER 14

The Jacob Cycle; Esau and Jacob

> Two nations are in your womb, two peoples are separating while still within you.
>
> —GENESIS 25:23

The Jacob Cycle

WITH ABRAHAM OFF THE stage, the narrator introduces the next patriarch with the usual *toledôt* phrasing: "these are the descendants of Isaac, son of Abraham" (Gen 25:19). However, Isaac plays a dominant role only in Genesis 26, the dominant character in the rest of the section is Jacob. The section Gen 25:19—36:43 is thus called the Jacob Cycle. Genesis 36 is a coda listing the line of Esau ("these are the descendants of Esau, that is, Edom," Gen 36:1) before the Esau line drops out of the story.

The story of the birth of the twins, Esau and Jacob (Gen 25:19–34), serves as a prologue that foreshadows and catalyzes the entire Jacob story. Four blocks of self-contained units have been brought together and arranged into an unfolding story of the fortunes of Jacob:

Jacob and Esau (Genesis 27–28);

Jacob and Laban (Genesis 29–31);

Jacob and Esau (Genesis 32–33);

Jacob's journeys in the Promised Land (Genesis 34–35).

The cycle is organized according to the *journey* motif of flight and return. The journey is geographical, psychological, and religious; it is also individual and communal, human and divine.[1] The narrative arc moves from conflict to reconciliation. Deception and rivalry permeate the entire story and its units. The bones of contention are *bᵉkôrah* and *bᵉrākah*—birthright and blessing.

The oracle of Gen 25:23 announces the birthright theme and plays the same role in the Jacob cycle that Gen 12:1–3 plays in the Abraham cycle.[2] The holy place of Bethel is the fulcrum of this journey. Jacob encounters God there during his flight (Gen 28:10–22) and again upon return when his name was changed (Gen 32:22–32; Gen 35:1–15). There is gradual conversion over the course of Jacob's life.

In contrast to the Abraham cycle, the Jacob cycle foregrounds human striving and human institutions. God works with and across these to fulfill divine purposes. A moral critique of Jacob is built into the story itself—his flight is a consequence of his stealing the blessing, and in Laban he met a match (dramatic justice). Particularly telling is Laban's saying to Jacob when he foisted Leah on him instead of Rachel: "it is not the custom in our country to give the younger daughter before the firstborn" (Gen 29:26).

Many outlines of the structure of the Jacob cycle exist, some in the form of a chiasm. The structure outlined by Blum[3] will do.

A Jacob and Esau—in Canaan, 25:19–34; 27

    C Jacob's encounter with God at Bethel, 28:10–22

  B Jacob and Laban—in Aram, 29–31 (32:1)

    C1 Jacob's encounter with God/gods at Mahanaim and Penuel, 32:2 3, 23 33

A1 Jacob and Esau—in Canaan, 32–33

Genesis 34 is late pro-Judahite thread; Genesis 36 lists the descendants of Esau.

---

1. Mann, *Story of Torah*, 65.
2. Fishbane, "Composition and Structure," 33.
3. Blum, "Jacob Traditions," 182. For other arrangements, see Fishbane, *Biblical Text and Texture*, 42; Mann, *Story of Torah*, 66.

Esau and Jacob Struggle in the Womb, 25:19–34

These are the descendants [toledôt] of Isaac, son of Abraham. Isaac was forty years old when he married Rebekah, the daughter of Bethuel, the Aramean of Paddan-aram[4] and the sister of Laban the Aramean.

Isaac now carries on the history of divine commitment and blessing. A variant in Gen 24:10 identifies the same place as Aram Naharaim, Aram of the Two Rivers.

Isaac entreated the Lord on behalf of his wife since she was sterile.

As Chrysostom noted, if he was forty when he married her and sixty when she gave birth, it follows that he kept beseeching God for twenty years.[5] This shows that the power of prayer eventually opened up the womb. Sarah was barren, and now Rebekah. Perry remarks that "God abuses precisely the fertility of his chosen ones. The gift bestowed upon the humans is partially taken away from them. That is why the wives of the elects are so often barren, pregnancies are delayed, and it is necessary to plead with God and thus to include him metonymically as a partner in procreation."[6] In other words, God makes it clear to the chosen ones that progeny and other blessings are by divine fiat, not by human striving.

The Lord heard his entreaty, and his wife became pregnant. But the children jostled each other in the womb so much ... If it is like this, why go on living!

Conflict marks the Jacob Cycle; the boys struggle already in the womb. The jostling makes for a painful pregnancy. The text actually reads, "if thus, why this, I." Modern translations have followed the Syriac version in filling out the phrase "why I living?"

She went to consult the LORD and the LORD answered her: two nations are in your womb, two peoples are separating while still within you. But the one will be stronger than the other, and the older will serve the younger.

The barren gives birth not to one child, but to twins! To consult the LORD is to seek guidance from him through his word, by prophet or priest. The oracle announces the theme of the unit—strife between

---

4. Paddan-Aram, meaning "Field of Aram," is P phrasing.
5. Chrysostom, *Homilies on Genesis* 48.12.
6. Perry, "Counter-Stories," 285.

brothers. The poetry stresses the verb "will be separated."[7] The strange thing is that twins will develop into conflicting nations. The superiority of the younger follows the pattern of reversal in the patriarchal narratives.[8] Rebekah received light about her infants even before they were born; did that influence her attitudes and actions in future?

The story is about two nations, Israel and Edom, as represented by their eponymous ancestors, Jacob and Esau. Edom preceded Israel as a nation in Canaan and hence was the elder; the nation was first mentioned by Egyptian sources around 1230 BCE.[9] To what extent does the divine word predetermine the future? Does it seize and control the freedom of the actors or rather leaves freedom intact, while harnessing behaviors towards the divine purpose?[10] Or, did the oracle transform history into prophecy, that is, portray the lived experience of rivalry between Israel and Edom as if fated from the start (prophecy from the event)?

When the time of her delivery came, there were twins in her womb. The first to emerge was reddish, and his whole body was like a hairy mantle, so they named him Esau.

The text so runs literally: and the days for her delivery were full, and behold (*we-hinneh*) twins in her womb—one part of the oracle has proven true! This raises expectations for the other part.[11] The etiologies here are based on wordplays. 'Adōm, red, signifies Edōm, whose soil is reddish. Śēʻār, hair, clangs with Śēʻîr, used for Edom in poetry. A body hairy all through signifies an animal and suggests beastly behavior.[12] His mother will put on Jacob the hairy skin of a kid to make him feel like Esau to Isaac.

Next his brother came out, gripping Esau's heel; so he was named Jacob.

---

7. The same root, *prd*, is used for the separation of Abraham and Lot in Gen 13:9, 11, 14.

8. Jeansonne, "Genesis 25:23," 148.

9. Gunkel, *Genesis*, 289.

10. Fretheim, "Genesis," 177 opines that "God's knowledge of future human behaviors is not absolute (evident in other texts; see 22:12). Moreover, the divine will can be frustrated by human behaviors (e.g., sin); though God's way into the future cannot, finally, be stymied."

11. Fokkelman, *Narrative Art in Genesis*, 89.

12. In the Epic of Gilgamesh, Enkidu, friend of Gilgamesh, was a hairy and wild man brought up by beasts until initiated into human ways by a harlot.

Gripping the heel is an act of contestation, of wrestling—the story will be about Jacob doing everything to contest the firstborn status of Esau. The one who grips the *'aqēb* (heel) is named *ya'aqōb*/Jacob (heel-grabber). The name Jacob is known outside the Bible. It occurs in the form *ya'aqub-alel* ("may El protect him" or "El will protect him").[13] Here, however, the etymology serves intertribal polemics. The given names foreshadow the character of the protagonists. The actual "telling" also "shows" the character of the protagonists, through their words and actions.[14]

When the boys grew up, Esau became a skillful hunter, a man of the open country, whereas Jacob was a simple man[15] *who stayed among the tents.*

'Ish śadeh, man of the field, in contrast with *yōshēb ōhalîm*, dwelling in tents,[16] suggests wildness and lack of culture. Reading backwards from Isaac's "by your sword you will live" (Gen 27:40), some ancient traditions even make Esau prone to war and violence.[17] The adjective *tām* would normally mean "sound," wholesome," but in contrast with *yōdea' ṣayîd*, skilled in the hunt, it suggests not just "simple," but "innocent," "blameless," "moral integrity." All other biblical occurrences of this word so understand it,[18] for example, God's qualification of Job as "blameless and upright" (*'ish tam we-yāshār*, Job 1:8).[19] Skill in the hunt begins to take on hues of violence and evil nature. Obviously, different etiologies have been gathered together in this piece.

---

13. Hamilton, *Genesis 18-50*, 178-79.
14. See Berlin, *Poetics*, 38-39.
15. NRSV and NJB: quiet; REB: lived quietly.
16. Midrash and Targum interpret dwelling in tents as engaging in Torah study. His choice is explained by his dedication to and knowledge of the Torah. *Tg. Onq.*: he attended the house of study; *Tg. Neof.*: he dwelt in the schoolhouses; *Tg. Ps.-J.*: ministering in the schoolhouses of Eber, seeking instruction from before the Lord.
17. Jub 19:14: Jacob learned to write, Esau did not learn, for he was a man of the field, and a hunter, and he learned war, and all his deeds were fierce. Jub 37:24—38:3 even reported a confrontation in which Jacob, in self-defense, had to bend his bow and kill his brother Esau. See Kugel, *Traditions*, 354, 371. A report in *Gen. Rab.* 61:7 says that Esau, because he came and attacked Jacob, received his deserts on his account.
18. Alter, *Art of Biblical Narrative*, 50.
19. Already *Jub.* 35:12: "you blessed your perfect and true son Jacob because he has virtue only and no evil" (see Kugel, *Traditions*, 353); *Tg. Onq.*: a perfect man; *Tg. Neof.*: a man perfect in good work; *Tg. Ps.-J.*: perfect in his works.

The depiction of Esau may have been influenced by experiences of conflict and violence. Amos 1:11 speaks of the sin of Edom, "because he pursued his brother with the sword, suppressing all pity, persisting in his anger, his wrath raging without end." In the catastrophe that led to the Babylonian exile, the Edomites stood at the crossroads to cut down the escapees of Judah (Obad 1:14). And so Edom shall fall: "because of violence to your brother Jacob, disgrace will cover you, you will be done away with forever!" (Obad 1:10).

Isaac preferred Esau, because he was fond of game, but Rebekah preferred Jacob.

We are not told whether Rebekah's preference for Jacob derived from the oracle, of which only herself was privy.[20] Anyway, Jacob was home and close enough to the mother to imbibe the art of cooking.

Once when Jacob was cooking a stew, Esau came in from the open country famished. He said to Jacob, "let me gulp down some of that red stuff; I am famished." That is why he was called Edom.

Literally, he was *'āyēf*, faint, weary; from the context, we interpret the fainting as caused by hunger. His hunting had come up short; he could not even feed himself. Again *'adōm*, red, explains the name Edom. There may be allusion to *dām*/blood—the "blood-red" stew enticed Esau, who as a killer is used to blood.[21] Humans do not gulp down food; the verb *lā'aṭ*, gulp down, is not used of humans but of beasts.

"First sell me your right as firstborn."[22] *"Look," said Esau, "I am on the point of dying. What good is the right as firstborn to me?"*

Esau had added the word "please" (enclitic *-na'*) to his request; Jacob uses the imperative: sell now (*ka-yōm*) . . . swear to me now (*ka-yōm*)[23]—showing his character and already illustrating the reversal of status. The key word *bekôrah*, birthright, enters the fray. The plot is driven by Jacob's

---

20. *Gen. Rab.* 63:11: the more she heard his voice engaged in study the stronger grew her love for him. The text says, not "loved," but "loves"—progressive present.

21. *Tg. Ps.-J.*: "skilled hunter able to hunt birds and wild beasts, a man who would go out into the field to kill people." *Gen. Rab.* 63:8: Abba b. Kahana: he was altogether a shedder of blood.

22. Hamilton, *Genesis 18–50*, 184 cites an example in the Nuzi tablets of a man who transferred his inheritance rights to a grove over to his brother in exchange for three sheep.

23. Alter, *Art of Biblical Narrative*, 51.

striving to displace Esau as firstborn. Esau is vulnerable; Jacob exploited his vulnerability.

But Jacob said, "Swear to me first!" So he sold Jacob his right as firstborn under oath.

The calculating Jacob will not take his brother's word. Esau must ratify the deed of conveyance by self-curse and invocation of the name of God, as usual in oaths. The oath confirms the sale of the birthright and makes it irreversible.

Jacob then gave him some bread and the lentil stew, and Esau ate, drank, got up, and went his way. So Esau treated his right as firstborn with disdain.

The staccato actions—ate, drank, got up, went away—portrayed Esau as a man of immediate gratification, with no forethought for the future, too much the slave of the moment.[24]

The narrator says that Esau did not care that much for his birthright; it serves him right. Esau lives for the present. Gunkel comments: "the narrator has no impression of ignobility or selfishness . . . but of cleverness and farsightedness."[25] Certainly, the narrator adopts ancient Israel's point of view concerning her erstwhile rival Edom. That was that Jacob did nothing wrong, for already at birth destiny conferred on him the rights of the firstborn. Besides, Esau's innate character disqualified him. Furthermore, he willingly and legally sold his birthright to Jacob.[26] In actual history, Edom was famous for wisdom (Jer 49:7; Bar 3:22-23). In "The Approach of This Commentary" (see ch. 1), I challenged the view that the biblical narrator "invests his dramatizations with the authority of an omniscience equivalent to God's own . . . this omniscience itself ultimately goes back to God."[27] I stated the case for sometimes separating the judgments of God and narrator. The behavior of both twins raises moral issues. Hosea actually condemned the Israel of his time as behaving like its eponymous ancestor: "the Lord will punish . . . Jacob for his conduct,

---

24. Alter, *Art of Biblical Narrative*, 52 comments that the episode shows him as not spiritually fit to be the vehicle of divine election, the bearer of the birthright of Abraham's seed.

25. Gunkel, *Genesis*, 292.

26. Obviously differing sources have been woven together here. Gunkel, *Genesis*, 289 distinguished them as follows: the divine oracle decreed it, Gen 25:21-23 is J; Jacob bought Esau's birthright, Gen 25:29-34, comes from E; Jacob appropriated the preferred blessing by deceit, Genesis 27, is JE.

27. Sternberg, *Poetics of Biblical Narrative*, 90.

and repay him for his deeds. In the womb he supplanted his brother . . ." He counsels: "you must return to your God. Maintain loyalty and justice, and always hope in your God" (Hos 12:3, 4, 7). The oracle raises questions concerning divine foreknowledge interacting with human freedom.

Tradition

Rom 9:10–13 referred to the Jacob-Esau story to defend the justice of God in choosing the Gentiles, the younger compared to the ancient people of Israel: "Also when Rebecca had conceived children by one husband, our father Isaac—before they had yet been born or had done anything, good or bad, in order that God's elective plan might continue, not by works but by his call—she was told, 'The older shall serve the younger' . . . Is there injustice on the part of God? Of course not!"

God is free to show mercy to whom he will, take pity on whom he will. God's choice cannot be questioned![28] Heb 12:16 knew the tradition that vilified Esau: "see that no one be an immoral or profane person like Esau, who sold his birthright for a single meal."

Some fathers of the church applied the oracle about the elder serving the younger to the Christian and Jewish faiths. "The older people of the Jews are proved to serve the younger, that is, the Christian people, for like servants of the Christians they are known to carry the books of the divine law throughout the world for the instruction of the nations. Therefore the Jews were scattered in every land, so that when we want to invite some pagan to faith in Christ by testifying that Christ was announced by all the prophets . . . to such a person we may say, if a doubt arises in you concerning my books, behold the books of the Jews, apparently our enemies, which I certainly could neither have written nor changed."[29] Many applied the oracle to good and bad in the church. "In the church, good and bad people are found, two peoples struggling as in the womb of the spiritual Rebeka—the humble, indeed, and the proud, chaste and adulterous, meek and irascible, kind and envious, merciful and avaricious."[30]

By the second century BCE, Jewish tradition said of Esau that he "learned war and all his deeds were fierce" (*Jub.* 19:14). And with the

---

28. See Clifford, "Genesis 25:19–25," 397–401.
29. Caesarius of Arles, *Sermon* 86.3, in ACCS 2:148.
30. Caesarius of Arles, *Sermon* 86.2, in ACCS 2:146.

wars of 66–70 CE and the Roman imposition on Palestine, Esau became a symbol of Rome and the Roman Empire. *4 Ezra* 6:8–10 interprets the heel-grabbing by Jacob eschatologically. Jacob's hand holding Esau's heel means that Esau, that is, the ascendancy of Rome, is the end of this age; Jacob, the ascendancy of Israel, is the beginning of the age that follows.[31] But even Esau's ascendancy is put on hold if Jacob's children observe the commandments of Torah.[32] In the fourth century, Rome, now Christian, claimed the very birthright and blessing that Israel understood to be hers alone. Esau became symbol of messianic Rome, Rome as surrogate for Israel, Rome as obstacle for Israel.[33]

In midrash, the birthright is interpreted religiously. The worship of YHWH, also the world to come, is the birthright of the people of God. That Esau despised his birthright meant that he despised the vivification of the dead (*Gen. Rab.* 63:14; *Tg. Neof.*) and the portion of the world to come (*Tg. Neof.*; *Tg. Ps.-J.*).

---

31. See Kugel, *Traditions*, 358.

32. *Tg. Ps.-J.*. *Gen. Rab.* 63:7: Rabbi Huna commented, "if he [Jacob] is deserving, he [Esau] shall serve him; if not, he [Esau] shall enslave him."

33. Neusner, *Genesis and Judaism*, 188, 189.

CHAPTER 15

Genesis 26

Traditions of Isaac

> For the sake of Abraham, my servant.
>
> —Genesis 26:24

Genesis 26 disrupts the flow of the story of Jacob and Esau. The chapter gathers together various Isaac traditions. Isaac takes the stage by name as the protagonist of the story, whereas elsewhere he had been referred to merely as "son of Abraham." Most of the stories in this chapter have doublets in prior stories about Abraham, for example, the "wife-sister" story in verses 6–11 (parallels Genesis 20 involving the same Abimelech) and the covenant with Abimelech in verses 26–31 (parallels Abraham's covenant with Abimelech in Gen 21:22–32). There are even verbal links and flashbacks to those earlier stories. Scholars debate whose story migrated to the other.[1]

Rebekah is still a young woman and Jacob and Esau have not yet been born, let alone grown up, otherwise Isaac's saying "she is my sister" would not be plausible.[2]

---

1. Boase, "Role and Function of Isaac," 322 argues, plausibly, for bidirectional movement between traditions associated with Isaac and Abraham.
2. Gunkel, *Genesis*, 293.

The narrative shows Isaac as inheritor of the divine blessings to Abraham.[3] YHWH's faithful love is now with Isaac. YHWH blesses him in all circumstances. A new note is introduced: the blessing YHWH confers on Isaac is "for the sake of Abraham, my servant" (26:24) and "because Abraham obeyed me, keeping my mandate, my commandments, my ordinances, and my instructions" (26:5). This sets Abraham up as mediator, one whose merit is applied to others; it raises the question of vicarious merit or redemption.

The LORD Appeared to Isaac in Gerar, 26:1–5

There was a famine in the land. Isaac went down to Abimelech, king of the Philistines in Gerar.

This is word-for-word the beginning of the story of Abram's descent to Egypt (Gen 12:10). The narrator adds that this famine is different from that in Abraham's time. Egypt is where one goes during a famine. Gerar is in the land and would be of no help (unless somehow the famine did not reach there),[4] but that is why the narrator invokes divine assistance. Abraham had dealings with an Abimelech, king of Gerar, seventy-five years earlier (Genesis 20).[5] That account, however, had nothing about Philistines in Gerar—here it is an anachronism, as the Philistines had not yet settled in Canaan.[6]

The Lord appeared to him and said: 'Do not go down to Egypt, but camp in this land wherever I tell you. Sojourn in this land.

"Wherever I tell you" patterns Isaac on Abram whom YHWH asked to go "to a land that I will show you" (Gen 12:1). Obedience to divine guidance is required of both patriarchs. Isaac is already in Gerar and does not need to be told to go there.[7] The command not to quit during a famine betokens a promise of special divine help. It would seem that the

---

3. The divine promises in 26:2–5 and 26:24 are latter additions which function to connect the Abraham and Isaac traditions.

4. Seters, *Abraham in History and Tradition*, 177.

5. Sarna, *Genesis*, suggests they are not the same person—Abimelech may have been a dynastic name.

6. Gunkel, *Genesis*, 296: the narrator confuses with the Philistine city of Gerar.

7. Seters, *Abraham in History and Tradition*, 182.

second divine appearance at the end of the chapter designates "the land I will show you" as the region of Beersheba.

I will be with you and bless you; for to you and your descendants I will give all these lands, in fulfillment of the oath I swore to your father Abraham . . . and I will give them all these lands.

The divine promise of "being with" is usual for one on a journey; it is characteristic of the Jacob narrative. "I will bless you" repeats the promise to Abram (Gen 12:2). As fruit of that blessing, his descendants will be as numerous as the stars in the sky (same image and terms as for Abraham in Gen 22:17).[8] A blessing promising the land is unsuitable in Gerar, for it is described as a Philistine city, an area that did not belong to ancient Israel.[9] The plural "all these lands" may thus refer to the promise of Canaan to Abram (Gen 12:7), but also to the more extensive promise of lands in Gen 15:18–21. This would confirm that these promises to Isaac are calqued upon those to Abraham.

In fulfillment of the oath that I swore to your father Abraham.

This is a clear reference back to Gen 22:16 where the angel of YHWH swore, saying, "I swear by my very self . . . I will bless you and make your descendants as countless as the stars of the sky and the sands of the seashore."

In your descendants all the nations of the earth will find blessing.

The only other place the exact string appears is Gen 22:18, with "nations" (not "families," as in Gen 12:3) and the reflexive *hitbarᵉkû*, "will bless themselves." In this phrase, as outlined in the commentary on Genesis 12, Abram becomes a paradigm or model of blessing. It is as if "a man says to his son, 'mayest thou become as Abraham.'"[10] It seems that the

---

8. See also Gen 15:5: "look up at the sky and count the stars, if you can. Just so, he added, will your descendants be."

9. Koch, *Growth of the Biblical Tradition*, 125.

10. Rosenbaum and Silbermann, *Pentateuch*, 49. Gen 48:20 illustrates this understanding, though using *yᵉbārēk*, the piel tense of the verb: "by you shall the people of Israel pronounce blessings, saying 'God make you like Ephraim and Manasseh.'" Jewish interpreters generally follow Rashi in this: Cassuto, *From Noah to Abraham*, 315: "the father of the Israelites will be privileged to become a source of benison to all the peoples of the world, and his merit and prayer will protect them before the Heavenly Court of Justice." However, several join the Targums in the mediatorial sense of the passage; Friedmann, *Commentary on Torah*, 50: "the result of the divine choice

diverse understandings of this promise derive from diverse contextualizations (see the discussion at Gen 22:15–18).

> The sense of mediator of blessings (using the passive tense) is used with *mishpaḥah* (clan) and *ha-adamah* (the ground), while the paradigm/model of blessing (using the reflexive tense) is used with *goyîm* (nations) and *ha-areṣ* (the earth).

Foreigners will recognize Abram's and his heirs' fame and blessing.[11]

This, because Abraham obeyed me, keeping my mandate, my commandments, my ordinances, and my instructions.

The promised blessings become rewards for obedience. The terms used here betray Deuteronomic language (see Deut 5:29–31; 6:2; 11:1) and its theology of righteousness as observance of Torah. Abraham is presented as exemplar of obedience, in contrast to the presentation in Gen 15:6, where he is a paragon of faith. Long before the Torah was revealed at Sinai, there is righteousness not based on law (think also of Noah being called "a righteous man and blameless in his generation," Gen 6:9). "Abraham is an example of one who shows the Law written on his heart (cf. Jer 31:33)."[12] So Paul could say: "when the Gentiles who do not have the law by nature observe the prescriptions of the law . . . they show that the demands of the law are written in their hearts" (Rom 2:14–15). This important principle enables interreligious dialogue.

The Wife-Sister Episode, 26:6–11

The wife-sister type-scene appeared already in Gen 12:10–20 and Genesis 20. Gunkel lays out a clear case for ongoing moral editing, whereby Genesis 20 and especially Gen 26:5–11 take pains to mitigate elements objectionable to later sensibilities. The chronological sequence is Gen 12:10–20; Genesis 20; and Gen 26:5–11 (though not every element in Genesis 20 is younger than Gen 12:10–20; for example, the lie, of necessity eliminated in Genesis 20, resurfaces in Genesis 26).[13]

---

of Abraham is supposed to be some good for all humankind."

11. Carr, *Reading the Fractures*, 158, 187.

12. Sailhamer, *Pentateuch as Narrative*, 187.

13. Gunkel, *Genesis*, 223–24. However, Hamilton, *Genesis 18–50*, 191 asserts that an increasing number of scholars think of these as not interdependent, but probably contemporaneous and each unique.

The moral danger. In Genesis 12, Pharaoh took Sarai to wife. In Genesis 20, nothing offensive took place, for God hindered it. Gen 26:5–11 omits the entire situation, only envisages the possibility that someone might have desired the ancestress.

The plagues. In Genesis 12, the plagues make Pharaoh aware of the sin that has taken place. In Genesis 20, they protect Abimelech from committing the sin. In Genesis 26, they are not necessary, for nothing evil has taken place. The narrator, nevertheless, reports the king's command that whoever touches the man or his wife shall be put to death—using the verb *naga'*, with the same root as the noun for plague, *nega'*. Since no one had considered harming Isaac or his wife, this means that the narrator alludes to other recensions where such harm took place.

The ancestors' wealth. In Genesis 12, the wealth consisted of the gifts for Abram's alleged sister, and that before Pharaoh took her. In Genesis 20, the gifts are subsequent and act as propitiation, also to declare Sarah's honor. In Genesis 26, Isaac is very rich because YHWH blessed his fields.

Treatment of the patriarch. In Genesis 12, Abram was escorted to the border. In Genesis 20, he was permitted to remain in the land wherever he pleased. But that he could be expelled had never come up, so this is tacit contrast to earlier recensions. In Genesis 26, Isaac was finally "sent away," but because of jealousy, for he had become too rich for his hosts.

The patriarch's lie. The lie in Genesis 12 becomes a mental reservation in Genesis 20, but Genesis 26 agrees with Genesis 12 on this point.

The religious character of the story. Gen 12:10–20 is a mixture of religious and worldly motifs: "the legend celebrates the clever ancestor, the beautiful ancestress, and the ever-faithful God."[14] There is a certain malicious glee over the misfortune of the mighty Pharaoh. Genesis 20 glorifies God and God's assistance; profane attitudes are entirely eliminated. Genesis 26 narrates a profane adventure in which the idea of God's protection only stands in the background (26:3a).

When the men of the place asked questions about his wife, he answered, "she is my sister."

---

14. Gunkel, *Genesis*, 224.

Why the men of the place should be asking about her is not said, nor does any action follow their questioning. However, Isaac entertained the fear that if he called her his wife, the men of the place would kill him on account of Rebekah, since she was beautiful. Had not YHWH said, "sojourn in this land, and I will be with you?" Isaac showed little trust in God. As in the case of Abraham, he will soon find out that she was safer as his wife than as unmarried sister. The people had moral standards and were better than he thought.

The king of the Philistines looked out of a window and saw Isaac fondling his wife Rebekah. How could you have said, "she is my sister?" Isaac replied, "I thought I might lose my life on her account." "How could you have done this to us! . . . It would have taken very little for one of the people to lie with your wife, and so you would have brought guilt upon us."

Isaac felt safe enough to dally in the public eye! There is no real crisis or complication. It was all in Isaac's mind. "What is this you have done to us" reproduces a similar charge of Abimelech to Abraham in Gen 20:9. The welfare of king and people would be at stake should one of the people unwittingly violate Rebekah—the whole kingdom would be guilty before God. They would have incurred 'ashām, guilt that called for expiation and compensation to boot. Lying with an unbetrothed woman was not as grave as lying with a married woman, which is both sin against God and damage to the husband.

Abimelech then commanded all the people: "anyone who maltreats this man or his wife shall be put to death."

"Anyone who touches/harms" (root *ng'* used of striking, injuring, even killing; from it is formed the noun, for plague)—the king's decree assures security to man and wife. God sometimes acts through just enactments of the people in charge.

Conflicts over Wells in Gerar, 26:12-22

Isaac sowed a crop in that region and reaped a hundredfold the same year.

"The same year" suggests that he planted during the famine and still received a hundredfold yield, thus exceeding even a bumper harvest. The Lord was true to his word to be with him and bless him.

Since the Lord blessed him, he became richer and richer all the time, until he was very wealthy . . . and so the Philistines became envious of him.

God's blessing materializes in an abundance of flocks and herds and a great work force.[15] The envy of the Philistines indicates that such wealth was not shared around, rather was result of divinely targeted blessing on Isaac.

And the Philistines stopped up all the wells which his father's servants had dug in the days of his father Abraham, filling them with earth.[16]

This action is vindictive; they did not just want him to leave—water is vital for the herds and humans—but never to return. They were willing to forego the use of the wells themselves! However, since Isaac's servants would clear the same wells a few verses on, one could render with NABRE in the pluperfect: *The Philistines had stopped up and filled with dirt all the wells that his father's servants had dug back in the days of his father Abraham.*

> Peace, therefore, does not mean "fellowship" in each and every case; it can also be to allow the other live in peace or withdraw in peace. (Westermann, *Genesis 18–36*, 430).

So Abimelech said to Isaac, "Go away from us; you have become far too numerous for us."

The verb *'āṣamtā* can also be rendered, "you have become far too big for us" (TNK), or better, "you have become too powerful for us" (NRSV). In other words, they feared domination or perhaps that the Isaac clan could become a fifth column should war or conflict arise. Isaac must have been there for a long time for such wealth to accumulate—the narrator telescopes.

Isaac left there and camped in the Wadi Gerar where he stayed. Isaac reopened the wells which his father's servants had dug back in the days of his father Abraham and which the Philistines had stopped up after Abraham's death; he gave them names like those that his father had given them.

---

15. In the case of Abraham (Gen 20:14), the "flocks and herds and male and female slaves" were given to Abraham by Abimelech on restoring his wife to him.
16. Reading with TNK Jewish version (1985).

A wadi is a stream that tends to dry up in summer. Wadi Gerar must be a valley in the vicinity, though outside the walls of Gerar. Most ancient cities had walls; the people farmed the surrounding fields. Isaac asserts continuity of lineage with Abraham. We do not know the names of these wells, but that he could reopen them suggests they were not in contested territory.

But when Isaac's servants dug in the wadi and reached spring water in their well, the shepherds of Gerar argued with Isaac's shepherds, saying, "The water belongs to us!"

The quarrel between the shepherds makes clear that at issue was the welfare of flocks and herds, the basis of wealth. Isaac's servants hit upon "living water," that is, spring water; this is like saying one struck gold—here is a permanent, not seasonal, supply of water.

So he named the well Esek, that is, "quarrel." Then they dug another well, and they argued over that one too; so he named it Sitnah, that is, "opposition." So he moved on from there and dug still another well, but over this one they did not argue. He named it Rehoboth, that is, "wide spaces," and he said, "The Lord has now given us ample room, we shall flourish in the land."

The divine promise of blessing and "being with" does not dispense with conflicts; the elect still has to make prudent responses to situations that arise.

The Lord Appears to Isaac in Beersheba, 26:23–25

From there Isaac went up to Beersheba. The same night the LORD appeared to him and said, "I am the God of Abraham, your father. Do not fear, for I am with you. I will bless you and multiply your descendants for the sake of Abraham, my servant."

In an earlier stage of religion, the patriarchs each worshiped a familial "god of the father"[17]; for the narrator this was identical with YHWH. "Do not fear" usually introduces a salvation oracle. YHWH reiterates the promise of "being with" and of a multitude of descendants, but now "for

---

17. Hence here the "god of Abraham," in Gen 31:42, the "Fear of Isaac," and in Gen 49:24, the "Mighty One of Jacob." See Alt, "God of the Father."

the sake of Abraham, my servant." "Here, for the first time, we encounter the notion that the righteousness of ancestors creates a fund of spiritual credit that may sustain their descendants."[18] In Jewish theology, this is called the *zekhût 'avôt*, the merit of the fathers. God initiated with Noah a principle of the solidarity of one man for others. Upon Noah's sacrifice, the LORD covenanted never again to curse the ground because of people. This means that "reconciliation occurs through the righteousness of one man."[19] In the section below on "Tradition," we will consider the figure of Abraham as counterpart to the Christian savior. For now, the question is how to understand "for the sake of Abraham" in relation to the "one mediator between God and the human race, Christ Jesus" (1 Tim 2:4). Is there a dual route to salvation—for Israel and others? "My servant"[20] (*'abdî*) relates Abraham especially to Moses, the paradigmatic servant of YHWH. There is reference to "my servants, the prophets" often in the Deuteronomist history; the "servant of the LORD" is a mysterious figure in Isaiah 40–53. All these had a special function in God's purposes for his people and the world. Abraham not only embodies a life of obedience, but also, "I have singled him out that he may direct his children and his household in the future to keep the way of the Lord by doing what is right and just, so that the Lord may put into effect for Abraham the promises he made about him" (Gen 18:19).

So Isaac built an altar there and invoked the Lord by name. After he had pitched a tent there, Isaac's servants began to dig a well nearby.

Abraham had planted a tamarisk in the same place and invoked by name the LORD, God the Eternal (*El 'Olam*), possibly the local deity (Gen 21:33). In effect, Abraham and Isaac dwelt in the same region.

A Covenant of Peace, 26:26–33

Then Abimelech came to him from Gerar, with Ahuzzath, his councilor, and Phicol, the general of his army. We clearly see that the Lord has been

---

18. Sarna, *Genesis*, 187.

19. Coats, "Strife and Reconciliation," 24.

20. In the Pentateuch, this title appears only for the patriarchs, Moses (some thirty-six times), and Caleb; elsewhere it is applied especially to David (some thirty-one times). The righteous are also collectively called "the servants of the LORD" (Ps 113:1; Isa 54:7 . . .). See Sarna, *Genesis*, 187.

with you, so we thought: let there be a sworn agreement between our two sides–between you and us.

A visit of Abimelech and his commander Phicol to Abraham in Beersheba for the purposes of a covenant is recorded in Gen 21:22–32. A delegation that includes the commander of the army is no private affair, rather the two groups represent two peoples. Isaac is treated as a king with equal power. The covenant is one between equals (parity treaty); one did not dictate terms to the other, rather *they exchanged oaths*. Isaac, with God standing with him, may soon prove mightier than the people of Gerar and might want to avenge the expulsion. The point of the oath is that "the descendants of the fathers are . . . bound to this covenant even now that they have become much stronger than Gerar."[21] The terms of the covenant are:

You shall do no harm to us, just as we have . . . always acted kindly toward you and have let you depart in peace. So now, may you be blessed by the Lord!

The reader knows that they did not quite act kindly toward Isaac, but the framing shows clearly who is now the weaker side. With peace covenanted, they have nothing more to fear from Isaac's greatness by reason of the LORD's blessing. By blessing Isaac, they even stand to gain for, "I will bless those who bless you" (Gen 12:3). Isaac was a gracious host; however, beyond hospitality, the meal was an essential part of reconciliation and good will through a covenant. Like Isaac, we must not return evil for evil. "He yielded to those who drove him out, but received them again when they were sorry, being neither harsh to insolence nor obdurate to kindness. When he went away from others, he fled to avoid strife."[22] That same day, Isaac's servants struck water. He called the well

Shibah, hence the name of the city is Beersheba to this day.

A double etiology of Beersheba is given in the story of Abraham—it derives from the seven ewe lambs Abraham set apart and from the oath he and Abimelech swore there (Gen 21:27–32).[23] The narrator clearly

---

21. Gunkel, *Genesis*, 296.
22. Ambrose, *On His Brother, Satyrus* 2.99, in ACCS 2:167.
23. *Shebaʿ* (seven), *nishbbaʿû* (they swore an oath).

alludes to this event: *Shibah* contains the root *šb'*, which is common to both "seven" and "oath."²⁴

Flash Forward: Esau Marries Canaanite Wives, 26:34–35

*When Esau was forty years old, he married Judith, daughter of Beeri the Hittite, and Basemath, daughter of Elon the Hivite. But these became a source of bitterness to Isaac and Rebekah.*²⁵

In Gen 28:9, Esau added a third wife, this time of the line of Abraham through Ishmael, son of Hagar: Mahalath, daughter of Ishmael and sister of Nebaioth.

> The Edomite genealogy at Gen 36:2 mentions the three wives as Adah, daughter of Elon the Hittite; Oholibamah, daughter of Anah, the son of Zibeon the Hivite; and Basemath, daughter of Ishmael and sister of Nebaioth. In one, the Hittite is Judith, daughter of Beeri; in the other, Adah, daughter of Elon; in Gen 28:9, the Ishmaelite is Mahalath, sister of Nebaioth; in Gen 36:2, she is Basemath, sister of Nebaioth. The divergences may issue from diverse sources used.

Any understanding of the inspiration of Scripture must take seriously the fact of such confusion (conflation?) in the text. The Hivites were among the nations of Canaan; marriage with them may lead to absorption and the disappearance of Israelite identity. The narrator prepares the reader for what is to come, but also presents Esau in a negative light that affects the reader's empathy with him in the affair of Jacob's stealing of his father's blessing.

Tradition

The Septuagint rendered Beer Lahai-roi where Isaac dwelled (Gen 24:62) as the "well of vision"; for the fathers, this well is a symbol of Scripture,

---

24. LXX: he called it Oath: therefore he called the name of that city, the Well of Oath.

25. Gen 28:8: Esau realized how displeasing the Canaanite women were to his father Isaac, so Esau went to Ishmael, and in addition to the wives he had, married Mahalath, the daughter of Abraham's son Ishmael and sister of Nebaioth.

the word of God.[26] "For what is a well of living water but a depth of profound instruction? . . . Therefore Isaac undertook to open wells out of a depth of vision and in good order, so that the water of his well might first wash and strengthen the reasoning faculty of the soul and its eye, to make its sight clearer."[27] Abraham dug wells, that is, the Scriptures of the Old Testament; they were filled with earth by the Philistines, that is, evil teachers, scribes and Pharisees, even hostile powers. Isaac, that is, Christ, has opened the wells for us. Just as Isaac called them by the same names Abraham gave them, so Christ did not change the names of the Scriptures, but the understanding.[28]

"Christianity maintained that salvation did not depend upon keeping the laws of the Torah. Abraham, after all, had been justified and he did not keep the Torah, which, in his day, had not yet been given. So the sages time and again would maintain that Abraham indeed kept the entire Torah even before it had been revealed."[29] Jewish theology posits both individual merit for obedience and individual punishment for disobedience, yet the "merit of the fathers" (*zekhût 'avôt*) assures Israel of the stability of God's covenant and Israel's special status before God. Punishment will never go so far as to annul the covenant itself on the part of God.[30] The merits of the fathers also guarantee God's bringing Israel a savior in the end (see the text box below).

> Praised are You, O Lord our God and God of our fathers, God of Abraham, God of Isaac, and God of Jacob, mighty, revered, and exalted God. You bestow loving-kindness and possesses all things. Mindful of the patriarchs' love for You, You will in your love bring a redeemer to their children's children for the sake of Your name. (Amida, Benediction 1, in *Siddur*, 21).

With the Christianization of the Roman Empire in early fourth century, the tendency increased to portray Abraham as having the mediative roles Christians associated with Christ. Abraham's suffering and sacrifice

---

26. Also in Jewish tradition, based on Isa 55:1–2, "all you who thirst come to the water . . . ," drawing water from the well symbolizes study of Torah.
27. Ambrose, *Isaac, or the Soul* 4.22, in ACCS 2:162.
28. Origen, *Homilies on Genesis* 13.3, in ACCS 2:163.
29. Neusner, *Genesis and Judaism*, 11.
30. Urbach, *Sages*, 1:496, 497.

of blood at his circumcision will bring forgiveness to his descendants when they sin (*Gen. Rab.* 48:5). His willingness to offer Isaac guarantees the future redemption of his descendants (*Gen. Rab.* 56:10). Christians interpreted Psalms 45 and 110 messianically in relation to Christ; the rabbis interpreted them in relation to Abraham. Abraham is the "anointed" of Psalm 45. "You are a priest forever according to the order of Melchizedek" (Ps 110:4) is applied to Abraham in relation to God's command to circumcise himself (*Gen. Rab.* 46:5; LevR 25:5). This downplays the role of the Davidic messiah, thus undercutting the Christian reading of these passages.[31]

---

31. See Himmelfarb, "Abraham and Messianism," 107–9.

CHAPTER 16

Genesis 27

Jacob Deceives Isaac, Receives Esau's Blessing

> God does not perfect people before deciding to work in and through them.[1]

Rebekah and Jacob, 27:1–17

THIS CHAPTER IS THE fulcrum of the Jacob narrative. It sets in motion the various forces that drive the plot. Jacob must flee from home and stay away till Esau's anger cools. In the end, he also had to flee from Laban and meet Esau face to face. The characters behave in ways that raise some moral issues which later Jewish and Christian exegesis sought to allay.

When Isaac was so old that his eyesight had failed him, he called his older son Esau and said to him. "My son!" "Here I am!" he replied. Now I have grown old. I do not know when I might die ... so that I may bless you before I die.

We know that Isaac loved Esau, but Rebekah loved Jacob (Gen 25:28). "Rebekah consistently calls Jacob 'my son,' and refers to Esau as Jacob's brother. In contrast, Isaac refers to Esau as 'my son' and never

---

1. Fretheim, "Which Blessing Does Isaac Give Jacob?," 284.

refers to Jacob as "son," except when he thinks Jacob is Esau."[2] Isaac even uses the term "your mother's sons" when he thought he was speaking to Esau about Jacob (27:29).

Esau is to take bow and arrow, kill game, and prepare delicacies (*mat'ammîm*), the type his father likes to eat. Behind the request for a dish may be early magical belief that one to pass on vital power through blessing must first replenish himself.[3] Balaam offered sacrifices before blessing or cursing (Numbers 22–24).

Rebekah had been listening while Isaac was speaking to his son Esau.

She did not just overhear; the narrator portrays her as eavesdropping. Each parent has the back of one twin and seeks to advance him in every way. This is recipe for serious conflict in any family. Some excuse Rebekah's action by saying that "revolt against a 'social' injustice lies behind her plan. She resists with all means at her disposal a privilege of the 'great' that excluded the 'small.'"[4] She objected to the blessing of the firstborn as exclusive privilege. The point, however, is that Scripture does not whitewash human behavior, not even of its heroes; the patriarchs are not "models for morality" but "mirrors for identity,"[5] with struggles like ours.

Rebekah said to her son Jacob, "Listen! I heard your father tell your brother Esau, 'Bring me some game . . . that I may bless you with the LORD's approval[6] before I die.'"

Rebekah adds a theological qualification; a blessing is actually a plea to God to grant the favor sought. She is sure the LORD will approve, and she wants it for her favorite. She sets up a counter-quest: "it is now a race against time: who will be the first to get to Isaac with a lovely dish of meat?"[7] The narration takes it for granted that Rebekah kept the content of the oracle to herself, that Isaac was not privy to it.

Go to the flock and bring me two choice young goats so that with these I might prepare a dish for your father in the way he likes. But Jacob said to his

2. Jeansonne, "Genesis 25:23," 149.
3. See Westermann, *Genesis 12–36*, 440.
4. Westermann, *Genesis 12–36*, 438.
5. Sanders, "Hermeneutics," 406.
6. So also TNK; literally, "before the LORD"; so LXX, NRSV.
7. Fokkelman, *Reading Biblical Narrative*, 83.

mother Rebekah, "But my brother Esau is a hairy man and I am smooth-skinned. Suppose my father feels me? He will think I am making fun of him, and I will bring on myself a curse instead of a blessing."

That's a whole lot of meat! Did the text envisage helpings over several days? She must have the art of making goat meat taste like venison, unless Isaac is considered so old that he could no longer distinguish between tastes!

Ever cautious and calculating, Jacob indicated the possible danger involved. Deception of the blind shows lack of the fear of the LORD: "You shall not insult the deaf or put a stumbling block in front of the blind, but you shall fear your God. I am the Lord" (Lev 19:14). In fact, Deut 27:18 adds a curse: "cursed be anyone who misleads the blind on their way. And all the people shall answer, 'Amen.'"

His mother, however, replied: "let any curse against you, my son, fall on me! Just obey me. Go and get me the young goats." Rebekah then took the best clothes[8] of her older son Esau that she had in the house, and gave them to her younger son Jacob to wear, and with the goatskins she covered up his hands and the hairless part of his neck.

Jacob brought them to her and she prepared the dish. Why the best or precious clothes? A change of clothing sometimes signifies new status (for example, judge, doctor, priest). Clothing Jacob in Esau's clothes is symbolic induction into his status. Besides, the clothes have a certain fragrance attached to Esau. Covering up the smooth parts of Jacob is necessary since Esau was at birth hairy all through. Later, Joseph's clothes dipped in the blood of a slaughtered goat would serve to deceive Jacob himself (Gen 37:32–33).

Isaac and Jacob, 27:18–29

Going to his father, Jacob said, "Father!" "Yes?" replied Isaac. "Which of my sons are you?" Jacob answered his father: "I am Esau, your firstborn. I did as you told me..."

Isaac actually asked, "who are you, my son?" (*mî 'attah bᵉnî*). This is a "who goes there?" The visitor could be anybody. Jacob then identified himself as Esau, the firstborn, said he was bringing the requested game to

---

8. The root *ḥamad* means "to desire," "to covet"; desirable garments are precious.

receive blessing. Did Jacob lie? Replying to Rebekah, he raised no moral concerns, only the possibility of being caught in deception. Did he believe that, having bought the birthright, he was now Esau as far as rights were concerned? But Isaac did not say that he was blessing Esau as the firstborn. Blessing is not a natural right, but rather depends on the good pleasure of the one who blesses.

But Isaac said to his son, "How did you get it so quickly, my son?" "Come closer, my son, that I may feel you, to learn whether you really are my son Esau or not . . ." When Isaac felt him, he said, "although the voice is Jacob's, the hands are Esau's."

The first flicker of doubt appears. Isaac applies two senses, hearing and touch, and they send conflicting signals. The blessing will not be given till Isaac thought he resolved the conflict by applying a third sense, smell. As such, the gloss at verse 23—

He failed to identify[9] him because his hands were hairy, like those of his brother Esau; so he blessed him

—is misplaced.

Again Isaac said, "Are you really my son Esau?" And Jacob said, "I am."

The repeated "whether you really are my son Esau" is more telling in the awkward Hebrew phrase: "whether you this/here my son Esau."[10] Isaac is, as it were, foreswearing Jacob. Isaac asked that food be served; he ate and drank.

Finally his father Isaac said to him, "Come closer, my son, and kiss me . . ." Isaac smelled the fragrance of his clothes. With that, he blessed him, saying.

A certain heathen met R. Ishmael and blessed him, to which he replied: "your answer has already been given." Then another met him and cursed him, and he again replied, "your answer has already been given." Said his disciples to him: "you have spoken to the one exactly the same as to the other!" "It is written thus," he returned, "Blessed be every one that blesses you; cursed be every one that curses you." (Gen. Rab. 66:6)

---

9. Using the same verb, *nakar*, as in Gen 37:23.
10. *'Attah zeh bᵉnî 'Eśāû*.

Rebekah was prescient in covering Jacob with Esau's precious clothes. Its fragrance dismissed Isaac's last doubts. From the blessing itself, we know the fragrance smacked of the field.

Ah, the fragrance of my son is like the fragrance of a field that the LORD has blessed! May God give to you of the dew of the heavens, and of the fertility of the earth, abundance of grain and wine. May peoples serve you, and nations bow down to you. Be master of your brothers, and may your mother's sons bow down to you. Cursed be those who curse you, and blessed be those who bless you.

The blessing is appropriately couched as a petition to God, but it is possible that this is later theologizing (witness Isaac's "I blessed him," v. 33). First, the *material* blessings—dew to soften the soil and water the crops results in the fat of the earth, that is, abundance of grain and wine. These blessings of a farmer hardly rhyme with Esau's profession as hunter. Then come *political* blessings. We knew from Gen 25:23 that the twins stood for two nations and that the elder will serve the younger. Isaac's blessing of Jacob in the guise of Esau confirms the oracle about the twins in the womb. But now the canvas widens to include the service/tribute of nations and peoples and lordship ($g^eb\hat{i}r$ is lord) over his brothers and his mother's sons. The blessing envisages ascendancy in the comity of nations: "peoples and nations" can refer to Israel only after it had become a state.[11] Except for the similarity of content (though not of phrasing) in "cursed be those who curse you . . . ,"[12] "the blessing is strangely independent of the otherwise uniformly formulated patriarchal promises."[13] "Your descendants will take possession of the gates of their enemies" (Gen 22:17) offers political domination, but the phrasing differs. Totally lacking is the part about "all the families of the earth will find blessing in you" (Gen 12:3). Lacking also is the blessing of numerous progeny and possession of the land—these he will supply when blessing Jacob before his flight to Mesopotamia (Gen 28:3–4). Isaac, it would seem, did not intend to transmit the blessing of Abraham. In ancient Israel, the firstborn replaced the father and took over the family holdings; a dying father's blessing assured abundance of wherewithals. When Jacob restored the

---

11. Westermann, *Genesis 12–36*, 441.
12. Gen 12:3 has: "I will bless those who bless you and curse those who curse you."
13. Von Rad, *Genesis*, 278.

blessing to Esau ("accept the gift[14] I have brought you," Gen 33:11), it was also in terms of herds and flocks he offered as gifts.

Rebekah achieved her aim. But are her actions justified because she helped to fulfill the prenatal oracle?[15] Does divine predestination need a helping hand? Her action led to conflict that could have resulted in fratricide. She had to whisk Jacob away into exile for twenty years. He later ran the risk of death at the hands of Laban and his kinsmen (Gen 31:23) and of Esau and his four hundred men (Gen 33:1).

Isaac "Blesses" Esau, 27:30–40

Jacob had scarcely left his father after Isaac had finished blessing him, when his brother Esau came back from his hunt . . . "Let my father sit up and eat some of his son's game, that you may then give me your blessing." His father Isaac asked him, "who are you?" He said, "I am your son, your firstborn son, Esau."

Had Esau encountered Jacob at the door, the story would have taken a different turn. The narrator constructs panels in which only two characters interact. Both Jacob and Esau name themselves as "firstborn"—the blessing is that of the firstborn.

Isaac trembled greatly. "Who was it then," he asked, "that hunted game and brought it to me? I ate it all just before you came, and I blessed him. Now he is blessed!"

Ḥarad, "be terrified," "tremble," denotes great fright, anxiety. The narrator indicates that Isaac was indeed deceived. Was Jacob really blessed? The narrator seems to concur with Isaac that Jacob was indeed blessed. However, Jacob's many attempts to secure blessing raise doubts about the blessing here. Besides, dominion over Esau never materialized in this story.

As he heard his father's words, Esau burst into loud, bitter sobbing and said, "Father, bless me too!" When Isaac said, "Your brother came here by a ruse and carried off your blessing," Esau exclaimed, "He is well named

---

14. The Hebrew actually has "my blessing."

15. Fokkelman, *Reading Biblical Narrative*, 83 asks the question, but leaves the reader to answer.

Jacob, is he not? He has supplanted me twice! First he took away my right at firstborn, and now he has taken away my blessing."

The reader feels Esau's pain as he sobs and asks that he too be blessed. "Your brother came by deceit" (*mirmah*) qualifies Jacob's action morally. A blessing given in deception is accounted effective all the same; the words of blessing have a concreteness, one can carry them off—a magical attitude? At birth, Jacob was gripping the heel of his brother, and was thus called Jacob—heel-grabber. Here he is *ya'aqōb* because *ya'aqēb*—Jacob because he Jacobs—supplanter is his name. Esau now qualifies the earlier sale of the birthright as trickery.

Then he said, "Have you not saved a blessing for me?" Isaac replied to Esau, "I have already appointed him your master, and I have assigned to him all his kindred as his servants; besides, I have sustained him with grain and wine. What then can I do for you, my son?" But Esau said to his father, "Have you only one blessing, father? Bless me too, father!" And Esau wept aloud.

Isaac reversed the order of blessing, placing first Esau's subjection to Jacob. In the peasant perspective of "limited good," there is a limited amount of good for all, so persons, with their family, can improve their social position only at the expense of others.[16] The family holding is one; both Esau and Jacob cannot grow rich from it simultaneously. Esau's loud sops again pierce the reader. The narrator presents him as a tragic hero floored by the one Achilles heel of improvidence. His father Isaac said in response:

"See, far from the fertile earth will be your dwelling; far from the dew of the heavens above! By your sword you will live, and your brother you will serve; But when you become restless, you will throw off his yoke from your neck."

> For both Jacob and Esau the text has "from the fat of the earth and from the dew of the heavens above." The Hebrew word for "from" is *min*; it can be used in a partitive or privative sense. The translation above understands it as privative for Esau ("far from"), though partitive for Jacob. Other translations, for example, TNK, understand both as partitive, hence: "See, your abode shall enjoy the fat of the earth, and the dew of heaven above. Yet by your sword you shall live . . ." In this translation, Esau is given the same material riches, though subordinated to Jacob.

---

16. See Malina, *New Testament World*, 95.

Isaac removes Esau from the Promised Land. "Far from the fertile earth" consigns him to the desert. Desert tribes do not have enough to live on, so they live by helping caravans or raiding them (live by your sword). "Your brother you will serve" confirms the blessing to "Jacob," also the oracle of birth. The yoke is metaphor for subjection to a power to whom one is obliged to pay tribute. The meaning of *tārîd* is unclear: "when you break loose" (NRSV); "when you win your freedom" (NJB). The story is told from a later point of view (prophecy from event) when Edom had secured freedom from Judah. David subdued Edom (2 Sam 8:14), she broke loose around 840 BCE.

> The title of this section, "Isaac 'blesses' Esau" (with "blesses" in quotations), invites discussion of the nature of blessing. Divine blessing is an act of creation available to all (God blesses humankind in Gen 1:28). Ishmael, although shunted from the line of promise, is blessed with twelve princes and multiple progeny (Gen 25:16).

Esau's Anger; Jacob Has to Flee, 27:41–46

Esau bore a grudge against Jacob because of the blessing his father had given him. Esau said to himself, "let the time of mourning for my father come, so that I may kill my brother Jacob."

The brothers reenact the case of Cain and Abel, though here parental partiality is the bone of contention. Esau felt too much for the father to cause him grief during his lifetime. He took his father's death to be imminent. In fact, Isaac lived another sixty years after this! Rebekah got news of what her older son Esau had in mind. The omniscient narrator informs us of what Esau had in mind, and Rebekah somehow discerned perhaps from Esau's behavior.

"Listen! Your brother Esau intends to get his revenge by killing you. So now, my son, obey me; flee at once to my brother Laban in Haran, and stay with him a while until your brother's fury subsides . . . Then I will send for you and bring you back. Why should I lose both of you in a single day?"

Rebekah seeks to minimize the fallout. There is a gap here; in the sequel, Rebekah never sent to bring Jacob back, rather Jacob decided on his own to flee Haran with his wives, children, and property.

Rebekah said to Isaac, "I am disgusted with life because of the Hittite women. If Jacob also should marry a Hittite woman, a native of the land, like these women, why should I live?"

Esau had married two women of the land (Gen 26:34), who became a source of bitterness to Isaac and Rebekah (Gen 26:35). Rebekah begins to talk Isaac into doing her bidding, as usual in this relationship. She is resourceful and manipulative. Jacob's flight to Haran becomes a sending away to procure the proper type of wife.

> *Nkwu puru taa, chaa taa, abughi ihe oma.*
> A palm tree that sprang out today and got ripe today, is not a good thing.
> Too much cleverness is not good.
> There should be adequate time given before a thing can be considered as good or well-done.
> (Davids, *Igbo Proverbs*, 157)

How do we evaluate the story morally? "God does not perfect people before deciding to work in and through them."[17] God already set the destiny of the boys before birth. Mal 1:3 says, "I loved Jacob, but rejected[18] Esau," and that is before they had done anything good or bad.[19] Hence, "the presence of the oracle constitutes a moral judgment on Jacob's behavior,"[20] striving to snatch what was already given by divine election.

On the other hand, "God's actions do not absolutely determine human decisions or life outcomes."[21] Rebekah, inspired by the oracle, may have sought to facilitate its fruition. Yet, God achieves his purposes in and through the decisions and actions of humans.

"The moral critique of Jacob's actions is textured into the cycle itself."[22] Jacob experiences mortal danger many times or Jacob-like types of deception are visited upon him. Hos 12:3 comments, "the LORD once indicted Judah, and punished Jacob for his conduct, requited him for his deeds" (TNK). And Jer 9:3 put his finger on it: "every brother *'āqôb*

---

17. Fretheim, "Which Blessing Does Isaac Give Jacob?" 284.
18. This is not the emotional feeling of love, but of election.
19. The reason is that God's elective plan might continue not by works, but by his call (Rom 9:13).
20. Sarna, *Genesis*, 397 (excursus 21).
21. Fretheim, "Which Blessing Does Isaac Give Jacob?" 280.
22. Fishbane, "Composition and Structure," 16.

yaʿaqōb" (takes advantage of), well rendered by NABRE as "every brother imitates Jacob, the supplanter." Heb 12:16–17 evinces a negative view of Esau. It exhorts the audience not to be immoral[23] or profane like Esau, who sold his birthright for a single meal. When later he wanted to inherit his father's blessing, he was rejected because he found no opportunity to change his mind, even though he sought the blessing with tears. Heb 11:20 posited a line pursued by later exegesis: "by faith regarding things still to come Isaac blessed Jacob and Esau." That is, Isaac was acting prophetically; he already believed in the future realities to come.

Tradition

Picking up from Heb 11:20, Augustine asserts that "Isaac undoubtedly knew what was happening since he had the spirit of prophecy, and he himself was acting symbolically . . . [otherwise he would be very angry with his son for deceiving him]. But he knew the mystery being enacted."[24] A thread of patristic exegesis is that Esau stands for the old dispensation, Jacob for the new dispensation and Christ. Jacob's gripping the heel of Esau means that by closely following the footsteps of the prophets the last peoples had to take hold of the right of primogeniture, since they are the first ones to be found in the New Testament.[25] Because Jacob is never shown as lord of Esau, rather ran away from him in fright and adored him seven times,[26] the words of Isaac must be seen as accomplished in the Savior. In fact, the field is the world, and the smell of his clothes are all those who believe in him, according to what the apostle says, "we are the aroma of Christ to God . . ." (2 Cor 2:15–16).[27]

Was Rebekah right in her preferential love of Jacob? "Rebekah did not prefer one son to another son but a just son to an unjust one . . . she offered him to the Lord, for she knew that he could protect the gift that the Lord had bestowed . . ."[28] Did the patriarch Jacob tell a lie? "It wasn't

---

23. "My brother Esau is a hairy man," that is, a sinner, "but I am a man of smooth skin." In fact, through these words the faultless and sinless character of the flesh of the Lord is revealed. Hippolytus, *On the Blessing of Isaac and Jacob*, in ACCS 2:170. That is, Jacob stands for Christ.
24. Augustine, *Sermon* 4.21, in ACCS 2:174.
25. Hippolytus, *On the Blessings of Isaac and Jacob* 8, in ACCS 2:178.
26. Hippolytus, *Blessing of the Patriarchs* 7, in ACCS 2:175.
27. Hippolytus, *On the Blessings of Isaac and Jacob* 7, in ACCS 2:174.
28. Ambrose, *Jacob and the Happy Life* 2.2 5–6, in ACCS 2:183.

a case of real guile, especially since he did not in fact lie when he said, 'I am your elder son Esau.' For that one had already made a bargain with his brother and sold him his rights as firstborn..."[29]

The rabbis of the third and fourth century saw Rome in Esau. "The voice is that of Jacob" alludes to the fact that Jacob wields power only by his voice (spiritual strength), whereas Esau wields dominion only by his hand (raw might). Abba son of Kahana says, "when the voice of Jacob rings out in the synagogue, Esau has no hands" (*Gen. Rab.* 65:20)—fidelity to worship and Torah study shields Jacob from the oppression of Esau. Blessing with the dew of heaven was because Jacob occupied himself with the study of Torah, which is compared to water[30] (*Gen. Rab.* 66:1).

Did Jacob lie? Jacob parsed his answer, "I am to receive the Ten Commandments,[31] [but] Esau is your firstborn" (R. Levi in *Gen. Rab.* 65:18). Was Isaac really deceived? "When he heard, 'the Lord your God sent me good speed,' he knew it was not Esau, for Esau does not mention the name of the Holy One, blessed be He" (*Gen. Rab.* 65:19). Isaac was feeling some misgiving, thinking, "perhaps I did not act rightly in making him the firstborn who is not so," but when Esau said, "he took away my birthright," he exclaimed, "rightly did I bless him" (R. Levi in *Gen. Rab.* 67:2). Jacob has one brother, while the blessing says, "may nations serve you ... be master of your brothers." "Nations" refer to the children of Ishmael and Keturah, "your brothers" to Esau and his chiefs (*Gen. Rab.* 66:1). "By your sword shall you live." R. Huna: "if Jacob is meritorious, you will serve (*taʿabōd*) him; if not, you shall destroy (*teʿabbed*) him. R. Jose son of R. Halfutha: if you see your brother Jacob throw off the yoke of the Torah from his neck, then decree his destruction and you will become his master" (*Gen. Rab.* 67:2).[32] This midrash exhorts to fidelity in face of Roman persecution.

---

29. Augustine, *Sermon* 4.23, in ACCS 2:179.

30. See Isa 55:1. Water was a common symbol (Jewish and Christian) of drawing from the word of God.

31. *'Anōkî* ("I") begins both Jacob's response and the Decalogue.

32. *Tg. Neof.* makes this clear: "And when the sons of Jacob study the Law and keep the commandments, they will place the yoke of their burden upon your neck. And when the sons of Jacob abandon the commandments and withhold themselves from studying the Law, you will rule over him and shall break the yoke of servitude from off your neck."

CHAPTER 17

Genesis 28

Divine Encounter at Bethel

> Truly, the LORD is in this place and I did not know it.
>
> —GENESIS 28:16

Narrative Structures

GENESIS 28-32 IS THE story of a journey. Bethel is significant for this journey—Jacob leaves from there and returns there, and later revisits it (Gen 35:10-12). Divine encounters (Gen 28:10-22 // Gen 32:23-33) frame Jacob's flight and return.[1] Literary features link one to the other. Both were theophanies and at night. Each encounter is introduced with the verb *paga'* ("to happen on"): Jacob came upon a certain place (28:11); God's angels came upon him (33:2). Each refers to angels of God: the angels of God were on the stairway (28:12); angels of God encountered him (32:2).[2] Both name a place with the phrase *zeh*, "here is..." (28:17; 32:3).[3]

---

1. See the schema in the commentary on Genesis 25.
2. Westermann, *Genesis 12-36*, 452 remarks that *mal'akê Elohim*, angels of God, do not occur again in the Hebrew Bible except at 2 Chr 16, though in a different sense.
3. Fishbane, *Text and Texture*, 53-54. See also Ross, "Jacob's Vision," 226; Westermann, *Genesis 12-36*, 452.

Jacob's journey is under God's protection and assistance, though in the end Jacob must reckon with the God who accompanied him. Jacob encounters God for the first time in this journey. God changes Jacob's name to Israel. The journey is a process of conversion, a gradual development towards righteousness, a growth marked by setbacks as well as advances.[4] God does not insist on holiness before engaging a person, though the interaction itself is transforming.

Abraham generated Isaac, Ishmael, and the children of Keturah; divine choice rested on Isaac. Isaac produced Esau and Jacob; again God chose one, Jacob. With Jacob it is different; all Jacob's children became Israel. The story tells how God prepared Jacob to become Israel and father of the twelve tribes of Israel. Jacob is presented as the starting point of Israel's relationship with YHWH and remembered for his decision to pursue the exclusive worship of YHWH.[5] On revisiting Bethel, he commanded his family to "get rid of foreign gods among you," and he buried them under the oak that is near Shechem (Gen 35:4).

Jacob is founder of the holy place of Bethel: "the true sanctity of the site commences only with God's self-revelation to the patriarch."[6] Bethel was a capital of the northern kingdom of Israel. "It appears to be beyond reasonable doubt that the primary home of our Story of Jacob was the kingdom of Israel."[7]

Isaac blesses Jacob and sends him off to Paddan-aram (Gen 28:1–9):

Isaac therefore summoned Jacob and blessed him, charging him: "You shall not marry a Canaanite woman. Go now to Paddan-aram,[8] to the house of your mother's father Bethuel, and there choose a wife for yourself from among the daughters of Laban, your mother's brother.

Rebekah had already told Jacob to flee to Laban to escape the wrath of Esau (27:44). To bring Isaac to embrace her decision, she feigned disgust with Esau's Hittite wives; she could not live to see Jacob marry a Hittite woman. But when Isaac spoke to Jacob, it was question of not marrying a

---

4. Mann, *Story of Torah*, 71.

5. Heckle, "Remembering Jacob," 55, 78. Speaking of the divine salvation in Egypt, Ezek 20:5–6 says, "the day I chose Israel, I swore to the descendants of the house of Jacob"—the Hebrew slaves in Egypt as descendants of Jacob.

6. Sarna, *Genesis*, 397 (excursus 21).

7. Blum, "Jacob Traditions," 209.

8. On the interchange of this and Aram-Naharaim, see the commentary at Genesis 25.

Canaanite woman. Canaan was the land promised to Abraham. The story perhaps reflects a period when mixed marriages threatened the purity of the religious community,[9] when intermarriages of the sort would lead to the disappearance of a minority population. The journey back to the kindred in Mesopotamia would be symbolic of journeying back to kindred in the exilic community. Is the narrator suggesting that Esau's mixed marriages were a factor in Isaac passing him over as heir? The Decalogue and other laws in the Torah did not take up the prohibition of mixed marriages. It is thus an example of a time-conditioned prohibition resulting from a particular historical situation.[10] This is an important principle in discriminating between the laws of Scripture as word of God.

Isaac summoned Jacob, blessed him, and sent him off to Laban to choose a wife from his daughters; in effect he transformed a flight from mortal danger into a quest for a wife. No reprimand for Jacob's deception of him in the last chapter! Were Isaac and Rebekah acting in tandem in the affair of Jacob's purloining of the blessing?[11] Or, perhaps, Isaac came to believe that Jacob was the right bearer of the blessing?[12]

May God Almighty bless you and make you fertile, multiply you that you may become an assembly of peoples. May God extend to you and your descendants the blessing of Abraham, so that you may gain possession of the land where you are residing, which he assigned to Abraham.

Compared with the blessing of Jacob disguised as Esau, there are two new elements—the blessing of fertility/numerous progeny, and that of possession of the land promised to Abraham. The blessing of fertility is couched in the language of the blessing of humanity in Gen 1:28, using the same verbs, *parah* and *rabah*. Isaac refers explicitly to the "blessing of Abraham," hence, he is consciously designating Jacob as bearer of the

---

9. Gunkel, *Genesis*, 372.

10. Westermann, *Genesis 12–36*, 449.

11. R. Levi said that Isaac felt misgivings about making one firstborn who was not so until he heard Esau say, "he took away my birthright," then he exclaimed, "rightly did I bless him" (*Gen. Rab.* 67:2). Zucker, "Restoring Rebekah," 116: "Isaac and Rebekah themselves plan out this scheme of deception...to achieve what they understand to be the greater good for the family, that Jacob becomes the link to the promised future..."

12. The impression that Isaac was somehow complicit derives from the use of different sources. The current source, P, either did not know of Jacob's ruse or discounted it; it also did not know of Rebekah's prior decision to have Jacob flee for his life and take refuge with her brother Laban.

blessings that God Almighty (*El Shaddai*) conferred on Abraham in Genesis 17.

Esau noted that Isaac had blessed Jacob when he sent him to Paddan-Aram... and that... he charged him, "You shall not marry a Canaanite woman," and that Jacob had obeyed his father and mother and gone to Paddan-aram.

"That Jacob had obeyed his father and mother" casts Esau's mixed marriage as disobedience and dishonoring of his parents. It also implicitly exhorts the readers to reject the way of Esau and follow Jacob's example in their marriages.

Esau realized how displeasing the Canaanite women were to his father Isaac, so Esau went to Ishmael, and in addition to the wives he had, married Mahalath, the daughter of Abraham's son Ishmael and sister of Nebaioth.

Esau's fault was therefore not calculated. He tried to make amends, even if that availed little. A midrash interpreted this as meaning that he made up his mind to be converted. R. Joshua b. Levi: the wife is named Mahalath because the Holy One forgave him his sins—*maḥal* means "to forgive" (*Gen. Rab.* 67:13).

Divine Encounter at Bethel, 28:10–22

> Praying at any place is like standing at the very foot of God's throne of glory, for the gate of heaven is there and the door is open for prayer to be heard. (Pirqe de Rabbi Eliezer 35, as cited in Plaut, *Torah*, 211). However, the original reads: "Everyone who prays in Jerusalem . . ."

Jacob departed from Beersheba and proceeded toward Haran. When he came upon a certain place, he stopped there for the night.

Midrash has it that Jacob was seventy-seven years old when he left his father's house.[13] He came upon a certain place—not by design, nor because it was a sacred place. The sun had set; he needed to pause for the night.

---

13. *Pirqe de Rabbi Eliezer*, 35. Sarna, *Genesis*, 364 n. 3 concluded that Jacob could not have been younger than seventy-one when he fled to Laban. In *Gen. Rab.* 68:5, R. Hezekiah said he was sixty-three years old when he received the blessings. See also b. Meg 17a.

Taking one of the stones at the place, he put it under his head and lay down in that place.

Away from home, and in the middle of nowhere, he is "betwixt and between"—a liminal stage. He must pull himself together, refashion his identity.

Then he had a dream[14]: a stairway rested on the ground, with its top reaching to the heavens; and God's angels were going up and down on it. And there was the Lord standing beside him[15] and saying.

The divine breaks into Jacob's world. For the first time, he becomes conscious of a world transcending his ego and its rivalries. "The dream challenges Jacob to acknowledge a connection to something that is larger than his personal desires, a connection that offers the potential for a new, more expansive personality."[16] A vital word, *hinneh* (behold), introduced each of the three sightings. The narrator followed Jacob's perceptual point of view: behold, a stairway! And behold, angels! And look, the Lord himself.[17] The imagery is that of the cosmic mountain, the center of the world where heaven and earth are opposite each other. Heaven is the realm of God, earth the realm of human beings. The *sullam*[18] is "the link between Heaven and Earth, the axial channel of communication between the human world and the superhuman realm."[19]

---

14. In Jungian psychology, "the dream gives a true picture of the subjective state, while the conscious mind denies that this state exists or recognizes it only grudgingly." Jung, *Modern Man in Search of a Soul*, 5.

15. So also NJB, NRSV, TNK; NIV: "here above it [stairway] stood the LORD."

16. Kille, "Jacob," 12.

17. Fokkelman, *Narrative Art in Genesis*, 51. See also Ross, "Jacob's Vision," 228.

18. NRSV, NIV, TNK also translate as stairway; NJB: ladder. The word is usually derived from the root *sll* meaning to heap up earth.

19. Garcia-Treto, "Jacob's Oath-Covenant," 2.

FIGURE 4

"Jacob's Dream" by Gustave Doré

Gen 28:12 And he dreamed, and behold a ladder set upon the earth, and the top of it reached to heaven: and behold the angels of God ascending and descending on it.

Babylonian temples tried to establish such links through ziggurats, stepped towers with a shrine at the top representing the abode of the gods. In the Akkadian Myth of Nergal and Ereshkigal, a *simmiltu*, long stairway, leads to the gate of Anu, Enlil, and Ea.[20] YHWH had frustrated the human attempt to build a tower with its top reaching heaven (Gen 11:4); by divine initiative, this stairway was let down from heaven. Angels usually descended from heaven for a mission, then ascended back to heaven. Here the angels of God were moving in the reverse direction,

20. Hurowitz, "New Light on Jacob's Dream," 437.

ascending and descending, drawing Jacob's attention to YHWH. YHWH was standing *niṣṣab 'ālāw*, that is, over against the stairway, or over against/beside Jacob? YHWH had come down to the human realm and precisely to Jacob, a man fleeing from the elder brother he had cheated of the birthright! It can also be translated as YHWH was standing on the stairway.[21] That is, YHWH remained above, while the angels' movement directed Jacob's attention to YHWH. For the first time, Jacob becomes aware of a world transcending his ego and its conflicts.

I am the Lord, the God of Abraham, your father and the God of Isaac; the land on which you are lying I will give to you and your descendants. Your descendants will be like the dust[22] of the earth, and through them you will spread to the west and the east, to the north and the south. In you and your descendants all the families of the earth will find blessing. I am with you and will protect you wherever you go, and bring you back to this land. I will never leave you until I have done what I promised you.

The reader waited for divine reproof, but hears instead divine assurances! In this first encounter, YHWH confirms the "blessing of Abraham" that Isaac just conferred on Jacob; it includes possession of the land and multiple progeny. For someone on a journey to secure a wife, the blessing of multiple progeny assures resounding success. YHWH self-presents as God of Abraham and God of Isaac; the story concerns the process by which YHWH became the God of Jacob also, and through Jacob, of Israel.

A parallel self-presentation in Exod 20:2, "I am the LORD your God who brought you out of the land of Egypt," outlined stipulations of the covenant that made the Hebrew escapees from Egypt "my treasured possession among all peoples" (Exod 19:5). Diverse traditions of YHWH's self-revelation to Israel[23] appear in Exodus—to Moses at the burning bush (Exod 3:14), to the patriarchs but under the name El Shaddai (Exod 6:3).

---

21. Hence the NIV: "here above it stood the LORD."

22. For similar phrasing, see Gen 13:16. There also spreading in all directions is mentioned.

23. Scholars increasingly posit a dual tradition of Israel's origin: origin in the land with the patriarchs, with gods of Canaan identified with YHWH, and origin in Egypt, with YHWH as jealous and exclusive God of Israel. See Schmid, "Genesis and Exodus," 188. See also his *Genesis and the Moses Story*, especially 92–151.

What Jacob needed most in his current situation was protection on the way and the success of his undertaking. YHWH assured him of support and constancy: "I will never leave you until I have done what I promised you." YHWH never quits; he walks with fractured human beings for their good: "he makes his sun rise on the bad and the good, and causes rain to fall on the just and the unjust" (Matt 5:45). "All families of the earth will be blessed [using the passive *nibraku*] in him and in his descendants" takes up the exact language of the promise to Abraham in Gen 12:3. Like Abram, Jacob becomes a source or mediator of blessing to all families of the earth.

Jacob's Vow

When Jacob awoke from his sleep, he said, "Truly, the Lord is in this place and I did not know it." He was afraid and said, "How awesome this place is! This nothing else but the house of God, the gateway to heaven."

If Bethel was an ancient sacred site, Jacob did not experience it so. There is deliberate dissociation from any earlier sacred status; the theophany provides the sole basis for the sanctity of Bethel.[24] Human beings can encounter God where they are!

The human posture before the Holy is fear and dread. The metaphor "house of God" does not refer to a building; the place itself is abode of God. The stairway with its top in the heavens links this place and heaven, hence an appropriate moniker is "gate of heaven."

Early the next morning, Jacob took the stone that he had put under his head, set it up as a sacred pillar, and poured oil on top of it. He named the place Bethel, whereas the former name of the town had been Luz.[25]

Sacred objects were consecrated by anointing with oil (tabernacle and altar in Exod 40:9–11).[26] Assyrian kings restored dilapidated temples and replaced inscriptions by anointing them with oil.[27] The pillar

---

24. Sarna, *Genesis*, 199.

25. Josh 18:13: "it crossed over to the southern flank of Luz (that is, Bethel). Judg 1:23: "Bethel, which formerly was called Luz."

26. Abraham built an altar in Bethel, 12:8; 13:3–4. There is no memory of this here.

27. Hurowitz, "New Light on Jacob's Dream," 438.

(*maṣṣebah*) immortalizes the dream, reflects what he saw;[28] it becomes a post-figuration of the theophany.[29]

Beth-El means "house of God" or "house of El."[30] Abraham built an altar in Bethel (Gen 12:8; 13:3–4). There is no memory of that here. Upon his return, Jacob will build an altar at Bethel (Gen 35:7).[31] The naming concretizes his experience.

Jacob then made this vow: "If God will be with me and protect me on this journey I am making and give me food to eat and clothes to wear, and I come back safely to my father's house, the Lord will be my God. This stone that I have set up as a sacred pillar will be the house of God. Of everything you give me I will return a tenth part to you without fail."

"If God will be with me"—but God already promised to be with him! The ever-calculating grasper cannot take God at his word? To soften the paradox, some suggest that the protasis is, not "the Lord will be my God," but "this stone . . . will be the house of God"[32]—Jacob will no longer appear to be choosing his God. However, we know that each patriarch related personally and intimately to a "god of the father": Abraham to El Shaddai, Isaac to the Fear of Isaac (Gen 31:42), and Jacob himself to "the Mighty One of Jacob" (Gen 49:24). His dream presents the image of the ascent to something higher, but Jacob is not quite ready to set out on that path. At this point, his pact with God is conditional.[33] "Jacob bargains with God: if God performs properly—and performs first—Jacob will be a loyal adherent."[34] He will respond with exclusive worship. He will establish the place of his encounter with YHWH as a place for worship of

---

28. This is shown linguistically. The same root is used for the stairway and the pillar: the stairway was *muṣṣāb* fixed on the ground, the pillar is a *maṣṣebah*, fixed structure.

29. Fokkelman, *Narrative Art*, 66.

30. Bethel was also the name of a god, as in Jer 48:13: "Chemosh shall disappoint Moab, just the house of Israel was disappointed by Bethel, in which they trusted"; the parallelism between Chemosh and Bethel shows Bethel to be a god. The Jews of Elephantine in Egypt (circa 400 BCE) invoked deities called Eshem-bethel, Anath-bethel, and Herem-bethel. A seventh-century treaty between Esarhaddon of Assyria and King Baal of Tyre has: "may Bethel and Anath-bethel deliver you to a man-eating lion." See Sarna, *Genesis*, 400.

31. A variant tradition.

32. Ross, "Jacob's Vision," 233.

33. Cf. Kille, "Jacob" 12.

34. Plaut, *Torah*, 209.

him. The tenth part promised is a once-for-all donation of all God would have given him.

> Three conceptions of a holy place are enshrined here.[35] There is the old idea of a holy stone or pillar as a house of God. In Sefire (eigth century BCE), stone stelae erected to seal or effect a treaty were called *bātê Alahaya* (houses of God).[36] The body of the story has the idea that God is at a particular place where he has appeared and that makes the place holy. The idea of stairway, however, posits God place in heaven and one needs some link for access.

> Conditional discipleship is much easier than unconditional surrender. The good news is that God is patient and does not despair or become disillusioned with this cautious covenant partner. God will be faithful even when doubt and timidity overshadow human faith. (Whartenby, "Gen 28:10–22," 403)

Tradition

Jubilees 27 follows the Masoretic text closely. But already circa 50 BCE, Wis 10:10–12 reread the passage. "She [Wisdom], when a righteous man fled from his brother's anger, guided him in right ways." Jacob has become a righteous man. The divine presence could no longer be allowed into direct contact with humanity, so Wisdom, "a pure emanation of the glory of the Almighty" (Wis 7:25), replaces YHWH in the theophany. The "right ways" include moral integrity and knowledge of holy things. The stairway with its top in the heavens signifies nothing less than the revelation of the "kingdom of God"—probably the first time this term is used in our Scriptures.

The call of the first disciples in John ends with a direct allusion to the Jacob incident: "Amen, amen, I say to you, you will see the sky opened and the angels of God ascending and descending on the Son of Man." As in Genesis 28, the angels of God are "ascending and descending," but now the focus is not YHWH, but the Son of Man. The Son of Man is thus

---

35. Westermann, *Genesis 12–36*, 460.
36. Fokkelman, *Narrative Art*, 79; Garcia-Treto, "Jacob's Oath-Covenant," 5.

the "house of God," the divine presence on earth: "and the Word became flesh and made his dwelling among us" (John 1:14).

The LXX translated the Hebrew *sullam* with Greek *klimax*, which can mean ladder or stairway. The fathers of the church generally understood it as a ladder. The ladder fixed to the ground and reaching heaven is the cross of Christ, through which the access to heaven is granted to us, because it actually leads us to heaven.[37] For others, "the ladder that Jacob saw is the church, which has its birth from the earth but its way of life in heaven . . . evangelists ascend when [in their teaching] they pass to heavenly things to be contemplated by the mind, and they descend when they educate their listeners as to how they ought to live on earth."[38] Following a translation similar to that of the NIV, which read, "here above it [stairway] stood the LORD," Cyril of Alexandria says that Christ is firmly placed on top of the stairway for those holy spirits who can reach him, who have him as their overseer.[39] The stone also was Christ, the stone which the builders rejected (Ps 118:22); it is called Ebenezer, that is, stone of help (1 Sam 4:1; 7:12).[40]

The midrash generally reads *wayyifga'* (literally, "he happened upon a place") as "he prayed in the place"—the verb shares a similar root with "to pray." The movement of the angels was inverse of the usual. R. Hiyya the Elder debated with R. Jannai.[41] One said that the angels were ascending and descending *the ladder*, the other *they were ascending and descending on Jacob*. That means that some were exalting him (it is you they said whose features are engraved on God's throne on high) and others degrading him, dancing, leaping, and maligning him. In *Tg. Neof.*, the angels that accompanied him from the house of his father ascended to bear good tidings to the angels on high, saying: come and see the pious man whose image is engraved on the throne of Glory whom you desired to see. A tradition in *Tg. Ps.-J.* speaks of "the two angels who had gone to Sodom and had been banished from their apartment because they had revealed the secrets of the Lord[42] . . . they had accompanied him to Bethel and on that day they ascended to the heavens on high and said,

37. Chromatius, *Sermon* 1.6, in ACCS 2:188.
38. Bede, *Homilies on the Gospels* 1.17, in ACCS 2:190.
39. Cyril of Alexandria, *Glaphyra* on Gen 3.4, in ACCS 2:189.
40. Jerome, *Homilies on Psalms* 46, in ACCS 2:187.
41. *Gen. Rab.* 68:12.
42. The reference is to the two angels sent to Sodom in Gen 19:1, 13; that day they regained entrance to heaven.

come and see Jacob the pious, whose image is engraved on the throne of Glory." Jacob vowed saying, "If the LORD be with me" when the LORD already promised, "I will be with you." R. Aibu insisted that the passage is disarranged. R. Jonathan: it is not. He means that if all the conditions stipulated are fulfilled, *then* will he fulfill his vow. But the rabbis chose to read "this way" as referring to saving him from slander, adultery, bloodshed, and idolatry.[43] What did Jacob see? God showed him the temple built, destroyed, and rebuilt again.[44]

---

43. In fact, *Tg. Ps.-J.* reads: "and keeps me from shedding innocent blood, idol worship, and sexual immorality."

44. *Gen. Rab.* 69.7.

CHAPTER 18

Genesis 29–31

Jacob and Laban; The Twelve Tribes of Israel

> Whoever walks honestly walks securely, but the one whose ways are crooked will fare badly.
>
> —PROVERBS 10:9

THE THEME OF THIS BLOCK of chapters is deception and rivalry. The unit detailing the rivalry between Jacob's wives (29:31—30:24) has been inserted into the competition at deception between Jacob and Laban: Laban deceives Jacob (29:15-30); Jacob outwits Laban (30:25-43); Jacob escapes Laban (31:1-24); Jacob and Laban in Gilead (31:25—32:1).[1]

The section carries the history forward by describing how there came to be twelve tribes of Israel. Till now, divine election has functioned to choose one son of the patriarch (the younger) and not the other—Isaac, not Ishmael; Jacob, not Esau. With Jacob, election becomes inclusive—all sons, including the offspring of concubines, become Israel. A daughter, Dinah, makes up the number twelve. She holds the place for Benjamin, to be born later.[2]

---

1. Gunkel, *Genesis*, 316.

2. Gunkel, *Genesis*, 323 suggests that the tribe of Benjamin arose only after Israel's immigration into Canaan.

The Song of Deborah, Judges 5, mentions nine tribes: Ephraim, Benjamin, Machir, Zebulun, Isaachar, Reuben, Gilead, Dan, and Naphtali. Machir and Gilead do not appear here in Genesis 29, nor do Simeon, Levi, Judah, Gad, Asher, and Joseph appear in Judges 5. The list of the twelve tribes fluctuated, as can be seen from the lists in Genesis 49, Numbers 2, and Deuteronomy 33.[3]

Jacob at the Well, 29:1–14

After Jacob resumed his journey, he came to the land of the Kedemites.

The Kedemites are literally the "sons of the East," that is, easterners.

Looking about, he saw a well in the open country, with three flocks of sheep huddled near it, for flocks were watered from that well.

The last time someone arrived at a well, he was on a quest for a wife for Isaac (Gen 24:11). The reader is prepared for the betrothal type-scene, which calls for "travel to a foreign land, encounter there with the future bride (almost always referred to as *na'arah*, 'girl') at a well, drawing of water, 'hurrying' or 'running' to bring the news of the stranger's arrival, a feast at which a betrothal agreement is concluded."[4]

A large stone covered the mouth of the well. When all the shepherds were assembled there they would roll the stone away from the mouth of the well and water the sheep.

The stone was so heavy that rolling it away needed collaboration between the shepherds. The well served several owners of flocks and was thus under common control.[5]

Jacob said to them, "My brothers, where are you from?" We are from Haran," they replied. Then he asked them, "Do you know Laban, son of Nahor?" "We do," they answered. He inquired further, "Is he well?" "He is," they answered; "and here comes his daughter Rachel with the sheep."

Laban, brother of Jacob's mother Rebekah, was son of Bethuel, who was son of Nahor. God has led the one fleeing for his life to exactly the

---

3. Westermann, *Genesis 12–36*, 472: the twelve tribes of Israel occur in twenty-eight places in the Old Testament.

4. Alter, *Genesis*, 115.

5. Gunkel, *Genesis*, 316.

right place, just as he did Abraham's servant! Everything is under God's control.⁶ When Isaac dispatched Jacob he told him to "choose a wife for yourself from among the daughters of Laban, your mother's brother" (Gen 28:2). Here before him was one of the daughters of Laban; it was love at first sight. In many traditional cultures, one claims immunity and the right to protection among the kindred of one's mother.

While he was still talking with them, Rachel arrived with her father's sheep, for she was the one who tended them. As soon as Jacob saw Rachel, the daughter of his mother's brother Laban, and the sheep of Laban, he went up and rolled the stone away from the mouth of the well,⁷ and watered Laban's sheep.

He alone lifted the stone cover that needed several shepherds to lift. He had superhuman strength and was already proving to his kinsman how useful he could be.

Then Jacob kissed Rachel and wept aloud.

Tears of gratitude to God. Is the kiss already one of love? It appears to be the chaste greeting kiss of a kinswoman. Jacob explained to Rachel why the kiss and the emotion:

He was her father's relative, Rebekah's son. So she ran to tell her father. When Laban heard the news about Jacob, his sister's son, he ran to meet him. After embracing and kissing him, he brought him to his house. Jacob then repeated to Laban all these things, and Laban said to him, "You are indeed my bone and my flesh."

When Laban exuberantly welcomed Abraham's servant (Gen 24:31), the visitor had signs of great wealth. But Jacob lands here empty-handed; not even a camel is mentioned—he travelled on foot. Laban's portrait in midrash is dark: midrash has Laban kiss him, thinking he may have precious stones which he is hiding in his mouth (*Gen. Rab.* 70:13). Adam cried out concerning Eve, "bone of my bones and flesh of my flesh" (Gen 2:23); he recognized her sameness to him in her difference from the beasts. Laban and Jacob are of the same blood. Perhaps the narrator

---

6. Adeyemo, *Africa Bible Commentary*, 54.

7. *Tg. Ps.-J.*: "with one of his arms rolled the stone from the mouth of the well; and the well began to flow, and the waters came up before him ... and it continued to flow for twenty years"—that is, the period of his sojourn.

wanted also to signify that "Laban and Jacob are truly both of the same bone and flesh of chicanery."[8]

Laban Deceives Jacob, 29:15–30

After Jacob had stayed with him a full month, Laban said to him, "Should you serve me for nothing just because you are a relative of mine? Tell me what your wages should be.

The Hebrew can also read: "are you a kinsman that you should serve me for nothing?"[9] Either way, the key word, "serve" (*'abad*) appears and takes the memory back to the "blessing" in Gen 27:29, which read, "may peoples *serve* you, and nations bow down to you." Jacob is not being served, rather "doing time" for a wife. He becomes an indentured laborer working to pay off the bride-price.[10]

Now Laban had two daughters; the older was called Leah, the younger Rachel. Leah had dull eyes, but Rachel was shapely and beautiful.

The adjective *rāk* can mean weak or tender. *Tg. Onq.* understood it positively: "Leah's eyes were lovely"; but the eyes were all she had going for her. Most ancient versions understood it negatively: the eyes were dull, lacking luster, weak.[11]

> Deep waters cannot quench love, nor rivers sweep it away. Were one to offer all the wealth of his house for love, he would be utterly despised. (Songs 8:7)

Because Jacob loved Rachel, he answered, "I will serve you seven years for your younger daughter Rachel." Laban replied, "It is better to give her to you than to another man. Stay with me." So Jacob served seven years for Rachel, yet they seemed to him like a few days because of his love for her.

---

8. Abramsky, "Jacob Wrestles with Angel," 111.
9. Sarna, *Genesis*, 203.
10. Sarna, *Genesis*, 203.
11. *Gen. Rab.* 70:16: weak through weeping; *Tg. Neof.*: the eyes of Leah were raised in prayer, begging that she be married to the just Jacob.

It will take seven years working for Laban for Jacob to pay off the equivalent of the bride wealth! Forget all about Laban's protestations of kinship; the narrator indicates that Laban's demand was excessive. The apparent love at first sight was no infatuation, rather deep love.

Then Jacob said to Laban, "Give me my wife,[12] that I may consummate my marriage with her, for my term is now completed.

Seven years passed in a flash—indeed his love was so great they looked like no time at all. *'Ahavah* as a man's love for a woman appears here for the first time in the Bible.[13] Jacob is the first romantic in the Bible! Till death he will continue to show his preferential love for Rachel, even in ways that risk ruining his family, as we shall see in the Joseph Novella.

So Laban invited all the local inhabitants and gave a banquet. At nightfall he took his daughter Leah and brought her to Jacob, and he consummated the marriage with her. Laban assigned his maidservant Zilpah to his daughter Leah as her maidservant. In the morning, there was Leah!

The cheater is cheated! Leah was smuggled into the bridal bed under cover of darkness.[14] In the morning, behold it was Leah, not Rachel! Leah must have been desperate for a husband to collaborate with her father in such deceit. Was Rachel complicit? The narrator is silent. To highlight the dramatic irony, the midrash paints the picture as follows.

> The whole of that night he called her "Rachel," and she answered him. In the morning, however, *Behold it was Leah.* Said he to her: "What, you are a deceiver and the daughter of a deceiver!" "Is there a teacher without pupils," she retorted; "did not your father call you 'Esau' and you answered him! So did you too call me and I answered you!" (*Gen. Rab.* 70:19)[15]

So Jacob said to Laban, "How could you do this to me! Was it not for Rachel that I served you? Why did you deceive me?" Laban replied, "It is not the custom in our country to give the younger daughter before the firstborn.

---

12. *Gen. Rab.* 70:18 had Jacob then eighty-four years old.
13. Adam's poetry at the sight of Eve (Gen 2:23) is clearly motivated by love.
14. Sternberg, *Poetics of Biblical Narrative*, 243.
15. *Tg. Ps.-J.*: during the whole night he had thought that she was Rachel, because Rachel had entrusted to her all the things that Jacob had entrusted to her.

Finish the bridal week for this one, and then the other will also be given to you in return for another seven years of service with me.

Marriage festivities still last for a week in these cultures. "Why did you deceive me," with the verb *ramah* recalling the use of the same root in Isaac's "your brother came here by a ruse [*be-mirmah*] and carried off your blessing" (Gen 27:35). Further rubbing it in, Laban told Jacob that putting the younger before the elder is not accepted in his place! Jacob has no option but to do equal time for Rachel, if he is to have her. Notice again the motif of *serve* and the reversal of expectations that involves. Laban's real reason may have been transactional: he would not run the risk of losing out on the bride wealth if no man came for Leah.[16]

Jacob did so. He finished the bridal week for the one, and then Laban gave him his daughter Rachel as a wife . . . Jacob then consummated his marriage with Rachel also, and he loved her more than Leah. Thus he served Laban another seven years.

The narrator sets up a scenario of the "loved" and "hated" wife (see Deut 21:15), that is, the preferred and the unloved wife, thus prepares the reader for the rivalry and conflict to follow. Jacob received Rachel, the love of his life, but must serve another seven years for her. Lev 18:18 forbids marriage to two sisters.

Rivalry between Leah and Rachel, 29:31—30:24

When the Lord saw that Leah was unloved, he made her fruitful, while Rachel was barren.

Rachel's barrenness follows the type of the earlier matriarchs, though exclusive election no longer obtains here. The Lord demonstrates his power over life, but also his bent towards the disadvantaged and people on the margins. The narration accelerates. Leah gives birth to four sons as if in the twinkling of the eye—a few verses for a period of eight to ten years! All the children are named by the two sisters, including those born by the maids. The first son Leah names Reuben, as if to say, "look, a son" (*re'û bēn*); however, the etiology given is that of *ra'ah be-'onyî*, "the LORD saw my misery." The second she named Simeon, that is, *shama'*, "he heard":

---

16. Ephrem, *Commentary on Genesis* 27.2: because of Leah's unattractiveness, no one had come to marry her all the seven years of Rachel's betrothal.

> Israel has emerged out of the intense struggle between Rachel and Leah, just as Israel will emerge from the struggle between Jacob and God in ch. 32. (Mann, *Book of the Torah*, 72)

The LORD heard that I was unloved, and therefore he has given me this one also. The third son she named Levi, now at last my husband will become attached to me, since I have now borne him three sons.

The verbal root *lawah* means "to become attached." Leah craves Jacob's love, which she never received. In that culture, women valued themselves by their sons and the love and esteem of their husbands. Finally a fourth one whom she named Judah, saying

This time I will give thanks to the LORD—hodah is the verb for "to give thanks/praise." *Then she stopped bearing children. When Rachel saw that she had not borne children to Jacob, she became envious of her sister. She said to Jacob, "Give me children or I shall die!"*

Rachel's situation in Jacob's family would be precarious should she survive Jacob, as usually wives survive husbands. In most traditional societies, childlessness is blamed on the woman. Here it is Rachel who blames her husband, for had he not given Leah four sons? But the narrator already told us that the Lord made Leah fruitful, while Rachel was barren (Gen 29:31). When Rebekah was sterile, Isaac entreated the LORD on her behalf and she became pregnant (Gen 25:21). Rather than turn to God, Rachel turned against her husband. Ephrem read it otherwise: she thought that it was because Jacob had not prayed for her that her closed womb had not been opened. For this reason, she said in anger and in tears, "Give me children, or I shall die.[17]

Jacob became angry with Rachel and said, "Can I take the place of God, who has denied you the fruit of the womb?"

Rightly did Jacob reprove her—it is the LORD's doing.

She replied, "Here is my maidservant Bilhah. Have intercourse with her, and let her give birth on my knees, so that and I too may have children through her."

---

17. Ephrem, *Commentary on Genesis* 28.11, in ACCS 2:199.

The Sarah-Hagar scenario repeats itself. A father would take a newborn on his knees to confirm paternity; Rachel mimics this custom. A male child establishes her rights to inheritance. "I too may have children through her" may be rendered, "I too may be built up through her"[18]—the very words of Sarai in Gen 16:2. Rachel too wants a "house" after her name.

So she gave him her maidservant Bilhah as wife. Bilhah conceived and bore a son for Jacob. Rachel said, "God has vindicated me; indeed he has heeded my plea and given me a son." Therefore she named him Dan.

The phrase "for Jacob" is new. Leah had treated the children she bore so far as a possession that would win the love of Jacob. Dan in Hebrew means "judgment." The Hebrew for "he has heeded my plea" can also be rendered, "he has heard my cry" (*qôlî*)—of distress.

Rachel's maidservant conceived again and bore a second son for Jacob, and Rachel said, "I have wrestled strenuously with my sister, and I have prevailed." So she named him Naphtali.

The Hebrew has "wrestlings of God." The translators understood "of God" as a superlative. But it can be understood in terms of wrestling with God in prayer. For in what sense could Rachel vanquish her sister who already had four sons![19]

When Leah saw that she had ceased to bear children, she took her maidservant Zilpah and gave her to Jacob as wife. So Leah's maidservant Zilpah bore a son for Jacob. Leah then said, "What good luck!" So she named him Gad. Then Leah's maidservant Zilpah bore a second son to Jacob; and Leah said, "What good fortune, because women will call me fortunate!" So she named him Asher.

"Gad" in Hebrew means "luck," or the god of luck; "Asher" is denominative of *ashrei*, "happy/fortunate are."

One day, during the wheat harvest, Reuben went out and came upon some mandrakes in the field which he brought home to his mother Leah. "Was it not enough for you to take away my husband, that you must now take my son's mandrakes too?"

---

18. One is denominative of *bēn*, "son"; the other of *banah*, "to build."

19. Gunkel, *Genesis*, 325.

Mandrakes look like tomatoes. Its Hebrew name sounds like the word for breast and for sexual pleasure—it was considered an aphrodisiac. God can do with some little help. Rachel sought the mandrakes from Leah who gave her some on condition that Jacob would sleep with her that night. Leah's retort is revealing. Jacob's sibling rivalry with Esau resonates in the sibling rivalry between Leah and Rachel.[20]

That evening, when Jacob came in from the field, Leah went out to meet him. She said, "You must have intercourse with me because I have hired you with my son's mandrakes." So that night he lay with her, and God listened to Leah; she conceived and bore a fifth son to Jacob. Leah then said, "God has given me my wages for giving my maidservant to my husband"; so she named him Issachar.

We learn that Jacob customarily spent the night with Rachel,[21] when Exod 21:10 requires equity of treatment and conjugal rights in such situations. Leah must even *pay* to have Jacob sleep with her again.[22] Issachar is denominative of the verb *śakar*, "to hire."

Leah conceived again and bore a sixth son to Jacob; and Leah said, "God has brought me a precious gift. This time my husband will honor me, because I have borne him six sons"; so she named him Zebulun. Afterwards she gave birth to a daughter, and she named her Dinah. Then God remembered Rachel. God listened to her and made her fruitful. She conceived and bore a son, and she said, "God has removed my disgrace." She named him Joseph, saying "May the Lord add another son for me!"

A double etiology is given for Joseph—from the verb *'asaph*, "to gather/remove," and from the verb *yasaph*, "to add." Rachel already prays for another son after him. There are now twelve children, though one, Dinah, is a daughter. She is placeholder for Benjamin, but also mentioned because she will be the subject of Genesis 34. Rachel conceived because God remembered her. What about the mandrakes? Did they work for Leah and not for Rachel? Is God solely responsible for conception? There is much "interweaving of divine and human roles" in this story, suggesting that "non-divine factors might be effective in enhancing potency."[23] The result somewhat relativizes the narrator's view that it all depends on

---

20. Abramsky, "Jacob Wrestles the Angel," 112.
21. Gunkel, *Genesis*, 326.
22. Mann, *Book of the Torah*, 72.
23. Fretheim, "Genesis," 193, 194.

God.²⁴ To what extent may a believer avail of various processes to enable conception?

Two Deceivers Compete: Jacob Outwits Laban, 30:25–43

After Rachel gave birth to Joseph, Jacob said to Laban, "Allow me to go to my own region and land. Give me my wives and my children for whom I served you and let me go, for you know the service that I rendered you."

Clearly, Jacob is not free to leave. In one sentence, 30:26, the key root *serve* appears three times—despite the "blessing," he is the one serving, not the other way round! *Shalḥēnî* (send me forth) is the technical term for the manumission of one in service to another.²⁵ It also mirrors²⁶ Moses' request of Pharaoh in Exod 5:1–3: "let my people go . . ." The patriarch Jacob is about to experience in his own life what the Hebrews would experience in theirs, moving from oppression in a foreign land to their own God-given land. Deut 15:13–14 legislates that such a person not be sent away empty-handed, rather be weighed down with gifts from your flock, and threshing floor and wine press. But Laban was in no mood even to release Jacob from his service.

Laban answered him, "if you will please! I have learned through divination that the LORD has blessed me because of you." He continued, "State the wages I owe you, and I will pay them."

Laban's god is not YHWH, yet through his own religious means he learned of YHWH's blessing of his family through Jacob. This raises the question of the extent to which there may be revelation in traditional religions. The more Jacob stays, the more the blessing. So, Laban asked Jacob to name his price! The blessing promised Abraham for all families of earth is working for Laban, the deceiver, through Jacob.

Jacob replied, "You know the work I did for you and how well your livestock fared under my care; the little you had before I came has grown into an abundance, since the Lord has blessed you in my company. Now when can I do something for my household as well?"

---

24. *Tg. Neof.* at Gen 30:22: there are four keys that the master of all the world keeps to himself—rain, provision, sepulchers, and barrenness. See also *Gen. Rab.* 73:4.

25. Sarna, *Genesis*, 211.

26. See further to this in Fretheim, "Genesis, 199.

The case is plain. To Laban's question, *"What should I give you?"* Jacob proposes that his wages be every dark animal among the lambs and every spotted or speckled one among the goats. Lambs in the place are usually white or light grey, goats dark brown or black. Laban, whose name means "white," gets everything white among the flock. Jacob proposes to take the tiny minority that bear the colors he outlined. One reason: if in doubt about Jacob's probity, Laban can always crosscheck the color of the flock; besides, flocks of Jacob's description would be so few that Laban would jump for it. It was a master con act. Jacob had something up his sleeves.

Laban said, "Very well. Let it be as you say." [He] put them in the care of his sons, and put three days' journey between himself and Jacob.

Laban immediately separated the flock of Jacob's description. The rest of his flock Laban left for Jacob to pasture. The result: Jacob starts off with zero flock as his own! He is at his wits end to survive. He did two things. Firstly, he separated the weaker animals; these *would go to Laban, but the hardy ones to Jacob*. Secondly, he set up striped shoots in front of the goats while they mated, so the offspring came out striped. Jacob made mating lambs to face the streaked or completely dark flock of Laban. He responds to Laban's deceit with deceit of Laban concerning the division of the herd.[27]

So the man grew exceedingly prosperous, and he owned large flocks, male and female servants, camels, and donkeys.

How do we evaluate Jacob's actions morally? That "His cunning is the use of ingenuity against the one who has superior power. It cannot be described as deception"?[28] The narrator seems to concur, for at 31:9–10 Jacob attributed his artifice to a vision in a dream from God. He said, "God took away your father's livestock and gave it to me." This may be a theological justification, but does it excuse Jacob? God has his ways of working through and around the actions of humans, good and evil. "God does not inspire the brothers [Jacob and Esau] to their immoral deed, but makes creative use of desires and acts that were self-serving or destructive . . . any more than later God had decided to have Jesus betrayed and therefore somehow inspired Judas to betray him. In such events, both

---

27. Abramsky, "Jacob Wrestles the Angel," 112.
28. Westermann, *Genesis 12–36*, 482.

God's design and human design are involved, but the former is working against the latter."[29]

Jacob Escapes Laban, 31:1–24

Jacob heard that Laban's sons were saying, "Jacob has taken everything that belonged to our father, and he has produced all this wealth from our father's property. Jacob perceived too, that Laban's attitude toward him was not what it had previously been.

The relationship was never cozy, but it has now become hostile. We later learn that Laban tried to fix this by altering the arrangements for Jacob's wages several times, but Jacob always managed to outwit him.

Then The LORD said to Jacob: Return to the land of your ancestors, where you were born, and I will be with you.

The Lord confirms Jacob's premonitions and commands him to return home. This may have been a later theologizing of Jacob's decision, as often happens in this unit. The promise of "being with" is a reminder of the promise, "I am with you and will protect you wherever you go and bring you back to this land" (Gen 28:15). The reader waits for the LORD to do some accounting with Jacob. Point is, "God's promise, 'I will be with you,' is as much terror as consolation; it is an awful thing to fall into the hands of the living God."[30] "Jacob faces his fate through faith. He follows God's wish to return to Haran, alone to face Esau's wrath and his 400 soldiers."[31]

> Not fulfilled was Rebekah's saying (Gen 27:45) that she would send for Jacob when Esau's anger cooled. In fact, Rebekah is not mentioned at Jacob's return to Isaac in Hebron and Isaac's burial by Jacob and Esau (Gen 35:27–29).

So Jacob sent for Rachel and Leah to meet him in the field where his flock was.

---

29. Goldingay, *Israel's Gospel*, 258, 260.
30. Wink, "On Wrestling with God," 140.
31. Abramsky, "Jacob Wrestles the Angel," 113.

Their going forth to him would arouse no suspicion; it could be seen as conjugal visit. Jacob laid out the case. He has served their father with all his strength,

Yet your father cheated me and changed my wages ten times. God, however, did not let him do me any harm.

If he apportioned Jacob the speckled animals, the entire flock would bear speckled young; if streaked animals, the entire flock would bear streaked animals. What he did not mention was how he engineered all this. Rather it was all God's work:

So God took away your father's livestock and gave it to me. "All the he-goats that are mating are streaked, speckled and mottled, for I have seen all the things that Laban has been doing to you."

All his efforts to engineer the conception of desired flock give way to revelation in a dream by an angel! It was the hand of God; God has been with me. He did not defraud Laban, rather his riches resulted from divine guidance and assistance. The angel merges with God:

I am the God of Bethel, where you anointed a sacred pillar and made a vow to me. Get up now! Leave this land and return to the land of your birth. Rachel and Leah answered him: "Do we still have an heir's portion in our father's house? Are we not regarded by him as outsiders? He not only sold us; he has even used up the money that he got for us! All the wealth that God took away from our father really belongs to us and our children. So do whatever God has told you.

The wives buy into Jacob's thesis. They have their own scores to settle with their father. They accuse him of alienation, of treating them as a commodity to be bought and sold. He viewed their marriage in transactional terms; his relationship with Jacob was transactional and not familial as it should be between a father-in-law and a son-in-law, the husband of his daughters. He used up all their bride wealth, when a decent father gives his daughter at least part of the *mohar* (bride wealth) to take with her into the marriage.[32] Having secured the agreement of his wives,

Jacob proceeded to put his children and wives on camels, and he drove off all his livestock and all the property he had acquired in Paddan-aram, to go to his father Isaac in the land of Canaan.

---

32. Gunkel, *Genesis*, 326.

Paddan-aram is a name for the area other sources call Haran. "He tries another escape, exiting the community to resolve his problems, another failed attempt to deal with issues by running."[33] He cannot keep running; he will soon encounter himself. When to his wives Jacob presented the increase of his flock as all work of God,[34] his grasping nature begins to open up to gratuitousness, his character begins to change.

Now Laban was away shearing his sheep, and Rachel had stolen his father's household gods . . . Once he was across the Euphrates, he headed for the hill country of Gilead.

Jacob availed of Laban's absence to flee in secret. The omniscient narrator gives advance notice of the theft of the household gods. These *teraphîm* in human shape functioned as *tutela domus*, guardian of the house, assuring good luck and protection from evil; they may also feature in inheritance claims.

On the third day, word came to Laban that Jacob had fled. Taking his kinsmen with him, he pursued him for seven days until he caught up with him in the hill country of Gilead. But that night God appeared to Laban the Aramean in a dream and said to him, "Take care not to say anything to Jacob."

That he took his kinsmen with him signals hostile intent, but God intervened with a warning against doing harm to Jacob.

Jacob and Laban in Gilead, 31:25—32:1

Laban said to Jacob, "how could you hoodwink me and carry off my daughters like prisoners of war? Why did you dupe me by stealing away secretly? You did not tell me! . . . You did not even allow me a parting kiss to my daughters and grandchildren . . . I have it in my power to harm all of you; but last night the God of your father said to me, "Take care not to say anything to Jacob! Granted that you had to leave because you were longing for your father's house, why did you steal my gods?"

Laban pitched his tent on the hill opposite Jacob's tent—a usual battle formation. Prisoners of war are carried off unceremoniously; Laban accused

---

33. Abramsky, "Jacob Wrestles the Angel," 112.

34. We mentioned above this might have come from a theologizing hand working over the material.

Jacob of not allowing him the usual parting rituals. Deflecting possible critique, he asserts that he could have given Jacob no cause for such stealth behavior. Jacob must have become so homesick as to act irrationally. His stealth in leaving is like that of a thief—the root "to steal" occurs thrice.[35] In fact, the punch line ends with the accusation of theft—"why did you steal my gods?" One is amused at gods who cannot defend themselves! Worse will follow.

Jacob replied to Laban, "I was frightened at the thought that you might take your daughters away from me by force."

Laban accused Jacob of theft (*ganab*, steal); Jacob feared he intended to kidnap (*gazal*, kidnap) his daughters and their children. With the kinsmen of both as witnesses, Laban is welcome to identify and carry off whatever belongs to him.

As for your gods, the one you find them with shall not remain alive! . . . Jacob had no idea that Rachel had stolen the household images.

Laban rummaged through Jacob's tent, then Leah's and the maidservants' before Rachel's tent. Meanwhile Rachel had taken the household images, put them inside the camel's saddlebag, and seated herself upon them. She said to her father,

"Do not let my lord be angry that I cannot rise in your presence; I am having my period." "What crime or offense have I committed that you should hound me?"

The images are not only impotent, they suffer pollution and desecration. It was now Jacob's turn. Laban should produce for the kinship as witness whatever of his he found in Jacob's keep. We learn more about the conditions of his twenty-year service.

No ewe or she goat of your ever miscarried, and I have never eaten rams of your flock.

A shepherd who lost flock to a wild beast and brings evidence of the mangled animal is not bound to restitution (Exod 22:12). But Jacob rather bore the loss himself. Further,

---

35. Literally: "you have stolen my heart," v. 26 (you have deceived me); "you have stolen me," v. 27 (hoodwinked me); "why have you stolen my gods?" v. 30.

"You held me responsible for anything stolen by day or night." Besides, "You changed my wages ten times. If the God of my father, the God of Abraham and the Fear of Isaac had not been on my side, you would now have sent me away empty-handed. But God saw my plight and the fruits of my toil, and last night he reproached you."

Jacob's was not just indentured service; Laban was an unjust and mean employer, even of his very son-in-law. Each patriarch related personally and intimately to a "god of the father": Abraham to El Shaddai, Isaac to the Fear of Isaac (Gen 31:42), and Jacob himself to "the Mighty One of Jacob" (Gen 49:24). *Paḥad Isaac* can also be rendered "the one whom Isaac reveres," or "the one of Isaac who causes terror"—as in Laban's dream.[36] Laban replied to Jacob,

"The daughters are mine, their children are mine, and the flocks are mine; everything you see belongs to me. What can I do now for my own daughters and for the children they have born? Come, now, let us make a covenant, you and I; and it will be a treaty between you and me."

It is as if Laban is saying that all he could have given his daughters and grandchildren are now in Jacob's hands. All he can now do is provide for their future peace and welfare through a covenant. From this point the characters Jacob and Laban change. The story is no longer about two individuals, but about two nations, Israel and Aram. Boundary demarcation by treaty is between peoples, not individuals.

> Some confusion about who does what here derives perhaps from diverse traditions. Jacob took a stone and set it up as a *maṣṣebah*, sacred pillar ... gathered stones and made a cairn, (v. 45, 46); in verse 51, Laban said, "here is this mound, and here is the sacred pillar that I have set up ..." Cairn and sacred pillar serve as witness[37] to the treaty (vv. 45, 46); in verse 48, they serve as boundary markers.

The treaty is a parity treaty between equals; each swears by his god and names the cairn by his own language. Laban called it in Aramaic, *Jegar-sahadutha*, Jacob called it, in Hebrew, *Galeed*. Both mean "the mound of witness." The mound was also called Mizpah,

---

36. Sarna, *Genesis*, 220.
37. See Josh 24:27 for mound of stones serving as witness to a covenant.

For he [Laban] said, "May the Lord keep watch between you and me when we are out of each other's sight. If you mistreat my daughters or take other wives besides my daughters know that even though no one else is there God will be a witness between you and me."

Mizpah is a town in Gilead; literally it means "an observation post." The root *ṣaphah* means "to look out." A similar contract from Nuzi stipulates: "if Wullu takes another wife, he shall forfeit the lands and houses of Nashwi [his father-in-law]."[38] Laban to Jacob:

"This mound will be a witness, and this sacred pillar will be a witness, that, with hostile intent, I may not pass beyond this mound into your territory, nor may you pass beyond it into mine. May the God of Abraham and the God of Nahor, the God of their father, judge between us!" Jacob took the oath by the Fear of his father Isaac.

The covenant is ratified by a meal (v. 46) and a sacrifice on the mountain (v. 54).

Early the next morning, Laban kissed his grandchildren and his daughters and blessed them; then he set out on his journey back home.

Laban kissed his daughters and grandchildren, no kiss or embrace for Jacob—the family simply breaks.[39] There is peace secured by treaty, but no reconciliation. As Jacob returns to the land, its eastern boundary is secured. Securing the southern border will hang on Jacob's dealings with Esau in Genesis 32–33.

Tradition

The question that still comes up today when the gospel meets agrarian cultures for the first time is: should a polygamous husband have to dismiss all wives except one before baptism? What obligation has he to the dismissed wives and their children? The fathers of the church faced similar questions in respect of the marriage of the patriarchs to several wives. The response below does not answer all the questions.

"In those times, you see, since it was the very beginning, people were allowed to live with two or three wives or more so as to increase the race; now, on the contrary, because through God's grace the human race

---

38. Sarna, *Genesis*, 222.
39. Coats, "Strife and Reconciliation," 31.

has expanded into a vast number, the practice of virtue has also increased ... since the practice itself was evil, see how it has been rooted out, and no one is free now to propose it."[40]

Laban's search of Jacob's household gave rise to allegory. Laban, whose name means "'lie that has been purified'—and even Satan transfigures himself into an angel of light—came to Jacob and began to demand his possession from him." Jacob answered him, "identify whatever of yours I may have," that is, "I have nothing of yours. See if you recognize any of your vices and crimes..."[41]

Can Rachel's stealing of the household gods be justified?[42] Her purpose was a noble one, for she said, "what, shall we go and leave this old man in his errors!" (*Gen. Rab.* 74:5). It might also be, lest they tell Laban that Jacob was leaving with his wives and children. Josephus gives a very practical reason: should Laban catch up with them, they might have recourse to the *teraphîm* in order to obtain a pardon.[43]

---

40. Chrysostom, *Homilies on Genesis* 56.12, in ACCS 2:197.
41. Ambrose, *Jacob and the Happy Life* 5.24, in ACCS 2:210.
42. On this, see Kugel, *Traditions*, 383-84.
43. Josephus, *Ant.* 1:310.

CHAPTER 19

Genesis 32–33

Jacob Renamed Israel; Jacob Encounters Esau

> The cycle that began with two brothers "crashing together" reaches its climax with Jacob and Yahweh fighting together.[1]

THE STORY OF JACOB and Esau has been one of rivalry and conflict. The long-running tension between the two is resolved in these chapters.

Jacob fled from home because his twin had resolved to kill him once the obsequies of the father was over. He absconded from Laban and his children furious at manipulations with the herd that enriched Jacob at their expense. The Lord stuck with Jacob all along, having promised, "I am with you and will protect you wherever you go, and bring you back to this land. I will never leave you until I have done what I promised you" (Gen 28:15). The narrator let the story itself comment obliquely on the morality of Jacob's conduct. Now at the boundary of the Promised Land, Jacob finds he cannot become Israel until he reckons with both the protecting God and the angry brother. The remarkable intersection of the human and the divine in these chapters shows clearly that "the life one lives with God and the life one lives with other human beings are two sides of the same coin."[2]

---

1. Mann, *Story of Torah*, 78.
2. Fretheim, "Genesis," 210.

Jacob Sends Messengers to Esau, 32:1–22

Early the next morning, Laban kissed his grandchildren and his daughters and blessed them; then he set out on his journey back home.

Laban kissed his daughters and grandchildren, no kiss or embrace for Jacob—the family simply breaks.³ There is peace secured by treaty, but no reconciliation.

Meanwhile Jacob continued on his way and God's angels encountered him.

> The angel of the Lord encamps around those who fear him, and he saves them. (Ps 34:8)

Angels appear without saying or doing anything.⁴ In his flight (Genesis 28) and now at his return, God's angels encounter him. They symbolize God's promised presence and protection.⁵

When Jacob saw them he said, "This is God's encampment." So he named the place Mahanaim.

The etiology plays on the term *maḥaneh* (camp). Mahanaim means "two camps": God's angels form "God's camp" over against and protecting Jacob's camp. Jacob will himself soon divide into two camps (vv. 8 and 11).

Jacob sent messengers ahead to his brother Esau in the land of Seir, the country of Edom, ordering them: Thus you shall say to my lord Esau: 'Thus says your servant Jacob . . . I have sent my lord this message in the hope of gaining your favor.'"

Angels are *mal'akîm*; the messengers sent are also *mal'akîm*. The semantic range of the word continues the intersection of the human and the divine.⁶ The "messenger formula," through which messengers speak in the person of the sender, enables Jacob to present himself to Esau in

---

3. Coats, "Strife and Reconciliation," 31.
4. Gunkel, *Genesis*, 342.
5. Westermann, *Genesis 12–36*, 504: *mal'akê Elohîm* (angels of God) occur in only these two places—Genesis 28 and 32. *Mal'ak YHWH* (angel of the LORD) is always singular.
6. See Anderson, "Intersection of Human and Divine," 33.

terms of "my lord"/"your servant." This language incidentally reverses the blessing of Gen 27:27–29; it is the language of a vassal towards the great king. Jacob makes it clear from the outset that he retains no pretensions to superiority or rule over his twin. Every gesture speaks of his desire for forgiveness and reconciliation. "To find favor in your sight" introduces the leitmotif of *ḥēn* (favor) with its root, *ḥanan* (to show favor, to be favorably disposed towards someone). These terms speak of gratuitousness—favor is not based on merit. Jacob, who all along relied on his acumen and strength, is beginning to discover grace.

When the messengers returned to Jacob, they said, "We found your brother Esau. He is now coming to meet you, and four hundred men are with him."

The verb "to meet" (*li-qr'āt*) may signal the positive sense of peaceful encounter or the negative sense of attack. The four hundred men with Esau suggested the latter sense to Jacob. He took it for granted that Esau was coming for revenge.

Jacob was very much frightened. In his anxiety, he divided the people who were with him, as well as his flocks, herds and camels, into two camps.

His reason was to cut his losses; if Esau attacks the first camp, the other may yet escape, with Jacob. He would not have to meet Esau face to face.

Then Jacob prayed. "God of my father Abraham and God of my father Isaac! . . . I am unworthy of all the acts of kindness and faithfulness that you have performed for your servant: although I crossed the Jordan here with nothing but my staff, I have now grown into two camps. Save me from the hand of my brother, from the hand of Esau! . . . You yourself said, 'I will be very good to you, and I will make your descendants like the sands of the sea, which are too numerous to count.'"

The text did not call it a prayer; it simply had, "and Jacob said." It is the prayer of someone in need. He began with an *invocation*[7] of the God of his fathers, Abraham and Isaac. In Gen 28:20–21 he had vowed that if the LORD protected him on the journey and he came back safe, "the LORD will be my God." We are about to learn how the LORD became Jacob's God. Next was *confession*. God held steadfastly to his promise (*emeth*) and showed him much *ḥesed*. This word has no direct English equivalent, but it is in the field of lovingkindness, merciful love, unmerited love.

---

7. For analysis of this prayer, see Sarna, *Genesis*, 225.

Jacob professes himself unworthy of all this divine graciousness, using the term *qāṭonti min,* "I am more little than,"[8] I in no way deserve this. "No longer bargaining, he acknowledges that all he has comes as a gift from God and, while he asks for protection in going to meet Esau, he is ready to accept whatever happens without conditions, trusting in God's continued goodness."[9] He had absolutely nothing when he fled from home; now he was so wealthy. "With only my staff I crossed *this Jordan.*" But he was standing at the River Jabbok![10] In Judg 11:13, 22, the Jabbok is the eastern frontier of Israel; hence "this Jordan" resonates with "cross this Jordan" used of entering to possess Canaan (Deut 31:2; Josh 1:2). Now comes *supplication.* His urgent need was that of rescue from the hands of Esau. He feared that in rage Esau might kill all—Jacob, his wives and children—and take over the herd and flock. The basis for his petition is God's own command to return home and God's promise of protection; besides, the promise of countless descendants calls for a future. Jacob is unworthy; God has been good and is trusted to deliver on his promises. God's promise to him of descendants appears nowhere in the Jacob story; it was rather given to Abraham and confirmed to Isaac (Gen 15:4; 26:4).

"Pray as if all depended on God. Work as if all depended on you."[11] Ever the man to pray and plan, Jacob set himself to confront the situation.

Jacob selected from what he had with him a present for his brother Esau.

The presents numbered 550 herds of cattle and flock. He put them in separate droves in the charge of servants, with some distance between the droves. When Esau asks,

"To whom do you belong? Where are you going? To whom do these animals ahead of you belong?" Tell him: *"To your servant Jacob, but they have been sent as a gift to my lord Esau. Jacob himself is right behind us."* For Jacob reasoned: *"If I first appease him with a gift that precedes me, then later, when I face him, perhaps he will forgive me."*

---

8. Significant, for *ha-qāṭon* is the younger brother, something Jacob fought off till now.

9. Kille, "Jacob," 15.

10. Sarna, *Genesis,* 225: standing on the banks of the Jabbok, he can point to the Jordan clearly visible in the distance.

11. This saying is attributed to St. Augustine. The *Catechism* no. 2834 attributed it to St. Ignatius of Loyola. Cf. Guibert, *Jesuits,* 148, no. 55.

Esau's anticipated questions imply that he controlled the right of passage. Jacob continues the "lord/servant" language. The presents are designated as *minḥah*, a word also used for a tribute from a vassal to an overlord! The text plays with the motif of "face" (*pānîm*)—the face-to-face encounter will be decisive for the antagonists.

> Go before my face—*le-pānai* (32:17); whose are these animals before your face—*le-pānekā* (32:19); perhaps he will lift up my face = be gracious, forgive (32:20); let me appease his face—*pānāw*—with gifts (32:21); the gift went before his face = ahead (32:21); Peniel = face of God (32:30); I see your face as seeing the face of God (33:10).

"If I first appease him with a gift" (32:21) borrows from the ritual of sacrifice. The expression "cover the face" (*kipper pānîm*) is usual for "to atone" and always involves guilt[12]—Jacob recognized that Esau's wrath was justified and so was making atonement, but in the Eastern manner uses the language of gestures.

The Wrestling at Night: Jacob Becomes Israel, 32:23-33

So the gifts went on ahead of him, while he stayed that night in the camp. That night, however, Jacob arose, took his two wives, with the two maidservants and his eleven children, and crossed the ford of the Jabbok . . . Jacob was left there alone. Then a man wrestled with him until the break of dawn.

"His eleven children" strangely leaves out of account Dinah, daughter of Leah, who brought the number to twelve (Gen 30:21). Genesis 34 will be all about her.

> The LORD has a dispute with Judah, and will punish Jacob for his conduct, and repay him for his deeds. In the womb he supplanted his brother, and in his vigor he contended with a divine being; He contended with an angel and prevailed, he wept and entreated. At Bethel he met with him, and there he spoke with him. (Hos 12:3-5)

---

12. Westermann, *Genesis 12-36*, 510 remarks that only here and in Prov 16:17 is this term used for something that happens between humans.

The parallel in Hos 12:4-5 (see text box above) calls the antagonist both *Elohim* (God, divine being) and *mal'āk* (angel); the verb *śarah*, which underlies the name Israel, occurs only in these. Jacob himself identified the adversary with God when he spoke of seeing God face to face. Elements of the story suggest that "originally, the legend was independent and had nothing to do with the Jacob-Esau narrative."[13] The god who must disappear before dawn cannot be YHWH. An ancient legend has been updated, but left ambiguous and mysterious in order to symbolize spiritual realities. It thus operates on different levels at once. The stranger may be an angel, God's emissary, representing God's will. Election calls for wrestling with the divine will and purpose. He may be the guardian prince (angel) of Esau—nations and individuals had patron angels presiding over their destiny and protecting them (*Gen. Rab.* 77:3). A psychologist may see Jacob wrestling with his shadow.[14] He uses his strength, talents, and tenacity to obtain legitimately what he got before through deception—this is genuine transformation.[15] At another level of meaning, the adversary represents Esau; shedding deception as the way to handle his desires, Jacob meets Esau face to face. Jacob himself interpreted his encounter with the adversary in terms of his encounter with Esau: "to see your face is for me like seeing the face of God" (Gen 33:10). The struggle is symbolic—it displaces conflict with Esau.[16] Proleptic of what will happen in the encounter with Esau, it symbolizes that Jacob will not only be spared, but will come back into the graces of his twin brother.

When the man saw that he could not prevail over him, he struck Jacob's hip at its socket, so that Jacob's socket was dislocated as he wrestled with him.

This maneuver should have been decisive, but it failed to settle the score. We know that Jacob had suprahuman strength (Gen 29:10). Jacob apparently now had the advantage, especially as the being was anxious to beat the dawn.[17] However, Jacob was no longer the same: the verb *yq'* ("to dislocate") inverts the very letters of Jacob's name (*y'qb*)! The adversary had touched him at his most sensitive point: his rugged tenacity and self-confidence. For the first time, Jacob learns to ask for the graces of another.

---

13. Gunkel, *Genesis*, 353.
14. Wink, "On Wrestling with God," 137.
15. For these suggestions see Abramsky, "Jacob Wrestles the Angel," 113.
16. Barthes, "Struggle with the Angel," 134.
17. Barthes, "Struggle with the Angel," 131.

The man then said, "Let me go, for it is daybreak." But Jacob said, "I will not let you go until you bless me." "What is your name," the man asked. He answered, "Jacob." Then the man said, "You shall no longer be named Jacob, but Israel, because you have contended with divine and human beings and have prevailed." Jacob then asked him, "Please tell me your name." He answered, "Why do you ask for my name?" With that, he blessed him.

> For it is God who sets before us our need for healing, God who meets us in the wound, God the terror that frightens us in the darkness of the unknown life that wells up from our own depths, God who needs our healing, God who heals us. (Wink, "On Wrestling with God," 141–42)

Recognizing "the man" as an otherworldly being, Jacob asked for blessing. Some read this as a request for the transfer of the rival's superhuman strength.[18] Rather, Jacob is in quest of blessing; his guilty conscience doubted the stolen blessing, and anxiety about what to expect at the hands of his brother plagued him. Yet, this is quintessence Jacob—trying by effort to grasp what can be obtained only by grace.[19] Following linguistic rules, "Isra-el" should mean something like "God rules" or "God strives" or "he whom God fights"—El/God as subject of the verb. However, the etiology understands El/God as the object. But, what does it mean to "contend" (using the root, *śarah*) with God (*Elohim*) and prevail?[20] This made sense in the earlier levels of the legend, but not if Elohim stands for the God Jacob worships. In the immediate context, it signified success at Jacob's coming encounter with Esau. The believer asks:

> is it possible for man to obtain God's blessing through strictly human efforts? Does there come a time in each believer's life when he is forced to lean completely on God and cling to him in helplessness and so receive the blessing that God desires to give him? Often believers are tempted to rely on their own strength and cunning when it comes to temporal things and on God only

---

18. Westermann, *Genesis 12–36*, 518. He adds that in no other place in the Old Testament can blessing be won through a struggle. Sarna, *Genesis*, 227 thinks that the bestowal of the new name constitutes the essence of the blessing and climax of the whole episode. My point is that "with that he blessed him" comes *after* the change of name.

19. Kaiser, "Jacob Wrestles with God," 85.

20. The root *śarah* appears only here and in Hos 12:4–5.

as a last resort. Examples of the failure of such reliance are plentiful throughout Scripture, but in Genesis 32 Jacob finds himself physically wrestling with God in an attempt to secure his blessing and protection.[21]

The narrative operates on two levels: Jacob, the man, is about to become Israel,[22] the nation.[23] Rashi comments: it will no longer be said that the blessing came to you through deviousness (*'oqbah*), but instead through lordliness (*serarah*). The Jacob to inherit the blessing will be a transformed Jacob who must beg for the blessing. God's opposition finally raises the moral question the reader has been waiting for. Yet, it shows how far God is willing to go with even a deceitful crook. Theologically, "this event . . . [is] a type of that which Israel experienced from time to time with God. Israel has here presented its entire history with God almost prophetically as such a struggle until the breaking of the day."[24]

Jacob named the place Peniel, "because I have seen God face to face," he said, "yet my life has been spared." At sunrise, as he left Penuel, Jacob limped along because of his hip. That is why, to this day, the Israelites do not eat the sciatic muscle that is on the hip socket . . .

Peniel or Penuel means "the face of God," hence the name enshrines Jacob's experience. But, did Jacob really see the "face of God" since the struggle was all in the dark? Besides, "face to face" with God is said only of Moses: "if there are prophets among you, in visions I reveal myself to them . . . not so with my servant Moses! . . . face to face I speak to him" (Num 12:6–7). And Deut 34:10 has it that "since then no prophet has arisen in Israel like Moses, whom the Lord knew face to face." See the discussion below in Ambrosiaster, *Questions on the Old and New Testaments*.

> Complicating the matter is that within the one chapter of Exodus 33 it is said both, "The Lord used to speak to Moses face to face as a person speaks to a friend" (v. 11), and later the Lord said to him, "but you cannot see my face, for no one can see me and live" (v. 20). Such juxtapositions happen when a later

21. Vawter, "Jacob's Experience at Jabbok," 1.
22. Geller, "Struggle at Jabbok," 50.
23. The first historical documentation of the existence of Israel in Canaan is in the Merneptah Stele around 1230 BCE.
24. Von Rad, *Genesis*, 325. See also Ross, "Jacob at the Jabbok," 351.

conception seeks to correct an earlier one, or when two views are purposely crashed together to induce further reflection.

Realizing that God was his adversary, Jacob saw himself as graced and saved from death—for one who saw God should die instantly. Reference to a dieting custom of the "sons of Israel" (Gen 32:33) is the first time "Israel" appears as a nation in this narrative. The prohibition detailed here does not occur in the laws at Sinai. The rabbis explain this by saying that before Sinai any meat could be eaten. In the continuing narrative, Jacob will be called both Jacob and Israel, depending on the point of view.

The point of the story for the nation of Israel entering the land of promise is clear: Israel's victory will come not by the usual ways nations gain power, but by the power of the divine blessing. And later in her history Israel would be reminded that the restoration to the land would not be by might, nor by strength, but by the Spirit of the Lord God, who fights for his people (Zech 4:6).[25]

Jacob Encounters Esau, 33:1–11

Jacob looked up and saw Esau coming, and with him four hundred men. So he divided his children among Leah, Rachel, and the two maidservants, putting the maidservants and their children first, Leah and her children next, and Rachel and Joseph last.

The fateful encounter is upon Jacob, for better or for worse. Esau's intentions are unknown. Jacob lined up his wives and children in order of preference, his beloved Rachel and her son last. With resolution and courage derived from his experience, he put himself at the head of the procession—a gesture of self-sacrifice. Should Esau's intentions be hostile, he, Jacob, would be the first casualty; the rest may escape or be abducted.

He himself went on ahead of them,[26] bowing to the ground seven times, until he reached his brother. Esau ran to meet him, embraced him, and flinging himself on his neck, kissed him as he wept.

---

25. Ross, "Jacob at the Jabbok," 351.
26. *Tg. Ps.-J.* adds that he was praying and beseeching mercy from the LORD.

"The Meeting of Jacob and Esau" by Gustave Doré

Gen 33:3–4 ... bowed himself to the ground seven times, ...
And Esau ran to meet him, and embraced him, and fell on his
neck, and kissed him: and they wept.

FIGURE 5: Jacob Meets Esau

Rather than nations bowing before Jacob (Gen 27:29), it is Jacob who bows to Esau. A sevenfold prostration of the vassal approaching an overlord is documented in the Amarna Letters: "at the feet of my lord, my sun, I fall seven times and seven times."[27] Esau greets Jacob as one brother greets another after a long separation;[28] Jacob sticks to the gestures of a vassal encountering his overlord. Esau calls him "brother"; Jacob calls him "my lord" and himself "your servant." The dramatic tension begins to resolve. Whatever he initially intended with the four hundred men,

27. Gunkel, *Genesis*, 347.
28. Westermann, *Genesis 12–36*, 524.

Esau does not retain the will for revenge. He takes the initiative in the process of reconciliation: his kiss writes off Jacob's deceitful kiss by which he angled for the birthright (Gen 27:26).[29] The Hebrew text has "and they wept"—Esau for joy at seeing his brother after such a long time, Jacob perhaps as emotional release of tension.

"Who are these with you?" Jacob answered, "They are the children with whom God has graciously favored your servant.

So focused was Esau on his brother that he hardly noticed the family in tow. The verb *ḥanan* (be gracious to, favor) returns on Jacob's lips—his horizons have opened up to the world of giving and receiving. Jacob's family drew up and made obeisance.

Then Esau asked, "What did you intend with all those herds that I encountered?" Jacob answered, "It was to gain my lord's favor." Esau replied, "I have plenty; my brother, you should keep what is yours."

For Esau, forgiveness is by nature a free offer and, therefore, cannot be exchanged for anything, no matter how grandiose.[30] Besides, he has suffered no disadvantage through the loss of his firstborn status, rather has even prospered.[31] Of the two, he was obviously the more powerful. Jacob had to try another tack.

"No, I beg you!" said Jacob. "If you will do me the favor, accept this gift from me, since to see your face is for me like seeing the face of God–and you have received me so kindly. Accept the gift I have brought you. For God has been generous toward me, and I have an abundance." Since he urged him strongly, Esau accepted.

Verses 10 and 11 are parallel; one defines the gift as my *minḥah* (present, tribute), the other as my *berakah* (blessing, gratitude). The *minḥah* is no longer to buy Esau's goodwill (freely given), rather to thank him for the gracious and kind reception. The encounter with Esau's face he linked with his encounter with God face to face, yet remaining alive. Esau's face brought home to him the graciousness of God; God's face symbolized Esau's gracious welcome. The *berakah* is a restitution with interest of the blessing stolen from his brother. What is more, he is so

---

29. See Sarna, *Genesis*, 229.
30. Agyenta, "Reconciliation More than 'Re-Membering,'" 125 n. 23.
31. Westermann, *Genesis 12–36*, 526.

blessed that it does not dent his resources—*yesh lî kōl* (I have everything) responds to Esau's earlier *yesh lî rāb* (v. 9: I have much).

Forgiveness and Reconciliation, 33:12–20

Then Esau said, "Let us break camp and be on our way; I will travel in front of you." But Jacob replied: "As my lord knows, the children are too young ... Let my lord, then go before his servant, while I proceed more slowly at the pace of the livestock before me and at the pace of my children, until I join my lord in Seir. So on that day Esau went on his way back to Seir, and Jacob broke camp for Succoth. There Jacob built a home for himself and made booths for his livestock. That is why the place was named Succoth.

Esau offered to put some of his men at Jacob's disposal, but Jacob gently refused. Jacob's continued use of vassalage language and the ever-cautious and deft manner in which he avoided Esau's company, even escort by Esau's men, suggests lingering misgivings, as though he was uncertain of how this newly found camaradie would work out.[32] Coats suggests that:

> Esau offers reconciliation. Jacob still offers the gift which Esau graciously accepted. Yet there is anticlimax. Esau presses for dialogue along the way home. Jacob promises to meet him later in Seir, but went on to Succoth. He rejects physical reunion, a sign of reconciliation. The brothers are separated: the strife between them becomes permanent division.[33]

> Nga mmadu abuo riri nta rie imo, otu n'ime ha nwe nta, nke ozo nwe imo.
> (Where two people ate "this" and "that" one of them owns "this" and the other owns "that").
> People move together and are happy because both of them agree and sacrifice their individual differences. (Davids, *Ilulu Igbo*, 156)

He argues that "reconciliation cannot occur if the reconciled parties continue to live apart." Jacob cannot claim reconciliation then choose to

---

32. Sarna, *Genesis*, 230.
33. Coats, "Strife without Reconciliation," 103.

ignore his brother, reject the need to confront each other.[34] However, forgiveness differs from reconciliation. Forgiveness is basically an act, reconciliation a process (which may include the act of forgiveness). Jacob's non-verbal request for pardon is unexpectedly met with Esau's renunciation of revenge (to speak of reconciliation at this point is inappropriate).[35] Reconciliation is more than a physical "re-membering" of former enemies; rather it is fundamentally a matter of attitudinal change (*metanoia*), especially from the desire to eliminate or dispossess each other to mutual respect and collaboration between former rivals. People emerging from long-standing conflict may not be expected to move to physical community without a period of trust and confidence building.[36] The brothers needed time to readjust to each other and to the changed circumstances. "The narrator [may have wanted] to say that a reconciliation between brothers need not require that they live side by side; it can also achieve its effect when they separate and each lives his own life in his own way."[37] But there must be the mutual will for a transformed relationship. The brothers may also have perceived reconciliation differently: Esau as an opportunity to blend their lives together, Jacob differently. In the end, each recognized the legitimate claim to leadership in their respective realms, allowing each to make his unique contribution without being cramped by the other.[38]

Their destinies had already been decided—Esau outside the land, Jacob within the land of Canaan. Jacob now built a home for himself and settled within his assigned portion. Succoth means "booths"—the town derives its name from the booths Jacob made for his livestock.

Jacob Settles in the Land, 33:18–20

In what must be a variant,[39] it is said that:

---

34. Coats, "Strife and Reconciliation," 26.
35. Agyenta, "Reconciliation More than Re-Membering," 127.
36. Agyenta, "Reconciliation More than Re-Membering," 132.
37. Westermann, *Genesis 12–36*, 527.
38. See Greenberger, "Esau and Jacob," 143, 153.
39. The use of Paddan-aram suggests that this variant is P.

Jacob arrived safely[40] *at the city of Shechem which is in the land of Canaan, when he came from Paddan-aram. He encamped in sight of the city. He set up an altar there and invoked "El, the God of Israel."*

This sets up the story in Genesis 34. He purchased the ground on which he pitched his tent from the descendants of Hamor, the father of Shechem. In Genesis 34, Shechem will be the prince to violate Dinah, Hamor his father. All the patriarchs have now rooted themselves in the land with a pied-à-terre. Abraham acquired the field of Machpelah facing Mamre (Genesis 23), Isaac in Beersheba (Gen 26:23–25), now Jacob in Shechem. Joseph will be buried in this field purchased by Jacob (Josh 24:32).

"Israel" here names the people, not the man Jacob. El is the supreme god in the Canaanite religion. And did Jacob not vow that if he returned safely, YHWH will be his God (Gen 28:21)? In the same piece, though, he said that this stone that I have set up as a sacred pillar will be the House of God, Beth-El (28:22). "The setting up of the altar means the beginning of the permanent cult of the cult of the God of Israel who is now 'El,' that is, God absolutely. It sees as the goal of the patriarchs' journeying the cult of the God of Israel which takes the place of the El cult."[41] The name of El is appropriated by YHWH; the worship of the God of Israel replaces the cult of the Canaanite El.

Tradition

The Struggle. In the book of Wisdom, it was Wisdom herself that engaged Jacob, not fighting against him, but aiding him in what was a spiritual struggle: "in his arduous contest she gave him the victory [helped him to victory], so that he might learn that godliness is more powerful than anything else" (Wis 10:12, NRSV). Wisdom read the preposition *'im*/with in the phrase "then a man wrestled with him" as meaning "in the company of," "with the help of."[42] In the Christian tradition, this spiritual struggle is often understood as intense prayer. Origen explained:

---

40. *Shalem*, translated as an adverb, "safely," can also be the name of a city, hence "Jacob came to Salem, the city of Shechem ..." Midrash reads it as his returning bodily whole, having been healed in the meantime, or perhaps he was whole in respect of his children or his wealth, or his learning (*Gen. Rab.* 79:5); *Tg. Neof.*: perfect in good work.

41. Westermann, *Genesis 12–36*, 529.

42. Kugel, *Traditions*, 386.

To wrestle with Jacob does not mean to wrestle against Jacob, but that the angel, who was present in order to save him, and who after learning of the progress he had made gave him the additional name of Israel, wrestled together with him, that is, was on his side in the contest and helped him in the struggle; for undoubtedly it was some other against whom Jacob was fighting and against whom his struggle was being waged.[43]

That "the man" was later in the text called "God" did not escape Christian apologists: "you struggle with a man, but you behold God face to face. You do not see with your bodily eyes what you perceive with the glance of your faith ... You recognize God in the weakness of his flesh in order to foreshadow the mystery of his blessing in the spirit."[44]

The name Israel. Philo already interpreted "Israel" as one who sees God:[45] "for seeing is the lot of the freeborn and firstborn Israel, which [name] translated is 'the one seeing God.'"[46] Origen capitalized on this for the Christian claim: "it is this people alone which is said to 'see God,' for the name Israel when translated has this meaning.[47]

Ambrosiaster says that if Jacob was called the man who sees God and Moses saw God face to face (Exod 33:11), also Isa 6:5 says, "I have seen with my own eyes the God of Hosts," then there is contradiction with the evangelist Saint John, who says, "No man has ever seen God" (1 John 4:12). His answer:

> To speak the truth, no man really saw God, neither the Father nor the Son. If the Scripture tells us that men have seen him, it is through intellect, for it can only appear to them in the figure. Just as without knowing the emperors we see them in image and not in reality, so God was seen in the sense that men understood that God appeared to them in a rational and not substantial way, for God cannot be seen in his nature. To put the difficulty of this question into all its light, let us endeavor to explain the meaning of the words of St. John. For he has wished to reveal to us a hidden truth that is part of the doctrine of salvation: "No man," he says, "has ever seen God; the only begotten Son who is in the bosom of the Father has manifested himself." (John 1:18). Let us

---

43. Origen, *On First Principles*, 3.2.5.
44. Hilary of Poitiers, *On the Trinity*, 5.19, in ACCS 2:222.
45. Philo wrote in Greek; in Hebrew this translates as *ish ra'ah El*.
46. Philo, *On Flight and Finding* 208; translation in Kugel, *Traditions*, 387.
47. Origen, *On First Principles* 4.3.2.

examine the meaning of these words of the Evangelist. To show us that it is of all truth that no man has ever seen God, he places this declaration on the lips of the Son himself who cannot be deceived because he is in the bosom of the Father. Now, what is the breast of the Father except the love of the true Father for his Son by the unity of nature that is common to them? No one, then, has ever seen God, except the only begotten Son, . . . "It is not that anyone has seen the Father, only the one who is of God has seen the Father" (John 6:46) . . . Indeed, denying that God the Father was ever seen, and yet declaring that God appeared to the patriarchs, the Son of God wants to reveal himself and show that it was he who appeared as God to their fathers . . . There is, then, no contradiction in saying that God has been both seen and invisible.[48]

The Vulgate saw in the name Israel a prophecy of victory over Esau: "for if you have been strong against God, how much more shall you be powerful against men" (see also the LXX). Jerome expanded this tradition: "moreover, if you have been able to wrestle with me, who am God or an angel, how much more shall you be able to do so with men, that is with Esau, from whom you ought to fear nothing."[49]

Philo had one of God's angels named Jacob or Israel—a heavenly counterpart to the earthly Jacob: "God's firstborn [cf. Exod 4:22], the *Logos*, who holds the eldership among the angels, their ruler, as it were. And many names are his, for he is called 'the Beginning,' and the Name of God, and his Lord, and the Man after his image, and 'he that sees,' that is, Israel."[50] *Tg. Onq.* derived the name from *śar*, prince: "for you are a prince before the Lord and among men, therefore you have prevailed." *Tg. Ps.-J.*: Israel, because you have gained superiority over the angels of the Lord and over men, and you have prevailed against them—also rejecting the idea that Jacob wrestled with God. *Elohim* in some texts can mean "divine beings." The angel wanted release before dawn because it was the time for the angels on high to praise God and he was the chief of those who praise (*Tg. Neof.*). In *Tg. Ps.-J.*, he was just one of the angels of praise, however, from the time the world was created his time to praise did not come until then. Both Targums try in this way to explain why the adversary must leave before dawn (see also *Gen. Rab.* 78:2).

48. Ambrosiaster, *Questions on the Old and New Testaments*.

49. Jerome, *Hebrew Questions on Gen* 32:28–29; for translation, see Kugel, *Traditions*, 395.

50. Philo, *Confusion of Tongues* 146, translation in Kugel, *Traditions*, 397.

Jacob's prostrations. Jacob prostrated seven times before Esau. R. Hanina: he did not cease from repeatedly prostrating himself until he converted judgment to mercy (*Gen. Rab.* 78:8). In short, the prostrations were not to Esau, but to God in prayer. The result was the mollified face of Esau.

The offer to march together. The midrash gives a completely spiritual reading of Esau's offer to march together. Esau requested partnership in Jacob's world, that is, in the future world, while in return Jacob would share this world's pleasure and greatness with him (*Gen. Rab.* 78:14). Jacob: we cannot share. I will walk *le-iṭṭî*—meekly. In this world, Israel is content not to seek material and military greatness. "Until I come to my lord in Seir" refers to the messianic era, when according to Obadiah 21 saviors shall come up on Mount Zion to judge the mount of Esau. Underlying this interpretation is the fact that "throughout tannaitic and amoraic literature, Rome is known as Edom,"[51] notwithstanding the fact that the Hasmonean priest, John Hyrcanus, erased Edom from history in the second century BCE, forcibly converting Edomites to Judaism. Rome had destroyed the temple (66–70 CE), and eventually banished Jews from Palestine after the Bar Kockba War (132–135 CE). With the decline of Rome as empire and the emergence of Christendom after Constantine, the Roman church became Edom—the persecuting brother.

---

51. Freedman, "Jacob and Esau," 114.

CHAPTER 20

Genesis 34

Dinah at Shechem

> The dilemma raised by the story is so complex and each choice so problematic that [the narrator] cannot fully identify with any of the positions taken.[1]

IN THE INTRODUCTION TO this commentary, I examined Genesis 34 in terms of how perplexing a theological reading can be. Also discussed was the role of the narrator. Sternberg speaks of "foolproof" composition:

> By foolproof composition I mean that the Bible is difficult to read, easy to underread and overread and even misread, but virtually impossible to, so to speak, counterread ... The essentials are made transparent to all comers: the story line, the world order, the value system ... The Bible always tells the truth in that its narrator is absolutely and straightforwardly reliable ... the reader cannot go far wrong even if he does little more than follow the statements made and the incidents enacted on the narrative surface. For the narrator who conveys them to him cannot go wrong himself ... nor is the narrator mendacious ... But follow the biblical narrator ever so uncritically, and by no great exertion you will be making tolerable sense of the world

---
1. Sternberg, "Delicate Balance," in *Poetics of Biblical Narrative*, 475.

you are in, the action that enfolds, the protagonists on stage, and the point of it all.[2]

He believes that vacillation between options there may be, though the narrator always indicates where his sympathies lie.[3] However, as the close reading will show, parts of the story are inconsistent, anachronisms and other features suggest a rereading of the text in a different setting with meanings not exactly consistent with or flowing from earlier ones. The narrator(s) appear(s) conflicted; the suture between readings is evident. In relation to the role of the narrator for the truth of Scripture, I concluded in that examination as follows: "Our perplexity with this text shows that the biblical text does not always give clear guidance to conduct, that theological interpretation is a drama in which one ever seeks to ponder God's word in relation to concrete circumstances that can sometimes be messy and unclear."

Shechem "Takes" Dinah, Asks for Her Hand, 34:1–12[4]

The last chapter ended with Jacob camping over against the city of Shechem and buying from them the plot of ground on which he pitched his tent. He set up an altar there and invoked "El, the God of Israel"—he meant to settle there. Nomadic group and city dwellers exchange wares. An incident leads to high tension.

Dinah, the daughter whom Leah had borne to Jacob, went out to visit some of the women of the land. When Shechem, son of Hamor the Hivite, leader of the region, saw her, he seized her and lay with her by force.

Why mention that Dinah was daughter of Leah, the unloved wife? Did this factor into Jacob's behavior in the matter? Dinah went out, not

---

2. Sternberg, *Poetics of Biblical Narrative*, 50–51. He adds, somehow under the breath: "the narrator does not tell the whole truth either." His statements about the world are rarely complete, fall much short of what his elliptical text suggests between the lines; "his *ex cathedra* judgments are valid as far as they go, but then they seldom go far below the surface of the narrative, where they find their qualification and shading."

3. "Yet his rhetorical maneuvers throughout, the final set of oppositions, and, above all, his giving the last word–and what a last word!–to Simeon and Levi, leave no doubt where his sympathy lies." Sternberg, *Poetics of Biblical Narrative*, 475.

4. This title allows room for discussion of the extent to which what happened could be called "rape" in our modern take on the matter.

"to see" any man, but the women of the land.⁵ But Shechem saw her—a different type of seeing. In the previous chapter, Shechem was the city in which Jacob settled; its inhabitants descended from an ancestor called Hamor (Gen 33:18–19). Here Shechem is a person, a Hivite, and his father is Hamor, the *nasi'*, prince or leader of the area. There is conflation between individual and tribe.

> The Hivites are one of the peoples of Canaan (Gen 10:17), whom YHWH will wipe out before Israel (Exod 23:23) and whom Israel, upon entry into Canaan, must put under the ban of destruction (Deut 7:3; 20:17). We watch for resonances of this point of view.

> In Hebrew, *hamor* means an ass. Rather than implied insult, "sons of Hamor" may mean those bound together by treaty, members of a confederacy—in Mari texts, to kill the foal of a donkey signifies to conclude a covenant.⁶

Shechem was head over heels in precipitous action: saw—took—laid her—violated her. *Laqah*, "to take," often signifies taking a woman for wife; for the moment, he takes Dinah to his private quarters.⁷ He then laid her. The usual term for sexual relations is *shakab 'im* (lie with someone—verb with preposition). The narrator used *shakab 'othah* (lay someone—verb with object). This is what Amnon did in 2 Sam 13:14, and may suggest self-regarding pleasure-taking.⁸ The next verb, *'innah*, is debated. Westermann believes that *we-'innah* underscores a forceful violation—the three verbs of increasing severity underscore the brutality of Shechem's assault on Dinah.⁹ Perhaps it is better at this stage to leave open the question whether this is statutory rape.

> LXX: "humbled her"; NIV: "violated her"; Alter: "debased her"¹⁰; NJB: "forced her"; NABRE, NRSV, TNK: "by force." The same verb occurs in the law at Deut 22:28, where NABRE renders:

---

5. Some modern readers blame her for going out without a male chaperon, but that is reading into the text. The narrator obviously thinks she should be safe with fellow women.

6. Sarna, *Genesis*, 233.

7. He will in verse four ask his father to "take me this girl for wife."

8. Sternberg, *Poetics of Biblical Narrative*, 446; he also thinks this signifies an "unequivocal condemnation of the assault."

9. Westermann, *Genesis 12–36*, 538; Sarna, *Genesis*, 234.

10. Alter, *Genesis*, 189.

"because he has violated her." On the other hand, the context of force is clear in Amnon's behavior in 2 Sam 13:14: "he was too strong for her: he forced her down [*we-'innah*] and raped her [*wa-yishkab 'othah*]." And *'innah* is used for exerting power over, oppressing a people.

Perhaps the sense is that of taking her virginity, thus debasing her in the eyes of society. Anyway, biblical law distinguishes forced from consensual sex only for betrothed or married women. In contrast to Amnon, whose hatred for Tamar surpassed the love he had for her,

He [Shechem] was strongly attracted to Dinah, daughter of Jacob, and was in love with the young woman. So he spoke affectionately to her. Shechem said to his father Hamor, "Get me this young woman for a wife."

It is strange to modern ears to speak of love of one's sexual victim. However, the narrator moves the reader to sympathy with the young man by piling up verbs of love (cleave to, love, speak to her heart). Shechem was indeed in love; his very self clung to Dinah[11] (now called "daughter of Jacob" in anticipation of the negotiations to come), and he "spoke to her heart," that is, comforted her (cf. Isa 40:2; Ruth 2:13). In effect, he promised to marry her,[12] and so restore her honor in the eyes of all. Indeed, the next thing Shechem does is ask his father to get her for wife. Some suggest that "he spoke to her heart" is perlocutionary expression, that is, a successfully completed action—means that she responded positively and stayed willingly.[13] We do not know. There are many facts an author could include but choose not to; these are *blanks*. What concerns the interpreter are *gaps*, namely, inferences and questions that arise from what a writer does say.[14] Unfortunately Dinah utters nary a word all through, nor are her feelings ever expressed.[15]

Meanwhile, Jacob heard that Shechem had defiled his daughter Dinah, but since his sons were out in the field with his livestock, Jacob kept quiet until they came home.

---

11. Alter, *Genesis*, 190.
12. Gunkel, *Genesis*, 363.
13. Thus Fewell and Gunn, "Tipping the Balance", 196.
14. For this distinction, see Sternberg, *Poetics of Biblical Narrative*, 236.
15. In the culture of the time, decisions concerning a girl are taken by the men in the family—her father and/or her brothers.

The narrator characterizes Shechem's behavior with a very negative evaluation, "defiled" (*ṭimmē'*). This term evokes the language of Ezekiel, the Priestly writer, and the Holiness Code; it rests upon the idea of the impurity of the nations of the land (Ezra 6:21), and of the land made impure through idolatry.[16] The perspective has changed from individual history to national identity—the story is now being read from the perspective of Israel as a holy nation. In fact, Gunkel and Westermann consider the motif of defilement a late gloss.[17] Frankel asserts that most references to "defiling" of Dinah can be recognized as removable appendages.[18]

In biblical law, *ṭimmē'* applies to married or betrothed women only—so it is inappropriately used here. "The seduction or rape of a virgin in the biblical milieu did not signify her being defiled."[19]

> In biblical law, adultery refers to sexual relations between a man and a married or betrothed woman only. Biblical law about unattached virgins makes no distinction between rape and consensual sex. "No laws require the death of the male, in stark contrast to such an act with either a betrothed virgin or married woman."[20] For attached women, the offense and the punishment of death are not so much for rape as the violation of the rights of the father and the groom.

When Jacob heard, he kept silent; when his sons heard, they were indignant and extremely angry. The contrast jars. Could Jacob not feel the pain of a daughter, even if of the unloved wife? The narrator put in a word for Jacob: he kept silent until the sons, whose duty it was to avenge the honor of their sister, returned.

Now Hamor ... went out to discuss the matter with Jacob.

It was the father of the prospective groom who asked the father of the prospective bride for her hand. Meantime Jacob's sons arrived and showed great pain and anger at the news,

For [kî] Shechem had committed an outrage in Israel by lying with Jacob's daughter; such a thing is not done.

---

16. Rofé, "Defilement of Virgins," 371.
17. Gunkel, *Genesis*, 362; and Westermann, *Genesis 12–36*, 543.
18. Frankel, "Proto-Story of Shechem," 2.
19. Rofé, "Defilement of Virgins," 375.
20. Wagner, "Politico-Juridical Proceedings," 152, 153.

The narrator and the sons of Jacob concur in this judgment. *Nebalah*, "outrage," is a senseless and disgraceful act of folly. The use of the term "Israel" is anachronistic—Jacob had not yet become the nation Israel—but it is hindsight; the sacred norms that constituted the moral underpinnings of the later people[21] were being read into the earlier situation.

Hamor appealed to them, saying: "My son Shechem has his heart set on your daughter. Please give her to him as a wife. Intermarry with us; give your daughters to us, and take our daughters for yourselves. Thus you can live among us. The land is open before you. Settle and move about freely in it and acquire holding here."

Hamor makes a clever political speech. He not only asks for the betrothal of Dinah to his son Shechem, but proposes a mutually advantageous political alliance, in which both sides would intermarry and the Jacobites would become full citizens (verb *yashab*, to dwell, no longer as alien, *gûr*), able to acquire land and move about freely. He can offer this because he was in charge of the place. One thing, though, was lacking: any reference to the pain caused by Shechem's deed and the shame accruing to Jacob and his sons for not adequately protecting Dinah or avenging her honor. The talk about intermarriage is couched in the language of Deut 7:3, which forbids such!

Then Shechem appealed to Dinah's father and brothers: "Do me this favor, and whatever you ask from me, I will give. No matter how high you set the bridal price and gift, I will give you whatever you ask from me; only give me the young woman as a wife."

The bridal price (*mohar*) is given to the father of the bride, the gift (*mattan*) is given to the bride. Shechem's first words, "let me find favor in your eyes," possibly struck the wrong note—he needed to acknowledge the dishonor to Jacob's family. Was his offer of a bridal price and gift far in excess of the normal amount a tacit recognition of the need to make reparation?[22] How did the brothers view this? An attempt to buy them off?

---

21. Sarna, *Genesis*, 234.
22. Sarna, *Genesis*, 235.

Deceit and Massacre, 34:13-29

Jacob's sons replied to Shechem and his father with guile, speaking as they did because he had defiled their sister Dinah.

Here Jacob's sons reply; at verse 25 only Simeon and Levi begin the execution. The LXX fills this gap by having the pair respond here: "And Symeon and Levi, the brothers of Dina, said to them." Jacob's sons or the pair of brothers sideline their father and take over the negotiations. The narrator raises a red flag with the phrase "with guile" (*be-mirmah*).[23]

> The last time we met this phrase was Gen 27:35: "your brother came here with guile and carried off your blessing." Jacob himself used the verb to complain to Laban who switched Leah for Rachel on the bridal night: "why did you deceive me?" (*rimîtanî*). The man of deceits meets with deceits.

They talk religion, but their real motives are other. They talk circumcision, but do not follow through with the law of circumcision, which in Exod 12:43-49 allowed circumcised aliens to participate in the cult, and so intermarry.[24] In terms of the story in its time, the sons acted with guile; in terms of a later rereading, there may have been religious concerns. For the Holiness Code, having combined the Priestly laws with the separatist views of the Deuteronomistic historian[25] would prohibit marriage with the circumcised foreign population. Even then, it would be deceptive to proffer circumcision as the solution.

They said to them, "We are not able to do this thing: to give our sister to an uncircumcised man. For that would be a disgrace for us. Only on this condition will we agree to that: that you become like us by having every male among you circumcised. Then we will give you our daughters and take your daughters in marriage; we will settle among you and become one people. But if you do not listen to us and be circumcised, we will take our daughter and go.

---

23. To wriggle out of the difficulty, *Tg. Onq.* and *Tg. Neof.* has them answering Hamor "with wisdom."

24. Scholars assign this to the Priestly source.

25. See Amit, "Polemics in Genesis 34," 211.

> *Onye kporo nkita oku jide osisi na aka, o si ya bia, ka osi ya abiala?*
> "He who calls a dog and carries a stick in his hand, does he want the dog to come or not to come?"
> Saying one thing and doing another is hurtful. (Okezie, *Role of Quoting*, 265)

Shechem took Dinah; the brothers will take Dinah and leave. That will end all communication between the two groups and frustrate Shechem's impassioned love. Biblical law on the violation of unbetrothed virgins in fact conforms to Shechem's request. Deut 22:28–29 (see also Exod 22:15–16) says:

> If a man comes upon a young woman, a virgin who is not betrothed, seizes her and lies with her, and they are discovered, the man who lay with her shall give the young woman's father fifty silver shekels and she will be his wife, because he has violated[26] her. He may not divorce her as long as he lives.

Compensation and marriage (without possibility of divorcing the woman) would be enough. No question of killing or massacre. The brothers, however, pitched the matter on the religious issue of circumcised versus uncircumcised, with its idea of defilement. They may have envisioned punishment starting exactly where the sexual crime did.[27] They cite Hamor's words about intermarriage and political relationships, adding, with tongue in cheek, "and become one people"—well "you will become as we are."[28] This would suggest the fear of assimilation and loss of national identity[29] something the story so far has striven against.

Their proposal pleased Hamor and his son Shechem. The young man lost no time in acting on the proposal, since he wanted Jacob's daughter.

Hamor and his son fell for it. Shechem wasted no time in getting himself circumcised—he loved Jacob's daughter that much, the narrator tells us. Because he was very highly regarded in the city, it was possible

---

26. The verb in the phrase, "because he has violated her," is the same verb '*innah* in verse 2 of our chapter.
27. See Sternberg, *Poetics of Biblical Narrative*, 266.
28. Fretheim, "Genesis," 212.
29. Amit, "Polemics in Genesis 34," 194.

for him and his father to convince the men at the gate of the city, that is, the city square at the gates where assemblies were held, saying that the men are friendly, we have ample room, let them settle with us and move about as they wish.

We can take their daughters in marriage and give our daughters to them. But only on this condition will the men agree to live with us and form one people with us: that every male among us be circumcised as they themselves are. Would not their livestock, their property, and all their animals then be ours? Let us just agree with them, so that they will settle among us.

To sway the people, they invoke greed. The tables will be turned when it is their property and animals that will be looted: "they thought to despoil them and were themselves despoiled" (*Gen. Rab.* 80:8). They agreed,

And all the males, all those who went out of the gate of the city, were circumcised.

That this did not include the children we learn from verse 29. "All who went out of the gate of the city" means either free citizens or perhaps men of military age who go out of the gates to war.[30]

On the third day, while they were still in pain, two of Jacob's sons, Simeon and Levi, brothers of Dinah, each took his sword, advanced against the unsuspecting city and massacred all the males. After they killed Hamor and his son Shechem with the sword, they took Dinah from Shechem's house and left.

The protagonists, Simeon and Levi, were full brothers of Dinah, but so were Reuben, Judah, Issachar, and Zebulon—all Leah's sons too. Was the singling out of Simeon and Levi read back into the story from Jacob's reproof of them in Gen 49:5–7? The midrash answers that Dinah is called by their name because they risked their lives for her sake (*Gen. Rab.* 80:10).[31] The narrator dissociates Simeon and Levi from the looting by the brothers. They took Dinah and left—what other choice could she have in the circumstances? We learn incidentally that Dinah was in Shechem's house all along. The narrator does not say whether she was there willingly or detained against her will. This hostile confrontation

---

30. Sarna, *Genesis*, 234.

31. Just as Miriam was called sister of Aaron who pleaded for her, though she was also sister of Moses.

with the surrounding peoples is out of character for the patriarchal stories, for the patriarchs are usually portrayed as living peacefully with them, even adopting their altars for the worship of YHWH.

For Sternberg, Simeon and Levi emerge as the real heroes: "their concern has been selfless and single-minded—to redress the wrong done to their sister and the whole family, which includes the prevention of an exogamous marriage, by hook or by crook."[32] A slight problem for this assertion concerning exogamous marriage is that not long after this Judah saw the daughter of a Canaanite named Shua and married her (Gen 38:2)—with no repercussions. "By hook or by crook" raises moral issues. A contract offered and willingly accepted has been unilaterally and deceitfully broken. The religious rite of circumcision, which incorporates adherents into Israel, has become a ploy for the massacre of the very people who painfully got themselves circumcised. Lack of proportionality: the crime of one person is visited upon a whole city. It would have preserved a certain proportionality had the brothers killed only Shechem and even his father (see below).

Then the other sons of Jacob followed up the slaughter and sacked the city because their sister had been defiled. They took their sheep, cattle and donkeys, whatever was in the city and in the surrounding country. They carried off all their wealth, their children, and their women, and looted whatever was in the houses.

That Simeon and Levi took Dinah and left should have done it. The other sons of Jacob add looting to massacre. The narrator tells us why: "because *they* defiled their sister." This is collective punishment: the entire city becomes guilty for the crime of one person. We already showed that the idea of defilement belongs to a later rereading in which intimate relations with uncircumcised people defiles Israel. There is irony: all this was because Shechem "took" a daughter of Jacob; after massacring the men, the sons of Jacob "took" everything, including the women and children! Defilement here appears a one-way street—they obviously did not consider that the women of Shechem would defile them.

---

32. Sternberg, *Poetics of Biblical Narrative*, 472.

Jacob and His Sons, 34:30–31

Jacob said to Simeon and Levi: "You have brought trouble upon me by making me repugnant to the inhabitants of the land, the Canaanites and the Perizzites. I have so few men that, if these people unite against me and attack me, I and my household will be wiped out." But they retorted, "Should our sister be treated like a prostitute?"

A prostitute offers her wares without discrimination to all who pay. For the brothers, accepting any gifts for Dinah in the circumstances reduces her to the status of a prostitute. Why Simeon and Levi and not all the sons?

> Westermann suggests that in the family narrative, Simeon and Levi killed Shechem only to atone for the outrage to their sister.[33] In fact, in *T. Levi* 6:4–5, Levi says he killed Shechem first and Simeon killed Hamor; only after did the brothers come and smite the city with the edge of the sword. Dinah entered the story as daughter of Jacob and ended as sister of Simeon and Levi. She disappears from the Bible. In midrash, she became the wife of Job (*Gen. Rab.* 57:4); a variant is that Simeon buried her in the land of Canaan (*Gen. Rab.* 80:11). Still another, *Jub.* 34:14, is that she expired from mourning over the news that a beast had devoured Joseph and was buried over against the tomb of Rachel.

The brothers seem to censure the passivity of their father and suggest he would have acted differently were Dinah daughter of Rachel. Some see Jacob as self-regarding and selfish. However, the threat was real, and Jacob had the duty of protecting his family. In fact, were it not for the terror from God that fell upon the surrounding towns (Gen 35:5), what Jacob feared would have come to pass. Therein the question of consequences—the brothers acted without thinking through the likely consequences of their action. Jacob in Gen 49:5–7 roundly condemns the passion and trickery of the brothers Simeon and Levi and rejects community with them; their later demise was viewed as just punishment.[34]

Shechem was a city hallowed by the patriarchs and regarded as sacred even in Joshua and Judges. "Abraham passed through the land as far

---

33. Westermann, *Genesis 12–36*, 542. Westermann divides the narrative into two: narrative A, the family narrative; and narrative B, the tribal narrative. In one the characters functions in their individual persona, in the other as tribes.

34. Gunkel, *Genesis*, 362.

as the sacred place at Shechem, by the oak of Moreh . . . he built an altar there to the LORD who had appeared to him" (Gen 12:6, 7). At Shechem, Joshua gathered together all the tribes of Israel and there they put away their foreign gods and swore: "We will serve the LORD, our God, and will listen to his voice" (Josh 24:24). Shechem did not become "unholy" till the Deuteronomistic movement condemned Jeroboam and his apostasy. The present form of the text knows of the Deuteronomistic attitude to the people of the land, and emphasizes Shechem as Hivite, one of the seven nations of Canaan. "In the background stands the command of Deut 7:1–5 which forbids intermarriage with the Canaanites and demands their extermination."[35] That "the prohibition of marriage with the inhabitants of the land applies even to those who are circumcised"[36] may contain hidden polemic concerning marriage between the inhabitants of the state of Judah and "those that dwell in Samaria," known in Ezra 4:1, 7. Of note is that Ezra 9:2 defines the population of Samaria as Canaanite.[37] In the return, the elites, including priests (Neh 13:8), were marrying women of the land.

What's the Drift of the Story?

How this narrative advances the plot of the patriarchal story is not clear. Because of Jacob's vow in Gen 28:20–22, the reader expected him to proceed straight back to Bethel—that's what happened in the variant account in Gen 35:9–14,[38] but not here. Here, after separating from Esau, Jacob landed in Succoth and built a home there and booths for his livestock (33:17). He must have settled over against Shechem (33:18–19). Following the Dinah incident at Shechem, God had Jacob going up to Bethel, reminding him of his vow. It is clear that the Tale of Dinah is an independent piece with loose links to the context. Dinah is mentioned again only in 46:15, the list of the seventy who went down with Jacob to Egypt. The incident receives oblique reference only in Jacob's Testament (49:5–7) and his severe reproof there of the excessive violence of Simeon and Levi.

---

35. Westermann, *Genesis 12–36*, 537.
36. Amit, *Hidden Polemics*, 195.
37. Amit, *Hidden Polemics*, 211 suggests that "Genesis 34 serves the polemic of the separatists and even becomes a basis for the anti-Samaritan polemic."
38. Scholars assign this to P.

But, while Genesis 34 concerns the deed of the brothers, 49:5–7 concerns the tribes and their demise.[39]

> The demise of these tribes and their scattering may have had something to do with the narrative here. Simeon is associated with Judah already in Judges 1, and apparently was absorbed in her. Levi, missing in the Song of Deborah (Judges 5), was scattered in families among the tribes (Josh 21:1–8). Gunkel suggests that at the origin of the story, "Dinah was an Israelite tribe related to Simeon and Levi, overpowered by Shechem and forced to join it, but avenged by the fraternal tribes."[40]

Sarna believes that, as with the book of Jonah, the closing rhetorical question provides an irresistible argument.[41] Sternberg at first opines that "The dilemma raised by th[is] story is so complex and each choice so problematic that [the narrator] cannot fully identify with any of the positions taken."[42] But then he comes down on a judgment similar to Sarna: "Yet his [narrator's] rhetorical maneuvers throughout, the final set of oppositions, and, above all, his giving the last word—and what a last word!—to Simeon and Levi, leave no doubt where his sympathy lies."[43] Fretheim, on the other hand, believes that in so doing the narrator throws negative light on the brothers: "by leaving the reader with the sons' question, standing over against the word of the head of the family oriented toward life and promise, the narrator shows how narrow and self-serving their perspective and actions have been. The question also leaves the reader with an agenda to consider: How would they respond?"[44] For Sailhamer, Jacob's words in Gen 34:30 ("you have brought trouble on me . . .") express the writer's own final judgment on the actions of the sons. The writer[45] then let the sons' reply stand to show that their motive was not plunder but the honor of their sister.[46]

---

39. See Westermann, *Genesis 12–36*, 545.
40. Gunkel, *Genesis*, 360.
41. Sarna, *Genesis*, 238.
42. Sternberg, "Delicate Balance," in *Poetics of Biblical Narrative*, 475.
43. Sternberg, "Delicate Balance," in *Poetics of Biblical Narrative*, 475.
44. Fretheim, "Genesis," 213.
45. For writer, I would say narrator; this inquiry is not on the level of writer and his intention.
46. Sailhamer, *Pentateuch as Narrative*, 202.

I am not so sure that the narrator comes out so clearly on one side or the other, for I agree with Rofé that Genesis 34 is internally inconsistent.[47] The narrator vacillates all along. He now ranges the reader alongside Shechem (he indeed loved Dinah, spoke to her heart, was willing to do anything, even to getting himself circumcised, the sons, on the other hand spoke "with guile"), now with the brothers, with the intonation of "defiled," "because they defiled their sister."

A similar inconsistency occurs in Genesis 17 where the addition of verses 15–22 in order to remove any doubt about the ascendancy of Isaac and his line over that of Ishmael introduces a restriction that narrows the scope of the covenant! The result is that Ishmael, though circumcised and thus bearing the sign of the covenant, is nevertheless excluded from those aspects of the same covenant that touch possession of the land and having YHWH as his God! This can only mean that the term *berît* ("covenant") takes on different fields of meaning in different parts of that text.

Besides, "*all* the characters are seriously flawed, although they all have some admirable qualities too."[48] In fact, Sternberg himself arrives at pretty much the same conclusion when he writes:

> After all, whatever Jacob's callousness and selfishness, he does right to think of the safety of his house. Whereas the brothers do right to champion Dinah; but they pay the price in deceit and bloodshed, they increasingly act from personal motives rather than horror of exogamy and in disregard for consequences rather than trust in God's providence, which validates their proceeding (35:5) after the event. From the narrator's vantage point, therefore, none of the dramatized views rises above the level of stuff for plot and polyphony.[49]

As they set out, a great terror fell upon the surrounding towns, so that no one pursued the sons of Jacob. (35:5)

Did God validate the proceeding? "Great terror" is literally "terror from God." God protected his protégé from an obliterating counter-massacre that would have frustrated God's promise. And that was not the first time God would appear to turn a blind eye to Jacob's ruses. Right after Jacob's stealing Esau's birthright and fleeing for his life, God encountered

---

47. Rofé, "Defilement of Virgins," 370.
48. Noble, "'Balanced' Reading," 195.
49. Sternberg, *Poetics of Biblical Narrative*, 475.

Jacob at Bethel only to promise to be with him and protect him wherever he goes (Gen 28:15). It is, however, true that the narrative evinces dramatic justice whereby "what goes round comes round." And later an *'ish* (man, being) struggled mightily with Jacob (Gen 32:23–33). In the case of Cain, YHWH clearly condemned the murder and punished Cain for it, even while sparing his life and putting a mark of protection on him. Did God here condone the evil in order to save them, or did he save them despite the evil? God's elect must be protected by all means?

So what is the "textual intention," what the text as constituted wants to say to the reader? Noble may not be exactly correct to affirm that "Genesis 34 is chiefly concerned with exploring complex issues of crime and punishment, and does so through an evaluative portrayal of how the principal characters (mis)handled the situation."[50] "Chiefly concerned with" might suggest authorial intention. But we have seen that varying intentions conflict in this text. Noble is more correct when he writes that Genesis 34:

> is a story about *issues*: through pondering, under the guidance of the narrator, upon the (largely unsatisfactory) ways in which the characters handle their situation, the reader's own moral sensibilities are sharpened. What one gains thereby is not, primarily, a straightforward set of rules, but a heightened awareness of the complexity of the situation, a deeper understanding of the terms in which such problems must be thought about ("crime," "punishment," "recompense," "just proportion," "lack of self-interest," "consequences"), and experience of thinking in such terms.[51]

To these we may add the need for prudence in conflictual situations and considerations of restorative justice.

Intentions conflict with each other in this text, but not by design. Noble's perspective is the response of a reader to "the complexity of the situation." The biblical narrator is no James Joyce; he does not write intricate and internally conflicting novels. The very laws of the Pentateuch adduce norms and principles that both affirm and challenge aspects of this story. The narrator empathizes with Shechem, but sides with the brothers, even if not fully condoning the methods used. Fretheim sees here

---

50. Noble, "'Balanced' Reading," 187.
51. Noble, "'Balanced' Reading," 195.

another instance in which the community of faith fails to serve as a chance for the blessing of God to outsiders. Rather than treat the rape of Dinah according to the law, as Hamor's family was openly willing to do, Israel takes the way of anarchy and violence. Rather than honor a genuine change on the part of Dinah's victimizers, the brothers ignore it and take a sharply overdrawn retributive form of behavior that serves to alienate the outsider . . . Israel loses the opportunity to bring good out of suffering, and Dinah becomes even more of a victim.[52]

Sailhamer gives a judicious canonical account. In the narrative, "God's purpose in setting apart the seed of Abraham comes into jeopardy with the proposal of marriage between Dinah and Shechem."[53] The request to be "one people" reverses God's intention, which is separation from the rest of the nations. The story shows that God works through and often in spite of the limited and self-serving plans of human beings. Jacob and his family have continuously been characterized as those who attempted to carry out God's intentions by means of their own plans and schemes.[54] The narratives show that in spite of these plans running counter to God's own, they could not thwart the eventual success of his intentions.[55]

"Separation from the rest of the nations" may feature in some strands of Israel's story, but is not the full story. Judah married a Canaanite woman, who became ancestor of the Messiah. Joseph married the daughter of the high priest of On, and his children from her, Ephraim and Manasseh, became the dominant tribes in Israel. Israel is also called to be "a kingdom of priests" (Exod 19:6), ministering among the nations. There is also the tradition of "blessing for all families of the earth." The prophets entertain the hope of a pilgrimage of the nations to Zion (Isa 2:1–5; Mic 4:1–4), when "the Lord will be king over the whole earth; on that day, the LORD will be only one, and the LORD's name only one" (Zech 14:9). My contention has been that rereading the story from an ideology of "separation from the rest of the nations" has produced the conflicted narrator on display.

---

52. Fretheim, "Genesis," 214.
53. Sailhamer, *Pentateuch as Narrative*, 201.
54. Sailhamer, *Pentateuch as Narrative*, 201.
55. Sailhamer, *Pentateuch as Narrative*, 202.

Still, this narrative confirms the truth of the saying that "God does not perfect people before deciding to work in and through them."[56]

Tradition

The attack was justified. In her prayer, Judith (the book of Judith is late second century or early first century BCE) called on the "Lord, God of my father Simeon, into whose hand you put a sword to take revenge upon the foreigners who had defiled a virgin by violating her . . . therefore you handed over their rulers to slaughter . . . and all the spoils you divided among your favored children who burned with zeal for you and in their abhorrence of the defilement of their blood called on you for help" (Jdt 9:2–4). Foreigners had defiled a daughter of Israel; the whole city was guilty. God himself gave the swords to Simeon and Levi. This reading hews closely to what I called the reread text of Genesis 34. Similarly, *Jub.* 30:5: the verdict was ordered in heaven against them, that they might annihilate with a sword all of the men of Shechem because they committed a disgrace in Israel. In fact, this was the pattern of behavior of the people of Shechem: God smote the inhabitants of Shechem, for they did not honor whoever came to them, whether evil or noble.[57]

Intermarriage with Gentiles is defilement. Jubilees was written in the second century BCE in the context of struggle with the people of the land and of fear of loss of national identity through assimilation. *Jub.* 30:7–10 highlights the implicit problematic in Genesis 34:

> If there is a man in Israel who wishes to give his daughter or his sister to any man who is from the seed of the gentiles, he shall surely die. He is to be stoned because he has committed a disgrace in Israel. And also the woman shall be burned with fire because she has defiled the name of her father's house and so she will be uprooted from Israel . . . For Israel is holy to the Lord, and any man who causes defilement shall surely die . . . the man who has so defiled his daughter shall be rooted out of

---

56. Fretheim, "Which Blessing Does Isaac Give Jacob?," 284.

57. Theodotus, frag. 7 in Eusebius, *Praeparatio Evangelica* 9.22.9; translation from Kugel, *Traditions*, 412.

the midst of Israel, because he has given of his seed to Molech, and acted impiously so as to defile it.[58]

Giving seed to Molech refers to Lev 18:21: "you shall not offer any of your offspring for immolation to Molech, thus profaning the name of your God, I am the LORD." Molech was the god of the Phoenicians and Canaanites, to whom people sacrificed their children. The text assimilates giving one's daughter to a Gentile to sacrificing her to Molech.

The fathers of the church did not know what to make of this material. Sheridan writes: "the story of the revenge, deceit and violence practiced by the sons of Jacob, Simeon and Levi in particular, against Hamor and the inhabitants of Shechem was a cause of scandal rather than edification to Christian readers of these Scriptures. This probably accounts for the little attention given to it by commentators. Dinah could be interpreted on a moral allegorical level to represent the soul, but violence must be avoided, for it is in conflict with the teaching of Christ (Cyril of Alexandria)."[59] Cyril warns against leaving the tabernacle of the Father, that is, the house of God, to be received into the herds of the heretics.

---

58. Translation of Kugel, *Traditions*, 408.
59. ACCS 2:227.

CHAPTER 21

Genesis 35–36

Jacob Becomes Israel; Esau Becomes Edom

> The God of Abraham is the God who blesses and saves even the nations.[1]

JACOB/ISRAEL IS THE ANCESTOR who gave his name to the people of Israel.[2] The narrator shows the reader how Jacob became Israel—the twelve tribes of Israel. And just as notices about the twelve encampments and chieftains of Ishmael (Gen 25:12–18) round off the story of Abraham, so also here the story of the clans and chiefs of Edom (line of Esau) round off the story of Jacob. Until now, an individual patriarch, usually the younger, was chosen as the bearer of divine blessing; now all the twelve sons of Israel become equal bearers of that blessing. Even the "non-chosen" are not left aside: the God of Abraham is the God who blesses and saves even the nations.

---

1. Westermann, *Genesis 12–36*, 574.
2. Heckle, "Remembering Jacob," 38.

Jacob Names Bethel Again, 35:1-7

God said to Jacob: Go up now to Bethel. Settle there and build an altar there to the God who appeared to you when you were fleeing from your brother Esau.

Bethel is some three hundred meters higher, so one goes up from Shechem. However, the language of "going up" is that of pilgrimage, as becomes clear in the preparations Jacob orders. God reminds Jacob of his own vow at Bethel (Gen 28:20) that if God protected and looked after him on the journey, "the LORD will be my God" and he will set up the stone as the house of God. God asks Jacob to build him an altar—everywhere else the raising of an altar is the free volition of the patriarch. Instead of saying, "an altar to me," God speaks in the third person of an altar to "the God who appeared to you." Told to settle (*yashab*) in Bethel, Jacob moves on to Hebron. These signals, and others to come, suggest that Gen 35:1-7 is an insertion that responds to expectations raised by Jacob's vow, but also qualifies the name change.

> The covenant with all his forebears was confirmed, and the blessing rested upon the head of Israel. God acknowledged him as the firstborn, and gave him his inheritance. He fixed the boundaries for his tribes and their division into twelve. (Sir 44:23)

So Jacob told his household and all who were with him: "Get rid of the foreign gods among you; then purify yourselves and change your clothes. Let us now go up to Bethel so that I might build an altar there to the God who answered me in the day of my distress and who has been with me wherever I have gone."

The narrator marks an important milestone in Israelite religion: "for the first time in the Bible, there now appears a recognition of tension between the religion of Israel and that of its neighbors."[3] Jacob represents the starting point of Israel's relationship with YHWH; he was remembered in his decision to pursue exclusive worship of YHWH.[4] Hitherto the patriarchs moved comfortably within the milieu of the Canaanite El

---

3. Sarna, *Genesis*, 239.
4. Heckle, "Remembering Jacob," 55, 78.

religion, with the narrator equating El and YHWH. Now, the gods of the nations are "foreign," that is, not Israelite—the perspective of later orthodoxy. Ezek 20:5–6 (see also the text box above of Sir 44:23) recalls this: "Thus says the Lord God: The day I chose Israel, I swore to the descendants of the house of Jacob . . . to bring them out of the land of Egypt . . . Then I said to them: throw away, each of you, the detestable things that held your eyes; do not defile yourselves with the idols of Egypt. I am the LORD, your God." Divine election calls for the rejection of all other gods.

> In the assembly of the tribes, also at Shechem, the people proclaimed, "far be it from us to forsake the LORD to serve other gods . . . we also will serve the LORD, for he is our God" (Josh 24:16, 18). Joshua then bade them: "now, therefore, put away the foreign gods that are among you and turn your hearts to the LORD, the God of Israel" (Josh 24:23).

Contact with idols pollutes, so purification is needed—they are entering YHWH's realm and his sanctuaries.[5] "God who is in Bethel" evokes the counterpart, "YHWH who dwells in Zion" (Isa 8:18). Focus on Bethel implies an audience for whom it is a living reality.[6] For the northern kingdom of Israel, Jacob was the primary patriarch and founder of its holy places[7]; Bethel was a hallowed and renowned Yahwistic sanctuary. The idols refer to Rachel's household gods (*teraphîm*) and the gods of the women and children captives of Shechem. Usually the washing of clothes is an act of purification. It may be that "changing clothes also works as a symbol of moving from the old to the new."[8]

They gave Jacob all the foreign gods in their possession and also the rings they had in their ears and Jacob buried them under the oak that is near Shechem.

The earrings possibly had images of the gods or were dedicated to them. The burial of idols is peculiar; the law commands them to be burned (Deut 7:5, 25). Burial under the oak possibly defiled a tree that was held as sacred.

As they set out, a great terror fell upon the surrounding towns, so that no one pursued the sons of Jacob.

5. See Westermann, *Genesis 12–36*, 550.
6. Carr, *Fractures*, 265.
7. Heckle, "Remembering Jacob," 65.
8. Fretheim, "Genesis," 218.

For "great terror," the Hebrew text has "terror from God," indicating the source. The sons of Jacob had sacked and looted Shechem. Jacob's fears of revenge massacre would have materialized had God not cast immobilizing terror upon the surrounding cities. This gives some closure to the story of Dinah, though Jacob will take it up in Genesis 49. Did God validate the treachery and massacre? See commentary in previous chapter.

Thus Jacob and all the people who were with him arrived in Luz (now Bethel) in the land of Canaan.

The locating phrase "in the land of Canaan" signals that in the original account Jacob first settled in Bethel (clearly implied in verse 9), and hence God's command to go to Bethel was, in that account, made in Mesopotamia. The reader already heard that Jacob "named the place Bethel [house of God], whereas the former name of the town had been Luz" (Gen 28:19).

There he built an altar and called the place El-Bethel, for it was there that God had revealed himself to him when he was fleeing from his brother.

The Hebrew text has the verb in the plural: "there that the gods/divine beings revealed themselves to him"—an oblique reference to the vision of angels at Genesis 28.[9] At Bethel on his way out, Jacob set up a sacred pillar (*maṣṣebah*), poured oil on top of it (Gen 28:18), and promised that this stone that I have set up as a sacred pillar will be the house of God (Gen 28:22); now upon return, he built an altar (*mizbeaḥ*) and called the place El-Bethel (God of Bethel), that is, he equates the place with the God worshiped there.

> El simply means god, but is also the name of the head of the Canaanite pantheon, in which capacity he is given the title El Elyon (Most High God). Several shrines combine the name El with the place name. To the LORD who spoke to her, Hagar gave the name, El Roi (the God of my seeing, the God who sees me, Gen 16:13). At Beersheba, Abraham invoked by name the LORD, El Olam (God Eternal, 20:13). In Priestly texts before the Sinai revelation, God is known as El Shaddai (God Almighty).

Bethel becomes firmly linked with Jacob's experience of God and his gratitude for God's protection of and kindness to him.

---

9. Sarna, *Genesis*, 241.

The God who answered me in the day of my distress and who has been with me wherever I have gone. (v. 3)

The text says nothing about his promise of tithes—a gap that later texts try to fill.

Jacob's Name Is Changed Again, 35:8–15

Deborah, Rebekah's nurse died. On Jacob's arrival from Paddan-aram, God appeared to him again and blessed him. God said to him: Your name is Jacob. You will no longer be named Jacob, but Israel will be your name. So he was named Israel.

Rebekah's nurse accompanied her to Canaan from Aram Naharaim (Gen 24:59); she was unnamed there. Did she accompany Jacob to Mesopotamia, or was she sent from Rebekah to meet Jacob on the way upon his return? They buried her under the oak below Bethel, and so it was named Allon-Bacuth, which means Oak of Weeping. Burial under the oak protects from scavengers; naming of the oak after her obsequies preserves her memory and the memory of her faithful service.

Jacob requested blessing from the being who wrestled with him at Peniel; that being changed Jacob's name to Israel (32:29), meaning "you have contended with divine and human beings and have prevailed." This rationale is unacceptable to the present writer, who portrays God himself as freely giving both blessing and name change from Jacob to Israel. In fact, for this writer, Bethel is no longer "house of God," but the place at which God spoke with him (vv. 14, 15),[10] for God dwells in heaven.

Then God said to him: I am God Almighty; be fruitful and multiply. A nation, indeed an assembly of nations, will stem from you, and kings will issue from your loins. The land I gave to Abraham and Isaac I will give to you; and to your descendants after you I will give the land.

"Be fruitful and multiply"—when all his children were already born or conceived![11] This promise seems to belong with Jacob's journey to Aram, when he did not yet have children.[12] The Hebrew text has: a

---

10. Blum, "Jacob Traditions," 190.

11. Midrash noted this and referred the promise to the future—the kings to come (*Gen. Rab.* 82:4).

12. Gunkel, *Genesis*, 373.

nation and an assembly [*qehāl*] of nations will stem from you, which cites Isaac's blessing before Jacob departed: "that you may become an assembly [*qehāl*] of peoples" (Gen 28:3).

> Gen 28:3 correctly used *qehāl* (assembly) with *'ammîm* (peoples), for *qāhāl* is the technical term for Israel assembled in worship or to hear the word of God, or to decide an important communal matter, and *'am* is the usual term for the people of Israel (see also Gen 48:4: *qehāl 'ammîm* in Jacob's blessing of Joseph). From this point of view, the use here (35:11) of *qāhāl* with *gōyîm* (assembly of nations) causes difficulty, for *gōyîm* is usual for foreign nations and the word *qāhāl* is not usual for them. Abraham as "father of a multitude of nations" (17:5) is in Hebrew *'ab* (father) *hamōn gōyîm*, where *gōyîm* includes Israel and other nations.[13]

Our passage is calqued on the promises to Abram in Gen 17:1–8. There too, as here, God promises the land, changes Abram's name to Abraham, Abraham will become father of a multitude of nations, God will make nations of him, and kings will stem from him. What such parallelism says is that "Jacob, by becoming also Israel, is the true heir to the Abrahamic promises, the one through whom the nation of Israel is to come into being."[14]

Then God departed from him. In the place where God had spoken with him, Jacob set up a sacred pillar, a stone pillar, and upon it he made a libation and poured out oil. Jacob named the place where God spoke to him Bethel.

At Gen 28:18 too, Jacob had poured oil on the stone pillar. At 28:22, he promised that "this stone that I have set up as a sacred pillar will be the house of God [*Beth Elohim*]." Here God does not dwell in the stone, rather the place is called Bethel, House of God. There has been demythologization; the stone pillar is no longer residence of God. This is now the third report of the naming of Bethel (Gen 28:19; 35:7, 15).

Then they departed from Bethel; but while they still had some distance to go to Ephrath, Rachel went into labor and suffered great distress . . . with her last breath . . . she named him Ben-oni; but his father named him Benjamin. Thus Rachel died; and she was buried on the road to Ephrath (now

---

13. *Tg. Ps.-J.* reflects the difficulty when it applies all to Israel: "a holy people and an assembly of prophets and priests shall come from the sons you have begotten, and two kings shall also issue from you."

14. Sarna, *Genesis*, 242.

Bethlehem). Jacob set up a sacred pillar on her grave, and the same pillar marks Rachel's grave to this day.

A gloss wrongly identifies Ephrath here with the Ephrathah (Bethlehem) in Mic 5:1 (see also Ruth 1:2). *"Ben-ŏni"* means "son of my affliction." His father renamed him Benjamin, son of the right hand, that is, son of good fortune or one that will support his father.

Israel moved on and pitched his tent beyond Migdal-eder. While Israel was encamped in that region, Reuben went and lay with Bilhah, his father's concubine. When Israel heard of it, he was greatly offended.

> The Hebrew text stops at "when Israel heard of it"; "he was greatly offended" has been supplied from the LXX. *Tg. Ps.-J.* rendered: "Reuben went and disarranged the couch of Bilhah, his father's concubine, which had been arranged opposite the couch of Leah his mother; and it was reckoned to him as if he had lain with her."

Migdal-eder means tower of the flock. The name Israel is used in this passage, but the name Jacob will continue. Only from Genesis 37 on will he mostly be called Israel; Chronicles retains only the name Israel. Lying with the concubine of one's father is both affront and claim to succession (see 2 Sam 16:22: "and Absalom went to his father's concubines in view of all Israel")—the struggle for leadership has begun in the house of Jacob. Jacob will give judgment on this in Gen 49:3-4. 1 Chr 5:1 informs the reader: "He was indeed the firstborn, but because he defiled the couch of his father his birthright was given to the sons of Joseph, son of Israel, so that he is not listed in the family records according to his birthright."

The Jacob story now reaches a climax in the naming of the twelve ancestors of Israel, named according to their mothers, all born in Paddan-aram—glossing over the fact that the reader just heard of the birth of Benjamin in the land of Canaan.[15] Dinah is not mentioned.

The sons of Jacob were now twelve. The sons of Leah: Reuben, Reuben, Jacob's firstborn, Simeon, Levi, Judah, Issachar, and Zebulun; the sons of Rachel: Joseph and Benjamin; the sons of Rachel's maidservant Bilhah: Dan and Naphtali; the sons of Leah's maidservant Zilpah: Gad and Asher. These are the sons of Jacob who were born to him in Paddan-aram.

---

15. Benjamin as the only son born in Canaan perhaps signifies that the Benjamin tribes were the last to become part of the Israelite tribal league. See Sarna, *Genesis*, 243.

The national story is about to begin. But the narrator must first bring Jacob back to Isaac and round off Jacob's story with the fortunes of the Esau tribes.

Jacob went home to his father Isaac at Mamre, in Kiriath-arba (now Hebron), where Abraham and Isaac had resided. The length of Isaac's life was one hundred and eighty years; then he breathed his last. He died as an old man and was gathered to his people. After a full life, his sons Esau and Jacob buried him.

The text consciously draws parallels between Jacob's journey and that of Abraham.[16] The journey begins with a similar command (cf. Gen 12:1; 35:1); both journey from Haran to Shechem to Bethel and toward the Negeb (Gen 12:6–9; 33:18; 35:6, 27); both journeys include a promise of land (Gen 12:7; 35:12) and travel in stages to Mamre (Gen 13:18; 35:27), with references to oaks and altars all along the way. Notable also is the separation of Jacob and Esau because "their possessions were too great to live together" (Gen 36:7), just as was the case for Abraham and Lot (Gen 13:6), and that Esau and Jacob buried Isaac rhymes with Isaac and Ishmael burying Abraham (Gen 25:9). Isaac, portrayed as dying in Genesis 27, lived even to see Jacob's children.

The Descendants of Esau, 36:1-19, 31-43

Nothing negative is conveyed about Edom. The patriarchal story is aware that Esau too is blessed. He had become wealthy and had four hundred men under his command (Gen 32:7). The genealogy of Esau rounds off the line of Isaac by tracing the historical links between Israel and Edom.

These are descendants [toledôt] of Esau, that is Edom.

Despite years of enmity, especially following the catastrophe of 586 BCE, Israel sticks to the memory of Edom as a brother: "Do not abhor the Edomite: he is your brother" (Deut 23:8). In the entry into Canaan, Israel must not come into conflict with the descendants of Esau, "for I will not give you so much as a foot of their land, since I have already given Esau possession of the highlands of Seir" (Deut 2:5). The descent of Esau is traced according to his wives.

---

16. See Carr, *Fractures*, 177, 211; especially Fretheim, "Genesis," 216.

> *Esau took his wives from among the Canaanite women: Adah, daughter of Elon the Hittite; Oholibahmah, the daughter of Anah the son of Zibeon the Hivite; and Basemath, daughter of Ishmael and sister of Nebaioth.*

Esau first married Canaanite wives, but when he saw this displeased his parents, he married a daughter of Ishmael (Gen 26:34–35). In the commentary on Genesis 26, we touched upon the contradictions in the genealogy of Esau, as follows.

> In Gen 28:9, Esau added a third wife, this time of the line of Abraham through Ishmael, son of Hagar: Mahalath, daughter of Ishmael and sister of Nebaioth.
>
> The Edomite genealogy at Gen 36:2 mentions the three wives as: Adah, daughter of Elon the Hittite; Oholibamah, the daughter of Anah the son of Zibeon the Hivite, and Basemath, daughter of Ishmael and sister of Nebaioth. In one, the Hittite is Judith, daughter of Beeri; in the other, Adah, daughter of Elon; in Gen 28:9, the Ishmaelite is Mahalath, sister of Nebaioth; in Gen 36:2, she is Basemath, sister of Nebaioth. The contradictions derive perhaps from different sources.

Esau took his wives, his sons, his daughters, and all the members of his household, as well as his livestock, all his cattle, and all the property he had acquired in the land of Canaan, and went to the land of Seir, away from his brother Jacob. Their possessions had become too great for them to dwell together, and the land in which they were residing could not support them because of their livestock. So Esau settled in the highlands of Seir (Esau is Edom). These are the descendants of Esau, ancestor of the Edomites, in the highlands of Seir.

Esau may have come from Seir to meet with Jacob and after "went on his way back to Seir" (Gen 33:16). The report that it is only now that he went to the land of Seir may be a variant from another source.

> The matter is complicated by the report that Esau and Jacob buried Isaac in Hebron, with no mention that Esau came there from elsewhere. Could it be that as a nomad he wandered the areas of Canaan and Seir until finally settling in Seir?[17] Deut 2:22 reports that the descendants of Esau dispossessed the Horites and dwelt in their place down to the present.

---

17. See Sarna, *Genesis*, 249.

In leaving the land, Esau fulfilled the "blessing" in 27:39: "see, far from the fertile earth will be your dwelling." In ceding the land of Canaan to his younger brother, he behaves in the same gracious manner as we saw him do in Genesis 32–33. Divine promises are being fulfilled; the land is effectively left for Jacob and his descendants. The reason given: "their possessions had become too great for them to dwell together" recalls the case of Abraham and Lot in Gen 13:6. It also shows that Esau too has been blessed abundantly. "The rise and development of the Edomite tribes, like the fortunes of Israel, are determined by the workings of God's Providence and are part of his grand design of history."[18]

These are the names of the sons of Esau.

The segmented genealogy traces the families and is given according to the sons of the wives: Adah, Basemath, and Oholibamah. Deviating slightly from the form, the text mentions a concubine of Eliphaz, firstborn of Esau:

Timna was a concubine of Eliphaz, the son of Esau, and she bore Amalek to Eliphaz.

The denigration of Amalek already begins. After the battle with Amalek (Exod 17:8-13), YHWH asked Moses to commit to memory: "I will completely destroy Amalek from under the heavens" (Exod 17:14). Some motivation for this is given in Deut 25:17-19: "bear in mind what Amalek did to you on the journey after you left Egypt, how he surprised you along the way, weak and weary, as you were, and, and struck down at the rear all those who lagged behind; he did not fear God . . . you shall blot out the memory of Amalek from under the heavens. Do not forget!" In terms of the word of God about loving your enemies, how is the believer to deal with this denigration of a whole people and the eternal hate of Amalek?

These are the clans of the sons of Esau.

The Edomite development into clans is outlined, the term for clan being *'alluf*.

> The word occurs in Exod 15:15, where because of the context *'allufê Edom* refers to the "chieftains of Edom." In other places, however, for example, Josh 22:14, it means clan. The clans are named after the names of the sons of Esau already detailed

---

18. Sarna, *Genesis*, 246.

above. The only difference refers to the sons/clans of Eliphaz. In verse 11: *the sons of Eliphaz were Teman, Omar, Zepho, Gatam, and Kenaz . . . Amalek* [son of Timna, a concubine of Eliphaz]. Now (verses 15–16) we have: the clans of *Teman, Omar, Zepho, Kenaz, Korah, Gatam, and Amalek*—Korah added.

These are the kings who reigned in the land of Edom before any king reigned over the Israelites. (36:31)

Eight kings are profiled. The Edomites preceded Israel in Canaan and developed the political structure of kingship even before Israel emerged. David subjected Edom in 2 Sam 8:13–14: "David made a name for himself by defeating eighteen thousand Edomites in the Valley of Salt. He set up garrisons in Edom, and all the Edomites became David's subjects." We are reminded of the saying, "the older will serve the younger" (Gen 25:23), also "your brother you will serve" (Gen 27:40)—Isaac's "blessing" of Esau. Notable in the kings list is that the seat of government rotates; each king reigns from a different city. Were these kings local leaders like the "judges" in Israel? The second king was

Jobab, son of Zerah, from Bozrah.

The LXX does intertextual exegesis when it identifies this Jobab with Job and Eliphaz, son of Esau, with Eliphaz, one of the friends of Job:

> And Job died, an old man and full of days: and it is written that he will rise again with those whom the Lord raises up. This man is described in the Syriac book as living in the land of Ausis, on the borders of Idumea and Arabia: and his name before was Jobab; . . . And he himself was the son of his father Zare, one of the sons of Esau, and of his mother Bosorrha, so that he was the fifth from Abraam. And these were the kings who reigned in Edom, which country he also ruled over: first, Balac, the son of Beor, and the name of his city was Dennaba: but after Balac, Jobab, who is called Job. . .And his friends who came to him were Eliphaz, of the children of Esau, king of the Thaemanites, Baldad son of the Sauchaeans, Sophar king of the Minaeans. (Job 42:17)

Two of the kings are named Hadad. Hadad is the name of a storm god, later identified with Baal, the head of the Canaanite pantheon.[19] It is interesting that 2 Sam 8:13–14 mentions that David overcame Edom

---

19. See Sarna, *Genesis*, 252.

under Hadad II (the last king in the Edomite list of kings here), while another Hadad of Edom attempted revolt against Solomon (2 Kgs 11:14). Verses 40–43 are a summary.

These are the names of the clans of Esau identified according to their families and localities . . . those are the clans of the Edomites according to their settlements in the their territorial holdings–that is, of Esau, the ancestor of the Edomites.

The Hebrew noun underlying "in their territorial holdings," *'ahuzzah* (possession), is consistently used of permanent possession through purchase (cave of Machpelah, Gen 23:9, 20) and of the land of Canaan as eternal possession allotted to the patriarchs (Gen 17:8; 48:4; 49:30; 50:13). The subtle hint here is that the Edomites took hold of Seir, their allotted portion, leaving the land of Canaan for Jacob and his progeny.[20]

The Horites of Seir, 36:20–30

These are the sons of Seir the Horite, the inhabitants of the land.

Seir is here regarded as the ancestor of the Horites, whereas in the Esau story Seir is a location. Seven clans are given. We saw above that the sons of Esau dispossessed the original Horite population of Edom.

He is the Anah who found water in the desert while he was pasturing the donkeys of his father Zibeon.

The exact meaning of *yēmîm*, (translated as "water"), is not known; some render "hot springs" (Vulgate), others "mules."[21]

Tradition

Jacob severely blamed his sons. Jacob "reproached them because they had put the city to the sword; for he feared those who dwelt in the land, the Canaanites and the Perizzites" (*Jub.* 30:25). Josephus (*Ant.* 1.21.2) wrote that, "Now while Jacob was astonished at the greatness of this act, and

---

20. See also Lowenthal, *Joseph Narrative*, 14.
21. *Tg. Onq.*: "Anah who had found the mighty ones in the wilderness"; *Tg. Ps.-J.* gives a double translation: "that was Anah who crossed wild asses, and in due time found the mules that had come forth from them."

was severely blaming his sons for it, God stood by him, and bid him be of good courage; but to purify his tents, and to offer those sacrifices which he had vowed to offer when he went first into Mesopotamia, and saw his vision."

Changing of garments. Some fathers of the church saw a clear allusion to the Christian dispensation in the changing of garments. Jacob "plainly sets out for those coming after him the proper manner of coming to the house of God ... when we are called into the presence of God or brought into his divine temple, especially at the time of holy baptism. For it is necessary, by way of casting the foreign gods from our midst and abandoning such falsehood, that we should say, 'I renounce you, Satan, with all your pomp and all your worship.' Furthermore, we must all change our clothes by stripping off the old man that is corrupt through deceitful lusts, and putting on the new that is being renewed according to the image of its creator ... Whenever, therefore, we go up to Bethel, that is, to the house of God, we shall there acknowledge the stone, the elect stone that has become the head of the corner, which is Christ."[22]

The promise to Jacob. St. Augustine noted that among the promises made to Jacob is the following: for nations and gatherings of nations shall be of you (Gen 35:11). He asks: "Are 'nations' according to the flesh, and 'gatherings of nations' according to faith, or both by the faith of the Gentiles, if the nations cannot be called a single nation of Israel according to the flesh?"[23]

Jacob gave the tithes promised. For *Jubilees*, Jacob did indeed give the promised tithes: "he clothed [Levi] in the garments of the priesthood and filled his hands ... and he gave a tithe of all that came with him, both of men and cattle, both of gold and every vessel and garment, yea, he gave tithes of all" (*Jub.* 32:3, 2). "To fill the hands" is an expression for the ordination of a priest.

Some Traits of the Patriarchal Story

Before moving on, we wish to underline three traits of the patriarchal story among those noted by Westermann.[24]

---

22. Cyril of Alexandria, *Glaphyra on Genesis* 5.5.
23. Augustine, *Questions on Genesis* q. 115.
24. See Westermann, *Genesis 12-36*, 570-77.

"Blessing is never counterbalanced by curse (as in Deut 28), promise never by the announcement of judgment; as far as the patriarchs are concerned, God's judgment and punishment are almost entirely absent."[25]

"The patriarchal stories are not yet aware of the holiness of God; the idea of [*qadosh*, holy and tremendous] is not found . . . there is still no specifically theological language."[26]

"Most significant is the absence of an institutional cult and the cult mediator; the action or talk between God and the person takes place directly . . . there is the gradual but clearly traced path from nature's holy places to those made by humans."[27]

---

25. Westermann, *Genesis 12-36*, 575.
26 Westermann, *Genesis 12-36*, 576.
27. Westermann, *Genesis 12-36*, 576.

CHAPTER 22

Genesis 37

The Joseph Narrative; Joseph Is Sold into Egypt

> The coat given to confirm love, becomes a confirmation of death.[1]

The Story Thread

OUR STORY BEGAN IN the Primeval History (Genesis 1–11)[2] with God creating the universe and dealing with all nations in salvation and judgment. That story concerned the universe and all humanity, though pivoted on unique individuals—Adam, Noah, and Abram—each ten generations distant from the other. With Abraham, the future Israel appeared on the horizon.

In the Abraham Cycle (Gen 12:1—25:18), YHWH focused on one man, Abraham, blessing him and promising a homeland that will become a great nation, all this so that through him all families of earth will be blessed. Though all progeny of Abraham share aspects of his blessing, possession of the land of Canaan and having YHWH as God accrue to the younger, not the firstborn, son—Isaac, not Ishmael (Genesis 17). Before

---

1. Fretheim, "Genesis," 228.
2. See Okoye, *Genesis 1–11*.

he died, Abraham "gave everything that he owned to his son Isaac" (Gen 25:5). To the rest, he gave gifts and sent them away eastward,

Away from his son Isaac.

The Jacob Cycle (Gen 25:19—37:1) repeats the paradox of the unchosen firstborn—Jacob is chosen, not Esau. With time, Esau took all he had and went to the land of Seir,

Away from his brother Jacob.

So he settled in the highlands of Seir, that is, Edom (Gen 36:6, 8). Genesis 36 concludes the Jacob Cycle with the *toledôt Esau*, genealogy of Esau; Esau's line developed into families, clans, and kingdoms.

The Genealogy of Jacob

Having phased out Esau, the narrator picks up the *toledôt Ya'akob*, genealogy of Jacob, and shows how Jacob's line in turn developed into families, clans, and kingdoms. The story moves from Jacob/Israel as an individual, to Israel as a family, to Israel as a people.[3] However, a real genealogy does not occur till Gen 46:8–25, and, at that, it is more a register of the people descending into Egypt than a genealogy! Rather, the announcement of the genealogy is followed by an account of some of Jacob's sons (Joseph, Judah, Reuben) with focus on the story of Joseph, "an artfully designed complex."[4]

> This unified Joseph narrative has now been inserted into the broader story of Jacob. Many see the proper Joseph narrative in Gen 37:3–36; 39–45; 46:28–47:31; 50:1–21.[5]

The focus on Joseph suggests that the Joseph narrative originated in a milieu that held Joseph up as leader of the particular group. The conflicts in the story may reflect the jockeying for position by the other sons of Jacob (and the tribes associated with them).

---

3. See Fretheim, "Genesis," 222.
4. Humphreys, *Joseph and his Family*, 8.
5. See Redford, *Study*, 2. Scholars differ on this issue, but Genesis 37; 39–45 are constant.

The Joseph narrative is usually characterized as a novella.[6] Novella (short novel) is a literary form that stands between novel and short story. Like both, novella is intended as fiction,[7] not history. It is built around a plot that moves from tension to resolution, even if there may be more than one stressful situation or event. It is prose, not poetry, and generally the conscious creative work of a single author. It is thus an artistic written composition designed to be read, rather than heard. It depicts not so much what *happened*, as what *happens* in life. While the short story tends to *reveal* the nature of a character or situation, both novel and novella *develop* characters or situations—characters evolve and shape and are shaped by events.

The Joseph Novella

"Genesis 37 sets the narrative in motion; the complication is defined and the main characters carefully sketched."[8] There is twofold tension and strife—between Joseph and his brothers, and between Jacob and his sons. Driven by envy and rivalry, the brothers sell Joseph into slavery in Egypt. There his fortune reverses; he becomes governor of the land and Jacob took all his other children and went down to Joseph in Egypt (Gen 46:8)—foreshadowing the story of Exodus. One outline of the plotline is as follows.[9]

Resolution (Gen 45:1–15)

Further complications (Gen 42–44) Denouement (Gen 45:16—50:21)

Interludes (Gen 38–41)

Complication (Gen 37:5–36)

Exposition (Gen 37:1–4)   Conclusion (Gen 50:22–26)

The unit begins with Joseph at the age of 17 and ends with his death in 50:26 at the age of 117. The reader "savor[s] the reconciliation of Joseph

---

6. Humphreys, "Joseph Story as a Novella," in *Joseph Story*, 15–31.

7. As literary fiction, not history, its inspiration and truth as Scripture are judged by its intention, not by conformity to the actual historical events and personages. In the Bible, the religious meaning intended by God goes through the various genres and their function.

8. Humphreys, *Joseph Story*, 23.

9. Humphreys, *Joseph Story*, 32. See also the detailed outline on pp. 56–67.

with his brothers, of the father with his sons, and especially the reunion of Joseph and Jacob after so many years."[10]

The Joseph narrative is now framed by stories that focus on a gradually ascendant Judah—Genesis 38 and 49. While the original Joseph Novella derives from the Joseph tribes of northern Israel[11] and presents Joseph's destiny to rule, the present form of the text redirects the story to predict Judah's future dominance and destiny to rule over all, including Joseph: "Joseph once ruled, but Judah rules now."[12] The canonical context does something further: it subordinates Joseph to Jacob, the Joseph story to the Jacob story. The plot of the Joseph story is moved forward by acts of favoritism, perpetrated by Jacob in the beginning, middle, and end points of the story.[13] Despite his royal robes, Joseph is not running this show. Joseph is not one of the patriarchs; he receives no direct vision or word from God. "Jacob does what God does: he by-passes the older for the younger"[14] He sets the agenda. It is through him that the divine plan is carried out.[15] In giving his last will and testament in Genesis 48 and 49, Jacob accords Joseph firstborn status. Reversing the pattern of the story hitherto, he decides that all his twelve sons—no longer just the younger or the firstborn—become Israel (inheriting Jacob's changed name), that all share in his election (Genesis 49)—and the narrator and God (apparently) concur.

> Some tensions in the story point to variants or may be the result of the insertion of the Joseph story into the Jacob story.[16]

---

10. Humphreys, *Joseph Story*, 53

11. Humphreys, *Joseph Story*, 198 wrongly, in my judgment, denies this when he writes: "yet too much emphasis should not be placed on the fact that the novella centers in critical ways on Joseph, for it cannot be said to manifest a clear critical perspective toward Judah, and most important, it is simply not colored by a strong political polemic of any sort." He leaves the focus on Joseph unexplained.

12. Carr, *Fractures*, 247, 304. Joseph was the eponymous ancestor of the Joseph tribes, Ephraim and Manasseh, who dominated the northern kingdom of Israel. Sarna, *Genesis*, 264 put it this way: "Judah became the name of the southern kingdom, while the northern kingdom of Israel was known as Joseph (cf. Zech 10:6). The present chapter, then, provides a foil to the Joseph-centered episodes. It hints, ever so obliquely, at the future Joseph-Judah polarity in the history of the people of Israel."

13. Mandolfo, "You Meant Evil Against Me," 453.

14. Mandolfo, "You Meant Evil Against Me," 456.

15. Other authors who argue equally that Jacob, not Joseph, is the dominant character are Clifford, "Genesis 37–50"; Golka, "Genesis 37–50."

16. See Carr, *Fractures*, 271.

Joseph is said to be son of Jacob's old age (37:3); there is nothing about this in 30:23-24 and 31:41, besides the story itself posits Benjamin as the youngest. Rachel is presumably alive (37:10), while she already died in 35:20. Jacob's sons and daughters tried to console him (37:35), while he had only one daughter, Dinah, in 30:21.

The brothers saw a caravan of Ishmaelites and decided to sell Joseph to them (37:25). Next we hear, Midianites pulled Joseph out of the cistern and sold him to the Ishmaelites (37:28). Instead of the Ishmaelites, 37:36 has the Midianites sell Joseph in Egypt to Potiphar, though in 39:1 Potiphar buys him from the Ishmaelites!

"When Joseph was taken down to Egypt" (39:1) resumes "The Midianites sold Joseph in Egypt" (37:36). This marks Genesis 38 as an insertion; nevertheless, effort was made to construct linguistic bridges between it and the wider Joseph story.[17]

For example, there are many parallels between chapters 37 and 38: both Joseph and Judah *went down* (*yarad*), away from their brothers; the brothers *send* Joseph's robe to the father (37:32) / Tamar *sends* word and items to Judah (38:25); they killed *a kid* and dipped his tunic in the blood (37:31) / Judah will send *a kid* to Tamar (38:17); *discern* (*hakker-na'*) if is this your son's robe / *discern* (*hakker-na'*) whose these are; Jacob *recognized* it (*wa-yakkirah*) and said (37:33) / Judah *recognized* them (*wa-yakker*) and said; deception occurs in both, the flashpoint being proved by production of tangible evidence.

Theology in the Joseph Novella

The image of God changes in the Joseph Novella. Hitherto, God intervened directly in history; miracles abounded. God conversed with humans sometimes in bodily form; God was seen and heard. The Joseph Novella portrays God differently. Besides not mentioning covenant or promise, the narrator in this story makes no theological comments on

---

17. See Alter, *Art of Biblical Narrative* (2011), 2, 9-10; Ackermann, "Jacob, Judah, and Joseph," 96; Golka, "Genesis 37-50," 153; Clifford, "Genesis 37-50," 219; Sarna, *Genesis*, 263.

matters and issues and nowhere uses the term YHWH (except in Genesis 39).[18]

"These accounts also characteristically omit the theophanies . . . The narrator lives in another religious world. In it the gods no longer appear bodily, but the deeper insight recognizes the hand of the ruling God in natural events. Belief in providence has taken the place of belief in theophanies . . . Only dreams, the least sensory form of revelation, still indicate the deity's will. But even in them the deity no longer appears to speak (exceptions 46:2ff.)."[19]

Some speak of a somewhat "secular mode"—something more in line with the modern experience of readers.

> The miraculous or supernatural element being conspicuously absent. There are no direct divine revelations or communications to Joseph. He builds no altars. He has no associations with cultic centers. God never openly and directly intervenes in his life. No wonder that Joseph is not included among the patriarchs (cf. Exod 2:24) and that Jewish tradition restricts that category to Abraham, Isaac, and Jacob (Ber 16b). Nevertheless, the secularity of the story is superficial, for the narrative is infused with a profound sense that God's guiding hand imparts meaning and direction to seemingly haphazard events.[20]

That "guiding hand" is able to work with and around evil and human failure: "The narrative as a whole witnesses to a God who uses even the evil designs of people to bring about good, indeed leads to events constitutive of the very character of Jacob's sons. Sinful behaviors do indeed frustrate the divine purposes in the world, but they do not, finally, stymie them."[21]

The Story of Joseph Elsewhere in the Bible

Outside of the book of Genesis, there is not much recall in the Bible of the story of the person Joseph. Josh 24:31 reports that Israel brought up the bones of Joseph from Egypt and buried them in Shechem—referenced in Sir 49:15. Ps 105:17–18 speaks of his feet being shackled and his neck

---

18. See Redford, *Study*, 247.
19. Gunkel, *Genesis*, 382.
20. Sarna, *Genesis*, 254.
21. Fretheim, "Genesis," 228–29.

collared in prison (see here on Genesis 39). Mattathias in his farewell speech recalls that "Joseph, when in distress, kept the commandment, and he became master of Egypt."[22] Otherwise, what we find are references to the "house of Joseph," "remnant of Joseph," "affliction of Joseph." In all these, Joseph refers to the tribe, not the person. An example is Ps 80:2: "O shepherd of Israel lend ear, you who guide Joseph like a flock." Here "Joseph" refers to the tribes of Ephraim, Benjamin, and Manasseh. Joseph was a northern hero, so was Jacob.[23]

Conflict in Jacob's Family, 37:1-11

Jacob settled in the land where his father had sojourned, the land of Canaan.

All rival claimants to this land have now been shunted off or settled elsewhere. Jacob is the first patriarch to actually settle in the land of Canaan — the promise of the possession of Canaan is beginning to be fulfilled.

This is the story of the family of Jacob.

This is one of the editor's signals that the canonical context makes the Joseph story a phase of the Jacob story. So the whole is properly the *toledot* (genealogy) of Jacob.

When Joseph was seventeen years old, he was tending the flocks with his brothers; he was an assistant to the sons of his father's wives Bilhah and Zilpah, and Joseph brought their father bad reports about them.

The text contains a *double entendre*: it may mean shepherding the flock with his brothers or shepherding his brothers.[24] It may even sustain the meaning, "he used to lord it over his brothers."[25] *Naʿar* (here "assistant," though usually "young man") is best understood as attendant boy

---

22. For postbiblical literature, see JUB. 39–43; *1 En.* 89:13-14; Philo, *On Joseph*; and Josephus, *Ant.* ii.20.

23. It appears that a northern Jacob-Joseph story was formed by integrating the core Joseph narrative with the Jacob narrative prior to its incorporation into the larger patriarchal narrative and the broader Exodus narrative. See Bekins, "Tamar and Joseph," 379.

24. Redford, *A Study*, 15. The preposition, *ʾeth*, placed before "his brothers" can function as accusative or designate the preposition, "with": "he was shepherding with his brothers" or "he was shepherding his brothers."

25. Sarna, *Genesis*, 255.

or apprentice shepherd. The evil report may not be a unique event, rather the habitual way of things[26]—Joseph used to tattle on them.

Israel loved Joseph best of all his sons, for he was the child of his old age; and he made him a long ornamented tunic.

Jacob's acts of favoritism have caused trouble in his family before (between his two wives); now he is at it again. His preferential love of Joseph, son of his beloved Rachel, drives the plot. Chrysostom wondered, "son of his old age even after Benjamin born?"[27] Benjamin was born during Jacob's return from Mesopotamia (Gen 35:18). So some read "son of old age" as "son with the wisdom of age."[28] However, this interpretation strives to base the father's predilection on some inherent quality in Joseph. But, the narrator portrays the father's love as gratuitous; it was this that fanned the jealousy of the siblings. *Ketōnet passim* was worn by princess Tamar in 2 Sam 13:18. Did it betoken Joseph's ascendancy over his brothers? Was it a signal of Jacob's intent to make Joseph his direct heir? For, hitherto election fell on one son, the younger, and not the elder. The coat may also be a long coat with sleeves that reach the wrists or the ankles, the type worn by those who need not work.[29] When the brothers go shepherding (v. 12), Joseph remained at home with the father. The brothers already hated Joseph for his reports; now

they hated him so much that they could not say a kind word to him. Once Joseph had a dream, and when he told his brothers, they hated him even more. My sheaf rose to an upright position, and your sheaves formed a ring around my sheaf and bowed down to it.

In the dream, it was the time of harvest and the brothers were binding sheaves. Joseph's dreams drive the plot of the entire narrative; the dreams come in pairs. This first dream foreshadows Genesis 42. It introduces the leitmotif of obeisance or "bowing down" that will characterize the future relationships of Joseph and his siblings. None of the characters

26. Humphreys, *Joseph and His Family*, 23.

27. Chrysostom, *Homilies on Genesis* 61.3, in ACCS 2:230.

28. Hence Cyril of Alexandria, *Glaphyra on Genesis* 6.2: He already had the reasoning powers of an older person, possessing a well-advanced mind, and employing the speech of the mature, so giving an anticipation of the wonderful nature of his brilliance. Already Philo, *On Joseph* 4: his father, observing in him a noble mind greater than the usual, marveled at him and admired him, and he loved him more than his other sons. Translation in Kugel, *Traditions*, 439.

29. Gunkel, *Genesis*, 390.

know this yet, but the future will reveal that the sheaves portend the nurture of the family to keep it alive.

His brothers said to him, "Are you really going to make yourself king over us? Will you rule over us? So they hated him all the more because of his dreams and his reports.

Obeisance is what subjects do towards a king. The brothers suspect Joseph of overweening ambition. Perhaps they echo the later jockeying for leadership among the tribes?[30]

Then he had another dream, and told it to his brothers . . . the sun and the moon and eleven stars were bowing down to me.

Some believe that this dream foreshadows Genesis 43—47:27[31]; however, it can be questioned whether this dream was fulfilled in the narrative or even repudiated (see Genesis 48). Jacob understood the import of the dream and reproved Joseph:

"Can it be that I and your mother[32] *and your brothers are to come and bow to the ground before you?" His brothers were furious at him.*

With addition of "to the ground," he underlined how preposterous such a gesture would be. Dreams were seen as messages from God, so, though perplexed, the father kept (*shamar*) the matter in mind. To keep, *shamar*, is to attend to, guard, as in guarding the Sabbath or keeping the law.[33] Jacob was ruminating over this to discern what all this could be saying.

The die is cast. The brothers are angry with their father for singling out Joseph and furious with Joseph for what they consider arrant self-aggrandizement. The arc of anger and jealousy grows: they hated him so much they could not say a word to him (v. 4); they hated him even more (v. 5); they hated him all the more for his dreams (v. 8); they were furious at him (v. 11).

---

30. Carr, *Fractures*, 274: Joseph's destiny to rule argues for northern claims to rule both northern and southern Israelite groups.

31. Coats, *From Canaan*, 13.

32. This presumes that Rachel was alive, but she died at Gen 35:19. This tension and others show that the Joseph Novella was originally independent of the Jacob story.

33. Mandolfo, "You Meant Evil Against Me," 457: Jacob here as "caretaker of the conception of reality posited by Joseph's dream."

The Brothers Sell Joseph into Slavery, 37:12–36

One day, when his brothers had gone to pasture their father's flock at Shechem, Israel said to Joseph. "Are your brothers not tending our flocks at Shechem? Come and I will send you to them."

"Joseph Sold by His Brethren" by Gustave Doré

Gen 37:28 ... lifted up Joseph out of the pit, and sold Joseph to the Ishmeelites for twenty *pieces* of silver: and they brought Joseph into Egypt.

FIGURE 6: His Brothers Sell Joseph into Slavery in Egypt

Joseph no longer went to pasture with his brothers! Was the father reacting to the brothers' animus with him? If so, why send him to the lion's den? A few chapters back, at Genesis 34, the brothers had sacked Shechem. Did Jacob fear for their safety?[34]

"Go then," see if all is well with your brothers and the flocks, and bring back word."

He is to inquire into the welfare/*shalom* of brothers who could not speak to him in peace/*shalom*! The last time Joseph brought word, it was a bad report, and they hated him for it. Is Jacob willfully blind to his other sons' reaction?[35]

When Joseph reached Shechem, a man came upon him as he was wandering about in the fields . . . they have moved on from here. In fact, I heard them say, "Let us go on to Dothan."

This man is an agent that helps the story forward; more, he is a symbol of divine providence that suggests divine intent behind Joseph's fateful encounter with his brothers.[36] The man had exact information. Dothan is some twelve kilometers from Shechem.

So Joseph went after his brothers and found them in Dothan. They saw him from a distance, and before he reached them, they plotted to kill him. They said to one another: "Here comes that dreamer! Come now, let us kill him and throw him into one of the cisterns here; we could say that a wild beast devoured him. We will see then what comes of his dreams."

The dreams were on their minds; hatred was pushing them to fratricide. Their new nickname for Joseph was "lord of dreams." He may in his dreams imagine himself their lord and master, but his elimination will surely show they were just the futile dreams of a fertile and arrogant imagination! The irony is that Joseph will soon prove to be lord of dreams and their interpretation. A little detail shows the depth of their contempt: they will not just throw, but *cast him* into one of the pits. No one will ever see his remains, the crime will never be found out. What happens next is slightly confused, perhaps due to combining of variants.

---

34. It is possible that this account of the Joseph story did not know or reckon with the detail about Shechem in Genesis 34. *Tg. Ps.-J.* takes this detail for granted: "I am afraid lest the Hivites come and smite them for having smitten Hamor and Shechem and the inhabitants of the city."

35. See Mandolfo, "You Meant Evil Against Me," 458.

36. Mandolfo, "You Meant Evil Against Me," 458: "Jacob and God are in cahoots here."

But when Reuben heard this, he tried to save him from their hands, saying: "We must not take his life." Then Reuben said, "Do not shed blood! Throw him into this cistern in the wilderness, but do not lay a hand on him." His purpose was to save him from their hand and restore him to his father.

Reuben, the firstborn who has prime responsibility for Joseph with their father, was apparently not part of the conspiracy. The brothers had already laid hands on Joseph when Reuben came upon the scene and saved him with a peremptory "do not lay hands on him!" His counsel to cast him into a pit agreed with the expressed wish of the brothers, but for a different purpose—he would clandestinely rescue him and return him to his father.

So when Joseph came up to his brothers, they stripped him of his tunic, the long ornamental tunic he had on; then they took him and threw him into the cistern. The cistern was empty; there was no water in it.

Then they sat down to eat. Joseph will prove to be a man whose status at various moments is defined by clothing and unclothing. The tunic symbols leadership and represents his father's favor. Stripping the tunic symbolically cancels these pretensions and brings him to measure. That there was no water in the pit means that he was saved from instant death; the story can continue. That they sat down to eat demonstrates deep and murderous callousness.

Looking up they saw a caravan of Ishmaelites coming from Gilead, their camels laden with gum, balm, and resin to be taken down to Egypt. Judah said to the brothers: "What is to be gained by killing our brother and concealing his blood? Come, let us sell him to these Ishmaelites, instead of doing away with him ourselves. After all, he is our brother, our own flesh." His brothers agreed.

The evocation of Ishmaelites is an anachronism—Ishmael, uncle of Joseph, was still alive![37] Judah did not want Joseph dead, but out of the way and no longer to be reckoned with. The rivalry between Reuben and Judah will issue in the ascendancy of Judah in Genesis 43–44. Judah begins a trajectory in the Joseph story that sees him sharing the firstborn status with Joseph in Genesis 49. Judah got no gain from the sale.

---

37. Some see no ethnic designation here; for them Ishmaelites refers generally to merchants of the desert.

Midianite traders passed by and they pulled Joseph up out of the cistern. They sold Joseph for twenty pieces of silver to the Ishmaelites, who took him to Egypt.

It appears that Midianite traders have been introduced to clear the brothers from the crime of kidnapping and selling a brother. Exod 21:16 legislates: "a kidnapper, whether he sells the person or the person is found in his possession, shall be put to death" (see similar in Deut 24:7). Twenty pieces of silver is the price for a half-grown youth (Lev 27:4–5).

"What happens to Joseph foreshadows all that will happen to the sons of Jacob. They will be carried down into Egypt and there put into slavery."[38]

When Reuben went back to the cistern and saw that Joseph was not in it, he tore his garments, and returning to his brothers, he exclaimed: "The boy is gone! And I–where can I turn?" They took Joseph's tunic, and after slaughtering a goat, dipped the tunic in its blood. Then they sent someone to bring the long ornamented tunic to their father, with the message: "We found this. See whether it is your son's tunic or not."

Tearing one's garment is a rite of mourning for the dead; Reuben assumed that Joseph was no more. "The coat given to confirm love, becomes a confirmation of death." The coat was distinctive of Joseph; kid's blood resembled human blood. That they sent someone else with such a message illustrates the chasm of disaffection between them and the father. To speak of "your son's tunic," not "our brother's" or even "Joseph's," turns Jacob's pet love on its head—he apparently referred to Joseph as "my son" even in their presence.[39]

He recognized it and exclaimed: "My son's tunic! A wild beast has devoured him. Jacob has been torn to pieces!" Jacob tore his garments, put sackcloth on his loins and mourned for his son many days.

Some dramatic justice here. Long ago, Jacob deceived his father Isaac by killing a kid and disguising himself in the clothes of his brother Esau (Gen 27:9, 15). In fact, he was inconsolable; he prolonged his mourning

---

38. Sailhamer, *Pentateuch as Narrative*, 209.

39. He will tell them of Benjamin who took Joseph's place in his heart: "my son shall not go down with you" (Gen 42:38).

to the point that his sons and daughters[40] tried to console him, but failed. He refused all consolation, saying,

"No, I will go down mourning to my son in Sheol . . . thus did his father weep for him."

He will continue mourning rites till he dies. This is the first occurrence in the Bible of Sheol, the abode of the dead in ancient eschatology before belief in the resurrection arose. The father's mourning enshrined the memory of Joseph, highlighting his enduring place in the father's affection. If the brothers' goal was to pry Joseph from this affection, their strategy did the very opposite.

The Midianites, meanwhile, sold Joseph in Egypt to Potiphar, an official of Pharaoh and his chief steward.

We pointed out the slight confusion in the text. If in verse 28 the Midianites sold Joseph to the Ishmaelites, then Ishmaelites should bring him to Egypt, which is exactly what Gen 39:1 envisages. Potiphar has two titles. He is *sarîs* of Pharaoh, eunuch of Pharaoh; in ancient societies, eunuchs were important officers placed in charge of the king's harem, among other duties. He is also *rab tabbaḥîm*, chief steward. This title designates Nebuzaradan as captain of the bodyguard of Nebuchadnezzar, king of Babylon (2 Kgs 25:8), and as such in charge of all executions.

Tradition

The fathers of the church quite early saw Joseph as a figure of Christ: "Joseph, again, himself was made a figure of Christ in this point alone . . . that he suffered persecution at the hands of his brethren, and was sold into Egypt, on account of the favor of God; just as Christ was sold by Israel—(and therefore,) 'according to the flesh,' by his 'brethren'-when He is betrayed by Judas."[41] Caesarius later drew this out.

> Upon seeing Joseph, his brothers discussed his death; just as when the Jews saw the true Joseph, Christ the Lord, they all resolved with one plan to crucify him. His brothers robbed Joseph of his outside coat that was of diverse colors; the Jews

---

40. In the Jacob narrative, he had only one daughter, Dinah.
41. Tertullian, *Adversus Judaeos* 10; translation from the online *Patristic Bible Commentary*.

stripped Christ of his bodily tunic at his death on the cross . . .
Upon the advice of Judah, Joseph is sold for thirty pieces of
silver [he remarks that for Joseph some say 20, others 30 pieces
of silver]; Christ is sold for the same amount upon the counsel
of Judas Iscariot . . . Joseph went down to Egypt; Christ went
into the world. Joseph saves Egypt from want of grain; Christ
frees the world from a famine of the Word of God.[42]

Augustine used Jacob's "my sadness will lead me to hell with my son" to reflect on hell. He somehow confounds Hades with Hell as developed in Christian doctrine.

There is often a serious problem in interpreting the word
"hell." Do only the bad or the good ones go down there? If
only the bad guys come down, how does Jacob say he wants
to come down crying where his son is? Obviously, he does not
believe that his son is in the pains of hell. Or is it the words of a
disturbed person who laments and therefore exaggerates their
evils?[43]

Cyril of Alexandria makes the distinction between Hades and Hell, somewhat straightening out Augustine's thinking.

The pit was empty; there was no water in it. By this means it
indicates to us most clearly that Hades is here being symbolized. And how is this, I ask? Because water in actual fact represents life, since it sustains life. So it says that there was no water
in the pit, for Hades is not unreasonably understood to be a
dwelling place that lacks life. Yet the youth was brought up. So
also Christ came back to life from the dead, for the pit could
not hold on to him. Neither did Christ remain in Hades, but
rather he emptied it out, for to those who were in bonds God
says, "Come out!" (cf. Isa 49:9).[44]

Midrash pondered why a person of seventeen years was called a *na'ar*/youth. It opined that Joseph was vain and did deeds of youthful foolishness—daubed his eyes and smoothed back his hair and raised his heel (*Gen. Rab.* 84:7). As such, he became occasion of temptation for Potiphar's wife. Another tradition interpreted it positively: he was seventeen

---

42. Caesarius of Arles, *Sermon* 89.2, in ACCS 1:240.
43. Augustine, *Questions on Genesis* q. 126.
44. Cyril of Alexandria, *Glaphyra on Penteuch: Genesis*, bk. 6.5.

when he went forth from the schoolhouse (*Tg. Ps.-J.*), where he learnt Torah.

Attempt was made to explain Jacob's love for Joseph: his father loved him above the rest of his sons, both because of the beauty of his body and the virtues of his mind, for he excelled the rest in prudence.[45] Or it may be because his features were like his own features (*Gen. Rab.* 88:8).

Reuben had not been with them to eat when they sold him, since he was sitting (and) fasting because he had disarranged his father's couch. And he had gone and sat in the mountains (intending) to return to the pit to raise him up (and restore him) to his father, hoping that he might win his favor (*Tg. Ps.-J.* on Gen 37:29; see also *Gen. Rab.* 84:19). "Disarranging his father's couch" refers to the incident of Gen 35:22 where Reuben lay with Bilhah, his father's concubine. "When Reuben went back to the cistern" uses the verb *shûb*. This root can mean "return/go back," but also "return/repent." The midrash opted for the second meaning.

---

45. Josephus, *Ant.* 2.9.

CHAPTER 23

Genesis 38

Judah and Tamar

> She is in the right rather than I.
>
> —Genesis 38:26

Genesis 38 is an interlude; it focuses on Judah, and not on Joseph. Allowing time for Joseph to be brought to Egypt, it reports on Judah who in the last chapter counseled the sale of Joseph. Judah's profile grows all through the Joseph Novella. Genesis 38 forms a frame with Genesis 49 around the story of the rise of Joseph; together they function to redirect the leadership of Joseph towards that of Judah in the present of the readers.[1]

---

1. Sarna, *Genesis*, 264: "So these narratives, while they recount the rise of Joseph, subtly register as well the ascendancy of Judah . . . Judah became the name of the southern kingdom, while the northern kingdom of Israel was known as Joseph (cf. Zech 10:6). The present chapter, then, provides a foil to the Joseph-centered episodes. It hints, ever so obliquely, at the future Joseph-Judah polarity in the history of the people of Israel."

> When brothers live together and one of them dies without a son, the widow of the deceased shall not marry anyone outside the family; but her husband's shall come to her, marrying her and performing the duty of a brother-in-law. The firstborn son she bears shall continue the name of the deceased brother, that his name may not be blotted out from Israel. (Deut 25:5–6)

The setting of this chapter is Palestine, that of Genesis 37 and 39 is Egypt. In Genesis 37, Judah is a young man, apparently without children and shepherding together with his brothers; here in Genesis 38, he appears to be an old grandfather.[2]

Although Genesis 38 was independent narrative, some literary features attach it to Genesis 39 and the Joseph story. Both share the theme of faithfulness practiced in spite of grave difficulties; both dramatize the perils and pitfalls to which the divine promises were subjected on their way to fulfillment.[3] These two chapters are the only ones to feature a female character, a seductress. Both are the only ones in the wider story of Joseph to feature the divine name YHWH. In distinction from the usual theology of the Joseph story, both portray a degree of overt divine involvement in human affairs.[4]

Tamar and Tragedy, 38:1–11

About that time Judah went down, away from his brothers, and pitched his tent near a certain Adullamite named Hirah. There Judah saw the daughter of a Canaanite named Shua; he married her, and had intercourse with her.

The narrator tells the story from Judah's point of view—his intentions and actions drive the plot. Here Judah separates from his brothers, whereas in the rest of the Joseph Novella he remains with them. "Judah left his family and settled in what was eventually designated as his tribal land."[5] This may preserve the memory that the Judah tribe was already settled

---

2. See Redford, *Study*, 17.
3. Cook, "Four Marginalized Foils," 116.
4. See Bekins, "Tamar and Joseph," 387.
5. Cook, "Four Marginalized Foils," 123.

independently in Canaan during the patriarchal period.[6] Adullam is an ancient Canaanite royal city that was conquered by Joshua (Josh 12:15). Judah's mixing with Canaanites is not condemned,[7] nor his marriage with a Canaanite woman, as was the case in Genesis 24 and Gen 28:8.[8]

She conceived and bore a son whom she called Er. Judah got a wife named Tamar for his firstborn Er. But Er, Judah's firstborn, greatly offended the LORD, so the LORD took his life.

In quick succession, she also bore Onan and Shelah. Tamar is Canaanite; the clans of Judah arose from a mixture of Israelite and Canaanite elements.[9] The narrator does not tell us what Er's offense was. He merely says that he was evil in the eyes of the LORD. It is possible that his early death was construed as deriving from culpability.

Then Judah said to Onan, "Have intercourse with your brother's wife, in fulfillment of your duty as brother-in-law, and thus preserve your brother's line.

The levirate custom appears elsewhere only in Ruth 4 and Deut 25:5–10. Apparently in earlier times, as in this story, the obligation rested with the father-in-law to give the widow to the surviving brother; later, as in Deuteronomy 25, the obligation was restricted to the brothers of the deceased. One takes the widow of his dead brother, and the first son of this union continues the line of the dead brother and inherits him.

Onan, however, knew that the offspring would not be his; so whenever he had intercourse with his brother's wife, he wasted his seed on the ground, to avoid giving offspring to his brother. What he did greatly offended the Lord, and the Lord took his life too.

The usually laconic narrator is here profuse about intentions. The offspring would not be his; besides, he would inherit the firstborn status

---

6. Bekins, "Tamar and Joseph," 385. See also Gunkel, *Genesis*, 396, who cites Judges 1 where Judah left the common camp to conquer its later tribal territory.

7. Cook, "Four Marginalized Foils," 117 thinks that use of the verb *naṭah*, turn aside, connotes deviation from the right or loyal path, that Judah turned geographically, but also morally.

8. *Pace* Clifford, "Genesis 38," 525, who says that Judah's marriage with a Canaanite woman was sin against God and cursed by God.

9. Gunkel, *Genesis*, 396.

over Onan and his own sons.[10] As the custom of the land, the levirate was deemed to have divine sanction. Twice the narrator assigned the death of the sons to divine causality. The reader knows that Tamar is not to blame; Tamar is no witch killing off her husbands. But Judah is not privy to this knowledge.

Then Judah said to his daughter-in-law Tamar, "Remain a widow in your father's house until my son Shelah grows up"–for he feared that Shelah also might die like his brothers. So Tamar went to live in her father's house.

In voicing Judah's fear for the life of his son Shelah, the narrator is excusing him somewhat. It was not animus towards Tamar, rather to preserve his son's life. As a widow, Tamar's bonds to Judah's family remained intact. Even in her own father's house, she would wear widow's garments and was under the authority of Judah, her father-in law.

Further Reflections

The Sin of Onan. What Onan did was evil in YHWH's eyes. The narrator faults Onan for wasting his seed to avoid giving offspring to his brother. He would be righteous had he followed through with the levirate custom and given Tamar a son. That custom was considered the right and honorable thing to do, for one to fulfill obligations to the family. Onan had no loyalty to his deceased brother, no intention of giving up the inheritance, yet slept with Tamar. The narrator's evaluation seems based on the socio-religious context of the levirate obligation.[11] See "Tradition" for the discussion of onanism.

Tamar and Righteousness, 38:12–30

In this unit, Tamar's intentions and actions drive the plot. She held all the cards.

Time passed, and the daughter of Shua, Judah's wife died. After Judah completed the period of mourning, he went up to Timnah, to those who were shearing his sheep, in company with his friend Hirah the Adullamite.

---

10. See Clifford, "Genesis 38," 528.
11. See Meyer, "Judah and Tamar," 3. Sarna, *Genesis*, 267 believes that evading his obligation in such manner places Onan's relationship with Tamar in the category of incest.

The narrator lauds Tamar, yet excuses Judah. He completed mourning duties for his wife, he did not know the woman was her daughter-in-law, he did not take advantage of her and renege on his pledge, and he never again touched her.[12] Tamar learnt that Judah was passing her way.

So she took off her widow's garments, covered herself with a shawl, and having wrapped herself sat down at the entrance to Enaim,[13] which is on the way to Timnah, for she was aware that, although Shelah was now grown up, she had not been given to him in marriage.

The narrator ranges the reader on her side by revealing that she was not after pleasure, rather acting out of fidelity towards the deceased.

When Judah saw her, he thought she was a harlot . . . So he went over to her at the roadside and said, "Come, let me have intercourse with you," for he did not realize that she was his daughter-in-law.

She asked for payment and a pledge.

He answered, "I will send you a young goat from the flock." Your seal, and cord, and the staff in your hand. So he gave them to her and had intercourse with her, and she conceived by him. After she got up and went away, she took off her shawl and put on her widow's garments again.

The seal and staff are personalized! She has set Judah up. Just one stand and she conceived—the hand of God was there. All she wanted was seed, and here it was. The narrator makes no comment about Judah's tryst with a prostitute.

Judah sent the young goat by his friend the Adullamite to recover the pledge from the woman; but did not find her.

He even asked the men of the place where the cult prostitute[14] by the roadside in Enaim was. They knew of none. He went back to Judah with the news. Judah replied,

"let her keep the things, otherwise we will become a laughingstock. After all, I did send her this young goat, but you did not find her." About three months later, Judah was told, "Your daughter-in-law Tamar has acted like a harlot,

---

12. See Gunkel, *Genesis*, 399.

13. *Petaḥ Enaîm* means "the opening of the eyes." Is there symbolism in this name?

14. Judah thought the woman was a prostitute (*zônah*); his Canaanite friend took her to be a cult prostitute (*qᵉdēshah*), perhaps in service of a fertility deity.

and now she is pregnant from her harlotry." Judah said, "Bring her out; let her be burned."

The stuff of which irony is made! The pledge in Tamar's possession will seriously and publicly compromise Judah. Because of continuing bonds to Judah's family, Tamar's pregnancy could only be defined as adultery. Deut 22:23-24 stipulates stoning as the punishment for adultery. Apparently in early Israel, the punishment was burning.[15] As head of the family, Judah had the power of life and death over its members. We saw Jacob himself wield this right when in Gen 31:32 he promised Laban, "as for your gods, the one you find them with shall not remain alive!" In later times, there would be need for a judicial inquiry with witnesses. The pledge Judah had given Tamar now served in lieu of witnesses:

"See whose seal and cord and staff these are." Judah recognized them and said, *"She is in the right rather than I, since I did not give her to my son Shelah." He had no further sexual relations with her.*

It was Judah's moment of truth. Judah used the root *ṣdq* usually translated as "righteous," "just," "in the right." The preposition *mimmenî* can mean "than me." The NIV renders: "She is more righteous than I." This translation places the transaction on the religious plane of conformity to the will of God; both pursued worthwhile goals, but Tamar adhered closer to God's will. *Mimmenî*, in context, can also be rendered "from me," "not me." This would be a comparison of exclusion, whereby the subject alone possesses the quality enumerated.[16] The NJB toes this line: "she was right and I was wrong."[17] Judah was on the legal plane—only Tamar's behavior conformed to the levirate relationship. Judah went against it in refusing her to Shelah. Judah's confession is the beginning of his redemption in the narrative. His profile will continue to grow until he becomes ascendant over the brothers.

The narrator lauded Tamar's foresight and scheming. Modern readers struggle with ethical questions involved, like does the end justify the means? Did Tamar commit adultery, even incest? Levirate marriage was an aspect of the culture of the ancient Near East. Indeed, it is practiced by many peoples of Africa. Is it among "statutes that were not good" (Ezek

---

15. Lev 21:9 prescribes this for adultery by a priest's daughter. Sarna, *Genesis*, 270 cites the analogy of Achan (Josh 7:15, 25) ordered burned, but who was first stoned.

16. Cf. Clifford, "Genesis 38," 530.

17. Westermann, *Genesis 37-50*, 55: "she is within her rights rather than I."

20:25) that God gave to his people? In relation to the social status of women in Pauline churches, the Pontifical Biblical Commission invites reflection on what "should be considered perennially valid and what should be considered relative, linked to a culture, a civilization, or even the mentality of a specific period of time."[18] So perhaps here also?

Tamar Becomes Ancestor of David

When the time of her delivery came, there were twins in her womb.

The birth of twins can be regarded as sign of blessing from God. While she was giving birth, one put out his hand. The midwife tied a crimson thread on his hand before he pulled it back.

But as he withdrew his hand, his brother came out; and she said, "What a breach you have made for yourself!" So he was called Perez. Afterward his brother, who had the crimson thread on his hand, came out; he was called Zerah.

We are back to the choice of the younger over the elder. The relevance of this little story can be seen from Ruth 4:18–22: "These are the descendants of Perez: Perez was the father of Hezron, Hezron was the father of Ram, Ram was the father of Amminadab, Amminadab was the father of Nahshon, Nahshon was the father of Salma, Salma was the father of Boaz, Boaz was the father of Obed, Obed was the father of Jesse, and Jesse became the father of David."

Tamar, the Canaanite, through union with Judah, became ancestor of David, eventually of Jesus. The continuing story may focus on the leadership of Joseph, but the rule of David and the southern tribe of Judah is already in the wings.

Tradition

How could Judah marry the daughter of a Canaanite? *Tg. Ps.-J.* took "Canaanite" not as ethnic term, but as designating a profession—Shua was a merchant. And in line with Genesis 24, *Jub.* 41:1 makes Tamar an Aramean: Judah took as wife for his firstborn Er one of the Aramean

---

18. Pontifical Biblical Commission, *Inspiration and Truth of Sacred Scripture*, no. 132.

women, whose name was Tamar. That way, Judah would not be seen as breaking the prohibition against marrying people of the land. *Tg. Ps.-J.* accordingly makes her daughter of Shem the Great. The narrator did not say why Er was evil in the eyes of YHWH; midrash (*Tg. Ps.-J.*; *Gen. Rab.* 85:4), on the analogy of Onan, opined that Er did not have intercourse with his wife according to the manner of all the earth.

Augustine lays out an early Christian understanding of the episode: "Intercourse even with one's own legitimate wife is unlawful and wicked where conception of the offspring is prevented. Onan, the son of Judah, did this and the Lord killed him for it."[19] Jerome in a diatribe against Jovinian wrote: "But I wonder why he [Jovinian] set Judah and Tamar before us for an example, unless perchance even harlots give him pleasure; or Onan who was slain because he grudged his brother seed. Does he imagine that we approve of any sexual intercourse except for the procreation of children?"[20] Also for Jerome, Onan's sin was *coitus interruptus*.

Tertullian condemned Tamar when he wrote: "That done, you will condone incests, too, for Lot's sake; and fornications combined with incest, for Judah's sake."[21] But Ephrem records a prayer of Tamar that suggests that her action had divine sanction.[22]

> Grant also that an invitation to lie with him might be found in his mouth, so that I may know that it is acceptable to you that the treasure, which is hidden in the circumcised, might be transmitted even through a daughter of the uncircumcised ... the prayer of Tamar inclined him, contrary to his usual habit, to go to a harlot.[23]

In the manner of "o happy fault" of the *Exultet* on Holy Saturday, Ephrem sang:

---

19. Augustine, *De Conjugiis Adulterinis*, 2.12; cited by Pius XI in *Casti Connubii*, no. 55.

20. Jerome, *Against Jovinian* 1.20.

21. Tertullian, *On Modesty* 6.

22. Jewish midrash recorded in *Tg. Onq.* and *Tg. Ps.-J.* at Gen 38:25 also records a long prayer of Tamar after asking and not finding three witnesses, followed by a long address of Judah that included, "Tamar, my daughter-in-law is innocent, by me she is with child." In *Tg. Ps.-J.* a heavenly voice then came down from heaven and said, "the matter has come from before me." *Tg. Onq.* has a *Bath Qol* proclaim, "they are both just, from before the Lord the thing has come about."

23. Ephrem, *Commentary on Genesis* 34.3, 4, in ACCS 2:243-44.

> For holy was the adultery of Tamar, for thy sake. Thee it was she thirsted after, O pure Fountain. Judah defrauded her of drinking thee ... She was a widow for thy sake. Thee did she long for, she hasted and was also an harlot for thy sake. Thee did she vehemently desire, and was sanctified in that it was thee she loved.[24]

Augustine has a long theological reflection on the moral evaluation of Tamar and Judah. What he refers to as "compensative sins" may evoke the morality of double effect.

> But why do these persons think they may imitate Tamar telling a lie, and not think they may imitate Judah committing fornication? For there they have read both, and none of these did that Scripture either blame or praise, but has merely narrated both, and to our judgment dismissed both; but it is marvelous if it has permitted anything of these to be imitated with impunity. For, that Tamar not through lust of playing the harlot, but through wish of conceiving seed, did tell the lie, we know. But fornication also, howbeit Judah's was not such, yet some man's may be such whereby to procure that a man may be delivered, just as her lie was in order that a man might be conceived. Is it right then to commit fornication on this account, if on that account it is thought that it was right to lie? Not therefore concerning lying only, but concerning all works of men in which there arise, as it were compensative sins, must we consider what sentence we ought to pass, lest we open a way not only to small sins whatsoever, but even to all wickedness, and there remain no outrageous, flagitious, sacrilegious deed, in which there may not arise a cause upon which it may rightly seem a thing meet to be done, and so universal probity of life be by that opinion subverted.[25]

Augustine speaks of her lie and Judah's fornication. What of her fornication? Was the birth of twins, one of whom became ancestor of David, indication of God's blessing? We face again the question of divine concurrence in acts of humans that may not seem moral.

What Onan did has entered the moral books as *onanism* or interrupted intercourse, with the implication that YHWH killed him because of this sexual sin. The dictionary defines onanism as a) masturbation and b) *coitus interruptus*. The *Catechism of the Catholic Church* nos. 2351–56 lists offenses against chastity as: lust, masturbation, fornication,

---

24. Ephrem, Hymn 7.
25. Augustine, *To Consentius, Against Lying* 30.

pornography, prostitution, and rape.[26] Offenses against the dignity of marriage are: adultery, divorce, polygamy, incest, "so-called free union," and "trial marriage" (nos. 2380–91).[27] A search for onanism and *coitus interruptus* turned up blank. It appears that the *Catechism* includes such when it speaks of the "inseparable connection, established by God . . . between the unitive significance and the procreative significance which are both inherent to the marriage act" (no. 2666). As such, "every action which, whether in anticipation of the conjugal act, or in its accomplishment, or in the development of its natural consequences, proposes, whether as an end or as a means, to render procreation impossible" is intrinsically evil" (no. 2370, citing *Humanae Vitae* 14). Does this answer all the questions above?

---

26. Nos. 2357–58 deal with homosexuality and homosexual acts.

27. No. 2370 approves of periodic continence and use of infertile periods as legitimate methods of controlling birth; contraception is proscribed.

CHAPTER 24

Genesis 39

Joseph and Potiphar's Wife

> For wisdom will enter your heart ... saving you from a stranger, from a foreign woman with her smooth words.
>
> —PROVERBS 2:10, 16

AFTER THE INTERLUDE OF the story of Judah and Tamar in Genesis 38, Genesis 39 picks up the story of Joseph from Genesis 37. Genesis 39 has been daubed "the theological entrance piece to the Joseph story."[1] It is framed with the motif of "YHWH with" Joseph (39:2-3; 22-23). Although there are no theophanies or overt divine exertions of presence and power, the reader is made to understand that God's hand still guides Israel's destiny through what is happening in Joseph's life.

The story also emphasizes Joseph's moral integrity, showing his resilience against the danger of the "strange woman" of Proverbs. Genesis 22 showed that Abraham was worthy of divine favor, so promises earlier made unconditionally became reward of his obedience. Genesis 39 performs a comparable function in the Joseph story; divine blessing is here linked with righteousness, and pious behavior is not without its reward.[2]

---

1. Westermann, *Genesis 37-50*, 62.
2. See Levin, "Righteousness in the Joseph Story," 228 for what he calls the "righteousness edition" in the Pentateuch.

The LORD Was with Joseph, 39:1–6

> How is it that the chief steward, a eunuch, had a wife? The terms "eunuch" and "castrated male" are frequently employed to mean more than one thing. But it was not unusual even for one who was truly a eunuch to have a wife in his house to attend to domestic affairs. (Theodoret of Cyrus, *Questions on the Octateuch*, Gen. q. 100)

When Joseph was taken down to Egypt, an Egyptian, Potiphar, an official of Pharaoh and his chief steward, bought him from the Ishmaelites who had brought him there.

This takes up the story of Joseph from Gen 37:28 where Midianites sold Joseph to the Ishmaelites who took him to Egypt, ignoring the information in Gen 37:36.[3] The meaning of the word *sarîs*, here translated "an official," is ambivalent. It is used in many places for a high court official, though literally it appears to mean "eunuch." The title is not strictly Egyptian; such officers appear in courts in Israel, Syria, and Babylonia.[4] Eunuchs, retained as overseers of the king's harem, often became confidants of the ruler and achieved high status and power.[5]

The LORD was with Joseph and he enjoyed great success and was assigned to the household of his Egyptian master.

"Grace from on high stood by him, it is saying, and smoothed over all his difficulties. It arranged all his affairs; it made those traders well-disposed to him and led them to sell him to the chief steward so that he should advance gradually and, by proceeding through those trials, manage to reach the throne of the kingdom."[6] It was also the LORD's doing that the courtier assigned him to the household and not to the fields, where we probably would have heard no more of him. The "LORD being with" is a feature of the Jacob saga in his travels and return home;

---

3. The Midianites sold Joseph in Egypt to Potiphar, an official of Pharaoh and his chief steward.

4. Redford, *Study*, 200.

5. See Kedar-Kopfstein, "Sarîs," 347. At Gen 40:1–2, Pharaoh's officials were first designated as cupbearer and baker before they were called his "eunuchs."

6. Chrysostom, *Homilies on Genesis* 62.13, in ACCS 2:248.

here it designates more covert divine guidance and assistance. With such assistance, everything Joseph touched was gold. Joseph found favor in the eyes of his master, who made him his personal attendant.

he put him in charge of his household and entrusted to him all his possessions . . . the Lord's blessing was on everything he owned, both inside the house and out. Having left everything he owned in Joseph's charge, he gave no thought, with Joseph there, to anything but the food he ate.

The same motif of putting everything under Joseph's care will recur with the prison jailer. According to Gen 43:32, Egyptians may not eat with Hebrews; so perhaps touching the food would defile it for his master. But, because Joseph later used a similar phrase in telling his master's wife that "he has withheld from me nothing *but you*," some understand "the food he ate" as equivalent to "you," that is, only Potiphar's wife was not placed in Joseph's hands.[7]

The Seduction, 39:7–20

Now Joseph was well-built and handsome.

This is the exact description of his mother Rachel in Gen 29:17. Joseph is the only male so described. The narrator seems to suggest that Potiphar's wife was drawn by Joseph's beauty. One may not, however, rule out the will for conquest and the casting of such a powerful servant of the master under her spell.

After a time, his master's wife looked at him with longing and said, "Lie with me." But he refused and said to his master's wife.

This woman is never named; she is merely "his master's wife"—the story is told from Joseph's point of view. "Lie with me" is two words in Hebrew. In Hebrew style it is coarse language and signals crass desire, yet it is the command of the mistress of the house to a slave. Joseph's response in twenty-eight words is verbose; the "verbosity is supposed to portray his gravity and zeal."[8] The Masoretes, who furnished the biblical text with vowels and cantillation signs, suggest otherwise. They marked "he refused" with the *shalshelet* sign, which denotes lingering, hesitation,

---

7. See Lowenthal, *Joseph Narrative*, 34.
8. Gunkel, *Genesis*, 407.

sustained deliberation[9] (see "Tradition" for views of Joseph as sorely tempted and almost yielding).

"Look, as long as I am here, my master does not give a thought to anything in the house, but has entrusted to me all he owns. He has no more authority in this house than I do. He has withheld from me nothing but you, since you are his wife. How, then, could I do this great wrong and sin against God?"[10]

Joseph invokes loyalty and fidelity to his beneficent master and fear of the all-seeing God. Most ancient peoples considered adultery a great sin and made severe laws against it. And in so far as general morality was under God's protection and sanction, adultery was also a great sin against God.

Although she spoke to him day after day, he would not agree to lie with her, or even be near her.

The sense of the text is better rendered by the NRSV, which reads, "to lie beside her or to be with her." In order to trap him, she went from "lie with me," to "lie beside me," to "just be with me." And this harassment went on daily and for quite some time! Joseph managed never to be alone with her.

One such day, when Joseph came into the house to do his work, and none of the household servants were then in the house, she laid hold of him by his cloak, saying, "Lie with me!" But leaving the cloak in her hand, he escaped and ran outside.

Joseph was about his duties. The woman's attack was sudden and unexpected, or is the narrator indicating vacillation in reporting that not one of the servants was then in the house? She laid hold of him by his *begged*, which usually denotes the inner garment as contrasted with *me'il*, the outside garment. Joseph had no choice but to slip out of the garment and flee naked, leaving the garment in her hands. She knew herself in mortal danger should the servants accost Joseph and hear his story first. There is nothing as burning as scorned love.

When she saw that he had left his cloak in her hand as he escaped outside, she cried out to her household servants and told them.

---

9. See Bakon, "Subtleties in the Story," 172; Lowenthal, *Joseph Narrative*, 35.

10. In speaking with a non-Hebrew, Joseph uses the common name for God, *Elohim*, and not the specific name of the Hebrew God, YHWH.

There is considerable artistry in the report of what follows.[11] Thrice the lady reported the scene with Joseph to the household servants, to her husband, and a further report to the husband—each time altering the story just slightly enough to address the susceptibilities of the particular audience. To the household servants:

"Look! My husband has brought us a Hebrew man to mock us! He came in here to lie with me, but I cried out loudly. When he heard me scream, he left his cloak beside me and escaped and ran outside."

She plays the ethnic card (a Hebrew man), highlighted in the TNK translation: "look, he had to bring us a Hebrew fellow." This foreigner has the effrontery to try to mock us (you and me). The verb used, *ṣaḥeq*, can mean "to play with" or "dally with." He even attempted rape. When I let out a scream (she was lying, of course), he left his cloak beside me (not in my hands). The timing is important. The narrator already reported that she cried out *after* Joseph escaped her; she put the cry *before*. Legally, a victim of rape in an urban area proves no consent by crying out for help according to Deut 22:23–24: "If there is a young woman, a virgin who is betrothed, and a man comes upon her in the city and lies with her, you shall bring them both out to the gate of the city and there stone them to death: the young woman because she did not cry out though she was in the city, and the man because he violated his neighbor's wife."

She refrains from calling Joseph a servant or slave, for they too were servants and she wanted them on her side, besides that a servant would raise lustful eyes towards the lady of the house would compromise her. Finally, "we" (you men of the household and I) must stand together against Joseph and his master, my husband, who brought this Hebrew man to us in the first place.

She kept the cloak with her [literally, "beside her"] *until his master came home. Then she told him the same story.*

This time, the picture changes somewhat. Joseph is now *the Hebrew slave whom you brought us*—"us" now being her husband and herself. The way she put it betrays studied ambiguity:

---

11. Among several who have dealt with this, the reader may follow Sternberg, *Poetics of Biblical Narrative*, 423–27. See also Pirson, "Twofold Message," 256.

There came the Hebrew slave (that you brought us to play games with
me)—Potiphar intended this[12] or at least enabled it.

There came the Hebrew slave (that you brought us) to play games with
me—instead of doing his assigned duty.

*When the master heard his wife's story in which she reported, "Thus and so
your servant did to me," he became enraged.*

In the third instance, the wife kept nagging about this, pressing the
point that the offender is a slave who thus betrayed the position of trust
placed in him. As Joseph's master, Potiphar had to do something. The
narrator says that he was enraged, naturally, but the object of his anger
remains unstated.

Joseph's master seized him and put him into the jail where the king's prisoners were confined. And there he sat in jail.

"The nature of the punishment is a sign that he was not convinced of
Joseph's guilt. The appropriate punishment for the crime would be death,
or at least sale into a lower degree of servitude."[13] In fact, Gen. Rab. 87:9
has the master admit: "I know that you are innocent . . . but [I must do
this] lest a stigma fall upon my children." It may also be that she did
not explicitly report that Joseph intended to rape her[14]; she did not use
the verb *shakab*, "lie with." Israel did not have the prison institution; this
aspect belongs to the Egyptian context of the story. A surprising twist
is that Joseph said nothing in his own defense; was he denied defense
because a slave? The fathers of the church found in his silence under false
witness one of his resemblances to Christ.

The LORD Was with Joseph, 39:21–23

*But the Lord was with Joseph, and showed him kindness by making the
chief jailer well-disposed toward him.*

12. For an interesting theory that Potiphar, being a eunuch, bought Joseph, the
good-looking slave, precisely to father a son with his wife, see Pirson, "Twofold Message." The scheme was designed by Potiphar and his wife. But in the end, Joseph, like
Onan, committed *coitus interruptus*. The garment served as proof of the great lengths
to which she went to bring the scheme to fulfillment.

13. Westermann, *Genesis 37–50*, 67.

14. Sarna, *Genesis*, 275.

The jail was in an enclosure housed on Joseph's master's property. "This, after all is ever God's way, not to free virtuous people from dangers or preserve them from trials but, in the midst of such trials, to give evidence of his characteristic grace to such an extent that the very trials prove an occasion of festivity for them."[15] "His characteristic grace," which the text renders as "kindness," is here found in the *ḥesed* God gave Joseph in the eyes of the jailer: God's loyalty and faithfulness to Joseph worked for favor before the chief jailer (see text box below). It appears that the chief jailer is responsible to the chief steward, Joseph's master (but see 40:4 where it was the chief steward who assigned the king's prisoners to Joseph, hence identifying him with the jailer).

The chief jailer put Joseph in charge of all the prisoners in the jail. Everything that had to be done there, he was the one to do it.

> So then the Sun of Righteousness rises upon us when God makes his face to shine upon us and gives us strength. Joseph in Egypt was shut up in prison, and we next hear that the keeper of the prison, believing in his fidelity, committed everything to his hand. And the reason is given: Genesis 39:23, Because the Lord was with him: and whatsoever he did, the Lord made it to prosper. (Jerome, *Dialogue against Pelagians* 3.8)

Just as in his master's house, so also here in prison, everything is put under Joseph's charge,

since the LORD *was with him and was bringing success to whatever he was doing.*

Wis. 10:13–14 recounts the story as follows:

> when the righteous man was sold, Wisdom did not desert him, but delivered him from sin. She descended with him into the dungeon and when he was in prison she did not leave him until she brought him the scepter of a kingdom and authority over his masters. Those who accused him she showed to be false, and she gave him everlasting honor.

Wisdom takes over the function of "the Lord being with" Joseph. New is that his master's wife and the household servants were shown to be false. In the context of persecution, 1 Macc 2:51–53 reads the story as

---

15. Chrysostom, *Homilies on Genesis* 62.15, in ACCS 2:249.

the testing and reward of Joseph: "was not Abraham found faithful when tested . . . Joseph in the time of his distress kept a commandment and became lord of Egypt."

Tradition

For the fathers of the church, Joseph became the hero of chastity and virtue: "The noble Samson was overcome by the harlot, and by another woman was shorn of his manhood. But Joseph was not thus beguiled by another woman. The Egyptian harlot was conquered. And chastity, assuming to itself bonds, appears superior to dissolute license."[16] He accomplished all this with little struggle: "Grace from on high stood by him, it is saying, and smoothed over all his difficulties" (see Chrysostom in note 6 above). In Chrysostom's retelling, Joseph is a martyr put to the test by a satanic female, and prevailing through a combination of effort and grace:

> he was in constant fear, lest his mistress should set upon him, and worse than any prison was the fear that lay upon him: but after the accusation he was in security and peace, well rid of that beast, of her lewdness and her machinations for his destruction . . . Here he comforted himself, that for chastity's sake he had fallen into it: there he had been in dread, lest he should receive a death-blow to his soul . . . So that the fact was not that he got into prison, but that he got out of prison. She made his master his foe, but she made God his friend: brought him into closer relation to Him who is indeed the true Master; she cast him out of his stewardship in the family, but made him a familiar friend to that Master.[17]

He becomes "the ideal of sexual purity—his name the topos for chastity and modesty."[18] Christology inhibited exploring the inner struggle of Joseph as happened in Jewish and Muslim tradition. Joseph as Christ-type cannot have been tempted, since sexual attraction and desire are not understood to be among those challenges confronted by Jesus.[19]

---

16. Clement of Alexandria, *Christ the Educator* 3.11.

17. Chrysostom, *Homilies on the Acts of the Apostles*, hom. 49, In *Patristic Bible Commentary*.

18. Gregg, "Joseph with Potiphar's Wife," 340.

19. Gregg, "Joseph with Potiphar's Wife," 342.

> A matron asked R. Jose: "Is it possible that Joseph, at seventeen years of age, with all the hot blood of youth, could act thus?" Thereupon he produced the Book of Genesis and read the stories of Reuben and Judah. If Scripture did not suppress aught in the case of these, who were older and in their father's home, how much the more in the case of Joseph, who was younger and his own master. (*Gen. Rab.* 87:6)

Jewish midrash had two trends. First, Joseph as a bastion of moral strength, illustrating the Hellenistic ideals of self-control and passionlessness (see text box above on *Gen. Rab.* 87:6, which illustrates that Scripture does not generally present its characters as models to imitate, but mirrors in which to contemplate human strivings and desire). *Jub.* 39:6–9 (second century, BCE) put it as follows.

> But he did not surrender his soul, and he remembered the Lord and the words which Jacob, his father, used to read from amongst the words of Abraham, that no man should commit fornication with a woman who has a husband; that for him the punishment of death has been ordained in the heavens before the Most High God, and the sin will be recorded against him in the eternal books continually before the Lord.[20] And Joseph remembered these words and refused to lie with her. And she besought him for a year, but he refused and would not listen. But she embraced him and held him fast in the house in order to force him to lie with her, and closed the doors of the house and held him fast; but he left his garment in her hands and broke through the door and fled without from her presence.

That she besought him for a year and that she embraced him and held him fast and closed the doors of the house are new. The *Testament of Joseph*[21] magnifies Joseph's integrity by expanding on various strategies Potiphar's wife indulged in to conquer Joseph. Dispute continues whether this work is basically a Jewish work or a Christian work based on Jewish material.

A second trend presented Joseph as a man of flesh and blood liable to temptation, but saved by adherence to Jewish tradition and culture.

---

20. This explains how before Sinai Joseph knew the divine prohibition of adultery. See Gregg, "Joseph with Potiphar's Wife," 330.

21. Some date it to the second century BCE, though it did not reach final form till the second century CE.

Rabbis of the Amoraim period (200–600 CE) presented Joseph as ambivalent, if not a willing collaborator, in keeping with the general rabbinic anthropology that privileges spiritual struggle over passive acceptance.[22] His initial vacillation would help justify the ordeal of his lengthy imprisonment. Besides, a Joseph who was tempted but not yielding was a more relatable model for ethical conduct.[23] She availed of a public festival: "So, on the approach of a public festival, when it was customary for women also to join the general assembly, she made illness an excuse to her husband, in quest of solitude and leisure to solicit Joseph."[24] In *Gen. Rab.* 87:7, R. Judah said this was the festival of the Nile, R. Nehemiah that it was a day of theater. Though some traditions read "he came into the house to do his work" (39:11) as to examine his masters account books (*Gen. Rab.* 87:7; all Targums), others read it as to do his work, not the master's; that is, he went in for sexual intercourse. However, he saw his father's face, at which his blood cooled (*Gen. Rab.* 87:7)—memory of, and adherence to, the tradition are ramparts against the temptation to alterity as symbolized by this foreign woman.

In their fight against the inroads of pagan festivals and the Roman theater (that often parodied synagogue and church), the rabbis saw in Potiphar's wife a symptom of the threat to national culture: the sexual struggle (*enkrateia*) becomes a trope for cultural continence, and the battle for cultural identity is intertwined with the conflict for sexual identity.[25] B. Sotah 36b is to be understood in this context:

> R. Yohanan said: this [verse] teaches that the two of them had planned to sin together. *And Joseph went to the house to do his work* (39:11). Rav and Shmuel–one said: it means literally to do his work, the other said that he went to satisfy his desires [his work, and not his master's]. *And not one of the members of the household were present* . . . R. Ishmael: that particular day was their festival, and they had all gone to their idolatrous rites, and she said to everyone, 'I am ill." Saying [to herself] she has no day to fornicate with Joseph like this day. *And she seized him by his garment saying, "lie with me."* This teaches that they both went to bed naked.[26] At that moment the image of his father appeared

---

22. Levinson, "Joseph and Potiphar's Wife," 279.
23. See Kugel, *In Potiphar's House*, 98.
24. Josephus, *Ant.* 2.45.
25. Levinson, "Joseph and Potiphar's Wife," 294.
26. Reading his *begged*/garment as his *bagdo*/betrayal—the root *bgd* appears as

to him in the window, and said, "Joseph, Joseph, your brothers will have their names written on the priestly breastplate (*ephod*) and yours among them. Do you want it effaced, and yourself called a shepherd of prostitutes," as it says *a man who loves wisdom will please his father but a shepherd of prostitutes loses his wealth* (Prov 29:3). At once *his bow stayed taut* (Gen 49:24)—R. Yohanan said, this teaches that his bow returned to its natural state.[27]

---

noun in garment, and as verb "to betray/deal treacherously."

27. Bow stands here for the phallus.

CHAPTER 25

Genesis 40–41

From Prison to Power

> Do you see how important it is to bear trials thankfully? . . . So take note: Joseph bore distress with endurance, endurance gave him character, having such character he acted in hope, and hope did not disappoint him [cf. Rom 5:3–5].[1]

SOME INTERPRETERS RELY ON these chapters to postulate Joseph's rise during the Hyksos period[2] in ancient Egypt.[3] Genre is important to meaning; as narrative, not history, the Joseph Novella's truth depends on what the narrative itself intends to reveal about God's purposes for his people. It seems that "the immediate objective of the two Pharaoh-dominated chapters (40–41) is to get Joseph into position as vice-ruler of Egypt so that his family may be able to take refuge there."[4]

---

1. Chrysostom, *Homilies on Genesis* 63.17, in ACCS 2:268.
2. The Hyksos or "shepherd kings" were a Semitic dynasty that ruled Egypt between 1700 and 1550 BCE. An early advocate of the connection was Josephus in *Against Apion* 1.86–94, reporting from the Greek historian, Manetho, that not fewer than 240,000 of these left Egypt and built up Jerusalem (*Against Apion* 1.89–90, 94).
3. Redford, *Study*, 241–42 argued that the parallels here and elsewhere in the Joseph Novella point rather to the writer's acquaintance with a much later Egypt, namely, of the seventh to the fifth centuries BCE, that is, Saite, Persian and Ptolemaic Egypt.
4. Green, "Determination of Pharaoh," 151.

Joseph Interprets the Dreams of Pharaoh's Officials, Genesis 40

Some time afterward, the royal cupbearer and baker offended their lord, the king of Egypt. Pharaoh was angry with his two officials ... and he put them in custody in the house of the chief steward, the same jail where Joseph was confined. The chief steward assigned Joseph to them, and he became their attendant.

Prisons and imprisonment were unique to ancient Egypt; Israel had no such institutions. The Pharaoh portrayed here and in the rest of the story is an absolute monarch whose fiat may result in life or death. The narrator says that these officials "sinned" against the king of Egypt; the chief cupbearer later in 41:9 speaks of "my sin." The offense is not mentioned, but it was such as could attract the death penalty. The jail was in the compound of the "chief steward," that is, Potiphar, Joseph's master. He had imprisoned Joseph there, assigning him a place with Pharaoh's officials.[5] Verse 7 is explicit that these officials were in custody with Joseph in his master's house. We get the sense later that resolution in Joseph's case depended on the Pharaoh, and not on Joseph's master.

> In Gen 39:22, the chief jailer put Joseph in charge of all the prisoners in the jail and of everything done there. Here, the chief steward assigned Joseph to serve the king's chief cupbearer and chief baker. The different traditions brought together here make the chief jailer the same person as the chief steward, namely, Joseph's master Potiphar.

After they had been in custody for some time, the cupbearer and the baker of the king of Egypt ... both had dreams on the same night, each his own dream and each dream with its own meaning.

Dream interpretation was a specialty in ancient Egypt, a feature of "Egyptian wisdom."[6] The Hebrew Scriptures contain contrasting views on dreams.[7] On the one hand is Num 12:6: "if there are prophets among you, in visions I reveal myself to them, in dreams I speak to them." In Gen 15:13-16, Abram received revelation in a dream about Israel's future

---

5. See Lowenthal, *Joseph Narrative*, 41. Lowenthal is trying to bring out the sense of "he assigned Joseph with them (*'ittam*)," rather than "to them." In 41:12, the cupbearer refers to Joseph as "a slave of the chief steward."

6. Gunkel, *Genesis*, 412.

7. Discussed by the rabbis in b. Ber. 55b.

enslavement and oppression in Egypt. The dream here was "not an illumination of the past and the present but of the future . . . [it] projects a divine scenario . . . a foreshadowing on the part of the narrator."[8] On the other hand, Zech 10:2 declares that "the diviners have seen false visions; deceitful dreams they have told." A rabbi asserts that "a man is shown in a dream only what is suggested by his own thoughts."[9]

When Joseph came to them in the morning, he saw that they looked disturbed. Upon inquiry, they answered: *"We have had dreams, but there is no one to interpret them." Joseph said to them, "Do interpretations not come from God? Please tell me the dreams."*

Human mediation in the matter is not denied. Not all dreams come from God, neither does all interpretation: "The initiative and the 'showing' come from God, but human wisdom and discernment remain necessary. Joseph's gifts are not irrelevant . . . His abilities come into play and are *used* by God in the interpretive process."[10]

Then the chief cupbearer told Joseph his dream. Pharaoh's cup was in my hand; so I took the grapes, pressed them out into his cup, and put it in Pharaoh's hand.

A vine with three branches barely budded when it blossomed, and the clusters ripened into grapes. Joseph gave him the interpretation:

"The three branches are three days; within three days Pharaoh will single you out and restore you to your post . . . Only think of me when all is well with you, and please do me the great favor of mentioning me to Pharaoh, to get me out of this place. The truth is that I was kidnapped from the land of the Hebrews, and I have not done anything here that they should have put me into a dungeon."

The phrase "single you out" is literally "lift up your head." A suppliant prostrated and bowed the head before Pharaoh; the lifting of the head signified graciousness. For the baker, Joseph adds "from you," meaning death by decapitation/impaling. Diviners and dream interpreters

---

8. Sternberg, *Poetics of Biblical Narrative*, 395. However, to say that it is "objective and infallible" seems to discount necessary human synergy.

9. Sternberg, *Poetics of Biblical Narrative*, 395. This last is close to the modern psychology of the interpretation of dreams, whereby dreams are held to express internal states and stresses.

10. Fretheim, "Genesis," 239.

normally expected some token of thanks. Joseph would accept nothing, but only asked to be remembered to Pharaoh. That he was kidnapped from his homeland seems to agree with Gen 37:28, 36 according to which Midianite traders, not his brothers, pulled Joseph out of the cistern and sold him into slavery in Egypt to Potiphar. Joseph may also be dissimulating to save his honor and that of his family (cf. 45:4, where he tells his brothers, "I am your brother Joseph, whom you sold into Egypt").

> In the commentary on Genesis 37, we indicated the variant according to which the Midianite traders sold Joseph to the Ishmaelites, Gen 37:28, who brought him to Egypt, Gen 39:1. Such variants indicate that biblical inspiration is not alien to the composition of a story by piecing together varying and sometimes contrasting strands.

> R. Bana'ah: There were twenty-four interpreters of dreams in Jerusalem. Once I dreamt a dream and I went round to all of them and they all gave different interpretations, and all were fulfilled, thus confirming that which is said: All dreams follow the mouth [= interpretation] . . . For R. Eleazar said: Whence do we know that all dreams follow the mouth? Because it says, and it came to pass, as he interpreted to us, so it was (Gen 41:13). Raba said: This is only if the interpretation corresponds to the content of the dream: for it says, to each man according to his dream he did interpret, Gen 41:12. (b. Ber. 55b)

"The land of the Hebrews" is an anachronism if the story were placed before Israel's arrival in Canaan. Some interpreters thus suggest that "Hebrew" here is no ethnic, but sociological, designation, recalling groups of uprooted and classless persons, called the *apiru* or *Habiru*, who roamed between Egypt and Syria in the Amarna Period (1400–1300 BCE), hiring themselves out as mercenaries. It appears, however, that the term "Hebrew" for Palestine belongs to the Persian period and after.[11] For the first time, Joseph reacts about the false charge of Potiphar's wife and Potiphar's throwing him into prison—he is guilty of no crime. The dungeon or pit recalls the cistern into which his brothers threw him (37:24). "Joseph seems to hope or expect, even to suggest, that if Pharaoh hears

---

11. Redford, *Study*, 201–2. For example, it is an ethnic term in Exod 2:11, where Moses saw an Egyptian man striking a Hebrew man.

of the unjust imprisonment, the great man would free him, would be fair, merciful."[12] The narrator does not disclose why Pharaoh should bother about Joseph at all.

When the chief baker saw that Joseph had given a favorable interpretation, he said to him: "I too had a dream. In it I had three bread baskets on my head; in the top one were all kinds of bakery products for Pharaoh, but the birds were eating them out of the basket on my head."

It was a bad omen when birds of prey swooped down on Abram's sacrifice in Gen 15:11.

"The three baskets are three days; within three days Pharaoh will single you out [lift up your head from you] and will impale you on a stake, and the birds will be eating your flesh.

As the narrator foretold in verse 5, each dream had its own meaning, although the pattern was similar. The art of the interpreter is to discern the difference.

And so on the third day, which was Pharaoh's birthday, when he gave a banquet to all his servants, he singled out the chief cupbearer and chief baker in the midst of his servants. He restored the chief cupbearer to his office ... but the chief baker he impaled ... Yet the chief cupbearer did not think of Joseph; he forgot him.

Events corresponded exactly with Joseph's interpretation. In ancient belief, the fate of the soul after death is tied to the care of the corpse—this explains the Egyptian art of mummification and the pyramids. The impaling of someone and leaving his corpse for the birds was tantamount to annihilation.

Both the fathers of the church and Jewish rabbis debated whether Joseph showed lack of trust in God. Citing Ps 40:5, "Happy the man that hath made the Lord his trust ... ," *Gen. Rab.* 89:3 opines that because he said to the chief butler, "but have me in remembrance ... and make mention of me," two years were added to his sufferings.[13] Chrysostom

---

12. Green, "Characterization of Pharaoh," 153.

13. *Tg. Neof.* to Gen 40:23: "Joseph forsook the favor that is from above and the favor that is from below, and the favor which had accompanied him from his father's house, and he trusted in the chief cup-bearer, in flesh that passes, in flesh that tastes the cup of death ... wherefore the cup-bearer did not remember Joseph and he forgot him until the appointed time to be redeemed had arrived."

added: "And for this he was suffered to remain, that he might learn not to place hope or confidence in men, but to cast all upon God."[14] When and how should one rely wholly in God? God does not always do it alone: "Although Joseph has the God-given ability to interpret dreams, he still needs *human* help . . . Human help will finally be a key to Joseph's future, as it will be for virtually everybody."[15]

In retelling this story, Ps 105:17–22 wrote:

> He had sent a man ahead of them, Joseph, sold as a slave. They shackled his feet with chains; collared his neck in iron, till his prediction came to pass, and the word of the LORD proved him true. The king sent and released him; the ruler of peoples set him free. He made him lord over his household, ruler over all his possessions, to instruct his princes as he desired, to teach his elders wisdom.

Being confined in fetters and having the neck collared in iron are new, so also that Joseph taught Egyptian elders wisdom—the tradition is growing.

Pharaoh Dreams, Joseph Interprets, Genesis 41

After a lapse of two years, Pharaoh had a dream. He was standing by the Nile, when up out of the Nile came seven cows, fine-looking and fat; they grazed in the reed grass. Behind them seven other cows, poor-looking and gaunt, came up out of the Nile; and standing on the bank of the Nile beside the others, the poor-looking, gaunt cows devoured the seven fine-looking, fat cows. Then Pharaoh woke up.

In derision, his brothers called Joseph "master of dreams" (Gen 37:17); ironically he proves to be master of dreams. Dreams and their interpretation drive his rise to power. The Nile is the lifeline of Egypt and symbolizes it; in flood, its waters irrigate the fields. The adjective used for "fat," *barî*, is usual for humans and not for animals.

He fell asleep again and had another dream. He saw seven ears of grain, fat and healthy, growing on a single stalk. Behind them sprouted seven ears of grain, thin and scorched by the east wind; and the thin ears swallowed up

---

14. Chrysostom, *Homilies on Genesis* 63.17, in ACCS, 2:268.
15. Fretheim, "Genesis," 240.

the seven fat, healthy ears. Then Pharaoh woke up–it was a dream! Next morning his mind was agitated.

What so agitated Pharaoh's mind we are not told here; the narrator will later give him word to express his fright. Dreams were held to be messages from the other world that revealed what was about to happen, and these ones do not seem to augur well for the country (symbolized by the Nile).

So Pharaoh had all the magicians and sages of Egypt summoned and recounted his dream to them; but there was no one to interpret it for him.

> **THE BEE AND THE PIGEON**
> One day, a bee and a pigeon that were good friends went to the river to draw some water. When they came to the river's edge, the bee fell into the water. His friend the pigeon helped him by throwing him a branch to climb onto. When the bee was safe, the pigeon flew away and perched in a nearby tree. A short time later, a man arrived. He was carrying a gun. He saw the pigeon and carefully aimed at it. When the bee saw this, he knew he had to help his friend. Quickly, he flew over to the man and stung him in the leg. The hunter jumped and the gun went off into the air. Thanks to his friend, the pigeon was able to fly away. (Schaefer, *Central African Folk Tales*, 19)

"He recounted his dream" suggests that Pharaoh already discerned that the two dreams were one. Magicians occur in the Bible only in connection with Egypt and Babylon[16]; dream interpretation was one of their specialties. The magicians applied their art, but no interpretation seemed right to Pharaoh—perhaps because the dream seemed to foretell misfortune, and no one had the courage to say so.[17]

Then the chief cupbearer said to Pharaoh: "Now I remember my negligence! Once, when Pharaoh was angry with his servants, he put me and the chief baker in custody in the house of the chief steward."

He recounted how he and the chief baker had dreams the same night and how a Hebrew youth with them in custody interpreted the dreams.

---

16. Sarna, *Genesis*, 281.

17. Westermann, *Genesis 37–50*, 85. Lowenthal, *Joseph Narrative*, 48 suggested that they saw them as two different dreams with different portents, when Pharaoh already realized they were really one dream.

"Things turned out just as he had told us: I was restored to my post, but the other man was impaled."

Pharaoh had Joseph hurried to him. He shaved, changed clothes, and came before Pharaoh. Egyptians grew beards and hair only when mourning a near relative; otherwise, only prisoners and slaves were unshaved as sign of humiliation and dishonor.[18] Joseph is a man whose fortunes change with clothing; he begins to take on new status. Pharaoh said to Joseph,

"I hear it said of you, 'If he hears a dream he can interpret it.'" "It is not I," Joseph replied to Pharaoh, "but God who will respond for the well-being of Pharaoh."

Both Pharaoh and Joseph share belief in dreams as media of revelation. Here also, Joseph accredited the divine with his ability to interpret dreams. The interpretation will satisfy Pharaoh and quieten his agitation (literally, will be for the "peace of Pharaoh").

Pharaoh related his dream to Joseph. In doing so, he gave vent to his fright and disturbance. The seven scrawny cows were such that

never have I seen such bad specimens as these in all the land of Egypt.

When they had devoured the fat cows,

No one could tell that they had consumed them, no one could tell that they had done so, because they looked as bad as before.

The Pharaoh was puzzled that eating so much made no difference for the scrawny cows; the same for the ears of grain. And what could all this mean?

Joseph said to Pharaoh: "Pharaoh's dreams have the same meaning. God has made known to Pharaoh what he is about to do ... Seven years of great abundance are now coming throughout the land of Egypt; but seven years of famine will rise up after them, when all the abundance will be forgotten in the land of Egypt. When the famine has exhausted the land, no trace of the abundance will be found in the land because of the famine that follows it, for it will be very severe. That Pharaoh had the same dream twice means that the matter has been confirmed by God and that God will soon bring it about.

---

18. Lowenthal, *Joseph Narrative*, 49. On the contrary, for Semites the beard was a mark of dignity, long hair an ornament of warriors and heroes.

The point of the dream concerned the coming famine. Something must be done if this is to be averted. So, Joseph suggested that a discerning and wise man be put in charge of organizing the storage of food during the years of plenty:

"*This food will serve as a reserve for the country against the seven years of famine that will occur in the land of Egypt, so that the land may not perish in the famine.*"

> Let Pharaoh act and appoint overseers for the land to organize it during the seven years of abundance (v. 34). The verb used, *himmesh*, is uncertain. If it derives from the word for five, it calls for one-fifth of the harvest to be stored during the time of plenty—something that seems to become permanent policy in Gen 47:24.[19] Some people derive the verb from *hamush*, armed, equipped, prepared—hence the translation, "organize."[20] Gen 41:35, however, speaks of gathering all the food during the time of plenty (what would the people eat then?).

Joseph's advice pleased Pharaoh and all his servants. Pharaoh did not wait to verify Joseph's interpretation or see the years of plenty begin.

"*Could we find another like him,*" Pharaoh asked his servants, "*a man so endowed with the spirit of God?*" So, Pharaoh said to Joseph: "*Since God has made all this known to you, there is no one as discerning and wise as you are. You shall be in charge of my household, and all my people will obey your command. Only in respect to the throne will I outrank you.*"

Joseph called for a "discerning and wise man"; Pharaoh and his servants found the discerning and wise man in Joseph, one endowed with the spirit of God. "True wisdom, the ability to discern between 'good and evil,' comes only from God."[21] For the first time in the Bible, we hear of endowment of the people by the spirit of God (*ruah Elohim*). The spirit of God "impels one to undertake a mission, imparts extraordinary energy and drive and produces uncommon intelligence and practical wisdom."[22] It does not dispense with the person's abilities, rather incites and maximizes particular gifts suitable to the task at hand.[23] This is the third time

19. Gunkel, *Genesis*, 419.
20. Sarna, *Genesis*, 285.
21. Sailhamer, *Pentateuch as Narrative*, 215.
22. Sarna, *Genesis*, 286.
23. See Fretheim, "Genesis," 243.

that everything is left in Joseph's hands, except one particular item—Potiphar put the entire household in Joseph's hand, except the food he ate (Joseph qualified it as except his wife). The jailer put the prisoners and everything under Joseph's charge; Pharaoh now puts all his household and the whole of Egypt under Joseph, except for the throne. For his installation as vizier of Egypt, Pharaoh put his own signet ring on Joseph's finger, dressed him in fine linen, and put a gold chain around his neck.[24]

He then had him ride in his second chariot, and they shouted "Abrek!" before him.

Just as in Gen 13:17 YHWH asked Abram to "get up and walk through the land..." as symbol of taking possession, so here Joseph rides around Egypt in Pharaoh's second chariot. The meaning of *Abrek* is disputed. It is a call for homage and may mean "stand at attention."

Pharaoh also bestowed the name of Zaphenath-paneah on Joseph, and he gave him in marriage Asenath, the daughter of Potiphera, priest of Heliopolis. And Joseph went out over the land of Egypt. Joseph was thirty years old when he entered the service of Pharaoh, king of Egypt.

That means that Joseph has been thirteen years in Egypt, since he was seventeen years when sold into slavery. His change of status is completed with the change of name—he became an Egyptian noble. His Egyptian name means "the god speaks and he (the newborn child) lives." Asenath means "belonging to the Neith (Egyptian goddess)." The narrator does not evaluate Joseph's marriage into the priestly family of the religion of Egypt. As a high official, he would have to participate in the state cult. What lessons can be drawn for religious minority officials and politicians who have to serve where the dominant religion is other?

Both Joseph and his brother Judah (see chap. 38) marry women outside the family and its religious heritage. Later legends speak of Asenath's conversion, but Genesis has no interest in this.

> The text attests to a remarkable capacity for the integration of Yahwistic faith and other religious communities and expressions (similarly 2 Kgs 5:15-19). Many OT texts do not tolerate such practices, but the reasons are contextual rather than normative

---

24. The same three insignia are found in Ashurbanipal's installation of Necho as vassal king of Egypt: "I clad him in a garment of multicolored trimmings, placed a golden chain on him (as the) insigne of his kingship and put golden rings on his hands." *ANET* 295. See also Redford, *Study*, 225.

(e.g., dangers of syncretism). Joseph functions as an ideal for Israel at this point, demonstrating that the later intolerance is not characteristic of the *Yahwistic faith in and of itself*. Joseph illustrates that such integration can be a positive experience and need not carry negative effects.[25]

In other words, biblical injunctions and prohibitions should be understood in their particular contexts and compared with one another before one can discern what the Bible intends as binding.

During the seven years of plenty, Joseph

collected all the food of these years of plenty . . . and stored in the cities, placing in each city the crops of the fields around it.

It was so much that he stopped measuring it. Before the famine set in he became the father of two sons, born to him by the Egyptian Asenath.

Joseph named his firstborn Manasseh, meaning, "God has made me forget entirely my troubles and my father's house"; and the second he named Ephraim, meaning, "God has made me fruitful in the land of my affliction."

Do we have here "studied forgetfulness"?[26] Trauma victims generally suppress memory of the trauma-inducing experience. Joseph understandably blocked out his siblings, but his father also? Why speak of "the land of my affliction"? In Egypt he rose from slave to vizier; that was hardly affliction. Perhaps being fruitful in the land of affliction foreshadows the experience of Israel in Egypt (Exod 1:12)? There entered the seven years of famine.

Although there was famine in all the other countries, food was available throughout the land of Egypt. When all the land of Egypt became hungry and the people cried out for food

The apparent contradiction between the two statements is eased if it is taken for granted that food was available in Egypt but locked up in silos. With time Egypt too felt the famine and the people cried out to Pharaoh for food and he directed them to Joseph.

Joseph opened all the cities that had grain and rationed it to the Egyptians . . . Indeed, the whole world came to Egypt to Joseph to buy grain, for famine had gripped the whole world.

---

25. Fretheim, "Genesis," 244–45.
26. Sternberg, *Poetics of Biblical Narrative*, 286.

The scene is set for the encounter between Joseph and his siblings.

Tradition

St. Stephen recalled Joseph's story (Acts 9:7, 9–10): "And the patriarchs, jealous of Joseph, sold him into slavery in Egypt; but God was with him and rescued him from all his afflictions. He granted him favor and wisdom before Pharaoh, the king of Egypt, who put him in charge of Egypt and [of] his entire household." For Augustine, the sale of Joseph calls for meditation on "how God uses well the evil works of men, as they on the other hand use ill the good works of God."[27] He raised the question how a eunuch could have a wife and daughter. Showing where his interest lies, he answered that "it is believed that he became a eunuch or because of some injury or of his own volition . . . [in the long run] neither of these two hypotheses that one admits is dangerous to faith or contrary to the truth of the Scriptures of God." He recalls that the name Pharaoh gave Joseph means "revealed things hidden." "Obviously it is because Joseph revealed to the king his dreams. They say that in the Egyptian language this name means 'savior of the world.'"[28]

We find similar reference to revealing secrets from Josephus, who explained Joseph's name as "Psothom Phanech, out of regard to his prodigious degree of wisdom; for that name denotes the revealer of secrets."[29] Equating Potiphar, Joseph's master, and Potiphera, the priest of Heliopolis, midrash has Joseph marry the daughter of his master's wife (*Gen. Rab.* 89:2). In addition, the Targums have Potiphera not as priest of Heliopolis, but as master or chief (*Tg. Neof./Tg. Ps.-J.*)—they could not see Joseph embracing Egyptian religion!

---

27. Augustine, *Exposition on the Psalms*, Ps 105:17.
28. Augustine, *Questions on Genesis*, q. 135.
29. Josephus, *Ant.* 2.6.1.The secret concerned Asenath's pedigree. She was indeed offspring of Dinah and Shechem, and the wife of Potiphera had reared her (*Tg. Neof./Tg. Ps.-J.*). In *Gen. Rab.* 90:4, Jacob drove her out, tying a disc round her neck to mark her as of his family. Joseph saw the disc and hid it, so her real identity remained unknown. All these say that Asenath really was no Egyptian, but had Israelite blood.

CHAPTER 26

Genesis 42–44

Joseph Encounters His Brothers

> Joseph is not only angry, but also capable of compassion... The whole psychological portrayal of Joseph, in whom two attitudes struggle with one another, is the most complicated and complete characterization in all of Genesis.[1]

THESE THREE CHAPTERS NARRATE two journeys to Egypt by Joseph's brothers. Escalating dramatic tension is broken only by Judah's speech in 44:18–34. Denouement is reached in 45:1–15 when Joseph finally reveals himself to his brothers.

Joseph's behavior in this unit is much debated. The reader knows that Joseph immediately recognized his brothers upon sight of them. His brothers did not recognize him and were left wondering the why of their experiences, what they could mean.

Some understand Joseph's actions positively. He intended to produce repentance and so make reconciliation possible.[2] He put on a show

---

1. Gunkel, *Genesis*, 426.
2. Midrash generally follows this script, for example, Lowenthal, *Joseph Narrative*, 70: Joseph "persists, for at stake is not his but God's forgiveness... Instead, Joseph now embarks upon an amazing and protracted strategy of 'testing' them, i.e., to actualize through their true repentance their potential brotherliness. That is why Joseph decides to purge them first with a 'show' of anger, God's anger and God's retribution." An

of anger and put the brothers through loops in order to arouse and reform their consciences. An example:

> We need to be very certain that what Joseph put his brothers through is not a protracted scheme of revenge but a course of education: a brief version of the process by which he himself learned that his gifts–good looks, authority, the prodigious abilities to interpret dream and deliver the land from a seven-year famine–were all presents from God, gifts with the power to save human lives ... beginning with Joseph's own.[3]

Others understand him as "a deeply flawed character, as his brothers were in chap. 37 ... [and] like them ... much in need of transformation."[4] Moved by revenge, at least initially, he knowingly set his brothers up and played the tension to breaking point. He behaved like a tyrannous lord, using power to deceive, manipulate, and agonize the prey.[5]

This commentary sees Joseph "caught in a maelstrom of conflicting emotions ... the instinctive desire for revenge is tempered by the knowledge that his father and brothers back in Canaan may be starving and are depending on the acquisition of provisions in Egypt ... above all, he feels he must find out conclusively whether or not his brothers regret their actions and have truly reformed themselves."[6] Decisive for him will be the brothers' relation to Benjamin, whether the brothers were equally treacherous to him.

---

example from the fathers of the church: "Truly he was so holy that he could not have hated them. Therefore, we must believe that he wearied them with so many tribulations, in order to arouse them to a confession of their sin and the healing of repentance ... Since blessed Joseph knew that his brothers could not be forgiven their sin of murder without much penance, once, twice and a third time he worried them with salutary trials as with a spiritual fire. His purpose was not to vindicate himself but to correct them and free them from so grave a sin ..." Caesarius of Arles, *Sermon* 91.6, in ACCS 2:277.

3. Prose, "Story of Joseph," 200-201. Cited in Humphreys, *Character of God in Genesis*, 225.

4. O'Brien, "Judah's Speech," 440.

5. See Coats, *From Canaan to Egypt*, 37-38. Gunkel, *Genesis*, 422: "Before, he was in their power; now they are in his. He also has the upper hand in that he recognizes them but they do not recognize him ... He thoroughly punishes and torments them. They go from one fear and distress to another, just as they deserve in relation to him. The narrator's sense of justice is expressed here. After punishing them sufficiently, he pardons them and becomes their benefactor."

6. Sarna, *Genesis*, 293. Westermann, *Genesis 37-50*, 111 speaks of the "inextricable intertwining of harshness and readiness for reconciliation."

The First Journey to Egypt, Genesis 42

When Jacob learned that grain rations were for sale in Egypt, he said to his sons: "Why do you keep looking at one another?" He went on, "I hear that grain is for sale in Egypt. Go down there and buy some for us, that we may stay alive and not die."

The seven years of plenty were over and the seven years of famine had set in. People were going to Egypt and returning with provisions. The brothers were looking at one another, implying hesitation. The Syriac version had the father ask, "why are you afraid?"[7] The narrator gives a hint that ever since the sale of Joseph the brothers were ill at ease hearing of Egypt. "To live and not die" is one of the recurring motifs of the Joseph story.

So, ten of Joseph's brothers went down to buy grain from Egypt. But Jacob did not send Joseph's brother Benjamin with his brothers, for he thought some disaster might befall him.

Benjamin is "Joseph's brother," the siblings are "Joseph's brothers"—such usage highlights the question of the presence or lack of fraternal solidarity dramatized by the story. There is narrative focus on Benjamin, called the "youngest brother" (*ha-qātōn*) six times in chapter 42 alone, besides three references by name or as prepositional object. Benjamin has become the surrogate Joseph; he has taken up Joseph's place in the father's affections. All ten brothers needed to go to Egypt in order to bring enough supplies for their families. They arrived in Egypt as "sons of Israel," as a nation in embryo; the journey to Egypt has national import.[8]

Joseph, as governor of the country, was the one who sold grain to all the people of the land. When Joseph's brothers came, they bowed down to him with their faces to the ground. He recognized them as soon as he saw them . . . and spoke harshly to them . . . When Joseph recognized his brothers, although they did not recognize him, he was reminded of the dreams he had about them.

He recognized them though they did not recognize him. These were the brothers who sent Joseph's blood-soaked garment to their father saying, "see whether it is your son's tunic," and he recognized it (Gen 37:32–33). Then Joseph was in their power; now they are in his. "They bowed

---

7. *Tg. Ps.-J.*: "why then are you afraid to go down to Egypt?"
8. Sarna, *Genesis*, 292.

to him with their faces to the ground"—the dream of sheaves (Genesis 37) is being fulfilled, reinforced by the court language of "your servants" and "my lord." The brothers understood the dream as a threat to rule over them, so sought to frustrate it. The sheaves, however, symbolized nurture, nurturing the family so it may live and not die. Joseph, who had correctly interpreted other people's dreams, may have been overtaken by the surge of suppressed memories of the trauma he experienced at the hands of his brothers. He was harsh to them.

He said to them: "You are spies. You have come to see the weak points of the land." "No, my lord," they replied. "On the contrary, your servants have come to buy food. All of us are sons of the same man. We are honest men; your servants have never been spies."

The charge of spying carried the death penalty. Joseph used to bring his father bad reports about the sons of Bilhah and Zilpah (Gen 37:2)—he spied on them. The brothers first wanted to kill him, but ended up throwing him into a cistern. Joseph first levelled a charge of capital crime, but eventually threw them into prison. "You have come to see the nakedness of the land" casts the brothers in the role that the wife of Potiphar cast him and for which he was thrown into prison—they were would-be Hebrew rapists.[9] This may also allude to his being undressed when they undressed him of the tunic given by the father. The brothers answered that they were upright men, sons of one man, though of different mothers. No family would risk the demise of all its sons on the dangerous mission of spying. Joseph continued to pressure them until they blurted out,

We your servants . . . are twelve brothers, sons of a certain man in Canaan; but the youngest one is at present with our father, and the other one is no more.

In speaking of twelve brothers, they included Joseph as "the other one [who] is no more."[10] The father was still alive. He has kept Benjamin by him, just as he had Joseph. Joseph doubted the brothers' word about Benjamin. Had they done away with him also? He needed to see Benjamin with his own eyes. That would prove them both honest (in regard to the charge of spying) and upright (in regard to behavior), and as having evolved from earlier wickedness.

9. See Sternberg, *Poetics of Biblical Narrative*, 288.
10. Reporting him as a missing person; they could neither confirm his death nor speak about their involvement in his disappearance.

"This is how you shall be tested: I swear by the life of Pharaoh that you shall not leave here unless your youngest brother comes here. So send one of your number to get your brother, while the rest of you stay here under arrest. Thus will your words be tested for their truth; if they are untrue, as Pharaoh lives, you are spies!" With that, he locked them up in the guardhouse for three days.

The brothers are given a taste of the arbitrariness of unchecked power. There is no logic to locking them all up in jail for three days,[11] except to ruffle and crack them up, and perhaps induce recriminations with each other.

On the third day Joseph said to them: "Do this, and you shall live; for I am a God-fearing man. If you are honest men, let one of your brothers be confined in this prison, while the rest of you go and take home grain for your starving families. But you must bring me your youngest brother. Your words will thus be verified, and you will not die." To this they agreed.

Joseph relented after three days. The imprisonment has not advanced his purpose of bringing Benjamin. He too has a conscience and fears God, who defends the stranger and the weak and before whom he will render an account. They can bring supplies home, but they must bring their youngest brother under pain of death. Failure to bring him would prove that they had also done away with the remaining son of the beloved Rachel. It would prove them not only liars, but also unrepentant murderers. The chain of events beyond their control cut the brothers to the quick.

To one another . . . they said: "Truly we are being punished because of our brother. We saw the anguish of his heart when he pleaded with us, yet we would not listen. That is why this anguish has now come upon us."

Asham refers to both guilt and its punishment; the two went together in the ancient mind. Retribution for past sins can be channeled through the ordinary events of life. They too remember, and now see "a connection between the mortal peril that they themselves brought on Joseph and the mortal peril in which they now stand through no fault of their own."[12] For the first time they recognize Joseph as "our brother."

---

11. Joseph himself was in jail for three years, the same term, *mishmar*, being used.
12. Westermann, *Genesis 37–50*, 110.

Then Reuben responded, "Did I not tell you, 'Do no wrong to the boy'? But you would not listen! Now comes the reckoning for his blood." They did not know, of course, that Joseph understood what they said, since he spoke with them through an interpreter. But turning away from them, he wept. When he was able to speak to them again, he took Simeon from among them and bound him before their eyes.

The narrator conveys delayed information: Joseph had pleaded with them for mercy, but they turned a deaf ear to him. Joseph's machinations have cracked open the consciences of his brothers: "in this moment of common adversity, their long-smoldering, tortured consciences erupt."[13] He learns that Reuben was not part of the conspiracy against him. Reuben connected their entrapment to their sin against Joseph. Like the blood of Abel, Joseph's unjustly spilled blood (they took Joseph for dead) cried to heaven for vengeance. Unknown to the brothers, Joseph understood all they were saying in Hebrew. His resolve for revenge began to melt, his defenses cracked open. He experienced the first feelings of brotherliness and compassion. He withdrew and wept. Before it is all over, he will have wept three times. Passing over Reuben, the firstborn, whom he now knows to be innocent, he had the next in seniority bound before their eyes and thrown into prison.

Then Joseph gave orders to have their containers filled with grain, their money replaced in each one's sack, and provisions given them for their journey. After this had been done for them, they loaded their donkeys with the grain and departed.

Joseph begins the role of nurture foreshadowed by the dream of sheaves. Was placing the money in their sacks an act of generosity? Was it intended as a temptation for the brothers or an eye-opener for the father?[14]—for the brothers would again return without a brother and with strange money in their sacks. Was it to shock them into relating this mystery of money in their bags to their guilt?[15]

At the night encampment, when one of them opened his bag to give his donkey some fodder, he saw his money there in the mouth of his bag. He cried out to his brothers, "My money has been returned! Here it is in my

---

13. Sarna, *Genesis*, 295.
14. Sternberg, *Poetics of Biblical Narrative*, 299.
15. See Lowenthal, *Joseph Narrative*, 74.

bag!" At that their hearts sank. Trembling, they asked one another, "What is this that God has done to us?"

"Suspicion always haunts the guilty mind; the thief doth fear each bush an officer."[16] For the first time they utter the word God, thought of whom they had so far suppressed.[17] God must have miraculously put the money in their sacks in order to punish them. Their fear was precisely what Joseph wanted to cause[18] To their father they reported:

"The man who is lord of the land . . . spoke to us harshly and put us in custody on the grounds that we were spying on the land."

Discrepancies with the narrator's report may be because they wished to spare their father more anxiety. They glossed over the imprisonment of Simeon ("the man" only held him back as surety) and that "the man" threatened them with death if Benjamin did not come with them. They did not mention that already on the way one of them saw his money returned in his sack.

When they were emptying their sacks, there in each one's sack was his moneybag! At the sight of their moneybags, they and their father were afraid. Their father Jacob said to them: "Must you make me childless? Joseph is no more, Simeon is no more, and now you would take Benjamin away! All these things have happened to me!"

It is possible they conspired to "discover" the money in their sacks right before their father.[19] But the effect on him was deep. He began to suspect something sinister: "this mysterious money explains why sons of mine keep disappearing from your company. Would you have me now entrust my youngest son to you as well? No. I had better cut my losses!"[20]

Then Reuben told his father: "You may kill my own two sons if I do not return him to you! Put him in my care, and I will bring him back to you." But Jacob replied: "My son shall not go down with you. Now that his brother is dead, he is the only one left. If some disaster should befall him on the journey you must make, you would send my white head down to Sheol in grief."

16. Shakespeare, *Henry VI*, part 3, act 5, scene 6.
17. Lowenthal, *Joseph Narrative*, 75.
18. See Gunkel, *Genesis*, 426.
19. See, Alter, *Genesis*, 249.
20. Sternberg, *Poetics of Biblical Narrative*, 298.

Ineffective Reuben is eclipsed from leadership in favor of Judah, whose portrait grows till he shares the leadership with Joseph in Genesis 49. In Gen 46:9 Reuben has four sons. He may have meant "two of my sons"—in replacement for Joseph and Benjamin. He was totally insensitive to Jacob's emotions that could not bear to hear of the loss of Benjamin, nor of any more of his grandchildren. Midrash has Jacob say: "he is indeed a foolish firstborn! Are not your sons my sons?" (*Gen. Rab.* 91:9). Benjamin as "my son . . . the only one left" confirms Benjamin as surrogate Joseph. Jacob's preferential love for the sons of his beloved wife is as strong as ever; the brothers will have to live with that.

The Second Journey to Egypt, Genesis 43

Now the famine in the land grew severe. So when they had used up all the grain they had brought from Egypt, their father said to them, "Go back and buy us a little more food." But Judah replied: "The man strictly warned us, 'You shall not see me unless your brother is with you.' If you are willing to let our brother go with us, we will go down to buy food for you. But if you are not willing, we will not go down, because the man told us, 'You shall not see me unless your brother is with you.'"

In this chapter, Joseph's father is consistently called Israel (three times). Judah effectively takes up the leadership position among the brothers. They felt no urgency about freeing Simeon, since they had reported him as not bound in prison but merely held back as surety. Judah dissimulated somewhat; the man actually threatened death if the youngest brother did not come with them (Gen 42:20). Israel faced the crisis of choice—continue grasping on to his love or giving him up for the good of the family.

Israel demanded, "Why did you bring this trouble on me by telling the man that you had another brother?" They answered: "The man kept asking about us and our family: 'Is your father still living? Do you have another brother?' We answered him accordingly. How could we know that he would say, 'Bring your brother down here'?"

In the narrator's report, Joseph did not ask them about the father, nor whether they had another brother; they blurted these out themselves. For Israel, merely telling the man of Benjamin was incalculable evil; he felt about to lose another favorite son, the only one left of his beloved wife.

Then Judah urged his father Israel: "Let the boy go with me, that we may be off and on our way if you and we and our children are to keep from starving to death. I myself will serve as a guarantee for him. You can hold me responsible for him. If I fail to bring him back and set him before you, I will bear the blame before you forever. Had we not delayed, we could have been there and back twice by now!"

The choice is between life and death; survival of the entire family is at stake. Judah, the man of pledges (see Gen 38:18), pledges himself for the boy. He will bring him back to the father or bear the guilt before the father all his days.[21]

Israel their father then told them: "If it must be so, then do this: Put some of the land's best products in your baggage and take them down to the man as gifts: some balm and honey, gum and resin, and pistachios and almonds . . . May God Almighty grant you mercy in the presence of the man, so that he may let your other brother go, as well as Benjamin. As for me, if I am to suffer bereavement, I shall suffer it."

> If Benjamin goes, he may be seized and he may not be seized; but if he does not go with us, we must all die. It is not good to avoid a doubtful evil and plunge into a certain one. (*Gen. Rab.* 91:6)

It was the first step towards reconciliation when the brothers acknowledged a beloved son of Rachel as "our brother," not just "your son." Israel himself now takes the second step—relinquishment. Having done the best in his power, he is resigned and leaves the rest to God. He gives his blessing, asking that God Almighty (El Shaddai) give them *raḥamim* (womb feelings, a mother's feelings for her baby) before the man. The brothers are to bring to Joseph a *minḥah*, the gift a subject makes to the king or a vassal to the lord. The Ishmaelites who brought Joseph to Egypt were laden with gum, balm, and resin (Gen 37:25); the brothers bringing the younger brother to Egypt are to be laden with the same, in addition to pistachios, almonds, and honey—the best products of the land. This is plot doubling: "the allusion to the items of transport suggests that this time the brothers are reenacting the role of the Ishmaelite traders,

---

21. In *Gen. Rab.* 93:8, he says, "I will be under a ban in the future world which is called 'days' if I do not bring him back."

bringing the other son of Rachel to an uncertain fate."[22] What they do in relation to Benjamin will determine the process of reconciliation in this broken family.

So the men took those gifts and double the money and Benjamin. They made their way down to Egypt and presented themselves before Joseph. When Joseph saw them and Benjamin, he told his steward, "Take the men into the house, and have an animal slaughtered and prepared, for they are to dine with me at noon."

The brothers had not forgotten the harsh reception on their first meeting with the man. They became apprehensive:

"It must be," they thought, "on account of the money put back in our bags the first time, that we are taken inside—in order to attack us and take our donkeys and seize us as slaves."

They went up to the steward and recounted to him how each one found money in his sack, money they have brought with them in addition to money for new purchases.

He replied, "Calm down! Do not fear! Your God and the God of your father must have put treasure in your bags for you. As for your money, I received it." With that, he led Simeon out to them.

We learn that Joseph had Simeon in prison for the two years it took the brothers to return (Gen 45:6 says that there have been two years of famine). The steward uttered the word of peace: "peace be with you." His equivocation was no lie; he indeed received the money. That it found its way into their sacks was the hidden largess of their God, aided by a trick of Joseph. He brought them into the house. When Joseph came home,

they presented him with the gifts they had brought inside, while they bowed down before him to the ground.

For a second time, they fulfilled the dream of sheaves by prostrating before the man.

After inquiring how they were, he asked them, "And how is your aged father, of whom you spoke? Is he still alive?" "Your servant our father is still alive and doing well," they said, as they knelt and bowed down.

This is the third time they are prostrating to Joseph.

22. Ackerman, "Joseph, Judah, and Jacob," 92; Redford, *Study*, 73.

Then Joseph looked up and saw Benjamin, his brother, the son of his mother. He asked, "Is this your youngest brother, of whom you told me?" Then he said to him, "May God be gracious to you, my son!"[23]

Using the same root, *ḥnn*, used of him pleading with his brothers in 42:21-22, he prays they will listen this time and show Benjamin favor.

With that, Joseph hurried out, for he was so overcome with affection for his brother that he was on the verge of tears. So he went into a private room and wept there.

For the second time, Joseph wept. Benjamin must have been at least twenty years old. The story presumes that Joseph never had set eyes upon him.[24] Israel had prayed that God Almighty give the brothers *raḥamîm* before the lord of the land; indeed Joseph's *raḥamîm* (intense fraternal emotion) grew hot upon sight of Benjamin. Israel's prayers were being answered. Something is changing, but reconciliation has ways to go; the compassion needs to extend to all the brothers. After withdrawing and calming himself, Joseph has the meal served.[25] Another surprise for the brothers:

> Everything he does is to test their attitude out of his wish to discover if they had been like that in dealing with Benjamin. (Chrysostom, *Homilies on Genesis* 64.11, in ACCS 2:277)

When they were seated before him according to their age, from the oldest to the youngest, they looked at one another in amazement; and as portions were brought to them from Joseph's table, Benjamin's portion was five times as large as anyone else's.

Seating them according to their ages upset the brothers—the man must have the gift of divination.[26] Benjamin's portion was five times as

---

23. Uses the same root, *ḥnn*, used of Joseph pleading with his brothers in 42:21-22.

24. In the Joseph story, Rachel is presumably alive (37:10), while she already died in 35:20. In the Joseph story, Benjamin was apparently born by or after the sale of Joseph.

25. The Egyptians ate apart, for eating with Hebrews was abhorrent to them. *Tg. Onq./Tg. Ps.-J.* gives the reason: "for the Hebrews eat the cattle which the Egyptians worship." Gen 46:34 has it that "all shepherds are abhorrent to the Egyptians."

26. *Tg. Ps.-J.* gave a different arrangement, showing Joseph using the silver cup

large, an intentional sign of preferential love (at 45:22 he will give each brother a set of clothes, but to Benjamin five sets of clothes). The brothers have passed the test of truth, have shown themselves to be honest men. But they need pass the test of *emeth* (cf. 42:16), sibling faithfulness.

The Silver Goblet in Benjamin's Sack; Judah's Speech, Genesis 44

Then Joseph commanded his steward: "Fill the men's bags with as much food as they can carry, and put each man's money in the mouth of his bag. In the mouth of the youngest one's bag put also my silver goblet, together with the money for his grain." The steward did as Joseph said. The men had not gone far when Joseph sent his steward after them: 'Why did you repay good with evil? Why did you steal my silver goblet? Is it not the very one from which my master drinks and which he uses for divination? What you have done is wrong.'"

Ambrose comments that "Joseph . . . sent the cup so that he might by a holy trick recall the brother whom he loved."[27] Much more than "holy trick" is in play. Silver (*keseph*) occurs twenty times in Genesis 42–45. They sold Joseph for twenty pieces of silver, he now harasses and tests them with silver.[28]

"We even brought back to you from the land of Canaan the money that we found in the mouths of our bags . . . If any of your servants is found to have the goblet, he shall die, and as for the rest of us, we shall become my lord's slaves." But he replied, "Now what you propose is fair enough, but only the one who is found to have it shall become my slave, and the rest of you can go free."

Sure of themselves, the brothers spoke death to the one with whom the goblet would be found, enslavement for the rest of themselves. They somehow felt implicated, or perhaps they would prefer enslavement to

---

for divining: "He took the silver cup in his hand, and striking (it) like a diviner, he arranged the sons of Leah on one side, the sons of Zilpah on another side, the sons of Bilhah on another side, and he placed Rachel's son Benjamin beside himself." This summarizes *Gen. Rab.* 93:7 where he called out and seated them according to their mothers, leaving Benjamin. "Said he: he is motherless and I am motherless, so he and I will sit together."

27. Ambrose, *On Joseph* 11.62, in ACCS 2:288.
28. Sarna, *Genesis*, 303.

again reporting to their father the loss of yet another son. The steward appeared to agree, but subtly commuted the sentence to enslavement for the culprit, freedom for the rest. In a quick search beginning with the eldest, the goblet was found in Benjamin's bag. The die is cast. The brothers have the option of abandoning the favored brother to enslavement and once more bringing their father news of the disappearance of a favored one. But much has happened since they sold Joseph to slavery. "They risk, and offer to risk themselves, rather than once more ridding themselves of the beloved youngest to avoid facing a situation they find discomforting."[29]

At this, they tore their garments. Then, when each man had loaded his donkey again, they returned to the city.

When Jacob saw Joseph's blood-stained tunic, he tore his garments in mourning (Gen 37:34). Now the brothers enact the same ritual of mourning. Judah and his brothers—Judah is clearly the leader now—return to the city and flung themselves on the ground before Joseph, the fourth time they prostrate to him.

"How could you do such a thing?" Joseph asked them. "Did you not know that such a man as I could discern by divination what happened?" Judah replied: "What can we say to my lord? How can we plead or how try to prove our innocence? God has uncovered your servants' guilt. Here we are, then, the slaves of my lord–the rest of us no less than the one in whose possession the goblet was found." Joseph said, "Far be it from me to act thus! Only the one in whose possession the goblet was found shall become my slave; the rest of you may go back unharmed to your father."

The reader knows that Benjamin did not steal the goblet, but the brothers did not. Still, Judah could not be saying that they knowingly stole the goblet.[30] Suffering in circumstances such as theirs called for examination of conscience. Judah concedes guilt seeing that one of the brothers was caught with the evidence; but also, a real guilt incurred some two decades earlier (cf. 42:21). He thus "expresses a real sense that God has at last exacted retribution for that act of fraternal betrayal."[31] "The brothers have come in the course of the story to choose unity over separation, even if it means a shared slavery that could easily be avoided."[32] Jo-

29. Humphreys, *Joseph and His Family*, 84.
30. Alter, *Art of Biblical Narrative*, 174.
31. Alter, *Genesis*, 261, 262.
32. Ackerman, "Joseph, Judah, and Jacob," 98.

seph intentionally separates their fate and Benjamin's.[33] Will they choose solidarity with a favored son of Rachel or again abandon him to slavery? What would Joseph do then? Recover his full brother (perhaps his father also) and abandon the rest to death by famine? Benjamin's situation is an instance of plot doubling: the narrator intends to make clear in this way that the brothers face the same options as in Genesis 37, but that something has changed.[34]

Judah then stepped up to him and said: "I beg you, my lord, let your servant appeal to my lord, and do not become angry with your servant, for you are the equal of Pharaoh.

Judah's intervention plays a critical role. His speech is the longest in Genesis, a masterpiece of indirection and rhetorical persuasion. The point at issue is to obtain that Benjamin be allowed to go home and Judah take his place, but this is carefully tucked in at the end of the speech, with the "so now" of verse 33. Judah cannot try to show that Benjamin is innocent or plead mitigating circumstances. He rather pleads the clemency of the court—Benjamin is a minor; the judge has shown good heart. He focuses on pathos: the father is old and Benjamin is a beloved son of his old age; some catastrophe already happened in the family; breaking the bond between father and son will result in a similar catastrophe.[35] He mentions the father fourteen times, and it is the last word of the last phrase: "the anguish that would overcome my father."[36]

My lord asked his servants, "Have you a father, or another brother?" So we said to my lord, "We have an aged father, and a younger brother, the child of his old age. This one's full brother is dead,[37] and since he is the only one by his mother who is left, his father is devoted to him." Then you told your servants, "Bring him down to me that I might see him." We replied to my lord, "The boy cannot leave his father; his father would die if he left him." But you told your servants, "Unless your youngest brother comes down with you, you shall not see me again."

---

33. Gunkel, *Genesis*, 433.
34. See Westermann, *Genesis 37–50*, 137.
35. Joosten, "Biblical Rhetoric and Judah's Speech," 21, 25.
36. Lowenthal, *Joseph Narrative*, 101.
37. *Gen. Rab.* 93:8: Judah reasoned thus, "if I tell him that he is alive, he will order me to go and bring him, as he did in respect of Benjamin."

Joseph hears for the first time of the father's grief, how his loss was a tragedy and cause of great distress for the father. He hears Judah offering himself as slave in place of Benjamin, all out of compassion for his father.[38] But Judah twists the record somewhat. He insinuates that the vizier is partially to blame for what happened, for had he not insisted on the boy being brought before him to "set eyes on him"? This, despite dire warnings that the boy cannot leave the father or the father would die. The above exchange, however, is lacking in the narrator's report in Genesis 42; for there, accused of being spies, Judah and his brothers were in no position to bargain.

There is eloquent reticence.[39] Judah skips entirely the crime Benjamin is accused of—in no way can he make it appear less grievous. He avoids any negative event that happened between the vizier and the brothers—the hostile atmosphere of the first visit, the charge of spying, the imprisonment of Simeon, even the long period between the two visits—as if the second followed immediately upon the first. With Near Eastern indirection, he avoids any explicit appeal to the vizier's compassion—the nouns mercy, pity, compassion, grace, goodwill and the cognate verbs are lacking! Rather, the vizier must feel he is being gracious, noble, and prompted to act from within.

"Then your servant my father said to us, 'As you know, my wife bore me two sons. One of them, however, has gone away from me,' and I said, "He must have been torn to pieces by wild beasts!" I have not seen him since. If you take this one away from me too, and a disaster befalls him, you will send my white head down to Sheol in grief."

Judah put in his father's mouth the words: "you know that my wife bore me two sons." He said that to us, ten of us of a different wife, but still we love him and worry about him.[40] His eloquent plea "shows that they can now take the part of their father, understand what he feels, and can accept that it is apparently in his nature to have favorites. They can now accept this even as it still pains them. They have changed."[41]

---

38. See McConville, "Forgiveness as Private and Public Act," 645.

39. Joosten, "Biblical Rhetoric and Judah's Speech," 23-24. See also Westermann, *Genesis 37-50*, 135-36; Sternberg, *Poetics of Biblical Narrative*, 304-6; O'Brien, "Judah's Speech," 435.

40. Joosten, "Biblical Rhetoric and Judah's Speech," 27.

41. Humphreys, *Character of God in Genesis*, 221.

"So now, if the boy is not with us when I go back to your servant my father, whose very life is bound up with his, he will die as soon as he sees that the boy is missing; and your servants will thus send the white head of your servant our father down to Sheol in grief. Besides, I, your servant, have guaranteed the boy's safety for my father by saying, 'If I fail to bring him back to you, father, I will bear the blame before you forever.' So now let me, your servant, remain in place of the boy as the slave of my lord, and let the boy go back with his brothers. How could I go back to my father if the boy were not with me? I could not bear to see the anguish that would overcome my father."

Judah who initiated the sale of Joseph offers himself as slave to set Joseph's brother free. "Here, at the climax and turning point of the Joseph story, the Bible speaks for the first time of vicarious suffering."[42] Judah "leaves it to Joseph to decide whether the old man would die if he were separated from Benjamin, or whether Benjamin could not survive without his father, or whether both dire possibilities might be probable."[43]

Tradition

For the fathers of the church, Joseph was a type of Christ (see this commentary at Genesis 37). His apparent lack of bother to contact his father even after his elevation was troubling. "God refused to notify blessed Jacob that his son was living, likewise did not allow holy Joseph to declare his glory to his father . . . God wanted to consume the small offenses in this world by the fire of tribulation . . . in order that our God might present holy Jacob as purified gold at the future judgment, he first removed all the stains of sin from him."[44] Caesarius applies the doctrine of the *fomes peccati* and of sufferings accepted for God's sake quittling down punishments for sin. If Joseph wept, it was "that they ever treated me thus. This man let us also imitate. Let us mourn and weep for those who have injured us. Let us not be angry with them. For truly they are worthy of tears, for the punishment and condemnation to which they make themselves liable."[45] How was it that the brothers did not recognize Joseph? It was the Lord's doing that he remained hidden from them until

---

42. Westermann, *Genesis 37–50*, 137.
43. Alter, *Genesis*, 264.
44. Caesarius of Arles, *Sermon* 91.3.4, in ACCS 2:279.
45. Chrysostom, *Homily 4 on First Thessalonians*, 3:5–8.

his dreams should be fulfilled in them;[46] for the rabbis it was because Joseph was beardless when they sold him (*Gen. Rab.* 91:7; *Tg. Ps.-J.* at Gen 42:8). Washing the feet of the brothers and setting the table before them had a spiritual meaning: "so too the Jews, having been so afflicted and oppressed by an unbearable famine, a spiritual one that is, will eventually forsake their haughtiness and arrogance, and they will come to Christ desiring to be fed by him with holy and spiritual food that gives life. Yet he will not receive them unless they are accompanied by the new people of God, of which Benjamin was a type."[47]

Jewish midrash has Jacob asking his sons not to enter Egypt through one gate for fear of the evil eye (envy) (*Gen. Rab.* 91:2).[48] Joseph had set guards at the ten gates and ordered them to record the names of all who entered. The records contained the names of his brothers. He ordered that when they came they were to be brought to him. Hence, they were arrested and brought to Joseph, who said to them, "If you are upright, why did you not all enter through one gate?" Midrash gives a more positive portrait of Joseph and his brothers. To begin with, they regretted selling him and were transformed even before meeting him: "every day they would say, 'let us go and inquire about him and restore him to his father.'" When Jacob bade them go down to Egypt, they all resolved to show him brotherly love."[49] It was through the holy spirit that they said to Joseph: "You and we are the sons of the same man . . . We have indeed come down with that purpose–to be killed or to kill [you]" (*Gen. Rab.* 91:7). Joseph bound Simeon before their eyes "because it was he who had pushed him into the pit" (*Gen. Rab.* 91:6).

---

46. Ephrem, *Commentary on Genesis* 37.7, in ACCS 2:286.

47. Cyril of Alexadria, *Glaphyra on the Pentateuch: Genesis*, 304.

48. *Tg. Ps.-J.*: "the sons of Israel came, each by a different gate, lest the evil eye should have power over them if they came together."

49. *Gen. Rab.* 91:6.

CHAPTER 27

Genesis 45

Joseph Reveals Himself to His Brothers

> How good and how pleasant it is, when brothers dwell together as one!
>
> —Psalm 133:1

THE TENSION HAS REACHED breaking point. Joseph can no longer hold himself back. He turns everyone out before he reveals himself to his brothers. With this revelation and forgiveness, the Joseph Novella reaches its climax.

> But God chooses to work within the framework of the brothers' decisions—not overriding these but reworking their results ... God does not inspire the brothers to their immoral deed, but makes creative use of desires and acts that were self-serving or destructive (though the First Testament itself is generally not so troubled at the idea that YHWH inspires acts that look immoral) ... any more than later God had decided to have Jesus betrayed and therefore somehow inspired Judas to betray him. In such events, both God's design and human design are involved, but the former is working against the latter. (Goldingay, *Israel's Gospel*, 258, 260)

Repetitions in this chapter seem more than "progressive heightening"[1]; rather they suggest the work of an author splicing different accounts.[2] For example, twice the brothers are to tell their father of Joseph's high position (vv. 45:9, 13); Pharaoh arranged the resettlement of Jacob and his family (vv. 17-18), while in 46:31, 47:1 Pharaoh is informed of their arrival and where they were; Pharaoh's command to Joseph to send wagons (vv. 18-19) is linked with their leaving their possessions behind, whereas in 46:6 they took those possessions along.

Joseph could no longer restrain himself in the presence of all his attendants, so he cried out, "Have everyone withdraw from me!" So no one attended him when he made himself known to his brothers ... "I am Joseph," he said to his brothers. "Is my father still alive?" But his brothers could give him no answer, so dumbfounded were they at him. "Come closer to me," Joseph told his brothers. When they had done so, he said: "I am your brother Joseph, whom you sold into Egypt. But now do not be distressed, and do not be angry with yourselves for having sold me here. It was really for the sake of saving lives that God sent me here ahead of you. The famine has been in the land for two years now, and for five more years cultivation will yield no harvest. God, therefore, sent me on ahead of you to ensure for you a remnant on earth and to save your lives in an extraordinary deliverance. So it was not really you but God who had me come here; and he has made me a father to Pharaoh, lord of all his household, and ruler over the whole land of Egypt.

The brothers' reaction to Joseph's dream had been, "will you rule over us?" (37:8). To frustrate the dream they sold him into slavery, only to meet him now as "ruler over the whole land of Egypt" and providential sustainer of the family. Considering his own honor and to save his brothers' face, Joseph arranged to be alone with them when he revealed himself. Yet, he wept so loudly that news reached Pharaoh of the advent of his brothers.

---

1. Westermann, *Genesis 37-50*, 143.
2. Gunkel, *Genesis*, 434-35.

FIGURE 7: Joseph Makes Himself Known to His Brothers (Gen 45:1-5)

His brothers were in utter disbelief. He needed to give them a sign for self-identification, so he said, "I am your brother Joseph, whom you sold into Egypt." In saying, "it was not really you, but God who had me come here,"[3] Joseph is not denying his brothers' responsibility for their crime, for he says clearly, "your brother Joseph, whom you sold into Egypt." Rather, he sees a higher design in the events: "Intended evil is neither excused nor avoided, but is caught up into a larger design that is shaped by divine will for good and life."[4] A similar pattern recurs in the crucifixion of Jesus (see above textbox). Joseph acts with extreme magnanimity

---

3. Ps 105:16-17 harps on this: "Then he called down a famine on the land, destroyed the grain that sustained them. He had sent a man ahead of them, Joseph, sold as a slave."

4. Humphreys, *Joseph and His Family*, 125. Hindsight may be operative here, but one can hardly say that "the Joseph story knows nothing of a concept of [God's providence]," as in Westermann, *Genesis 37-50*, 143. In fact, one of the theological contributions of the Joseph story is this very idea of God's hand at work in ordinary daily events.

when, far from reproaching them for what they did to him, he even comforts them, "Do not grieve so!"⁵ With subtle Near Eastern indirection, he acts out his forgiveness in tears and kisses. While incognito, he already had proof of their repentance and transformation.

> The NRSV gives a closer translation of verse 7: "God sent me before you to preserve for you a remnant on earth, and to keep alive for you many survivors." $Sh^e\bar{e}r\hat{\imath}t$/remnant occurs only here in the Pentateuch; with $p^el\hat{e}tah$/survivor, it appears mainly in late prophecy and in situations of war. This verse was probably written from the point of view of a later time.⁶

"Hurry back, then, to my father and tell him: 'Thus says your son Joseph: God has made me lord of all Egypt; come down to me without delay. You can settle in the region of Goshen, where you will be near me—you and your children and children's children, your flocks and herds, and everything that you own . . .'" Then he threw his arms around his brother Benjamin and wept on his shoulder. Joseph then kissed all his brothers and wept over them; and only then were his brothers able to talk with him.

With kisses and weeping, Joseph initiates the process of reconciliation.⁷ For, "it is through the victim that the wrongdoer is called to repentance and forgiveness; repentance and forgiveness are not the preconditions for reconciliation, but are rather the consequences of it."⁸ Forgiveness does not mean ignoring or forgetting the past, but deciding for a different future; the victim is liberated from the hold of the past. "Forgive and forget" may trivialize a traumatic experience; rather, "in forgiving, we do not forget; we remember in a different way."⁹ In reaction to his dreams, his brothers had hated him so much they could not even speak with him (37:4). Joseph's gestures restored communication, the heartbeat of true and substantial communion.¹⁰ They opened the way to reconcilia-

---

5. Gunkel, *Genesis*, 436.
6. See Westermann, *Genesis 37–50*, 144.
7. Coats, *From Canaan to Egypt*, 83, 86 sees no reconciliation here as the restored relation seemed imposed by the innocent party on the guilty party, the brothers' "confession" having been made before they recognized the man as Joseph. He opines that "Reconciliation for Jacob's family lies in the future, a dangerous future, a future built on mutual commitment among people who already showed their true colors."
8. Schreiter, *Ministry of Reconciliation*, 15.
9. Schreiter, *Ministry of Reconciliation*, 66.
10. See Berthoud, "Reconciliation of Joseph," 9.

tion, for "reconciliation does not necessarily entail full erasure of the past or newly perfected characters, rather, it involves a commitment to live the relationship differently than one did in the past."[11] We shall take up this question in the commentary on 50:15-21. For an earlier treatment, see the commentary at 33:12-20.

> *The news reached Pharaoh's house: "Joseph's brothers have come." Pharaoh and his officials were pleased. So Pharaoh told Joseph: "Say to your brothers: 'This is what you shall do: Load up your animals and go without delay to the land of Canaan. There get your father and your households, and then come to me; I will assign you the best land in Egypt, where you will live off the fat of the land.' Instruct them further: 'Do this. Take wagons from the land of Egypt for your children and your wives and bring your father back here. Do not be concerned about your belongings, for the best in the whole land of Egypt shall be yours'" . . . Joseph gave them the wagons, as Pharaoh had ordered, and he supplied them with provisions for the journey. He also gave to each of them a set of clothes, but to Benjamin he gave three hundred shekels of silver and five sets of clothes. Moreover, what he sent to his father was ten donkeys loaded with the finest products of Egypt and another ten loaded with grain and bread and provisions for his father's journey. As he sent his brothers on their way, he told them, "Do not quarrel on the way."*

Pharaoh's order to leave behind their possessions in Canaan envisages permanent residence in Egypt. The brothers needed new garments after having torn their garments in 44:13; besides, the change of clothing symbolizes the new transformed status and the joy of restored relationship. Benjamin is again singled out for preferential treatment: "the gift of clothing and the preference shown to Benjamin are Joseph's subtle hint that the old quarrel over the coat of many colors is shown to have been futile."[12] The three hundred shekels may be a final gesture of "restitution" for the twenty pieces of silver the brothers took for the sale of Joseph![13] "The quarrel which he forbade them was that one say to another, 'It was you who counseled us to throw him into the pit,' while another would contend with his brother, saying, 'It was you who urged us to sell him naked and in chains to the Arabs.' As I have forgiven all of you, you forgive each other."[14]

11. Kaminsky, "Reclaiming a Theology of Election," 146.
12. Plaut, *Torah*, 330, citing Toldot Yitzchak.
13. Alter, *Genesis*, 270.
14. Ephrem, *Commentary on Genesis* 40.2, in ACCS 2:295.

So they went up from Egypt and came to the land of Canaan, to their father Jacob. When they told him, "Joseph is still alive–in fact, it is he who is governing all the land of Egypt," he was unmoved, for he did not believe them. But when they recounted to him all that Joseph had told them, and when he saw the wagons that Joseph had sent to transport him, the spirit of their father Jacob came to life. "Enough," said Israel. "My son Joseph is still alive! I must go and see him before I die."

What is the liar's fate? Even when he speaks the truth he is not believed (*Gen. Rab.* 94:3: R. Ḥiyya). But seeing the wagons, Jacob's spirit came alive. His spirit was dead, only waiting to meet Joseph down in Sheol (37:35). "Enough" is shorthand for his willingness to put the past behind him and get on with the new possibilities presented by the surprising good news.[15]

Tradition

> His Holiness recalled how Joseph could no longer contain what had been the yearning of his heart and . . . he cried out: "It is I—Joseph, your brother!" . . . To be honest, there is a large gap between those who accept only the Old Testament and those who add the New Testament to it as well, as [their] supreme law and guidance. This distinction does not, however, impede the brotherhood that derives from our common origin, since we are all children of the same heavenly Father, and so this should always shine forth before all people, and should be put into practice through charity. (*L'Osservatore Romano*, October 19, 1960)

St. John XXIII as much as used the declaration, "I am Joseph, your brother," to welcome a U.S. delegation of 130 of the "United Jewish Appeal: Jewish Study Mission" on October 18, 1960 (see text box above).

The narrator created a gap by not presenting whether or how Jacob reconciled with his sons. Ephrem imagines the scenario as follows.

"Their father asked them and said, 'Did you not ask Joseph how or why he went down to Egypt?' Then, when they all looked at each other and did not know what to say, Judah opened his mouth and said to his father, 'We are recalling our crime today before our father.' Because of the

---

15. Fretheim, "Genesis," 257.

dreams of Joseph, Joseph's brothers thought, in their simplicity, that you and they would soon serve him as slaves. They also imagined, in their foolishness, that 'it was better that he alone should be the servant than that we and our father should serve him as slaves.' They did this because they took pity on you and on Benjamin, and not because you loved Joseph. You also loved Benjamin, but because he did not say that we would become servants to him, all of us love him. 'Forgive us then for having humiliated Joseph, for it is on account of our humiliating him that he has come to this exalted state.' Their father then accepted their apology."[16]

The fathers of the church also grappled with how Joseph could say that it was God who sent him ahead to Egypt. Preaching on Philemon, Chrysostom said:

> And he has not said, he separated himself, but, "he was separated." For it was not his own arrangement that he should depart either for this purpose or for that. Which also Joseph says, in making excuse for his brethren, "For God did send me hither," that is, he made use of their wickedness for a good end. "Therefore," he says, "he was parted for a season." Thus he contracts the time, acknowledges the offense, and turns it all to a providence.[17]

---

16. Ephrem, *Commentary on Genesis* 40.4, in ACCS 2:297-98.
17. Chrysostom, *Homily 2 on Philemon*, 1:4-6.

CHAPTER 28

Genesis 46

Jacob Migrates to Egypt

> Do not be afraid to go down to Egypt, for there I will make you a great nation.
>
> —GENESIS 46:3

THE JOSEPH NOVELLA REACHED its climax in Genesis 45. The remaining chapters of Genesis weave the story of Joseph into the patriarchal story of Jacob. Family history transitions into national history—the "sons of Jacob" become "sons of Israel" or Israelites. The emerging nation inherits the earlier divine promises to the patriarchs. In contrast to Abraham and Isaac, all Jacob's offspring remain together, none is excluded from divine blessing and parental inheritance.[1] From here on, the story looks forward, and constructs a bridge to Israel's stay in, and exodus from, Egypt.

Inconsistencies reveal the splicing of two traditions.[2]

> In the Joseph story, Jacob dwells around Beersheba, while in 46:1 Israel moves there ostensibly for the first time, from an unnamed location. In 46:1 Jacob is robust, breaks camp, while in 46:5 he is a feeble old man, who has to be borne in a cart.

---

1. See Lowenthal, *Joseph Narrative*, 114.
2. Redford, *Study*, 19. See also Westermann, "Genesis 46–50: Survey," in *Genesis 37–50*, 211–14.

Especially striking is that in the Joseph story the trip is temporary, to alleviate the rigors of the famine in Canaan, while in 46:1–4 the trip is understood as permanent, in fact, Israel is to increase and become a "great nation" in Egypt. In 45:20 Pharaoh instructed that the Jacob family leave their possessions behind in Canaan, while in 46:6 they took with them their livestock and all the possessions they had acquired in the land of Canaan.

The Migration, 46:1–7, 28–34

A register of the people who migrated to Egypt with Jacob now interrupts the story of the migration. We shall consider the migration, then the register.

Israel set out with all that was his. When he arrived at Beersheba, he offered sacrifices to the God of his father Isaac. There God, speaking to Israel in a vision by night, called: Jacob! Jacob! He answered, "Here I am." Then he said: I am God, the God of your father. Do not be afraid to go down to Egypt, for there I will make you a great nation. I will go down to Egypt with you and I will also bring you back here, after Joseph has closed your eyes.

The shifting between the names Jacob and Israel suggests the transition from family to national history, such that "these are the names of the sons of Israel" (v. 8) is rightly translated, "these are the names of the Israelites." Had not Jacob vowed that if God will be with him and protect him, "the LORD will be my God" (28:21)? And did he not acknowledge this God when he set up an altar at Bethel to "the God who answered me in the day of my distress and who has been with me wherever I have gone" (35:3)? Why does God here self-introduce as "God of your father"? God is including him in the line of promise and conveying to him the promise of "great nation" made to Abraham in Genesis 12. That promise appeared tied to Canaan; here Israel is told he will become a great nation in Egypt. This implies that the migration will be somewhat of long duration. "A family visit is thereby transformed into an event of national significance with its preordained place in God's scheme of history."[3] Isaac was forbidden to go to Egypt during a similar famine (26:2), so Jacob may have feared contravening divine command and losing the promises should he leave Canaan. The dangers of the road may have worried him; he may have feared death on the way before seeing Joseph. Hence the

---

3. Sarna, *Genesis*, 313.

promise of "being with" him and the assurance of meeting with Joseph, who will close his eyes in death. The promise "I will also bring you back here" can hardly mean bringing him back in a coffin for burial in Canaan. Rather, it already looks towards the exodus of Israel from Egypt. "Visions of the night," as stylized expression for revelation, appears only in Ezekiel, hence is late usage—there is no vision here, only words.[4] Only here and in Gen 15:13–16 do the promises to the patriarchs say something of descent to Egypt and the exodus—both are late expansions of the promise tradition and presuppose the Pentateuch story.[5]

So Jacob departed from Beersheba, and the sons of Israel put their father and their wives and children on the wagons that Pharaoh had sent to transport him. They took with them their livestock and the possessions they had acquired in the land of Canaan.

In this account, Jacob first arrived Beersheba from elsewhere, whereas in the Joseph narrative he dwelt in Beersheba. In 45:20 Pharaoh instructed that the Jacob family leave their possessions behind in Canaan, but here they took all their possessions with them (see above).

Israel had sent Judah ahead to Joseph, so that he might meet him in Goshen. On his arrival in the region of Goshen, Joseph prepared his chariot and went up to meet his father Israel in Goshen. As soon as Israel made his appearance, Joseph threw his arms around him and wept a long time on his shoulder. And Israel said to Joseph, "At last I can die, now that I have seen for myself that you are still alive."

Judah has been the leader ever since the brothers' second journey to Egypt. Was Judah sent ahead to point the way,[6] to inform Joseph of his father's imminent arrival,[7] or to ask Joseph to appear before him in Goshen?[8] "As soon as Israel made his appearance" is literally "and he [Joseph] appeared to him [Jacob]." The verb for "to appear" is usual for divine apparitions to humans. The narrator may be suggesting that Joseph in all his glory appeared "divine" to his father. Jacob had proclaimed, "I will go down mourning to my son in Sheol" (37:35). He did go down, but

---

4. Westermann, *Genesis 37–50*, 155.
5. Redford, *Study*, 20; Westermann, *Genesis 37–50*, 157, 214.
6. Tg. Ps.-J., followed by Alter, *Genesis*, 276.
7. Josephus, *Ant.* 2.184.
8. Peshitta and Samaritan Pentateuch—by altering the vowels of the verb from *le-hôrôt* to the niphal, *le-hērā'ôt*. NABRE adopts this translation.

to Egypt, to see his son alive. He could now die in peace. The tears were tears of joy for people who so loved each other and had been separated for years.

Joseph then said to his brothers and his father's household: "I will go up and inform Pharaoh, telling him: 'My brothers and my father's household, whose home is in the land of Canaan, have come to me. The men are shepherds, having been owners of livestock; and they have brought with them their flocks and herds, as well as everything else they own.' So when Pharaoh summons you and asks what your occupation is, you must answer, 'We your servants, like our ancestors, have been owners of livestock from our youth until now,' in order that you may stay in the region of Goshen, since all shepherds are abhorrent to the Egyptians."

Pharaoh actually sent the wagons to bring them from Canaan (45:17-19) promising to settle them in the best land in Egypt. Goshen is on the border and grassy; Pharaoh's own flocks pasture there. Joseph must be dissimulating somewhat when he put words in the mouth of his brothers![9] There is no extrabiblical evidence that shepherding was a taboo profession among the Egyptians.[10] At play may be the city dwellers' disdain for shepherds on hygienic grounds.

The Register of the Sons of Israel, 46:8-27

These are the names of the Israelites, Jacob and his children, who came to Egypt . . . Jacob's people who came to Egypt–his direct descendants, not counting the wives of Jacob's sons–numbered sixty-six persons in all. Together with Joseph's sons who were born to him in Egypt—two persons—all the people comprising the household of Jacob who had come to Egypt amounted to seventy persons in all.

The sons of Israel are numbered according to the order of his wives: Leah, her maidservant, Zilpah, then Rachel, and her maidservant, Bilhah. This also parallels the descending number of progeny.[11] Similar lists in Numbers 26 and 1 Chronicles 7 show variants in the names of offspring and the number of progeny. Surprising is that Benjamin suddenly has ten sons, when at Gen 43:29 Joseph greeted him as a mere lad! It is unclear how the number seventy results from the sixty-six given in

---

9. Gunkel, *Genesis*, 440. If it was all transparent, why instruct them what to say?
10. Alter, *Genesis*, 278.
11. Sarna, *Genesis*, 314.

verse 26. R. Nahman was perplexed: "have you ever seen a man give his neighbor sixty-six glasses, then give him another three and count them seventy?" (*Gen. Rab.* 94:9). Is Jacob included in the seventy or not? Verse 12 gives the sons of Judah as Er, Onan, Shelah, Perez, and Zerah. But Er and Onan had died in the land of Canaan; the sons of Perez were Hezron and Hamul. Were Er and Onan counted? Verse 15: "these were the sons whom Leah bore to Jacob in Paddan-aram, along with his daughter Dinah—thirty-three persons in all, sons and daughters," seems to count Dinah. Many suggest that the number seventy here is symbolic—suggests completion, also that Israel represents the seventy nations of the earth (cf. Genesis 10) before God. The new nation of Israel [is portrayed] as a new humanity and Abraham as a second Adam.[12] The LXX, followed by Stephen in Acts 7:14, has the number seventy-five. To be noted is the absence of names compounded with the divine element YHWH and that the names parallel those in the book of Judges[13]—pointer to early date?

Tradition

Tg. Ps.-J. solved the question of the number seventy as follows: "Thus with Joseph, who was already in Egypt, and Jochebed, the daughter of Levi, who was born between the walls when they were going into Egypt, the sum total of the persons in the household of Jacob who came into Egypt was seventy."

Augustine had problems calculating the number of people migrating to Egypt.

> How could young people under the age of twenty-six have grandchildren? This question cannot be resolved by any Hebrew text. For how could Jacob have so many grandchildren before entering Egypt, even of his son Benjamin, who at that time came to his brother Joseph? For the Scripture not only speaks of Jacob having children, but also grandchildren and great-grandchildren, all of whom must be added to those sixty-six persons with whom Jacob entered into Egypt, as it says even the Hebrew text itself. It is also necessary to consider the

---

12. See Sailhamer, *Pentateuch as Narrative*, 225. See also Deut 32:8: "When the Most High gave the nations their inheritance, when he divided all mankind, he set up boundaries for the peoples according to the number of the sons of Israel" (NIV; TNK: children of Israel).

13. Westermann, *Genesis 37–50*, 159.

fact that while Joseph and his children are only eight, Benjamin and his children are eleven in all, not nineteen among all, as indeed eight are eleven plus, but the sum throws the figure of eighteen. And besides, Joseph and his children are not eight people, but they are said to be nine, when in reality only eight appear. These problems, which seem unsolvable, undoubtedly contain a great meaning; but I do not know if I will be able to agree all things literally, especially the numbers that in the Scriptures are absolutely sacred and are full of mysteries, as we believe with all reason, based on some numbers that we have been able to know by them.[14]

The early fathers of the church applied their principle that all appearances of God in the Old Testament were appearances of the Logos incarnate. The one saying, "Fear not to go down into Egypt," was God, the Word, the Educator (*paidagogue*). See how the Instructor follows the righteous man, and how he anoints the athlete, teaching him to trip up his antagonist.[15] The athlete is anointed before games or a bout; the antagonist comprises the evil forces—Egypt is cipher for the forces of evil. Origen uses this symbolism when he interprets: "Fear not to descend into Egypt": "that is to say, you shall contend "against principalities and powers and against the rulers of this world of this darkness" (cf. Eph 6:12)—which is figuratively called Egypt . . . He therefore with whom God shall go down into the struggles is not afraid 'to go down into Egypt.' He is not afraid to approach the struggles of this world and the battles with resisting demons."[16] In another move, Origen observes that "I will also bring you back here" (46:4) does not seem to have been fulfilled. It rather points to the Christian mystery:

"Who is it who is made 'into a great nation' in Egypt and is recalled 'in the end'? . . . For he was not recalled from Egypt 'in the end,' since he died in Egypt . . . Let us consider therefore whether there may be depicted in this statement a figure of the Lord who descends into this world and is made 'into a great nation,' that is, the church of the Gentiles, and after all things were completed, returned to the Father."[17]

---

14. Augustine, *Questions on Genesis*, q. 152.
15. Clement of Alexandria, *Christ the Educator* 1.7.
16. Origen, *Homilies on Genesis* 15.5, in ACCS 2:300.
17. Origen, *Homilies on Genesis* 15.5, in ACCS 2:300.

CHAPTER 29

Genesis 47

Israel Settles in Goshen; Joseph's Agrarian Policy

> Thus the land passed over to Pharaoh, and the people were reduced to slavery, from one end of Egypt's territory to the other.
>
> —GENESIS 47:20, 21

JOSEPH'S AGRARIAN POLICY (47:13–26) interrupts the story of the presentation of Jacob and his sons to Pharaoh and their settlement in Goshen. I deal with the presentation as a unit before commenting on Joseph's agrarian policy.

Some inconsistencies suggest the splicing of traditions.[1] In verse 1 Joseph announces their arrival to Pharaoh, while in verse 5 Pharaoh seems to announce it himself.[2] Pharaoh says no word to Joseph after he informed him about his family's arrival. Pharaoh does not address the brothers after they answered his question about their occupation. Pharaoh's subsequent granting of the brothers' petition is directed to Joseph. This is preceded by the seemingly superfluous "your father and your brothers have come to you"—when Joseph already announced their arrival in verse 1. The text of verse 5 is literally, "and Pharaoh said to Joseph

---

1. Lowenthal, *Joseph Narrative*, 122.
2. Mann, *Book of the Torah*, 91 n. 197.

saying . . ."—tautological. The LXX transposed verses 6 and 5 to take care of some of the text problems mentioned.

Joseph Presents His Family to Pharaoh; They Settle in Goshen, 47:1–12, 27–31

Joseph went and told Pharaoh, "My father and my brothers have come from the land of Canaan, with their flocks and herds and everything else they own; and they are now in the region of Goshen."

True, Goshen being at the border would be a point of arrival, but Joseph did not tell Pharaoh that he himself asked them to stop there. They came with all their possessions, when Pharaoh had counseled they leave their belongings behind (45:20).

When Pharaoh asked them, "What is your occupation?" they answered, "We, your servants, like our ancestors, are shepherds. We have come," they continued, "in order to sojourn in this land, for there is no pasture for your servants' flocks, because the famine has been severe in the land of Canaan. So now please let your servants settle in the region of Goshen."

They gave the answer that Joseph prompted them to give in 46:33. Settlement in Goshen would bring them near to Joseph (45:10). It would also allow them to stay apart, unaffected by Egyptian disdain for shepherds (46:34). They request sojourn (*la-gûr*), temporary stay, because of lack of pasture for the sheep in Canaan. The use of the verb "to sojourn" may be one link to the prophecy in 15:13,[3] "know for certain that your descendants will reside as aliens in a land not their own, where they shall be enslaved and oppressed for four hundred years." Husbandry has been the family occupation and they have no higher ambitions, thus will not disturb the social balance.

Pharaoh said to Joseph, "Now that your father and your brothers have come to you, the land of Egypt is at your disposal; settle your father and brothers in the pick of the land. Let them settle in the region of Goshen. And if you know of capable men among them, put them in charge of my livestock."

---

3. See Sarna, *Genesis*, 319.

Ramses III is said to have had 3,264 men, mostly foreigners, take care of his herds,[4] and that in the Goshen area. Mention of the land of Goshen prepares the reader for the distinction between Egypt and Goshen in some of the plagues, for example, the plague of the flies (Exod 8:18): "But on that day I will make an exception of the land of Goshen, where my people are, and no swarms of flies will be there, so that you may know that I the LORD am in the midst of the land." The LXX reordered verses 4–6 as follows, supplying what it thought had fallen out:

> Then Pharao said to Joseph, "Let them settle in the land of Gesem, and if you know that there are capable men among them, appoint them as rulers of my livestock." And Iakob and his sons came into Egypt to Joseph, and Pharao king of Egypt heard. And Pharao spoke to Joseph, saying, "Your father and your brothers have come to you. See the land of Egypt is before you; settle your father and your brothers in the best land."

Then Joseph brought his father Jacob and presented him to Pharaoh. And Jacob blessed Pharaoh. Then Pharaoh asked Jacob, "How many years have you lived?" Jacob replied: "The years I have lived as a wayfarer amount to a hundred and thirty. Few and hard have been these years of my life, and they do not compare with the years that my ancestors lived as wayfarers." Then Jacob blessed Pharaoh and withdrew from his presence.

The audience begins and ends with Jacob blessing Pharaoh (some render the root *brk* here as "to greet").[5] The ambiguity may derive from the greeting usual for a king, namely, "may the king live forever," which is both greeting and blessing.

> *Tg. Ps.-J.* articulates the blessing as follows: "And Jacob blessed Pharaoh and said, "May it be the will (of Heaven) that the waters of the Nile be full, and that the famine may cease from the world in your days."

As blessing, there may be link with 12:3, where Abram and his offspring are to be a blessing. This functions in 39:5 when "the LORD blessed the Egyptian's house for Joseph's sake." Chrysostom comments on "few and hard have been these years of my life":

---

4. Sarna, *Genesis*, 319.
5. TNK: "And Jacob greeted Pharaoh . . . Then Jacob bade Pharaoh farewell." NJB: "Jacob paid his respects to Pharaoh . . . Jacob then took leave of Pharaoh."

Here he is referring to the years of servitude he endured under Laban in consequence of the flight made on account of his brother, and as well, following his return from there, the grief he suffered for so long on account of Joseph's death and all the misfortunes in the meantime. After all, how great do you think was the fear he had when in retribution for their sister the company of Symeon and Levi in one fell swoop wiped out wiped out a city and took everyone captive in Shekim?[6]

Jacob recalls the fact that though promised possession of the land of Canaan, it is "the land of their sojourning" (Gen 36:7), and he has had to displace himself the most.

Joseph settled his father and brothers and gave them a holding in Egypt on the pick of the land, in the region of Rameses, as Pharaoh had ordered. And Joseph provided food for his father and brothers and his father's whole household, down to the youngest.

In giving them property in the land, Joseph goes beyond their request for sojourn. The "land of Ramses" must be equivalent to Goshen. In Exod 1:11, Israel did forced labor building for Pharaoh the garrison cities of Pithom and Ramses. At the beginning of the exodus (Exod 12:37), "The Israelites set out from Ramses for Succoth." Ramses II (thirteenth century BCE) enlarged the city of Tanis and made it his capital, naming it after himself. The use of the name Ramses here is anachronistic, but may be another link to the exodus.

Thus Israel settled in the land of Egypt, in the region of Goshen. There they acquired holdings, were fertile, and multiplied greatly. Jacob lived in the land of Egypt for seventeen years; the span of his life came to a hundred and forty-seven years. When the time approached for Israel to die, he called his son Joseph and said to him: "If it pleases you, put your hand under my thigh as a sign of your enduring fidelity to me; do not bury me in Egypt. When I lie down with my ancestors, take me out of Egypt and bury me in their burial place." "I will do as you say," he replied. But his father demanded, "Swear it to me!" So Joseph swore to him. Then Israel bowed at the head of the bed.

"They were fertile and multiplied greatly" recalls El Shaddai's blessing of Israel in 35:11 and foreshadows Exod 1:7, which immediately

---

6. Chrysostom, *Homilies on Genesis* 65.10.

precedes the rise of a new king worried about Israel being too mighty for Egypt.[7] Jacob lived seventeen years in Egypt, Joseph's age when his brothers sold him into slavery. The oath to bury him in the ancestral burial place in Canaan highlights Jacob's hope that the people will eventually come into possession of that land. The mode of solemn swearing is similar to that between Abraham and his servant in Genesis 24. "Then Israel bowed at the head of the bed" does not indicate fulfillment of Joseph's second dream—Joseph's mother was already dead (see commentary on next chapter).

> The LXX renders: "And Israel did reverence, leaning on the top of his staff." As Augustine points out, the manuscripts of LXX and the Vulgate vacillate between Joseph's staff and Jacob's staff.[8] In LXX, Israel worshiped in an act of thanksgiving to God.

Joseph's Agrarian Policy, 47:13–26

This unit deals with internal Egyptian matters and at first does not seem to advance the story of Jacob or the story of Joseph. However, it seems to have been inserted here as flashback to Joseph's administrative exploits in Genesis 41 and as foreshadowing Israel's future history.

Since there was no food in all the land because of the extreme severity of the famine, and the lands of Egypt and Canaan were languishing from hunger, Joseph gathered in, as payment for the grain that they were buying, all the money that was to be found in Egypt and Canaan, and he put it in Pharaoh's house.

He put the money into Pharaoh's house, did not enrich himself thereby—portrait of a faithful servant. In the very first year, Joseph takes in all the money from Egypt and Canaan—hyperbole. The die is cast for the next round.

---

7. Ron, "Joseph's Agrarian Policy," 257. He cites Or. Hachaim to the effect that the Egyptians complained that the Israelites were multiplying and becoming great because they were not enslaved to Pharaoh as the Egyptians were.

8. "What does it mean then: 'He bowed to the end of the rod of his,' that is to say, of his son Joseph? Would it be by chance that Jacob had received his son's scepter while he was swearing, and that after Joseph's oath, still holding the scepter in his hands, he worshiped God immediately?" Augustine, *Questions on Genesis*, q. 162.

When all the money in Egypt and Canaan was spent, all the Egyptians came to Joseph, pleading, "Give us food! Why should we perish in front of you? For our money is gone." "Give me your livestock if your money is gone," replied Joseph. "I will give you food in return for your livestock." So they brought their livestock to Joseph, and he gave them food in exchange for their horses, their flocks of sheep and herds of cattle, and their donkeys.

Gunkel is right to ask, "What did Pharaoh do with all the cattle"? "How did the people plow"?[9] The narrator is trying to explain a custom in Egypt that diverges from Israelite private ownership of land, a situation in which everything belongs to Pharaoh; he credits Joseph with its origins.

That year ended, and they came to him in the next one and said: "We cannot hide from my lord that, with our money spent and our livestock made over to my lord, there is nothing left to put at my lord's disposal except our bodies and our land. Why should we and our land perish before your very eyes? Take us and our land in exchange for food, and we will become Pharaoh's slaves and our land his property; only give us seed, that we may survive and not perish, and that our land may not turn into a waste." So Joseph acquired all the land of Egypt for Pharaoh ... Thus the land passed over to Pharaoh, and the people were reduced to slavery, from one end of Egypt's territory to the other.

TNK correctly renders the MT text as follows: "And he removed the population town by town,[10] from one end of Egypt's border to the other."[11] Was this because food had been stored in silos in the cities? Or was it by conscious design to break the power of the feudal nobility in favor of the king and the poor?[12]

Joseph told the people: "Now that I have acquired you and your land for Pharaoh, here is your seed for sowing the land. But when the harvest is in, you

9. Gunkel, *Genesis*, 444.

10. *Tg. Neof.* (similar *Tg. Ps.-J.*): "And, as for the people that slandered with evil tongue, Joseph displaced them and exiled them, and changed them from one city to another and from one end of the territories of the Egyptians to the other. And the people who were in the city he settled in the provinces; and the people of the provinces he settled in the cities ... so that the Egyptians would not taunt the brothers of Joseph and say to them: 'Homeless strangers.'"

11. NABRE (also NRSV, NJB, NIV) adopted the LXX reading of "slaves" instead of "cities"—*le-ʿavadim* instead of *le-ʿārîm*.

12. See Lowenthal, *Joseph Narrative*, 128, citing Delitzsch, *Genesis II*, 352.

must give a fifth of it to Pharaoh, while you keep four-fifths as seed for your fields and as food for yourselves and your households and as food for your children." "You have saved our lives!" they answered. "We have found favor with my lord; now we will be Pharaoh's slaves." Thus Joseph made it a statute for the land of Egypt, which is still in force, that a fifth of its produce should go to Pharaoh. Only the land of the priests did not pass over to Pharaoh.

There is extrabiblical evidence that the priests of Egypt were exempt from taxation[13] and that generally from Ptolemaic times (third century BCE) Pharaoh was regarded theoretically as owner of the land of Egypt. The text says literally, "They came to him [Joseph] in the second year." Is this the second year of the famine or two years after the arrival of Jacob? Is it even the seventh and last year of the famine, since they ask for seed?[14] Twenty percent tax on produce was reasonable; in Ptolemaic times it was roughly thirty-three to forty percent.[15] The people interpreted Joseph's policy as an act of salvation, applying to it the motif "that we may live and not die" associated with the divine salvation of the family of Jacob through Joseph. Sarna avers that:

> Joseph's actions cannot be measured by the moral standards that the Hebrew Bible, especially the prophetic tradition, has inculcated in Western civilization. Rather, they must be judged in the context of the ancient Near Eastern world, by whose norms Joseph emerges here as a highly admirable model of a shrewd and successful administrator.[16]

Von Rad adds, in this vein, the meaning that the ancient narrator himself wanted to convey as follows:

> The nation is grateful; it praises Joseph as its savior. Joseph, therefore, has accomplished the gigantic task of preserving the people throughout the period of distress. The narrative shows us Joseph's wisdom which is capable of mastering every new complication . . . The ancient narrator is honestly amazed and wants the reader also to be amazed at the way an expedient was found to save the people from a gigantic catastrophe. In this respect there pervades in the narrative a naïve pleasure in the possibilities of human wisdom which can conquer economic

---

13. Redford, *Study*, 237 cites Herodotus and Diodorus for Ptolemaic times.
14. See Sarna, *Genesis*, 321.
15. Redford, *Study*, 237.
16. Sarna, *Genesis*, 322–23.

difficulties by a venturesome shift of values, money for bread, manpower and land for seed corn, etc.[17]

In fact, an author argues that Joseph's agrarian reform "was intended to fulfill a theological role by demonstrating that substantial blessing came to Pharaoh"[18] in line with the mandate of blessing in 12:3, and that this explains their inclusion.

However, the reader cannot but try to square all this with the moral standards of the Bible and the prophetic tradition. Sarna admits as much in pointing out that, "Nonetheless, a moral judgment on the situation is subtly introduced into the narrative by shifting the onus of responsibility for the fate of the peasants from Joseph to the Egyptians themselves."[19] From the biblical point of view, what Joseph does here looks like using an emergency to secure permanent restructuring of society to Pharaoh's advantage. Justly does Fretheim reflect that "there may be some irony in that, as Joseph makes 'slaves' of the Egyptians (though not to himself), so the later Pharaohs–who do not have the wisdom and commitments of Joseph–will make 'slaves' of his family. While we cannot be certain, this reversal raises the question of whether later pharaohs extend Joseph's economic policy to include the Israelites."[20]

Tradition

Why were all the patriarchs so desirous of burial in Eretz Israel? Because the dead of Israel will be the first to be resurrected in the days of the Messiah and to enjoy the years of the Messiah (*Gen. Rab.* 96:5). R. Simon asked, "Have the righteous who are buried without the Land lost thereby? What does God do? He makes cavities like channels for them in the earth, and they roll along in them until they reach Eretz Israel, when the Holy One, blessed be he, will infuse into them a spirit of life and they will arise." That is, what really matters is faithful and righteous living.

Augustine picks this up: we must not believe "that men of God of such importance and status so frivolously worried that their bodies were buried, being and ought to be for the faithful, a total security, the fact that wherever their bodies are buried or even if they are buried even by

---

17. Von Rad, *Genesis*, 410.
18. McKenzie, "Jacob's Blessing on Pharaoh," 398.
19. Sarna, *Genesis*, 323.
20. Fretheim, "Genesis," 263.

the hatred of the enemies, or even if they are dismembered to procure pleasure for those same enemies, this does not mean that their resurrection will be less complete or less glorious."[21] Chrysostom adds that "it was to let them have a glimpse of returning themselves some day to the Promised Land. The fact that he gave this direction for that reason his son teaches us quite clearly by saying: 'God will visit you in person, and you will all bring my bones from here' (50:24) . . . Let him not think it a misfortune for someone to end his days in a foreign land or to pass from this life in solitude. After all, it is not such a person who deserves to be thought to be unfortunate but the one who dies in sin, even if he dies in bed, at home, in the bosom of his family."[22]

Chrysostom asked how Joseph's second dream came true since his mother had died before, and did not bow down to her son: "It is invariably Scripture's way to offer the explanation of the whole from the principle example. So since 'the man is the head of the woman' and 'the two will come to be one flesh,' if the head bowed, obviously the whole body followed it. That is to say, if the father did it, much more would she also have done so, had she not been snatched from this life ahead of time . . . 'He bowed,' the text says, 'to the tip of his staff.' Hence Paul also said: 'By faith, Jacob at death's door praised each of Joseph's sons and "bowed to the tip of his staff"' (Heb. 11:21)."[23] Jacob in this act "bowed" to his son Joseph, which act included Rachel, since the man is the head of the woman.

---

21. Augustine, *Questions on Genesis*, q. 161.
22. Chrysostom, *Homilies on Genesis* 66.3.
23. Chrysostom, *Homilies on Genesis* 66.6.

CHAPTER 30

Genesis 48

Jacob Adopts Joseph's Sons, Ephraim and Manasseh

> By faith, Jacob, when dying, blessed each of the sons of Joseph and "bowed in worship, leaning on the top of his staff.
>
> —HEBREWS 11:21

GEN 47:28 REPORTS THAT Jacob lived 147 years. Such information usually follows or precedes the announcement of a protagonist's death. The next verse, v. 29, reports that "when time approached for Israel to die," he called Joseph and arranged to be buried in the ancestral grave in Canaan. Thus "Israel bowed at the head of the bed" (47:31) suggests a report of Israel's death, a report appearing two chapters later, in 49:33. This suggests that Genesis 48–49 have been inserted. The profile of the tribes in them fills in the transition from Israel as a person to Israel as a nation of twelve tribes. Further, the division of Joseph into two tribes here is not consistently carried out in the next chapter where Joseph stands alone.

The following inconsistencies appear. In 48:8 Israel notices the sons of Joseph, but does not know them, when according to 47:28 Israel had lived in Egypt for seventeen years.[1] The original context may have been

---

1. Westermann, *Genesis 37–50*, 186 remarks that since Jacob died shortly thereafter, he did not stay seventeen years in Egypt as in 47:28 (P).

Jacob's arrival in the second year of the famine, and not at his deathbed.[2] In 49:27 Joseph is summoned to his father, while in 48:1 he comes on hearing news of his illness. In 47:29-31 Israel and Joseph already discuss Israel's burial and grave, while in 48:1 Joseph learns for the first time that Jacob is ill and could die. In 48:10 Israel can no longer see, while in 48:8, 11 he sees Joseph and his sons. Twice Joseph brings his sons to Jacob—in 48:10 (he places them on Jacob's knees, Jacob kisses and embraces them) and in 48:13 (he brings Manasseh to Jacob's right, Ephraim to Jacob's left).[3] Twice Israel blesses Joseph's sons, in 48:15-16 and 48:20. "Thus he placed Ephraim before Manasseh" (48:20) is not borne out by the actual words of blessing, but rather refers to Jacob's gesture of crossing his hands and the explanation of this in 48:19.

Some time afterward, Joseph was informed, "Your father is failing." So he took along with him his two sons, Manasseh and Ephraim . . . Jacob then said to Joseph: "God Almighty appeared to me at Luz in the land of Canaan, and blessing me, he said, 'I will make you fertile and multiply you and make you into an assembly of peoples, and I will give this land to your descendants after you as a permanent possession.' So now your two sons who were born to you in the land of Egypt before I joined you here, shall be mine; Ephraim and Manasseh shall be mine as much as Reuben and Simeon are mine."

Joseph never received a direct theophany of God and as such is not one of the patriarchs. Divine appearances and words of promise link Abraham, Isaac, and Jacob as patriarchs of Israel. Jacob refers precisely to God's appearance to him at Bethel (35:11-12), where God changed his name to Israel. The theophany is the legal basis for what he is about to do: as heir to the blessings, Jacob claims the right to decide who is to be included in the "community of peoples" that will be known as Israel.[4] Jacob adopts Joseph's sons, Ephraim and Manasseh (note that he named Ephraim before Manasseh), as his own sons and counts them with his other children among the tribes of Israel. Any offspring of Joseph thereafter will not become individual tribes, rather share with their brothers. God's promise of multiple offspring and making him into an assembly (*qehāl*) of peoples (*'ammîm*) harps back to the blessing by his father Isaac

---

2. See Redford, *Study*, 24.
3. Gunkel, *Genesis*, 445.
4. See Sarna, *Genesis*, 325.

just before he fled to Mesopotamia (28:3). *Qāhāl* is the technical term for Israel assembled in worship, to hear the word of God or to take a common decision; *'am* is the usual term for the people of Israel.

Implied is Israel's continuing fidelity to her God. Israel's permanent possession will be Canaan, hence the land holdings in Egypt given by Joseph and Pharaoh (47:11, 27) can only be temporary.

"I do this because, when I was returning from Paddan, your mother Rachel died, to my sorrow, during the journey in Canaan, while we were still a short distance from Ephrath; and I buried her there on the way to Ephrath [now Bethlehem]."

Adopting Rachel's two grandsons is an act of loving faithfulness to his beloved wife; it compensates symbolically and legally for the additional sons she did not live to bear.[5] This in itself is a double portion and confers on Joseph the status of firstborn, as noted in 1 Chr 5:1, alluding to Jacob's dispositions in the next chapter: "The sons of Reuben, the firstborn of Israel. (He was indeed the firstborn, but because he defiled the couch of his father his birthright was given to the sons of Joseph, son of Israel, so that he is not listed in the family records according to his birthright. Judah, in fact, became powerful among his brothers, so that the ruler came from him, though the birthright had been Joseph's)."[6]

Now Israel's eyes were dim from age; he could not see well . . . Then Israel said to Joseph, "I never expected to see your face again, and now God has allowed me to see your descendants as well!" Joseph removed them from his father's knees and bowed down before him with his face to the ground.

"Face to the ground" repeats exactly Jacob's retort to Joseph's second dream (37:11), while Joseph's report of the dream lacked this phrase! In contradiction to this dream, it is Joseph who prostrates to the ground before Jacob. Does the repudiation suggest that only the first dream revealed divine intentions, while the second derived from a puffed-up

---

5. See Alter, *Genesis*, 288.

6. Jacob in Genesis 49 and Moses in Deuteronomy 33 still count Joseph as one of the tribes of Israel. Numbers 2 and 26, though, count Ephraim and Manasseh as two tribes, even if Numbers 26 names Manasseh before Ephraim. It should be noted that such exaltation of the northern tribes does not know of the strictures in the Deuteronomistic History against the northern kingdom of Israel as idolatrous.

sense of self?⁷ Anyway, this is another indication of the subordination of Joseph to Jacob, the Joseph story to the Jacob story.

From this point to the end of the chapter, Jacob is named Israel—the patriarch is in process of becoming Israel the nation.⁸ Joseph led his sons to Israel for blessing in such manner that Manasseh, the firstborn, would be on Israel's right, Ephraim on the left. But in giving the blessing, Israel crossed his hands, laying the right on Ephraim, the left hand on Manasseh. The verb for crossing his hands, *śikkel*, can also mean "acting wisely," in wisdom hidden from Joseph. Jacob asserts one more time his position as architect of this tale and of Israel's tale in general.⁹

Then he blessed them¹⁰ with these words:

> *May the God in whose presence*
>   *my fathers Abraham and Isaac walked,*
> *The God who has been my shepherd*
>   *from my birth to this day,*
> *The angel who has delivered me from all harm,*
>   *bless these boys*
> *That in them my name be recalled,*
>   *and the names of my fathers, Abraham and Isaac,*
> *And they may become teeming multitudes*
>   *upon the earth!*

Jacob articulates a spirituality of the presence of God. God Almighty directed Abraham to "walk in my presence and be blameless" (17:1). Jacob affirms that this has indeed been so: "the whole life of Abraham and Isaac is described as a path before God, as a path vis-à-vis God. This includes every conceivable relationship to God, every event mutually affecting the patriarchs and God."¹¹ He prays that this history of the patriarchs with God continue in the offspring. Jacob before relied on his prowess and cunning. Matured by experience, he recognizes the grace of the God who "has been my shepherd from my birth to this day." This God accompanied him as an angel on all his journeying and has delivered him

---

7. Mandolfo, "You Meant Evil Against Me," 457.

8. In this account, the sons of Joseph are still boys who can be placed on their grandpa's knees, in another account they would be at least twenty years old.

9. Mandolfo, "You Meant Evil Against Me," 462.

10. NABRE corrected the Hebrew text following LXX, Syr. and Vulg.; the Hebrew text had: "and he blessed Joseph."

11. Westermann, *Genesis 37–50*, 190.

from all harm."¹² The crossing of Israel's hand "was evil in his [Joseph's] eyes," says the text. It seemed against justice and fairness—and he knows a thing or two about what havoc upsetting standards of justice can cause in a family.

> But his father refused. "I know it, son," he said, "I know. That one too shall become a people, and he too shall be great. Nevertheless, his younger brother shall surpass him, and his descendants shall become a multitude of nations."

Why does Jacob persist in privileging the younger over the elder? "That Jacob might be manipulating events in collusion with YHWH's 'will' is completely beyond [Joseph's] grasp."¹³ The struggle for primogeniture has played itself out in this story right from Cain and Abel. The Joseph story is indeed one of sustained meditation on "undeserved chosenness," a theme that reflects "a deep-seated Israelite perception that the nation itself is blessed, but has not earned this blessedness primarily on its own merit."¹⁴ Anyway, both inherit the blessing of "great nation" (cf. 12:2), only that Ephraim will be greater.

> Manasseh will become a people (*'ām*); *'ām* is marked by consanguinity and common racial parentage. Ephraim will become "a multitude of nations" (*mᵉlō'-ha-gôyîm*, literally "fullness of the nations"). *Gôy* highlights political structure and territorial affiliation.¹⁵ Ephraim never grew into a multitude of nations, so the versions sought various ways to understand the text. TNK: "and his offspring shall be plentiful enough for nations"; similarly, NJB: "his offspring will be sufficient to constitute nations." *Tg. Onq.* speaks of rule: "and his descendants shall rule over nations" (similar, *Tg. Neof.*). I wonder whether there is here a subtle reference to "Galilee of the nations" (Isa 8:23) and reference to the mixed population of "Ephraim" (as the northern

---

12. In fidelity to his word which said, "I am with you and will protect you wherever you go" (28:15).

13. Mandolfo, "You Meant Evil Against Me," 456. Mandolfo uses Bakhtin's category of dialogic truth to argue that Joseph and Jacob represent two competing theologies—a worldview in which God's dealings with humanity support a consistent and benevolent cosmic order and another in which God is not above inflicting evil on humanity to forward divine purposes.

14. Kaminsky, "Reclaiming a Theology of Election," 151.

15. See Clements, "Gôy," in *TDOT* 2:427.

kingdom is known in poetry) induced by Shalmaneser, king of Assyria (2 Kgs 10:24).

So he blessed them that day and said, "By you shall the people of Israel pronounce blessings, saying, 'God make you like Ephraim and Manasseh.'"

"By you" is singular in the Hebrew. By Joseph? By each of you—distributive? God's blessing of Abraham is to be so concentrated in the Joseph tribes that the other tribes will use their names for blessing! And Israel must never give up hope of the Promised Land, no matter how long the sojourn in Egypt may prove to be.

Then Israel said to Joseph: "I am about to die. But God will be with you and will restore you to the land of your ancestors. As for me, I give to you, as to the one above his brothers, Shechem, which I captured from the Amorites with my sword and bow."

In making Joseph's two sons into two tribes, Israel already assigned him the firstborn's double portion; here he gives him a further mark of distinction from his brothers. The verse bristles with difficulties. Conjectures for the Hebrew word *Shekhem 'aḥad* range from "a mountain slope" to "a portion" to the city of Shechem. Gunkel believes it refers to the shoulder piece of divided meat portions,[16] the shoulder being an additional and choice piece for Joseph. The versions try their best to make sense of the context.

> "and now, I assign to you one portion more than to your brothers, which I wrested from the Amorites with my sword and bow" (TNK, similar the NRSV); "as for me, I have given you with single intent over your brothers what I took from the hand of the Amorites with my sword and my bow."[17] The LXX makes a double translation: "and I give to thee Sicima, a select portion above thy brethren, which I took out of the hand of the Amorites with my sword and bow."

Augustine rightly wonders: "If now, rejoicing in that victory, he gives that land to his son Joseph, why then did the sons who did this act

---

16. Gunkel, *Genesis*, 449.

17. Alter, *Genesis*, 291. He relies on the adverbial meaning *Shekhem 'aḥad* in the context of in Zeph 3:9, where the parallelism seems to dictate the sense, "with one accord": for all of them to invoke the name of the LORD / to serve him with one accord.

[Genesis 34] displease him?"[18] And there is no account in our texts of Jacob fighting with sword and bow.

The New Testament sees Jacob's act here as an expression of that faith which is the evidence of things not seen: "By faith, Jacob, when dying, blessed each of the sons of Joseph and "bowed in worship, leaning on the top of his staff" (Heb 11:21).

Tradition

Augustine answered his own question (see note 18) by uncovering prophetic mystery hidden there: since Joseph prefigured Christ and was from that land where Jacob had destroyed and annihilated the foreign gods, it would be understood that Christ would possess the Gentiles, who would renounce the gods of their fathers and believe in him. Cyril of Alexandria says it clearly: "That is to say, they would be among the firstborn sons, and also be placed with those who render obedience, for Reuben was the firstborn, and Simeon means 'obedience.' Through faith we who are the last have become the first, and the people taken from among the Gentiles have inherited the glory of the firstborn."[19] Ambrose concluded that "Jacob himself approved the deed; for when he had possession of Shechem he gave it at his death to his most beloved son Joseph and said to him, 'I give to you above all your brothers Shechem in particular, which I took from the hands of the Amorites with my sword and bow.'" Spiritually, however, "by 'Shechem' are meant 'shoulders' and by 'shoulders' are meant works. Therefore Jacob chose the holy Joseph before the others as heir to his good works, for the other brothers could not match his works. Who indeed could match Christ's deeds?"[20] The fathers, of course, saw Joseph as type of Christ. Since Jacob had twelve sons, replacing Joseph with his two sons makes the tribes thirteen! In mystery, this alludes to Paul himself: "After being chosen among the tribes, he was counted the thirteenth after the apostles, and so he was sent to the Gentiles as apostle."[21]

Tg. Neof. dealt with the difficulty of Jacob's sword and bow as follows: "And now, I give you a part more than your brothers: Shechem,

---

18. Augustine, *Questions on Genesis*, q. 167.
19. Cyril of Alexandria, *Glaphyra on Genesis*, 307.
20. Ambrose, *Patriarchs* 3.11–12, in ACCS 2:323.
21. Hippolytus, *On the Blessings of Isaac and Jacob* 11, in ACCS 2:314.

which I took from the hands of the Amorites, by my merits and my good works, which are better for me than my sword and my bow."[22]

---

22. *Tg. Ps.-J.* has Jacob assisting in the slaughter of Genesis 34: "behold I give you the city of Shechem, one portion as a gift more than your brothers, which I took from the hands of the Amorites when you went into it, and I arose and assisted you with my sword and with my bow."

CHAPTER 31

Genesis 49

The Testament of Jacob

> The patriarchal period began with a divine promise of nationhood to Abraham (12:2), and the fulfilment of that promise is expressed here through "the twelve tribes of Israel" (49:28).[1]

WE SUGGESTED IN THE last chapter that Genesis 48 and 49 were inserted. The profile of the tribes they contain fills in the transition from Israel as a person to Israel as a nation of twelve tribes. The division of Joseph into two tribes in Genesis 48 does not feature in this chapter; rather Joseph is treated as one of the twelve tribes.

These tribal sayings do not have a common background; they arose at different times and in different circumstances. They enshrine the common origin of the tribes and the basic unity of the nation of Israel.[2] They portray Jacob as eponymous ancestor "prophesying" and almost predetermining the nature and destiny of the tribes. Some believe this is prophecy from the event (the situation current at the time of production was projected backwards as prophecy from Jacob's lips) or that "what is to happen to you in days to come" is the understanding of a later editor. The persons of Reuben, Simeon, and Levi may be directly addressed, but the

---

1. Sarna, *Genesis*, 331.
2. See Sarna, *Genesis*, 331.

tribes named after them bear the consequences of their actions. Above all, the tribal sayings focus on Judah and Joseph; these have by far the longest sayings. Jacob assigns rule (political power) to Judah, numbers and fertile fields to Joseph, but nothing about rule as the reader expected. Thus "Jacob's Testament takes a distinctly Judahite view of the divided monarchy."[3] The collection as we have it stems from the time of Judah's dominion over Israel.[4] The tribes are listed in the order of the six sons of Leah, then the two sons of Bilhah, the two of Zilpah, and finally the two of Rachel.

In these sayings, the tribe of Levi is still a secular tribe, with martial qualities still evident in Exodus 32. The tribe is in disfavor, while elsewhere it is a priestly tribe that enjoys privileged status (Num 3:12–13). Here the lack of territory is punishment, while elsewhere (Num 18:20–24) it is because of the tribe's spiritual destiny and special status.[5] Notable is that the Song of Deborah (Judges 5) does not mention Judah or Simeon or Levi, though she mentions a tribe of Machir (in Gen 50:23 Joseph adopts Machir, a son of Manasseh, as one of his own children) among the levy, and blames Reuben, Gilead, Dan, and Asher for not showing up for battle (does Gilead = Gad?). Deuteronomy 33 also does not mention Simeon—it was absorbed in Judah—while Levi is portrayed as a priestly tribe dispersed among the other tribes. The table below indicates something of the evolution of the tribes.

The piece is poetry. Jacob puns on the names of the tribes and uses animal metaphors to describe some of them. Some words are uncertain, so the versions differ considerably in rendering some verses. I lay these out to indicate the possible fields of meaning. Even experts find Genesis 49 difficult. I shall relegate some of the discussion to the footnotes.

---

3. Fretheim, "Genesis," 226, 228.
4. Gunkel, *Genesis*, 453.
5. Sarna, *Genesis*, 334.

Judges 5	Gen 49:1–22	Num 2:3–79; 7:12–83	Deut 33:1–29	Joshua 13–19
Ephraim	Reuben	Judah	Reuben	Judah
Benjamin	Simeon	Issachar	Judah	Manasseh
Machir = Manasseh?	Levi	Zebulun	Levi	Ephraim
Zebulun	Judah	Reuben	Benjamin	Reuben
Issachar	Zebulun	Simeon	Joseph = Ephraim/ Manasseh	Gad
Naphtali	Issachar	Gad		Benjamin
Reuben	Dan	Ephraim	Zebulun	Simeon
Gilead = Gad?	Gad	Manasseh	Issachar	Zebulun
Dan	Asher	Benjamin	Gad	Issachar
Asher	Naphtali	Dan	Dan	Asher
	Joseph	Asher	Naphtali	Naphtali
	Benjamin	Naphtali	Asher	Dan
no Judah, Simeon, Levi Reuben, Gilead, Dan, Asher—no show for battle		no Levi	no Simeon; Levi as priestly	Levi as priestly

Jacob's Testament for the Tribes of Israel, 49:1–27

Jacob called his sons and said: "Gather around, that I may tell you what is to happen to you in days to come. "Assemble and listen, sons of Jacob, listen to Israel, your father.

It is usual for a hero to gather his offspring for a last will and testament before passing off the stage. People close to death are often credited with prophetic vision; Jacob's words are so couched. *Be-'aḥarit ha-yammîm* ("in the latter days") literally means "in the future."[6] It, however, became a technical term for the end-time and is so used especially in late prophecy.

---

6. See Sarna, *Genesis*, 332: it means this in the cognate language of Akkadian.

You, Reuben, my firstborn, my strength and the first fruit of my vigor, excelling in rank and excelling in power! Turbulent as water, you shall no longer excel, for you climbed into your father's bed and defiled my couch to my sorrow.

When the incident was reported in 35:22, Jacob said nothing ("he was greatly offended" is supplied from the LXX). Now he gives his verdict. Lying with the concubine of one's father is both affront and claim to succession (see 2 Sam 16:22: "and Absalom went to his father's concubines in view of all Israel"). It was part of Reuben's struggle for the leadership of the house of Jacob; it cost him the firstborn status. 1 Chr 5:1 informs the reader that "he was indeed the firstborn, but because he defiled the couch of his father his birthright was given to the sons of Joseph, son of Israel, so that he is not listed in the family records according to his birthright." Later legislation (Deut 21:15–17) forbids the father from disinheriting the firstborn, but in the early period a father could annul the firstborn status of his son. Moses voices a prayer for Reuben: "May Reuben live and not die out, but let his numbers be few" (Deut 33:6). It appears that the tribe of Reuben was gradually consumed in battles with the Moabites and Ammonites.[7]

Simeon and Levi, brothers indeed, weapons of violence are their knives . . . For in their fury they killed men, at their whim they maimed oxen . . . I will scatter them in Jacob, disperse them throughout Israel.

The only event in which Simeon and Levi acted violently together was the sack of Shechem (Genesis 34), but there they carried off the sheep, cattle, and donkeys (34:28) rather than maim them. In the Blessing of Moses (Deuteronomy 33), Simeon is not mentioned (absorbed into Judah) and Levi's scattering among the tribes is because of its priestly status. Jacob condemns the excessive fury that went beyond all measure. We discussed in the last chapter the dilemma that Jacob claimed to have captured Shechem himself with his sword and bow. At a certain period, a man's sin could be punished in his offspring to the third and fourth generation (Exod 20:5); later, however, it was felt to be unjust for children's teeth to be set on edge when it was their parents who ate sour grapes (Ezek 18:2).

You, Judah, shall your brothers praise—your hand on the neck of your enemies; the sons of your father shall bow down to you. Judah is a lion's cub,

---

7. Gunkel, *Genesis*, 454.

you have grown up on prey, my son . . . The scepter shall never depart from Judah, or the mace from between his feet, until tribute comes to him, and he receives the people's obedience. He tethers his donkey to the vine, his donkey's foal to the choicest stem. In wine he washes his garments, his robe in the blood of grapes.

Name is destiny. Judah (praise) will draw praise from his brothers for military prowess and for routing his enemies and pursuing after them. "Your father's sons shall bow down to you" subtly inverts Joseph's first dream using the same verb! Joseph's dream may have proven true in Egypt, but now Judah rules.[8] The lion is the king of the beasts and the most daring. Balaam applied the lion imagery to the people of Israel (Num 23:24; 24:9). Rev 5:5 will speak of the Lamb as the "lion of the tribe of Judah." Scepter and mace are paraphernalia of a king. The meaning of what follows is greatly disputed between those who favor a messianic interpretation and those who reject it. Westermann resists a messianic interpretation of 49:10: "it is not a messianic prophecy in the sense that it promises a king of salvation at the end-time."[9] He takes Shiloh in *'ad kî yabō' Shîloh* (literally, "until Shiloh comes") as the one who wins the obedience of the nations. A sort of dominion over the tribes remains with Judah until (*'ad kî* taken inclusively) one comes who wins the obedience of the nations (the surrounding Canaanite peoples), and this refers to the monarchy under David and Solomon. But the messianic interpretation already appeared in the LXX, which speaks of an individual, not the tribe of Judah: "A ruler shall not fail from Juda, nor a prince from his loins." This renders "scepter" in personal terms, as ruler, also *mḥqq* (here rendered "mace") as prince/leader, *Shiloh* as *hôi apokeitai* ("what is stored up for him"), and *yipphat 'ammîm* as "hope/expectation of the nations" (as if from *tiqwah*, "expectation," "hope").[10] The Vulgate built on the messianic interpretation by rendering *Shiloh* with "who is to be sent" (*qui mittendus est*), as if from the root *shalaḥ*, "to send." The LXX translators may have seen an intertext in Isa 42:4, where the Servant will not wilt "until he establishes justice on the earth, the coastlands *will wait* [emphasis mine] for his teaching."[11] Justin Martyr debated with Jews as to

---

8. *Pace* Westermann, *Genesis 37–50*, 228, who denies the claim of kingship for Judah or that the tribes of Israel acknowledge him as lord.

9. Westermann, *Genesis 37–50*, 232.

10. See Smyth, "Prophecy Concerning Judah," 295.

11. The Samaritan Pentateuch, with forty Hebrew manuscripts, read *Shiloh* as *she*

who the referent of this saying might be (see "Tradition"). Most English versions today, Jewish and Christian, concur in breaking Shiloh into *shai lō* (tribute to him) and reading *yipphat* as a noun meaning "obedience."[12] Hope for dominion over the nations is a messianic theme that one encounters across the Bible—Psalms 2, 72, and 110; Isa 2:1–4; 11:10; Mic 5:3; Zech 9:10.[13] In fact, the LORD says of his servant: "I will make you a light to the nations that my salvation may reach to the ends of the earth" (Isa 49:6). Balaam's oracle in Num 24:17 applies the imagery to Israel: "a star shall advance from Jacob, and a scepter shall rise from Israel, that will crush the brows of Moab and the skull of all the Sethites . . . and Jacob will rule his foes." "In wine, he washes his garments" points to both the purple color of his robes and the abundance of wine, so abundant that a donkey may have his fill. Dark eyes and white teeth are metaphors of beauty and health.

Zebulun shall dwell by the seashore; he will be a haven for ships, and his flank shall rest on Sidon.

In Josh 19:10–16, Zebulun was landlocked, blocked from the sea by Asher.[14]

Issachar is a rawboned donkey, crouching between the saddlebags. When he saw how good a settled life was, and how pleasant the land, he bent his shoulder to the burden and became a toiling serf.

Jacob puns on the name Issachar—*'ish sakar* means a hired laborer. Issachar was one of the tribes that responded to Deborah's call to battle. Jacob blames it for forfeiting freedom and independence for a life of ease as hirelings.

Dan shall achieve justice for his people as one of the tribes of Israel. Let Dan be a serpent by the roadside, a horned viper by the path, that bites the horse's heel, so that the rider tumbles backward.

lō ("that is his," that is, to whom the scepter and mace belong).

12. NRSV: until tribute comes to him; and the obedience of the peoples is his / TNK: So that tribute shall come to him, and the homage of peoples be his / NJB: until tribute be brought him and the peoples render him obedience. As mentioned, the ancient versions rendered differently. LXX: until there come the things stored up for him; and he is the expectation of nations / Vulg.: until there come who is to be sent (*qui mittendus est*).

13. See Gunkel, *Genesis*, 457.

14. See Sarna, *Genesis*, 338.

The pun on the name of Dan is like saying the judge will judge! Some take "his people" as Dan's own people, and not Israel—Dan will maintain its independence like the other tribes.[15] Others read it as that Dan will become active in seeking justice for the tribes of Israel.[16] Dan, being small, lived by guerilla warfare, like a viper by the roadside that bites the horse's heel and topples the rider.[17]

I long for your deliverance, O Lord!

Is this an editor's gloss using the exact words of Ps 119:166, or a heartfelt prayer by Jacob for the promised salvation?

Gad shall be raided by raiders, but he shall raid at their heels.

Gad, means "good luck" (Gen 30:11), but also "raider." The prophecy puns on this: the raider shall be raided by raiders, but he shall raid at their heels. Gad settled in Gilead (Josh 13:24–28) where it sharpened military skill dealing with raiding groups (1 Chr 5:18–22).

Asher's produce is rich, and he shall furnish delicacies for kings.

As noted in Judg 1:31–32, Asher could not dispossess the inhabitants of Acco or those of Sidon, so he settled among the Canaanite inhabitants of the land.

Naphtali is a hind let loose, which brings forth lovely fawns.

LXX read the key words differently and rendered: "Nephthalim is a spreading stem, bestowing beauty on its fruit."

Joseph is a wild colt, a wild colt by a spring, wild colts on a hillside. Harrying him and shooting, the archers opposed him[18]*; But his bow remained taut, and his arms were nimble, by the power of the Mighty One of Jacob, because of*[19] *the Shepherd, the Rock of Israel, the God of your father, who*

---

15. Gunkel, *Genesis*, 459; Sarna, *Genesis*, 340.
16. Fretheim, "Genesis," 269.
17. Sarna, *Genesis*, 340 remarks that the genealogies of Chronicles ignore Dan altogether. Josh 19:40–48 does not define the borders of the tribe, only allots to it a list of cities. There are no reports of the Danites having captured any of their allotted cities, however, they marched up and attacked Leshem, which they captured and put to the sword.
18. Only here do we hear of archers attacking the Joseph tribes and of their prowess with the bow. See Sarna, *Genesis*, 343.
19. Reading *mi-shēm* ("by the name of"); the Hebrew has *mi-shām* ("from there").

helps you, God Almighty, who blesses you, with the blessings of the heavens above, the blessings of the abyss that crouches below, the blessings of breasts and womb, the blessings of fresh grain and blossoms, the blessings of the everlasting mountains, the delights of the eternal hills. May they rest on the head of Joseph, on the brow of the prince among his brothers.

Joseph is named here as a tribe in his own name and not as Ephraim and Manasseh. A wild ass is strong and indomitable—the Joseph tribes will be indomitable. However, the reading "wild colt" is unsure.

> Depending on which version you take, Joseph is compared to a son, a wild colt, or fruitful plant.[20]

LXX: Joseph is a son increased; my dearly loved son is increased; my youngest son, turn to me / *Tg. Onq.*: Joseph is my son who shall be numerous; my son who shall be blessed like a vine that is planted near a spring of water.

TNK (= NABRE): Joseph is a wild ass, a wild ass by a spring—wild colts on a hillside.

NRSV: Joseph is a fruitful bough, a fruitful bough by a spring; his branches run over the wall

NJB: Joseph is a fruitful plant near a spring whose tendrils reach over the wall.

Jacob is effusive in his blessing of Joseph. On him he conferred fecundity of man, beast, and field, and permanent sources of living water from the heavens above and the abyss below. All nature (merism of the heavens and the abyss) conspires together for Joseph's enrichment and welfare. Joseph is set up in a relation of *nāzîr* to his brothers (Moses' Blessing, Deut 33:16, repeats the phrase word for word).[21] The basic meaning of the word is "to withdraw from ordinary use," "to set apart." The particular context shows what the setting apart or the consecration is for. Amos 2:11, "I who raised up prophets among your children, and nazirites among your young

---

20. The initial *bēn pōrāt* is a puzzle. *Bēn* is a son (used with another noun, it can signify a type, class, or quality), *pō'rah* is a bough (though some read *pōrat* as feminine of *pere'*, wild ass)—the versions have focused on a term to give meaning to the whole context.

21. Westermann, *Genesis 37–50*, 241 opines that *nāzîr* cannot refer to the king, and never designates a king, rather one is consecrated to a special act among his brothers. However, Sarna, *Genesis*, 345 thinks that *nāzîr* can mean one who wears the *nezer*, symbol of royal power.

men," has nazirites in parallelism with prophets as YHWH's emissaries. Thus the *nāzîr* seems to be a charismatic figure called by YHWH, just like the prophet. The consecration of such nazirites may have initially been for the holy war.[22] It appears, however, that naziriteship later became a special act of devotion to YHWH; this is described in Num 6:1–21.[23] The term ascribes to Joseph a certain leadership and preeminence over the tribes, but not in terms of rule and political power (assigned to Judah). In poetry, especially of Second Isaiah, Jacob appears in parallelism with Israel to represent the nation. *'Abbîr* usually means "bull," but in the five passages where it is used of God it is written *'abîr* (without the doubling of -b), as signal to exclude the meaning "bull" for the underlying meaning of "power," "strength," and "might."[24] The Canaanite cult represented Baal, the storm god, as a bull! The Mighty One of Jacob is ranged with four other epithets of Israel's God: Shepherd, the Rock of Israel, the God of your father, God Almighty (*El Shaddai*). The northern Ps 80:2 fills in the context of the epithet Shepherd: "O shepherd of Israel, lend an ear, you who guide Joseph like a flock! . . . Stir up your power, and come and save us." Personal piety later adopted the epithet as we read in Ps 23:1: "the LORD is my shepherd; there is nothing I lack." "Rock,"[25] as symbol of firmness and invincibility, appears in many psalms, for example, Ps 18:3: "I love you, Lord, my strength, Lord, my rock, my fortress, my deliverer." Apparently each patriarch related personally and intimately to a "god of the father": Abraham to *El Shaddai*, Isaac to the Fear of Isaac (*Paḥad Isaac*, Gen 31:42),[26] and Jacob himself to "the Mighty One of Jacob" (Gen 49:24). In line with the Judahite redirection of the blessing of Joseph is Ps 78:67-68: "He rejected the tent of Joseph, chose not the tribe of Ephraim.

---

22. Mayer, "*Nāzîr*," *TDOT*, IX, 306-311, here 307, 308. Mayer holds that in Gen 49:26 and Deut 33:16, "the word characterizes Joseph's special relationship to God that sets him apart from his brothers; there is no need to invent the meaning of 'prince.'" Gunkel, *Genesis*, 460 (referring to Samson) opines that the *nāzîr* was an Israelite champion and partisan who single-handedly fought YHWH's wars. This would mean that Joseph battled Israel's common enemies singlehandedly, was Israel's champion. This image does not necessarily point to Joseph's monarchy, but is better understood against the Judges period.

23. Mayer, "*Nāzîr*," in *TDOT* 9:309.

24. Kapelrud, "*Abbîr*/*Abîr*," in *TDOT* 1:43. The five instances are Gen 49:24; Isa 1:24; 49:26; 60:16; and Ps 132:2, 5.

25. However, the term used here is *'eben* (stone), not the usual *ṣûr* (rock).

26. *Paḥad Isaac* can also be rendered "the one whom Isaac reveres" or "the one of Isaac who causes terror."

God chose the tribe of Judah, Mount Zion which he loved." As regards the inspiration and truth of Scripture, we recall that "there is no program that can be constructed on the basis of the Bible which can escape the challenge of other portions of it."[27]

Benjamin is a ravenous wolf; mornings he devours the prey, and evenings he distributes the spoils.

The prey is so much that this wolf is at it the whole day. The Benjamin here who lives by plunder (perhaps setting upon passing caravans) does not match the image of the tender Benjamin of the Joseph story, nor of the Benjamin of the Blessing of Moses (Deut 33:12): "the beloved of the LORD, he abides in safety beside him; he shelters him all day long; the beloved abides at his breast."

Jacob's Farewell and Death, 49:28-33

All these are the twelve tribes of Israel, and this is what their father said about them, as he blessed them. To each he gave a suitable blessing.

For the first time, the twelve tribes of Israel are referred to as such. "The patriarchal period began with a divine promise of nationhood to Abraham (12:2), and the fulfilment of that promise is expressed here through 'the twelve tribes of Israel' (49:28)."[28]

Then he gave them this charge: "Since I am about to be gathered to my people, bury me with my ancestors in the cave that lies in the field of Ephron the Hittite, the cave in the field of Machpelah . . . When Jacob had finished giving these instructions to his sons, he drew his feet into the bed, breathed his last, and was gathered to his people.

The purchase of the burial cave in the field of Machpelah as a personal holding was a pledge of the possession of the Promised Land. At the end of his life, Jacob reaffirms his hope in God's promise and signals that however long the Egyptian sojourn may be, Israel's home is in Canaan. Mentioned here for the first time is the death and burial of Sarah, Rebekah, and Leah.[29]

---

27. Sanders, *Canon and Community*, 37.
28. Sarna, *Genesis*, 331.
29. Sarna, *Genesis*, 346.

Tradition

Micah 5:1 picks up the theme of the ruler to come from Judah: "but you, Bethlehem-Ephrathah least among the clans of Judah, from you shall come forth for me one who is to be ruler in Israel; whose origin is of old, from ancient times." Bethlehem is the home of David, so the ruler will be of the House of David. The Oracle of Nathan to David takes center piece in this: "I will raise up your offspring after you . . . and I will establish his kingdom . . . Your house and your kingdom are firm forever before me; your throne shall be firmly established forever" (2 Sam 7:12, 16). A fragment from Qumran Cave IV (4Q252 on Gen 49:10) dated to first half of the first century BCE comments on Jacob's oracle on Judah:

> The scepter [shall not] depart from the tribe of Judah . . . Whenever Israel rules, there shall [not] fail to be a descendant of David upon the throne (Jer 33:17). For the ruler's staff is the Covenant of kingship, [and the clans] of Israel are the divisions, until the Messiah of Righteousness comes, the Branch of David. For to him and his seed is granted the Covenant of kingship over his people for everlasting generations which he is to keep . . .[30]

Writing on the Jewish Revolt of 66–70 CE, Josephus said:

> But now, what did most elevate them in undertaking this war, was an ambiguous oracle that was also found in their sacred writings, how, "about that time, one from their country should become governor of the habitable earth." The Jews took this prediction to belong to themselves in particular and many of the wise men were thereby deceived in their determination. Now, this oracle certainly denoted the government of Vespasian, who was appointed emperor in Judea.[31]

Matthew's genealogy of Jesus (Matthew 1) and the entire New Testament take it for granted that the Messiah was to be of the tribe of Judah and "son of David." In the debates of the early church fathers with Jews, both sides agreed that the Messiah was to be of David. The debate was who and when, with Jews insisting that the coming of the Messiah will be at the end-time only. Some Jews insisted that the prophecy was about Judah, not an individual; if individual, it would refer to a line of

---

30. Vermes, *Complete Dead Sea Scrolls*, 462–63. Vermes comments (p. 462): that royal power belongs to descendants of David implies that all non-Davidic rulers, such as the contemporary Hasmonaean priest-kings, unlawfully occupy the throne.

31. Josephus, *Jewish Wars* 6.5.4.

ethnarchs who represented Jews before the Romans. Even as late as 132 CE, the prophecy was applied to Bar Kockba, who led the last Jewish Revolt against Rome. The fathers countered this with LXX's messianic rendering. "A prince shall not fail from Judah and a ruler from his loins, until what is laid up for him shall come; and he shall be the expectation of the Gentiles. And that this was said not of Judah but of the Christ, is plain. For all we who are of all the Gentiles are not expecting Judah, but Jesus, who also brought up your fathers out of Egypt . . . Now, Gentlemen, I could contend with you about the passage, which you interpret by affirming that it runs: *until those things that are laid up for him come.* This is not the interpretation of the Seventy [LXX], but, *until he come for whom it is laid up.*"[32]

Some Jews applied the saying to their current ethnarchs[33] under Roman rule. "And these predictions we employ to answer those who, in their perplexity as to the words spoken in Genesis by Jacob to Judah, assert that the Ethnarch, being of the race of Judah, is the ruler of the people, and that there will not fail some of his seed, until the advent of that Christ whom they figure to their imagination. But if 'the children of Israel are to sit many days without a king, or ruler, or altar, or priesthood, or responses'; and if, since the temple was destroyed, there exists no longer sacrifice, nor altar, nor priesthood, it is manifest that the ruler *has* failed out of Judah, and the leader from between his thighs. And since the prediction declares that 'the ruler shall not fail from Judah, and the leader from between his thighs, until what is reserved for him shall come,' it is manifest that he is come to whom (belongs) what is reserved— the expectation of the Gentiles. And this is clear from the multitude of the heathen who have believed on God through Jesus Christ."[34] Generally Herod's reign was seen as the signal: "'There shall not be lacking a prince out of Judah, nor a teacher from his loins, until he shall come for whom it is reserved; and he is the expectation of the nations.' There lacked not therefore a Jewish prince of the Jews until that Herod, who was the first king of a foreign race received by them. Therefore it was now the time

---

32. Justin, *Dialogue with Trypho*, 120.3-4. Was Justin reading from a variant LXX manuscrip? For our current LXX text corresponds to the text he criticizes.

33. In 1 Macc 14:47; 15:1-2, Simon_s referred to as high priest and ethnarch, that is, leader/governor of an ethnic group, in this case the Judeans. With the debacle of 70 CE, Rome gave this title to Jewish leaders who reorganized Jewish life and represented them before Rome.

34. Origen, *First Principles* 1.3.

when he should come for whom that was reserved which is promised in the New Testament, that he should be the expectation of the nations."[35]

Some fathers placed the prophesied time under Herod Antipas: "For Jews exercised authority, and there were rulers of Israelite descent among them until the time of Herod son of Antipas, a native of Palestine, who claimed the right to rule and was called a tetrarch. It was in his days that Christ, *'the expectation of the nations,'* was born. It is not necessary to demonstrate that the multitude taken from the nations were saved when he was born, since the matter is patently obvious."[36]

Justin found the words "tying his foal to the vine" fulfilled in the incident in Mark 11:1-6 where Christ declares himself the lord of the foal tied up:

> and the words, "tying his foal to the vine, and washing his robe in the blood of the grape," allegorically signified the things that would befall Christ, and the deeds he would perform. For the foal of a donkey stood tied to a vine at the entrance to a village, and he ordered his disciples to lead it to him . . . after this he was crucified, in order that the rest of the prophecy be verified, for the words, "washing his robe in the blood of the grape," were a forewarning of the passion he was to endure, purifying with his blood those who believe in him . . . "His robe" are those believers in Christ, in whom dwells the seed of God, namely, the Word.[37]

Hippolytus saw the union between Father and Son signified in the lion and lion's whelp: "By saying 'lion' and 'lion's whelp,' he has clearly pointed toward the two persons: that of the Father and that of the Son. He said, 'From a shoot, my son, you have gone up' in order to show the generation of Christ according to the flesh."[38]

---

35. Augustine, *City of God.*
36. Cyril of Alexandria, *Glaphra on Genesis* 7.3 (p. 329).
37. Justin, *First Apology* 32. See also Blenkinsopp, "Oracle of Judah," 60.
38. Hippolytus, *On the Blessings of Isaac and Jacob* 16, in ACCS 2:328.

CHAPTER 32

Genesis 50

The Joseph Story Dovetails with the Jacob Story; Reconstruction of Memory

> We know that all things work for good for those who love God, who are called according to his purpose.
>
> —Romans 8:28

THE CLOSING CHAPTER OF Genesis pulls the strings together. The genealogy of Jacob (37:2), in which the story of Joseph played a significant part, attains narrative closure with the death and burial of both Jacob and Joseph. Israel transits into the twelve tribes of Israel. The last two words of the chapter, "in Egypt," prepare us for the next phase of the story—Israel's sojourn in Egypt and eventual liberation from there.

Jacob's Funeral, 50:1–14

Joseph flung himself upon his father and wept over him as he kissed him. Then Joseph ordered the physicians in his service to embalm his father.

Jacob was embalmed and mourned according to Egyptian custom; the mourning of seventy days approximates to the seventy-two days mourning for Pharaoh! Egyptians did not wear hair on their heads or beards except when mourning a close relative. Joseph could not appear as such before Pharaoh, so he sent members of Pharaoh's household to speak on his behalf. His father put him on oath to bury him in the patriarchal grave in Canaan. He would go and return. Pharaoh acceded.

So Joseph went up to bury his father; and with him went all of Pharaoh's officials who were senior members of his household and all the other elders of the land of Egypt, as well as Joseph's whole household, his brothers, and his father's household; only their children and their flocks and herds were left in the region of Goshen. Chariots, too, and horsemen went up with him; it was a very imposing retinue.

It was a funeral procession befitting a king. They even had chariots and horsemen ready for defense against any attack by caravans or other marauders. This contrasts in advance with Israel's negative relationship with the Egypt and Pharaoh of the exodus. Elsewhere, Egypt is called "my people": "on that day Israel shall be a third party with Egypt and Assyria, a blessing in the midst of the earth, when the Lord of hosts gives this blessing: 'Blessed be my people Egypt, and the work of my hands Assyria, and my heritage, Israel'" (Isa 19:24–25). The divine election of Israel does not mean rejection of other peoples and nations.

When they arrived at Goren-ha-atad, which is beyond the Jordan, they held there a very great and solemn memorial service; and Joseph observed seven days of mourning for his father.

It appears that Goren-ha-Atad is east of the Jordan; this is the only place in the Bible where peoples east of the Jordan are called Canaanites. Goren-ha-Atad means "threshing floor of Atad" or "threshing floor of the brambles." From Joseph's party's mourning rites there, it received the name Abel-mizraim, which means "mourning of the Egyptians." It appears that the Egyptian escort waited here to rejoin Joseph and his brothers on the way back. Meantime Joseph and his brothers proceeded to the burial of their father in the cave in the field of Machpelah, as he had enjoined.

After Joseph had buried his father he returned to Egypt, together with his brothers and all who had gone up with him for the burial of his father.

One went up from Egypt to Canaan, but the use here of 'alah ("to go up") is a subtle nod to Israel's definitive "going up" from Egypt.

The Reconstruction of Memory, 50:15-21

Now that their father was dead, Joseph's brothers became fearful and thought, "Suppose Joseph has been nursing a grudge against us and now most certainly will pay us back in full for all the wrong we did him!" So they sent[1] to Joseph and said: "Before your father died, he gave us these instructions: 'Thus you shall say to Joseph: Please forgive the criminal wrongdoing of your brothers, who treated you harmfully.' So now please forgive the crime that we, the servants of the God of your father, committed." When they said this to him, Joseph broke into tears. Then his brothers also proceeded to fling themselves down before him and said, "We are your slaves!"

Josephus told it this way: "Now his brethren were at first unwilling to return back with him, because they were afraid lest, now their father was dead, he should punish them for their secret practices against him; since he was now gone, for whose sake he had been so gracious to them."[2] *Tg. Ps.-J.* reconstructed the situation as follows: "When Joseph's brothers saw that their father was dead, and that (Joseph) did not sit together with them to eat bread, they said, 'Perhaps Joseph bears hatred against us, and he will surely pay us back for all the evil that we have done to him.' So they commanded *Bilhah* to say to Joseph . . ." These are all attempts to read what happens here in light of the apparent reconciliation in Genesis 45. In fact, some find that "there is no basis at all for their fear in what has gone before. The reconciliation narrated in ch. 45 implies a forgiveness that is definitive."[3] We argued there, however, that Joseph only initiated reconciliation, for "reconciliation does not necessarily entail full erasure of the past or newly perfected characters, rather, it involves a commitment to live the relationship differently than one did in the past."[4] In the meeting of Jacob with Esau (Genesis 33), we argued that forgiveness differs from reconciliation. Forgiveness is basically an act, reconciliation a process (which includes the act of forgiveness). Reconciliation is more than a physical "re-membering" of former enemies; rather it is

---

1. The Hebrew has "so they commanded."
2. Josephus, *Ant.* 2.8.1-2.
3. Westermann, *Genesis 37-50*, 204.
4. Kaminsky, "Reclaiming a Theology of Election," 146. Fretheim, "Genesis," 273: "This is the only text in which Jacob gives a clear indication that he knows what the brothers did to Joseph (cf. 43:26). Nothing suggests it is a fabrication, spun out of the brothers' anxiety . . . This high consciousness of their crime suggests that the encounter in chap. 45 did not resolve the matter for the brothers."

fundamentally a matter of attitudinal change (*metanoia*), especially from the desire to eliminate or dispossess each other to mutual respect and collaboration between former rivals. People emerging from long-standing conflict may not be expected to move to physical community without a period of trust and confidence building.[5] The brothers needed time to readjust to each other and to the changed circumstances. Apparently, the readjustment has been uncomfortable and not was carried through. Joseph never mentioned forgiveness, though he acted it out; the brothers never asked for forgiveness either. The narrator never mentioned a report to Jacob—by Joseph or the brothers. Either they fabricated their father's supposed plea to Joseph or he must somehow have known of what they did. Did Joseph break into tears because he was distressed that his brothers must assume that it was he who revealed their crime?[6] Or did the whole trauma come rushing back to him? The brothers make their plea on religious grounds—the common belonging to "the God of your father." Memory must be healed, reconstructed: "The reconstruction of memory, however, is not simply a retrieval of memory . . . That is done by repeating the narrative of the violence over and over again to ease the burden of trauma that it carries. Such an activity begins to put a boundary around the violence, as it were, to separate it from memory."[7] Over and over, they speak of the evil they did to him, the crime, the sin. For the first time perhaps, they confront the dastardly betrayal of brotherhood in its enormity and ask forgiveness. They suggest due reparation in becoming his slaves. This is the last stage of repentance and shows that they truly have turned the page.[8]

But Joseph replied to them: "Do not fear. Can I take the place of God? Even though you meant harm to me, God meant it for good, to achieve this present end, the survival of many people. So now, do not fear. I will provide for you and for your children." By thus speaking kindly to them, he reassured them.

---

5. Agyenta, "Reconciliation More than Re-Membering," 132.
6. See Lowenthal, *Joseph Narrative*, 155.
7. Schreiter, *Reconciliation*, 38.
8. Schimmel, "Joseph and His Brothers," 64.

> The Bible does not claim that all suffering is the will of God or that no suffering is the will of God. Or, that all suffering is due to sin or that no suffering is due to sin. Or, that all suffering is bad and to be avoided at all costs or that no suffering is bad. (Fretheim, "Genesis," 346)

"I will provide for you" means that the famine was not over yet. Forgiveness of sin belongs to God alone; humans can show favor and reconciliation, not forgiveness.[9] The way Joseph explained matters here raises some questions. He did not just say that "God can write straight with crooked lines" or "you devised evil against me, but God devised good." The verb *hashab* (devise, plan) purports purposeful action. What he said sounds as if "God *devises* evil to bring about salvation."[10] The brothers deliberately devised and executed an evil plan; Joseph did not condone this—"you devised evil against me." Human choices fall within the order of causes that propel history forward.[11] But they are somehow subsumed under God's sovereign will, are even used by God, for the good of Jacob's family and great multitudes.[12] Goldingay's text is worth repeating:

> But God chooses to work within the framework of the brothers' decisions–not overriding these but reworking their results . . . God does not inspire the brothers to their immoral deed, but makes creative use of desires and acts that were self-serving or destructive (though the First Testament itself is generally not so troubled at the idea that YHWH inspires acts that look immoral) . . . any more than later God had decided to have Jesus betrayed and therefore somehow inspired Judas to betray him. In such events, both God's design and human design are involved, but the former is working against the latter."[13]

---

9. Lowenthal, *Joseph Narrative*, 156.
10. Mandolfo, "You Meant Evil Against Me," 462.
11. Maxfield, "Divine Providence," 356.
12. However, the Hebrew Bible did not have a single coherent view of divine providence and its relationship to human action. Except in a few late books, the idea of providence did not encompass the full-blown idea that all history was being orchestrated towards some final consummation. See Kaminsky, "Reclaiming a Theology of Election," 147.
13. Goldingay, *Israel's Gospel*, 258, 260.

Death of Joseph, 50:22–26

Joseph remained in Egypt, together with his father's household . . . He saw Ephraim's children to the third generation, and the children of Manasseh's son Machir were also born on Joseph's knees.

One hundred and ten was considered the fullness of a blessed life. Joseph adopted the children of Ephraim and Manasseh as his own, just as his father had adopted Ephraim and Manasseh. The Song of Deborah (Judg 5:14) mentions Machir as one of the tribes that brought commanders to the battle. When time came for him to die, Joseph put the sons of Israel under oath to return his bones to Canaan, assuring them that

God will surely take care of you and lead you up from this land to the land that he promised on oath to Abraham, Isaac and Jacob."

The story already looks forward to the exodus from Egypt. Joseph himself, for the first time in the Bible, confirms the triad of the patriarchs of Israel. Though God's instrument of salvation at a particular time, Joseph was not graced with theophany and divine promise and is not one of them.

Joseph died at the age of a hundred and ten. He was embalmed and laid to rest in a coffin in Egypt.

Exod 13:19 reports that leaving Egypt, "Moses also took Joseph's bones with him, for Joseph had made the Israelites take a solemn oath . . ." Josh 24:32 reports the eventual burial of Joseph's bones in Shechem in the plot of ground Jacob had bought from the sons of Hamor, father of Shechem, which plot fell in the heritage of the descendants of Joseph.

In his speech in Acts 7:16, Stephen mixed things up a bit: "And he and our ancestors died and were brought back to Shechem and placed in the tomb that Abraham had purchased for a sum of money from the sons of Hamor at Shechem." Not Abraham, but Jacob, purchased this piece.

Tradition

The fathers reminded Christians that undue and prolonged mourning for the dead was out of place.

> The gates of the underworld were still not broken nor the bonds of death loosed, nor was death yet called sleep. Hence because

they feared death, they acted this way; today, on the contrary, thanks to the grace of God, since death has been turned into slumber and life's end into repose, and since there is a great certitude of resurrection, we rejoice and exult at it like people moving from one life to another . . . From a worse to a better, from a temporary to an eternal, from an earthly to a heavenly.[14]

Joseph had two reasons for commanding about his bones: "one, in case the Egyptians when recalling his wonderful beneficence and being disposed to deify human beings, should make the good man's corpse the occasion of impiety; and the other, so that they would be certain of returning without hindrance."[15]

Theology maintains the complete foreknowledge of God and the total responsibility of the human will for good and evil. Augustine of Hippo thought long and hard about the providence of God. All history, even the antithetical evil actions of fallen man, moves under that providence of God, which puts such creatures to good use.[16] The earthly city and the City of God both develop under the loving care of God. Providence is not for material blessings of the good and the judgment of the evil, but for the eternal beatitude of all.[17] And so, "we know that all things work for good for those who love God, who are called according to his purpose" (Rom 8:28).

---

14. Chrysostom, *Homilies on Genesis* 67.17.
15. Chrysostom, *Homilies on Genesis* 67.21.
16. See Maxfield, "Divine Providence," 346.
17. Maxfield, "Divine Providence," 355.

CHAPTER 33

By Way of Conclusion

Some Themes of the Narrative

A Message about God

THE STORY IS MORE about dysfunctional families. Beyond Cain and Abel, Lamech and the sons of God, we hear of Jacob and Esau, Laban and Jacob, Leah and Rachel struggling for Jacob's attention, Simeon and Levi masterminding the massacre and sack of a whole city, Reuben laying his father's concubine, and the brothers selling Joseph into slavery. And this is the elect family, destined by God for blessing for all families of the earth! There may be twists and turns, but this is God's story, and his purposes prevail. The "memory" of Abraham enshrines the gratuitousness of God's choice of Israel. God's choice and predilection is steadfast—this is grace. "God does not perfect people before deciding to work in and through them"[1] Imperfect as we all are, God can still carry out his purposes through us, provided we let him.

---

1. Fretheim, "Which Blessing Does Isaac Give Jacob?," 284.

God's Purpose: Blessing for all Families of the Earth

"Blessing and curse have been wrestling for dominance in the world... God declares that blessing will [win], first in Abram's family, but then through Abram's family in the wider world... YHWH's direct intent is blessing."[2] "Blessing" opens the narrative at Gen 12:2 and runs through the life of the patriarchs: "you will be a blessing... All the families of the earth will be blessed[3] in you." Sir 44:21 makes clearer the import: "God promised him with an oath to *bless the nations* [emphasis mine] through his descendants, to make him numerous as grains of dust, and to exalt his posterity like the stars, giving them an inheritance from sea to sea, and from the River to the ends of the earth."

So, does the narrative attain to universal blessing? Abraham was not much of a blessing in Egypt (12:10-20), rather the cause of severe plagues. He did plead with YHWH on behalf of Sodom and Gomorrah (18:16-33), though the crimes of these cities got in the way. He pleaded successfully for Ishmael: "now as for Ishmael, I will heed you: I hereby bless him. I will make him fertile and will multiply him exceedingly. He will become the father of twelve chieftains, and I will make of him a great nation" (17:20; cf. 21:18). The fulfillment for Ishmael is recorded at 25:12-16—Ishmael did grow into twelve chieftains of as many tribal groups. The Esau we meet in Genesis 33, with four hundred fighting men under his command, and who averred that "I have plenty, my brother; you should keep what is yours" (33:1, 9), was a blessed man. Further, Esau and Jacob had to separate because "their possessions had become too great for them to dwell together" (36:7). Esau's genealogy in Genesis 36 evinces a vast multitude and "kings who reigned in the land of Edom before any king reigned over the Israelites" (36:31). In Joseph, blessing begins to move outside the family circle. He is a source of blessing for Potiphar (39:1-6), and for Pharaoh (Genesis 41). Egypt and the surrounding countries benefited from his foresight about the famine (though his agrarian policy, Genesis 47, may have benefitted Pharaoh at a cost to the citizens of Egypt). At first he interprets his sale as follows: "God sent me before you to preserve for you a remnant on earth, and to keep alive for you many survivors" (45:7).[4] Later, he realized that the

---

2. Goldingay, *Israel's Gospel*, 214.

3. For this acceptation, see the commentary at Genesis 12.

4. NRSV. *Sh^{e}ērît*/remnant occurs only here in the Pentateuch; with *p^{e}lêtah*/survivor, it appears mainly in late prophecy and in situations of war.

canvass went beyond the family: "even though you meant harm to me, God meant it for good, to achieve this present end, the survival of many people" (50:20). *'Am-rāb*, many people, can also be rendered as "a multitude of people."

Still, "blessing for all families of the earth" awaits fulfillment beyond Genesis. The tradition enshrines the hope that Israel as a power under God will bring peace and righteous government to the world. Ps 2:7 tells YHWH's king on Zion: "ask it of me, and I will give you the nations as your inheritance, and as your possession, the ends of the earth." Psalm 72 prays God to give his justice to the king's son, not only to "govern your people with justice" (v. 2), but "may he rule from sea to sea, from the River to the ends of the earth" (v. 8). In days to come, the nations will stream to the LORD's mountain in Zion "that he may instruct us in his ways, and we may walk in his paths. For from Zion shall go forth instruction [*torah*] and the word of the LORD from Jerusalem" (Isa 2:2–5//Mic 4:1–5). In that time, "Israel shall be a third party with Egypt and Assyria, a blessing in the midst of the earth, when the LORD of Hosts gives this blessing: 'Blessed be my people Egypt, and the work of my hands Assyria, and my heritage Israel'" (Isa 19:24–25). For indeed, "the LORD shall make himself known to Egypt, and the Egyptians shall know the LORD" (Isa 19:21). All this may demand *vicarious suffering*: "my servant, the just one shall justify the many, their iniquity he shall bear" (Isa 53:11).

Representing Israel, Jesus "drove out the spirits by a word and cured all the sick, to fulfill what had been said by Isaiah the prophet, 'he took away our infirmities and bore our diseases'" (Matt 8:17). Yes, "Christ also suffered for you, leaving you an example that you should follow in his footsteps . . . He himself bore our sins in his body upon the cross, so that, free from sin, we might live for righteousness. By his wounds you have been healed" (1 Pet 2:21–25). And Paul concludes: "realize then that it is those who have faith who are children of Abraham. Scripture which saw in advance that God would justify the Gentiles by faith, foretold the good news to Abraham saying, 'through you shall all the nations be blessed.' Consequently, those who have faith are blessed along with Abraham who had faith" (Gal 3:7–9).

I Will Make of You a Great Nation

YHWH promises Abraham: "I will make of you a great nation" (12:2). Again, God promised him: "I will make nations of you; kings will stem from you" (17:6), and to Sarah, "she will give rise to nations, and rulers of peoples will issue from her" (17:16). The "great nation" will become a world empire not by war or conquest, but by becoming a blessing and mediator of blessings for all the families of the earth.[5] One searches Genesis in vain for nations and kings springing from Sarah! This promise of "great nation" lies beyond the book of Genesis. 38:27-30 casually records the birth of Perez and Zerah. These two feature again as sons of Judah in the register of Jacob's children who went to Egypt (46:12). The relevance of their little story begins to appear only in Ruth 4:18-22" "These are the descendants of Perez: Perez was the father of Hezron, Hezron was the father of Ram, Ram was the father of Amminadab, Amminadab was the father of Nahshon, Nahshon was the father of Salma, Salma was the father of Boaz, Boaz was the father of Obed, Obed was the father of Jesse, and Jesse became the father of David." So, one can say that the book of Genesis hints at the "great nation" that eventuated in David. God's promise to David (2 Samuel 7) aroused messianic hopes on the line of David, even through times of foreign rule.

The mysterious verse of 49:10 speaks of scepter and mace not departing from Judah until *yabō' Shīloh* (literally, "until Shiloh comes") and he will win the obedience of the nations (see the discussion there). Some believe this refers to the monarchy under David and Solomon. But the LXX speaks of an individual, not the tribe of Judah, and of the hope/expectation of the nations. The Vulgate made it more clearly messianic by rendering *Shiloh* with "who is to be sent" (*qui mittendus est*). Justin Martyr debated with Jews as to who the referent of this saying might be. Hope for dominion over the nations is a messianic theme that one encounters across the Bible—Psalms 2; 72; and 110; Isa 2:1-4; 11:10; Mic 5:3; Zech 9:10.[6] In fact, the LORD says of his servant: "I will make you a light to the nations that my salvation may reach to the ends of the earth" (Isa 49:6). Balaam's oracle in Num 24:17 applies the imagery to Israel: "a star shall advance from Jacob, and a scepter shall rise from Israel, that will crush the brows of Moab and the skull of all the Sethites . . . and Jacob will rule his foes."

---

5. Albertz, *Israel in Exile*, 257.
6. See Gunkel, *Genesis*, 457.

Matthew seized upon the genealogy of Perez to introduce Jesus as the Davidic Messiah: "Judah became the father of Perez and Zerah, whose mother was Tamar. Perez became the father of Hezron . . . Boaz became the father of Obed, whose mother was Ruth. Obed became the father of Jesse, Jesse the father of David the king . . . thus the total number of generations from Abraham to David is fourteen generations; from David to the Babylonian exile, fourteen generations; from the Babylonian exile to the Messiah, fourteen generations" (Matt 1: 3, 5–6, 17).

The Promised Land

An essential part of YHWH's promises to Abraham has to do with possession of land, and it is promised "for ever" (Genesis 17). That this was not open land posits a problem, for as Ps 44: 3, 4 says: "you rooted out nations to plant them, crushed peoples and expelled them . . . for you favored them." Christian interpreters gloss over the promise of land, for two reasons: it touches current political issues in the Middle East and raises questions of divine justice.

However, the biblical evidence needs be examined. The extent of the land varies in parts of Scripture. In 13:15 it is "all the land you see"—very much the extent of the boundaries of Yehud after the exile. Two boundaries of the land appear in Genesis 15 alone. The first boundary reaches from the Wadi of Egypt to the River Euphrates (15:18). These most extensive borders of the land appear also in Deut 11:24 and Josh 1:4; they correspond to the borders of the Garden of Eden (Gen 2:10–14).[7] This may mean that the whole Persian province of Transeuphrates, the territory where the Jews lived, has become homeland for Abraham's offspring.[8] Is this another way of saying that "the promise is fulfilled through the Diaspora, where Judeans—beginning to become the Jewish communities—could live all in all an acceptable life."[9] The second comprises a list of ten nations (usually seven are given) all within Palestine (15:19). Torah, which "[designates]. . .the Mosaic age as a constitutive and normative narrative,"[10] ends with Israel on the Plains of Moab overlooking the

---

7. See Sailhamer, *Pentateuch as Narrative*, 152.

8. Römer, "Abraham, the Law and the Prophets," 95. See also Romer, "Exodus in Genesis," 19: "the whole Persian empire may be a homeland for Abraham's offspring."

9. Bechmann, "Genesis 12," 74.

10. Fretheim, *Pentateuch*, 57, citing Blenkinsopp, *Pentateuch* (1992), 51.

Promised Land. Moses himself died outside the land. That seems to say that the land is not constitutive of Jewish faith: one can be a Jew whether in the land or in the Diaspora. Deuteronomy even conditions possession of the land upon obedience to the commandments of Torah. This means that whereas a specific land was promised to Israel, this promise came largely to symbolize a place or condition of perfect harmony with God. Heb 11:9 transfers all speech of the promised land to the heavenly homeland.[11]

Righteous "Pagans" are Part of the Story

Abimelech is consistently righteous and gracious in his dealings with Abraham and Isaac. Abraham thought "there would be no fear of God in this place," but Abimelech and his folk showed deep religion in listening to God and being filled with fear. In the heat of passion at Jacob's stealing of his birthright, Esau may have thought of killing his brother upon his father's imminent death. However, the Esau we meet in Genesis 33 is gracious, magnanimous, and forgiving, willing to put the past behind him and take up fraternal bonds again; in fact, he comes across better compared with Jacob in that scene. Whatever about the "rape" of Dinah, Shechem and Hamor, in their willingness to do everything to remedy a conflictual situation, come out more dignified than the sons of Israel who allowed their revenge to run riot. Potiphar showed class in entrusting his entire household to Joseph and not quite believing his wife's defamations. And the Pharaoh of the Joseph story cared for his people and was gracious and hospitable to foreigners, especially the house of Jacob. As Paul says, God's grace has no boundaries, "so that people might seek God, even perhaps grope for him and find him, though indeed he is not far from any one of us. 'For in him we live and move and have our being'" (Act 17:27–28).

The Image of God

The image of God evolves through the text, corresponding to the theology of the particular era. Inspiration does not guarantee the truth of

---

11. See Pontifical Biblical Commission, *Jewish People and Their Scriptures*, nos. 54–57.

every verse in the Bible taken on its own, rather as understood within the unfolding divine revelation, which abuts in Christ.

God is portrayed as sovereign of the universe and just to all and sundry. He recognized Abimelech's innocence: "yes, I know you did it with a pure heart" (20:6). As such, he intervened to prevent him sinning: "it was I who kept you from sinning against me." However, when "the LORD struck Pharaoh and his household with severe plagues" (12:17), one can wonder why a just God would so strike an unwitting Pharaoh and why include Pharaoh's innocent household. Sarai oppressed Hagar, yet the messenger of YHWH tells her to return and submit herself to oppression. The reader is perplexed that a God who elsewhere responds to the cry of the oppressed, here asks the oppressed to submit to oppression. Accordingly, scholars struggle with the narrative intention—was this for Hagar's liberation and salvation or advocacy for the claims of Isaac? Sherwood compares the story to an inverted exodus[12]: "Like the Israelites at the beginning of the Exodus, she is fertile and conceives easily, finds water in the desert and is found by a messenger/angel of God."[13] Dozeman interprets Hagar as prototype of Moses: "Each is a founder of a nation, each flees (*baraḥ*) to a well in the wilderness to escape oppression. There each encounters a messenger of God, is commanded to return to the threatening situation, receives a word of promise and leaves with a special name for God."[14] But Trible severely criticizes God's apparent partiality in favor of Sarah: "Hagar foreshadows Israel's pilgrimage of faith through contrast, experiences exodus without liberation, revelation without salvation, wilderness without covenant, wanderings without land, promise without fulfillment, and unmerited exile without return."[15] Not to be forgotten: God heard the boy's voice and promised: "I will make of him a great nation" (21:18)—just as YHWH promised Abraham!

Genesis 19 presents this side of YHWH's heart. He came down to investigate and his investigation confirmed what he suspected. He responds, measure for measure, to the oppression of the weak, but not

---

12. Sherwood, "Hagar and Ishmael," 290

13. Perry, "Counter-Stories in the Bible," 286 speaks of Ishmael's banishment to the desert (Gen 21:4–21) as "Ishmael's Aqedah." He points to opposing details between the two culminating in the angel calling out from heaven in each. Abraham not to reach out his hand to the lad (Gen 22:12) contrasts with Hagar asked to lift up the lad and hold him by the hand (Gen 21:18).

14. Cf. Dozeman, "Wilderness and Salvation," 29–30.

15. Trible, *Texts of Terror*, 28.

before he agreed "that the righteous few can often save a city,"[16] thus launching the idea of vicarious redemption.[17] He did not decree the punishment; the outcome was still open depending on evidence. He was open to Abraham's postulation and would not destroy the city should even ten righteous people be found in it. Here is a patient and forbearing God. God's dealings with Jacob were delicate. Jacob, apparently, could do anything yet retain the protection and care of God. The Lord stuck with him: "I am with you and will protect you wherever you go, and bring you back to this land. I will never leave you until I have done what I promised you" (28:15). God was content to teach and transform him through reverberations from his behavior. Eventually, God, apparently in the guise of Esau, wrestled with him, dented his self-assuredness, and opened him up to justice and gratuitousness.

Divine Providence

The conception oracle of Jacob and Esau seemed to have set their history on an inevitable trajectory. Joseph in 50:20 did not say just "you devised evil against me, but God devised good." Rather, using the verb, *ḥashab* (devise, plan, purposeful action), he seemed to be saying that "God *devises* evil to bring about salvation."[18] Human choices fall within the order of causes that propel history forward.[19] "But God chooses to work within the framework of the brothers' decisions–not overriding these but reworking their results . . . God does not inspire the brothers to their immoral deed, but makes creative use of desires and acts that were self-serving or destructive (though the First Testament itself is generally not so troubled at the idea that YHWH inspires acts that look immoral) . . . any more than later God had decided to have Jesus betrayed and therefore somehow inspired Judas to betray him. In such events, both God's design and human design are involved, but the former is working against the latter."[20]

---

16. Fretheim, "Genesis," 143.

17. However, in Ezek 14:14, YHWH maintains that "even if these three were in it, Noah, Daniel, and Job, they could only save themselves by their righteousness."

18. Mandolfo, "You Meant Evil Against Me," 462.

19. Maxfield, "Divine Providence," 356.

20. Goldingay, *Israel's Gospel*, 258, 260.

The Dialectic of Grace and Works

The narratives of Genesis 15 and 22 posit the dialectic of grace and works. "Abraham put his faith in God who attributed it to him as an act of righteousness" (15:6) reflects the background of the exile and the theological questions of the postexilic community.[21] The catastrophe of 586 and the exile shattered hopes founded on the bilateral Sinai covenant. A fresh and different way to the heart of God must be found. Jer 31:31–34 held out a new covenant in which "I will place my law within them and write it upon their hearts; I will be their God and they shall be my people." This leaves the Sinai covenant in place, only that God's surgical operation will assure fidelity in the future; the danger of infringement remains. Deut 4:30–31[22] promised that "in your distress, when all these things shall have come upon you, you shall finally return to the LORD, your God, and listen to his voice. Since the LORD, your God, is a merciful God, he will not abandon or destroy you, nor forget the covenant with your ancestors that he swore to them." This relies on the mercy of God, but also introduces a shift in the covenant. The basis of divine mercy rests on *covenant as oath sworn* to the fathers[23] (not covenant cut with Moses and the exodus generation). The language of covenant as sworn oath is exactly what appears in Genesis 15!

In 22:15–18, what was given as free blessing becomes predicated on the merit of Abraham. The text posits a dialectic between free gift and merit, grace and human endeavor! In the classic words of St. Augustine: "God who created you without you, will not save you without you" (*Sermon* 169, 13). We find grace and freedom juxtaposed in Phil 2:12–13: "work out your salvation with fear and trembling. For God is the one who, for his good purpose, works in you both to desire and to work." We find Paul and James standing on different sides of the coin. In Rom 4:13–16, Paul reads Gen 15:6 in the light of Gen 12:3: "It was not through the law that the promise was made to Abraham and his descendants that he would inherit the world, but through the righteousness that comes from faith . . . For this reason, it depends on faith, so that it may be a gift,

---

21. Bechmann, "Genesis 12," 67: "the stories of Abraham are theological texts, but they use the form of a historical narrative."

22. A postexilic addition to the book of Deuteronomy.

23. Westermann, *Genesis 12–36*, 215 cites Perlittt, *Bundestheologie im Alten Testament* as demonstrating that the patriarchal oath (*berît*) as reinforcing the old and simple promise to the patriarchs belongs to the Deuteronomic theology, and in Genesis 12–50 is always related to the gift of the land.

and the promise may be guaranteed to all his descendants, not to those who only adhere to the law but to those who follow the faith of Abraham, who is the father of all of us." James, however, read Gen 15:6 in the light of Genesis 22: "because you acted as you did in not withholding from me your son, your only one, I will bless you and make your descendants as countless as the stars of the sky and the sands of the seashore . . . and in your descendants all the nations of the earth will find blessing, because you obeyed my command" (Gen 22:15–8). He throws out the challenge: "demonstrate your faith to me without works, and I will demonstrate my faith to you from my works . . . Was not Abraham our father justified by works when he offered his son Isaac upon the altar? You see that faith was active along with his works, and faith was completed by the works. . ." (Jas 2:17–22).[24] Christian theology has split along the same lines of emphasis!

Forgiveness and Reconciliation

We reflected on this theme a propos Esau and Jacob (Genesis 33), and Joseph and his brothers (45:1–5; 50:20). Coats suggests that: "Esau offers reconciliation. Jacob still offers the gift which Esau graciously accepted. Yet there is anticlimax. Esau presses for dialogue along the way home. Jacob promises to meet him later in Seir, but went on to Succoth. He rejects physical reunion, a sign of reconciliation. The brothers are separated: the strife between them becomes permanent division."[25] He argues that: "reconciliation cannot occur if the reconciled parties continue to live apart." Perhaps one needs to distinguish forgiveness from reconciliation. Forgiveness is basically an act, reconciliation a process (which may include the act of forgiveness). Reconciliation takes time and effort. It is fundamentally a matter of attitudinal change (*metanoia*), especially from the desire to eliminate or dispossess each other to mutual respect and collaboration between former rivals. People emerging from long-standing conflict may not be expected to move to physical community without a period of trust and confidence building.[26] The brothers needed time to readjust to each other and to the changed circumstances. So with

---

24. Moberly, "Abraham's Righteousness," 130 mentions Gen 15:6 as a case study of how different traditions developed differing implications of the text because of their differing theological contexts.

25. Coats, "Strife without Reconciliation," 103.

26. Maxfield, "Divine Providence," 132.

the case of Joseph and his brothers. The readjustment must have been uncomfortable and not carried through while the father lived. Joseph never mentioned forgiveness, though he acted it out; the brothers never asked for forgiveness either. At their father's death, the brothers make their plea, but on the religious grounds of their belonging to "the God of your father." They appeal to a higher authority. Memory must be healed: "The reconstruction of memory, however, is not simply a retrieval of memory . . . That is done by repeating the narrative of the violence over and over again to ease the burden of trauma that it carries. Such an activity begins to put a boundary around the violence, as it were, to separate it from memory."[27] For the first time perhaps, they confront the dastardly betrayal of brotherhood in its enormity and ask forgiveness. They suggest due reparation in becoming his slaves. This is the last stage of repentance and shows that they truly have turned the page.[28]

Reception: Christian and Jewish

Patristic and rabbinic interpretations varied from era to era depending on issues confronted in debates with opponents, also even in the same fathers or rabbis, depending on the occasion. Both Jewish and Christian exegetes used the literal and spiritual sense. We still lack, as far as I know, comprehensive studies of patristic interpretation of topoi that show how contemporary debates affected the interpretation of certain key passages; the same obtains for early rabbinic exegesis.[29] In Genesis 18–19 I illustrate with the interpretation of the "three angels" visiting Abraham. The christological interpretation was almost universal till the late fourth century. The principle, already in Justin Martyr, was that every divine appearance in the Old Testament was of the Logos incarnate. The debate with the Arians showed a weakness of this thesis. The way Justin put it sounded subordinationist (made Christ subordinate to God) and played into the hands of the Arians, who seized upon it to deny Christ the title "God."[30] The First Council of Sirmium, 347 CE, failed in the attempt at a compromise with the Arians. Anathema 15–16, 5 has this: "Whoever

---

27. Schreiter, *Reconciliation*, 38.
28. Schimmel, "Joseph and His Brothers," 64.
29. However, this is remedied to some extent by the two volumes of Urbach's *The Sages*, though that treatise is more theological than exegetical.
30. See Watson, "Abraham's Visitors," 5.

shall say that Abraham saw, not the Son, but the Ingenerate God or part of him, let him be anathema! Whoever shall say with Jacob, not the Son as man, but the Ingenerate God or part of him, has wrestled, let him be anathema . . . he it is to whom the Father said, 'let us make man in our image, after our likeness' (Gen 1:26), who also was seen in his own Person by the patriarchs, gave the law, spoke by the prophets, and at last, became man . . ."[31] Meantime, the Council of Constantinople (381 CE) set on firm foundations the divinity of both the Son and the Holy Spirit. Justin's Logos-centric exegesis was now seen as deficient. Augustine, who earlier[32] had embraced the christological exegesis of Genesis 18, now argued against it in favor of a Trinitarian one. In the treatise on the Trinity, he followed a critique of Justin's position with the Trinitarian affirmation: "How, then, before he had done this [virgin birth], did he appear as one man to Abraham? Or, was not that form a reality? I could put these questions, if it had been one man that appeared to Abraham, and if that one were believed to be the Son of God. But since three men appeared, and no one of them is said to be greater than the rest either in form, or age, or power, why should we not here understand, as visibly intimated by the visible creature, the equality of the Trinity, and one and the same substance in three persons?"[33]

A final word: "if your theology doesn't agree with your life experiences, it's time to take a second look at your theology. Life doesn't lie."[34]

---

31. Text courtesy of Bucur, "Early Christian Reception," 352.

32. Augustine, *City of God* 16:29.

33. Augustine, *On the Trinity* 2.11.20. About the same time, Trinitarian interpretations appear in Cyril of Alexandria (375–444), *Against Julian*. Ambrose, *On Abraham* 1:33: the three visitors and the three measures of flour point to God as Trinity.

34. McLean, "Thinking Out Loud," 304.

Bibliography

Abegg, Martin, Jr., Peter Flint, and Eugene Ulrich, translators. *Dead Sea Scrolls: The Oldest Known Bible Translated for the First Time into English*. New York: HarperOne, 2002.
Abbot, Walter, editor. *The Documents of Vatican II*. London: Chapman, 1966.
Abramsky, Michael. "Jacob Wrestles the Angel: A Study in Psychoanalytic Midrash." *International Journal of Transpersonal Studies* 29/1 (2020) 106–17.
Achtemeier, Elizabeth R. "Righteousness in the OT." *IDB*, 4:80–85. Nashville: Abingdon, 1962.
Ackerman, James S. "Joseph, Judah, and Jacob." In *Literary Interpretation of Biblical Narratives*, 2:85–113. Nashville: Abingdon, 1982.
Adeyemo, Tokunboh, editor. *Africa Bible Commentary: A One-Volume Commentary Written by 70 African Scholars*. Nairobi: WordAlive, 2006.
Agyenta, Alfred. "When Reconciliation Means More than the 'Re-Membering' of Former Enemies: The Problem of the Conclusion to the Jacob-Esau Story from a Narrative Perspective (Gen 33, 1–17)." *ETL* 83/1 (2007) 123–34.
Aitken, Kenneth T. "The Wooing of Rebekah: A Study in the Development of the Tradition." *JSOT* 30 (1984) 3–23.
Albertz, Rainer. "The Exilic Patriarchal History." In *Israel in Exile: The History and Literature of the Sixth Century B.C.E.*, 246–71. Atlanta: SBL, 2003.
———. *Israel in Exile: The History and Literature of the Sixth Century B.C.E.* Atlanta: SBL, 2003.
Alexander, Philip S. "'Pre-Emptive Exegesis': Genesis Rabbah's Reading of the Story of Creation." *JJS* 43 (1992) 230–45.
———. "The Rabbis and Messianism." In *Redemption and Resistance: The Messianic Hopes of Jews and Christians in Antiquity*, edited by Markus Bockmuehl and James Carleton Paget, 227–44. London: T. & T. Clark, 2007.
Alexander, T. Desmond. "Genesis 22 and the Covenant of Circumcision." *JSOT* 25 (1983) 17–22.
Alt, Albrecht. "The God of the Father." In *Essays on Old Testament History and Religion*, 3–100. New York: Doubleday, 1967.
Alter, Robert. *The Art of Biblical Narrative*. New York: Basic, 1981. 2nd ed: 2011.
———. *Genesis: Translation and Commentary*. New York: Norton, 1996.
Alter, Robert, and Frank Kermode, editors. *The Literary Guide to the Bible*. Cambridge, MA: Harvard University Press, 1987.
Ambrosiaster. *Questions on the Old and New Testaments*. Translated by John Litteral. In *Patristic Bible Commentary*. https://sites.google.com/site/aquinasstudybible/home/genesis/ambrosiaster-questions-and-answers-on-genesis.

Amit, Yairah. *The Book of Judges: The Art of Editing*. Leiden: Brill, 1999.
———. *Hidden Polemics in Biblical Narrative*. Leiden: Brill, 2000.
———. *Reading Biblical Narratives: Literary Criticism and the Hebrew Bible*. Minneapolis: Fortress, 2001.
Anderson, Bradford A. "The Intersection of the Human and the Divine in Genesis 32–33." *ZAW* 128/1 (2016) 30–41.
André, G. "Paqad." *TDOT*, 12:30–63. Grand Rapids: Eerdmans, 2003.
Augustine of Hippo. *City of God*. Translated by Gerald G. Walsh and Mother Grace Monahan. Fathers of the Church 14. New York: Fathers of Church, 1952.
———. *Exposition on the Book of Psalms*. Christian Classics Ethereal Library. https://www.ccel.org/ccel/schaff/npnf108.toc.html.
———. *Homilies on the First Letter of John*. Nicene and Post-Nicene Fathers 7. Edited by Philip Schaff. Edinburgh: T. & T. Clark, 1888. http://newadvent.org/fathers/170207.htm.
———. *On the Trinity*. Nicene and Post-Nicene Fathers 3. Edited by Philip Schaff. Edinburgh: T. & T. Clark, 1887. http://www.newadvent.org/fathers/130102.htm accessed September 30, 2018.
———. *Questions on the Book of Genesis*. Translated by John Litteral. In *Patristic Bible Commentary*. https://sites.google.com/site/aquinasstudybible/home/genesis/augustine-questions-on-genesis.
———. *Teaching Christianity* (*De Doctrina Christiana*). Translated by Edmund Hill. New York: New City, 1996.
Bakhos, Carol. "The Family of Abraham in Genesis Rabbah." In *Genesis Rabbah in Text and Context*, edited by Sarit Kattan Gribetz, David M. Goldberg, and Martha Himmelfarb, 115–27. Tübingen: Mohr Siebeck, 2016.
Bakon, Shimon. "Subtleties in the Story of Joseph and Potiphar's Wife." *JBQ* 41/3 (2013) 171–74.
Barclay, John M. G. "Paul and Philo on Circumcision: Romans 2:25–9 in Social and Cultural Context." *NTS* 44 (1998) 536–56.
Bar-Efrat, Shimeon. *Narrative Art in the Bible*. Sheffield, UK: Almond, 1989.
Barthes, Roland. "The Struggle with the Angel: Textual Analysis of Gen 32:22–32." In *Image, Music, Text*, 125–41. New York: Hill and Wang, 1977.
Bechmann, Ulrike. "Genesis 12 and the Abraham-Paradigm Concerning the Promised Land." *ERev* 68/1 (2016) 62–80.
Bekins, Peter. "Tamar and Joseph in Genesis 38 and 39." *JSOT* 40/4 (2016) 375–97.
Ben Zvi, Ehud. "The Dialogue between Abraham and YHWH in Gen 18.23–32: A Historical-Critical Analysis." *JSOT* 53 (1992) 27–46.
———. "The Memory of Abraham in Late Persian/Early Hellenistic Yehud/Judah." In *Remembering Biblical Figures in the Late Persian and Early Hellenistic Periods: Social Memory and Imagination*, edited by Ehud ben Zvi and Diana V. Edelman, 3–37. Oxford: Oxford University Press, 2013.
Benedict XVI. *Verbum Domini*. Post-Synodal Apostolic Exhortation. Libreria Editrice Vaticana, 2010. http://www.vatican.va/content/benedict-xvi/en/apost_exhortations/documents/hf_ben-xvi_exh_20100930_verbum-domini.html.
Berlin, Adele. *Poetics and Interpretation of Biblical Narrative*. Winona Lake, IN: Eisenbrauns, 1994.
Berlin, Adele, and Marc Zvi Brettler, editors. *Jewish Study Bible*. Jewish Publication Society. Oxford: Oxford University Press, 1999.

Berthoud, Pierre. "The Reconciliation of Joseph with His Brothers: Sin, Forgiveness and Providence, Genesis 45. 1–11 (42.1–45.11) and 50.15–21." *EuroJTh* 17/1 (2008) 5–11.
BiblIndex. *Index of Biblical Quotations in Early Christian Literature*. http://www.biblindex.info/.
Blenkinsopp, Joseph. "Abraham and the Righteous of Sodom." *JJS* 33/1–2 (1982) 119–32.
———. "Abraham as Paradigm in the Priestly History in Genesis." *JBL* 128/2 (2009) 225–41.
———. "The 'Covenant of Circumcision' (Gen 17) in the Context of the Abraham Cycle (Gen 11:27—25:11). Preliminary Considerations." In *The Post-Priestly Pentateuch*, edited by Federicl Giuntoli and Konrad Schmid, 145–56. Tübingen: Mohr Siebeck, 2015.
———. *Creation, Un-Creation, Re-Creation: A Discursive Commentary on Genesis 1—11*. London: T. & T. Clark, 2011.
———. "The Midianite-Kenite Hypothesis Revisited and the Origins of Judah." *JSOT* 33/2 (2008) 131–53.
———. "Oracle of Judah and the Messianic Entry." *JBL* 80/1 (1961) 55–64.
———. *The Pentateuch: An Introduction to the First Five Books of the Bible*. Anchor Reference Library. New Have, CT: Yale University Press, 1992.
Blum, Erhard, "Jacob Tradition." In *The Book of Genesis: Composition, Reception, and Interpretation*, edited by Craig A. Evans, Joel N. Lohr, and David L. Petersen, 181–212. Leiden: Brill, 2012.
Boase, Elizabeth. "Life in the Shadows: The Role and Function of Isaac in Genesis—Synchronic and Diachronic Readings." *VT* 51/3 (2001) 312–35.
Bridge, Edward J. "Slave Is Master": Jacob's Servile Language to Esau in Genesis 33.1–17." *JSOT* 38/3 (2014) 263–78.
Brown, Francis, with S. R. Driver and Charles A. Briggs. *A Hebrew and English Lexicon of the Old Testament*. With an appendix containing the biblical Aramaic based on the Lexicon of William Gesenius, as translated by Edward Robinson. Oxford: Clarendon, 1951.
Brueggemann, Walter. *Genesis*. Interpretation. Atlanta: John Knox, 1982.
———. *Theology of the Old Testament: Testimony, Dispute, Advocacy*. Minneapolis: Fortress, 1997.
Bucur, Bogdan G. "Early Christian Reception of Genesis 18: From Theophany to Trinitarian Symbolism." *JECS* 23/2 (2015) 245–72.
Caesarius of Arles. *Sermons*. 3 vols. Translated by Sister Mary Magdeleine Mueller. Fathers of the Church: A New Translation. Washington, DC: Catholic University of America Press, 1972.
Carr, David M. *Fractures of Genesis. Reading the Fractures of Genesis: Historical and Literary Approaches*. Louisville: Westminster John Knox, 1996.
Cassuto, Umberto. *A Commentary on the Book of Genesis*. 2 vols. Jerusalem: Magnes, 1961, 1964.
Catechism of the Catholic Church. New York: Doubleday, 1998.
Charlesworth, James H. *Old Testament Pseudepigrapha*. 2 vols. New York: Doubleday, 1985.
Chilton, B. D., and P. R. Davies. "The Aqedah: A Revised Tradition History." *CBQ* 40 (1978) 514–46.

Chinpeng Ho, Andrew. "A Paragon of Faith? Doubting Abraham." *Themelios* 42/3 (2017) 452–64.
Chrysostom, John. *Homily 4 on First Thessalonians*. Translated by John A. Broadus. Nicene and Post-Nicene Fathers 13. Edited by Philip Schaff. Grand Rapids: Eerdmans, 1888. http://newadvent.org/fathers/230404.htm.
———. *Homilies on Genesis 18–45*. Translated by Robert C. Hill. FC 82. Washington, DC: Catholic University of America Press, 1990.
———. *Homilies on the Gospel of Matthew*. Nicene and Post-Nicene Fathers 10. Edited by Philip Schaff. Grand Rapids: Eerdmans, 1888. http://www.newadvent.org/fathers/2001.htm.
Clement of Alexandria. *Christ the Educator*. Translated by Simon P. Wood. Fathers of the Church 23. New York: Fathers of Church, 1954.
Clements, Ronald E. *Old Testament Theology: A Fresh Approach*. London: Marshall, Morgan & Scott, 1978.
Clifford, Richard J. "Genesis 25:19–34." *Int* 45 (1991) 397–401.
———. "Genesis 37–50: Joseph Story or Jacob Story?" In *The Book of Genesis: Composition, Reception, and Interpretation*, edited by Craig A. Evans, Joel N. Lohr, and David L. Petersen, 213–29. Leiden: Brill, 2012.
———. "Genesis 38: Its Contribution to the Jacob Story." *CBQ* 66 (2004) 519–32.
Clines, David. "Noah's Flood I: The Theology of the Flood Narrative." *Faith and Thought* 100/2 (1972–3) 128–42.
Coats, George W. "The Curse in God's Blessing.": Gen 12:1–4a in the Structure and Theology of the Yahwist." In *Die Botschaft und die Boten: Festschrift für Hans Walter Wolff zum 70. Geburtstag*, edited by Jörg Jeremias and Lothar Perlitt, 31–41. Neukirchen-Vluyn: Neukrchener, 1981.
———. *From Canaan to Egypt: Structural and Theological Context for the Joseph Story*. CBQMS 4. Washington, DC: Catholic Biblical Association of America, 1976.
———. "Strife and Reconciliation. Themes of a Biblical Theology in the Book of Genesis." *HBT* 2 (1980) 15–37.
———. "Strife Without Reconciliation: A Narrative Theme in the Jacob Traditions." In *Werden und Wirken des alten Testaments. Festschrift für Claus Westermann zu 70. Geburtstag*, edited by Rainer Albert et al., 82–106. Göttingen: Vandenhoeck & Ruprecht, 1980.
Cohen, Aryeh. "Hagar and Ishmael: A Commentary." *Int* 68/3 (2014) 247–65.
Cohen, Jeffrey M. "The Jacob-Esau Reunion." *JBQ* 21/3 (1993) 159–63.
Collins, John J. "Modern Theology." In *Reading Genesis: Ten Methods*, edited by Ronald Hendel, 196–214. Cambridge: Cambridge University Press, 2010.
Commission for Religious Relations with the Jews. *A Reflection on the Theological Questions pertaining to Catholic-Jewish Relations on the Occasion of the 50th Anniversary of "Nostra Aetate" (no. 4)*. Vatican City: Libreria Editrice Vaticana, 2015. http://www.vatican.va/roman_curia/pontifical_councils/chrstuni/relations-jews-docs/rc_pc_chrstuni_doc_20151210_ebraismo-nostra-aetate_en.html.
Cook, Joan E. "Four Marginalized Foils"—Tamar, Judah, Joseph and Potiphar's Wife: A Literary Study of Genesis 38–39." *Proceedings EGL & MWBS* 21 (2001) 115–28.
Cotter, David. *Genesis*. Berit Olam. Collegeville, MN: Liturgical, 2003.
Crenshaw, James. "Journey into Oblivion: A Structural Analysis of Gen 22:1–19." *Soundings* 58/2 (1975) 243–56.

Cyril of Alexandria. *Glaphyra on the Pentateuch*, vol. 1: *Genesis*. Book 6. Translated by Nicholas P. Lunn. Fathers of the Church 137. Washington, DC: Catholic University of America Press, 2018.

Cyril of Jerusalem. *The Works of Saint Cyril of Jerusalem*. Translated by Leo P. McCauley. Fathers of the Church 61. Washington, DC: Catholic University of America Press, 1969.

Danby, Herbert, translator. *The Mishnah*. Oxford: Clarendon, 1933.

Davids, P. K. *Ilulu Igbo: Textbook of Igbo Proverbs*. Onitsha: University Publishing, 1980.

Davies, Eryl W. *The Immoral Bible: Approaches to Biblical Ethics*. London: T. & T. Clark, 2010.

Derouchie, Jason S. "Circumcision in the Hebrew Bible and Targums: Theology, Rhetoric, and the Handling of Metaphor." *BBR* 14/2 (2004) 175–203.

DiTommaso, Lorenzo, and Gerbern S. Oegema, editors. *New Vistas on Early Judaism and Christianity: From Enoch to Montreal and Back*. New York, Bloomsbury T. & T. Clark, 2016.

Doerfler, Marie E. "Entertaining the Trinity Unawares: Genesis XVIII in Western Christian Interpretation." *JEH* 65/3 (July 2014) 485–503.

Dozeman, Thomas. "The Wilderness and Salvation History in the Hagar Story." *JBL* 117 (1998) 23–43.

Dozeman, Thomas, Konrad Schmid, and Baruch Schwartz, editors. *The Pentateuch: International Perspectives on Current Research*. Forschungen zum Alten Testament 78. Tübingen: Mohr Siebeck, 2011.

Drey, Philip R. "The Role of Hagar in Genesis 16." *AUSS* 40/2 (2002) 179–95.

Dunn, James D. G. *The Theology of Paul the Apostle*. Grand Rapids: Eerdmans, 2006.

Ephrem the Syrian. *Commentary on Genesis*. In *Ephrem the Syrian: Selected Prose Works*, translated by Edward G. Matthews Jr. and Joseph P. Amar. Fathers of the Church 91. Washington, DC: Catholic University of America Press, 1994.

Fishbane, Michael. *Biblical Text and Texture: A Literary Reading of Selected Texts*. New York: Schoken, 1979.

———. "Composition and Structure in the Jacob Cycle (Gen 25:19—35:22)." *JJS* 26 (1975) 15–38.

Fitzmyer, Joseph. *The Genesis Apocryphon of Qumran Cave 1 (1Q20): A Commentary*. 3rd rev. ed. Rome: Biblical Institute Press, 2004.

———. "The Sacrifice of Isaac in Qumran Literature." *Bib* 83 (2002) 211–29.

Floriani, Wagner. "Benefits and Pitfalls of Narrative Criticism." Masters essay. The Master's Seminary, Los Angeles, February 1, 2019. https://www.academia.edu/38458548/Benefits_and_Pitfalls_of_Narrative_Criticism_in_Biblical_Studies.

Fokkelman, Jan P. "Genesis 37 and 38 at the Interface of Structural Analysis and Hermeneutics." In *Literary Structure and Rhetorical Strategies in the Hebrew Bible*, edited by L. J. de Regt, J. de Waard, and J. P. Fokkelman, 152–87. Assen: Van Gorcum, 1996.

———. *Narrative Art and Poetry in the Books of Samuel: A Full Interpretation Based on Stylistic and Structural Analyses*. 4 vols. Assen: Van Gorcum, 1981–1993.

———. *Narrative Art in Genesis: Specimens of Stylistic and Structural Analysis*. Studia Semitica Neerlandica 17. Assen: Van Gorcum, 1975.

———. *Reading Biblical Narrative: An Introductory Guide*. Translated by Ineke Smit. Louisville: Westminster John Knox, 1999.

Fox, Everett. *The Five Books of Moses: Genesis, Exodus, Leviticus, Numbers, Deuteronomy: A New Translation with Introductions, Commentary, and Notes.* New York: Schocken, 1995.

———. "'The Sign of the Covenant': Circumcision in the Light of the Priestly 'ōt Etiologies." *RB* 81/4 (Oct 1974) 557–96.

———. "Wisdom in the Joseph Story." *VT* 51/1 (2001) 26–41.

Francis, Pope. *Laudato Si': On Care for Our Common Home.* Encyclical letter, May 24, 2015. Vatican City: Libreria Editrice Vaticana, 2016. http://www.vatican.va/content/francesco/en/encyclicals/documents/papa-francesco_20150524_enciclica-laudato-si.html.

Frankel, David. "The Proto-Story of Shechem and Jacob's Daughter." *TheTorah.com*, 2015. https://thetorah.com/the-proto-story-of-shechem-and-jacobs-daughter/.

Freedman, Harry. "Jacob and Esau: Their Struggle in the Second Century." *JBQ* 23/2 (1995) 107–15.

Freedman, Harry, and Maurice Simon, editors. *Midrash Rabbah: Genesis.* London: Soncino, 1977.

Fretheim, Terence. "Genesis." In *The New Interpreter's Bible*, 1:17–276. Nashville: Abingdon, 2015.

———. "The Jacob Traditions. Theology and Hermeneutic." *Int* 26 (1972) 419–36.

———. *The Suffering of God: An Old Testament Perspective.* Minneapolis: Fortress, 1984.

———. "To Say Something—About God, Evil, and Suffering." *WW* 19/4 (1999) 339, 346–50.

———. "Which Blessing does Isaac Give Jacob?" In *Jews, Christians, and the Theology of the Hebrew Scriptures*, edited by Alice Ogden Bellis and Joel S. Kaminsky, 289–91. Atlanta: SBL, 2000.

Friedman, Richard Elliot. *Commentary on the Torah: With a New English Translation.* New York: HarperOne, 2003.

Garcia-Treto, Francisco O. "Jacob's 'Oath-Covenant' in Genesis 28." *Trinity University Studies in Religion* 10 (1975) 1–10.

Garsiel, Moshe. *The First Book of Samuel: A Literary Study of Comparative Structures, Analogies and Parallels.* Ramat-Gan, Israel: Revivim, 1985.

Gaston, Lloyd. "Abraham and the Righteousness of God." *HBT* 2 (1980) 39–68.

Geller, Stephen A. "The Struggle at the Jabbok: The Use of Enigma in a Biblical Narrative." *JANES* 14 (1982) 37–60.

Goldingay, John. *Israel's Gospel.* Vol. 1 of *Old Testament Theology.* Downers Grove, IL: IVP Academic, 2003.

———. *Psalms 90–150.* Baker Commentary on the Old Testament Wisdom and Psalms. Grand Rapids: Baker Academic, 2008.

———. "Significance of Circumcision." *JSOT* 88 (2000) 3–18.

Golka, Friedemann W. "Genesis 37–50: Joseph Story or Israel-Joseph Story?" *CBR* 2/2 (2004) 153–77.

Good, Edwin M. "The "Blessing" on Judah, Gen 49 8–12." *JBL* (1963) 427–32.

Goodnick, Benjamin. "Rebekah's Deceit or Isaac's Great Test." *JBQ* 23/4 (1995) 221–28.

Goppelt, Leonhard. *Typos: The Typological Interpretation of the Old Testament in the New.* Translated by Donald H. Madvig. Eugene, OR: Wipf & Stock, 2002.

Graves, Michael. *The Inspiration and Interpretation of Scripture: What the Early Church Can Teach Us.* Grand Rapids: Eerdmans, 2014.

Green, Barbara. "The Determination of Pharaoh: His Characterization in the Joseph Story (Genesis 37-50)." In *The World of Genesis: Persons, Places, Perspectives*, edited by P. R. Davies and D. J. A. Clines, 150-71. JSOTSup 257. Sheffield: Sheffield Academic, 1998.

Greenberg, Moshe. "Jewish Conceptions of the Human Factor in Biblical Prophecy." In *Jewish Bible Theology: Perspectives and Case Studies*, edited by Isaac Kalimi, 63-77. Winona Lake, IN: Eisenbrauns, 2012.

Greenberger, Chaya. "Esau and Jacob: Brothers Clash, Reconcile, and Separate." *JBQ* 46/3 (2018) 143-57.

Greenspahn, Frederick E. "Jewish Theologies of Scripture." In *Jewish Bible Theology: Perspectives and Case Studies*, edited by Isaac Kalimi, 13-29. Winona Lake, IN: Eisenbrauns, 2012.

Gregg, Robert C. "Joseph with Potiphar's Wife: Early Christian Commentary Seen against the Backdrop of Jewish and Muslim Interpretations." *StPatr* 34 (2001) 326-46.

Gregory of Nyssa. *Dogmatic Treatises*. Nicene and Post-Nicene Fathers, 2nd ser., 5. Edited by Philip Schaff and Henry Wace. Peabody, MA: Hendrickson, 1995.

Groenewald, Alphonso. "Old Testament Exegesis: Reflections on Methodology." *TS* 63/3 (2007) 1017-31.

Grossfeld, Bernard, translator. *Targum Onqelos to Genesis*. The Aramaic Bible: The Targums 6. Collegeville, MN: Liturgical, 1988.

Grossman, Jonathan. "The Story of Joseph's Brothers in Light of the 'Therapeutic Narrative' Theory." *BibInt* 21/1 (2013) 171-95.

Grypeou, Emmanouela, and Helen Spurling. "Abraham's Angels: Jewish and Christian Exegesis of Genesis 18—19." In *The Exegetical Encounter between Jews and Christians in Late Antiquity*, edited by Emmanouela Grypeou and Helen Spurling, 181-203. Leiden: Brill, 2009.

Guibert, Joseph de. *The Jesuits: Their Spiritual Doctrine and Practice*. Translated by William J. Young, edited by George E. Ganss. Chicago: Institute of Jesuit Sources, Loyola University Press, 1964.

Gunkel, Hermann. *Genesis*. Mercer Library of Biblical Studies. Macon, GA: Mercer University Press, 1997.

Gunn, David. *The Fate of Saul: An Interpretation of a Biblical Story*. JSOTSup 14. Sheffield: JSOT, 1980.

———. "New Directions in the Study of Biblical Hebrew Narrative." *JSOT* 39 (1987) 65-75.

Gunn, David, and Danna Fewell. *Narrative in the Hebrew Bible*. New York: Oxford University Press, 1993.

———. "Tipping the Balance: Sternberg's Reader and the Rape of Dinah." *JBL* 110/2 (1991) 193-211.

———. "Varieties of Interpretation: Genesis 4 through 2000 Years." In *Narrative in the Hebrew Bible*, 12-33. New York: Oxford University Press, 1993.

Habel, Norman C., editor. *The Birth, the Curse and the Greening of Earth: An Ecological Reading of Genesis 1-11*. Sheffield: Sheffield Phoenix, 2011.

———, editor. *Readings from the Perspective of Earth*. The Earth Bible 1. Sheffield: Sheffield Academic, 2000.

Habel, Norman C., and Peter Trudinger, editors. *Exploring Ecological Hermeneutics*. Atlanta: SBL, 2008.

Hamilton, Victor P. *The Book of Genesis*. 2 vols. New International Commentary on the Old Testament. Grand Rapids: Eerdmans, 1990, 1995.

Haydon, Ron. "A Survey and Analysis of Recent 'Canonical' Methods 10/1 (2000–2015)." *JTI* 10/1 (2016) 145–55.

Heck, Joel D. "A History of Interpretation of Genesis 49 and Deuteronomy 33." *BSac* 147 (1990) 16–31.

Heckle, Raik. "Remembering Jacob in the Late Persian/Early Hellenistic Era." In *Remembering Biblical Figures in the Late Persian and Early Hellenistic Periods. Social Memory and Imagination*, edited by Ehud ben Zvi and Diana V. Edelman, 38–80. Oxford: Oxford University Press, 2013.

Helyer, Larry R. "The Separation of Abram and Lot: Its Significance in the Patriarchal Narratives." *JSOT* 26 (1983) 77–88.

Hendel, Ronald. "Historical Context." In *The Book of Genesis: Composition, Reception, and Interpretation*, edited by Craig A. Evans, Joel N. Lohr, and David L. Petersen, 51–81. Leiden: Brill, 2012.

Himmelfarb, Martha. "Abraham and the Messianism of Genesis Rabbah." In *Genesis Rabbah in Text and Context*, edited by Sarit Kattan Gribetz, David M. Goldberg, and Martha Himmelfarb, 99–114. Tübingen: Mohr Siebeck, 2016.

Hippolytus. *Fragments on Genesis*. In *Patristic Bible Commentary*. https://sites.google.com/site/aquinasstudybible/home/genesis/st-hippolytus-on-genesis.

Horrel, David, et al., editors. *Ecological Hermeneutics: Biblical, Historical and Theological Perspectives*. New York: T. & T. Clark, 2010.

House, Paul. "God's Design and Postmodernism: Recent Approaches to Old Testament Theology." In *The Old Testament in the Life of God's People: Essays in Honor of Elmer A. Martens*, edited by Jon Isaak, 29–54. Winona Lake, IN: Eisenbrauns, 2009.

Humphreys, W. Lee. *The Character of God in the Book of Genesis*. Louisville: Westminster John Knox, 2001.

———. *Joseph and His Family: A Literary Study*. Columbia: University of South Carolina Press, 1988

Hurowitz, Victor Avigdor. "Babylon in Bethel—New Light on Jacob's Dream." In *Orientalism, Assyrology and the Bible*, edited by David Clines, J. Cheryl Exum, Keith W. Whitelam, et al., 436–448. Sheffield: Sheffield Phoenix, 2006.

Irenaeus. *Against Heresies*. In *The Faith of the Early Fathers*, edited by William A. Jurgens, 1:84–107. Collegeville, MN: Liturgical, 1970.

———. *Proof of the Apostolic Preaching*. Translated and Annotated by Joseph P. Smith. London: Longmans, Green, 1952.

Isaak, Jon, editor. *Old Testament in the Life of God's People: Essays in Honor of Elmer A. Martens*. Winona Lake, IN: Eisenbrauns, 2009.

Iser, Wolfgang. *The Art of Reading: A Theory of Aesthetic Response*. Baltimore: John Hopkins University Press, 1978.

———. "The Reading Process: A Phenomenological Approach." *New Literary History* 3 (1972) 279–99.

Jeansonne, Sharon Pace. "Genesis 25:23—the Use of Poetry in the Rebekah Narratives." In *The Psalms and Other Studies on the Old Testament, Presented to Joseph I. Hunt*, edited by Jack C. Knight and Lawrence A. Sinclair, 145–52. Nashotah, WI: Nashotah House Seminary, 1990.

Jerome. *Against the Pelagians*. Translated by W. H. Fremantle, G. Lewis, and W. G. Martley. Nicene and Post-Nicene Fathers, 2nd ser., 6. Edited by Philip Schaff and

Henry Wace. Buffalo, NY: Christian Literature, 1893. http://www.newadvent.org/fathers/30111.htm.
———. *Hebrew Questions on Genesis*. Translated by C. T. R. Hayward. Oxford: Clarendon, 1995.
John of the Cross. *The Dark Night*. In *The Collected Works of St. John of the Cross*m, translated by Kieran Kavanaugh and Otilio Rodriguez. Washington, DC: Institute of Carmelite Studies, 1973.
Joosten, Jan. "Biblical Rhetoric as Illustrated by Judah's Speech in Genesis 44.18–34." *JSOT* 41/1 (2016) 15–30.
Josephus, Flavius. *Antiquities of the Jews*. In *The Works of Josephus: Complete and Unabridged*, translated by William Whiston, 27–542. New ed. Peabody, MA: Hendrickson, 1987.
Jurgens, William A., editor. *The Faith of the Early Fathers*. 3 vols. Collegeville, MN: Liturgical, 1970, 1979.
Justin Martyr. *Saint Justin Martyr*. Translated by Thomas B. Falls. Fathers of the Church 6. Washington, DC: Catholic University of America Press, 1948.
Kaiser, Walter C., Jr. "Narrative." In *Cracking Old Testament Codes: A Guide to Interpreting the Literary Genres of the Old Testament*, edited by D. Brent Sandy and Ronald L. Giese Jr., 81–86. Nashville: B&H Academic, 1995.
Kalimi, Isaac, editor. *Jewish Bible Theology: Perspectives and Case Studies*. Winona Lake, IN: Eisenbrauns, 2012.
———. "Joseph between Potiphar and His Wife: The Biblical Text in the Light of a Comparative Study on Early Jewish Exegesis." *BN* 107/108 (2001) 55–64.
Kaminsky, Joel S. "Election Theology and the Problem of Universalism." *HBT* 33 (2011) 34–44.
———. "New Testament and Rabbinic Views of Election." In *Jewish Bible Theology: Perspectives and Case Studies*, edited by Isaac Kalimi, 119–46. Winona Lake, IN: Eisenbrauns, 2012.
———. "Reclaiming a Theology of Election: Favoritism and the Joseph Story." *PRS* 31/2 (Summer 2004) 135–52.
Kant, Immanuel. *The Conflict of the Faculties/Der Streit der Facultäten*. New York: Abaris, 1979.
———. "Religion within the Boundaries of Mere Reason." In *Religion and Rational Theology*, translated and edited by Allen W. Wood, 39–216. Cambridge: Cambridge University Press, 1996.
Kaunfer, Rabbi Elie. "Torah Reading as a Weapon: Rosh Hashanah and the Akedah." http://livelyseders.com/sitebuildercontent/sitebuilderfiles/rhandakedaharnowfinal.pdf.
Kawashima, Robert S. "Sources and Redaction." In *Reading Genesis: Ten Methods*, edited by Ronald Hendel, 47–70. Cambridge: Cambridge University Press, 2010.
Kedar-Kopfstein, Benjamin. "Sarîs." *TDOT*, 10:344–50. Grand Rapids: Eerdmans, 1999.
Kelly, Declan. "Discuss and Evaluate the Strengths and Weaknesses of Narrative Criticism as a Tool for a Theological Reading of the Old Testament." https://www.academia.edu/10033083/Narrative_Criticism_and_a_Theological_Reading_of_the_Old_Testament.
Kierkegaard, Soren. *Fear and Trembling*. New York: Penguin Classics, 1986.
Kille, Andrew, "Jacob—A Study in Individuation." Originally in *Jung and the Study of the Bible*, edited by David L. Miller, 40–54. New York: Continuum, 1995. https://www.academia.edu/1610237/Jacob_A_study_in_individuation.

Kim, Hyun Chul Paul. "Reading the Joseph Story (Genesis 37–50) as a Diaspora Narrative." *CBQ* 75 (2013) 219–38.
Kling, David W. *The Bible in History: How the Texts Have Shaped the Times*. Oxford: Oxford University Press, 2004.
Koch, Klaus, *The Growth of Biblical Tradition*. New York: Scribner, 1969.
Kugel, James L. *The Bible as It Was*. Cambridge, MA: Harvard University Press, 1997.
———. *Traditions of the Bible: A Guide to the Bible as It Was at the Start of the Common Era*. Cambridge, MA: Harvard University Press, 1999.
Kugel, James L., and Rowan A. Greer. *Early Biblical Interpretation*. Library of Early Christianity 3. Philadelphia: Westminster, 1986.
Kuruvilla, Abraham. "The Aqedah (Genesis 22): What Is the Author Doing with What He Is Saying?" *JETS* 55/3 (2012) 489–508.
Kurz, William. "Patristic Interpretation of Scripture within God's Story of Creation and Redemption." Marquette University e-Publications@Marquette, January 2011. https://pdfs.semanticscholar.org/3303/05215d978500f5f1e89234ce77e111f13ea8.pdf. Published in *The Bible and the Church Fathers: The Liturgical Context of Patristic Exegesis*, edited by Scott Hahn, 35–50. Letter & Spirit 7. Steubenville, OH: St. Paul Center for Biblical Theology and Emmaus Road, 2011.
Lambdin, Thomas O. *Introduction to Biblical Hebrew*. London: Darton, Longman, & Todd, 1973.
Landy, Francis. "Narrative Techniques and Symbolic Transactions in the Akedah." In *Signs and Wonders: Biblical Texts in Literary Focus*, edited by J. Cheryl Exum, 1–40. SBL Semeia Studies. Atlanta: SBL, 1989.
Lauterbach, Jacob Z., translator. *Mekilta de-Rabbi Ishmael*. Vol. 1. Philadelphia: Jewish Publication Society of America, 1933.
Lester, G. Brooke. "Admiring Our Savvy Ancestors: Abraham's and Jacob's Rhetoric of Negotiation (Gen 23, 33)." *Koinonia* 15 (2003) 81–94.
Letellier, Robert Ignatius. *Day in Mamre, Night in Sodom: Abraham and Lot in Genesis 18–19*. Leiden: Brill, 1995.
Levenson, Jon Douglas. *Creation and the Persistence of Evil: The Jewish Drama of Divine Omnipotence*. Princeton, NJ: Princeton University Press, 1988.
———. *The Death and Resurrection of the Beloved Son*. New Haven, CT: Yale University Press, 1993.
———. *Inheriting Abraham: The Legacy of the Patriarch in Judaism, Christianity, and Islam*. Princeton, NJ: Princeton University Press, 2012.
———. "The Universal Horizon of Biblical Particularism." In *Ethnicity and the Bible*, edited by Mark G. Brett, 146–69. Leiden: Brill, 1996.
———. "Why Jews Are Not Interested in Biblical Theology." In *Judaic Perspectives on Ancient Israel*, edited by Jacob Neusner, Baruch Levine, Ernest Frerichs, 281–307. Philadelphia: Fortress, 1987.
Levin, Christoph. "Righteousness in the Joseph Story: Joseph Resists Seduction (Genesis 39)." In *The Pentateuch: International Perspectives and Current Research*, edited by Thomas Dozeman, Konrad Schmid, and Baruch Schwartz, 223–40. Tübingen: Mohr Siebeck, 2011.
Levinson, Joshua. "An-Other Woman: Joseph and Potiphar's Wife. Staging the Body Politic." *JQR* 87/3 (1997) 269–301.

Liber Antiquitatuum Biblicarum (*The Book of Biblical Antiquities*, also called Pseudo-Philo). Translated by D. J. Harrington. In *OTP*, 2:297–377. New York: Doubleday, 1985.

Lockwood, Peter F. "Tamar's Place in the Joseph Cycle." *LTJ* 26/1 (1992) 35–43.

Long, Jesse. "Wrestling with God to Win: A Literary Reading of the Story of Jacob at the Jabbok in Honor of Don Williams." *Stone-Campbell Journal* 15 (Spring 2012) 47–61.

Louth, Andrew, editor. *Genesis 1–11*. ACCS, Old Testament 1. Downers Grove, IL: InterVarsity, 2001.

Lowenthal, Eric I. *The Joseph Narrative in Genesis: An Interpretation*. New York: Ktav, 1973.

MacDonald, Nathan. "Listening to Abraham—Listening to Yhwh: Divine Justice and Mercy in Genesis 18:16–33." *CBQ* 66/1 (2004) 25–43.

Maher, Michael, translator. *Targum Pseudo-Jonathan: Genesis*. Aramaic Bible: The Targums 1B. Collegeville, MN: Liturgical, 1992.

Malina, Bruce J. *The New Testament World: Insights from Cultural Anthropology*. 3rd ed. Philadelphia: Westminster John Knox, 2001.

Malina, Bruce J., and John J. Pilch. *Biblical Social Values and Their Meaning: A Handbook*. Peabody, MA: Hendrickson, 1993.

Mandolfo, Carlene. "'You Meant Evil Against Me': Dialogic Truth and the Character of Jacob in Joseph's Story." *JSOT* 28/4 (2004) 449–65.

Mann, Samuel J. "Joseph and His Bothers: A Biblical Paradigm for the Optimal Handling of Traumatic Stress." *Journal of Religion and Health* 40/3 (Fall 2001) 335–42.

Mann, Thomas. *The Book of the Torah: The Narrative Integrity of the Pentateuch*. 2nd ed. Eugene, OR: Cascade, 2013.

Marcus, David. "Traditional Jewish Responses to the Question of Deceit in Genesis 27." In *Jews, Christians, and the Theology of the Hebrew Scriptures*, edited by Alice Ogden Bellis and Joel S. Kaminsky, 293–305. Atlanta: SBL, 2000.

Matthews, Victor H., and Don C. Benjamin. *Old Testament Parallels*. Rev. ed. New York: Paulist, 1991.

Maxfield, John A. "Divine Providence, History, and Progress in Saint Augustine's City of God." *CTQ* 66/1 (2002) 339–60.

McConville, Gordon. "Forgiveness as Private and Public Act: A Reading of the Biblical Joseph Narrative." *CBQ* 75 (2013) 635–48.

McDonald, Nathan, et al., editors. *Genesis and Christian Theology*. Grand Rapids: Eerdmans, 2012.

McEvenue, Sean E. "A Comparison of Narrative Styles in the Hagar Stories." *Semeia* 3 (1975) 64–80.

———. *The Narrative Style of the Priestly Writer*. Analecta Biblica, Investigationes scientificae in Res biblicas 5. Rome: Biblical Institute Press, 1971.

Mckenzie, Brian Alexander. "Jacob's Blessing on Pharaoh: An Interpretation of Gen 46:31—47:26." *WTJ* 45 (1983) 386–99.

McKenzie, Steve. "'You Have Prevailed': The Function of Jacob's Encounter at Peniel in the Jacob Cycle." *ResQ* 23 (1980) 225–31.

McLean, Haydn J. "Thinking Out Loud: Pondering the Providence of God." *Journal of Pastoral Care & Counseling* 62/3 (Fall 2008) 303–7.

McNamara, Martin, translator. *Targum Neofiti 1: Genesis*. Aramaic Bible: The Targums 1A. Collegeville, MN: Liturgical, 1992.

Meyer, Esias. "Old Testament Stories and Christian Ethics: Some Perspectives from the Narrative of Judah and Tamar." *Stellenbosch Theological Journal* 2/1 (2016) 241–59.

Milgrom, Jacob. "Repentance." In *IDB* 5:736–38.

Miller, Patrick D. *They Cried to the Lord: The Form and Theology of Biblical Prayer.* Minneapolis: Fortress, 1994.

Moberly, R. W. L. "Abraham's Righteousness (Genesis XV 6)." In *Studies in the Pentateuch*, edited by John Adney Emerton, 103–30. VTS 41. Leiden: Brill, 1990.

———. "The Earliest Commentary on the Akedah." *VT* (1988) 302–23.

———. *The Old Testament of the Old Testament.* Minneapolis: Fortress, 1992.

———. *Old Testament Theology: Reading the Hebrew Bible as Christian Scripture.* Grand Rapids: Baker Academic, 2013.

———. *Theology of the Book of Genesis.* Cambridge: Cambridge University Press, 2009.

Muilenburg, James. "Abraham and the Nations: Blessing and World History." *Int* 19 (1965) 387–98.

Nelson-Pallmeyer, Jack. *Jesus Against Christianity: Reclaiming the Missing Jesus.* Harrisburg, PA: Trinity, 2001.

Neusner, Jacob. *Genesis and Judaism: The Perspective of Genesis Rabbah. An Analytical Anthology.* Atlanta: Scholars Press, 1985.

———. "Genesis Rabbah as Polemic: An Introductory Account." *HAR* 9 (1985) 253–65.

———. *A Theological Commentary to the Midrash*, vol. 2: *Genesis Rabbah.* Lanham, MD: University Press of America, 2001.

———. *The Theological Foundations of Rabbinic Midrash.* Lanham, MD: University of America Press, 2006.

Neusner, Jacob, Baruch Levine, and Ernest Frerichs, editors. *Judaic Perspectives on Ancient Israel.* Philadelphia: Fortress, 1987.

Nicholson, E. *The Pentateuch in the Twentieth Century: The Legacy of Julius Wellhausen.* Oxford: Clarendon, 1998

Nickelsburg, George W. E. *Jewish Literature between Bible and the Mishnah.* 2nd ed. Minneapolis: Fortress, 2005.

Nickelsburg, George W. E., and James C. VanderKam, translators. *1 Enoch: A New Translation.* Minneapolis: Fortress, 2004.

Niehoff, Maren. "Circumcision as a Marker of Identity: Philo, Origen and the Rabbis on Gen 17:1–14." *JSQ* 10 (2003) 89–123.

———. "Origen's Commentary on Genesis as a Key to Genesis Rabbah." In *Genesis Rabbah in Text and Context*, edited by Sarit Kattan Gribetz et al., 129–53. Texts and Studies in Ancient Judaism 166. Tübingen: Mohr Siebeck, 2016.

Noble, Paul. "A 'Balanced' Reading of the Rape of Dinah: Some Exegetical and Methodological Observations." *BibInt* 4/2 (1996) 173–204.

Noth, Martin. *A History of Pentateuchal Traditions.* Atlanta: Scholars, 2000.

Oblath, Michael. "'To Sleep, Perchance to Dream . . .' What Jacob Saw at Bethel (Genesis 28.10–22)." *JSOT* 95 (2001) 117–26.

O'Brien, Mark A. "The Contribution of Judah's Speech, Genesis 44:18–34, to the Characterization of Joseph." *CBQ* 59 (1997) 429–47.

Okezie, Joyce Ann. *The Role of Quoting Behavior as Manifested in the Use of Proverbs in Igbo Society.* Buffalo: State University of New York, 1977.

Okoye, James Chukwuma. "An Examination of the Non-Literal Exegesis in Genesis 1—11 in the Pseudo-Jonathan Targum." PhD diss., Oxford University, 1980.

———. *Genesis 1–11: A Narrative-Theological Commentary*. Eugene, OR: Cascade, 2018.

———. *Israel and the Nations: A Mission Theology of the Old Testament*. Maryknoll, NY: Orbis, 2006.

———. "The PBC, the Old Testament, and Christ as the Key to all Sacred Scripture." *CBQ* 80/4 (October 2019) 670–86.

———. Review of *A Reflection on the Theological Questions pertaining to Catholic-Jewish Relations on the Occasion of the 50th Anniversary of "Nostra Aetate" (no. 4)*. *Spiritan Horizons* 11 (Fall 2016) 157.

———. "Sarah and Hagar: Genesis 16 and 21." *JSOT* 32/2 (2007) 163–75.

———. *Scripture in the Church: The Synod on the Word of God and the Post-Synodal Exhortation Verbum Domini*. Collegeville, MN: Liturgical, 2011.

Ollenburger, Ben C., editor. *Old Testament Theology: Flowering and Future*. Rev. ed. Sources for Biblical and Theological Study 1. Winona Lake, IN: Eisenbrauns, 2004.

Origen. *Contra Celsum (Against Celsus)*. Translated by Henry Chadwick. Cambridge: Cambridge University Press, 1953.

———. *Homilies on Genesis and Exodus*. Translated by Ronald E. Heine. Fathers of the Church 71. Washington, DC: Catholic University of America Press, 1996.

———. *On First Principles*. Translated by G. W. Butterworth. Gloucester, MA: Peter Smith, 1973.

Oswalt, John N. "Righteousness in Isaiah: A Study of the Function of Chapters 55–66 in the Present Structure of the Book." In *Writing and Reading the Scroll of Isaiah: Studies of an Interpretive Tradition*, edited by Craig Broyles and Craig Evans, 177–91. VTSup 70. Leiden: Brill, 1997.

Otto, Eckart. "A Hidden Truth behind the Text or the Truth of the Text: At a Turning Point of Biblical Scholarship Two Hundred Years after De Wette's *Dissertatio critico exegetica*." In *Die Tora: Studien zum Pentateuch*, 1–8. Beihefte zur Zeitschrift für altorientalische und biblische Rechtsgeschichte 9. Wiesbaden: Harrassowitz, 2009.

Palmquist, Stephen R., and Philip McPherson Rudisill. "Three Perspectives on Abraham's Defense against Kant's Charge of Immoral Conduct." *JR* 89/4 (2009) 467–97.

Patristic Bible Commentary: Genesis. https://sites.google.com/site/aquinasstudybible/home/genesis.

Pedersen, Johs. *Israel: Its Life and Culture*. 2 vols. Translated by A. Moller and A. I. Fausbell. London: Oxford University Press, 1926.

Perlittt, Lothar. *Bundestheologie im Alten Testament*. WMANT 36. Neukirchen-Vluyn: Neukirchener, 1969.

Perry, Menahem. "Counter-Stories in the Bible: Rebekah and Her Bridegroom, Abraham's Servant." *Prooftexts* 27 (2007) 275–323.

Perry, Menahem, and Meir Sternberg. "The King through Ironic Eyes." *Ha-Sifrut* 1–2 (Summer 1968) 263–292 (Hebrew). Published as "Gaps, Ambiguity, and the Reading Process," in *The Poetics of Biblical Narrative*, by Meir Sternberg, 186–229. Bloomington: Indiana University Press, 1984.

Pilch, John J., and Bruce J. Malina, editors. *Biblical Social Values and their Meaning: A Handbook*. Peabody, MA: Hendrickson, 1993.

Pirson, Ron. "The Twofold Message of Potiphar's Wife." *SJOT* 18/2 (2004) 248–59.

Plaut, W. Gunther, editor. *The Torah: A Modern Commentary*. Rev. ed. New York: Union for Reform Judaism Press, 2006.

Pontifical Biblical Commission. *The Interpretation of the Bible in the Church*. Vatican City: Libreria Editrice Vaticana, 1993.

———. *The Inspiration and Truth of Sacred Scripture: The Word That Comes from God and Speaks of God for the Salvation of the World*. Collegeville, MN: Liturgical, 2014.

———. *The Jewish People and Their Sacred Scriptures in the Christian Bible*. Vatican City: Libreria Editrice Vaticana, 2002. http://www.vatican.va/roman_curia/congregations/cfaith/pcb_documents/RC_CON_CFAITH_DOC_20020212_popolo-ebraico_en.html

Pontifical Council for Justice and Peace. *Compendium of the Social Doctrine of the Church*. Vatican: Libreria Editrice Vaticana, 2004. http://www.vatican.va/roman_curia/pontifical_councils/justpeace/documents/rc_pc_justpeace_doc_20060526_compendio-dott-soc_en.html.

Preuss, "'ôlām." In *TDOT*, edited by G. Johannes Botterweck, Helmer Ringgren, and Heinz-Josef Fabry, translated by Douglas W. Stott, 10:530–45. Grand Rapids: Eerdmans, 1999.

Pritchard, James B., editor. *Ancient Near Eastern Texts Relating to the Old Testament*. 3rd ed. Princeton, NJ: Princeton University Press, 1969.

Pury, Albert de. "The Jacob Story and the Beginning of the Formation of the Pentateuch." In *A Farewell to the Yahwist?: The Composition of the Pentateuch in Recent European Interpretation*, edited by Thomas B. Dozeman and Konrad Schmid, 51–72. SBL Symposium Series 34.

Rashkow, Ilona N. "Intertextuality, Transference, and the Reader in/of Genesis 12 and 20." In *Reading Between Texts: Intertextuality and the Hebrew Bible*, edited by Danna Nolan Fewell, 57–73. Louisville: Westminster John Knox, 1992.

Redford, Donald B. *A Study of the Biblical Story of Joseph (Genesis 37–50)*. VTSup 20. Leiden: Brill, 1970.

Rendtorff, Rolf. "Isaiah 56:1 as a Key to the Formation of the Book of Isaiah." In *Canon and Theology: Overtures to an Old Testament Theology*, translated and edited by Margaret Kohl, 181–89. Minneapolis: Fortress, 1993.

———. *Problem of the Process of Transmission in the Pentateuch*. Library of Hebrew Bible/Old Testament Studies. Berlin: de Gruyter, 1977.

Rimmon-Kenan, Shlomith. *Narrative Fiction: Contemporary Poetics*. London: Routledge, 1989.

Rofé, Alexander. "Defilement of Virgins in Biblical law and the case of Dinah (Genesis 34)." *Bib* 86 (2004) 369–75.

Römer, Thomas. "Abraham, the 'Law and the Prophets.'" In *The Reception and Remembrance of Abraham*, edited by Pernille Carstens and Niels Peter Lemche, 87–101. Perspectives on Hebrew Scriptures and Its Contexts 13. Piscataway, NJ: Gorgias, 2011.

———. "Abraham's Righteousness and Sacrifice: How to Understand (and Translate) Genesis 15 and 22." *CV* 54/1 (2012) 3–15.

———. "The Exodus in the Book of Genesis." *SEÅ* 75 (2010) 1–20.

———. "Genèse 15 et les tensions de la communauté juive postexilique dans le cycle d'Abraham." *Transeuphratene* 7 (1994) 107–21.

———. "Isaac et Ismaël: Concurrents ou coheritiers de la promesse? Une lecture de Genèse 16." *ETR* 74/2 (1999) 161–72.

———. "The Joseph Story in the Book of Genesis: Pre-P or Post-P?" In *The Post-Priestly Pentateuch: New Perspectives on Its Redactional Development and Theological*

Profiles, edited by Federico Giuntoli and Konrad Schmid, 185–202. Forschungen zum Alten Testament 101. Tübingen: Mohr Siebeck, 2015.

Römer, Thomas, and Israel Finkelstein. "Comments on the Historical Background of the Abraham Narrative Between 'Realia' and 'Exegesis.'" *Hebrew Bible and Ancient Israel* 3 (2014), edited by Gary N. Knoppers et al, 3–23. Tübingen: Mohr Siebeck, 2014.

Rom-Shiloni, Dalit. "Hebrew Bible Theology: A Jewish Descriptive Approach." *JR* 96/2 (April 2016) 165–84.

Ron, Zvi. "The Significance of Joseph's Agrarian Policy." *JBQ* 28/4 (2000) 256–59.

Rosenbaum, M., and A. M. Silbermann, translators. *Pentateuch: With Targum Onkelos, Haphtaroth and Rashi's Commentary*, vol. 1: *Genesis*. New York: Hebrew Publishing, 1935.

Ross, Allen P. "Jacob's Vision: The Founding of Bethel." *BSac* 142 (1985) 224–37.

———. "Studies in the Life of Jacob Part 2: Jacob at the Jabbok, Israel at Peniel." *BSac* 137 (1980) 223–40.

Roth, Wolfgang M. W. "The Wooing of Rebekah: A Tradition-Critical Study of Genesis 24." *CBQ* 34 (1972) 177–87.

Sailhamer, John H. *Introduction to the Old Testament Theology: A Canonical Approach*. Grand Rapids: Zondervan, 1995.

———. *The Meaning of the Pentateuch: Revelation, Composition, and Interpretation*. Downers Grove, IL: IVP Academic, 2009.

———. *The Pentateuch as Narrative: A Biblical-Theological Commentary*. Grand Rapids: Zondervan, 1992.

Sanders, James. "Hermeneutics." *IDB Supplementary Volume*, 402–7. Nashville: Abingdon, 1976.

Sandy, D. Brent, and Ronald L. Giese Jr., editors. *Cracking Old Testament Codes: A Guide to Interpreting the Literary Genres*. Nashville: B&H Academic, 1995.

Saner, Andrea D. "Of Bottles and Wells: Hagar's Christian Legacy." *JTI* 11/2 (2017) 199–215.

Sarna, Nahum M. *Genesis*. JPS Torah Commentary. Philadelphia: Jewish Publication Society, 1991.

———. *Understanding Genesis: The World of the Bible in the Light of History*. Heritage of Biblical Israel 1. New York: Schoken, 1966.

Sasson, Jack M. "The Servant's Tale: How Rebekah Found a Spouse."In *JNES* 65/4 (October 2006) 241–65.

Schimmel, Sol. "Joseph and His Brothers: A Paradigm for Repentance." *Judaism* 37/1 (Winter 1988) 60–65.

Schmid, Konrad. "Abraham's Sacrifice: Gerhard von Rad's Interpretation of Genesis 22." *Int* (July 2008) 268–76.

———. "Genesis and Exodus as Two Formerly Independent Traditions of Origins for ancient Israel." *Bib* 93/2 (2012) 187–208.

———. *Genesis and the Moses Story: Israel's Dualo Origins in the Hebrew Bible*. Siphrut 3. Winona Lake, IN: Sifrut, 2009.

———. "What Is the Difference between Historical and Theological Exegesis?" https://www.academia.edu/13866464/What_is_the_Difference_Between_Historical_and_Theological_Exegesis. Translation of "Sind die Historisch-Kritischen kritischer geworden? Überlegungen zu Stellung und Potential der Bibelwissenschaft." *JBT* 25 (2011) 63–78.

Schökel, Luis Alonso. *A Manual of Hebrew Poetics*. Rome: Editrice Pontificio Istituto Biblico, 1988.

Shaefer, Thomas G. *Central African Folk Tales. Les Contes Centralafricains*. Ashland, OH: Bookmasters, 2014.

Shreiter, Robert J. *Reconciliation: Mission and Ministry in a Changing Social Order*. Maryknoll, NY: Orbis, 1992.

Schwartz, Baruch J. "Reexamining the Fate of the 'Canaanites' in the Torah Traditions." In *Sefer Moshe: The Moshe Weinfeld Jubilee Volume: Studies in the Bible and the Ancient Near East, Qumran, and Post-Biblical Judaism*, edited by Chaim Cohen et al., 151–70. Winona Lake, IN: Eisenbrauns, 2004.

Seebass, Horst. "The Joseph Story, Genesis 48 and the Canonical Process." *JSOT* 35 (1986) 29–43.

Segal, Alan. "The Sacrifice of Isaac in Early Judaism and Christianity." In *The Other Judaisms of Late Antiquity*, 109–30. Atlanta: Scholars, 1987.

Shakespeare, William. *The Works of William Shakespeare: Henry VI, Parts I–III, King Richard III, King Henry VIII*. BibioBazaar, 2015.

Sheridan, Mark, editor. *Genesis 12–50*. ACCS, Old Testament 2. Downers Grove, IL: InterVarsity, 2001.

Sherwood, Yvonne. "Hagar and Ishmael: The Reception of Expulsion." *Int* 68/3 (2014) 286–304.

Siddur: Sabbath and Festival Prayer Book. With a New Translation, Supplementary Readings and Notes. Rabbinical Assembly of America and the United Synagogue of America, 1946.

Simkovich, Malka Z. "Interpretations of Abraham's Circumcision in Early Christianity and Genesis Rabbah." In *New Vistas on Early Judaism and Christianity: From Enoch to Montreal and Back*, edited by Lorenzo DiTomasso and Gerbern S. Oegema, 249–68. Jewish and Christian Texts in Contexts and Related Studies 22. London: Bloomsbury T. & T. Clark, 2018.

Simonetti, Manlio. *Biblical Interpretation in the Early Church: An Historical Introduction to Patristic Exegesis*. Edinburgh: T. & T. Clark, 1994.

Ska, Jean Louis. "The Call of Abraham and Israel's Birth-Certificate (Gen 12:1–4a)." In *The Exegesis of the Pentateuch: Exegetical Studies and Basic Questions*, 46–66. Tübingen: Mohr Siebeck, 2009.

———. "Essay on the Nature and Meaning of the Abraham Cycle (Gen 11:29—25:11)." In *The Exegesis of the Pentateuch: Exegetical Studies and Basic Questions*, 23–45. Tübingen: Mohr Siebeck, 2009.

———. "L'Ironie de Tamar (Gen 38)." *ZAW* 100/2 (1988) 261–63.

———. "Some Groundwork on Genesis 15." In *The Exegesis of the Pentateuch: Exegetical Studies and Basic Questions*, 67–81. Tübingen: Mohr Siebeck, 2009.

Skinner, John. *A Critical and Exegetical Commentary on Genesis*. New York: Scribner, 1910.

Smyth, Kevin. "The Prophecy Concerning Judah, Gen 49:8–12." *CBQ* (1945) 290–305.

Sommer, Benjamin D. "Dialogical Biblical Theology: A Jewish Approach to Reading Scripture Theologically." In *Biblical Theology: Introducing the Conversation*, edited by Leo G. Perdue, Robert Morgan, and Benjamin D. Sommer, 1–54 (notes on 265–285). Nashville: Abingdon, 2009.

———. "Psalm 1 and the Canonical Shaping of Jewish Scripture." In *Jewish Bible Theology: Perspectives and Case Studies*, edited by Isaac Kalimi, 199–221. Winona Lake, IN: Eisenbrauns, 2012.

———. "Prophecy as Translation: Ancient Israelite Conceptions of the Human Factor in Prophecy." In *Bringing the Hidden to Light: The Process of Interpretation: Studies in Honor of Stephen A. Geller*, edited by Kathryn F. Kravitz and Diane M. Sharon, 271–90. Winona Lake, IN: Eisenbrauns, 2007.

Speiser, E. A. *Genesis*. New York: Doubleday, 1964.

Spero, Shubert. "Jacob and Esau: The Relationship Reconsidered." *JBQ* 32/4 (2004) 245–50.

Spiekermann, Hermann, and David M. Carr. "Abraham: Hebrew Bible/Old Testament." In *Encyclopedia of the Bible and Its Reception*, edited by Steven L. McKenzie et al., 1:149–56. Berlin: de Gruyter, 2009.

Spurrell, George James. *Notes on the Hebrew Text of the Book of Genesis*. Oxford: Clarendon, 1887.

Sternberg, Meir. "The Double Cave and the Bible's Art of Dialogue (Genesis 23)." *Stuttgarter theologische Themen* 6 (2011) 83–92.

———. *The Poetics of Biblical Narrative: Ideological Literature and the Drama of Reading*. Bloomington: Indiana University Press, 1985.

Sternberg, Naomi. "The Sarah-Hagar Cycle: Polycoity." In *Kinship and Marriage in Genesis: A Household Economics Perspective*, 35–86. Minneapolis: Fortress, 1993.

Strack, Hermann Leberecht, and Paul Billerbeck. *Kommentar zum Neuen Testament aus Talmud und Midrasch*. 5 vols. Munich: Beck, 1922.

Sugirtharajah, R. S., editor. *Voices from the Margin: Interpreting the Bible in the Third World*. Rev. ed. Maryknoll, NY: Orbis, 1995.

Sweeney, Marvin A. "Jewish Biblical Theology: An Ongoing Dialogue." *Int* 70/3 (2016) 314–25.

———. "Form Criticism: The Question of the Endangered Matriarchs in Genesis." In *Method Matters: Essays on the Interpretation of Hebrew Bible in Honor of David L. Petersen*, edited by Joel L. LeMon and Kent Harold Richards, 17–38. Atlanta: SBL, 2009.

———. "The Jacob Narratives: An Ephraimitic Text?" *CBQ* 78 (2016) 236–55.

Teugels, Lieve. "The Background of the Anti-Christian Polemics in Aggadat Bereshit." *Journal for the Study of Judaism* 30 (1999) 178–208.

Theodoret of Cyrus. *Questions on the Octateuch*. Vol 1: *On Genesis and Exodus*. Edited by John F. Petruccione, translated by Robert C. Hill. Washington, DC: Catholic University of America, 2007.

Thompson, Thomas. "Conflict Themes in the Jacob Narratives." *Semeia* 15 (1979) 5–26.

Trible, Phyllis. "Hagar: The Desolation of Rejection." In *Texts of Terror: Literary-Feminist Readings of Biblical Narratives*, 9–35. Philadelphia: Fortress, 1984.

Tsevat, M. "Hagar and the Birth of Ishmael." In *The Meaning of the Book of Job and Other Biblical Studies: Essays on the Literature and Religion of the Hebrew Bible*, 56–69. New York: Ktav, 1980.

Urbach, Ephraim E. *The Sages: Their Concepts and Beliefs*. Vol. 1. Jerusalem: Magnes, 1975.

Van Seters, Jan. *Abraham in History and Tradition*. New Haven, CT: Yale University Press, 1975.

———. "The Birth of Ishmael and Isaac." In *Abraham in History and Tradition*, 192–208. New Haven, CT: Yale University Press, 1975.

———. "Divine Encounter at Bethel (Gen 28,10–22) in Recent Literary Critical Study of Genesis." *ZAW* 110 (1998) 503–13.

VanMaaren, John. "The Adam-Christ Typology in Paul and its Development in the Early Church Fathers." *TynBul* 64/2 (2013) 275–97.

Vatican Council II. *Dei Verbum*. Dogmatic Constitution on Divine Revelation. November 18, 1965. http://www.vatican.va/archive/hist_councils/ii_vatican_council/documents/vat-ii_const_19651118_dei-verbum_en.html.

Vaux, Roland de. *Ancient Israel: Its Life and Institutions*. Translated by John McHugh. Grand Rapids: Eerdmans, 1997.

Vawter, Paul. "An Exposition of Jacob's Experience at Jabbok: Genesis 32:22–32." Maranatha Baptist Seminary, November 20, 2013. https://www.mbu.edu/seminary/journal/an-exposition-of-jacobs-experience-at-jabbok-genesis-3222-32/.

Vermes, Geza, translator. *The Complete Dead Sea Scrolls in English*. New York: Penguin, 1997.

———. "Redemption and Genesis XXII." In *Scripture and Tradition in Judaism*, 193–227. Studia Post-Biblica 4. Leiden: Brill, 1961.

Vermeylen, J. "Le Vol de la Bénédiction Paternelle. Une Lecture de Gen 27." In *Pentateuch and Deuteronomistic Studies: Papers read at the XIIIth IOSOT Congress, Leuven 1989*, edited by C. Brekelmans and J. Just, 23–40. Ephemerides theologicae Lovanienses / Bibliotheca 94. Leuven: Leuven University Press, 1990.

Von Rad, Gerhard. *Genesis: A Commentary*. Translated by John H. Marks. Rev. ed. Phildelphia: Westminster, 1972.

———. "Faith Reckoned as Righteousness." In *The Problem of the Hexateuch and Other Essays*, translated by E. W. Trueman Dicken, 125–30. Edinburgh: Oliver and Boyd, 1966.

Wagner, Angela B. "Considerations on the Politico-Juridical Proceedings of Genesis 34." *JSOT* 38/2 (2013) 145–61.

Walker, Andy. "The Role of Genesis 37:1–11 in the Joseph Novella." *Leaven* 24/4 (2016) 174–77. https://digitalcommons.pepperdine.edu/leaven/vol24/iss4/3/.

Warrior, Robert Allen. "A Native American Perspective: Canaanite, Cowboys, and Indians." In *Voices from the Margin: Interpreting the Bible in the Third World*, 277–285. edited by R. S. Sugirtharajah. Rev. ed. Maryknoll, NY: Orbis, 1995.

Watson, Francis. "Abraham's Visitors: Prolegomena to a Christian Theological Exegesis of Genesis 18—19." *Journal of Scriptural Reasoning* 2/3 (2002) 1–11.

Weingreen, J. *From Bible to Mishnah: The Continuity of Tradition*. Manchester: Manchester University Press, 1976.

Wenham, Gordon J. "The Akedah: A Paradigm of Sacrifice." In *Pomegranites and Golden Bells: Studies in Biblical, Jewish and Near Eastern Ritual, Law and Literature in Honor of Jacob Milgrom*, edited by David P. Wright, David Noel Freedman, and Avi Hurvitz, 93–102. Winona Lake, IN: Eisenbrauns, 1995.

———. "*Betulah*, A Girl of Marriageable Age." *VT* 22 (1972) 32–48.

———. "Some Problematic Tales." In *Story as Torah: Reading Old Testament Narrative Ethically*, 109–27. Grand Rapids: Baker Academic, 2004.

———. *Story as Torah: Reading Old Testament Narrative Ethically*. Grand Rapids: Baker Academic, 2004.

Westermann, Claus. *Genesis 1–11*. Translated by John J. Scullion. Continental Commentary. Minneapolis: Fortress, 1994.

———. *Genesis 12–36*. Translated by John J. Scullion. Continental Commentary. Minneapolis: Fortress, 1995.

———. *Genesis 37-50*. Translated by John J. Scullion. Continental Commentary. Minneapolis: Augsburg, 1986.
Whartenby, Thomas J., Jr. "Genesis 28:10-22." *Int* 45/4 (1991) 402-5.
Wilson, Robert R. "Anthropological Perspectives on Old Testament Genealogies." In *Sociological Approaches to the Old Testament*, 54-66. Minneapolis: Fortress, 1984.
Wink, Walter. "On Wrestling with God: Using Psychological Insights in Biblical Study." *Religion in Life* 47/2 (1978) 136-47.
Yoo, Philip Y. "Hagar the Egyptian: Wife, Handmaid, and Concubine." *CBQ* 78 (2016) 215-35.
Zoob, Henry A. "A Positive Perspective on the Three Embarrassing Wife-Sister Stories in Genesis." *CCAR Journal*, Fall 2014, 5-33.
Zucker, David J. "Abraham, the Years of Frustration: Genesis 13-14 and 15 as a Literary Unit." *BTB* 48/1 (2018) 3-9.

Subject Index

Aaronide priests, 67, 68
Abel, 67, 115
Abimelech
    consistently righteous and gracious, 419
    covenant with Abraham at Beersheba, 142–44
    dialogue of God with, 128–30
    dialogue with Abraham, 130–32
    gifts to Abraham, 131, 132
    innocence of, 420
    representing studious and wise men, 133
    told Isaac to go away, 201
Abraham—*see also* Abram, 448
    Abram's name changed to, 94
    acquiring the cave of Machpelah in the Land of Canaan, 162–67
    as the "anointed" of Psalm 45, 207
    attempting to spare Sodom, 116
    becoming a great and mighty nation, 112
    becoming a monotheist, 52
    believed in future possession of the land of promise, 170
    believed in the LORD before the law of circumcision, 51
    bound his son Isaac and put him on top of the wood on the altar, 151–52
    built an altar in Bethel, 226n26, 227
    burial of, 77, 87, 146
    buried his wife Sarah, 166
    called Sarah his sister, 128
    circumcised Isaac, 135
    circumcised Ishmael, 101
    clear to him that the promised son would be by Sarah, 134
    commanded by God to relinquish his past and his future, 147
    commissioned a trusted servant to fetch a wife for Isaac, 169–71
    content to dwell in tents, 167
    covenant with Abimelech at Beersheba, 142–44
    death of, 180
    dialogue of Abimelech with, 130–32
    dies before the promise of land is realized, 166
    dug wells that Philistines filled with earth, 206
    faith of, 416, 422
    "father of a multitude of nations," 289
    fathered Ishmael and Isaac, 31
    fertility of burst forth, 181
    gave everything that he owned to Isaac, 182, 299
    genealogies of, 157
    as God's friend, 50
    having free access to God and his word, 149
    hosting YHWH, 110–12
    identification of Melchizedek as, 68
    inheriting the promises of, 80

Abraham (*continued*)
    invoked by name the LORD, El Olam (God Eternal) at Beersheba, 287
    justified by works when he offered his son Isaac, 423
    keeping the entire Torah before it had been revealed, 52n81, 206
    knew of Rebekah, daughter of Bethuel, 170
    laughter of, 100, 111
    leaving Isaac as sole heir of the Promised Land, 180
    left the choice of blessing of his sons to God, 185
    Lot and, 54–68
    meanness towards Ishmael, 145
    mediative roles associated with Christ, 206–7
    "memory" of Abraham, enshrining the gratuitousness of God's choice of Israel, 414
    "The Most High," as an epithet of the God of Israel, 64
    narrative narrowing the offspring of, 157
    needing ground to bury his wife, 163
    needing to show that he is worthy of God's beneficence, 148
    not giving Isaac the birthright or the blessing as customary at the end of life, 185
    not much of a blessing in Egypt, 415
    obedience of, 184, 198, 423
    pleaded successfully for Ishmael, 415
    professing YHWH as *El Elyon*, God Most High, 144
    promised by YHWH "I will make of you a great nation," 417–18
    promised with an oath to bless the nations through his descendants, 415
    receiving wayfarers with hospitality, 146
    reference to nations and kings in relation to, 99
    religious interpretation, of the blessing of Abraham, 50–51
    saw a ram caught by its horns in the thicket, 152–53
    securing his first piece of property in the land, 143
    set two conditions for his servant to find Isaac's wife, 171
    story of Abimelech in Gerar told from a religious perspective, 127
    swore not to deal falsely with Abimelech or his progeny and posterity, 143
    taught his offspring fidelity to God, 113
    question of theophany, 109
    took another wife, Keturah, 180
    took the knife to slaughter his son, 151–52
    trading his wife for his own welfare, 130
    true descendants of, 51
    true offspring of, 92
    as the type of all who have faith, 157
    united with Isaac in the same spirit, 159
    viewed by the Hittites as one in God's protection, 164–65
    willing to sacrifice his son, 155
Abraham Cycle, 35–36, 298
Abraham ibn Ezra, 45
Abram—*see also* Abraham, 447
    age of, 38
    alone with a barren Sarai, 57
    believed before any law of circumcision, 81
    call of, 36
    in Canaan, 44–45

claimed Sarai as his sister in
    Egypt, 127
counterfoil to Moses and Joshua,
    63
defeated the northern kings and
    recovered his kinsman Lot,
    58–63
dialogue with YHWH in two
    parallel panels, 69
disunity in his family, 82–83
in Egypt, 46–49
faith of, 73
God's election of, 50
holding on to his trust in
    YHWH, 72
Melchizedek and, 63–65, 65n38
name changed to Abraham, 94
named Hagar's son Ishmael, 88
never sacrificed in Bethel or
    Hebron, 55
not claiming hegemony over the
    Promised Land, 63
origins of, 34–35
rescued his nephew, 61–62
rich in livestock, silver and gold,
    55
righteousness of, 74–75
seeking survival in Egypt, 46
separation from Lot, 55–58
settled in the land of Canaan, 57
taking on a new identity, 37
YHWH appears to, 92
treated Hagar as he would a
    wife, 85
vocation and blessing of, 36–42
worry at leaving his father,
    38n26
Absalom, 290
"act-consequence" moral chain, 47
Adam, 34, 78
Adonizedek, pre-Israelite king of
    Jerusalem, 64
adultery, 90, 128, 270, 327
agents, moving the story along, 7
agrarian policy, of Joseph, 381–84
Ahuzzath, councilor of Abimelech,
    203

Akedah, Rosh Hashanah associated
    with, 161
all the nations of the earth, finding
    blessing in Abraham's
    descendants, 153
allegory, 23, 27, 28
Amalek, 293
ambiguities, in narrative criticism, 9
Ambrose
    distinguished precepts from
        counsels, 11
    on Jacob giving Joseph Shechem,
        392
    on Joseph sending the silver
        goblet, 358
    on Lot choosing deviation, 66
    preaching flight from the world,
        118
    remained close to allegorical
        interpretation of Philo and
        Origen, 28
    on the visitors of Genesis 18, 22
Ambrosiaster, 263
Ammon, 41
Ammonites, 121–22
Amoraic traditions, 161n62
Amorites, wickedness of, 79–80
Amos, 87, 191
Anabaptist Hetterites, 11
"And laughed," containing the name
    Isaac, 100
Aner, ally of Abram, 62
angel of the LORD, called to
    Abraham at the critical time,
    152
angels in Sodom, 116–19
    identified in the Talmud as
        Michael, Raphael, and
        Gabriel, 124
angels of God
    ascending and descending,
        224–25
    at Bethel, 219
    called to Hagar from heaven, 139
    encountered Jacob, 250
    occurrence in the Hebrew Bible,
        219n2
    visiting Abraham, 424

annunciation type-scene, promising
    offspring to a barren couple,
    110
Anthony of Egypt, 11
Antiochene school, 28
Antiochus Epiphanes, on leaving
    sons uncircumcised, 102
Aphrahat, on Abraham's
    circumcision, 105
Aqedah
    as the Binding of Isaac, 152
    doctrine of, 159, 160
    of Ishmael, 155–56, 420n13
Aram, Laban representing, 246
Arians, denying Christ the title
    "God," 125, 424
Asenath, wife of Joseph, 344,
    346n29
Asher, 238, 400
ass, as indomitable, 87
assembly of nations, stemming from
    Jacob, 289
Augustine
    on the analogy of Scripture, of
        faith, and the goal of love, 28
    calculating the number of
        people migrating to Egypt,
        375–76
    critique of Justin with a
        Trinitarian affirmation, 425
    on the crown of righteousness,
        156
    on "four generations," 79
    God created you without you
        but will not save you without
        you, 156, 422
    on God's gifts, 72
    on Isaac knowing what was
        happening, 217
    on Jacob giving Joseph Shechem,
        391–92
    on the Joseph Novella, 346
    on Joseph prefiguring Christ,
        392
    on the moral evaluation of
        Tamar and Judah, 322
    on nations of Jacob, 296
    on Onan, the son of Judah, 321
    on the providence of God, 413
    reflecting on hell, 312
    on resurrection, 384–85
    on second marriages, 185
    on the Trinity as one God,
        125–26
    on the visitors of Genesis 18,
        22–23

Balaam's oracle, 398, 417
Bar Kockba, led the last Jewish
    Revolt against Rome, 404
Bar Kockba Revolt, 102n39
barrenness, 35, 83, 99. See also
    childlessness
Basemath
    daughter of Elon the Hivite, 205
    sister of Nebaioth, 292
Beersheba, etiologies of the name,
    143
Beliar, 66
Pope Benedict XVI, 18
Benjamin
    brothers' relation to as decisive
        for Joseph, 348
    did not go to Egypt with his
        brothers, 349
    Jacob's blessing of, 403
    as "my son...the only one left,"
        354
    named by Jacob, 290
    as the only son born in Canaan,
        290n15
    singled out for preferential
        treatment by Joseph, 368
    suddenly having ten sons, 374
Bera, king of Sodom, 60
Beth-El, meaning "house of God,"
    227
Bethel
    altars built there, 44
    divine encounter at, 219–30
    as a hallowed and renowned,
        286
    importance of, 187
Bethlehem, home of David, 404
Bethuel
    death of, 176n28

Rebekah, daughter of, 155
betrothal type-scene, 168, 171, 232
Bible
    containing diverse views on many issues, 13
    containing variant forms of the text and some obscure passages, 18
    not always giving clear guidance to conduct, 267
biblical images of God, as not unitary, 19
biblical law, on the violation of unbetrothed virgins, 269, 273
biblical narrator. *See* narrator
Bilhah
    conceived and bore a son for Jacob named Dan, 238
    given to Jacob by Rachel, 83n5, 237
    Rachel's handmaid, 181
    Reuben lay with, 290, 313
birds of prey, 76, 339
Birsha, king of Gomorrah, 60
birthright and blessing, as bones of contention, 187
blessing
    of Abraham, Clements interpretations of, 50
    for all the families of the earth, 39, 415–16
    depending on the good pleasure of the one who blesses, 211
    determinative for Abraham's family self-consciousness, 42
    diverse understandings of the promise of, 39–40, 39n30
    Jacob asked for, 255
    of Joseph, Judahite redirection of, 402–3
    linking together Abraham-Isaac-Jacob, 36
    meaning of Abram's, 41
    moving outside the family circle with Joseph, 415
    never counterbalanced by curse, 297
    as reward for obedience, 198
    of the tribes of Israel, 396–403
Blessing of Moses, Benjamin of, 403
Book of Jubilees, retelling the biblical story, 23
boundaries, of the Promised Land, 77, 418
"bowing down," characterizing future relationships of Joseph and his siblings, 305
bread and wine, offered by Melchizedek pointing to the Eucharist, 68
breastfeeding, in traditional cultures, 135
bridal price, 271
bride, took off the veil only in the bridal chamber, 177
bride wealth, used up by Laban, 243
brother-in-law, duty of, 315
brothers of Joseph
    abandoning the favored brother to enslavement, 359
    angry with their father and with Joseph, 306
    became fearful after Jacob died and asked for forgiveness, 409
    blurted out that Benjamin was at home and the other brother is no more, 350
    bowed down before to the ground before Joseph, 356
    bowed down to him with their faces to the ground, 349–50
    choosing unity over separation, 359
    enacting the ritual of mourning, 359
    finally acknowledged the beloved son of Rachel as "our brother," 355
    given a taste of the arbitrariness of unchecked power, 351
    hated Joseph, 305, 306
    ill at ease hearing of Egypt, 349
    needed time to readjust to each other, 410

brothers of Joseph (*continued*)
    never asked for forgiveness, 424
    plotted to kill Joseph, 308
    reenacting the role of the Ishmaelite traders, 355–56
    selling Joseph into slavery, 307–11
    strife between, 189
Brueggemann
    his *Genesis Commentary* as discourse analysis, 2n6
    Bible as speech about God, *Theology of the OT*, 14–15
    on the metaphor of barrenness, 35
burnt offering, 151

Caesarius of Arles
    Abraham recognized one God in three persons, 126
    Isaac carrying wood prefigured Christ, 158
    Jews were scattered so their books lay ground for Gentile faith, 193
    Joseph's brothers discuss his death just as Jesus' brother Jews shout "crucify him," 311–12
    Joseph wept that the brothers ever treated him thus, 362
Cain, driven east of Eden, 57
Calvin, John, 11
camels, representing the irrational and perverse, 179
Canaan
    Abraham acquired the cave of Machpelah in, 162–67
    Abram in, 44–45
    Benjamin the only son of Jacob born in, 290n15
    boundaries of, 45
    Esau ceding to his younger brother, 293
    given to Abraham and his descendants, 95
    given to Abram's descendants, 45
    Isaac left in secure possession of, 35–36
    Jacob reaffirming as Israel's home, 403
    Jacob settled in the land of, 304
    Joseph requiring his bones to be returned to, 412
    kings from the north invading, 59
    memorial stones taking possession of, 44
    Sarah buried in, 162
canon of Scripture, 13
canon of the New Testament, 27
"canonical Pentateuch," written after Israel's failures, 15
captives, proclaiming liberty to, 66
Catechism of the Catholic Church
    biblical writers as true authors, 17
    books of the OT as divinely inspired, 106
    coitus interruptus, 322, 329n12
    pray as if all depended on God. Work as if all depended on you, 252
    offenses against chastity, 322–23
Catholic-Jewish-relations, reflections on, 106–7
cave in the field of Machpelah
    Abraham acquiring in the Land of Canaan, 162–67
    Abraham buried his wife Sarah in, 166
    for burials, 403
    Isaac and Ashmael buried Abraham in, 182
    Jacob buried in, 408
characters, in narrative criticism, 7
chief baker, 339
chief cupbearer
    not remembering Joseph until the appointed time, 339, 339n13
    restored to his office, 339
    told Joseph his dream, 337
    told Pharaoh about Joseph, 341–42

chief jailer, 326, 329, 330, 336
chief steward, of Pharaoh, 311
childlessness, 237. *See also* barrenness
children, of Rachel through Bilhah, 237
Christ
   established the church in place of the synagogue, 179
   fear of death done away with, 131
   as high priest, 67
   Justin's subordinationist interpretation, 424
   priesthood of not passing away, 68
   representing Israel, 416
   as the unique "seed" of Abraham, 157
Christian liturgy, Melchizedek as high priest, 68
Christianity, salvation not depending on keeping the laws of the Torah, 206
Christians, Torah Prophets seen as heralds of Christ, 13
christological interpretation, of "three angels" visiting Abraham, 424
Chrysostom
   on Abraham as a shadow of Christ, 158–59
   on Christians amassing possessions, 167
   on fear of death, 130–31
   on God sending Joseph to Egypt, 370
   on God strengthening the bonds of harmony between Abraham and Sarah, 137
   on Jacob's love of Joseph, 305
   on Joseph as a martyr put to the test, 331
   on Joseph learning not to place hope or confidence in men, 339–40
   on Joseph's second dream, 385
   on Lot considering the wickedness of the inhabitants, 57
   on returning to the Promised Land, 385
   on Sarai accusing Abram of injustice, 89
circumcision
   ceremony of, 102
   covenant of, 91–107
   of heart, 97
   kinds of in Scripture, 104
   law of, 51, 96–97
   opened the Jewish family to outsiders, 98
   as a ploy for massacre, 275
   as a site of Jewish resistance, 102
   as still the word of God, 107
   as the symbol of *enkrateia* (self-control, self-perfecting), 103
clashes, between herdsmen and farmers in Nigeria, 55
Clement of Alexandria
   salvation of the rich man—poverty of spirit, not poverty of possessions, 11
   Joseph through chastity overcame his master's wife, 331
   the Paidagogue, Christ, anoints Jacob, athlete, for spiritual struggles, 376
coat or tunic of Joseph, 305, 309
command, of God to sacrifice Isaac, 148–51
commentaries, on Genesis, 1
commissioning, of the trusted servant to fetch a wife for Isaac, 169–71
"compensative sins," evoking the morality of double effect, 322
concubines, Keturah and Hagar as, 181
conflict, in Jacob's family, 304–6
consciences of Joseph's brothers, cracked open, 352

SUBJECT INDEX

context, text never divorced from, 4–5
Cornelius, baptized by Peter, 103
Council of Constantinople, 125, 425
Council of Jerusalem, 103
Council of Sirmium, 125, 424
covenant
    with Abimelech, 143, 203–5
    with Abram, 93–96
    circumcision becoming a sign of, 97–98
    between Jacob and Laban, 247
    as oath sworn to the fathers, 71
    of Sinai, 43
"covenant between the pieces," 76
covenant formula, 95
covenant relationship, offer of, 32
creation, requiring perfection through human effort, 106
cursing, all who hold Abram in disdain, 41
cycles, of the story of Genesis, 31
Cyril of Alexandria
    on Christ as placed on top of the stairway, 229
    on Hagar seeing "a well of living water," 146
    on Joseph's reasoning powers, 305n28
    on the last becoming the first, 392
    making the distinction between Hades and Hell, 312
    on violence, 283

Dan, 238, 399–400
Dan (tribe of), Old Testament mentions of, 400n17
Dark Night of the Spirit, for Abraham, 156–57
daughter of Shua, Judah's wife, death of, 317
daughters
    considered part of the property of the father, 118
    of Lot, 121
David
    "great nation" eventuated in, 417
    as king of Judah first in Hebron, 164
    overcame Edom under Hadad II, 294–95
    Tamar becoming ancestor of, 320
Davidic messiah, downplayed by the rabbis, 207
dead of Israel, as the first to be resurrected, 384
Deborah, Rebekah's nurse, 177
defilement, intermarriage with Gentiles as, 282
deity, names for, 93n6
derash hermeneutic process, 25
deuterocanonical books, dealing with, 18n67
Deuteronomistic History, 112
Deuteronomy, on possession of the land, 419
Deuteronomy (siglum D) source, 3n8
dialectic, of grace and works, 422–23
"dialogical biblical theology," 21n85
dialogue, in narrative criticism, 7
Dinah
    compensation and marriage, as legally enough for Dinah, 273
    daughter of Leah, 239
    disappears from the Bible, 276
    feelings of never expressed, 269
    holding the place for Benjamin, 231
    Jacob's daughter from Leah, 11
    listing of, 375
    massacre, other sons of Jacob added looting to, 275
    point of view of, 12
    seized by Shechem, 267, 268
    taken from Shechem's house, 274
discernment, by the trusted servant of Abraham, 173
disunity, in Abram's family, 82–83
"divine beings," *Elohim*, 264

divine blessing, linked with
    righteousness, 324
divine commitment, depth of, 71
divine election, 13, 286
divine encounter, at Bethel, 219–30
divine mercy, resting on covenant,
    422
divine oath, guaranteeing the future,
    153–54
divine predestination, needing help,
    213
divine providence. *See* providence
divine will and purpose, wrestling
    with, 254
"Do not fear," introducing a
    salvation oracle, 202–3
"do not fear" formula, 72
Documentary Hypothesis, 3–4, n8
double genealogy, of Abraham, 184
doubt, as a necessary part of faith,
    76
drawing of water, establishing a
    male-female bond, 171
dream(s)
    ancients believed in the
        revelatory function of, 129
    following the mouth, 338
    held to be messages from the
        other world, 341
    indicating the deity's will, 303
    interpretation of in ancient
        Egypt, 336
    of Jacob of a stairway to the
        heavens, 223
    of Joseph, 8–9, 305, 306, 350,
        352, 362–63, 385, 388
    of Pharaoh, 340–46
    of Pharaoh's officials, 336–40
dwelling in tents, by Isaac, 190n16
dysfunctional families, in Genesis,
    414

early Christian hermeneutics, of the
    Old Testament, 26–29
Ebenezer, as stone of help, 229
"ecumenical" patriarch, Abraham
    as, 101
edification (*haggadah*), 26

Edom
    clans and chiefs of, 284
    descendants of Esau as, 291
    famous for wisdom, 192
    preceded Israel as a nation in
        Canaan, 189
    referring to the "chieftains of
        Edom," 293
    Rome known as, 265
    secured freedom from Judah,
        215
Edomites, 191, 294, 295
Egypt
    Abram in, 46–49
    benefited from Joseph's
        foresight, 415
    brothers' first journey to, 349–54
    brothers' second journey to,
        354–58
    as a cipher for the forces of evil,
        376
    everything belonging to
        Pharaoh, 382
    Jacob migrating to, 371–76
    as the natural refuge during
        famine, 46
Egyptians, ate apart from Hebrews,
    357n25
El, meaning god, 287
El Shaddai, as the divine name, 92
El-Bethel (God of Bethel), 287
elect, given a role to play in God's
    dispositions, 112
elect family, as dysfunctional, 414
election, 137
Elohist (siglum E) source, 3n8
Elyon, highest god of the Canaanite
    pantheon, 62
Emim in Moab, as tall like the
    Anakim, 61
encounter, of Abraham's servant
    with Rebekah, 171–74
Enosh, line of, 44
Ephraim
    becoming "a multitude of
        nations," 390
    Jacob adopting, 386–93

SUBJECT INDEX

  named by Jacob before
      Manasseh, 387
  son of Joseph, 345
  son of Joseph and daughter of
      priest of On, 281
  surpassing Manasseh, 390
Ephrem
  Melchisedek as Shem, 68
  Abraham took concubine after
      death of Sarah, 185
  Leah so unattractive no one has
      come to marry her, 236
  Rachel attributed her barrenness
      to Jacob not praying for her,
      237
  records a prayer of Tamar
      that makes her action
      providential, 321
  it was the Lord's doing that the
      brothers did not recognize
      Joseph, 363
  Joseph counsels brothers to
      avoid recriminations on way
      back, 368
  Jacob makes the brothers
      recount their crime to him,
      369–70
Ephron the Hittite, 165
Er, 316, 321
Eretz Israel, patriarchs desirous of
      burial in, 384
Esau
  became a skilful hunter, 190
  as a blessed man, 415
  buried Isaac, 291
  ceding the land of Canaan to
      Jacob, 293
  coming with four hundred men,
      251
  descendants of, 186, 291–95
  on the earlier sale of the
      birthrights as trickery, 214
  emerged first from the womb,
      189
  fragrance attached to, 210
  given material riches but
      subordinated to Jacob, 214
  as gracious, magnanimous, and
      forgiving, 419
  hairy body, suggesting beastly
      behavior, 189
  intending to kill Jacob, 215
  Isaac blessing, 213–15
  Jacob encountering, 257–60
  Jacob sending messengers to,
      250–53
  learned war, 190n17
  as a man of immediate
      gratification, 192
  negative view of, 217
  not part of Israelite identity, 41
  pressing for dialogue and
      reconciliation, 423
  renunciation of revenge, 261
  requested partnership in Jacob's
      world, 265
  sold Jacob his right as firstborn
      under oath, 191–92
  son of Isaac, 32
  standing for the old
      dispensation, 217
  struggle in the womb with Jacob,
      188–93
  as a symbol of Rome, 194
  tradition that vilified, 193
  tried to make amends, 222
  went to the land of Seir, 292, 299
  wielding dominion only by his
      hand, 218
  wives of, 205, 216, 222, 292
Eshcol, ally of Abram, 62
eunuch, having a wife, 325
eunuch of Pharaoh, 311
Eusebius of Emesa
  contemporary of Jerome,
      Chrysostom and Genesis
      Rabbah, 24
  was Abraham inhumane in
      dealings with Hagar? 145
  inhabitants of Shechem did not
      honor anyone who came,
      282
Evangelicals, support of the State of
      Israel, 43–44

everlasting covenant, with Abraham,
      94–95
exile, 78–80, 422
"exile" and "return," as a model, 76
exiles, 49, 95

"face to face" with God, said only of
      Moses, 256
"face to the ground," repeating
      Jacob's retort to Joseph's
      second dream, 388
face-to-face encounter, of Jacob and
      Esau, 253
faith
   of Abraham, 416, 422–23
   of Abram, 73
   active along with works, 51
   doubt as a necessary part of, 76
   Gentiles justified by, 416
   justifying one before God, 74
   making no distinction between
      Jew and Greek, 144
   as righteousness, 73
   as waiting for God, 149
Falwell, Jerry, support of the State of
      Israel, 43–44
families of the earth
   blessed in Abraham, 154
   blessing for all as God's purpose,
      415–16
family of Abraham, question of who
      belongs to, 184
family of Jacob, story of, 304
famine, dream pointing to, 343
"father of a multitude of nations,"
      Abraham as, 184
father-in-law, tradition to give a
      widow to the surviving
      brother, 316
fathers of the church
   on appearances of the Logos
      incarnate, 376
   applied the elder serving the
      younger to the Christian and
      Jewish faiths, 193
   on changing of garments, 296

on how Joseph could say that
      it was God who sent him
      ahead to Egypt, 370
   interpreting Sarah as virtue of
      the soul, 133
   on Joseph as a type of Christ,
      311, 362
   on Joseph as the hero of chastity
      and virtue, 331
   on Joseph showing lack of trust
      in God, 339
   on Joseph's treatment of his
      brothers, 348n2
   on mourning, 412–13
   on Rebekah as representing
      patience, 178
   on the tale of Dinah, 283
   on why God should want to test
      Abraham, 158
favoritism, Jacob's acts of, 305
fear of God, 130, 131, 158
fertility, 42, 96
fertility/numerous progeny, blessing
      to Jacob, 221
feudal nobility, breaking the power
      of in Egypt, 382
flat characters, 7
food, in Egypt, 343, 345
forgiveness
   differing from reconciliation,
      261, 409–10
   as a free offer for Esau, 259
   Joseph acting out of, 367
   reconciliation and, 423–24
   of sin, 411
Fragmentary Targum, 24
Francis of Assisi, forsook his wealth,
      11
fratricide, hatred pushing the
      brothers to, 308
friend of God, Abraham as, 50
full-fledged characters, 7
funeral procession befitting a king,
      for Jacob, 408
furnace ordeal, of Abraham, 52

Gabriel, role of, 124
Gad, 238, 400

Galatians
   advised to choose freedom, 145
   on failure of the Sinai covenant, 15
   justified by their faith independent of circumcision, 81
gaps, in narrative criticism, 9
Garden of Eden, borders of, 77
garments
   changing of, 296
   tearing of, 310
"gate of heaven," Bethel as, 226
gates of enemies, gaining possession, 177
Gebiah, son of Kosem, 185
genealogy(ies)
   of Abraham, 157, 184
   of Esau as a vast multitude, 415
   in Genesis, 33
   of Ishmael, 183
   of Jacob, 299–300
   of Perez, 418
   propelling the Genesis story, 31
   as records of perceived realities, 183
   of Sarah, 131
Genesis
   Christian and Jewish reception of, 424–25
   Jewish Midrash on, 24
   literary structure of, 33
   narrative theology of, 10–13
   recurring themes, 31–32
   Targums on, 24
   translations of 1:2, 30
Genesis Apocryphon, of Qumran, 23
Genesis Rabbah
   Palestinian compilation circa 400 CE, 24–25
   God exempted Abram from duty towards his parents, 38, n.26
   Abram made converts in Egypt, 44, n.49
   Pharaoh struck by skin disease, 48
   Nimrod cast Abram into a furnace, 52
   numerical value of name Eliezer is 318, 62
   Abram feared war from sons of the kings he defeated, 72
   Hagar among gifts Pharaoh gave Sarai, 83
   a man may remarry if wife bore him no child in 10 years, 90
   often reacts to Christian interpretations, 104
   Abraham's hospitality to strangers for conversion, 123
   Abraham's acts merit for descendants, 126, 207
   Ishmael tried to kill Isaac, 145
   God judges people according to their present deeds, 146
   Abraham and Isaac united in mind to sacrifice, 159
   identifies Keturah and Hagar, 181, 185
   Esau as shedder of blood, 191n21
   Esau despised the rising of the dead, 194
   the yoke of the Torah shields from persecution, 218
   four keys master of the world keeps to himself, 240n24
   patron angels guard destiny of nations and individuals, 254
   Jacob's 7 prostrations were to God, gained him mercy, 265
   Dinah became the wife of Job, 276
   Joseph preened himself, 312
   Potiphar knew Joseph was innocent, 329
   Joseph married the daughter of his master's wife, 346
   Simeon it was he who pushed Joseph into the pit, 363
   The dead of Israel will rise first, 384
Gentiles, 51, 80–81, 157, 416
Gnostics, 22, 27

SUBJECT INDEX 459

goat meat, cooking to taste like venison, 210
God
    achieving his purposes through humans, 216, 241, 411, 421
    acting in his own ways, 167
    affording repentance to Abimelech, 129
    announcing that Sarah will have a son, 99
    appearing to men in a rational way, 263
    asking Abraham to relinquish his future, 149
    asking Jacob to build him an altar in Bethel, 285
    blessing Abraham and his descendants, 95, 153, 183, 185
    as a character in narrative criticism, 6
    declaring that blessing will win for dominance in the world, 415
    defining "the father of many nations," 137
    demanding preferential love, 37
    dialogue with Abimelech, 128–30
    did not spare his own son, 158
    including Jacob in the line of promise, 372
    with Ishmael and Isaac, 141
    loving people individually, 142
    made Abimelech impotent, 132
    as mindful of his covenant with Abraham, Isaac, and Jacob, 43
    moral norms for, 155
    names of, 34n4
    not perfecting people before deciding to work in and through them, 216, 220, 282, 414
    portrayed differently in the Joseph Novella, 302–3
    prepared Jacob to become Israel, 220
    presenting holy Jacob at the future judgment, 362
    putting Abraham to the test, 148
    reaffirmed the promise of seed for Sarah, 134–35
    refused to notify Jacob that his son was living, 362
    restored health to Abimelech, 132
    sent Joseph to Egypt, 365
    showing mercy to whom he will, 193
    as sovereign of the universe, 420
    stood by Jacob and his sons, 295–96
    taking account of the present condition of a person, 146
    trusting in the power of, 73
    views of, 109
    wanting to know if Abraham really fears God, 147
    warned Laban against doing harm to Jacob, 244
God of Israel, beginning of the permanent cult of, 262
gods, associated with mountains, 92
God's angels. See angels of God
"God's camp," protecting Jacob's camp, 250
God's face, symbolized Esau's gracious welcome, 259
God's hand
    guiding Israel's destiny through Joseph's life, 324
    at work in ordinary daily events, 366n4
gods of the nations, as foreign, 286
Goldingay, John
    Examines the faith implied in the OT, 15
    Blessing and curse wrestling for dominance, 33, 415
    Musings of God about those he calls, 37
    Is land essential to biblical faith? 45
    God loves Israel, as he loves other peoples, 49, 142

Goldingay, John (*continued*)
    Jewish faith affirms world and body, 96
    How does God relate to human wrongdoing? 242, 364, 411
Gomorrah, 121–22
Good Friday Prayers, regarding Jews, 105, 106
Goshen, exempted from the plague of the flies, 379
grace, 70, 251
grace and works, dialectic of, 422–23
Graf-Wellhausen Hypothesis, 3n8
great name, offered to Abram, 39
"great nation"
    becoming a world empire as a mediator of blessings, 40, 417
    making of Abram, 38
    promise of given to Ishmael, 140
    promises of, 38n24
greed, invoked to favor circumscision, 274
gripping the heel, as an act of contestation, 190
guiding hand, of God, 303

Hadad, kings named as, 294–95
Hadad of Edom, attempted revolt against Solomon, 295
Hades, distinguishing from Hell, 312
Hadrian, made circumcision a capital crime, 102n39
Hagar
    Abraham taking back, 185
    in Abraham's power at the birth of Isaac, 135
    as captive Sinai, 157
    cast out with Ishmael, 138–40
    children of as children of the flesh, 144
    claiming rights over the child still in the womb, 84
    experiences exodus without liberation, 142

    expulsion, as an act of liberation for Hagar, 139
    expulsion of as an inverted exodus, 141, 420
    gave the name, El Roi, 287
    giving rise to nations, 87
    having marital rights, 90
    as powerless because God supported Sarah, 137
    ran away from Sarai, 85
    receives a divine oracle of salvation, 139
    receives a theophany, 85–89
    representing introductory knowledge, 89
    role of, 84
    Sarai and, 82–90
    saw and addressed YHWH and named him, 88
    as secondary wife, 84
    told to return and submit to oppression, 86, 420
Hagee, John, support of the State of Israel, 43–44
Ham, populating the earth, 31
Hamor the Hivite, 11, 267, 270, 271, 419
Haran, died before Terah, 52
heart, circumcision of, 97
Hebrew Bible, allowing diverse voices, 20
Hebrew Scriptures, contrasting views on dreams, 336
herdsmen, of Lot not muzzling their cattle, 66
Herod, as the first king of a foreign race, 405
Hezekiah, 68
Hippolytus
    Jacob's smooth skin reveals sinless body of Christ, 217n23
    Lion/lion's whelp signifies union between Father and Son, 406
historical critical approach, 3
historical critical exegesis, 10
Hittites, Abraham's negotiations with, 164–65

Hivites, as one of the peoples of
    Canaan, 268
Holiness Code, prohibiting marriage
    with the circumcised foreign
    population, 272
homosexual intercourse, as
    abomination, 117
homosexuality, Sodom story as a
    prime text against, 122–23
Horites, of Seir, 295
Hosea, condemned Jacob for his
    conduct, 192–93
hospitality
    of Abraham, 146
    at Mamre, 110–12
    as sacred, 117
    virtue of, 123
"house of God," 226
household gods, of Laban stolen by
    Rachel, 244
human choices, subsumed under
    God's sovereign will, 411
human design, God's design
    working against, 421
human help, Joseph needing, 340
human likeness to God, evaluation
    of, 19
human wisdom, conquering
    economic difficulties,
    383–84

idolatry, misleading Abraham into,
    133
idols, burial of, 286
image of God, evolving through
    Genesis, 419–21
"in the latter days," 396
indentured laborer, Jacob as, 234
inheritance, allotting to sons, 182
institutional cult and cult mediator,
    absence of in the patriarchal
    stories, 297
intended evil, caught up into a larger
    design shaped by divine
    will, 366
intermarriage, with Gentiles as
    defilement, 282

interpretation, layers of in biblical
    materials, 19
intertextuality, 12
Irenaeus
    first to use expression, "New
        Testament," 27
    developed criterion of "rule of
        faith," 27
    Abraham saw Son of God with
        two angels, 124
irony, 8
Isaac
    as Abraham's only son, 148, 152
    absent at the burial of Sarah in
        Hebron, 169
    acting prophetically in his
        blessings, 217
    age of according to the rabbis,
        159n52
    birth of, 134–37
    "blesses" Esau, 213–15
    blessing of Jacob, 210–13, 220
    burial of, 166
    called Esau to bless him, 208
    death of, 291
    deceived by Jacob, 213
    designating Jacob as bearer of
        the blessings of Abraham,
        221–22
    dominant role as brief, 186
    fathered Esau and Jacob, 32
    feared that men would kill him
        on account of Rebekah, 200
    fled to avoid strife, 204
    forbidden to go to Egypt during
        a famine, 372
    God's command to sacrifice,
        148–51
    God's covenant maintained
        through, 135
    as inheritor of the divine
        blessings to Abraham, 196
    left in secure possession of
        Canaan, 35–36
    lived to see Jacob's children, 291
    loved Esau, 208
    loved Rebekah, 178

Isaac (*continued*)
   name rooted in peals of laughter, 135
   never named in his marriage arrangements, 176
   never went back to his homeland, 170
   not intending to transmit the blessing of Abraham, 212
   not mentioned at his mother's funeral, 166, 169n5
   not returning evil for evil, 204
   obedience to divine guidance required of, 196
   as the only remaining son, 149
   opening wells, 206
   planted during the famine and still received a hundredfold yield, 200
   preferred Esau, 191
   promise of the land and of progeny, 52
   removing Esau from the Promised Land, 215
   seen as a willing victim, 159–60
   sent Jacob off to Laban to choose a wife from his daughters, 221
   showed little trust in God, 200
   smelled the fragrance of Isaac's clothes, 211–12
   son of Abraham, 31
   tradition of, 159, 195–207
   treated as a king with equal power, 204
   used the term "your mother's sons" when speaking to Esau about Jacob, 209
   walking in the field caught sight of camels approaching, 177
   went down to Abimelech, king of the Philistines in Gerar, 196
   wished to bless Esau with inheritance, 182
Isaac and Ishmael, buried Abraham in the cave of Machpelah, 166, 182

Isaachar, 239, 399
Ishmael
   Abraham pleaded for, 134, 415
   Aqedah of, 155–56, 420n13
   banishing from possession of the Promised Land, 136
   birth of, 83–85
   cast out, 138–40
   circumcised, 101, 135, 136–37
   excluded from aspects of the covenant, 100
   genealogy of, 183
   at home when Abraham died, 87n16
   improper actions of, 146
   inheritance rights, 84, 88
   lived in the same vicinity as Isaac, 183
   lived in the wilderness and became an expert bowman, 140
   making a nation of, 137
   making fertile, 100–101
   name proclaiming that "God hears," 86, 87
   nationhood, blessing of, to Ishmael, 101
   not part of Israelite identity, 41
   prayer on behalf of, 100
   saved by an angel of God, 152
   seeking to entice the spirit, 145
   son of Abraham, 31, 136
   treatment of Isaac, 145
   was "playing Isaac," 136
Ishmael and Isaac, buried Abraham, 146, 182
Ishmaelites, 183–84, 185, 309
Israel
   appearing as a nation for the first time, 257
   duty to be blessing for all families of the earth, 43
   God's covenant with as still intact, 106
   as a holy nation, 41, 282–83
   learning that God is free to act with Israel however God wishes, 152

SUBJECT INDEX   463

as a power under God for peace
and righteousness, 416
representing seventy nations of
the earth before God, 375
Israel (Jacob)
benefits accruing to, 154
content not to seek material and
military greatness, 265
faced the crisis of choice, 354
gained superiority over the
angels of the Lord and over
men, 264
laying his right on Ephraim for
the blessing, 389
loved Joseph best of all his sons,
305
naming of the twelve ancestors
of, 290
offered sacrifices to the God of
his father Isaac at Beersheba,
372
sent Judah ahead to Joseph, 373
told he will become a great
nation in Egypt, 372
told the brothers to "put some
of the land's best products in
your baggage" as gifts, 355
YHWH testing by affliction, 148
YHWH's self-revelation to, 225
Israelite patriarch, Abraham as, 101
Israelite religion, starting point of
Israel's relationship with
YHWH, 285–86

Jacob
according Joseph firstborn
status, 301
adopting Joseph's sons, Ephraim
and Manasseh, 386–93
age of when he fled to Laban,
222, 222n13
all sons becoming Israel, 220,
231
articulating the presence of God,
389
assigning inheritance, 181

assigning rule (political power)
to Judah and numbers and
fertile fields to Joseph, 395
avoided Esau's company, 260
becoming Israel, 253–57
blessed Pharaoh, 379
blessing of Judah, 404
"bowed" to his son Joseph, 385
bowing to Esau, 258
built an altar at Bethel, 44
burial of, 166
came out of the womb gripping
Esau's heel, 189–90
chose Joseph before the others
as heir to his good works,
392
as chosen, 32
clothing in Esau's clothes, 210
conflict in his family, 304–6
contesting the firstborn status of
Esau, 190
continued mourning rites till he
dies, 311
customarily spent the night with
Rachel, 239
deceived by Laban, 234–36
deciding who is to be included
in Israel, 387
demonstrated superhuman
strength, 233
departed from Beersheba, 373
disinheriting Reuben, 182
divided the people into two
camps out of fear, 251
effusive in his blessing of Joseph,
401
embalmed and mourned
according to Egyptian
custom, 407–8
encountering Esau, 257–60
encountering God for the first
time, 220
escaping Laban, 242–44
events in the life of, 380
experiencing mortal danger
many times or deceptions
are visited upon him, 216

Jacob (*continued*)
    explanations of his love for
        Joseph, 313
    farewell and death of, 403
    as father of righteous Israel, 184
    first indication of knowing what
        the brothers did to Joseph,
        409n4
    as the first romantic in the Bible,
        235
    following God's wish to return
        to Haran, alone to face
        Esau's wrath, 242
    funeral of, 407–8
    genealogy of, 299–300
    heard that Shechem had defiled
        his daughter Dinah, 11
    Hebrew slaves in Egypt as
        descendants of, 220n5
    hip socket dislocated as he
        wrestled, 254
    inconsolable over Joseph,
        310–11
    Isaac's blessing of, 210–13
    journey motif, of flight and
        return, 187
    kissed Rachel and wept aloud,
        233
    learned to write, 190n17
    leaving the rest to God, 355
    lived seventeen years in Egypt,
        380, 381
    love of Rachel, 233, 234
    memorial service, for Jacob, 408
    migrating to Egypt, 371–76
    name changed again, 288–91
    naming Bethel, 285–88, 289
    never shown as lord of Esau, 217
    not believing that Joseph is
        governing all the land of
        Egypt, 369
    outwitting Laban, 240–42
    pact with God as conditional,
        227
    physically wrestling with God,
        256
    point of view of stairway and
        angels and Lord himself, 223
    prayed for God to save him from
        the hand of his brother, 251
    presented to Pharaoh, 379
    professing himself unworthy of
        divine graciousness, 252
    proposing wages of every dark
        animal among the lambs and
        every spotted or speckled
        one among the goats, 241
    putting himself at the head of
        the procession as a gesture
        of self-sacrifice, 256
    reaffirming that Israel's home is
        in Canaan, 403
    recognized Joseph's tunic, 310
    recognized that Esau's wrath was
        justified, 253
    recognizing the grace of God,
        389
    rejecting physical reunion with
        Esau, 423
    relation with Rachel's
        maidservant Bilhah, 83n5
    reproached his sons for putting
        city to the sword, 295–96
    reproved Joseph for his sun
        and moon and eleven stars
        dream, 306
    requested blessing from the
        being who wrestled with
        him at Peniel, 288
    requested to be burred with
        ancestors, 380, 381
    response to Simeon and Levi,
        276–77
    retaining no pretensions to
        superiority or rule over his
        twin, 251
    retaining the protection and care
        of God, 421
    selected presents for his brother
        Esau, 252
    sending messengers to Esau,
        250–53
    sent Joseph to see if all was well
        with his brothers, 308
    sent the brothers to Egypt to buy
        grain, 349

served Laban another seven
years for Rachel, 236
setting the agenda in the Joseph
story, 301
settled in the land of Canaan,
261–62, 304
severe reproof of the excessive
violence of Simeon and Levi,
277
sons of replied to Shechem and
his father with guile, 272
spoke of seeing God face to face,
254
standing for the new
dispensation and Christ, 217
starting off with zero flock as his
own, 241
stayed among the tents, 190
superhuman strength of, 254
suspecting something sinister,
353
testament of, 394–406
told his household to get rid of
foreign gods, 285
as the true heir to the
Abrahamic promises, 289
trying to grasp what can be
obtained by grace, 255
visiting Bethel, 219
vow of, 226–28
at the well, 232–34
went home to his father Isaac at
Mamre, 291
wrestling to obtain legitimately
what he got before through
deception, 254
Jacob and Esau, needed time to
readjust to each other, 423
Jacob and Laban, in Gilead, 244–47
Jacob and the brothers, afraid at the
sight of their moneybags,
353
Jacob Cycle, 186–87, 188, 299
Jacob-Esau story, defending the
justice of God in choosing
the Gentiles, 193
Jacob's ladder, as cross of Christ, as
the church, 229

James, Letter of
on faith completed by works, 81
on the obedience of Abraham,
423
Japheth, populating the earth, 31
Jerome
on Abraham taking back Hagar,
185
on Abram being cast into a
furnace, 52
on Israel having victory over
Esau, 264
on Onan's sin as *coitus
interruptus*, 321
perplexed about God testing
Abraham, 158n46
prepared a fresh translation
of the Old Testament, the
Vulgate, 28
Jesse, father of David, 418
Jesus
bore our sins, 416
declared by God high priest
according to the order of
Melchizedek, 67
as a divine being, 67
as the fulfillment of Isaac's
sacrifice, 160
Jethro, 65n41, 181
Jewish Antiquities, of Philo, 23
Jewish exegetical works, referenced
in this commentary, 23–24
Jewish reformulation of doctrine,
in response to Christian
doctrine of atonement, 160
Jewish Sacred Scriptures, in
continuity with the Second
Temple period, 20
Jews
accused of deicide, 106
afflicted and oppressed by a
spiritual famine, 363
Jobab, son of Zerah, from Bozrah,
294
John 1:18, "No one has ever seen
God," 263–64

John Hyrcanus, erased Edom
    from history in the second
    century BCE, 265
Saint John Paul II, 107
St. John XXIII, 369
Jordan Plain, like the Garden of
    Eden to Lot, 56
Joseph
    abilities of used by God, 337
    accepted nothing from the
        cupbearer, 338
    accredited the divine with his
        ability to interpret dreams,
        342
    accused of attempted rape, 328
    acquired all the land of Egypt for
        Pharaoh, 382
    acting with extreme
        magnanimity, 366–67
    adopted the children of Ephraim
        and Manasseh as his own,
        395, 412
    agrarian policy of, 381–84
    appeared "divine" to his father,
        373
    arousing his brothers to a
        confession of their sin,
        348n2
    arranged to be alone with his
        brothers when he revealed
        himself, 365
    asked for livestock from the
        Egyptians, 382
    assigned to the household of his
        Egyptian master, 325
    assurance of meeting with for
        Jacob, 373
    became an Egyptian noble, 344
    became the father of two sons,
        345
    blessing operating through, 39
    bound Simeon, 352, 363
    bowed down before Jacob with
        his face to the ground, 388
    burial of, 262, 412
    caught in a maelstrom of
        conflicting emotions, 348
    collected all the food of the years
        of plenty, 345
    compared to a son, a wild colt,
        or fruitful plant in different
        translations, 401
    complete characterization of,
        347
    death of, 412
    defined by clothing and
        unclothing, 309
    as the "discerning and wise
        man," 343
    dreams of, 8–9
    encountering his brothers,
        347–63
    found favor in the eyes of his
        master, 326
    goblet, of Joseph found in
        Benjamin's bag, 359
    had the brothers seated before
        him according to their age,
        357
    hearing for the first time of his
        father's grief, 361
    inquired about his father, 356
    interpreting Pharaoh's dreams,
        340–46
    interpreting the dreams of
        Pharaoh's officials, 336–40
    invoking loyalty and fidelity to
        his beneficent master, 327
    Jacob's blessing of, 400–402
    journeys, of the brothers to
        Egypt, 349–58
    kept a commandment and
        became lord of Egypt, 331
    "lie with me," signaling crass
        desire, 326
    lording it over his brothers,
        304–5
    making "slaves" of the
        Egyptians, 384
    as a man of flesh and blood
        liable to temptation, 332–34
    married the daughter of the high
        priest of On, 281, 344
    master of dreams, Joseph proves
        to be, 340

national import, of the brothers' journey to Egypt, 349
needed to see Benjamin, 350
never mentioned forgiveness, 410, 424
never received a direct theophany of God, 387
not graced with theophany and divine promise, 412
not included among the patriarchs, 301, 303
Potiphar's wife and, 324–34
presenting his family to Pharaoh, 378–80
from prison to power, 335–46
punishes and torments his brothers, 348n5
put in charge of the household and entrusted to all possessions, 326
put the money into Pharaoh's house, 381
putting his brothers through a course of education, 348
putting the sons of Israel under oath to return his bones to Canaan, 412
rationed food to the Egyptians, 345
reacting for the first time about the false charge of Potiphar's wife, 338
readjustment with his brothers, 424
reassured his brothers, 410
recognized his brothers, 349
redirecting leadership towards that of Judah, 314
refusal of to Potiphar's wife, 327
remained hidden from his brothers until his dreams should be fulfilled in them, 362–63
resolve for revenge began to melt, 352
revealing himself to his brothers, 364–70
riding around Egypt in Pharaoh's second chariot, 344
said nothing in his own defense, 329
sent for his father, 368
set apart by Jacob, 401
sexual purity, Joseph as the ideal of, 331
sexual struggle, as a trope for cultural continence, 333
as a shrewd and successful administrator, 383
sold into slavery by his brothers, 307–11
son of Rachel, 239
spoke harshly to his brothers, 350
status of firstborn, 388
story of elsewhere in the Bible, 303–4
suggested that a discerning and wise man be put in charge of organizing the storage of food, 343
suspected of overweening ambition, 306
taking on new status, 342
taught Egyptian elders wisdom, 340
tending flocks at seventeen years old, 304
"testing" his brothers, 347n2
threw his brothers into prison, 350
tunic dipped in goat's blood, 310
tunic of Joseph, 305, 309
understood as a deeply flawed character, 348
understood what his brothers said, 352
as vain and doing deeds of youthful foolishness, 312
weeping of, 352, 357
well-built and handsome, 326
went up to meet his father Israel in Goshen, 373

Joseph Novella
  Augustine on, 346
  climax of, 364
  described, 300–302
  inserted into the broader story of Jacob, 299
  as originally independent of the Jacob story, 306n32
  theology in, 302–3
Joseph-Judah polarity, in the history of the people of Israel, 314n1
Josephus
  on Abraham as a monotheist, 52
  explaining Joseph's Egyptian name, 346
  on the Jewish Revolt of 66-70 CE, 404
  on Joseph's brothers being unwilling to return back with him to Egypt, 409
  on the land of the Sodomites, 122n31
  on Rachel's theft of Laban's household gods, 248
  works of, 23
Joshua
  Abram counterfoil to, 63
  Adullam conquered by, 316
  built an altar at Bethel, 44
  on putting away foreign gods, 286
jubilee, proclaiming releasing from the debt of sins, 66
Judah
  ascendance of, 301
  became powerful among his brothers, 388
  as clearly the leader now, 359
  father of Perez and Zerah, 418
  having power of life and death over his family, 319
  intervention and speech of, 360
  Jacob's blessing of, 397–99
  married a Canaanite woman, 275, 281, 315
  not wanting Joseph dead, 309
  offering himself as slave in place of Benjamin, 361, 362
  recognized his seal and cord that he had given Tamar, 319
  registering the ascendancy of, 314n1
  relating that "my wife bore me two sons," 361
  son of Leah, 237
  sons of, 375
  speaking with Jacob/Israel about selling Joseph, 369–70
  taking up the leadership position among the brothers, 354
  Tamar and, 314–23
  told Jacob that Benjamin must go back with them, 354
  urged his father Israel to let Benjamin go with him, 355
Judah's wife, bore Onan and Shelah, 316
Judaism, 16, 103
Judith, 205, 282
justice, meaning individual retribution, 115
Justin Martyr
  on Abraham seeing the Logos, 124
  on circumcision, 104–5, 106
  Dialogue with Trypho on Old Testament as prophecy of Christ, 27
  on every divine appearance in the Old Testament as the Logos incarnate, 424
  making Christ subordinate to God, 125
  on the meaning of Shiloh, 398–99, 417
  reproached Trypho, 68
  on "tying his foal to the vine," 406
  on the visitors of Genesis 18, 22

Kant, Immanuel, 155
Keturah, 180, 181, 181n4, 184n14
kidnapper, punishment of, 310
Kierkegaard, on Abraham's act as true faith, 155
"kingdom of God," 96, 228

kings
    reigned in the land of Edom, 294
    in righteousness or
        unrighteousness, 129
kings from the north, 59, 61
King's Valley, 64

L.A.B. (*The Book of Biblical
        Antiquities*), 159n54, 160
Laban
    accused Jacob of not allowing
        him the usual parting
        rituals, 244–45
    deceiving Jacob, 234–36
    Jacob escaping, 242–44
    as Jacob's match, 187
    kissed his daughters and
        grandchildren, 250
    in no mood to release Jacob
        from service, 240
    outwitted by Jacob, 240–42
    presented as selfish and greedy,
        174
    ran to meet Jacob, 233
    as an unjust and mean employer,
        246
Laban and Bethuel, replied that the
    servant should take Rebekah
    and go, 176
Jacob's ladder, as cross of Christ, as
    the Church, 229
land grant, as sworn oath, 75–78
land holdings, in Egypt as only
    temporary, 388
land of Canaan. *See* Canaan
language games, in Hebrew Text, 30
Leah
    brought to Jacob who
        consummated marriage with
        her, 235
    burial of, 166
    craving Jacob's love, 237
    death and burial of, 403
    Dinah daughter of, 267
    gave her maid-servant Zilpah to
        Jacob as wife, 238
    giving birth to four sons, 236
    having dull eyes, 234
    rivalry with Rachel, 236–40
    substituted for Rachel by Laban,
        177
Levenson, Jon Douglas, 16
Levi, 12, 237, 397
Levi (tribe), 395, 397
levirate marriage, 319
literal meaning, as an educative
    starting point for Origen,
    27–28
literary approaches, to commentary,
    4
Logos, Abraham saw, 124
Logos-centric exegesis, of Justin as
    deficient, 425
LORD
    appeared in human form to
        Abraham, 110
    appeared to Abram, 45
    appeared to Isaac in Beersheba,
        202–3
    appeared to Isaac in Gerar,
        196–98
    commanding Jacob to return
        home, 242
    inducting Abraham into his role
        as "blessing," 113
    not forgetting the covenant, 422
    rained down sulphur upon
        Sodom and Gomorrah, 119
    was with Joseph, 325–26, 329–31
"LORD being with," as a feature of
    the Jacob saga, 325
"lord/servant" language, Jacob
    continuing, 253
Lot
    Abraham and, 54–68
    Abram willing to rescue, 59
    chose the area of Sodom, 115
    greets angels in Sodom, 116–19
    lifted up his eyes to Sodom with
        lustful desire, 66
    looked eastward to the fertile
        Jordan Plain, 56
    not a citizen of Sodom, 120
    not part of Israelite identity, 41
    offering his two daughters,
        117–18

Lot (continued)
    as possible heir to Abram, 42, 54
    proved himself righteous, 118
    rich in flocks and herds, 56
    salvation of attributed to YHWH's fidelity to Abraham, 120
    separation from Abram, 55–58
    Terah's grandson, 35
Lot's wife, turned into a pillar of salt, 120
"loved" and "hated" wife, scenario of, 236
Luther, Martin, 11

Machir, Manasseh's son, 395, 412
Machpelah. *See* cave in the field of Machpelah
magicians, specialized in dream interpretation, 341
Mahalath, daughter of Ishmael and sister of Nebaioth, 205, 205n25, 292
Mahanaim, meaning "two camps," 250
maidservant, as not necessarily a slave, 83
Malchiresha (king of wickedness), also called Beliar and Satan, 66
Mamre, the Amorite, 62, 110
"the man," as an otherworldly being, 255
Manasseh, 281, 345, 386–93
mandrakes, considered an aphrodisiac, 239
Marcion, rejected the entire Old Testament, 27
married woman, lying with as sin, 200
material blessings, to Isaac as abundance of grain and wine, 212
matriarchs of Israel, most barren, 35
Matthew, used the genealogy of Perez to introduce Jesus, 418

Melchizedek
    Abram and, 63–65
    appeared without ancestry remaining a priest forever, 68
    appearing again in the Old Testament only in Psalm 110, 65
    blessed Abram, 68
    as a figure of Christ, the high priest, 67
    meaning "king of righteousness," 63
    offering of, 67
    professing YHWH as *El Elyon*, God Most High, 144
    representing the priesthood of the second temple, 65n41
memorial stones, taking possession of the land of Canaan, 44
memory, reconstruction of, 424
merchants of the desert, Ishmaelites as, 309n37
mercy and justice, as the nature of YHWH, 114
"merit of the fathers," 75, 203, 206
"messenger formula," enabling Jacob to present himself to Esau, 250–51
Messiah, to be of the tribe of Judah and "son of David," 404
messianic hopes, on the line of David, 417
Michael (archangel), 66, 124
Midianites, 9, 181, 310, 311
midrash, 185, 332, 363
Midrash Rabbah: Genesis, 24
migration, of Jacob (Israel) to Egypt, 372
migration and displacement, tradition of, 78
Milcah, 155
military ascendancy, promised over enemies, 154
"minim" (heretics), rejected paths of interpretation, 22
Mishnah, as rabbinic interpretation, 23

mixed marriages, 221
Moab, not part of Israelite identity, 41
Moabites, origin of, 121–22
Moberly, R. W. I., 13–14
    Christian theology, of the book of Genesis, 14
Molech, giving seed to, 283
moral imperatives, competing, 12
moral integrity, of Joseph, 324
moral performance, fulfillment of the covenantal promise contingent on, 113
moral standards, of the Philistines, 200
Moses
    accepted the obligations of God's covenant, 43
    asked to completely destroy Amalek, 293
    asked YHWH to be mindful of his promises to Abraham, 38n24
    died outside the Promised Land, 45, 58, 419
    face to face with God, 256
    Hagar as prototype of, 141, 420
    not writing the whole Torah, 45
    Pharaoh's command to, 48
    prayer for Reuben, 397
    requested Pharaoh to "let my people go," 240
    took Joseph's bones with him, 412
    tradition of holy war dominating the story of, 63
mourning, current Jewish practice of, 164n5
mourning rites, prohibiting excessive grief, 164
"multitude of nations"
    Abraham as the father of, 289
    Ephraim becoming, 390
    sprang from Abraham, 180, 184

NABRE (New American Bible, Revised Edition, 2011), 31
Nahor, 51, 155
names, for deity, 93n6
naming, in narrative criticism, 9
Naphtali, 238, 400
narration, 7, 19
narrative, themes of, 414–25
narrative approach, 3–10
narrative arc, 187
"Narrative Art" commentaries, examples of, 1–2
narrative commentaries, 1, 2–3
narrative criticism, concepts in, 5–10
narrative English commentaries, on Genesis, 2
narrative theology, of Genesis, 10–13
narratives of Genesis, 17–21
narrator
    accrediting God with complete trustworthiness, 19
    in narrative criticism, 5–6
    not telling the whole truth either, 267n2
    "omniscient narrator," 5–6
    role of for the truth of Scripture, 267
    separating the judgments of from those of God, 192
    showing and telling, 10
    telling the story from his point of view, 8
nazirites, consecration of, 402
Nephilim, 9
New Testament
    reading in the light of the Old, 17, 21
    treated the Old Testament as a prophecy of Jesus Christ, 26
Nimrod, casting Abram into the furnace, 52
Noah
    divine commitment to, 71
    in Genesis, 34
    as a new beginning, 31
    removed humankind from the threat of a further deluge, 154
    as righteous, 74, 93, 198

472 SUBJECT INDEX

Noble, Paul
    all characters in Dinah story flawed, though admirable qualities also, 279
    Gen 34 explores complex issues of crime and punishment, 280
Nostra Aetate, no.4 (dealing with Jews and Judaism), 106
novella. *See* Joseph Novella

oath, confirming the sale of the birthright, 192
oath of loyalty, between Abraham and Abimelech, 142
Obed, 418
obedience
    of Abraham, 37, 153, 184, 198
    of Abram, 36, 38
obeisance, as what subjects do towards a king, 306
Og, king of Bashan, 61
oil
    anointing with, 226
    pouring on the stone pillar at Bethel, 289
Old Testament
    books divinely inspired, 17
    debated between Christians and Jews, 22
    early Christian hermeneutics, 26–29
    early Jewish interpretation of, 23–26
    embodying various interpretive processes, 21–23
    "re-reading" in the light of Jesus Christ, 21
Onan, 316, 317
onanism, 322
"oral torah," in addition to "written torah," 25
"order of Melchizedek," LXX translation created, 67
Origen
    on Abraham's ascent of the mountain with Isaac, 149
    on the angel wrestling with Jacob in order to save him, 262–63
    dismissed physical circumcision as flesh, 104
    established Christian biblical hermeneutics as a real science, 27–28
    on "fearing not to descend into Egypt," 376
    on the literal sense of the Old Testament as "Jewish" or "Judaic," 22
    on the name Israel meaning to "see God," 263
    on Paul dubbing children's play a persecution, 145
    on things repeated which were previously promised, 158
    Trinitarian reading, 124–25

pagans, righteous, 419
Parable of the Sower, 10
patriarchal narratives, pattern of reversal in, 189
patriarchal story, traits of, 296–97
patriarchs
    as *gerim* (resident aliens) in Canaan, 45
    living peacefully with surrounding peoples, 275
    as "mirrors for identity," 209
    portraying, 49
    promises to, 32
patristic exegesis, 22, 29
Paul
    on the child of the flesh persecuting the child of the spirit, 145
    on Christians accepting circumcision, 144
    on circumcision of the heart as equivalent, 104
    counted the thirteenth after the apostles, 392
    on the crown of righteousness awaiting him, 156
    on exercising hospitality, 123

on genealogies of Abraham, 157
on Gentiles having the law
    written in their hearts, 198
on Gentiles sharing in the
    promise of Abraham, 144
on God's grace having no
    boundaries, 419
on Jacob at death's door, 385
on the law, 26
on promises made to Abraham,
    80–81
on righteousness coming from
    faith, 422–23
on those who have faith as
    children of Abraham, 416
Paul and Barnabas, mission of, 103
Peniel, meaning "the face of God,"
    256
*Pentateuch: With Targum Onkelos,
Haphtaroth and Rashi's
Commentary*, 24
Pentateuchal "sources," calling
    upon, 5
people of the land, 162–63, 165
Perez
    birth of, 417
    descendants of, 320, 417
    son of Tamar, 320
    sons of, 375
perspectives, interplay of, 8
peshat hermeneutic process, 25
pesher, of Qumran sectarians, 23
Peter, received and baptized
    Cornelius, 103
Pharaoh (Abram's)
    Abram and Sarai deceiving,
        46n60
    gave flocks and herds and male
        and female slaves to Abram,
        131
    God striking an unwitting and
        his household, 420
    and his household stricken with
        severe plagues, 47
    as really in the right, 48
    reproach of Abram, 47
    telling Abram to leave Egypt, 48
    took Sarai and YHWH sent
        plagues, 127
    took Sarai because of her beauty,
        128
    took Sarai to wife, 48, 199
Pharaoh of the Joseph story
    blessed by Jacob, 379
    cared for his people and was
        hospitable to foreigners, 419
    dreams interpreted by Joseph,
        340–46
    gave Joseph in marriage
        Asenath, 344
    giving a fifth to, 383
    had Joseph hurried to him, 342
    Joseph interpreting the dreams
        of, 336–40
    puts all his household and
        the whole of Egypt under
        Joseph, 343, 344
    regarded as owner of the land of
        Egypt, 383
    said to Joseph the land of Egypt
        is at your disposal, 378
Phicol, general of Abimelech's army,
    142, 203, 204
Philistines, became envious of the
    wealth of Isaac, 201
Philo
    on Abraham extending
        hospitality, 123
    on the incorporeal nature of the
        visitors, 123
    interpreted "Israel" as one who
        sees God, 263
    on Joseph's noble mind, 305n28
    on the land of the Sodomites,
        122n31
    on the meaning of circumcision
        as spiritual, 102–3, 103n42
    on Melchizedek as the high
        priest of God Most High, 67
    on one of God's angels named
        Jacob or Israel, 264
    used allegory, 23
Phinehas, 74, 74n18
physical circumscription, versus
    spiritual, 97

physical reunion, as a sign of
    reconciliation, 260
pilgrimage, of Jacob to Bethel, 285
plagues, 79, 199
plot, in narrative criticism, 8
point of view, 8–9, 8n28, 30
political blessings, to Isaac, 212
political interpretation, of the
    blessing of Abraham, 50
polygamous husband, duties of,
    247–48
Pontifical Biblical Commission, 18,
    320
possession of the land, blessing to
    Jacob, 221
postexilic community, theological
    questions of, 70
Potiphar
    bought Joseph, 325
    entrusting his entire household
        to Joseph, 419
    not convinced of Joseph's guilt,
        329
    purchased Joseph, 311
    seized Joseph and put him into
        the jail, 329
    titles of, 311
Potiphar's wife
    cried out to her household
        servants, 327
    drawn by Joseph's beauty, 326
    Joseph and, 324–34
    not placed in Joseph's hands, 326
    pressing the point that the
        offender is a slave, 329
Potiphera, theories about, 346
presents, designated as a tribute
    from a vassal, 253
Priestly (siglum P) source, 3n8
priests of Egypt, exempt from
    taxation, 383
Primeval History (Genesis 1-11),
    positing three beginnings of
    humanity, 33–34
primogeniture, struggle for, 390
prison jailer. *See* chief jailer
procreation, intrinsically evil to
    frustrate, 323

progeny, promise of, 69–70, 71–75,
    87
promise texts, in Genesis, 33
Promised Land
    boundaries of, 45
    Esau removed from, 215
    as the heavenly homeland in
        Hebrews, 58
    Lot chose land outside the
        boundaries of, 57
    promised "for ever," 418–19
    requiring the annihilation of the
        indigenous peoples, 78
promise-fulfillment pattern, 20
promises
    given to Abraham as conditional
        upon obedience, 51
    of God, 167
    looking beyond Abram to the
        people of Israel, 38
    to the patriarchs, 32
prostitute, reducing Dinah to by
    accepting any gifts, 276
providence, 303, 413, 421
purification, washing of clothes as
    an act of, 286

quarrels, between the herders of
    Abram and those of Lot's
    livestock, 65–66
Qumran scroll fragments, on
    Melchizedek, 66

"rabbi," as a title, 25
rabbinic exegesis, secondary
    material in the study of, 25
Rabbinic Judaism, 25
rabbis
    on Joseph showing lack of trust
        in God, 339
    on Potiphar's wife, 333
    "pre-emptive exegesis" by, 22
    saw Rome in Esau, 218
    on setting up signs for God to
        fulfill, 178
Rachel
    barrenness of, 236
    bowing to Joseph, 385

brought to Isaac and not
    introduced to Abraham,
    169n5
conceived and bore a son, 239,
    388
died and was buried on the
    road to Ephrath (now
    Bethlehem), 289–90
giving her maidservant Bilhah
    to Jacob, 83n5
Jacob's preferential love for, 235
stealing of the household gods of
    Laban, 248
wanting a "house" after her
    name, 238
went into labor and suffered
    great distress with Benjamin,
    289
Rachel and Leah, buying into Jacob's
    thesis, 243
rainbow, as a sign, 97–98
Ramses III, 379
Raphael, role of, 124
Rashi, 99, 256
reader-response approaches, to
    commentary, 4
reading strategies, for the Old
    Testament, 13–17
Rebekah
    on any curse falling on her, 210
    burial of, 166
    calls Jacob "my son" and refers
        to Esau as Jacob's brother,
        208
    caught sight of Isaac in the field,
        177
    death and burial of, 403
    as the dominant partner in
        relation to Isaac, 173n18
    eavesdropping on Isaac and
        Esau, 209
    foreshadowing of, 155
    gave water to Abraham's servant
        and watered his camels,
        172–73
    gives her consent, 176
    loved Jacob, 208
    not mentioned at Jacob's return
        to Isaac and Isaac's burial by
        Jacob and Esau, 242
    patience, Rebekah representing,
        178
    preferred Jacob, 191
    preferring a just son to an unjust
        one, 217
    prepared by God, 178
    prescient in covering Jacob with
        Esau's precious clothes, 212
    sending Jacob away to procure
        the proper type of wife, 216
    sent off with Abraham's servant
        and his men, 177
    sister of Laban the Aramean,
        188
    sterile for twenty years, 188
    takes the place of Sarah as the
        matriarch of the family, 178
    telling Jacob to flee Esau's
        revenge, 215
    told that two nations are in her
        womb and the older will
        serve the younger, 188
Rebekah's nurse, buried under the
    oak below Bethel, 288
reconciliation
    forgiveness and, 423–24
    Joseph initiating the process of,
        367–68
    as a matter of attitudinal change
        (*metanoia*), 261, 423
    not necessarily entailing full
        erasure of the past, 409
    occurring through the
        righteousness of one man,
        203
    rejected by Jacob, 260
reconstruction, of memory, 410, 424
redemption, theology of, 126
repentance
    brothers exhibiting, 410
    last stage of, 424
Rephaim, race of giants in the area
    of Ammon, 61
resident alien, 118, 164
retribution, for past sins, 351

Reuben
- birthright of given to the sons of Joseph, 290
- claim to succession, lying with the concubine of one's father as, 290
- connected their entrapment to their sin against Joseph, 352
- defiled the couch of his father, 290, 388, 397
- disinherited by Jacob, 182
- on doing no wrong to the boy Joseph, 352
- having prime responsibility for Joseph, 309
- insensitive to Jacob's emotions, 354
- Jacob's blessing of, 397
- named by Leah, 236
- not with the brothers when they sold Joseph, 313
- planned to rescue Joseph, 309
- told his father to put Benjamin in his care, 353

Reuben (tribe of), consumed in battles with the Moabites and Ammonites, 397

riches
- of Abram, 55
- of Esau, 214
- of Jacob, 243
- of Lot, 56
- regarding as a blessing, 11

"righteous Gentile," Abimelech as, 130

righteous "pagans," 419

righteousness
- of Abram, 74–75
- of ancestors, 203
- coming from faith, 51, 422–23
- crown of, 156
- divergent views on, 114
- divine blessing linked with, 324
- faith as, 73
- Israel as a power for, 416
- kings in, 129
- Melchizedek as king of, 63
- not based on law, 198
- Tamar and, 317–20
- as more righteous, 319

Roman church, became Edom after the decline of Rome, 265

Rome
- Esau as a symbol of, 194
- known as Edom, 265

Rosh Hashanah, began to be associated with the Akedah, 161

round characters, 7

royal figure, Abram as, 59

"rule of faith," see Irenaeus, 27

ruler, from the House of David, 404

rules for conduct (*halakah*), 26

rules of interpretation, *middot* of Hillel, 25

sacred objects, consecrated by anointing with oil, 226

sacrifice
- consisting in devotion and obedience to God, 152
- of Isaac, 151–53, 161
- purpose to remind God of merit, 160

Sailhamer, John H.
- Pentateuch, as quite close in meaning to the NT book of Galatians, 15
- assimilates Old Testament to the New, 16
- Gen 15 addresses Jews awaiting fulfilment of promises, 70
- Gen 15: boundaries of land correspond to those of Eden, 77, 418
- "father of many nations" points to being born of God, 94
- not plunder, but their sister's honor was motive, 278
- Abraham portrayed as second Adam, 375

Salem, in parallelism with Zion (Jerusalem), 63

salvation
   for Christians not depending
      on keeping the laws of the
      Torah, 206
   Hagar receiving a divine oracle
      of, 139
   of Lot, 120
   oracle of, 202–3
   paths to, 107
   working out with fear and
      trembling, 156
Sarah
   Abimelech putting the paternity
      of her child in doubt, 128
   bore Abraham a son, 134
   burial, of the first matriarch
      of Israel "in the land of
      Canaan," 162
   burial cave, in the field of
      Machpelah, 403
   buried in the land of Canaan,
      162
   death and burial of, 403
   death of, 154n31, 163–64
   forcing Abraham to drive away
      Hagar, 136
   as free Jerusalem, 157
   genealogy of, 131
   giving rise to nations and rulers,
      417
   God siding with, 137
   God's apparent partiality in
      favor of, 142, 420
   laughter of, 111, 135
   lied about laughing, 112
   noticed Ishmael playing with her
      son Isaac, 135
   representing virtue, 89, 145
   Sarai's name changed to, 99
   saw Ishmael displacing Isaac for
      the birthright, 135, 136
   as virtue of the soul, 133
Sarah-Hagar scenario, repeating
   itself, 238
Sarah's children, as children of the
   promise, 144
Sarai
   as Abram's sister, 47n61
   age of, 38
   barrenness of, 35, 57, 83
   burial, of the first matriarch
      of Israel "in the land of
      Canaan," 162
   burial cave, in the field of
      Machpelah, 403
   calling upon YHWH, 85
   concerned for herself, 84
   Hagar and, 82–90
   honor of in Egypt, 46
   mistreated Hagar, 85
   name changed to Sarah, 99, 134
   oppressed Hagar, 420
   requested Abram to "go in to"
      her maid, 83–84
Sarna, Nahum
   Abraham shows steadfast
      loyalty, 152
   acquiring field of Machpelah
      presages possession of the
      land, 167
   Abimelech probably dynastic
      name – not same person in
      Abraham and Isaac stories,
      196
   Israel's ancestors create fund
      of spiritual benefits for
      descendants, 203
   Jacob snatching what was
      already given by divine
      election, 216
   The theophany as sole basis for
      holiness of Bethel, 226
   Bestowal of name Israel as the
      essence of the blessing, 255
   narrator of Dinah story sides
      with her brothers, 278
   Jacob initiates Israel's pure
      worship of YHWH, 285
   God's guiding hand gives
      direction to Joseph story,
      303
   Joseph both harsh and ready for
      reconciliation, 348
Satan, 66, 154n31, 163n3
scepter, 398
scepter and mace, 417

Scripture
  authors of, 17
  as best explained from Scripture, 26
  earliest Christian interpretation of, 26
  pattern of redemption of many through the one, 154
  presenting its characters as mirrors, 332
  senses of, 27, 27n96
  as "word of God in the words of humankind," 20
Second Vatican Council (1962-65), Declaration on the Relation of the Church to Non-Christian Religions, 106
seduction, of Joseph, 326–29
Seir the Horite, sons of, 295
"separation from the rest of the nations," ideology of, 281
Septuagint, 22
servant of Abraham
  embodying the piety, loyalty, and trustworthiness of a good steward, 178
  prayer for guidance asking for a sign, 172
  tale told by, 174–76
sexual immorality, types of, 133
sheaves, of Joseph's dream, 350
Shechem
  promised to marry Dinah, 269
  son of Hamor the Hivite, 11
  "taking" Dinah and asking for her hand, 267–71
  wasted no time in getting himself circumcised, 273
  willingness to do everything to remedy a conflictual situation, 419
Shechem (city)
  all of the men of committed a disgrace in Israel, 282
  hallowed by the patriarchs and regarded as sacred, 276–77
  Jacob assisting in the slaughter of, 393n22

Shelah, Judah's fear for the life of, 317
Shem, son of Noah
  age of, 68n50
  identifying Melchizedek with, 68
  populating the earth, 31
  as a priest, 68n51
  toledot of, 34
Sheol, first occurrence in the Bible, 311
shepherds
  family of Israel as, 378
  of Gerar argued with Isaac's shepherds over water, 202
Shiloh, 398–99, 417
Shua, a merchant, 320
sibling faithfulness, brothers needing to pass the test of, 358
silver goblet, in Benjamin's sack, 358–62
Simeon
  Jacob's blessing of, 397
  no urgency about freeing, 354
  reaction to Dinah's defilement, 12
  son of Leah, 236
Simeon (tribe), 395, 397
Simeon and Levi
  acted violently together in the sack of Shechem, 397
  criticism of, 278
  Jacob's response to, 276–77
  massacred all the males and killed Hamor and his son Shechem, 274
  as real heroes, 275
Simon Maccabeus, as leader and high priest forever, 65
sin, of Onan, 317
sin of Sodom, as oppressive violence, 115
Sinai covenant
  danger of infringement, 422
  leaving in place, 70–71
  as no longer extant, 93
  substituting the covenant of Abraham for, 69–70

sinful behaviors, frustrating divine
    purposes but not stymieing
    them, 303
slaughter, defined, 152
slavery in Egypt, delaying possession
    of the land, 78–79
social justice, the LORD loving,
    113–14
Sodom
    as a cipher for corporate sin and
        punishment, 121–22
    destruction of as a hotly
        disputed text between the
        early fathers of the church
        and the rabbis, 119–20
    flouting God-given
        opportunities, 113
    inhabitants as wicked and great
        sinners against the Lord, 63
    midrash on the destruction of,
        112
    narrative of the destruction of
        for moral depravity, 119
    as totally corrupt, 117
Sodom and Gomorrah, plundered
    by the kings from the north,
    60
sojourn (temporary stay), requested
    by Israel's family, 378
sojourner, not having the rights of a
    citizen, 118
Son, eternal generation of by the
    Father, 67
Son of God, appeared as God to the
    fathers, 264
Son of Man, angels of God
    ascending and descending
    on, 228–29
Song of Deborah, tribes of Israel
    mentioned in, 232, 395, 412
sons, of concubines or secondary
    wives having no right to
    inherit, 181
"sons of Hamor," as those bound
    together by treaty, 268
sons of Israel
    register of, 374–75
    "sons of Jacob" becoming, 371

sons of Jacob
    followed up the slaughter and
        sacked the city of Shechem,
        275
    listing of, 290
soul, bringing to undivided love of
    God, 157
spirit of God, endowment of the
    people by, 343
spiritual circumcision, versus
    physical, 97
spiritual struggle, in the Christian
    tradition, 262
spring water, Isaac's servants hit
    upon, 202
spying, Joseph accusing his brothers
    of, 350
stairway, as the link between Heaven
    and Earth, 223
stars in the heavens, Abram's
    offspring as innumerable
    as, 73
St. Stephen, on Joseph's story, 346
stewards, required to be trustworthy,
    178
story of a people, reading the Old
    Testament as, 13–14
strife, between Joseph and his
    brothers, and between Jacob
    and his sons, 300
supersessionism, 106
supplication, of Jacob, 252
suspicion, haunting the guilty mind,
    353
swearing, mode of solemn, 381
symbolic struggle, displacing
    conflict with Esau, 254

Talmud
    Babylonian, 24
    Jerusalem, 23
Tamar
    acting out of fidelity towards the
        deceased, 318
    adhered closer to God's will, 319
    as Aramean, 320–21
    asked for payment and a pledge,
        318

Tamar (*continued*)
  under the authority of Judah, 317
  becoming ancestor of David and Jesus, 320
  behavior conformed to the levirate relationship, 319
  conceived from one stand with Judah, 318
  delivered twins, Perez and Zerah, 320
  Judah and, 314–23
  not to blame for the deaths of her husbands, 317
  pledge from Judah served in lieu of witnesses, 319
  prayer of in Jewish midrash, 321n22
  pregnancy defined as adultery, 319
  righteousness and, 317–20
  tragedy and, 315–17
  wife of Er, 316
Targum Neofiti 1, 24
Targum Onkelos, 24
Targum Pseudo-Jonathan, 24
Targums, as Aramaic translations of the Hebrew Bible, 24
ten trials of Abraham, in Jewish tradition, 159
tension, between the religion of Israel and that of its neighbors, 285–86
Terah, 31, 34, 35, 38n26, 51
terror from God, fell upon the surrounding towns after the massacre at Shechem, 276, 279–80, 286–87
Tertullian
  Joseph's brothers like Judas in relation to Christ, 311
  condemned Tamar, 321
testament, of Jacob, 394–406
Testament of Joseph, magnifying Joseph's integrity, 332
Testament of the Twelve Patriarchs, 23
testimony, becoming revelation, 14

text, difficulties and inconsistencies in, 18
themes
  of the narrative, 414–25
  recurring in Genesis, 31–32
Theodore, bishop of Mopsuestia, 28
Theodoret, on circumcision as a distinguishing mark, 105
theological exegesis, incorporating insights of historical exegesis, 10
theological interpretation, as a drama, 13, 267
theological reading, 10–11, 13–17
theology, in the Joseph Novella, 302–3
theophany
  of Abraham, 109
  of Abram, 92
  as the basis for the sanctity of Bethel, 226
  received by Hagar, 85–89
"three angels" visiting Abraham, 424
tithe
  Abram giving Melchizedek, 64–65
  described, 64n36
tithes, Jacob's promise of, 288, 296
toledot (begettings, genealogy), in Genesis, 33
Torah
  Abraham observing, 52
  ending with Israel overlooking the Promised Land, 418–19
  Jacob occupied himself with the study of, 218
  Joseph learning, 313
  observance of all the precepts of, 52
  Prophets and Writings interpreting for Jews, 13
  speaking in the language of humans, 25
  ways of as planted in Abram's heart, 53
Tosephta, as rabbinic interpretation, 23

SUBJECT INDEX 481

townspeople of Sodom, surrounded Lot's house, 117
translators, choosing between fields of meaning, 30
transliteration, drawing attention to features of the biblical text, 31
treaty, as a parity between equals, Laban and Jacob, 246
trials, bearing thankfully, 335
tribes of Israel
  evolution of, 395–96
  Jacob's testament for, 396–403
  lists of fluctuated, 232
Trinity, equality of, 425
type-scenes, 46, 168n1
typological reading, of Israel's history, 21–22
typology, 26, 28

Vatican II, *Dei Verbum* (Dogmatic Constitution on Divine Revelation), 17
Vespasian, appointed emperor in Judea, 404
vicarious suffering, 51, 362, 416
violence, 117, 283
virgin, seduction or rape of, 270
virginity, taking of, 269
virtue
  of hospitality, 123
  remaining with Abraham and circumcision, 133
vizier of Egypt, Joseph installed as, 344
voice of God, Abram discerning, 36
vow, of Jacob, 226–28
Vulgate, translation by Jerome, 28

Wadi Gerar, 202
water
  representing life, 312
  as a symbol of drawing from the word of God, 218n30
wayfarers, hospitality to, 110
wealth, of Abram on leaving Egypt, 48
well(s)
  conflicts over in Gerar, 200–202
  Jacob at in the land of the Kedemites, 232–34
  naming of by Isaac, 202
  at an oasis as a symbol of fertility, 171
  of water seen by Hagar, 140
widow, firstborn son continuing the name of the deceased brother, 315
wife, as property, 47
"wife-sister" stories, appearing in Genesis, 46
wife-sister type-scene, involving Isaac, 198–200
wisdom
  coming only from God, 343
  descended with Joseph into the dungeon, 330
  engaging Jacob in a spiritual struggle, 262
  of Joseph capable of mastering every new complication, 383–84
  replacing YHWH in the theophany of Jacob, 228
  taking over the function of "the Lord being with," 330
womb, Esau and Jacob struggle in, 188–93
works, 51, 422–23
wrestling, of Jacob, 253–57, 262–63

Yahweh, grace and wisdom of in the Abraham narratives, 184
Yahwist (siglum J) source, 3n8
YHWH
  appearing in human form and eating, 123
  assured Jacob of support and constancy, 226
  binding covenant with Abram to give the land to his descendants, 76
  came down to the human realm to Jacob, 225
  clarifying the promise of seed to Abram, 73

YHWH (*continued*)
    confirming the "blessing of Abraham" to Jacob, 225
    dialogue with, 80
    dialogue with Abram, 69
    dialogues with Abraham about Sodom, 112–16
    frustrated the attempt to build a tower with its top reaching heaven, 224
    investigation confirming what he suspected, 116
    Jacob as the starting point of Israel's relationship with, 220
    nature of, 114
    not treating wicked and righteous alike, 115
    as patient and forebearing, 421
    proving faithful to the very end, 180
    putting into effect for Abraham the promises he made, 154
    showing Abram the Promised Land, 57–58
    sought Hagar out, 86
    worship of linking the ancestors of Israel with the line of Enosh, 44

Zacchaeus, 11
Zebulun, 239, 399
Zerah, 320, 417
ziggurats, shrine at the top, 224
Zilpah, 181, 238
Zoar (town), spared for the sake of Lot, 119

Scripture Index

OLD TESTAMENT

Genesis

Ref	Pages
Genesis	417
1	19n78, 20, 41, 44n49, 123
1:2 NABRE	30
1:2 NIV	30
1:2 NJB	30
1:2 NRSV	30
1:2 REB	30
1:2 TNK	30
1–11	31, 33, 298
1:26	19, 125, 425
1:28	40, 93, 100, 215, 221
2–3	19n78
2:4	31
2:10–14	77, 418
2:21	78
2:23	233, 235n13
3:17	34
3:22	19
4:1–16	9
4:7	116
4:8	86
4:10	115
4:11	34
4:17	183
5:1	31
5:18	183
6:4	9
6:5	34
6:6	31
6:8–9	34
6:9	31, 74, 93, 198
6:11	34, 42
8:1	30
8:21	34, 71
9:8	93, 97
10	375
10:1	31
10:7	181
10:10	59
10–11	34
10:17	268
10:21	34
10:28	181
11	31
11:1–9	34
11:4	39, 224
11:7	116
11:10	31, 34
11:27	31, 171
11:27—25:18	35
11:28	34, 35n10
11:29	155
11:30	83
11:31	171n13
12	75, 80, 101, 112n10, 131, 197, 199, 372
12:1	35n12, 37, 57, 147, 196, 291
12:1–3	51, 112, 131, 187
12:1–3 LXX	131
12:1–4	36–42
12:1–4a	35
12:1—25:18	31, 298

483

Genesis (*continued*)

12:2	94, 101, 140, 153, 169, 183, 197, 390, 394, 403, 415, 417
12:2–3	73
12:3	80, 81, 84, 197, 204, 212, 212n12, 226, 379, 384, 422
12:4a	36
12:5	73
12:5–9	44–45
12:6, 7	277
12:6–9	291
12:7	197, 291
12:8	44, 226n26, 227
12:9	46, 55
12:10	196
12:10–12	127
12:10–20	41n39, 44, 46, 55, 198, 199, 415
12:16	55, 83
12:17	420
12–50	71n8, 422n23
13	55, 59
13:1	46, 54, 55
13:2	46
13:3–4	226n26, 227
13:4	44
13:6	291, 293
13:9, 11, 14	189n7
13:10	66
13:13	63, 115
13–14	54–68, 108
13:14–15	45
13:14–17	36n15
13:15	45, 95, 418
13:16	73, 83, 225n22
13:17	344
13:18	110, 291
14	58–63, 59n14, 61n26, 62n30, 143, 144
14:11, 12, 16, 21	71n10
14:12	59
14:12, 24	59
14:13	71n10, 110
14:13, 24	166n15
14:14, 16	59
14:15	71n10
14:17	63
14:18	67n45, 68n51
14:18–20	63–65, 65n38
14:20	71n10
14:21	63
14:22	62
14:23	72
15	69–81, 69n3, 70n3, 91n2, 93, 95, 96, 104n44, 156, 418, 422
15, 22	422
15:1	64
15:1, 7	69
15:1–6	69, 71–75, 100n36
15:1–7, 18	36n15
15:1–12, 17–18	92n3
15:2	170
15:2, 8	69
15:3	72
15:4	83, 128, 252
15:4–5, 9–21	69
15:5	83, 153, 197n8
15:6	51, 81, 81n39, 83, 103n44, 198, 422, 423, 423n24
15:6 LXX	80
15:7	35, 37n20, 52, 70, 92n5
15:7–8	74
15:7–12	75–78
15:11	339
15:12	75
15:13	85, 378
15:13–16	78–80, 336, 373
15:15	77, 182
15:16	79
15:17	75
15:18	45, 76, 77, 418
15:18–21	197
15:19	77, 418
15:20	71n10, 163
15:21	71n10
16	82–90, 128, 135, 151
16, 21	182
16:1–5	141
16:1–6	83–85

16:2	238	18	5, 45, 100n37, 125, 128, 136, 425
16:3	82	18:1	109, 124, 128
16:7	82, 140n15, 141	18:1–8	108
16:7–16	85–89	18:1–15	108, 110–12
16:9	83, 89	18:1–16	91n2
16:9, 10, 11	82	18:3	109
16:10	82	18:5	109, 110
16:11	82	18:5 NABRE	110n7
16:12	183	18:9	109
16:13	83, 85, 183, 287	18:9–19	36n15
16:13–14	151n14	18:10	109
16:14	82, 146	18:12	135
16:15	82	18:13	109
16:16	92	18:16–33	108, 112–16, 124, 415
17	5, 42n43, 51, 57, 73, 81, 91–107, 95n15, 104n44, 137, 154, 158, 222, 279, 298, 418	18:17	109
		18:18	38n24, 39, 40
		18–19	23
17:1	104, 389	18:19	42, 42n43, 52
17:1–2	92	18–19	108–26
17:1–8	92n3, 289	18:19	126, 154, 203
17:1–22	36n15	18–19	424
17:2	180	18:23–32	112
17:3, 9, 15, 19	91	18:24–29	108
17:4	91, 96, 180	18:25	108
17:4–8	91, 94–96	18:33	109
17:5	184, 289	19	130, 155, 420
17:6	94, 134, 417	19:1	109, 118
17:7	42, 92	19:1, 13	229n42
17:8	58, 295	19:1–3	108
17:9	91	19:1–10	168n1
17:9–14	96–97, 101	19:1–23	108, 116–19
17:11	136	19:1–25	41n39
17:15	91	19:16	109
17:15–17	91	19:16 NABRE	109
17:15–19	99–100	19:20	56
17:15–22	92n3, 100n38, 279	19:24	109, 119, 124
17:16	417	19:24–29	119–21
17:17	111	19:30–38	108, 121–22
17:19	92, 135, 182	20	46, 48n66, 127–33, 142, 195, 196, 198, 199
17:20	38n24, 91, 183, 415		
		20:1–7	128–30
17:20–22	100–101	20:4, 5	127
17:21	136	20:6	420
17:22	92	20:8–18	130–32
17:23–27	101	20:9	200
17:25	139		

Genesis (*continued*)

20:13	287
20:14	201n15
20:17	135n3
21	89, 90, 134–46, 155
21:1–13	134–37
21:3	88
21:4–21	141n20, 420n13
21:9–21	82
21:12	148
21:14	141, 142
21:14–21	138–42
21:17	139, 146, 152
21:18	38n24, 137n7, 141n20, 183, 415, 420, 420n13
21:19	146
21:21	24n90
21:22	140, 164
21:22–32	195, 204
21:22–33	163
21:22–34	142–34
21:27–32	204
21:32	142
21:33	44, 203
21:33–34	142
22	36, 50, 56, 75n23, 81, 138, 147–61, 169n5, 184, 324, 423
22:1–14	148–53
22:2	37, 147
22:8	160n55
22:12	141n20, 189n10, 420n13
22:14	150n11, 160n55
22:15–18	36n15, 39, 74n18, 81, 113, 126, 198, 422
?? not 15–8?	423
22:15–19	153
22:16	51, 197
22:17	197, 212
22:18	40, 177, 197
22:20–24	155
22:23	170
23	45, 159, 162–67, 169, 262
23:9, 20	295
23:19	162
24	155, 168–79, 316, 320, 381
24:1	174
24:1, 35	174n24
24:1–9	169–71
24:3, 6	163
24:4	35, 37n20
24:10	188
24:10–33	171–74
24:11	232
24:27	168
24:31	174n24, 233
24:34–49	174–76
24:35	180
24:42, 45	175n26
24:50	176
24:50–67	176–78
24:59	288
24:61	177n31
24:62	88, 169, 183, 205
25	94, 101, 220n8
25:1	84n9
25:1–18	180–85
25:5	35, 169n5, 175, 299
25:6	84n9, 139, 181
25:6 ??	184n14
25:7	87n16
25:9	87, 146, 166, 291
25:9 LXX	88n18
25:9 Vulgate	88n18
25:11	88, 146, 169
25:12	31, 181
25:12–16	415
25:12–18	284
25:16	215
25:18	87
25:19	186
25:19–34	186, 187, 188–93
25:19—36:43	31, 186
25:19—37:1	299
25:20	171n12
25:21–23	192n26, 237

SCRIPTURE INDEX

25:23	8, 186, 187, 212, 294	28:1–4	169
25:28	208	28:1–9	220
25:29	31	28:2	233
25:29–34	192n26	28:2, 6, 7	171n12
26	186, 195–207, 292	28:3	289, 388
26:1–5	196–98	28:3–4	212
26:1–11	46	28:8	205n25, 316
26:2	372	28:9	205, 292
26:2–5	196n3	28:10–22	187, 219, 222–26
26:3–6	126	28:11	219
26:3a	199	28:12	219, 224
26:4	40, 252	28:12 NABRE	8
26:4–5	36n15, 154n27	28:14	39
26:5	52, 113, 196	28:14–15	36n15
26:5–11	198, 199	28:15	242, 249, 280, 390n22, 421
26:6–11	195, 198–200	28:16	219
26:12–22	200–202	28:17	219
26:15–22	45	28:18	287, 289
26:23–25	202–3, 262	28:19	287, 289
26:24	195, 196, 196n3	28:20	285
26:25	44	28:20–21	251
26:26–31	195	28:20–22	277
26:26–33	203–5	28:21	262, 372
26:34	216	28:22	262, 287, 289
26:34–35	205, 292	28–32	219
26:35	216	29	232
27	182, 187, 192n26, 208–18, 291	29:1–14	232–34
27:1–17	208–10	29:5	174
27:9, 15	310	29:10	254
27:18–29	210–13	29:15–30	231, 234–36
27:23	211	29:17	326
27:26	259	29:23–25	177
27:27–29	251	29:26	187
27–28	186	29–31	186, 187, 231–48
27:29	36n15, 209, 234, 258	29:31	237
27:30–40	213–15	29:31—30:24	231, 236–40
27:33	212	30:3	83n5
27:35	236, 272	30:4	84n9, 181
27:39	293	30:9	181
27:40	190, 294	30:21	253, 302
27:41–46	215–17	30:22	240n24
27:43	171	30:23–24	302
27:45	242	30:25–43	231, 240–42
28	219–30, 250, 287	30:26	240
28, 32	250n5	31:1–24	231, 242–44
		31:9–10	241
		31:23	213

488 SCRIPTURE INDEX

Genesis (*continued*)

31:25—32:1	231, 244–47
31:26	245n35
31:27	245n35
31:30	245n35
31:32	319
31:41	302
31:42	202n17, 227, 246, 402
31:45, 46	246
31:46	247
31:48	246
31:51	246
31:54	247
32	86n11, 256
32, 35	55
32:1	187
32:1–22	250–53
32:2	219
32:2–3, 23–33	187
32:3	219
32:7	291
32:8, 11	250
32:17	253
32:19	253
32:20	253
32:21	253
32:22–32	187
32:23–33	219, 253–57, 280
32:29	288
32:30	253
32–33	186, 187, 247, 249–65
32:33	257
32–33	293
33	409, 415, 419, 423
33:1	213
33:1, 9	415
33:1–11	257–60
33:2	219
33:3–4	258
33:9	260
33:10	253, 254
33:10, 11	259
33:11	213
33:12–20	260–61, 368
33:16	292
33:17	277
33:18	44, 291
33:18–19	268, 277
33:18–20	261–62
34	11, 187, 239, 253, 262, 266–83, 277n37, 308, 308n34, 392, 393n22, 397
34:1–12	267–71
34:2	273n26
34:13–29	272–75
34:25	272
34:28	397
34:29	274
34:30	278
34:30–31	276–77
34–35	186
35:1	291
35:1–7	285–88
35:1–15	187
35:3	288, 372
35:4	44, 220
35:5	276, 279
35:6, 27	291
35:7	227
35:7, 15	289
35:8	177
35:8–15	288–91
35:9	171n12, 287
35:9–14	277
35:10–12	219
35:11	289, 296, 380
35:11–12	387
35:12	291
35:14, 15	288
35:18	305
35:19	306n32
35:20	302, 357n24
35:22	12, 84n9, 181, 313, 397
35:27	291
35:27–29	242
35–36	284–97
36	186, 187, 299, 415
36:1	186
36:1, 9	31
36:1–19, 31–43	291–95
36:2	205, 292

SCRIPTURE INDEX

36:6, 8	299
36:7	291, 380, 415
36:11	294
36:15–16	294
36:20–30	295
36:31	294, 415
36:40–43	295
37	8, 290, 298–313, 299n5, 315, 324, 338, 350, 360, 362
37, 38	302
37, 39	315
37:1–4	300
37:1–11	304–6
37:2	31, 84n9, 350, 407
37:3	302
37:3–36	299
37:4	306, 367
37:5	306
37:5–36	300
37:8	306, 365
37:10	302, 357n24
37:11	306, 388
37:12	305
37:12–36	307–11
37:17	340
37:19	9
37:24	338
37:25	302, 355
37:28	9, 302, 307, 311, 325, 338
37:28, 36	338
37:29	313
37:31	302
37:32	302
37:32–33	210, 349
37:33	302
37:34	359
37:35	302, 369, 373
37:36	302, 325
37–50	31
38	302, 314–23, 324
38, 49	301
38:1–11	315–17
38:2	275
38:12–30	317–20
38:17	302
38:18	355
38:25	302, 321n22
38:26	314
38:27–30	417
38–41	300
39	303, 304, 315, 324–34
39:1	302, 311, 338
39:1–6	315–26, 415
39:2–3, 22–23	
39:5	39, 379
39:7	66
39:7–20	326–29
39:11	333
39:14, 17	61
39:17	136n4, 145
39:21–23	329–31
39:22	336
39:23	330
39–45	299, 299n5
40	
40:1–2	325n5
40:4	330
40:5	339
40:7	336
40:23	339n13
40–41	335–46
41	340–46, 381, 415
41:9	336
41:12	336n5, 338
41:13	338
41:34	343
41:35	343
41:38	344
42	305, 349–54, 361
42:5, 6	9
42:8	363
42:11	175n26
42:13	175n26
42:16	358
42:20	354
42:21	359
42:21–22	357, 357n23
42:38	310n39
42–44	300, 347–63
42–45	358
43	354–58

Genesis (*continued*)

43:26	409n4
43:29	374
43:32	326
43–44	309
43—47:27	306
44	358–62
44:13	368
44:18–34	347
44:33	360
45	364–70, 371, 409, 409n4
45:1–5	366, 423
45:1–15	300, 347
45:4	338
45:6	356
45:7	367, 415
45:9, 13	365
45:10	378
45:16—50:21	300
45:17–18	365
45:17–19	374
45:18–19	365
45:20	372, 373, 378
45:22	358
45:33	378
46	371–76
46:1	371
46:1–4	372
46:1–7, 28–34	372–74
46:2–4	36n15
46:2ff	303
46:3	38n24, 371
46:3–4	33
46:4	376
46:5	371
46:6	365, 372
46:8	300, 372
46:8–25	299
46:8–27	374–75
46:9	354
46:12	417
46:15	277
46:26	375
46:28—47:31	299
46:31	365
46:34	357n25, 378
47	377–85, 415
47:1	365, 377
47:1–12, 27–31	378–81
47:4–6 LXX	379
47:5	377
47:5, 6	378
47:11, 27	388
47:13–26	377, 381–84
47:20, 21	377
47:28	386, 386n1
47:29	170, 386
47:29–31	387
47:31	386
47:34	343
48	306, 386–93
48, 49	301, 394
48:1	387
48:4	289, 295
48:8	386
48:8, 11	387
48:10	387
48:13	387
48:15–16	387
48:19	387
48:20	40n35, 197n10, 387
48:33	386
48–49	386
49	232, 287, 301, 309, 314, 354, 388n6, 394–406
49:1–22	396
49:1–27	396–403
49:3–4	182, 290
49:5–7	12, 274, 276, 277, 278
49:8–12	36n15
49:10	398, 404, 417
49:24	202n17, 227, 246, 334, 402, 402n24
49:26	402n22
49:27	387
49:28	394, 403
49:28–33	403
49:30	166, 295
50	407–13
50:1–14	407–8
50:1–21	299

50:3	164	19:5–6	51
50:13	166, 295	19:6	281
50:15–21	368, 409–11	20:2	70, 75, 225
50:20	416, 421, 423	20:5	397
50:22–26	300, 412	20:17	47
50:23	395	21:1–11	44
50:24	385	21:10	239
50:26	300	21:16	9, 310
		22:12	245
Exodus		22:15–16	12, 273
		23:23	268
1	85	32	395
1:7	380	32:6	136n4, 146
1:11	380	32:10	38n24
1:12	345	33:11	256, 263
2:1–10	141	33:20	256
2:11	338n11	33:23	88, 109
2:24	43, 303	40:9–11	226
3:1	181		
3:14	36n17, 225	Leviticus	24
3:22	79	18:18	236
4:22	264	18:21	283
5:1–3	240	18:22	117
6:2	36n17	19:14	210
6:3	92, 225	19:28	164
6:7a	95n13	20:13	122
6:11	139	20:19	131
8:18	379	24:30	117
11–12	86n11	27:4–5	310
12:5	93	31:9	319n15
12:13	160		
12:31	48	Numbers	
12:33	141	2	232
12:34	141	2, 26	388n6
12:35–36	48, 55	2:3–79	396
12:36	79	3:12–13	395
12:37	380	6:1–21	402
12:40	78n33	7:12–83	396
12:43–44	98	12:6	336
12:43–49	272	12:6–7	256
13:19	412	13:33	9
14:5	86	14:18	38n24
15:15	293	18:20–24	395
15:22	85	22–24	209
17:8–13	293	23:24	398
17:14	293	24:9	36n15
18:1	77	24:16	64
19:5	43, 225		

Numbers (continued)

24:17	399, 417
25:6–13	74
26	374, 388n6
32:12	77

Deuteronomy

19, 21, 45, 55n2, 56, 58, 70n7, 113, 143, 153n24, 422n22

2:5	291
2:9	121
2:9–14	61
2:10	61
2:12	61
2:19–20	121
2:20	61, 61n24
2:33	292
4:6–8	38n24
4:30–31	70, 422
5:29–31	198
6:2	198
7, 20	143
7:1–5	12, 277
7:3	170n10, 268, 271
7:5, 25	286
7:14	41
8:2	148
10:16	97
10:16 LXX	97n26
11:1	198
11:24	77, 418
15:12–18	44
15:13–14	240
20:17	268
21:13	164
21:15	236
21:15–17	182, 397
21:17	185
22:11	123
22:23–24	319, 328
22:28 NABRE	268
22:28–29	12, 273
23:8	291
24:7	9, 310
25	316
25:5–6	315
25:5–10	316
25:17–19	293
27:18	210
27:22	131
28	70, 297
30:6	15, 97
31:2	252
32:8	64, 375n12
32:11	30
33	232, 388n6, 395, 397
33:1–29	396
33:2	140
33:6	397
33:12	403
33:16	401, 402n22
34:10	256

Joshua

	56
1:2	252
1:4	77, 418
7:15, 25	319n15
8:9, 12	44
10:1, 3	64
12:15	316
13–19	396
14:5–15	77
14:15	163
15:13	164n4
18:13	226n25
19:10–16	399
19:40–48	400n17
21:1–8	278
22:14	293
24:2	51
24:16, 18	286
24:23	286
24:24	277
24:27	246n37
24:31	303
24:32	262, 412

Judges

	1, 375
1	278, 316n6
1:16	77
1:23	226n25
1:31–32	400

2:22	113	2 Chronicles	
5	232, 278, 395, 396	3:1	149
5:14	412	16	219n2
11:13, 22	252	20:2	61
18:29	61n25	20:7	50
		36:23	170
Ruth	49		
1:2	290	Ezra	
2:13	269	1:2	170
4	316	4:1, 7	277
4:18–22	320, 417	5:12	170
		6:9–10	170
1 Samuel		6:21	270
4:1	229	9:2	277
7:12	229		
15:11 NIV	30	Nehemiah	
15:11 NRSV	30	9	74
15:11 TNK	30	9:7	52
		9:7–8	74
2 Samuel		9:8	75n23
7	417	13:8	277
7:12, 16	404		
8:13–14	294	Judith	
8:14	215	8:26–27	159
13:14	268, 269	9:2–4	282
13:18	305		
13:21	12	1 Macabees	
16:22	290, 397	1:48	102
18:18	64	1:60–61	102
24:24	166	2:51–53	330
		14:41	65
1 Kings		14:47	405n33
1–2	7	15:1–2	405n33
		Job	24, 112
2 Kings		1:8	190
5:15–19	344	9:22	115
10:24	391	42:17	294
11:14	295		
19:35	86n11	Psalms	
25:8	311	2, 72, 110	399, 417
		2:7	50, 416
1 Chronicles		16:9–10	162
1:32	181, 181n4	18:3	402
5:1	290, 388, 397	22:18	26
7	374		

Psalms (continued)

23:1	402
24:3-4	129
33:5	113
33:5 NABRE	114
34:8	250
40:5	339
44:3, 4	418
45, 110	207
45:8	111
46:5	64
72:2	50, 416
72:8	50, 416
76:3	63
78:35, 56	64
78:67-68	402
80:2	402
88:11	61n22
105:16-17	366n3
105:17	346n27
105:17-18	303
105:17-22	340
106:30-31	74
106:31	74n17
110	65, 67
110 LXX	68
110:1, 4	67
110:1-4	65
110-1-4	66
110:3	67
110:4	67, 207
113:1	203n20
118:22	229
119:1	113
119:33, 32	113
119:166	400
132:2, 5	402n24
133:1	54, 364

Proverbs

2:10, 16	324
10:9	231
10:29	113
16:17	253n12
21:3	113
29:3	334

Song of Songs 28

8:7	234

Wisdom

7:25	228
10:6	122
10:7	120
10:10-12	228
10:12 NRSV	262
10:13-14	330

Sirach

16:8	122
44:21	39, 415
44:23	285, 286
49:15	303

Isaiah

1:10	122
1:15, 17	122
1:24	402n24
1-39	114
2:1-4	399, 417
2:1-5	281
2:2-5	50, 416
4:4	126
6:5	263
8:18	286
8:23	390
11:10	399, 417
16:5	114
19:21	50, 416
19:24-25	36n15, 50, 408, 416
28:17	114
29:22	52
32:16	114
33:5	114
40:2	269
40:3	113
40:9-10	79
40:26	73
40:31	70
40-53	203
41:8	50
42:4	398

45:8	114	20:25	319–20
46:12–13	114	22:11	131
49:6	399, 417	27:44	220
49:9	312	44:9	97
49:26	402n24		
51:1–3	41, 42	Daniel	
51:3	56	2:37	170
53:5, 10	122		
53:11	51, 416	Hosea	
54:7	203n20	11:8–9	122
55:1	218n30	12:3	216
55:1–2	206n26	12:3, 4, 7	193
56:1	114	12:3–5	253
56:1–8	50	12:4–5	254, 255n20
56:6	96	12:5	86n11
56–66	114		
60:16	402n24	Amos	
61:1	66	1:11	191
		2:11	401
Jeremiah	71	9:7	87
5:4, 5	113		
9:3	216	Obadiah	
9:24–25	97	1:10	191
12:1–6	112	1:14	191
12:2	112	21	265
23:14	122		
31:31–34	53, 70, 422	Jonah	49
31:33	198	1:9	61, 170
32	49	3	115
33:17	404		
34:10	76	Micah	
34:17–20	76	4:1–4	281
42–44	49	4:1–5	50, 416
48:13	227n30	5:1	290, 404
49:7	192	5:3	399, 417
Baruch		Habakkuk	
3:22–23	192	2:4	75n23
		3:3	140
Ezekiel	71, 373		
14:12–20	112	Zephaniah	
14:14	116n25, 421n17	3:9	391n17
16:2, 45	79		
16:49–50	122		
18	112		
18:2	397		
20:5–6	220n5, 286		

Zechariah

4:6	257
9:10	399, 417
10:2	337
10:6	301n12, 314n1
14:8	126
14:9	281

Malachi

1:3	216

ANCIENT NEAR EASTERN TEXTS

Epic of Gilgamesh	189n12

PSEUDOPIGRAPHA (OLD TESTAMENT)

1 Enoch

89:13–14	304n32

4 Ezra

6:8–10	194

Jubilees	23
11:16–17	52
13:10–12	47n61
13:25	65
15:26, 28, 34	102
16:8	121n29
17:15–18	159
18:16	158n47
19:8	159, 163
19:14	190n17, 193
27	228
30:5	282
30:7–10	282
30:25	295
32:3, 2	296
34:14	276
35:12	190n19

37:24—38:3	190n17
39:6–9	332
39–43	304n32
41:1	320

Testaments of the Twelve Patriarchs	23
Testament of Joseph	332

Testament of Levi

6:4–5	276

DEAD SEA SCROLLS

1Q20

Genesis Apocryphon	23
20:10–16	47n61
20:16–17	48n65
20.30–32	83n4

1Qap Gen

Genesis Apocryphon	46n60

4Q180

Pesher of the Periods

2:3–4	124n37

4Q225

psJub2	160, 160n58

4Q252

Commentary on Genesis A	404

4QPseudo-Jubilees	160

11Q13

Melchizedeek	66

Qoh

3:18	65n39
7:14	65n39
8:2	65n39

ANCIENT JEWISH WRITERS

Josephus
Against Apion
1.86–94　　　　　　　335n2
1.89–90, 94　　　　　335n2

Jewish Antiquities　　　23
1:310　　　　　　　　248n43
1.11.2　　　　　　　 124n37
1.154–157　　　　　　　52
1.164　　　　　　　　 48n65
1.192　　　　　　　　105n51
1.198　　　　　　　　122n31
1.21.2　　　　　　　　 295
2.184　　　　　　　　 373n7
2.45　　　　　　　　 333n24
2.6.1　　　　　　　　346n29
2.8.1–2　　　　　　　 409n2
2.9　　　　　　　　　313n45
14.163　　　　　　　　65n40
ii.20　　　　　　　　304n32

Jewish Wars
6.5.4　　　　　　　　404n31

Philo of Alexandria　　23, 102

On Abraham
23, 24　　　　　　　 123n36
26　　　　　　　　　 122n31
107–18　　　　　　　 123n34

Confusion of Tongues
146　　　　　　　　　264n50

On Flight and Finding
208　　　　　　　　　263n46

On Joseph　　　　　 304n32
4　　　　　　　　　　305n28

Questions on Genesis
3:48　　　　　　　　 103n40

Pseudo-Philo
L.A.B. (The Book of Biblical Antiquities)　159n54, 160
32:3　　　　　　　　　　159

RABBINIC WORKS

Mishnah　　　　　　　　23

Mishnah Kidd
4:13　　　　　　　　　　52

Tosephta　　　　　　　　23

Talmuds
Babylonian *Talmud*　　　24

Berakhot
16b　　　　　　　　　　303
55b　　　　　　　336n7, 338

Jerusalem *Talmud*　　　23

Megillah
17a　　　　　　　　　222n13

Pesahim
119b　　　　　　　　　184

Rosh Hashanah
16a　　　　　　　　　　161

Sanhedrin
74a　　　　　　　　　133n15
108b　　　　　　　　　 68

Shabbat
127a　　　　　　　　　110
137b　　　　　　　　　102

Sotah
36b   333

Yevamot
64a   90

Yoma
28b   52n81

Targums   24
Fragmentary Targum   24

Targum Neofiti   24, 39n30, 52,
                    65, 67n45, 68, 124,
                    146, 159n52, 159n53,
                    166n14, 190n16,
                    190n19, 194, 218n32,
                    229, 234n11, 240n24,
                    262n40, 272n23,
                    339n13, 346, 346n29,
                    382n10, 390, 392

Targum Onkelos   24, 39n30, 44n49,
                    60n18, 67, 73n15,
                    133, 146, 166n14,
                    176n30, 181n7,
                    190n16, 190n19,
                    234, 264, 272n23,
                    295n21, 321n22,
                    357n25, 390, 401

Targum Pseudo-Jonathan
                    24, 39n30, 44n49,
                    48n65, 52, 65, 66, 67,
                    68, 73n15, 76n25,
                    83n4, 90, 122n31,
                    124n37, 138n11,
                    145, 146, 154n31,
                    159n53, 163n3,
                    181n4, 181n7,
                    184n14, 190n16,
                    190n19, 191n21,
                    194, 194n32, 229,
                    230n43, 233n7,
                    235n15, 257n26,
                    264, 289n13, 290,

                    295n21, 308n34,
                    313, 320, 321,
                    321n22, 346,
                    346n29, 349n7,
                    357n25, 357n26,
                    363, 363n48, 373n6,
                    375, 379, 382n10,
                    393n22, 409
58 n. 44   67n46

Midrash
Genesis Rabbah   24
11:6   106n53
11:7   184
38:13   52
39:7   38n26
39:11   44n49
39:14   44n49
41:1   48
44:23   77n31
45:1   83n4
45:2   90
45:3   90
45:10   87n17
46   104
46:4   96n20
46:4, 5   104n47
46.5   207
48:9   124
48:10   126n49
48.5   207
49:4   123
49:9   111, 115n21
50:12   176n28
51:2   124
52:12   132
53:11   145
53:14   146
54:6   146
55:7   149
56:4   159
56:8   159n52
56:8–10   159n53
56.10   207
57:4   276
60:3   178
61:4   181n4, 185n17

61:6	185n21
61:7	190n17
63:3	184
63:7	194n32
63:8	191n21
63:11	191n20
63:14	194
65:18	218
65:19	218
65:20	218
66:1	218
66:6	211
67:2	218, 221n11
67:13	222
68:5	222n13
68:11	184
68:12	229n41
69:7	230n44
70:13	233
70:16	234n11
70:18	235n12
70:19	235
73:4	240n24
74:5	248
77:3	254
78:2	264
78:8	265
78:14	265
79:5	262n40
80:8	274
80:10	274
80:11	276
82:4	288
84:4	44n49
84:7	312
84:19	313
85:4	321
87:6	332
87:7	333–34
87:9	329
88:8	313
89:2	346
89:3	339
90:4	346n29
91:2	363
91:6	355, 363, 363n49
91:7	363
91:9	354
93:7	358n26
93:8	355n21, 360n37
94:3	369
94:9	375
96:5	384

Leviticus Rabbah

25:5	207

Mekilta of Rabbi Ishmael	160

Midrash Rabbah	24

Sifre to Deuteronomy

36:5	184

Amida

Benediction 1, in *Siddur*

21	206

Meforshim (Commentators)

Rashi	68, 149, 176n29

NEW TESTAMENT

Matthew

1	404
1:3, 5–6, 17	418
5:45	226
8:17	416
13:1–9	10
13:18–23	10
19:21	10
19:24	11

Mark

11:1–6	406
15:24	26

Luke

14:26	37

Luke (continued)

19:8–9	11
24:45	17, 21

John

1:13	94
1:14	229
6:46	264
8:56, 58	124
14:13	11
19:24	26

Acts

3:25	39n29
7:2–3	37n20
7:14	375
7:16	412
9:7, 9–10	346
10	103
15:1 ??	103
15:28–29	103
17:27–28	419

Romans

2:14–15	198
2:28–29	104
4	103n44
4:11–13, 16	157
4:13–16	51, 81, 422
5:3–5	335
8:19	120
8:21	120
8:22	120
8:28	407, 413
8:32	158
9:7–8	144
9:10–13	193
9:13	216n19
10:12	144
11:26	157
11:28–30	157
12:13	123

1 Corinthians

4:1	178
4:1–2	178

2 Corinthians

2:15–16	217

Galatians

	15
2:7	103
3	103n44
3:7–9	81, 157, 416
3:8	39n29
3:8–9	51
3:16	51, 80
3:24	26
4:21–31	144
4:22–31	157
4:29	145
5:1	145
5:2–4	103

Ephesians

6:12	376

Philippians

2:12–13	156, 422

Colossians

2:11–13	103n42

1 Timothy

2:4	203

2 Timothy

4:7–8	156

Hebrews

1:13	26
5, 7	67
5–7	67
5:10	67
7:3	68
7:7	68
7:25	68
11:8	50
11:9	45, 45n53, 58, 58n12, 167, 419
11:19	151
11:20	217

11:21	385, 386, 392
12:16	193
12:16–17	217
13:2	23n89, 123

James

2:17–22	51, 81, 423
2:23	50

1 Peter

2:21–25	416

2 Peter

2:6–8	122n32

1 John

4:4–12	125n45
4:12	263

Jude

7	122n33

Revelation

5:5	398

EARLY CHRISTIAN WRITINGS

Ambrose

On Abraham

1:33	126n46, 425n33
1:35	126n46
1.35, 33	22n88
1.4.23	90n29
2.10.77	94n11
2.6.35	66n42

On His Brothers, Satyrus

2.99	204n22

Isaac, or the Soul

4.22	206n27

Jacob and the Happy Life

2.2 5–6	217n28
5.24	248n41

On Joseph

11.62	358n27

Patriarchs

3.11–12	392n20

Aphrahat

Demonstrations

11.3	105n52

Apostolic Constitutions

8:12.23	68n47

Augustine

City of God

	406n35
16:29	125, 425n32
16.19	48n65
16.24	79n34
16.25	89n23
16.29	23n89
16.34	185n19

To Consentius, Against Lying

30	322n25

De Conjugiis Adulterinis

2.12	321n19

Exposition on the Psalms   346n27

On Grace and Free Will

6.15	72n13

Homilies on the First Letter of John

7.6	125n45

Quaestiones in Heptateuchum

2, 73	17n64

Questions on Genesis

q. 115	296n22
q. 126	312n43
q. 135	346n28
q. 152	376n14
q. 161	385n21
q. 162	381n8
q. 167	392n18

Sermon

4.21	217n24
4.23	218n29
169, 13	422
169.13	156n37
333.2, 5	156n38

On the Trinity	23
2.11.20	126n46, 425n33

Bede
Homilies on the Gospels

1.17	229n38

Caesarius of Arles
Sermon

83.4	126n47
84.3	158n48
85.5	179n18
86.2	193n30
86.3	193n29
89.2	312n42
91.3.4	362n44
91.6	348

Catena on Genesis

3.1206	145n28

Chromatius
Sermon

1.6	229n37

Chrysostom
Homilies on Genesis

33.15	57n7
45	131n10
46.5	137n9
46.6	139n13
47:13	152n18
47:14	159n50
47.12	158n47
47.3	148n4, 158n45
48:12	188n5
48.12	170
48.25	175
48.3-4	167n21
56.12	248n40
61.2	305n27
62.13	325n6
62.15	330n15
63:17	335n1, 340n14
64.11	357
65.10	380n6
66.3	385n21
66.6	385n21
67.17	413n14
67.21	413n14

Homiliies on the Acts of the Apostles

hom. 49	331n17

Homily 2 on Philemon

1:4-6	370n17

Homily 4 on First Thessalonians

3:5-8	362n45

"Homily 38"	89n26, 89n27, 90n28

Homily on Genesis 18-45

472	131n7

Clement of Alexandria
Christ the Educator

1.7	376n15

3.11	331n16

Cyprian
Letters

63.4	68n53

Cyril of Alexandria 283n59

Catena on Genesis

3.1026	95n12

Glaphyra on the Pentateuch: Genesis

3-4	229n39
3:10	146n31
5.5	296n22
6.2	305n28
6.5	312n44
7.3	406n36
304	363n47
307	392n19

Against Julian   126n46, 425n33

Didymus the Blind
On Genesis

242-43	89n24
245	89n25

Ephrem the Syrian
Commentary on Genesis

22:1	185n20
27.2	236n16
28,11	236n17
34.3, 4	321n23
37.7	363n46
40.2	368n14
40.4	370n16

Hymn 7   322n24

Eusbius of Emesa
Catena on Genesis

3.1216	145n29

Eusebius
Praeparatio Evangelica

9.22.9	282n57

Hilary of Poitiers
On the Trinity

5.19	263n44

Hippolytus
On the Blessing of Isaac and Jacob   217n23

Blessing of the Patriarchs

7	217n26

On the Blessings of Isaac and Jacob

7	217n27
8	217n25
11	392n21
16	406n38

Ignatius
Epistle to the Philadelphians

6:1	103n43

Irenaeus of Lyons
Demonstrations

44	124n40

Against Heresies

4.9.1	27

Jerome
Dialogue against Pelagians

3.8	330

Hebrew Questions on Genesis

25:1	185n18

Homilies on Psalms

1	158n46
46	229n40

Against Jovinian

1.20	321n20

John of the Cross
Dark Night

bk. 2 (p. 331)	156n39
bk. 2 (p. 333)	156n40
bk. 2 (p. 336, 338)	157n41

Justin Martyr
Dialogue with Trypho 22, 27

16	105n50
23	104n49
56:5	124
59	124n38
120.3–4	405n32

First Apology

32	406n37

Origen
Against Celsus

6.77	27

Commentary on John 27

On the First Principles

1, praef 3	27
1.3	405n34
3.2.5	263n43
4, 2:9	28
4, 3:4, 5	28
4.1–3	27
4.3.2	263n47

Homilies on Genesis

3:4	104n48
4.1–3	125n42
6.2	133n13
6.3	133n14
7.3	145n26
8.3	149n10
9.1	158n49
10.2	179n17
13.3	206n28
15.5	376n16, 376n17

Tertullian
Adversus Judaeos

10	311n41

On Modesty

6	321n21

Theodoret of Cyrus
Questions on the Octateuch

Gen. q. 100	325
q. 69 (p. 141)	105n51

Theodotus

frag. 7	282n57

Valentinian Heracleon
Commentary on John's Gospel 27

ROMAN CATHOLIC

Catechism of the Catholic Church

no. 121	106
nos. 251–56	322–23

Eucharistic Prayer

1	67

Pius XI
Casti Connubii

no. 55	321n19

www.ingramcontent.com/pod-product-compliance
Lightning Source LLC
Chambersburg PA
CBHW021230300426
44111CB00007B/486